Lecture Notes in Computer Science 10370

More information about this series at http://www.springer.com/series/7409

Giovambattista Ianni · Domenico Lembo
Leopoldo Bertossi · Wolfgang Faber
Birte Glimm · Georg Gottlob
Steffen Staab (Eds.)

Reasoning Web

Semantic Interoperability on the Web

13th International Summer School 2017
London, UK, July 7–11, 2017
Tutorial Lectures

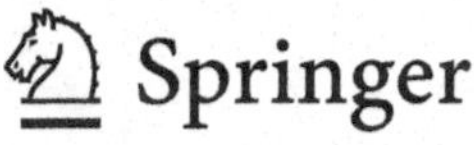

Springer

Editors
Giovambattista Ianni
University of Calabria
Rende
Italy

Domenico Lembo
Sapienza University of Rome
Rome
Italy

Leopoldo Bertossi
Carleton University
Ottawa, QC
Canada

Wolfgang Faber
University of Huddersfield
Huddersfield
UK

Birte Glimm
University of Ulm
Ulm
Germany

Georg Gottlob
St John's College
Oxford
UK

Steffen Staab
University of Koblenz
Koblenz
Germany

ISSN 0302-9743 ISSN 1611-3349 (electronic)
Lecture Notes in Computer Science
ISBN 978-3-319-61032-0 ISBN 978-3-319-61033-7 (eBook)
DOI 10.1007/978-3-319-61033-7

Library of Congress Control Number: 2017943075

LNCS Sublibrary: SL3 – Information Systems and Applications, incl. Internet/Web, and HCI

Printed on acid-free paper

This Springer imprint is published by Springer Nature
The registered company is Springer International Publishing AG
The registered company address is: Gewerbestrasse 11, 6330 Cham, Switzerland

Preface

This volume contains tutorial papers prepared for the 13th Reasoning Web Summer School (RW 2017), held during July 7–11, 2017, in London, United Kingdom.

The Reasoning Web series of annual summer schools was initiated in 2005 by the European Network of Excellence REWERSE. Since 2005, the school has become the prime educational event in the field of reasoning techniques on the Web, attracting both young and established researchers. Previous editions of the school were held in Malta (2005), Lisbon (2006), Dresden (2007 and 2010), Venice (2008), Bressanone-Brixen (2009), Galway (2011), Vienna (2012), Mannheim (2013), Athens (2014), Berlin (2015), and Aberdeen (2016). For each edition, a volume has been published containing the school lecture notes, which are today considered fundamental bibliographic references in the Semantic Web and Knowledge Representation areas.

Since 2011 the school has been co-located with the International Conference on Web Reasoning and Rule Systems (RR), and in 2015 it was also co-located with the International Web Rule Symposium (RuleML). Following this tradition, the 2017 edition of the school was held together with RuleML+RR, a conference that joined the RuleML and RR event series. In addition, it was also co-located with DecisionCAMP 2017 and the 11th International Rule Challenge. RW 2017 was hosted by Birkbeck, University of London, and was organized by University of Calabria and by Sapienza, University of Rome.

In 2017, the theme of the school was "Semantic Interoperability on the Web," which encompasses subjects such as data integration, open data management, reasoning over linked data, database to ontology mapping, query answering over ontologies, hybrid reasoning with rules and ontologies, and ontology-based dynamic systems. The RW 2017 lectures were focused on these topics and also addressed foundational reasoning techniques used in answer set programming and ontologies. This volume contains the following tutorial papers, each accompanying a school lecture:

- "Challenges for Semantic Data Integration on the Web of Open Data", in which Axel Polleres (presenter), Sebastian Neumaier, Jürgen Umbrich, and Simon Steyskal discuss main challenges related to the integration of open data over the Web (data formats, license and usage issues, data quality problems, etc.);
- "Ontological Query Answering over Semantic Data," in which Giorgos Stamou (presenter) and Alexandros Chortaras study data access mediated by an ontology, and present methods for data integration, query rewriting, and query answering when ontologies are specified in both tractable and expressive Description Logics;
- "Ontology Querying: Datalog Strikes Back," where Andrea Calì faces query answering over Datalog+/−, a family of ontology languages allowing for Datalog rules enriched with existential quantification in the head;
- "Integrating Relational Databases with the Semantic Web," in which Juan Sequeda surveys methods and standards to realize RDF access to relational databases and reviews how these standards can be used in practice for data integration;

- "Datalog Revisited for Reasoning in Linked Data," in which Marie-Christine Rousset describes a unifying Datalog-based framework for RDF ontologies and databases, and discusses modeling and reasoning over Linked Data within this framework;
- "A Tutorial on Hybrid Answer Set Solving," in which Torsten Schaub (presenter), Roland Kaminski, and Philipp Wanko introduce Answer Set Programming and show its usage in complex software environments and interaction with complementary forms of reasoning;
- "Answer Set Programming with External Source Access," in which Thomas Eiter (presenter), Tobias Kaminski, Christoph Redl, Peter Schüller, and Antonius Weinzierl continue the investigation on hybrid systems, and describe how ASP can interact with external resources in the DLVHEX system;
- "Uncertainty Reasoning for the Semantic Web," in which Thomas Lukasiewicz provides an overview of formalisms for handling uncertainty and/or vagueness in the Semantic Web;
- "Ontology-Based Data Access for Log Extraction in Process Mining," in which Marco Montali (presenter), Diego Calvanese, Tahir Emre Kalayci, and Ario Santoso show how semantic technologies, and in particular ontology-based data access, provide a viable solution for data preparation and log extraction for the task of process mining.

The tutorial papers are either in-depth surveys or shorter papers containing references to existing work. These papers have been written as accompanying material for the students of the summer school, in order to deepen their understanding and to serve as a reference for further detailed study.

We would like to thank everybody who contributed to the realization of this event. First and foremost, the school lecturers and their co-authors. We also want to thank the institutions of the school lecturers, which sponsored the school by covering the travel costs of the speakers. Furthermore, we would like to thank the general chairs of the RuleML+RR conference, Roman Kontchakov and Fariba Sadri, for their help in the logistic organization of the event, the sponsorship chair, Nick Bassiliades, and the Web chair, William Van Woensel, for taking care of the school website.

May 2017

Giovambattista Ianni
Domenico Lembo
Leopoldo Bertossi
Wolfgang Faber
Birte Glimm
Georg Gottlob
Steffen Staab

Organization

Chairs

Giovambattista Ianni University of Calabria, Italy
Domenico Lembo Sapienza University of Rome, Italy

Scientific Advisory Board

Leopoldo Bertossi Carleton University, Canada
Wolfgang Faber University of Huddersfield, UK
Birte Glimm Ulm University, Germany
Georg Gottlob Oxford University, UK
Steffen Staab University of Koblenz-Landau, Germany

Website Administrator

William Van Woensel Dalhousie University, Canada

Sponsorship Chair

Nick Bassiliades Aristotle University of Thessaloniki, Greece

Local Organization

Roman Kontchakov Birkbeck, University of London, UK
Fariba Sadri Imperial College London, UK

Additional Reviewers

Shqiponja Ahmentaj
Matthias Thimm

Sponsors

Birckbeck University

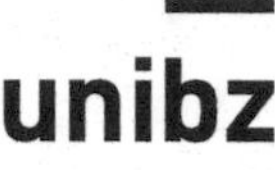

Free University of Bozen-Bolzano

Capsenta

University of Grenoble-Alpes

National Technical University of Athens

Oxford University

University of Potsdam

Vienna University of Technology

Vienna University of Economics and Business

University of Calabria

Sapienza University of Rome

Contents

Data Integration for Open Data on the Web

Sebastian Neumaier[1], Axel Polleres[1,2(✉)], Simon Steyskal[1], and Jürgen Umbrich[1]

[1] Vienna University of Economics and Business, Vienna, Austria
axel.polleres@wu.ac.at
[2] Complexity Science Hub Vienna, Vienna, Austria

Abstract. In this lecture we will discuss and introduce challenges of integrating openly available Web data and how to solve them. Firstly, while we will address this topic from the viewpoint of Semantic Web research, not all data is readily available as *RDF* or *Linked Data*, so we will give an introduction to different *data formats* prevalent on the Web, namely, standard formats for publishing and exchanging tabular, tree-shaped, and graph data. Secondly, not all *Open Data* is really completely open, so we will discuss and address issues around *licences*, terms of usage associated with Open Data, as well as documentation of data *provenance*. Thirdly, we will discuss issues connected with (meta-)data quality issues associated with Open Data on the Web and how Semantic Web techniques and vocabularies can be used to describe and remedy them. Fourth, we will address issues about *searchability* and *integration* of Open Data and discuss in how far *semantic search* can help to overcome these. We close with briefly summarizing further issues not covered explicitly herein, such as multi-linguality, temporal aspects (archiving, evolution, temporal querying), as well as how/whether OWL and RDFS reasoning on top of integrated open data could be help.

1 Introduction

Over the last decade we have seen the World Wide Web being populated more and more by "machines". The world wide Web has evolved from its original form as a network of linked Documents, readable by humans to more and more a Web of data and APIs. That is, nowadays, even if we interact as humans with Web pages, in most cases (i) the contents of Web pages are generated from Databases in the backend, (ii) the Web content we see as humans contains annotations readable by machines, and even (iii) the way we interact with Web pages generates data (frighteningly, even often without the users being aware of), collected and stored again in databases around the globe. It is therefore valid to say that the Web of Data has become a reality and – to some extent – even the vision of the Semantic Web. In fact, this vision of the Semantic Web has itself evolved over the decades, starting with Berners-Lee et al.'s seminal article in 2001 [13] that already envisioned the future Web as "federating particular knowledge bases and databases to perform anticipated tasks for humans and their agents". Based on these ideas a lot of effort and research has been devoted

G. Ianni et al. (Eds.): Reasoning Web 2017, LNCS 10370, pp. 1–28, 2017.
DOI: 10.1007/978-3-319-61033-7_1

to the World Wide Web Consortium (W3C) Semantic Web activity,[1] which in 2013 has been subsumed by – i.e., renamed to – "Data Activity".[2]

In many aspects, the Semantic Web has not necessarily evolved as expected, and the biggest success stories so far do less depend on formal logics [37] than we may have expected, but more on the availability of data. Another recent article by Bernstein et al. [14] takes a backwards look on the community and summarizes successes of the Semantic Web community such as the establishment of lightweight annotation vocabularies like Schema.org on Web pages, or praising the uptake of large companies such as Google, Yahoo!, Microsoft, and Facebook who are developing large knowledge graphs, which however, so far these companies mostly keep closed.

Thus, if Web researchers outside of these companies want to tap into the rich sources of Data available now on the Web they need to develop their own data workflows to find relevant and usable data. To their help, more and more Open Data is being published on the Web, that is, data that is made freely available by mostly public institutions (Open Government Data) both for transparency reasons and with the goal to "fuel" a Data Economy, pushed both by the EU [29] and the G8 [72].

The present lecture notes may be viewed as partially an experience report as well as – hopefully – a guide through challenges arising when using (Open) data from the Web. The authors have been involved over the past view years in several projects and publications around the topic of Open Data integration, monitoring, and processing. The main challenges we have come across in all these projects are largely overlapping and therefore we decided to present them in the present chapter:

1. **Where to find Open Data?** (Sect. 2) Most Open Data nowadays can be found on so called Open Data Portals, that is, data catalogs, typically allowing API access and hosting dataset descriptions and links to actual data resources.
2. **"Low-level" data heterogeneity** (Sect. 3) As we will see, most of the structured data provided as Open Data is not readily available as RDF or Linked Data – the preferred formats for semantic data access described in other chapters of this volume. Different formats are much more prevalent, plus encoding issues make it difficult to access those datasets.
3. **Licenses and Provenance** (Sect. 4) Not all *Open Data* is really completely open, since most data on the Web is attached to different licences, terms and conditions, so we will discuss how and whether these licenses can be interpreted by machines, or, respectively how the provenance of different integrated data sources can be tracked.
4. **Quality issues** (Sect. 5) A major challenge for data – also often related to its provenance – is quality; on the one hand the re-use of poor quality data is obviously not advisable, but on the other hand different applications might have different demands/definitions of quality.

[1] https://www.w3.org/2001/sw/, last accessed 30/03/2017.
[2] https://www.w3.org/2013/data/, last accessed 30/03/2017.

5. **How to find data – Searchability?** (Sect. 6) Last, but not least, we will look into current solutions for search in Open Data, which we pose as a major open research challenge: whereas crawling and (keyword-based search) of human readable websites work well, this is not yet the case for structured data on the Web; we will discuss why and sketch some routes ahead.

Besides these main questions, we will conclude with summarizing issues and open questions around integrating Open Data from the Web not covered explicitly herein in Sect. 7, such as multi-linguality, temporal aspects (archiving, evolution, temporal querying), as well as how/whether OWL and RDFS reasoning on top of integrated open data could be help.

2 Where to Find Web Data?

If we look for sources of openly available data that is widely discussed in the literature, we mainly can identify three starting points, which are partially overlapping:

- User-created open data bases
- The Linked Open Data "Cloud"
- Webcrawls
- Open Data Portals

User-created open data bases, through efforts such as Wikipedia, are large amounts of data and data-bases that have been co-created by user communities distributed around the globe; the most important ones being listed as follows:

- **DBpedia** [44] is a community effort that has created one of the biggest and most important cross-domain dataset in RDF [19] in the focal point of the so called Linked Open Data (LOD) cloud [6]. At its core is a set of declarative mappings extracting data from Wikipedia *infoboxes* and tables into RDF and it is accessible as well as through dumps also through an open query interface supporting the SPARQL [33] query language. DBpedia can therefore be well called one of the cornerstones of Semantic Web and Linked Data research being the subject and center of a large number of research papers over the past few years. Reported numbers vary as DBpedia is modular and steadily growing with Wikipedia, e.g. in 2015 DBpedia contained overall more than 3B RDF Statements[3], whereof the English DBpedia contributed 837 M statements (RDF triples). Those 837 M RDF triples alone amount to 4.7 GB when stored in the compressed RDF format HDT [30][4]. However, as we will see there are many, indeed far bigger other openly accessible data sources, that yet remain to be integrated, which are rather in the focus of the present chapter.

[3] http://wiki.dbpedia.org/about/facts-figures, last accessed 30/03/2017.
[4] http://www.rdfhdt.org/datasets/, last accessed 30/03/2017.

- **Wikidata** [74] a similar, but conceptually different effort has been started in 2012 to bring order into data items in Wikipedia, with the idea to – instead of extracting data from semi-structured Wikipages – build a database for data observations with fixed properties and datatypes, mainly with the idea to avoid extraction errors and provide means to record provenance directly with the data, with likewise 100s of millions of facts in the meantime: exact numbers are hard to give, but [71] report some statistics of the status of 2015, when Freebase was included into Wikidata; we note that counting RDF triples[5] is only partially useful, since the data representation of Wikidata is not directly comparable with the one from DBpedia [35,36].
- **OpenStreetmap** as another example of an openly available data base that has largely been created by users contains a vast amount of geographic features to obtain an openly available and re-usable map; with currently 739.7GB (uncompressed) data in OSM's native XML format (and still 33GB compressed).[6]

The Linked Open Data "Cloud" – already mentioned above – is a manually curated collection of datasets that are published on the Web openly, adhering to the so-called Linked Data principles, defined as follows [12] (cf. chapters of previous editions of the Reasoning Web book series for good overview articles):

LDP1: use URIs as names for things;
LDP2: use HTTP URIs so those names can be dereferenced;
LDP3: return useful – herein we assume RDF – information upon dereferencing of those URIs; and
LDP4: include links using externally dereferenceable URIs.[7]

The latest iteration of the LOD Cloud [1] contains – with DBpedia in its center – hundreds of datasets with equal or even larger sizes than DBpedia, documenting a significant growth of Linked Data over the past years. Still, while often in the Semantic Web literature the LOD cloud and the "Web of Data" are implicitly equated, there is a lot of structured data available on the Web (a) either, while using RDF, not being linked to other datasets, or (b) provided in other, popular formats than RDF.

Running Web crawls is the only way to actually find and discover structured Web Data, which is both resource intensive and challenging in terms of respecting politeness rules when crawling. However, some Web crawls have been made openly available, such as the Common Crawl corpus which contains "petabytes of data collected over the last 7 years"[8]. Indeed the project has already been used to collect and analyse the availability (and quality) of structured data on the Web, e.g. in the Web Data Commons Project [50,51] (Table 1).

[5] Executing the SPARQL query `SELECT (count(*) as ?C) WHERE {?S ?P ?O }` on https://query.wikidata.org/ gives 1.7B triples, last accessed 30/03/2017.

[6] http://wiki.openstreetmap.org/wiki/Planet.osm, last accessed 30/03/2017.

[7] That is, within your published RDF graph, use HTTP URIs pointing to other dereferenceable documents, that possibly contain further RDF graphs.

[8] http://commoncrawl.org/, last accessed 30/03/2017.

Table 1. Top-10 portals, ordered by datasets.

Domain of portal URL	Origin	Software	$\|\mathcal{D}\|$	$\|\mathcal{R}\|$
data.gov	US	CKAN	192,738	170,524
www.data.gc.ca	Canada	CKAN	147,364	428,141
transparenz.hamburg.de	Germany	CKAN	69,147	101,874
data.noaa.gov	US	CKAN	57,934	148,343
geothermaldata.org	US	CKAN	56,388	59,804
data.gov.au	Australia	CKAN	42,116	77,900
data.gov.uk	UK	CKAN	41,615	80,980
hubofdata.ru	Russia	CKAN	28,393	62,700
openresearchdata.ch	Switzerland	CKAN	20,667	161,259
govdata.de	Germany	CKAN	19,334	55,860

Open Data portals are collections or catalogs that index metadata and link to actual data resources which have become popular over the past few years through various Open Government Data Initiatives, but also in the private sector. Apart from all the other sources mentioned so far, most of the data published openly is indexed in some kind of Open Data Portal. We therefore will discuss these portals in the rest of this paper in more detail.

Open Data portals

Most of the current "open" data form part of a dataset that is published in Open Data portals which are basically catalogues similar to digital libraries (cf. Fig. 1): in such catalogues, a *dataset* aggregates a group of data files (referred to as *resources* or distributions) which are available for access or download in one or more formats (e.g., CSV, PDF, Microsoft Excel, etc.). Additionally, a dataset contains *metadata* (i.e., basic descriptive information in structured format) about these resources, e.g. authorship, provenance or licensing information. Most of these portals rely on existing software frameworks, such as CKAN[9] or Socrata,[10] that offer UI, search, and API functionalities. CKAN is the most prominent portal software framework used for publishing Open Data and is used by several governmental portals including data.gov.uk and data.gov.

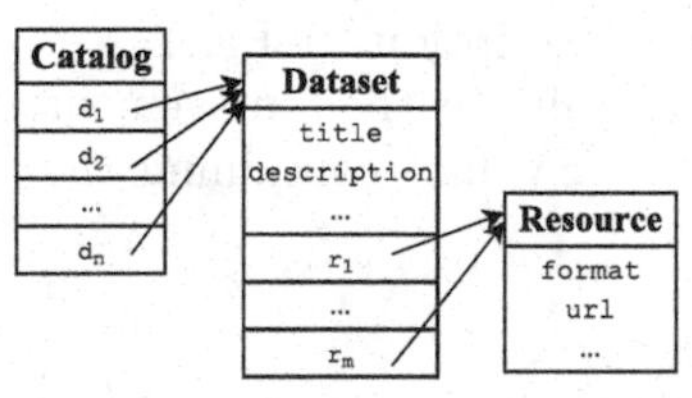

Fig. 1. High-level structure of a data catalog.

For example, the Humanitarian Data Exchange[11] (see Fig. 2) is a portal by the United Nations. It aggregates and publishes data about the context in which a humanitarian crisis is occurring (e.g., damage assessments and geospa-

[9] https://ckan.org/, last accessed 30/3/2017.

[10] https://socrata.com/, last accessed 30/3/2017.

[11] https://data.humdata.org/, last accessed 27/3/2017.

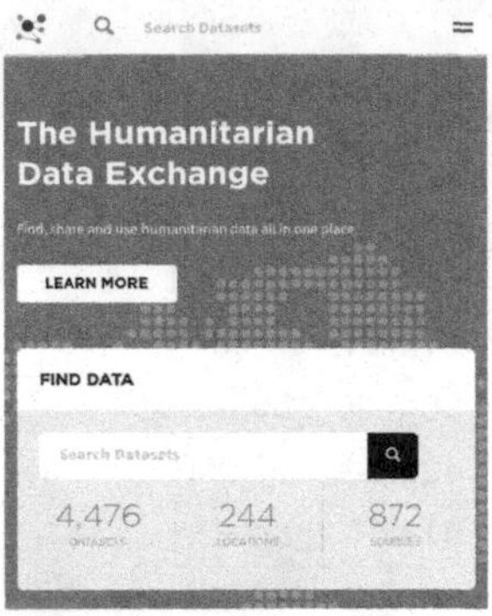

```
{
  "name":"amounts-paid-by-refugees-...",
  "title": "Amounts paid by refugees...",
  "license": "Creative Commons Attribution",
  "tags": [
    "europe",
    "mediterranean",
    "refugee"
  ],
  "resources": [
    {
      "format": "CSV",
      "name": "The Money Trail - South - Prices",
      "created": "2015-10-28T21:20:40.006453",
      "url": "https://docs.google.com/...",
    }
  ],
  ...
}
```


Fig. 2. Example dataset description from the humanitarian data exchange portal.

Table 2. The tabular content of the dataset in Fig. 2

Route	Period	Ref crossing	Total in EUR 2014
Central Med	2010–2015	285,700	3,643,000,000
East Borders	2010–2015	5,217	72,000,000
East Med Land	2010–2015	108,089	1,751,000,000
East Med Sea	2010–2015	61,922	1,053,000,000
West African	2010–2015	1,040	4,000,000
West Balkans	2010–2015	74,347	1,589,000,000
West Med	2010–2015	29,487	251,000,000

tial data) and data about the people affected by the crisis. The datasets on this portal are described using several metadata fields, and the metadata description can be retrieved in JSON format using the Web API of the data portal (cf. Fig. 2).

The metadata description of these datasets provide download links for the actual content. For instance, the particular dataset description in Fig. 2 – a dataset reporting the amounts paid by refugees to facilitate their movement to Europe – holds a URL which refers to a table (a CSV file) containing the corresponding data, displayed in Table 2.

3 Data Formats on the Web

When we discuss different available data on the Web, we already emphasized that – despite being subject of a lot of research – RDF and Linked Data are not necessary the prevalent formats for published data on the Web. An analysis of the datasets systematically catalogued in Open Data portals will confirm this. Likewise, we will have to discuss *metadata* formats on these portals.

Data Formats on Open Data Portals. Table 3 shows the top used formats and the number of unique resources together with their number of portals they appear, adapted from [58], where we analysed and crawled metadata from 260 Open Data Portals for cues to the data formats in which different datasets are provided. Note, that these numbers are based on available metadata information of the datasets and can be higher due to varying spellings, misspellings, and missing metadata. Therefore, these numbers should be considered as a lower bound for the respective formats. Bold highlighted values indicate that the format is considered as open as per the Open Definition [12]:[12] the open definition sets out several guidelines of which data formats are to be considered "open", according to which we have analysed assessed openness by a list of compliant formats, cf. [58].

Table 3. Most frequent formats.

	format	|*resources*|	%	|*portals*|
1	**HTML**	491,891	25	74
2	PDF	182,026	9.2	83
3	**CSV**	179,892	9.1	108
4	XLS(X)	120,703	6.1	89
5	**XML**	90,074	4.6	79
6	**ZIP**	50,116	2.5	74
	...			
11	**JSON**	28,923	1.5	77
16	**RDF**	10,445	0.5	28

A surprising observation is that ~10% of all the resources are published as PDF files. This is remarkable, because strictly speaking PDF cannot be considered as an Open Data format: while PDFs may contain structured data (e.g. in tables) there are no standard ways to extract such structured data from PDFs - or general-purpose document formats in general. Therefore, PDFs cannot be considered as machine-readable, nor as a suitable way for publishing Open Data. As we also see, RDF does not appear among the top-15 formats for Open Data publishing.[13] This underlines the previously stated hypothesis that – especially in the area of Open Government Data – openly available datasets on data portals are mostly not published as RDF or Linked Data.

Also, JSON does not appear among the top ten formats in terms of numbers of published data resources on Open Data portals. Still, we include those main formats in our discussion below, as

[12] http://opendefinition.org/ofd/, last accessed 30/03/2017.

[13] The numbers for the RDF serializations JSON-LD (8 resources) and TTL (55) are vanishingly small.

- particularly JSON and RDF play a significant role in metadata descriptions,
- JSON is the prevalent format for many Web APIs,
- RDF, as we saw, is apart from the Linked Data cloud prevalent in Web pages and crawls through its support as an annotation format by popular search engines.

In the following we introduce some of these popular, well known, data formats on the Web and categorize them by their structure, namely, graph-based, tree-shaped, and tabular formats.

3.1 Graph-Based Formats

RDF, W3C recommendation since 2004 [41] and "refurbished" in 2014 [19,23], was originally conceived as a metadata model language for describing resources on the web. It evolved (also through deployment) to a universal model and format to describe arbitrary relations between resources identified, typically, by URIs, such that they can be read and understood by machines.

RDF itself consists of statements in the form of *subject, predicate, object* triples. RDF triples can be displayed as graphs where the subjects and objects are nodes and the predicates are directed edges. RDF uses vocabularies to define the set of elements that can be used in an application. Vocabularies are similar to schemas for RDF datasets and can also define the domain and range of predicates. The graph in Fig. 3 represents the metadata description of the dataset in Fig. 2 in the DCAT (Data Catalog) vocabulary [48].[14]

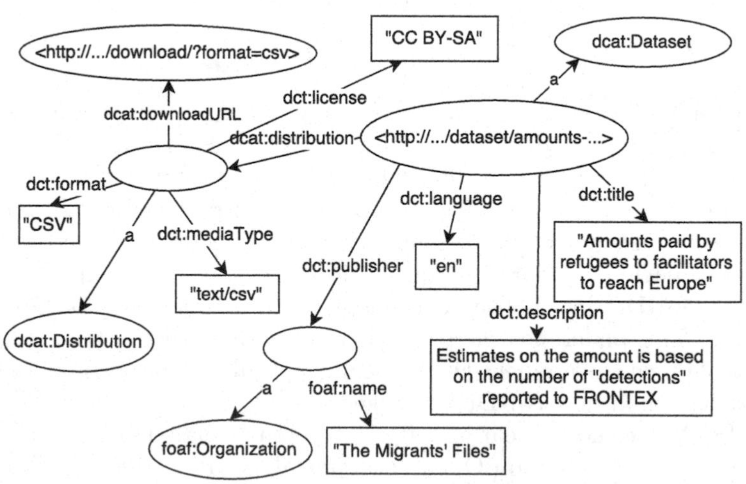

Fig. 3. RDF graph of DCAT metadata mapping of Fig. 2

[14] DCAT is a vocabulary commonly used for describing general metadata about datasets. See Sect. 5.2 for mapping and homogenization of metadata descriptions using standard vocabularies.

There exist several formats to serialize RDF data. Most prominent is RDF/XML, the XML serialization first introduced in the course of 1999 W3C specification of the RDF data model, but there are also a more readable/concise textual serialization formats such as the line-based N-Triples [21] and the "Terse RDF Language" TURTLE [10] syntax. More recent, in 2014, W3C released the first recommendation for JSON-LD [68]. JSON-LD is an extension for the JSON format (see below) mostly allowing to specify namespaces for identifiers and support of URIs (supporting Linked Data principles natively in JSON) which allows the serialization of RDF as JSON, or vice versa, the transformation of JSON as RDF: conventional JSON parser and databases can be used; users of JSON-LD which are mainly interested in conventional JSON, are not required to understand RDF and do not have to use the Linked Data additions.

3.2 Tree-Shaped Formats

The JSON file format [18] is a so-called semi-structured file format, i.e., where documents are loosely structured without a fixed schema (as for example data in relational databases) as attribute–value pairs where values can be primitive (Strings, numbers, Booleans), arrays (sequences of values enclosed in square brackets '[','], or nested JSON objects (enclosed in curly braces '{','}'), thus – essentially – providing a serialization format for tree-shaped, nested structures. For an example for JSON we refer to Fig. 2.

Initially, the JSON format was mainly intended to transmit data between servers and web applications, supported by web services and APIs. In the context of Open Data we often find JSON as a format to describe metadata but also to publish the actual data: also raw tabular data can easily be transformed into semi-structured and tree-based formats like JSON[15] and, therefore, is often used as alternative representation to access the data. On the other hand, JSON is the de facto standard for retrieving metadata from Open Data portals.

XML. For the sake of completeness, due to its long history, and also due to its still striking prevalence as a data exchange format of choice, we shall also mention some observations on XML. This prevalence is not really surprising since many industry standards and tools export and deliver XML, which is then used as the output for many legacy applications or still popular for many Web APIs, e.g., in the area of geographical information systems (e.g. KML,[16] GML,[17] WFS,[18] etc.). Likewise, XML has a large number of associated standards around it such as query, navigation, transformation and schema languages like XQuery,[19]

[15] For instance, see Converter Tools on https://project-open-data.cio.gov/, last accessed 24/03/2017.
[16] https://developers.google.com/kml/documentation/, last accessed 24/03/2017.
[17] http://www.opengeospatial.org/standards/gml, last accessed 24/03/2017.
[18] http://www.opengeospatial.org/standards/wfs, last accessed 24/03/2017.
[19] https://www.w3.org/TR/xquery-30/, last accessed 24/03/2017.

XPath,[20] XSLT[21], and XML Schema[22] which are still actively developed, supported by semi-structured database systems, and other tools. XML by itself has been subject to extensive research, for example in the fields of data exchange [4, Part III] or query languages [8]. Particularly, in the context of the Semantic Web, there have also been proposals to combine XQuery with SPARQL, cf. for instance [15,26] and references therein. The issue of interoperability between RDF and XML indeed is further discussed within the W3C in their recently started "RDF and XML Interoperability Community Group"[23] see also [16] for a summary. So, whereas JSON has probably better support in terms of developer-friendliness and recent uptake particularly through Web APIs, there is still a strong community with well-established standards behind XML technologies. For instance, schema languages or query languages for JSON exist as proposals, but their formal underpinning is still under discussion, cf. e.g. [17,63]. Another approach would be to adopt, reuse and extend XML technologies to work on JSON itself, as for instance proposed in [26]. On an abstract level, there is not much to argue about JSON and XML just being two syntactic variants for serializing arbitrary, tree-shaped data.

3.3 Tabular Data Formats

Last but not least, potentially driven also by the fact that the vast majority of Open Data on the Web originates from relational databases or simply from spreadsheets, a large part of the Web of Open Data consists of tabular data. This is illustrated by the fact that two of the most prominent formats for publishing Open Data in Table 3 cover tabular data: CSV and XLS. Note particularly that both of these formats are present on more Open Data portals than for instance XML.

While XLS (the export format of Microsoft Excel) is obviously a proprietary open format, CSV (comma-separated values) is a simple, open format with a standard specification allowing to serialize arbitrary tables as text (RFC4180) [67]. However, as we have shown in a recent analysis [54], compliance with this standard across published CSVs is not consistent: in Open Data corpus containing 200 K tabular resources with a total file size of 413 GB we found out that out of the resources in Open Data portals labelled as a tabular only 50% can be considered CSV files. In this work we also investigated different use of delimiters, the availability of (multiple) header rows or cases where single CSV files actually contain multiple tables as common problems.

Last, but not least, as opposed to tabular data in relational databases, which typically adhere to a fixed schema and constraints, these constraints, datatype information and other schema information is typically lost when being exported and re-published as CSVs. This loss can be compensated partially by adding this

[20] https://www.w3.org/TR/xpath-30/, last accessed 24/03/2017.
[21] https://www.w3.org/TR/xslt-30/, last accessed 24/03/2017.
[22] https://www.w3.org/XML/Schema, last accessed 24/03/2017.
[23] https://www.w3.org/community/rax/, last accessed 24/03/2017.

information as additional metadata to the published tables; one particular format for such kind of metadata has been recently standardized by the W3C [65]. For more details on the importance of metadata we refer also to Sect. 5 below.

3.4 Data Formats – Summary

Overall, while data formats are often only considered syntactic sugar, one should not underestimate the issues about conversions, scripts parsing errors, stability of tools, etc. where often significant amounts of work incurs. While any data can be converted/represented in principle into a CSV, XML, or RDF serialization, one should keep in mind that a canonical, "dumb" serialization in RDF by itself, does not "add" any "semantics".

For instance, a naive RDF conversion (in Turtle syntax) of the CSV in Table 2 could look as follows in Fig. 4, but would obviously not make the data more "machine-readable" or easier to process.

```
@prefix : <http://www.example.org/> .

:c1 rdfs:label "Route".
:c2 rdfs:label "Period".
:c3 rdfs:label "Ref_crossing".
:c4 rdfs:label "Total in EUR 2014".

[:c1 "Central Med"; :c2 "2010-2015", :c3 "285,700"; :c4 "3,643,000,000"].
[:c1 "East Borders"; :c2 "2010-2015"; :c3 "5,217"; :c4 "72,000,000" ].
[:c1 "East Med Land" ; :c2 "2010-2015"; :c3 "108,000" ; :c4 "1,751,000,000"].
[:c1 "East Med Sea", :c2 "2010-2015" ; :c3 "61,922"; :c4"1,053,000,000"].
[:c1 "West African"; :c2 "2010-2015"; :c3 "1,040"; :c4 "4,000,000"].
[:c1 "West Balkans"; :c2 "2010-2015"; :c3 "74,347"; :c4 "1,580,000,000"].
[:c1 "West Med"; :c2 "2010-2015"; :c3 "29,487"; :c4 "251,000,000"].
```

Fig. 4. Naive conversion of tabular data into RDF

We would leave coming up with a likewise naive (and probably useless) conversion to XML or JSON to the reader: the real intelligence in mapping such data lies in finding suitable ontologies to describe the properties representing columns c1 to c4, recognizing the datatypes of the column values, linking names such as "East Med Sea" to actual entities occurring in other datasets, etc. Still, typically, in data processing workflows more than 80% of the effort to data conversion, pre-processing and cleansing tasks.

Within the Semantic Web, or to be more precise, within the closed scope of Linked Data this problem and the steps involved have been discussed in depth in the literature [7,60]. A partial instantiation of a platform which shall provide a cleansed and integrated version of the Web of Linked Data is presented by the LOD-Laundromat [11] project: here, the authors present a cleansed unified store of Linked Data as an experimental platform for the whole Web of Linked Data, mostly containing the all datasets of the current LOD cloud, are made available. Querying this platform efficiently and investigating the properties of this subset of the Web of Data is a subject of active ongoing research, despite only Linked

RDF data has been considered: however, building such a platform for the scale of arbitrary Open Data on the Web, or even only for the data accumulated in Open Data portals would demand a solution at a much larger scale, handling more tedious cleansing, data format conversion and schema integration problems.

4 Licensing and Provenance of Data

Publishing data on the Web is more than just making it publicly accessible. When it comes to consuming publicly accessible data, it is crucial for data consumers to be able to assess the trustworthiness of the data as well as being able to use it on a secure legal basis and to know where the data is coming from, or how it has been pre-processed. As such, if data is to be published on the Web, appropriate metadata (e.g., describing the data's provenance and licensing information) should be published alongside with it, thus making published data as self-descriptive as possible (cf. [34]).

4.1 Open Data Licensing in Practice

While metadata about terms and conditions under which a dataset can be re-used are essential for its users, according to the Linked Open Data Cloud web page, only less than 8% of the linked data datesets provide license information[24].

Within Open data portals, the situation seems slightly better overall: more than 50% of the monitored datasets in the Open Data portals in the Portalwatch project (see Sect. 5 below) announce somehow in the metadata some kind of

Table 4. Top-10 licenses.

license_id	$\lvert datasets \rvert$	%	$\lvert portals \rvert$
ca-ogl-lgo	239662	32.3	1
notspecified	193043	26	71
dl-de-by-2.0	55117	7.4	7
CC-BY-4.0	49198	6.6	84
us-pd	35288	4.8	1
OGL-UK-3.0	33164	4.5	18
other-nc	27705	3.7	21
CC0-1.0	9931	1.3	36
dl-de-by-1.0	9608	1.3	6
Europ.Comm.[a]	8604	1.2	2
others	80164	10.8	

[a]http://open-data.europa.eu/kos/licence/EuropeanCommission, last accessed 24/03/2017

[24] http://lod-cloud.net/state/state_2014/#toc10, last accessed 01/05/2017.

license information [58]. The most prevalent license keys used in Open Data portals [58] are listed in Table 4.

While most of the provided license definitions lack a machine-readable description that would allow automated compatibility checks of different licenses or alike, some are not even compliant with *Open Definition* conformant data licenses (cf. Table 5).

Table 5. Open definition conformant data licenses [40]

License
Creative Commons Zero (CC0)
Creative Commons Attribution 4.0 (CC-BY-4.0)
Creative Commons Attribution Share-Alike 4.0 (CC-BY-SA-4.0)
Open Data Commons Attribution License (ODC-BY)
Open Data Commons Public Domain Dedication and Licence (ODC-PDDL)
Open Data Commons Open Database License (ODC-ODbL)

In order to circumvent these shortcomings, different RDF vocabularies have been introduced to formally describe licenses as well as provenance information of datasets, two of which (ODRL and PROV) we will briefly introduce in the next two subsections.

4.2 Making Licenses Machine-Readable

The Open Digital Rights Language (ODRL) [39] is a comprehensive policy expression language (representable with a resp. RDF vocabulary) that has been demonstrated to be suitable for expressing fine-grained access restrictions, access policies, as well as licensing information for Linked Data as shown in [20,69].

An *ODRL Policy* is composed of a set of *ODRL Rules* and an *ODRL Conflict Resolution Strategy*, which is used by the enforcement mechanism to ensure that when conflicts among rules occur, a system either grants access, denies access or generates an error in a non-ambiguous manner.

An *ODRL Rule* either permits or prohibits the execution of a certain action on an asset (e.g. the data requested by the data consumer). The scope of such rules can be further refined by explicitly specifying the party/parties that the rule applies to (e.g. Alice is allowed to access some dataset), using constraints (e.g. access is allowed until a certain date) or in case of permission rules by defining duties (e.g. a payment of 10 euros is required).

Listing 1.1 demonstrates how ODRL can be used to represent the *CreativeCommons* license `CC-BY 4.0`.

Listing 1.1. CC-BY 4.0 represented in ODRL

```
<http://purl.org/NET/rdflicense/cc-by4.0>
    a odrl:Policy ;
    rdfs:label"Creative Commons CC-BY";
    rdfs:seeAlso
      <http://creativecommons.org/licenses/by/4.0/legalcode> ;
    dct:source <http://creativecommons.org/licenses/by/4.0/> ;
    dct:hasVersion "4.0";
    dct:language <http://www.lexvo.org/page/iso639-3/eng> ;
    odrl:permission [
      odrl:action cc:Distribution,
                cc:Reproduction, cc:DerivativeWorks ;
      odrl:duty [
        odrl:action cc:Notice, cc:Attribution
      ]
    ] .
```

Policy Conflict Resolution. A rule that permits or prohibits the execution of an action on an asset could potentially affect related actions on that same asset. Explicit relationships among actions in ODRL are defined using a subsumption hierarchy, which states that an action α_1 is a broader term for action α_2 and thus might influence its permission/prohibition (cf. Fig. 5). On the other hand implicit dependencies indicate that the permission associated with an action α_1 requires another action α_2 to be permitted also. Implicit dependencies can only be identified by interpreting the natural language description of the respective *ODRL Actions* (cf. Fig. 6). As such, when it comes to the enforcement of access policies defined in ODRL, there is a need for a reasoning engine which is capable of catering for both explicit and implicit dependencies between actions.

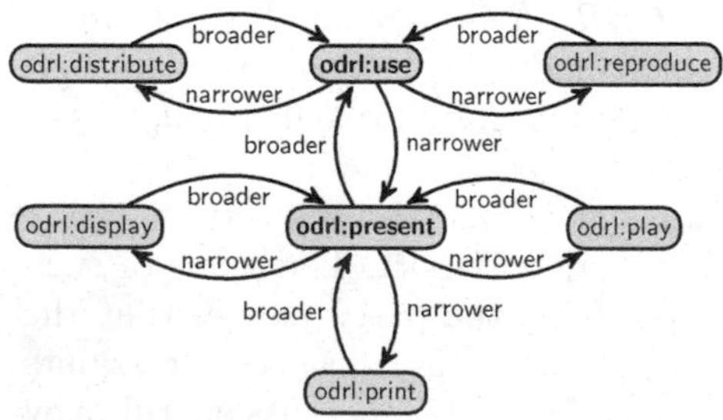

Fig. 5. Example of explicit dependencies in ODRL.

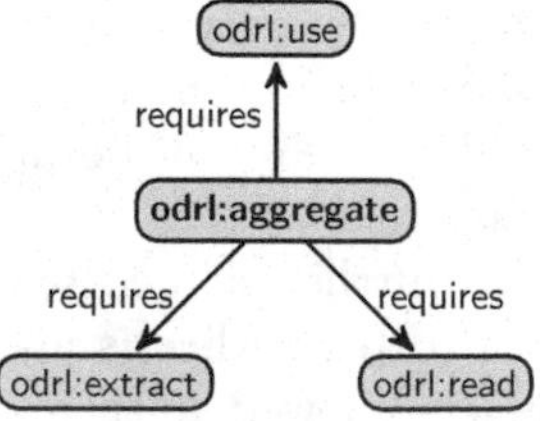

Fig. 6. Example of implicit dependencies in ODRL.

4.3 Tracking the Provenance of Data

In order to handle the unique challenges of diverse and unverified RDF data spread over RDF datasets published at different URIs by different data publishers across the Web, the inclusion of a notion of provenance is necessary. The W3C PROV Working Group [49] was chartered to address these issues and developed an RDF vocabulary to enable annotation of datasets with interchangeable provenance information. On a high level PROV distinguishes between entities, agents, and activities (see Fig. 7). A `prov:Entity` can be all kinds of things, digital or not, which are created or modified. Activities are the processes which create or modify entities. An `prov:Agent` is something or someone who is responsible for a `prov:Activity` (and indirectly also for an entity).

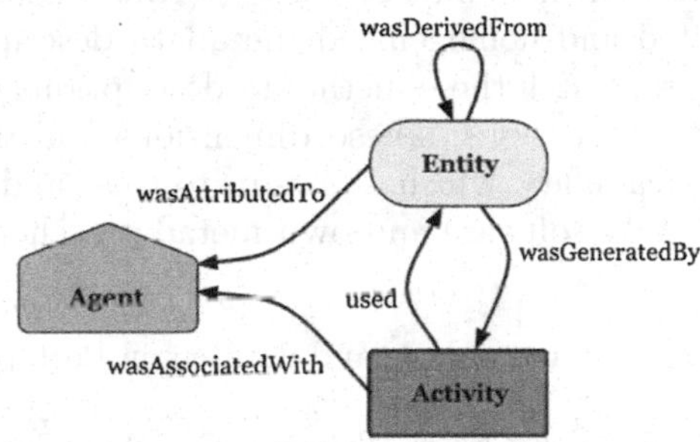

Fig. 7. The core concepts of PROV. Source: Taken from [49]

Listing 1.2 illustrates a PROV example (all other triples removed) of two observations, where observation `ex:obs123` was derived from another observation `ex:obs789` via an activity `ex:activity456` on the 1st of January 2017 at 01:01. This derivation was executed according to the rule `ex:rule937` with an agent `ex:fred` being responsible. This use of the PROV vocabulary models tracking of source observations, a timestamp, the conversion rule and the responsible agent (which could be a person or software component). The PROV vocabulary could thus be used to annotated whole datasets, or single observations (data points) within such dataset, or, respectively any derivations and aggregations made from open data sources re-published elsewhere.

Listing 1.2. PROV example

```
ex:obs123 a prov:Entity ;
   prov:generatedAtTime "2017-01-01T01:01:01"^^xsd:dateTime;
   prov:wasGeneratedBy ex:activity456 ;
   prov:wasDerivedFrom ex:obs789 .
ex:activity456 a prov:Activity;
   prov:qualifiedAssociation [
      a Association ;
      prov:wasAssociatedWith ex:fred ;
      prov:hadPlan ex:rule397 .
   ] .
```

5 Metadata Quality Issues and Vocabularies

The Open Data Portalwatch project [58] has originally been set up as a framework for monitoring and *quality assessment* of (governmental) Open Data portals, see http://data.wu.ac.at/portalwatch. It monitors data from portals using the CKAN, Socrata, and OpenDataSoft software frameworks, as well as portals providing their metadata in the DCAT RDF vocabulary.

Currently, as of the second week of 2017, the framework monitors 261 portals, which describe in total about 854 k datasets with more than 2 million distributions, i.e., download URLs (cf. Table 6). As we monitor and crawl the metadata of these portals in a weekly fashion, we can use the gathered insights in two ways to enrich the crawled metadata of these portals: namely, (i) we publish and serve the integrated and homogenized metadata descriptions in a weekly, versioned manner, (ii) we enrich these metadata descriptions by assessed quality measures along several dimensions. These dimensions and metrics are defined on top of the DCAT vocabulary, which allows us to treat and assess the content independent of the portal's software and own metadata schema.

Table 6. Monitored portals and datasets in Portalwatch

	Total	CKAN	Socrata	OpenDataSoft	DCAT
Portals	261	149	99	11	2
Datasets	854,013	767,364	81,268	3,340	2,041
URLs	2,057,924	1,964,971	104,298	12,398	6,092

The quality assessment is performed along the following dimensions: (i) The *existence* dimension consists of metrics checking for important information, e.g., if there is contact information in the metadata. (ii) The metrics of the *conformance* dimension check if the available information adheres to a certain format, e.g., if the contact information is a valid email address. (iii) The *open data* dimension's metrics test if the specified format and license information is suitable to classify a dataset as open. The formalization of all quality metrics currently assessed on the Portalwatch platform and implementation details can be found in [58].

5.1 Heterogeneous Metadata Descriptions

Different Open Data portals use different metadata keys to describe the datasets they host, mostly dependent on the software framework under which the portal runs: while the schema for metadata descriptions on Socrata and OpenDataSoft portals are fixed and predefined (they use their own vocabulary and metadata keys), CKAN provides a higher flexibility in terms of own, per portal, metadata schema and vocabulary. Thus, overall, the metadata that can be gathered from Open Data Portals show a high degree of heterogeneity.

In order to provide the metadata in a standard vocabulary, there exists a CKAN-to-DCAT extension for the CKAN software that defines mappings for datasets and their resources to the corresponding DCAT classes `dcat:Dataset` and `dcat:Distribution` and offers it via the CKAN API. However, in general it cannot be assumed that this extension is deployed for all CKAN portals: we were able to retrieve the DCAT descriptions of datasets for 93 of the 149 active CKAN portals monitored by Portalwatch [59].

Also, the CKAN software allows portal providers to include additional metadata fields in the metadata schema. When retrieving the metadata description for a dataset via the CKAN API, these keys are included in the resulting JSON. However, it is neither guaranteed that the CKAN-to-DCAT conversion of the CKAN metadata contains these extra fields, nor that these extra fields, if exported, are available in a standardized way.

We analysed the metadata of 749 k datasets over all 149 CKAN portals and extracted a total of 3746 distinct extra metadata fields [59]. Table 7 lists the most frequently used fields sorted by the number of portals they appear in; most frequent `spatial` in 29 portals. Most of these cross-portal extra keys are generated by widely used CKAN extensions. The keys in Table 7 are all generated by the harvesting[25] and spatial extension.[26]

We manually selected mappings for the most frequent extra keys if they are not already included in the mapping; the selected properties are listed in the "DCAT key" column in Table 7 and are included in the homogenized, re-exposed, metadata descriptions, cf. Sect. 5.2. In case of an ? cell, we were not able to choose an appropriate DCAT core property.

Table 7. Most frequent extra keys

Extra key	Portals	Datasets	Mapping
spatial	29	315,652	dct:spatial
harvest_object_id	29	514,489	?
harvest_source_id	28	486,388	?
harvest_source_title	28	486,287	?
guid	21	276,144	dct:identifier
contact-email	17	272,208	dcat:contactPoint
spatial-reference-system	16	263,012	?
metadata-date	15	265,373	dct:issued

[25] http://extensions.ckan.org/extension/harvest/, last accessed 24/03/2017.
[26] http://docs.ckan.org/projects/ckanext-spatial/en/latest/, last accessed 24/03/2017.

5.2 Homogenizing Metadata Using DCAT and Other Metadata Vocabularies

The W3C identified the issue of heterogeneous metadata schemas across the data portals, and proposed an RDF vocabulary to solve this issue: The metadata standard DCAT [48] (Data Catalog Vocabulary) describes data catalogs and corresponding datasets. It models the datasets and their distributions (published data in different formats) and re-uses various existing vocabularies such as Dublin Core terms [75], and the SKOS [52] vocabulary.

The recent DCAT application profile for data portals in Europe (DCAT-AP)[27] extends the DCAT core vocabulary and aims towards the integration of datasets from different European data portals. In its current version (v1.1) it extends the existing DCAT schema by a set of additional properties. DCAT-AP allows to specify the version and the period of time of a dataset. Further, it classifies certain predicates as "optional", "recommended" or "mandatory". For instance, in DCAT-AP it is mandatory for a `dcat:Distribution` to hold a `dcat:accessURL`.

An earlier approach, in 2011, is the VoID vocabulary [3] published by W3C as an Interest Group Note. VoID – the Vocabulary for Interlinked Datasets – is an RDF schema for describing metadata about linked datasets: it has been developed specifically for data in RDF representation and is therefore complementary to the DCAT model and not fully suitable to model metadata on Open Data portals (which usually host resources in various formats) in general.

In 2011 Fürber and Hepp [32] proposed an ontology for data quality management that allows the formulation of data quality, cleansing rules, a classification of data quality problems and the computation of data quality scores. The classes and properties of this ontology include concrete data quality dimensions (e.g., completeness and accuracy) and concrete data cleansing rules (such as whitespace removal) and provides a total of about 50 classes and 50 properties. The ontology allows a detailed modelling of data quality management systems, and might be partially applicable and useful in our system and to our data. However, in the Open Data Portalwatch we decided to follow the W3C Data on the Web Best Practices and use the more lightweight Data Quality Vocabulary for describing the quality assessment dimensions and steps.

More recently, in 2015 Assaf et al. [5] propose HDL, an harmonized dataset model. HDL is mainly based on a set of frequent CKAN keys. On this basis, the authors define mappings from other metadata schemas, including Socrata, DCAT and Schema.org.

Metadata mapping by the Open Data Portalwatch framework. In order to offer the harvested datasets in the Portalwatch project in a homogenized and standardised way, we implemented a system that re-exposes data extracted from Open Data portal APIs such as CKAN [59]: the output formats include a subset

[27] https://joinup.ec.europa.eu/asset/dcat_application_profile/description, last accessed 24/03/2017.

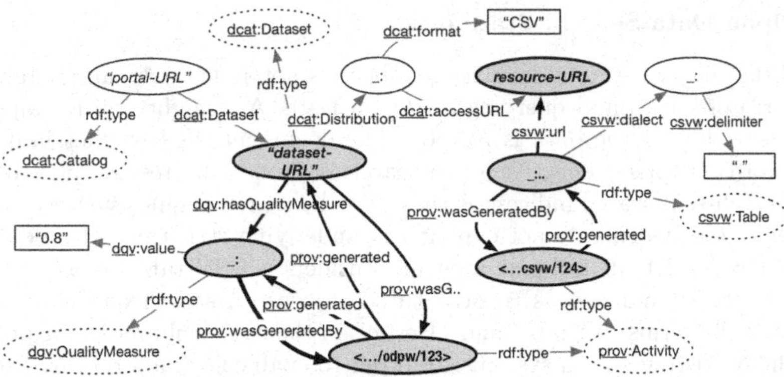

Fig. 8. The mapped DCAT dataset is further enriched by three additional datasets (indicated by the bold edges): (i) each DCAT dataset is associated to a set of quality measurements; (ii) there is additional provenance information available for the generated RDF graph; (iii) in case the corresponding distribution is a table we generated CSV specific metadata such as the delimiter and the column headers.

of W3C's DCAT with extensions and `Schema.org`'s Dataset-oriented vocabulary.[28] We enrich the integrated metadata by the quality measurements of the Portalwatch framework available as RDF data using the Data Quality Vocabulary[29] (DQV). To further describe tabular data in our dataset corpus we use simple heuristics to generate additional metadata using the vocabulary defined by the W3C CSV on the Web working group [65], which we likewise add to our enriched metadata. We use the PROV ontology (cf. Sect. 4.3) to record and annotate the provenance of our generated/published data (which is partially generated by using heuristics). The example graph in Fig. 8 displays the generated data for the DCAT dataset, the quality measurements, the CSV metadata, and the provenance information.

6 Searchability and Semantic Annotation

The popular Open Data portal software frameworks (e.g., CKAN, Socrata) offer search interfaces and APIs. However, the APIs typically allow only search over the metadata descriptions of the datasets, i.e., the title, descriptions and tags, and therefore rely on complete and detailed meta-information. Nevertheless, if an user wants to find data for a specific entity this search might be not successful. For instance, a search for data about "Vienna" at the Humanitarian Data Exchange portal gives no results, even though there are relevant datasets in the portal such as "World – Population of Capital Cities".

[28] Google Research Blog entry, https://research.googleblog.com/2017/01/facilitating-discovery-of-public.html, last accessed 27/01/2017.

[29] https://www.w3.org/TR/vocab-dqv/, last accessed 24/03/2017.

6.1 Open Data Search: State of the Art

Overall, to the best of our knowledge, there is not much substantial research in the area of search and querying for Open Data. A straightforward approach to offer search over the data is to index the documents as text files into typical keyword search systems. Keyword search is already addressed and partially solved by full-text search indices, as they exist by search engines such as Google. However, these systems do not exploit the underlying structure of the dataset. For instance, a default full-text indexer considers a CSV table as a document and the cells get indexed as (unstructured) tokens. A search query for tables containing the terms "Vienna" and "Berlin" in the same column is not possible using these existing search systems. In order to enable such a structured search over the content of tables an alternative data model is required.

In a current table search prototype[30] we enable these query use-cases while utilizing existing state-of-the-art document-based search engines. We use the search engine Elasticsearch[31] and index the rows and columns of a table as separated documents, i.e., we add a new document for each column and for each row containing all values of the respective row/column. By doing so we store each single cell twice in the search system. This particular data model enables to define multi-keyword search over rows and columns. For instance, queries for which the terms "Vienna" and "Berlin" appear within the same column.

Recently, the Open Data Network project[32] addresses the searchability issue by providing a search and query answering framework on top of Socrata portals. The UI allows to start a search with a keyword and suggested matching datasets or already registered questions. However, the system relies on the existing Socrata portal ecosystem with its relevant data API[33]. This API allows to programmatically access the uploaded data and apply filters on columns and rows.

The core challenge for search & query over tabular data is to process and build an index over a large corpus of heterogeneous tables. In 2016, we assessed the table heterogeneity for over 200 k Open Data CSV files [54]. We found that a typical Open Data CSV file has less than 100 kB (the biggest with over 25 GB) and consists of 14 columns and 379 rows. An interesting observation was that ~50% of the inspected header values were composed of camel case, suggesting that the table was exported from a relation table. Regarding the data types, roughly half of the columns consists of numerical data types. As such, Open Data CSV tables have different numbers of columns and rows and column values can belong to different data types. Some of the CSV files contain multiple tables and the tables itself can be non well-formed, meaning that there exists multiple-headers or the rows with aggregated values over the previous rows.

To the best of our knowledge, the research regarding querying over thousands of heterogeneous tables is fairly sparse. One of the initial work towards search

[30] http://data.wu.ac.at/csvengine, last accessed 24/03/2017.

[31] https://www.elastic.co/products/elasticsearch, last accessed 24/03/2017.

[32] https://www.opendatanetwork.com, last accessed 24/03/2017.

[33] https://dev.socrata.com, last accessed 24/03/2017.

and query over tables was the work by Das Sarma et al. in 2012 [25]. The authors propose a system to find for a given input table a set of related Web tables. The approach relies on the assumptions that tables have an "entity" column (e.g. the player column in a table about tennis players) and introduces relatedness metrics for tables (either for joining two tables or appending one table to the other). the authors propose a set of high-level features for *grouping* tables to handle the large amount of heterogeneous tables and to reduce the search space for a given input table. Eventually, the system itself returns tables which either can be joined with the input table (via the entity column) or can be append to the input table (adding new rows).

The idea of finding related tables is also closely relate to the research of finding inclusion dependencies (IND), that are relation such as column$A \subseteq$ column$B$. A core application for these dependencies is the discovery of foreign key relations across tables, but they are also used in data integration [53] scenarios, query optimization, and schema redesign [62]. The task of finding INDs gets harder with the number of tables and columns and the scalable and efficient discovery of inclusion dependencies across several tables is a well-known challenge in database research [9,43,62]. The state of the art research combines probabilistic and exact data structures to approximate the INDs in relational datasets. The algorithm guarantees to correctly find all INDs and only adds false positives INDs with a low probability [42].

Another promising direction is the work of Liu et al. in 2014 which investigates the fundamental differences between relation data and JSON data management [46]. Consequently, the authors derive three architectural principles to facilitate a schema-less development within traditional relation database management systems. The first principle is to store JSON as JSON in the RDBMS. The second principle is to use the query language SQL as a Set-oriented Query Language rather than a Structured Query Language. The third principle is to use available partial schema-aware indexing methods but also schema agnostic indexing. While this work focuses on JSON and XML, it would be interesting to study and establish similar principles for tabular data and how this can be applied and benefit for search and querying.

Enabling search and querying over Open Data could benefit from many insights from the research around semantic search systems. The earlier semantic search systems such as Watson [24], Swoogle [27] or FalconS [22] provided search and simple querying over collections of RDF data. More advanced systems, such as SWSE [38] or Sindice.com [61] focused on indexing RDF document at web-scale. SWSE is a scalable entity lookup system operating over an integrated data, while Sindice.com provided keyword search and entity lookups using an inverted document index. Surprisingly, published research around semantic search slowed down. However, the big search engine players on the market such as Google or Bing utilise semantic search approaches to provide search over their internal knowledge graph.

6.2 Annotation, Labelling, and Integration of Tabular Data

Text-based search engines such as Elasticsearch, however, do not integrate any semantic information of the data sources and therefore do not enable search based on concepts, synonyms or related content. For instance, to enable a search for the concept "population" over a set of resources (that do not contain the string "population"), it is required that the tables (and their columns, respectively) are labelled and annotated correctly.

There exists an extensive body of research in the Semantic Web community in semantic annotation and linking of tabular data sources. The majority of these approaches [2,28,45,55,66,70,73,76] assume well-formed relational tables and try to derive semantic labels for attributes in these structured data sources (such as columns in tables) which are used to (i) map the schema of the data source to ontologies or existing semantic models or (ii) categorize the content of a data source.

Given an existing knowledge base, these approaches try to discover concepts and named entities in the table, as well as relations among them, and link them to elements and properties in the knowledge base. This typically involves finding potential candidates from the knowledge base that match particular table components (e.g., column header, or cell content) and applying inference algorithms to decide the best mappings.

However, in typical Open Data portals many data sources exist where such textual descriptions (such as column headers or cell labels) are missing or cannot be mapped straightforwardly to known concepts or properties using linguistic approaches, particularly when tables contain many numerical columns for which we cannot establish a semantic mapping in such manner. Indeed, a major part of the datasets published in Open Data portals comprise tabular data containing many numerical columns with missing or non human-readable headers (organisational identifiers, sensor codes, internal abbreviations for attributes like "population count", or geo-coding systems for areas instead of their names, e.g. for districts, etc.) [47].

Table 8. Header mapping of CSVs in open data portals

Portal	Tables	$\overline{cols}$	$\overline{num.cols}$	w/o Header	Num. H	Mapped
AT	968	13	8	154	6,482	1,323
EU	357	20	4	223	1,233	349

In [57] we verified this observation by inspecting 1200 tables collected from the European Open Data portal and the Austrian Government Open Data Portal and attempted to map the header values using the BabelNet service (http://babelnet.org): Table 8 lists our findings; an interesting observation is that the AT portal has an average number of 20 columns per table with an average of 8 numerical columns, while the EU portal has larger tables with an average of 4 out of 20 columns being numerical. Regarding the descriptiveness of possible column headers, we observed that 28% of the tables have missing header rows. Eventually, we extracted headers from 7714 out of around 10 K numerical columns and used the BabelNet service to retrieve possible mappings. We received only 1472 columns mappings to BabelNet concepts or instances, confirming our assumption that many headers in Open Data CSV files cannot easily be semantically mapped.

Therefore, we propose in [57] an approach to find and rank candidates of semantic labels and context descriptions for a given bag of numerical values, i.e., the numerical data in a certain column. To this end, we apply a hierarchical clustering over information taken from DBpedia to build a background knowledge graph of possible "semantic contexts" for bags of numerical values, over which we perform a nearest neighbour search to rank the most likely candidates. We assign different labels/contexts with different confidence values and this way our approach could potentially be combined with the previous introduced textual labelling techniques for further label refinement.

7 Conclusions, Including Further Issues and Challenges

In this chapter we gave a rough overview over the still persisting challenge of integrating and finding data on the Web. We focused on Open Data and provided some starting points for finding large amounts of nowadays available structured data, the processing of which still remains a major challenge: on the one hand, because the introduction of Semantic Web Standards such as RDF and OWL did not yet find adoption and there is still a large variety in terms of formats to publish structured data on the Web. On the other hand, even the use of such standard formats alone would not alleviate the issue of findability of said data. Proper search and indexing techniques for structured data and its metadata need to be devised. Moreover, metadata needs to be self-descriptive, that is, it needs to not only describe what published datasets contain, but also how the data was generated (provenance) or under which terms it can be used (licenses). Overall, one could say that despite the increased availability of data on the Web, (i) there are still a number of challenges to be solved before we can call it a Semantic Web, and (ii) one often needs to be ready to manually pre-process and align data before automated reasoning techniques can be applied. Projects such as the Open Data Portalwatch, a monitoring framework for Open Data portals worldwide, from which most of our insights presented in this paper were derived, are just a starting point in the direction of making this Web of data machine-processable: there is a number of aspects that we did *not* cover herein, such as monitoring the evolution of datasets, archiving such evolving data, or querying Web data over time, cf. [31] for some initial research on this topic. Nor did we discuss attempts to reason over Web data "in the wild" using OWL and RDFS, which we had investigated on the narrower scope of Linked Data some years ago [64], but which will impose far more challenges when taking into account the vast amounts of data not yet linked to the so called Linked Data cloud, but available through Open Data Portals. Lastly, another major issue we did not discuss in depth is multi-linguality: data (content) as well as metadata associated with Open Data is published in different languages with different language descriptions and thereby a lot of "Open" information is only accessible to speakers of the respective languages, leave aside impossible to integrate for machines: still recent progress in machine translation or multi-lingual Linked Data corpora like Babelnet [56] could contribute to solving this puzzle.

You will find further starting points in these directions in the present volume, or also previous editions of the Reasoning Web summer school. We hope these starting points serve as an inspiration for further research on making machines understand openly available data on the Web and thus bringing us closer to the original vision of the Semantic Web, an ongoing journey.

Acknowledgements. The work presented in this paper has been supported by the Austrian Research Promotion Agency (FFG) under the projects ADEQUATe (grant no. 849982) and DALICC (grant no. 855396).

References

1. Abele, A., McCrae, J.P., Buitelaar, P., Jentzsch, A., Cyganiak, R.: Linking open data cloud diagram 2017 (2017)
2. Adelfio, M.D., Samet, H.: Schema extraction for tabular data on the web. Proc. VLDB Endow. **6**(6), 421–432 (2013)
3. Alexander, K., Cyganiak, R., Hausenblas, M., Zhao, J.: Describing linked datasets with the VoID Vocabulary, March 2011. https://www.w3.org/TR/void/
4. Arenas, M., Barceló, P., Libkin, L., Murlak, F.: Foundations of Data Exchange. Cambridge University Press, New York (2014)
5. Assaf, A., Troncy, R., Senart, A.: HDL - towards a harmonized dataset model for open data portals. In: PROFILES 2015, 2nd International Workshop on Dataset Profiling & Federated Search for Linked Data, Main conference ESWC15, 31 May-4, Portoroz, Slovenia, Portoroz, Slovenia, 05 2015. CEUR-WS.org., June 2015
6. Auer, S., Bizer, C., Kobilarov, G., Lehmann, J., Cyganiak, R., Ives, Z.: DBpedia: a nucleus for a web of open data. In: Aberer, K., et al. (eds.) ASWC/ISWC - 2007. LNCS, vol. 4825, pp. 722–735. Springer, Heidelberg (2007). doi:10.1007/978-3-540-76298-0_52
7. Auer, S., Lehmann, J.: Creating knowledge out of interlinked data. Semant. Web **1**(1–2), 97–104 (2010)
8. Bailey, J., Bry, F., Furche, T., Schaffert, S.: Web and semantic web query languages: a survey. In: Eisinger, N., Małuszyński, J. (eds.) Reasoning Web. LNCS, vol. 3564, pp. 35–133. Springer, Heidelberg (2005). doi:10.1007/11526988_3
9. Bauckmann, J., Abedjan, Z., Leser, U., Müller, H., Naumann, F.: Discovering conditional inclusion dependencies. In 21st ACM International Conference on Information and Knowledge Management (CIKM 2012), Maui, HI, USA, October 29 - November 02, 2012, pp. 2094–2098 (2012)
10. Beckett, D., Berners-Lee, T., Prud'hommeaux, E., Carothers, G.: RDF 1.1 turtle: the terse RDF triple language. W3C Recommendation, February 2014. http://www.w3.org/TR/turtle/

11. Beek, W., Rietveld, L., Schlobach, S., van Harmelen, F.: LOD laundromat: why the semantic web needs centralization (even if we don't like it). IEEE Internet Comput. **20**(2), 78–81 (2016)
12. Berners-Lee, T.: Linked Data. W3C Design Issues, July 2006. http://www.w3.org/DesignIssues/LinkedData.html. Accessed 31 Mar 2017
13. Berners-Lee, T., Hendler, J., Lassila, O.: The semantic web. Sci. Am. **5**, 29–37 (2001)
14. Bernstein, A., Hendler, J., Noy, N.: The semantic web. Commun. ACM **59**(9), 35–37 (2016)
15. Bischof, S., Decker, S., Krennwallner, T., Lopes, N., Polleres, A.: Mapping between RDF and XML with XSPARQL. J. Data Semant. **1**(3), 147–185 (2012)
16. Borriello, M., Dirschl, C., Polleres, A., Ritchie, P., Salliau, F., Sasaki, F., Stoitsis, G.: From XML to RDF step by step: approaches for leveraging xml workflows with linked data. In: XML Prague 2016 - Conference Proceedings, pp. 121–138, Prague, Czech Republic, February 2016
17. Bourhis, P., Reutter, J.L., Suárez, F., Domagoj Vrgoc, J.: Data model, query languages and schema specification. CoRR, abs/1701.02221 (2017)
18. Bray, T.: The JavaScript Object Notation (JSON) Data Interchange Format. Internet Engineering Task Force (IETF) RFC 7159, March 2014
19. Brickley, D., Guha, R.V.: RDF Schema 1.1. W3C Recommendation, February 2014. http://www.w3.org/TR/rdf-schema/
20. Cabrio, E., Palmero Aprosio, A., Villata, S.: These are your rights. In: Presutti, V., d'Amato, C., Gandon, F., d'Aquin, M., Staab, S., Tordai, A. (eds.) ESWC 2014. LNCS, vol. 8465, pp. 255–269. Springer, Cham (2014). doi:10.1007/978-3-319-07443-6_18
21. Carothers, G., Seaborne, A.: RDF 1.1 N-triples: a line-based syntax for an RDF graph. W3C Recommendation, February 2014. http://www.w3.org/TR/rdf-schema/
22. Cheng, G., Ge, W., Qu, Y.: Falcons: searching and browsing entities on the semantic web. In: Proceedings of the 17th International Conference on World Wide Web (WWW 2008), pp. 1101–1102, New York, NY, USA. ACM (2008)
23. Cyganiak, R., Wood, D., Lanthaler, M., Klyne, G., Carroll, J.J., Mcbride, B.: RDF 1.1 concepts and abstract syntax. Technical report (2014)
24. d'Aquin, M., Motta, E.: Watson, more than a semantic web search engine. Semant. Web **2**(1), 55–63 (2011)
25. Sarma, A.D., Fang, L., Gupta, N., Halevy, A., Lee, H., Wu, F., Xin, R., Yu, C.: Finding related tables. In: Proceedings of the 2012 ACM SIGMOD International Conference on Management of Data, pp. 817–828. ACM (2012)
26. Dell'Aglio, D., Polleres, A., Lopes, N., Bischof, S.: Querying the web of data with XSPARQL 1.1. In: ISWC2014 Developers Workshop, vol. 1268 of CEUR Workshop Proceedings. CEUR-WS.org, October 2014
27. Ding, L., Finin, T., Joshi, A., Pan, R., Scott Cost, R., Peng, Y., Reddivari, P., Doshi, V., Sachs, J.: Swoogle: a search and metadata engine for the semantic web. In: Proceedings of the Thirteenth ACM International Conference on Information and Knowledge Management (CIKM 2004), pp. 652–659, New York, NY, USA. ACM (2004)
28. Ermilov, I., Auer, S., Stadler, C.: User-driven semantic mapping of tabular data. In: Proceedings of the 9th International Conference on Semantic Systems (I-SEMANTICS 2013), pp. 105–112, New York, NY, USA. ACM (2013)
29. European Commission. Towards a thriving data-driven economy, July 2014

30. Fernández, J.D., Martınez-Prieto, M.A., Gutiérrez, C., Polleres, A., Arias, M.: Binary RDF representation for publication and exchange (HDT). J. Web Semant. **19**(2), 22–41 (2013)
31. Fernández Garcia, J.D., Umbrich, J., Knuth, M., Polleres, A.: Evaluating query and storage strategies for RDF archives. In: 12th International Conference on Semantic Systems (SEMANTICS), ACM International Conference Proceedings Series, pp. 41–48. ACM, September 2016
32. Fürber, C., Hepp, M.: Towards a vocabulary for data quality management in semantic web architectures. In: Proceedings of the 1st International Workshop on Linked Web Data Management (LWDM 2011), pp. 1–8, New York, NY, USA. ACM (2011)
33. Harris, S., Seaborne, A.: SPARQL 1.1 Query Language. W3C Recommendation, March 2013. http://www.w3.org/TR/sparql11-query/
34. Heath, T., Bizer, C.: Linked Data: Evolving the Web into a Global Data Space. Synthesis Lectures on the Semantic Web. Morgan & Claypool Publishers, San Rafael (2011)
35. Hernández, D., Hogan, A., Krötzsch, M.: Reifying RDF: what works well with wikidata? In: Proceedings of the 11th International Workshop on Scalable Semantic Web Knowledge Base Systems Co-located with 14th International Semantic Web Conference (ISWC 2015), Bethlehem, PA, USA, October 11, 2015, pp. 32–47 (2015)
36. Hernández, D., Hogan, A., Riveros, C., Rojas, C., Zerega, E.: Querying wikidata: comparing SPARQL, relational and graph databases. In: Groth, P., et al. (eds.) ISWC 2016. LNCS, vol. 9982, pp. 88–103. Springer, Cham (2016). doi:10.1007/978-3-319-46547-0_10
37. Hitzler, P., Lehmann, J., Polleres, A.: Logics for the semantic web. In: Gabbay, D.M., Siekmann, J.H., Woods, J. (eds.) Computational Logic, vol. 9 of Handbook of the History of Logic, pp. 679–710. Elesevier, Amsterdam (2014)
38. Hogan, A., Harth, A., Umbrich, J., Kinsella, S., Polleres, A., Decker, S.: Searching and browsing linked data with SWSE: the semantic web search engine. J. Web Sem. **9**(4), 365–401 (2011)
39. Iannella, R., Villata, S.: ODRL information model. W3C Working Draft (2017). https://www.w3.org/TR/odrl-model/
40. Open Knowledge International. Open Definition Conformant Licenses, April 2017. http://opendefinition.org/licenses/. Accessed 28 Apr 2017
41. Klyne, G., Carroll, J.J.: Resource description framework (RDF): concepts and abstract syntax. Technical report (2004)
42. Kruse, S., Papenbrock, T., Dullweber, C., Finke, M., Hegner, M., Zabel, M., Zöllner, C., Naumann, F.: Fast approximate discovery of inclusion dependencies. In: Datenbanksysteme für Business, Technologie und Web (BTW 2017), 17. Fachtagung des GI-Fachbereichs, Datenbanken und Informationssysteme (DBIS), 6.-10. März 2017, Stuttgart, Germany, Proceedings, pp. 207–226 (2017)
43. Kruse, S., Papenbrock, T., Naumann, F.: Scaling out the discovery of inclusion dependencies. In: Datenbanksysteme für Business, Technologie und Web (BTW), 16. Fachtagung des GI-Fachbereichs "Datenbanken und Informationssysteme" (DBIS), 4.-6.3.2015 in Hamburg, Germany. Proceedings, pp. 445–454 (2015)
44. Lehmann, J., Isele, R., Jakob, M., Jentzsch, A., Kontokostas, D., Mendes, P.N., Hellmann, S., Morsey, M., van Kleef, P., Auer, S., et al.: DBpedia-a large-scale, multilingual knowledge base extracted from wikipedia. Semant. Web **6**(2), 167–195 (2015)
45. Limaye, G., Sarawagi, S., Chakrabarti, S.: Annotating and searching web tables using entities, types and relationships. PVLDB **3**(1), 1338–1347 (2010)

46. Liu, Z.H., Hammerschmidt, B., McMahon, D.: JSON data management: supporting schema-less development in RDBMS. In: Proceedings of the 2014 ACM SIGMOD International Conference on Management of Data (SIGMOD 2014), pp. 1247–1258, New York, NY, USA. ACM (2014)
47. Lopez, V., Kotoulas, S., Sbodio, M.L., Stephenson, M., Gkoulalas-Divanis, A., Aonghusa, P.M.: QuerioCity: a linked data platform for urban information management. In: Cudré-Mauroux, P., et al. (eds.) ISWC 2012. LNCS, vol. 7650, pp. 148–163. Springer, Heidelberg (2012). doi:10.1007/978-3-642-35173-0_10
48. Maali, F., Erickson, J.: Data Catalog Vocabulary (DCAT), January 2014. http://www.w3.org/TR/vocab-dcat/
49. McGuinness, D., Lebo, T., Sahoo, S.: The PROV Ontology (PROV-O), April 2013. http://www.w3.org/TR/prov-o/
50. Meusel, R., Petrovski, P., Bizer, C.: The WebDataCommons microdata, RDFa and microformat dataset series. In: Mika, P., et al. (eds.) ISWC 2014. LNCS, vol. 8796, pp. 277–292. Springer, Cham (2014). doi:10.1007/978-3-319-11964-9_18
51. Meusel, R., Ritze, D., Paulheim, H.: Towards more accurate statistical profiling of deployed schema.org microdata. J. Data Inf. Qual. **8**(1), 3:1–3:31 (2016)
52. Miles, A., Bechhofer, S.: Simple knowledge organization system reference. W3C Recommendation (2009)
53. Miller, R.J., Hernández, M.A., Haas, L.M., Yan, L., Howard Ho, C.T., Fagin, R., Popa, L.: The clio project: managing heterogeneity. SIGMOD Rec. **30**(1), 78–83 (2001)
54. Mitlöhner, J., Neumaier, S., Umbrich, J., Polleres, A.: Characteristics of open data CSV files. In: 2nd International Conference on Open and Big Data, Invited Paper, August 2016
55. Mulwad, V., Finin, T., Joshi, A.: Semantic message passing for generating linked data from tables. In: The Semantic Web - ISWC 2013–12th International Semantic Web Conference, Sydney, NSW, Australia, 21–25 October, 2013, Proceedings, Part I, pp. 363–378 (2013)
56. Navigli, R., Ponzetto., S.P.: Babelnet: the automatic construction, evaluation and application of a wide-coverage multilingual semantic network. Artif. Intell. **193**, 217–250 (2012)
57. Neumaier, S., Umbrich, J., Parreira, J.X., Polleres, A.: Multi-level semantic labelling of numerical values. In: Groth, P., et al. (eds.) ISWC 2016. LNCS, vol. 9981, pp. 428–445. Springer, Cham (2016). doi:10.1007/978-3-319-46523-4_26
58. Neumaier, S., Umbrich, J., Polleres, A.: Automated quality assessment of metadata across open data portals. J. Data Inf. Qual. **8**(1), 2:1–2:29 (2016)
59. Neumaier, S., Umbrich, J., Polleres, A.: Lifting data portals to the web of data. In: WWW 2017 Workshop on Linked Data on the Web (LDOW 2017), Perth, Australia, 3-7 April, 2017 (2017)
60. Auer, S., Lehmann, J., Ngonga Ngomo, A.-C.: Introduction to linked data and its lifecycle on the web. In: Polleres, A., d'Amato, C., Arenas, M., Handschuh, S., Kroner, P., Ossowski, S., Patel-Schneider, P. (eds.) Reasoning Web 2011. LNCS, vol. 6848, pp. 1–75. Springer, Heidelberg (2011). doi:10.1007/978-3-642-23032-5_1
61. Oren, E., Delbru, R., Catasta, M., Cyganiak, R., Stenzhorn, H., Tummarello, G.: Sindice.com: a document-oriented lookup index for open linked data. IJMSO **3**(1), 37–52 (2008)
62. Papenbrock, T., Kruse, S., Quiané-Ruiz, J.-A., Naumann, F.: Divide & conquer-based inclusion dependency discovery. PVLDB **8**(7), 774–785 (2015)

63. Pezoa, F., Reutter, J.L., Suárez, F., Ugarte, M., Vrgoc, D.: Foundations of JSON schema. In: Proceedings of the 25th International Conference on World Wide Web (WWW 2016), Montreal, Canada, 11–15 April, 2016, pp. 263–273 (2016)
64. Polleres, A., Hogan, A., Delbru, R., Umbrich, J.: RDFS & OWL reasoning for linked data. In: Rudolph, S., Gottlob, G., Horrocks, I., van Harmelen, F. (eds.) Reasoning Web. Semantic Technologies for Intelligent Data Access (Reasoning Web 2013), volume 8067, pp. 91–149. Springer, Mannheim (2013)
65. Pollock, R., Tennison, J., Kellogg, G., Herman, I.: Metadata vocabulary for tabular data, W3C Recommendation, December 2015. https://www.w3.org/TR/2015/REC-tabular-metadata-20151217/
66. Ramnandan, S.K., Mittal, A., Knoblock, C.A., Szekely, P.: Assigning semantic labels to data sources. In: Gandon, F., Sabou, M., Sack, H., d'Amato, C., Cudré-Mauroux, P., Zimmermann, A. (eds.) ESWC 2015. LNCS, vol. 9088, pp. 403–417. Springer, Cham (2015). doi:10.1007/978-3-319-18818-8_25
67. Shafranovich,Y.: Common Format and MIME Type for Comma-Separated Values (CSV) Files. RFC 4180 (Informational), October 2005
68. Sporny, M., Kellogg, G., Lanthaler, M.: JSON-LD 1.0A JSON-based Serialization for Linked Data, January 2014. http://www.w3.org/TR/json-ld/
69. Steyskal, S., Polleres, A.: Defining expressive access policies for linked data using the ODRL ontology 2.0. In: Proceedings of the 10th International Conference on Semantic Systems (SEMANTICS 2014) (2014)
70. Taheriyan, M., Knoblock, C.A., Szekely, P., Ambite, J.L.: A scalable approach to learn semantic models of structured sources. In: Proceedings of the 8th IEEE International Conference on Semantic Computing (ICSC 2014) (2014)
71. Tanon, T.P., Vrandecic, D., Schaffert, S., Steiner, T., Pintscher, L.: From freebase to wikidata: the great migration. In: Proceedings of the 25th International Conference on World Wide Web (WWW 2016), Montreal, Canada, 11–15 April, 2016, pp. 1419–1428 (2016)
72. The Open Data Charter. G8 open data charter and technical annex (2013)
73. Venetis, P., Halevy, A.Y., Madhavan, J., Pasca, M., Shen, W., Fei, W., Miao, G., Chung, W.: Recovering semantics of tables on the web. PVLDB **4**(9), 528–538 (2011)
74. Vrandecic, D., Krötzsch, M.: Wikidata: a free collaborative knowledgebase. Commun. ACM **57**(10), 78–85 (2014)
75. Weibel, S., Kunze, J., Lagoze, C., Wolf, M.: Dublin core metadata for resource discovery. Technical report, USA (1998)
76. Zhang, Z.: Towards efficient and effective semantic table interpretation. In: Mika, P., et al. (eds.) ISWC 2014. LNCS, vol. 8796, pp. 487–502. Springer, Cham (2014). doi:10.1007/978-3-319-11964-9_31

Ontological Query Answering over Semantic Data

Giorgos Stamou(✉) and Alexandros Chortaras

School of Electrical and Computer Engineering,
National Technical University of Athens, 15780 Zografou, Athens, Greece
gstam@cs.ntua.gr

1 Introduction

Modern information retrieval systems advance user experience on the basis of concept-based rather than keyword-based query answering. In particular, efficient user interfaces involve terminological descriptions of the domain of interest, expressed in formal knowledge representation formalisms. Ontological representation and reasoning based on Description Logics (DLs) [7,9,10] play an important role, providing expressive concept-level query languages with formal semantics and reasoning support. On the other hand, most real-life applications use huge amounts of data, consequently, efficient data storage and retrieval focuses on methodologies that take advantage of the physical storage using simple rather than sophisticated data models. Trying to combine the requirements for highly expressive queries and efficient data storage, ontology-based query answering is one of the widely used approaches, especially for web applications, involving data from different sources, in different formats [25,27,29,31,32,34].

Here, we present methods for data integration, query rewriting and query answering based on both tractable and expressive Description Logics. Specifically, we focus on semantic data representation based on relational schemas to ontology mappings, ontology-based query rewriting for tractable Description Logics and approximate query answering techniques for expressive Description Logics.

The rest of the paper is structured as follows. Section 2 presents some basics of semantic data technologies. First, relational databases are introduced as a paradigm of disk-oriented data storage that misses a vocabulary-based semantic interpretation. Then, thing descriptions that are based on terminological assertions (ABoxes) are presented as a simple way to store and access semantic data. Finally, Sect. 2 concludes with a short presentation of semantic databases that are based on relational to terminology mappings, an important technology widely used in practice, especially in cases where systems already use relational database management systems. Section 3 provides the reader with a short introduction to Description Logics and how Description Logic ontologies can be used to extend the vocabulary of data descriptions, thus providing a formal terminological data access framework. Moreover, automated ontology reasoning problems introduce the reader to ontology-based data access that is the subject of Sect. 4. Starting

G. Ianni et al. (Eds.): Reasoning Web 2017, LNCS 10370, pp. 29–63, 2017.
DOI: 10.1007/978-3-319-61033-7_2

from standard reasoning and instance retrieval problems, the main technologies of semantic data access are presented, with emphasis to optimised query rewriting in tractable fragments of web ontology languages. Finally, Sect. 5 briefly describes the current technologies and standards that enable ontology based data access methods, discussed in the previous sections, to be used in real web applications, while Sect. 6 concludes the paper.

2 Semantic Data Representation

Data access in real life applications is usually based on storage oriented technologies that focus on the efficient retrieval of information from the disks, taking advantage of the specific technological restrictions of the physical layer. Sophisticated, analytical data modelling that represents the knowledge of the domain, is usually avoided for the sake of efficiency. A typical example is the relational database management model.

Definition 1. *Let $\Delta_{\mathcal{V}}$ be a value domain and $\Delta_{\mathcal{F}}$ a name domain for subsets of the values in $\Delta_{\mathcal{V}}$. The n-tuple $\mathcal{D} = \langle \mathcal{F}_1, \mathcal{F}_2, ..., \mathcal{F}_n \rangle$ is a* data structure *defined on $\Delta_{\mathcal{V}}$; $\mathcal{F}_i \in \Delta_{\mathcal{F}}$ ($i \in \mathbb{N}_n$ (we write $\mathbb{N}_n$ for the set $\{1, 2, ..., n\}$)) are the* fields *of $\mathcal{D}$; $v = \langle v_1, v_2, ..., v_n \rangle$, with $v_i \in \Delta_{\mathcal{V}}$ ($i \in \mathbb{N}_n$), is a* record *of $\mathcal{D}$. A* database *is a tuple $\mathcal{B} = \langle \mathbf{D}, \mathcal{V} \rangle$, where $\mathbf{D} = \{\mathcal{D}_1, \mathcal{D}_2, ..., \mathcal{D}_m\}$ is a non-empty set of data structures and $\mathcal{V}$ a set of their records. We say that $\mathbf{D}$ is the* database schema *and $\mathcal{V}$ is the* data.

An expression of the form

```
SELECT fields
FROM   structures
WHERE  conditions
```

is an SQL query *against the database $\mathcal{B}$, where* structures *are elements of $\mathbf{D}$ (some $\mathcal{D}_i$),* fields *are some fields of the* structures *(some $\mathcal{F}_{ij}$) and* conditions *are conditions for the values of these* fields. *The* answer *to the SQL query is the set that contains all the* fields *value vectors of $\mathcal{V}$, that satisfy* conditions. □

Definition 1 presents a simple form of relational databases and SQL queries, covering the basic ideas. More sophisticated relational models and query languages have been introduced in the literature (see for example [2,3]).

Example 1. Table 1 summarises the database schema of an example database from the cinema domain. The schema consists of five data structures providing information for directors, movies and awards. For example, the data structure DIRECTORS, after a unique number for each record that is usually called *primary key* (here underlined), stores the name, place of birth and a short bio of a director, while her possible movies and awards are stored in the data structures DIRECTOR-OF and AWARDED-WITH, respectively.

Some data following this database schema is given in Table 2. It contains information about two directors and two movies; it is stored in different records of the database. For example, the movie 'Manhattan Murder Mystery' is described (its title is stored in the field Title of the first record of the data structure MOVIES). The movie is a 'Comedy' (see the value of the field Genre of MOVIES), its duration is 104 min (field Duration), its director is 'Woody Allen' (we join the information from the first record of DIRECTOR-OF and the field Name of the first record of DIRECTORS).

With the following SQL query q, we may find all directors of comedies.

```
SELECT DIRECTORS.Name
FROM   DIRECTORS, MOVIES, DIRECTORS-OF
WHERE  DIRECTORS.DirID = DIRECTORS-OF.DirID
       MOVIES.MovID = DIRECTORS-OF.MovID
       MOVIES.Genre = "Comedy"
```

The query involves three structures of the database, as we can see in its FROM clause, namely the DIRECTORS, the MOVIES and the DIRECTORS-OF. The query answer returns only director names, from the field DIRECTORS.Name (see the SELECT clause), however finding the correct answer set involves condition checking that needs information from the three structures (see the WHERE clause). In particular, the first two conditions ensure that the movies of all directors will be checked against the third condition. Thus, the relevant set of tuples is constructed with appropriate joins of DIRECTORS, MOVIES and DIRECTORS-OF, and then only tuples that satisfy the condition "the movie is a comedy" are selected. In this case, only M1 has M1.Genre= "Comedy", thus only D1 is "director of a comedy" and thus only D1 will be an answer of the query. Formally, we write $\mathsf{ans}(q) = \{\langle \text{WoodyAllen} \rangle\}$. □

Collecting information from the data is not always a straight-forward process. It presupposes a good understanding of the database schema and the value domains, and involves conditions that are difficult to be expressed in the query language. In some cases, a sophisticated information extraction procedure may be needed to mine semantically rich information out of semi-structured or unstructured data, stored in some of the fields of the database. For instance (in Example 1) the field ShortBio of DIRECTORS may contain useful information in an unstructured form.

The syntax of relational databases is suitable for efficient data storage, on the other hand it does not provide rich semantic information. For example, the position of a symbol in a statement (schema, record, field, value) is not informative

Table 1. Database schema for Example 1

DIRECTORS(<u>DirID</u>, Name, PlaceOfBirth, ShortBio)
MOVIES(<u>MovID</u>, Title, Year, Duration, Genre)
AWARDS(<u>AwID</u>, Type, Category)
AWARDED-WITH(DirID, AwID, Year, Type)
DIRECTOR-OF(DirID, MovID)

Table 2. Example 1 database values

DIRECTORS

DirID	Name	PlaceOfBirth	ShortBio
D1	Woody Allen	New York, USA	ex/waBio.pdf
D2	Theo Angelopoulos	Athens, Greece	ex/taCV.pdf

MOVIES

MovID	Title	Year	Duration	Genres
M1	Manhattan Murder Mystery	1993	104	Comedy
M2	Eternity and a day	1998	137	Drama

AWARDS

AwID	Type	Category
A1	BAFTA Film Award	Best Actress in a Supporting Role
A2	Cannes Film Festival	Palme d'Or

AWARDED-WITH

MovID	AwID	Year	Type
M1	A1	1995	Nomination
M2	A2	1998	Win

DIRECTOR-OF

DirID	MovID
D1	M1
D2	M2

for the nature of the entity that the specific symbol stands for (individual, concept, property, relationship, constant or datatype). An alternative of relational modelling is the object-oriented one that focus on representing *thing descriptions* in a clear syntactic form of statements classifying things to categories and describing their properties and roles (for example manhattan is a feature film, a comedy, has director 'Woody Allen' etc.). The first ingredient of this modelling is the use of an extended set of names that is clearly distinguished into three subsets, the individual, the concept and the role names. It constitutes the *vocabulary* or the *terminology* of the data representation. The second ingredient is the use of very simple syntax rules: statements *classify* individuals to concepts, based on their properties or relations to other individuals. Then, data access is based on queries that use the vocabulary to formally describe conditions and bring 'individuals that are members of a specific class'.

Definition 2. *Let* $\mathcal{L} = \langle \mathsf{IN}, \mathsf{CN}, \mathsf{RN} \rangle$ *be a* vocabulary, *i.e. mutually disjoint sets of names for individuals, concepts and roles of the world, respectively. We call* individual equality assertion *the statement* $a \approx b$, individual inequality assertion *the statement* $a \not\approx b$, concept assertion *the statement* $A(a)$ *and* role assertion *the statement* $r(a, b)$, *where* $a, b \in \mathsf{IN}$, $A \in \mathsf{CN}$ *and* $r \in \mathsf{RN}$. *A set of (equality, inequality, concept or role) assertions is called* assertion box *or simply* ABox. *The set of names involved in the assertions of an ABox* $\mathcal{A}$ *is the* signature *of* $\mathcal{A}$, *written as* $\mathsf{Sig}(\mathcal{A})$.

Let VN *be a set of* variable *names, taking values on* IN. *An* atomic query *for the ABox* $\mathcal{A}$ *is an expression of the following forms (the symbol* $|$ *is used to summarise alternatives):*

$$q = C(a) \mid r(a, b) \tag{1}$$

$$q(x) = C(x) \mid r(x, a) \mid r(a, x) \tag{2}$$

$$q(x, y) = r(x, y) \tag{3}$$

where $C \in \mathsf{CN}$, $r \in \mathsf{RN}$ $a, b \in \mathsf{IN}$, $x, y \in \mathsf{VN}$ *are concept, role, individual and variable names, respectively. We refer to the individual names involved in the query as* constants. *We refer to the set of the variables of a query* q *with* $\mathsf{var}(q)$. *In case the query has no variable (form 1), it is called* boolean.

A conjunctive query *is an expression of the form:*

$$q(\boldsymbol{x}) = \{q_1, ..., q_n\}, \tag{4}$$

where q_i, $i \in \mathbb{N}_n$ *are atomic queries.* $q(\boldsymbol{x})$ *is the* head *and* $\{q_1, ..., q_n\}$ *is the* body *of the query. We say that* $\boldsymbol{x}$ *is the* variable vector *of* q *and its elements are called* answer variables. *The set of answer variables is written as* $\mathsf{avar}(q)$. *Answer variables should be also in the body (in at least one* q_i*). The variables appear in the body of* q *and not in its head are called* free variables *(*$\mathsf{fvar}(q)$ *is the set of free variables). The free variables that appear at least twice are called* existential join variables *(the set of existential join variables is written as* $\mathsf{ejvar}(q)$*). A conjunctive query with no answer variables is called* boolean.

Example 2. [example 1 cont.] Table 3 presents an ABox representing information from the movies domain, also contained in the database example of the previous section (see Table 2). In particular, the set of assertions

$$\mathcal{A} = \{\alpha_1, \alpha_2, ..., \alpha_8\}$$

describes individuals like manhattan, woodyAllen and their properties, for example it is stated that manhattan is a Comedy (assertion α_1). The same information can be extracted from the database (the first record of the structure Movies, that has title manhattan, has the value Comedy in the field Genre). Additionally, the Abox contains information for the individual interrelationships, for example the assertion hasDirector(manhattan, woodyAllen) states that 'Woody Allen is a director of the movie 'Manhattan Murder Mystery'. It is not difficult to see that this information is also in the database, in a more complicated manner, specifically from the first record of the structure DIRECTOR-OF we find the keys and then we get the names from the structures DIRECTORS and MOVIES. Suppose now that we would like to find all directors of comedies (the same query as in Example 1), from the information of ABox. The conjunctive query

$$q(x) = \{\mathsf{Director}(x), \mathsf{isDirector}(x, y), \mathsf{Comedy}(y)\}, \tag{5}$$

uses the ABox signature, in particular the concepts Director, Comedy and the role isDirector. In this case, x is an answer variable and y a free variable, specifically an existential one. Intuitively, the answer that we would get is woodyAllen, knowing the meaning of the vocabulary names. However, looking more carefully, this is not the case, since it is not explicitly stated in the ABox that woodyAllen is a director (although from assertion α_2 we can conclude that since he has directed a movie, he obviously *is* a director). In the next sections, we will see how this problem can be handled by representing domain knowledge on the basis of terminological axioms. □

Table 3. ABox of Example 2

α_1	Comedy(manhattan)
α_2	hasDirector(manhattan, woodyAllen)
α_3	FeatureFilm(manhattan)
α_4	nominatedFor(manhattan, baftaBestActressSupporting)
α_5	hasAward(eternityAndAday, cannesPalmeDor)
α_6	woodyAllen $\not\approx$ theoAngelopoulos

The development of efficient disk-oriented storage and retrieval of ABoxes has been an attractive area of research during the last years, especially in the framework of the Semantic Web. As a result, several systems, known as *triple stores* have been proposed in the literature, some of them really efficient. However, even state-of-the-art triple stores face difficulties when they try to scale to big data. Moreover, in several applications, existing systems use relational database management systems and it is difficult to swap to other technologies. Thus, some applications call for vocabulary-based, semantic information access on the one hand, with relational database storage on the other hand. This requirement can be achieved with *semantic databases*, that need to connect the terms of vocabularies with the information stored in the database.

Consider the first record of the structure MOVIES in Table 2, that stores the fact that the movie with ID M1 and title 'Manhattan Murder Mystery' is an instance of the concept Comedy (defined in the vocabulary). The same information is given in the ABox of Table 3 (assertion α_1):

$$\mathsf{Comedy}(\mathsf{manhattan}). \tag{6}$$

In order to represent the same information by simply connecting the individual described in the database with the term Comedy, we need to first *identify* individuals that are described in the structure MOVIES and then *filter* only those individuals that are instances of the class Comedy.

Definition 3. *Let $\mathcal{B}$ be a database and $\mathcal{F}$ the set of fields of all structures of $\mathcal{B}$. An* object identifier *is a function* id *of any order $n \leq |\mathcal{F}|$ defined as:*

$$\mathsf{id}(v_1, v_2, ...v_n) = a, \tag{7}$$

where v_1*,* v_2*,...,*v_n *values form n fields of* $\mathcal{F}$ *and* $a \in \mathsf{IN}$ *an individual name.*

Similarly, a concept classifier *is a function* ccl *of order* $m \leq |\mathcal{F}|$ *defined as:*

$$\mathsf{ccl}(v_1, v_2, ...v_m) = C, \tag{8}$$

where v_1*,* v_2*,...,*v_m *form m fields of* $\mathcal{F}$ *and* $C \in \mathsf{CN}$ *an individual name.*

Finally, a role classifier *is a function* rcl *of order* $k \leq |\mathcal{F}|$ *defined as:*

$$\mathsf{rcl}(v_1, v_2, ...v_k) = r, \tag{9}$$

where v_1*,* v_2*,...,*v_k *form k fields of* $\mathcal{F}$ *and* $r \in \mathsf{RN}$ *an individual name.*

Definition 4. *Let* $\mathcal{B}$ *be a database and* $\mathcal{L}$ *a vocabulary, with* IN, CN *and* RN *the set of names, concepts and roles, respectively. Let also* $p(\boldsymbol{x})$ *be an SQL query for* $\mathcal{B}$*,* id, ccl *and* rcl*, individual, concept and role identifier, respectively,* $\boldsymbol{x}$ *a nonempty variable vector on* $\mathcal{V}$*, and* $q(\boldsymbol{y})$ *an instance query. An expression of the form:*

$$p(\boldsymbol{x}) \overset{(\mathsf{id},\mathsf{ccl},\mathsf{rcl})}{\rightsquigarrow} q(\boldsymbol{y}) \tag{10}$$

is a semantic mapping *from the database* $\mathcal{B}$ *to the vocabulary* $\mathcal{L}$*. A set of semantic mappings,* $\mathcal{M}$*, is a* semantic mapping box *or MBox.*

The triple $\mathcal{S} = \langle \mathcal{L}, \mathcal{B}, \mathcal{M} \rangle$ *is a* semantic database.

The intuitive meaning of the identifiers id, ccl and rcl is the following. They are used to define fresh names for individuals, concept and roles respectively, if they are not already in the vocabulary. For practical reasons, these names should be intuitive for humans (i.e. informative enough for humans to refer to the specific entity) and uniquely identify the entity. id, ccl and rcl are necessary in practice, since database IDs are not always appropriate as entity identifiers. Indeed, database IDs do not fulfil the first requirement (they are not informative for humans) and moreover, the entities described in the knowledge base are not always formally identified in the database schema (see for example the award category).

Example 3. [example 2 cont.] Following Examples 1 and 2, an identifier dir(DIRECTORS.Name) can be defined as a function of order 1, that takes as input the value of the field Name of the structure DIRECTORS (see Table 2) and gives output object names, as:

$$\mathsf{dir}(\text{Woody Allen}) = \mathsf{woodyAllen}.$$

Moreover, the function mov can be defined similarly, as a function of order 1, taking as input the title of a movie (or parts of it for simplicity reasons) to define movie names, giving at the output for example manhattan as an movie identifier for the movie 'Manhattan Murder Mystery'. If the context suggest for more information in the name to identify, the function mov could do so by concatenating the title and the first release date:

$$\mathsf{mov}(\mathsf{MOVIES.Title}, \mathsf{MOVIES.Year})$$

giving the output:

$$\mathsf{mov}(\text{Manhattan Murder Mystery}, 1993) = \mathsf{manhattanMurderMystery1993}.$$

Finally, we define the semantic mapping

$$\begin{array}{lll} m: & \mathsf{SELECT} & \mathsf{DIRECTORS.Name} \\ & \mathsf{FROM} & \mathsf{DIRECTORS, MOVIES, DIRECTORS\text{-}OF} \\ & \mathsf{WHERE} & \mathsf{DIRECTORS.DirID} = \mathsf{DIRECTORS\text{-}OF.DirID} \\ & & \mathsf{MOVIES.MovID} = \mathsf{DIRECTORS\text{-}OF.MovID} \\ & & \mathsf{MOVIES.Genre} = \text{“Comedy”} \\ & \mapsto & \mathsf{DirectorOfComedy}(\mathsf{dir}(x)), \end{array} \tag{11}$$

that maps to the concept DirectorOfComedy. In this case, we can get the assertion

$$\mathsf{DirectorOfComedy}(\mathsf{woodyAllen}),$$

since Woody Allen is the only answer to the SQL query of the mapping (11). □

Definition 4 presents a simple form of semantic mappings. More general mapping frameworks, especially mapping relational databases to terminologies have been studied in the literature, especially in the framework of data integration [4–6].

3 Ontological Data Descriptions

Information retrieval using vocabularies and semantic data forms a basis for user friendly systems, however it does not meet *all* user requirements. Users sometimes expect that the system will employ logical procedures during the retrieval process in order to be more precise and effective. For example, users expect that ‘directors’ should be answers to a query that asks for ‘creators’, simply because ‘all directors are creators’. Formal knowledge representation can be very helpful within this context, enriching the vocabularies with additional terms (not directly mapped to the data, but connected with other entities that are mapped), and expressing the restrictions of the domain that are helpful during the data retrieval process. Ontologies expressed in Description Logics play an important role here, as a rich terminological knowledge representation framework, supported by efficient automated reasoning services [7–12].

Definition 5. *Let* IN, CN *and* RN *be mutually disjoint sets of individual, concept and role names, respectively.*

A role $r \in \mathsf{RN}$ *is a* named role expression *or* atomic role. *Let* r, s *be atomic roles. The expressions* r^-, $r \circ s$, *recursively defined using the* role constructors $^-$ (inverse role constructor) *and* $\circ$ (role composition constructor), *are* role expressions *or* complex roles *or simply* roles. *Moreover, we use the symbol* U *for the* universal role.

A concept $C \in \mathsf{CN}$ *is a* named concept expression *or* atomic concept. *Let C, D be atomic concepts, r an atomic role, a an individual name and n a natural number. The expressions* $\neg C$, $C \sqcap D$, $C \sqcup D$, $\exists r.C$, $\forall r.C$, $\geq nr.C$, $\leq nr.C$, $\{a\}$, *recursively defined using the* concept constructors $\neg$ (negation), $\sqcap$ (conjunction), $\sqcup$ (disjunction), $\exists$ (existential), $\forall$ (universal), $\geq n$ (at-least number restrictions), $\leq n$ (at-most number restrictions), $\{\}$ (nominal), *are called* concept expressions *or* complex concepts *or simply* concepts. *Moreover,* $\top$ *(named* Top*) and* $\bot$ *(named* Bottom*) are concepts. Finally,* Self *can be used in expressions of the form* $\exists r.\mathsf{Self}$.

An expression of the form $C \sqsubseteq D$ $(C \equiv D)$ *is a* concept subsumption axiom *(*concept equivalence axiom). *Similarly, an expression of the form* $r \sqsubseteq s$ $(r \equiv s)$ *is a* role subsumption axiom (role equivalence axiom).

A set of concept or role subsumption or equivalence axioms is a terminological box *or TBox or* ontology. *The individual, concept and role names used in the axioms of a TBox $\mathcal{T}$ is the* signature *of $\mathcal{T}$, written as* $\mathsf{Sig}(\mathcal{T})$.

The tuple $\mathcal{K} = \langle \mathcal{T}, \mathcal{A} \rangle$, *where $\mathcal{T}$ is a TBox and $\mathcal{A}$ an ABox, with* $\mathsf{Sig}(\mathcal{T}), \mathsf{Sig}(\mathcal{A}) \subseteq \mathsf{IN} \cup \mathsf{CN} \cup \mathsf{RN}$ *is a* knowledge base *or simply* knowledge, *with* signature $\mathsf{Sig}(\mathcal{K}) = \mathsf{Sig}(\mathcal{T}) \cup \mathsf{Sig}(\mathcal{A})$.

Example 4. The set of axioms $\mathcal{T} = \{\tau_1, \tau_2, ..., \tau_{13}\}$, where

τ_1. $\mathsf{Director} \sqsubseteq \mathsf{Creator}$,
τ_2. $\mathsf{Movie} \equiv \mathsf{Film}$,
τ_3. $\mathsf{Director} \sqcap \mathsf{Movie} \sqsubseteq \bot$,
τ_4. $\mathsf{Movie} \equiv \mathsf{ShortFilm} \sqcup \mathsf{FeatureFilm}$,
τ_5. $\mathsf{FeatureFilm} \equiv \mathsf{Film} \sqcap \mathsf{LongFilm}$,
τ_6. $\mathsf{FeatureFilm} \equiv \mathsf{Film} \sqcap \neg\mathsf{ShortFilm}$,
τ_7. $\mathsf{Director} \equiv \exists \mathsf{isDirector}.\mathsf{Movie}$,
τ_8. $\mathsf{Movie} \sqsubseteq \forall \mathsf{hasDirector}.\mathsf{Director}$,
τ_9. $\mathsf{MultiAwardWinning} \equiv \geq 3 \mathsf{hasAward}.\mathsf{MajorAward}$,
τ_{10}. $\top \sqsubseteq \forall \mathsf{hasDirector}.\mathsf{Director}$,
τ_{11}. $\mathsf{hasDirector} \sqsubseteq \mathsf{hasCreator}$,
τ_{12}. $\mathsf{isDirector} \equiv \mathsf{hasDirector}^{-}$,
τ_{13}. $\mathsf{hasCollaboration} \sqsubseteq \mathsf{isDirector} \circ \mathsf{hasActor}$,

is a TBox, with signature

$$\begin{aligned}\mathsf{Sig}(\mathcal{T}) = \{&\mathsf{Director}, \mathsf{Creator}, \mathsf{Movie}, \mathsf{Film}, \mathsf{ShortFilm}, \mathsf{FeatureFilm},\\ &\mathsf{LongFilm}, \mathsf{MultiAwardWinning}, \mathsf{MajorAward},\\ &\mathsf{isDirector}, \mathsf{hasDirector}, \mathsf{hasAward}, \mathsf{hasCreator},\\ &\mathsf{hasCollaboration}, \mathsf{hasActor}, \mathsf{hasRunningTime}\}.\end{aligned}$$

Axioms τ_1, τ_3, τ_8 and τ_{10} are concept inclusion axioms, τ_2, τ_4–τ_7 and τ_9 are concept equivalence axioms, τ_{11} and τ_{13} are role inclusion axioms and τ_{12} is a role equivalence axiom. □

Ontologies and knowledge bases are practically useful because reasoning services can extract logical entailments of their axioms, by applying simple semantic rules. For example, based on the TBox of Example 4 we can conclude using simple reasoning rules that if an individual a is director of an individual b that has actor an individual c, then a is a director, b is a movie and a has a collaboration with c. Consequences like the above, are based on formal semantics of axioms and assertions.

Definition 6. *Let $\mathcal{K} = \langle \mathcal{T}, \mathcal{A} \rangle$ be a knowledge base, with signature* $\mathsf{Sig}(\mathcal{K}) \subseteq \mathsf{IN} \cup \mathsf{CN} \cup \mathsf{RN}$, *where* IN, CN, RN *mutually disjoint sets of individual, concept and role names, respectively.* Interpretation *of the knowledge, is a tuple $\mathcal{J} = \langle \Delta^{\mathcal{I}}, \cdot^{\mathcal{I}} \rangle$, where $\Delta^{\mathcal{I}}$ a nonempty (possibly infinite) set of objects, called* domain *and $\mathcal{I}$ the* interpretation function, *that maps elements of $\mathcal{K}$ to $\Delta^{\mathcal{I}}$ structures as follows:*

- *Individuals are interpreted as elements of $\Delta^{\mathcal{I}}$, i.e. if $a \in \mathsf{IN}$, then $a^{\mathcal{I}} \in \Delta^{\mathcal{I}}$.*
- *Atomic concepts are interpreted as subsets of $\Delta^{\mathcal{I}}$, i.e. if $A \in \mathsf{CN}$, then $A^{\mathcal{I}} \subseteq \Delta^{\mathcal{I}}$.*
- *Atomic roles are interpreted as subsets of $\Delta^{\mathcal{I}} \times \Delta^{\mathcal{I}}$, i.e. if $r \in \mathsf{RN}$, then $r^{\mathcal{I}} \subseteq \Delta^{\mathcal{I}} \times \Delta^{\mathcal{I}}$.*
- *Complex roles are interpreted as subsets of $\Delta^{\mathcal{I}} \times \Delta^{\mathcal{I}}$ ($(x, y) \in \Delta^{\mathcal{I}} \times \Delta^{\mathcal{I}}$) recursively on their structure, as follows:*
  - *For every $x, y \in \Delta^{\mathcal{I}}$ it is $(x, y) \in \mathsf{U}^{\mathcal{I}}$.*
  - *$(x, y) \in (r^-)^{\mathcal{I}}$ if and only if $(y, x) \in r^{\mathcal{I}}$.*
  - *$(x, y) \in (r \circ s)^{\mathcal{I}}$ if and only if there exists $z \in \Delta^{\mathcal{I}}$ such that $(x, z) \in r^{\mathcal{I}}$ and $(z, y) \in s^{\mathcal{I}}$.*
- *Complex concepts are interpreted as subsets of $\Delta^{\mathcal{I}}$, recursively on their structure, as follows:*
  - *For every $x \in \Delta^{\mathcal{I}}$ it is $x \in \top^{\mathcal{I}}$.*
  - *There does not exist $x \in \Delta^{\mathcal{I}}$ such that $x \in \bot^{\mathcal{I}}$.*
  - *$x \in (\neg C)^{\mathcal{I}}$ if and only if $x \notin C^{\mathcal{I}}$.*
  - *$x \in (C \sqcap D)^{\mathcal{I}}$ if and only if $x \in C^{\mathcal{I}}$ and $x \in D^{\mathcal{I}}$.*
  - *$x \in (C \sqcup D)^{\mathcal{I}}$ if and only if $x \in C^{\mathcal{I}}$ or $x \in D^{\mathcal{I}}$.*
  - *$x \in (\exists r.C)^{\mathcal{I}}$ if and only if there exists $y \in \Delta^{\mathcal{I}}$, such that $(x, y) \in r^{\mathcal{I}}$ and $y \in C^{\mathcal{I}}$.*
  - *$x \in (\forall r.C)^{\mathcal{I}}$ if and only if for every $y \in \Delta^{\mathcal{I}}$ with $(x, y) \in r^{\mathcal{I}}$, it is $y \in C^{\mathcal{I}}$.*
  - *$x \in (\geq n\ r.C)^{\mathcal{I}}$ if and only if there exist at least n different elements $y_1, ..., y_n$ of $\Delta^{\mathcal{I}}$ such that $(x, y_i) \in r^{\mathcal{I}}$ and $y_i \in C^{\mathcal{I}}$, $i \in \mathbb{N}_n$.*
  - *$x \in (\leq n\ r.C)^{\mathcal{I}}$ if and only if there exist at most n different elements $y_1, ..., y_n$ of $\Delta^{\mathcal{I}}$, such that $(x, y_i) \in r^{\mathcal{I}}$ and $y_i \in C^{\mathcal{I}}$, $i \in \mathbb{N}_n$.*
  - *$x \in (\exists r.\mathsf{Self})^{\mathcal{I}}$ if and only if $(x, x) \in r^{\mathcal{I}}$.*
  - *$x \in \{a\}^{\mathcal{I}}$ if and only if $x = a^{\mathcal{I}}$.*

The interpretation $\mathcal{I}$ of the knowledge $\mathcal{K}$, satisfies*:*

- *a concept assertion $C(a)$ of $\mathcal{A}$ if and only if $a^{\mathcal{I}} \in C^{\mathcal{I}}$,*
- *a role assertion $r(a, b)$ of $\mathcal{A}$ if and only if $(a^{\mathcal{I}}, b^{\mathcal{I}}) \in r^{\mathcal{I}}$,*
- *an individual equality $a \approx b$ of $\mathcal{A}$ if and only if $a^{\mathcal{I}} = b^{\mathcal{I}}$,*
- *a concept inequality $a \not\approx b$ of $\mathcal{A}$ if and only if $a^{\mathcal{I}} \neq b^{\mathcal{I}}$.*

An interpretation $\mathcal{I}$ satisfies *an ABox $\mathcal{A}$ if and only if it satisfies all of its assertions. In this case, we say that $\mathcal{I}$ is a* model *of $\mathcal{A}$.*

An interpretation $\mathcal{I}$ of a knowledge $\mathcal{K}$, satisfies*:*

- *a concept subsumption axiom $C \sqsubseteq D$ if and only if $C^{\mathcal{I}} \subseteq D^{\mathcal{I}}$,*
- *a concept equivalence axiom $C \equiv D$ if and only if $C^{\mathcal{I}} = D^{\mathcal{I}}$,*
- *a role subsumption axiom $r \sqsubseteq s$ if and only if $r^{\mathcal{I}} \subseteq s^{\mathcal{I}}$,*
- *a role equivalence axiom $r \equiv s$ if and only if $r^{\mathcal{I}} = s^{\mathcal{I}}$.*

The interpretation $\mathcal{I}$ satisfies *the TBox $\mathcal{T}$ if and only if it satisfies all of its axioms. Then, we say that $\mathcal{I}$ is a* model *of $\mathcal{T}$. Additionally, $\mathcal{I}$ satisfies a concept C of $\mathcal{T}$, if and only if $C^{\mathcal{I}}$ is nonemply.*

Finally, the interpretation $\mathcal{I}$ satisfies *the knowledge $\mathcal{K}$ (is a* model *of $\mathcal{K}$), if and only if it is a model of both its Abox and Tbox. We say that $\mathcal{K}$ is* satisfiable *if there exists a model of $\mathcal{K}$.*

Table 4. Complex concept and role semantics

Constructor	Syntax	Semantics
Top	$\top$	$\Delta^{\mathcal{I}}$
Bottom	$\bot$	$\emptyset$
Negation	$\neg C$	$\Delta^{\mathcal{I}} \backslash C^{\mathcal{I}}$
Conjunction	$C \sqcap D$	$C^{\mathcal{I}} \cap D^{\mathcal{I}}$
Disjunction	$C \sqcup D$	$C^{\mathcal{I}} \cup D^{\mathcal{I}}$
Existential	$\exists r.C$	$\{x \mid \exists y$ such that $r(x,y)\}$
For-all	$\forall r.C$	$\{x \mid \forall y$ with $r(x,y)$ it is $C(y)\}$
At-least n	$\geq n.C$	$\{x \mid \exists y_1, ..., y_n$ with $y_i \neq y_j, r(x,y_i), i,j \in \mathbb{N}_n\}$
At-most n	$\leq n.C$	$\{x \mid \nexists y_1, ..., y_{n+1}$ with $y_i \neq y_j, r(x,y_i), i,j \in \mathbb{N}_{n+1}\}$
Reflexivity	$\exists r.\mathsf{Self}$	$\{x \mid$ it is $r(x,x)\}$
Nominals	$\{a\}$	$a^{\mathcal{I}}$
Universal role	U	$\Delta^{\mathcal{I}} \times \Delta^{\mathcal{I}}$
Inverse role	r^{-}	$\{(x,y) \mid$ it is $r(y,x)\}$
Role composition	$r \circ s$	$\{(x,y) \mid \exists z$ such that $r(x,z)$ and $s(z,y)\}$

A great advantage of DLs is that the expressive power of concept and role constructors can be used in a pay-as-you-go manner. The more expressive the language that is used in the axioms, the more difficult the problem of automated reasoning. Less expressive DLs are supported by very efficient reasoning services and are used in applications that need fast response, while more expressive ones are used in applications where sophisticated reasoning is needed. We say that the former DLs are of *low expressivity*, while the latters are *very expressive*. An example of a very expressive DL is $\mathcal{SROIQ}$ [16] underpinning the Web

Table 5. Semantics of concept and role axioms

Axiom	Syntax	Model condition
Concept assertion	$C(a)$	$a^{\mathcal{I}} \in C^{\mathcal{I}}$
Role assertion	$r(a,b)$	$(a^{\mathcal{I}}, b^{\mathcal{I}}) \in r^{\mathcal{I}}$
Individual equality	$a \approx b$	$a^{\mathcal{I}} = b^{\mathcal{I}}$
Individual inequality	$a \not\approx b$	$a^{\mathcal{I}} \neq b^{\mathcal{I}}$
Concept subsumption	$C \sqsubseteq D$	$C^{\mathcal{I}} \subseteq D^{\mathcal{I}}$
Concept equivalence	$C \equiv D$	$C^{\mathcal{I}} = D^{\mathcal{I}}$
Role subsumption	$r \sqsubseteq s$	$r^{\mathcal{I}} \subseteq s^{\mathcal{I}}$
Role equivalence	$r \equiv s$	$r^{\mathcal{I}} = s^{\mathcal{I}}$

Ontology Language (OWL 2) [56], that uses all the constructors shown in Table 4. Examples of tractable DLs underpinning some tractable fragments of OWL 2, are DL-Lite [25,26], $\mathcal{ELHI}$ [27], and the DLP [17].

Automated reasoning for DLs has been studied by many researchers over the past 20 years [9,13–15]. The work mainly focused to the development of sophisticated algorithms and optimised systems for standard reasoning problems, directly following the semantics. Finally, several systems have been implemented for DL reasoning [18–21].

Definition 7. *Let $\mathcal{K} = \langle \mathcal{A}, \mathcal{T} \rangle$ be a knowledge base with signature* $\mathsf{Sig}(\mathcal{K}) \subseteq \mathsf{IN} \cup \mathsf{CN} \cup \mathsf{RN}$, *where* IN, CN, RN *mutually disjoint sets of individual, concept and role names, respectively. Let $C \in \mathsf{CN}$, α an assertion with* $\mathsf{Sig}(\alpha) \subseteq \mathsf{Sig}(\mathcal{K})$ *and τ an axiom with* $\mathsf{Sig}(\tau) \subseteq \mathsf{Sig}(\mathcal{K})$.

- Concept satisfiability *The concept C is* satisfiable *in $\mathcal{T}$, if and only if C is satisfied in some model of $\mathcal{T}$.*
- Logical entailment of axioms *The axiom τ is a* logical entailment *of $\mathcal{T}$ (we write $\mathcal{T} \models \tau$), if and only if τ is satisfied in every model of $\mathcal{T}$.*
- ABox consistency *The ABox $\mathcal{A}$ is* consistent *w.r.t. the TBox $\mathcal{T}$, if and only if there exists a model of $\mathcal{T}$ that is also a model of $\mathcal{A}$.*
- Logical entailment of assertions *The assertion α is a* logical entailment *of $\mathcal{K}$ (we write $\mathcal{K} \models \alpha$), if and only if α is satisfied in every model of $\mathcal{K}$.*

The above problems are not independent. An algorithm solving one of them can be used to solve others, as suggested by the following proposition.

Proposition 1. *Let $\mathcal{K} = \langle \mathcal{A}, \mathcal{T} \rangle$ be a knowledge base, C, D two concepts and a an individual of $\mathcal{K}$.*

1. *C is satisfiable in $\mathcal{T}$, if and only if $\mathcal{T} \models C \sqsubseteq \bot$.*
2. *It is $\mathcal{T} \models C \sqsubseteq D$, if and only if the concept $C \sqcap \neg D$ is non-satisfiable in $\mathcal{T}$.*
3. *It is $\mathcal{K} \models C(a)$, if and only if the ABox $\mathcal{A} \cup \{\neg C(a)\}$ is inconsistent w.r.t. $\mathcal{T}$.*

4. $\mathcal{T}$ entails that C is satisfiable in $\mathcal{T}$, if and only if the ABox $\{C(b)\}$ is consistent w.r.t. the TBox $\mathcal{T}$, where b is a fresh individual name.

The reasoning problems mentioned above are useful in applications where data retrieval is based on terminological description of the domain. Among them, the problem of logical entailment of assertions is of great importance. Indeed, it is not difficult to imagine a (naive) algorithm that, given a concept $C \in \mathsf{CN}$ checks for every individual $a \in \mathsf{IN}$ whether $\mathcal{K} \models C(a)$ holds or not, thus collecting all instances of C. This is a simple way to solve a problem that is called *instance retrieval*, which is actually semantic query answering for very simple query languages (only atomic concepts or roles). In the next, we will see how this problem can be efficiently solved, depending on the DL expressivity, as well as how it can be extended to conjunctive query answering over DL terminologies.

4 Semantic Data Access

Consider a semantic database $\mathcal{S} = \langle \mathcal{L}, \mathcal{B}, \mathcal{M} \rangle$, where $\mathcal{L}$ is a vocabulary with IN, CN, RN the sets of individuals, concept and role names respectively, $\mathcal{B}$ a database, and $\mathcal{M}$ a semantic mapping box. Assume also that we have a TBox $\mathcal{T}$ with $\mathsf{sig}(\mathcal{T}) \subseteq \mathsf{IN} \cup \mathsf{CN} \cup \mathsf{RN}$ and that we pose a conjunctive query of the form

$$q(\boldsymbol{x}) = \{q_1, ..., q_n\},$$

where $q_1, ..., q_n$ are atomic queries for concepts and roles of CN and RN. Since no explicit ABox is given, intuitively, to answer this query we need to find the elements in $\mathcal{B}$ that satisfy the constrains of query q and TBox $\mathcal{T}$, according to the mappings defined in $\mathcal{M}$. Thus, implicitly we assume that we have a knowledge base $\mathcal{K} = \langle \mathcal{T}, \mathcal{A} \rangle$ with an ABox $\mathcal{A}$, implicitly encoded in $\mathcal{S}$.

For answering such conjunctive queries in practice, two different strategies have been suggested. The first approach, following the above intuition, tries to solve the problem by *converting the semantic database into a knowledge base*, i.e. by computing explicitly the missing $\mathcal{A}$ from $\mathcal{S}$ using a forward-chaining procedure. In this case, the problem of answering a query over the semantic database can be solved as an instance retrieval problem. The second approach tries to solve the problem in a backward-chaining manner by *converting the conjunctive query to an SQL query*, using the TBox and the mappings. In this case, the data retrieval problem is solved as a database access problem of answering SQL queries. Both approaches have advantages and disadvantages, have been studied extensively in the literature and have been used in several systems.

The process of converting a semantic database into a knowledge base is relatively simple. Intuitively it can be described as follows: Starting from the mappings, we execute all SQL queries contained in the mappings, and record each answer in an ABox $\mathcal{A}$, specifically generated for this purpose. This conversion can be performed efficiently, and it can be proved that it does not affect the soundness and completeness of the answering system.

The second approach is based on converting the conjunctive query, that is expressed in terms of the TBox, into an SQL query, expressed in terms of the underlying database schema. In particular, using the mappings defined in $\mathcal{M}$, we check if each atomic query of the conjunctive query q is the righthand side of some element in $\mathcal{M}$. If this is the case, then the respective SQL query is transformed, so that its SELECT part returns the identifiers of the objects of the variables of the database structure that correspond to query answer variables. To complete the construction of the final SQL query from the individual SQL queries specified in $\mathcal{M}$, we join their FROM and WHERE clauses, and add in the WHERE clause any necessary additional conditions for the joining, in the case the same variable belongs to two different atomic queries. This approach does not explicitly construct the ABox $\mathcal{A}$.

In both approaches, we will not get the full, sound and complete, solution to the semantic data retrieval problem, if we limit ourselves to retrieving simply the instances of the atomic queries (in the first case) or to answering the SQL query (in the second case). This is because, this process does not take into account the information of the axioms in the TBox $\mathcal{T}$, which encode additional knowledge both explicit and implicit. If we take into account also $\mathcal{T}$, a right answer to the query should be compatible with a model of the implicit knowledge base $\langle \mathcal{T}, \mathcal{A} \rangle$. However, unlike relational databases, a knowledge base may in general have many models. So, we can consider as right answers to the query those answers that depend only on the information contained in $\mathcal{T}$, i.e. those that are obtained by evaluating the query over a database compatible with $\mathcal{T}$, but independently of which is the actually chosen database [34]. This leads to the following definition:

Definition 8. *Let $\mathcal{K} = \langle \mathcal{T}, \mathcal{A} \rangle$ be a knowledge base and $q(\boldsymbol{x})$ a conjunctive query for the particular knowledge base, where $\boldsymbol{x}$ (of size n) are the answer variables. Let also $\mathcal{I}$ be an interpretation for knowledge base $\mathcal{K}$. An* answer *$q^{\mathcal{I}}$ to the conjunctive query q in $\mathcal{I}$ is the set of the individual vectors $\boldsymbol{a}$, of size n, for which we have that $\mathcal{I} \models q(\boldsymbol{a})$.*

A vector of individuals $\mathbf{c}$ of size n is a certain answer *to q for $\mathcal{K}$, if and only if for each model $\mathcal{I}$ of $\mathcal{K}$ we have $\mathbf{c} \in q^{\mathcal{I}}$. The set of certain answers to the conjunctive query q is denoted by $\mathsf{cert}(q, \mathcal{K})$.*

Based on the above definition, in order to solve the query answering problem, we need to find the set of certain answers to q for $\langle \mathcal{T}, \mathcal{A} \rangle$, i.e., not only the answers obtained from the ABox directly derivable from $\mathcal{S}$, but also the answers that are obtained though the assertions that are consequences of the ABox, using the axioms in TBox. Finding all these assertions is a reasoning problem, which can be solved in two ways:

The first method, called *materialization*, or *saturation* is query-independent and is performed as a data preprocessing step. In particular, it uses the TBox $\mathcal{T}$ to extend the ABox $\mathcal{A}$ that has been derived directly from $\mathcal{S}$, making thus explicit all the implicit knowledge that can be derived from $\mathcal{S}$ and $\mathcal{T}$. In this way, when answering the query, the TBox in not needed any more, since its contribution has already been recorded by extending the ABox.

The second approach, called *query rewriting*, follows a different strategy and does not modify the database. Instead, it starts from the query and extends it using the TBox, trying to encode in this extension all the implicit knowledge related with the atomic queries that appear in the query. Then, the extended query is executed against the database, without needing the TBox. Of particular practical significance are the cases where the extended query can be expressed as an SQL query, so that it can be directly executed over the underlying relational database $\mathcal{B}$.

4.1 Implicit Knowledge Materialization

In the materialization approach introduced above, the contribution of the TBox to answering a query is determined through the expansion of the ABox, i.e. through computing and recording all relevant assertions. For this process to be effective, it should be guaranteed that all of the implicit knowledge are converted to explicit knowledge. In this case, the TBox is not any more necessary for finding the certain answers to a query, and the query answering process can be performed by simply retrieving the relevant individuals from the ABox. Materialisation is very effective in some Description Logics, but impossible to be applied on others [22]. In general, materialization applies a set of rules that encode the consequences of the TBox axioms. These rules, depending on the axiom expressions, add assertions for the ABox individuals, and if necessary, add also new individuals in the ABox.

Example 5. Consider a TBox $\mathcal{T}$ that contains only the axiom

$$\tau_1.\ \mathsf{Director} \sqsubseteq \mathsf{Creator},$$

that for the database $\mathcal{B}$ of Table 2 $\mathcal{M}$ contains only the mapping

$$\begin{array}{lll} m_1\colon & \mathsf{SELECT} & \mathsf{DIRECTORS.Name} \\ & \mathsf{FROM} & \mathsf{DIRECTORS} \\ & \mapsto & \mathsf{Director}(\mathsf{dir}(x)), \end{array}$$

where dir is the object identity function, and that we want to answer the query

$$q(x) = \{\mathsf{Creator}(x)\}.$$

In order to answer q, we will first construct an ABox $\mathcal{A}$ that corresponds to the materialization of $\mathcal{B}$ using $\mathcal{M}$. This results in $\mathcal{A} = \{\alpha_1, \alpha_2\}$, where α_1 is Director(woodyAllen) and α_2 is Director(theoAngelopoulos). Next, we have to extend $\mathcal{A}$, using the axioms of $\mathcal{T}$. This results in adding to $\mathcal{A}$ the assertions α_3. Creator(woodyAllen) and α_4. Creator(theoAngelopoulos); these are the results of applying τ_1 on α_1 and α_2. In this way, the certain answers for the new knowledge base $\mathcal{K} = \langle \mathcal{T}, \mathcal{A}' \rangle$, where $\mathcal{A}' = \{\alpha_1, ..., \alpha_4\}$, are the following: $\mathsf{cert}(q) = \{\langle \mathsf{woodyAllen} \rangle, \langle \mathsf{theoAngelopoulos} \rangle\}$.

Next, assume that we add to $\mathcal{T}$ the axioms

$$\tau_2.\ \mathsf{Director} \sqsubseteq \exists \mathsf{isDirector}.\mathsf{Movie}$$
$$\tau_3.\ \mathsf{Movie} \sqsubseteq \exists \mathsf{hasDirector}.\mathsf{Director}$$

and that we want to answer the same query q. In this case, when trying to expand the initial $\mathcal{A}$, we face the following problem: When we try to apply the axiom τ_2 on woodyAllen, which according to α_1 is an instance of Director, we have to add to the knowledge a new individual, say mov1, which will be an instance of Movie and will be connected to woodyAllen through the role isDirector. Thus, the following assertions will be added: α_5. Movie(mov1) and α_6. isDirector(woodyAllen, mov1). Then we can apply the axiom τ_3 on mov1, and obtain the assertions α_7. Director(dir1) and α_8. hasDirector(mov1, dir1), after adding the new individual dir1, in a way similar to mov1. After the addition of the new assertions, we can apply axiom τ_2 on the new individual dir1. This leads to the addition of a new individual mov2 for which we will then have to apply again axiom τ_3 to add a new individual dir2, etc. Hence, the process will not terminate.

As the above example shows, materialization cannot be applied to expressive Description Logics because it does not always terminate. Problems arise also in ontology languages with disjunction, which leads to alternative ABoxes, which are difficult to handle. For these reasons, materialization can be applied more successfully to Description Logics that do not allow representation of disjunctive knowledge and in which no references to new individuals are needed. Languages that do not allow representation of disjunctive knowledge have been studied extensively within the first-order logic framework and are known as Horn Logic. Accordingly, the Description Logics exhibiting similar properties are called Horn Description Logics and play an important role in developing practical semantic retrieval systems.

In such Description Logics, the inference procedure needed to perform the materialization can be encoded in a set of inference rules: the initial ABox is saturated by repeatedly applying the rules to the available data until no fresh data are derived. Optimizations can be applied on this naive approach, so as to avoid redundant derivations. The OWL 2 RL profile is a subset of OWL 2 designed specifically to allow reasoning using such a rule-based implementation.

A rule language that is commonly used to capture the consequences of TBox axioms is *datalog* [2], which is particularly useful because it underlies deductive databases.

Definition 9. *[adapted from [2]] A* datalog rule *is an expression of the form*

$$R_1(\boldsymbol{u}_1) \leftarrow R_2(\boldsymbol{u}_2), \ldots, R_n(\boldsymbol{u}_n),$$

where $n \geq 1$, $R_1, \ldots, R_n$ are relation names and $\boldsymbol{u}_1, \ldots, \boldsymbol{u}_n$ are tuples of appropriate arities. Each variable occurring in $\boldsymbol{u}_1$ must occur in at least one of $\boldsymbol{u}_2, \ldots, \boldsymbol{u}_n$. A datalog program *is a finite set of datalog rules.*

Using datalog, the TBox is converted into a datalog program that is executed to generate the inferred assertions. There are several systems that perform rule-based reasoning and materialization over OWL 2 RL knowledge bases using datalog or other rule-based methodologies, such as Apache Jena, Oracle 11g, GraphDB (formerly OWLIM) [24] and RDFox [23].

4.2 Query Rewriting

The query rewriting approach is based on the premise that the answers to a conjunctive query are affected by the axioms of the TBox that are related in some way with the query. Since the conjunctive query is a set of atomic queries, it is obvious, as a starting point, that any axiom that involves a concept or a role that is used in the conjunctive query is related with the query. Of course, other axioms may also affect the answers to the query. Hence, if we could encode in some way in the query itself, or to an expansion of it, the way that all relevant axioms affect the answers to the query, then we could possibly ignore the TBox.

Example 6. Consider the TBox $\mathcal{T} = \{\tau_1, \tau_2, \tau_3, \tau_4\}$ where

τ_1. $\mathsf{Director} \sqsubseteq \mathsf{Creator}$,
τ_2. $\mathsf{Movie} \sqsubseteq \mathsf{Film}$,
τ_3. $\mathsf{isDirector} \sqsubseteq \mathsf{isCreator}$,
τ_4. $\mathsf{MovieDirector} \sqsubseteq \exists \mathsf{isDirector}.\mathsf{Movie}$.

First, assume that we want to answer the query $q_1(x) = \{\mathsf{Creator}(x)\}$. Since τ_1 tells us that all Directors are Creators, the axiom is relevant to the query. In order to 'encode' it into the query, we need to produce the additional query $q_{1a}(x) = \{\mathsf{Director}(x)\}$, by 'replacing' Creator with its subconcept Director, so as to guarantee that we will retrieve also the individuals that have been declared to be directors but not creators. So, we can consider as answers to the original query q_1 the answers to both q_1 and q_{1a}, i.e. the answers to the query set $Q = \{q_1, q_{1a}\}$. Given Q, we do not need to consider any more τ_1 when answering the query. The encoding of τ into q_1 gave rise to the set of conjunctive queries Q, which is called *union of conjunctive queries*.

Now, assume that we want to answer the query $q_2(x) = \{\mathsf{isCreator}(x, y), \mathsf{Film}(y)\}$. By applying the same idea, we see that now τ_2 and τ_3 are relevant to the query and we can use them to extend the initial query, to produce the queries $q_{2a}(x) = \{\mathsf{isDirector}(x, y), \mathsf{Film}(y)\}$, $q_{2b}(x) = \{\mathsf{isCreator}(x, y), \mathsf{Movie}(y)\}$ and $q_{2c}(x) = \{\mathsf{isDirector}(x, y), \mathsf{Movie}(y)\}$. Similarly to the first query, we constructed the new queries by 'replacing' the concepts and roles of the original query with their subconcepts and roles; in this case, however, we have to take also their combinations.

At this point, we note that τ_4, that tells us that a MovieDirector is a director of movies, is now also relevant to the query, and we can use it in conjunction with the query q_{2c} to obtain the additional query $q_{2d}(x) = \{\mathsf{MovieDirector}(x)\}$. In this case we did not just 'replace' a concept or role of the original query with a subconcept or subrole, but we had to combine a concept and a role into a new concept, using a TBox axiom. Thus, in this case the answers to q_2 can be obtained by answering the union of conjunctive queries $\{q_2, q_{2a}, q_{2b}, q_{2c}, q_{2d}\}$.

Building on the idea illustrated in the above example, the query rewriting approach to query answering over semantic databases is to transform the query q using the TBox $\mathcal{T}$ into a set of sentences $\mathcal{R}$, which is called *rewriting*, such that for any Abox $\mathcal{A}$ the answers to q w.r.t. $\mathcal{A}$ and $\mathcal{T}$ coincide with the answers to q w.r.t. $\mathcal{A}$ and $\mathcal{R}$ discarding $\mathcal{T}$ [25,27]. More formally [30]:

Definition 10. *Let q be a conjunctive query, and $\mathcal{T}$ a TBox. A rewriting $\mathcal{R}$ of q w.r.t. $\mathcal{T}$ is a datalog program whose rules can be partitioned into two disjoint sets $\mathcal{R}_D$ and $\mathcal{R}_q$, such that $\mathcal{R}_D$ does not mention q, $\mathcal{R}_q$ is a union of conjunctive quries with query predicate q, and where for each $\mathcal{A}$ consistent w.r.t. $\mathcal{T}$ and using only predicates from $\mathcal{T}$ we have:*

$$\mathsf{cert}(q, \mathcal{T} \cup \mathcal{A}) = \mathsf{cert}(\mathcal{R}_q, \mathcal{R}_D \cup \mathcal{A}).$$

In Example 6, the rewriting of q was a union of conjunctive queries, and $\mathcal{R}_D = \emptyset$. In this case the rewriting can be answered over a semantic database $\langle \mathcal{L}, \mathcal{B}, \mathcal{M} \rangle$ and a TBox $\mathcal{T}$, for a relational database $\mathcal{B}$, directly by using the mappings in $\mathcal{M}$ to transform the union of conjunctive queries into an SQL query that can be executed directly over $\mathcal{B}$. As the above definition states, however, in the general case the rewriting $\mathcal{R}$ is a datalog program. In this case, a scalable deductive database system capable of executing the datalog part of the rewriting is needed on top of database $\mathcal{B}$.

Most of the current query rewriting systems use resolution-based calculi to compute rewritings. In this approach, the TBox axioms are first transformed into a set of Horn clauses, which, together with the query, are then saturated using resolution to derive new clauses. (A *Horn clause* is a clause that has at most one positive literal, and hence can be written as a logic rule with one head atom).

Example 7. The axioms in the TBox of Example 6 can be transformed into the following first-order clauses:

$$\begin{aligned}
&\pi_1.\ \mathsf{Creator}(x) \leftarrow \mathsf{Director}(x),\\
&\pi_2.\ \mathsf{Film}(x) \leftarrow \mathsf{Movie}(x),\\
&\pi_3.\ \mathsf{isCreator}(x,y) \leftarrow \mathsf{isDirector}(x,y),\\
&\pi_{4a}.\ \mathsf{isDirector}(x, f(x)) \leftarrow \mathsf{MovieDirector}(x),\\
&\pi_{4b}.\ \mathsf{Movie}(f(x)) \leftarrow \mathsf{MovieDirector}(x).
\end{aligned}$$

The conjunctive query $q_2(x)$ can be rewritten as the clause

$$q_2.\ q(x) \leftarrow \mathsf{isCreator}(x,y) \wedge \mathsf{Film}(y)$$

Resolving q_2 with π_3 and π_2 we get queries q_{2a} and q_{2b}, respectively, and by resolving q_{2a} with π_2 we get q_{2c}, which in clause form is

$$q_{2c}.\ q(x) \leftarrow \mathsf{isDirector}(x,y) \wedge \mathsf{Movie}(y).$$

Proceeding and resolving q_{2c} with π_{4a} and π_{4b}, respectively, we get the clauses

$$q_{2c1}.\ q(x) \leftarrow \mathsf{MovieDirector}(x) \wedge \mathsf{Movie}(f(x))$$
$$q_{2c2}.\ q(x) \leftarrow \mathsf{isDirector}(x, f(x)) \wedge \mathsf{MovieDirector}(x)$$

Resolving either q_{2c1} with π_{4b} or q_{2c1} with π_{4a}, we get $q(x) \leftarrow \mathsf{MovieDirector}(x, y)$, i.e. query q_{2d}.

The above example illustrates some of the key ideas in using resolution-based calculi for computing query rewritings. First, in the clausification step, i.e. in the conversion of the TBox to first-order clauses, the resulting clauses may either contain function terms or be function-free. Because of this, during the resolution process, intermediate clauses containing function terms may be derived, which should not included in the rewriting; the final rewriting consists only of function-free clauses. The number of such intermediate clauses that are produced and then discarded, but are potentially necessary to derive other clauses of the output rewriting, may be large and may even contain compositions of function terms. An intermediate non function-free clause may even not contribute at all to the derivation of new function-free clauses, as would be the case in the above example for clause q_{2c1} if π_{4b} was not part of $\mathcal{T}$.

Second, the size of the rewriting may be large, since it is necessary to preform all resolution steps in order to derive all clauses that contain all possible combinations of the subconcepts and subroles that can take the place of the atomic queries in the original query. In our particular example, with two atomic queries in the original query and two subconcept/subrole axioms we obtained four conjunctive queries in the rewriting. In general, the size of the resulting rewriting may be exponentially larger than the size of the initial query and the TBox.

Third, some of the intermediate clauses and output conjunctive queries may be computed several times, through different resolution chains. In the above example, q_{2d} has been obtained twice after resolving q_{2c1} with π_{4b} and q_{2c2} with π_{4a}. This means that during the resolution process many redundant recomputations may take place that do not contribute anything to the final rewriting. This negatively affects the efficiency of the rewriting process.

Finally, the exhaustive application of the resolution rule may create long derivations of clauses that are eventually subsumed by other clauses, and hence do not need to be included in the output rewriting. E.g. if in the above example the initial query was $q(x) \leftarrow \mathsf{Film}(x) \wedge \mathsf{Movie}(x)$, the resolution process would produce $q(x) \leftarrow \mathsf{Movie}(x)$, which subsumes the initial query; a compact rewriting should include the latter, but not the initial query.

The existence of a rewriting and whether it is possible to compute a rewriting that is a pure union of conjunctive queries part depends on the expressivity of the TBox. Computing rewritings has been studied for various ontology languages, in particular for ontologies expressed in $\mathcal{ELHI}$, Horn-$\mathcal{SHIQ}$ and in the DL-Lite family of languages. The DL-Lite family of languages introduced in [25] is essentially the maximal language fragment exhibiting the desirable computational properties that allows the construction of rewritings that can be expressed as unions of conjunctive queries, and hence the direct delegation of query answering to a relational database engine. In general, for the $\mathcal{ELHI}$ and Horn-$\mathcal{SHIQ}$ languages, rewritings containing a datalog part are produced, and hence a deductive database system is needed on top of the underlying relational database.

The first algorithm for computing rewritings for the DL-Lite family was proposed in [25] and implemented in the QuOnto system, which later evolved to Presto [26] and Mastro [5]. The algorithm encodes the TBox axioms as a set of custom rewriting rules, that are applied backwards on the query, and systematically replace concepts and roles in the query by concepts and roles that imply them. QuOnto does not produce a compact rewriting; the size of the produced rewriting can be very large and include many clauses subsumed by other clauses, which do not contribute anything to the query answers. Presto avoids this problem and generates a non-recursive datalog program instead of a union of conjunctive queries as a rewriting for DL-Lite ontologies. This essentially hides the exponential size of the rewriting inside the datalog rules. Requiem [27] proposed a resolution based approach, which rewrites the initial conjunctive query to a union of conjunctive queries which is, generally, smaller in size than the rewriting produced by QuOnto because systematic subsumption checking is applied to remove redundant clauses and produce a compact rewriting. Requiem supports also $\mathcal{ELHI}$ ontologies, for which it produces datalog rewritings. Rapid [29,30], which we will discuss in detail later, carefully applies an optimized resolution-based rewriting technique only in cases that lead to the generation of useful, non-redundant conjunctive queries, avoiding in this way many query subsumption tests. Of course, although the optimization techniques reduce the size of the rewriting in many practical cases by avoiding redundancies, the size of the rewriting remains worst case exponential in the size of the original query and the Tbox. Rapid supports also $\mathcal{ELHI}$ TBoxes, for which it produces datalog rewritings. Several other practical rewriting system have been developed for DL-Lite, including Quest [28], Nyaya [35], IQAROS [36], and Ontop [37]. Query rewriting techniques have also been developed for the more expressive Horn-$\mathcal{SHIQ}$ language in the Clipper system [31].

4.3 The Rapid Query Rewriting System

Rapid is an optimized resolution-based query rewriting system, which tries to avoid or to minimize the effects of the problems inherent in the general resolution process outlined above. The general idea on which it is based is to constrain the resolution process in such a way so as to avoid the production of clauses that will later be discarded and not included in the final rewriting, either because they are non-function-free or because they are subsumed by others. Avoiding the production of such clauses early, helps to avoid redundant resolution steps later in the process. Originally it was developed to support DL-Lite$_R$ ontologies [29], subsequently it has been extended to support $\mathcal{ELHI}$ ontologies [30], and currently it is being extended for Horn-$\mathcal{SHIQ}$ ontologies.

Rapid for DL-Lite$_R$. We will start the exposition of Rapid, discussing the query rewriting algorithm for DL-Lite$_R$, a DL-Lite family language. As in any resolution-based query rewriting algorithm, the first part is the conversion of the TBox axioms to first-order clauses. Table 6 shows the axioms that are allowed in DL-Lite$_R$ and their corresponding first-order clause form, which we call DL-Lite$_R$ clauses. Note that for each occurrence of a concept of the form $\exists R.B$ in the righthand side of a concept subsumption axiom, a distinct function symbol is used in the respective clauses. Thus, the same function symbol can occur at most twice in the clausified TBox.

Table 6. DL-Lite$_R$ axioms and their translation to clauses

Axiom	Clause
$B \sqsubseteq A$	$A(x) \leftarrow B(x)$
$\exists R \sqsubseteq A$	$A(x) \leftarrow R(x,y)$
$\exists R^- \sqsubseteq A$	$A(x) \leftarrow R(y,x)$
$A \sqsubseteq \exists R.B$	$R(x,f(x)) \leftarrow A(x)$
	$B(f(x)) \leftarrow A(x)$
$A \sqsubseteq \exists R^-.B$	$R(f(x),x) \leftarrow A(x)$
	$B(f(x)) \leftarrow A(x)$
$P \sqsubseteq R$	$R(x,y) \leftarrow P(x,y)$
$P \sqsubseteq R^-$	$R(x,y) \leftarrow P(y,x)$

The core part of Rapid implements a controlled resolution-based derivation process over the clausified TBox and a given conjunctive query. The crucial difference between Rapid and other resolution-based systems, such as Requiem, is that Rapid implements the resolution step by using as main premise always the initial conjunctive query or a query derived from it, and as side premise, or premises, clauses of the original clausified TBox $\mathcal{T}$, and not clauses that are resolvents of clauses of the clausified $\mathcal{T}$ (i.e. of the saturation of the clausified $\mathcal{T}$). The obvious benefit is that the clausified TBox is much smaller than its saturation. Moreover, Rapid performs in a controlled way resolution with the clauses of the clausified TBox that contain function symbols, taking advantage of the fact that the clausified TBox contains at most two clauses with the same function symbol. Finally, Rapid never produces, as resolvents, clauses than contain function symbols.

Formally, Rapid for DL-Lite$_R$ employs the $\mathcal{I}_{lite}$ resolution-based inference system, given in the following definition (all definitions in this section are adapted from [30]):

Definition 11. *Let q be a conjunctive query. $\mathcal{I}_{lite}$ is the inference system that consists of the following inference rules:*

– *Unfolding:*

$$\frac{q \quad \mathcal{C}}{q'\sigma} \quad \textit{where}$$

1. *the side premise* $\mathcal{C}$ *is a DL-Lite*$_R$ *clause,*
2. $q'\sigma$ *is function-free resolvent of* q *and* $\mathcal{C}$*, and*
3. *if* $x \mapsto f(y) \in \sigma$*, then* $x \notin \mathsf{ejvar}(q)$*.*

– *Shrinking:*

$$\frac{q \quad \mathcal{C}_1\ [\mathcal{C}_2]}{q'\sigma} \quad \textit{where}$$

1. *the side premises* $\mathcal{C}_1$ *and the optional* $\mathcal{C}_2$ *are DL-Lite*$_R$ *clauses,*
2. $q'\sigma$ *is a function-free resolvent of* q*,* $\mathcal{C}_1$ *and* $\mathcal{C}_2$*, and*
3. *there exists some* $x \mapsto f(y) \in \sigma$ *such that* $x \in \mathsf{ejvar}(q)$*.*

The rewriting of a conjunctive query q *w.r.t to a DL-Lite*$_R$ *TBox* $\mathcal{T}$ *is the set of all the (function-free) clauses derivable from* q *and the clausified* $\mathcal{T}$ *by* $\mathcal{I}_{lite}$*.*

The unfolding rule represents standard resolution inferences with a function-free resolvent. Since this rule essentially 'replaces' an atomic query of q with a subconcept or a subrole, the resolvent has the same size with the main premise of the query (unless the replacement already exists in the main premise). Hence this rule 'unfolds' the main premise.

The shrinking rule represents a controlled resolution process involving clauses with function symbols that eventually leads to a function-free resolvent. In particular, it represents a chain of inferences $q, q_1, \ldots, q_n, q'$, where q is a function-free conjunctive query, q_1 contains a function symbol, and the subsequent inferences eliminate all occurrences of the function symbol until the function-free conjunctive query q' is obtained. Because a function symbol f can occur in at most two DL-Lite$_R$ clauses, these inferences can involve at most the two different side premises that mention f (which according to Table 6 can only be of the form $R(x, f(x)) \leftarrow B(x)$ and $A(f(x)) \leftarrow B(x)$). Furthermore, since the resolvent is function-free, the variable of the query q that has been bound to the function symbol is eventually eliminated, and since DL-Lite$_R$ clauses do not introduce new variables in their bodies, the resolvent has fewer variables than the main premise. Hence this rule 'shrinks' the main premise.

$\mathcal{I}_{lite}$ produces a union of conjunctive queries since all queries in the rewriting are clauses having the query predicate as head. It can be proved that $\mathcal{I}_{lite}$ is correct, in the sense that it terminates and that it computes indeed a rewriting for obtaining the certain answers of q.

Example 8. In Example 7, the resolution of q_2 and π_3 to derive q_{2a} is an application of the unfolding rule:

$$\frac{q(x) \leftarrow \mathsf{isCreator}(x, y) \land \mathsf{Film}(y) \quad \mathsf{isCreator}(x', y') \leftarrow \mathsf{isDirector}(x', y')}{q(x) \leftarrow \mathsf{isDirector}(x, y) \land \mathsf{Film}(y)}$$

with $\sigma = \{x' \mapsto x, y' \mapsto y\}$. Similarly we obtain q_{2b} from q_2 and π_2. The resolution of q_{2a} and π_2 to derive q_{2c} is also an application of the unfolding rule:

$$\frac{q(x) \leftarrow \mathsf{isDirector}(x,y) \wedge \mathsf{Film}(y) \quad \mathsf{Film}(x') \leftarrow \mathsf{Movie}(x')}{q(x) \leftarrow \mathsf{isDirector}(x,y) \wedge \mathsf{Movie}(y)}$$

with $\sigma = \{x' \mapsto y\}$.

Then, conjunctive query q_{2d} can be derived from q_{2c} using the shrinking rule and π_{4a} and π_{4b} as side premises:

$$\frac{q(x) \leftarrow \mathsf{isDirector}(x,y) \wedge \mathsf{Movie}(y) \qquad \begin{array}{r}\mathsf{isDirector}(x', f(x')) \leftarrow \mathsf{MovieDirector}(x')\\ \mathsf{Movie}(f(x')) \leftarrow \mathsf{MovieDirector}(x')\end{array}}{q(x) \leftarrow \mathsf{MovieDirector}(x)}$$

with $\sigma = \{y \mapsto f(x), x' \mapsto x\}$, and y is the variable that is eliminated from q_{2c}.

The application of the shrinking step on clause q_{2c} to derive directly q_{2d} corresponds to a double saving, since it does not only avoid the production of the intermediate clauses q_{2c1} and q_{2c2}, but also produces q_{2d} only once.

Although $\mathcal{I}_{lite}$ avoids many eventually unneeded resolution steps, it does not always avoid the production of redundant queries, i.e. of queries that are subsumed by others and do not need to be included in the final rewriting. Checking queries for subsumption after all queries have been generated, in order to produce an as compact rewriting as possible, is very expensive and may lead to poor rewriting times. Redundant queries can be produced by the unfolding rule because different chains of applications of the unfolding rule on different atoms of the main premise may produce the same clause. Moreover, an unfolding may replace an atom of the main premise with an atom that already exists in the main premise, hence reducing the size of the query. In such a case the resolvent subsumes all queries of greater size that are supersets of the resolvent. Finally, queries produced using the shrinking rule are likely to subsume queries produced by the unfolding rule, since they 'shrinked' queries are shorter.

To efficiently address some of the above issues, the practical implementation of Rapid does not explicitly construct the queries that should normally be produced using the unfolding rule. Instead, it computes a structure that holds all the information that is needed to construct all queries derivable by the unfolding rule from the same starting conjunctive query. After this structure has been constructed, a redundant-free set of the queries unfoldings can automatically be generated.

Definition 12. *Let $\mathcal{T}$ be a DL-Lite TBox, q a conjunctive query, and A an atom of q. Let q_A be the query having A as body and* $\mathsf{avar}(q_A) = \mathsf{var}(A) \cap \mathsf{ejvar}(q)$. *The* unfolding set *of A w.r.t. q and $\mathcal{T}$ is the set that contains all atoms that are bodies of the queries derivable from the clausified $\mathcal{T}$ and q_A using only the unfolding rule, including the atom A.*

For a query q, the unfolding sets of its atoms fully represent the queries that can be derived from q by unfolding. Indeed, all such queries can be constructed by taking all possible combinations of atoms from the respective unfolding sets. However, the unfolding sets allow the generation of the minimum number of queries that represent all unfoldings of q, i.e. the generation only of the unfoldings that are not subsumed by other unfoldings and hence are redundant. This can be done by scanning the respective unfolding sets and cross checking for the presence of identical atoms (up to variable renamings) in the unfolding sets corresponding to different atoms of the query body, while producing the set of unfoldings. This process essential performs subsumption checking in a much more efficient way because it does not check for subsumption whole clauses, but carefully recasts the problem to comparing individual atoms.

Clearly, depending on the particular TBox and query, this step can still result in an exponential number of queries in the rewriting. As in other query rewriting systems, this exponential behaviour can be hidden by producing a datalog rewriting instead of a union of conjunctive queries rewriting. Rapid provides also this option; in this case the rules of the datalog program essentially encode the non explicitly generated unfoldings.

Example 9. For query q_2 of Example 7, Rapid calculates unfolding sets for atoms $\mathsf{isCreator}(x, y)$ and $\mathsf{Film}(y)$, which are the sets $\{\mathsf{isCreator}(x, y), \mathsf{isDirector}(x, y)\}$ and $\{\mathsf{Film}(y), \mathsf{Movie}(y)\}$, respectively. These are then used to actually generate the queries q_2, q_{2a}, q_{2b} and q_{2c}. Recall from Example 6 that the rewriting of q_2 as a union of conjunctive queries is $\{q_2, q_{2a}, q_{2b}, q_{2c}, q_{2d}\}$. If we choose not to explicitly perform the unfoldings and produce a datalog program instead, the rewriting would be $\{q_2, \pi_2, \pi_3, q_{2d}\}$.

Rapid for $\mathcal{ELHI}$. Moving from the DL-Lite family of languages to the $\mathcal{ELHI}$ language, we loose the property that the rewriting can always be a union of conjunctive queries. Table 7 shows the permissible axioms in $\mathcal{ELHI}$ and their clausifications, which we call $\mathcal{ELHI}$ clauses.

Table 7. $\mathcal{ELHI}$ axioms and their translation to clauses

Axiom	Clause
$B \sqsubseteq A$	$A(x) \leftarrow B(x)$
$B \sqcap C \sqsubseteq A$	$A(x) \leftarrow B(x) \wedge C(x)$
$\exists R \sqsubseteq A$	$A(x) \leftarrow R(x, y)$
$\exists R^- \sqsubseteq A$	$A(x) \leftarrow R(y, x)$
$A \sqsubseteq \exists R.B$	$R(x, f(x)) \leftarrow A(x)$
	$B(f(x)) \leftarrow A(x)$
$A \sqsubseteq \exists R^-.B$	$R(f(x), x) \leftarrow A(x)$
	$B(f(x)) \leftarrow A(x)$
$\exists R.C \sqsubseteq A$	$A(x) \leftarrow R(x, y) \wedge C(y)$
$\exists R^-.C \sqsubseteq A$	$A(x) \leftarrow R(y, x) \wedge C(y)$
$P \sqsubseteq R$	$R(x, y) \leftarrow P(x, y)$
$P \sqsubseteq R^-$	$R(x, y) \leftarrow P(y, x)$

The essential difference with respect to DL-Lite$_R$ is the permission of axioms of the form $\exists R.C \sqsubseteq A$, whose clausification takes the form $A(x) \leftarrow R(x,y) \wedge C(y)$. The distinguishing property of such clauses, which are called RA-clauses, is that when used as side premises of an inference they can produce resolvents containing more variables than the main premise. If there is a cyclicity in the axioms, this can lead to termination problems. E.g. rewriting the query $q(x) \leftarrow A(x)$ using the clause $A(x) \leftarrow R(x,y) \wedge A(y)$, produces the queries $q(x) \leftarrow R(x,y) \wedge A(y)$, $q(x) \leftarrow R(x,y) \wedge A(y) \wedge R(y,z) \wedge A(z)$, etc. Hence, to guarantee termination, the calculus for $\mathcal{ELHI}$ should not allow RA-clauses as side premises, but still produce the clauses that are derivable by RA-clauses. It turns out that to achieve this, the restriction not to perform resolution using clauses of the TBox as main premises must be lifted.

Consider e.g. the clausified TBox c_1. $C(x) \leftarrow S(x,y) \wedge D(y)$, c_2. $S(f(x),x) \leftarrow B(x)$ and c_3. $K(x) \leftarrow S(y,x) \wedge C(y)$, and the query q_1. $q(x) \leftarrow K(x)$ (the example is adapted from [30]). By resolving c_1 with c_2 we get c_4. $C(f(x)) \leftarrow B(x) \wedge D(x)$, by resolving c_3 with c_2 we get c_5. $K(x) \leftarrow B(x) \wedge C(f(x))$, by resolving c_5 with c_4 we get c_6. $K(x) \leftarrow B(x) \wedge D(x)$, and finally by resolving q_1 with c_6 we get q_{1a}. $q(x) \leftarrow B(x) \wedge D(x)$. The crucial clause here is c_4 which is needed to derive the rewriting, but can be produced only by performing resolution on clauses of the TBox. To account for this, the Rapid calculus for $\mathcal{ELHI}$ ontologies includes a new inference rule, called function rule, which can produce clauses like c_4 from RA-clauses and clauses of the form of c_2. It also extends the unfolding and shrinking rules so as to allow also RA-clauses as main premises, in order to be able to compute, e.g. clause c_6 from c_2, c_3, and c_4. Because the function rule can produce clauses with function symbols in the head, there can now be more than two clauses mentioning the same function symbol f. Hence, the extended shrinking rule allows for arbitrary number of side premises.

Definition 13. *Let Υ be either a conjunctive query or an RA-clause. With $\mathcal{I}_{\mathcal{EL}}$ we denote the inference system consisting of the following rules:*

- *Unfolding:*

$$\frac{\Upsilon \quad C}{\Upsilon'\sigma} \text{ where}$$

1. *the side premise C is an $\mathcal{ELHI}$, non RA-clause,*
2. *$\Upsilon'\sigma$ is a function-free resolvent of Υ and C, and*
3. *if $x \mapsto f(y) \in \sigma$ then $x \notin \mathsf{ejvar}(\Upsilon)$.*

- *n-Shrinking:*

$$\frac{\Upsilon \quad C_1 \; [C_2 \; \ldots \; C_n]}{\Upsilon'\sigma} \text{ where}$$

1. *the side premises $C_1, \ldots, C_n$, $n \geq 1$ are $\mathcal{ELHI}$, non RA-clauses,*
2. *$\Upsilon'\sigma$ is a function-free resolvent of Υ and all $C_1, \ldots, C_n$ for $n \geq 1$, and*
3. *some $x \mapsto f(y) \in \sigma$ exists such that $x \in \mathsf{ejvar}(\Upsilon)$.*

– *Function:*

$$\frac{B(x) \leftarrow R(x,y) \wedge [\boldsymbol{C}(y)] \quad R(f(x),x) \leftarrow A(x)}{B(f(x)) \leftarrow A(x) \wedge [\boldsymbol{C}(x)]} \quad or$$

$$\frac{B(x) \leftarrow R(y,x) \wedge [\boldsymbol{C}(y)] \quad R(x,f(x)) \leftarrow A(x)}{B(f(x)) \leftarrow A(x) \wedge [\boldsymbol{C}(x)]}$$

where $[\boldsymbol{C}(y)]$ *denotes an optional conjunction of atoms, all with argument* y.

The rewriting of a conjunctive query q *w.r.t a* $\mathcal{ELHI}$ *TBox* $\mathcal{T}$ *is defined as the set of all function-free clauses derivable from* q *and the clausified* $\mathcal{T}$ *by* $\mathcal{I}_{\mathcal{EL}}$.

The function rule is not expected to 'fire' often in practice since it models a rather complex interaction between a clause containing $R(x, f(x))$ or $R(f(x), x)$ and an RA-clause containing the inverse $R(y, x)$, or $R(x, y)$, respectively. In practice, the application of the $\mathcal{I}_{\mathcal{EL}}$ calculus on a conjunctive query q and a TBox $\mathcal{T}$ can be performed in two steps. The first saturates $\mathcal{T}$ using $\mathcal{I}_{\mathcal{EL}}$ and only the RA-clauses as main premises. Then, the second step collects all non RA-clauses from the clausified $\mathcal{T}$ and those produced in the previous step and uses them as side premises in the unfolding and shrinking rules with main premises only query clauses.

Example 10. Consider the TBox $\mathcal{T} = \{\tau_1, \tau_2, \tau_3, \tau_4\}$ where

τ_1. $\mathsf{Director} \sqsubseteq \mathsf{Creator}$,
τ_2'. $\mathsf{Movie} \equiv \mathsf{Film}$,
τ_3. $\mathsf{isDirector} \sqsubseteq \mathsf{isCreator}$,
τ_4'. $\mathsf{MovieDirector} \equiv \exists \mathsf{isDirector}.\mathsf{Movie}$.

The difference w.r.t. the TBox of Example 6 is that τ_2 and τ_4 have been replaced by τ_2' and τ_4', respectively, where the subconcept relations have been replaced by equivalence relations. These axioms can be transformed into the following $\mathcal{ELHI}$ clauses:

π_1. $\mathsf{Creator}(x) \leftarrow \mathsf{Director}(x)$,
π_{2a}'. $\mathsf{Film}(x) \leftarrow \mathsf{Movie}(x)$,
π_{2b}'. $\mathsf{Movie}(x) \leftarrow \mathsf{Film}(x)$,
π_3. $\mathsf{isCreator}(x,y) \leftarrow \mathsf{isDirector}(x,y)$,
π_{4a}'. $\mathsf{isDirector}(x, f(x)) \leftarrow \mathsf{MovieDirector}(x)$,
π_{4b}'. $\mathsf{Movie}(f(x)) \leftarrow \mathsf{MovieDirector}(x)$
π_{4c}'. $\mathsf{MovieDirector}(x) \leftarrow \mathsf{isDirector}(x,y) \wedge \mathsf{Movie}(y)$.

Consider that we want to answer the query $q_3 = \{\mathsf{MovieDirector}(x)\}$, which in clause form is $q_3(x) \leftarrow \mathsf{MovieDirector}(x)$. To apply $\mathcal{I}_{\mathcal{EL}}$, we need to saturate first the clausified TBox using only RA-clauses as main premises. The only RA-clause is π_{4c}', for which we can apply the unfolding rule with π_{2b}' as side premise:

$$\frac{\mathsf{MovieDirector}(x) \leftarrow \mathsf{isDirector}(x,y) \wedge \mathsf{Movie}(y) \quad \mathsf{Movie}(x') \leftarrow \mathsf{Film}(x')}{\mathsf{MovieDirector}(x) \leftarrow \mathsf{isDirector}(x,y) \wedge \mathsf{Film}(y)}$$

with $\sigma = \{x' \mapsto y\}$. Let π_5 be the resulting clause. The shrinking rule is also applicable on π'_{4c} with π'_{4a} and π'_{4b}, but it produces a tautology which is immediately discarded. No other resolution is possible using RA-clauses as main premise, so we proceed by applying the rules using only query clauses as main premise. Because no rule is applicable on $q_3(x) \leftarrow \mathsf{MovieDirector}(x)$ with a non RA-clause as side premise, the final rewriting is $\{q_3, \pi'_{4c}, \pi_5\}$, where the datalog part is $\{\pi'_{4c}, \pi_5\}$. Note that if we did not perform explicitly the unfolding, we could produce the equivalent rewriting $\{q_3, \pi'_{4c}, \pi'_{2a}\}$. Note also that, since no structural circularity exists in the TBox axioms, the rewriting could also be expanded into a union of conjunctive queries. In this case, the rewriting would be $\{q_3, q_{3a}, q_{3b}\}$, where $q_{3a}(x) = \{\mathsf{isDirector}(x, y), \mathsf{Movie}(y)\}$ and $q_{3b}(x) = \{\mathsf{isDirector}(x, y), \mathsf{Film}(y)\}$.

5 Semantic Data Representation in the Web

This section provides a brief overview of the current technologies that allow the use of the techniques discussed in the previous sections in real applications, in particular the construction of functional knowledge bases (i.e. of ABoxes and TBoxes) that possibly use data from an underlying relational database and support query answering. These technologies have been developed as part of the Semantic Web and are now standards of the W3C (World Wide Web Consortium).

5.1 RDF

In Semantic Web applications ABoxes are represented using RDF [50], which is a general framework for making statements about resources. An RDF statement always has the structure <subject><predicate><object>, where the subject and the object represent the two resources being related and the predicate represents the type of the relationship. RDF statements are called *(RDF) triples*.

To represent an ABox as a set of RDF statements we need statements for expressing concept and role assertions of the form $C(a)$ and $r(a, b)$, respectively, where C is a concept, r a role, and a, b individuals. In RDF each concept, role or individual is a resource having a IRI. Thus, assuming some namespace ns, a concept assertion $C(a)$ is represented by the triple

ns:C rdf:type ns:a

where rdf:type is a special property defined by the RDF standard (which can also be shorthanded as a), and the role assertion $r(a, b)$ is represented by the triple

ns:a ns:r ns:b

An RDF dataset, i.e. a set of RDF statements, is an *RDF graph*. RDF graphs are stored in triple stores, which are databases specifically build for storing and retrieving RDF triples.

For writing down RDF graphs there exist several serializations, such as N-Triples, Turtle, and RDF/XML. In our continuing example, assuming a namespace `cine` corresponding e.g. to <http://image.ece.ntua.gr/cinemaOntology/>, the triples stating that Woody Allen is a director and has directed the movie Manhattan can be written in Tutle syntax as following:

```
@prefix cine: <http://image.ece.ntua.gr/cinemaOntology/> .
@prefix rdf: <http://www.w3.org/1999/02/22-rdf-syntax-ns#> .

cine:woodyAllen
   cine:isDirector cine:manhattan;
   rdf:type cine:Director.
```

5.2 OWL 2

In Semantic Web applications, concepts, roles, individuals and axioms between them can be modeled using the OWL 2 language [56]. OWL 2 provides structures for expressing all constructors and axioms of Tables 4 and 5. Because OWL 2 is a very expressive ontology language (c.f. Sect. 3) and the use of its full expressivity in real applications poses computational problems, OWL 2 provides three profiles, which reflect compromises between expressivity and desirable computational properties. These profiles are OWL 2 QL, OWL 2 EL, and OWL 2 RL. OWL 2 QL is based on the DL-Lite family of languages [25] and hence can be used for answering conjunctive queries by translating them to SQL queries using query rewriting, as discussed in Sect. 4.2 and avoiding materialization. OWL 2 EL is based on the $\mathcal{ELHI}$ language and OWL 2 RL on DLP [17]. As discussed in Sect. 4.1, OWL 2 RL consequences can be modeled using rule-based techniques.

OWL 2 axioms can be written down as RDF triples and stored in a triple store, along with other RDF triples corresponding to ABox assertions. In this way, the triple store can represent a knowledge base of the form $\langle \mathcal{T}, \mathcal{A} \rangle$. However, in order for to guarantee that a set of OWL 2 axioms constitutes a TBox under the model theoretic-semantics of Sect. 3, some additional syntactic conditions must be imposed on the OWL 2 structures. These conditions are specified by the OWL 2 Direct Semantics, and guarantee that the knowledge base is compatible with the $\mathcal{SROIQ}$ language. OWL 2 ontologies that satisfy these syntactic conditions are called OWL 2 DL ontologies.

There are several serializations of OWL 2, the more reader friendly of which is the functional syntax. In this syntax, the TBox of Example 6 is written as follows:

```
Prefix(cine:=<http://image.ece.ntua.gr/cinemaOntology/>)
Ontology(<http://image.ece.ntua.gr/cinemaOntology/>
   SubClassOf(cine:Director cine:Creator)
   SubClassOf(cine:Movie cine:Film)
   SubObjectPropertyOf(cine:isDirector cine:isCreator)
   SubClassOf(cine:MovieDirector
               ObjectSomeValuesFrom(cine:isDirector cine:Movie) )
)
```

5.3 R2RML

R2RML [57] is a language for expressing mappings from relational databases to RDF datasets. Every R2RML mapping is constructed for a specific database schema and target vocabulary. The input to an R2RML mapping is a relational database that conforms to the database schema. The output is an RDF dataset, that uses roles and concepts from the target vocabulary. R2RML mappings are expressed as RDF graphs and written down in Turtle syntax.

R2RML allows us to model the semantic mappings defined in Sect. 4: $\mathcal{L}$ corresponds to the target vocabulary, $\mathcal{B}$ is the input relational database, and the semantic mapping box $\mathcal{M}$ corresponds to the actual mappings defined in an R2RML document. Note, however, that unlike Definition 4, R2RML mappings cannot contain object identifier, and concept or role classifier functions, other that the functions allowed by the SQL language supported by the underlying database.

The mappings defined in an R2RML document is conceptual; An R2RML implementation may either materialize the mappings, or access directly the underlying database when answering queries. These two strategies correspond to the options of explicitly converting the semantic database into an RDF dataset representing the ABox, or of converting the queries to SQL queries without explicitly constructing the ABox, that we have discussed in Sect. 4.

An R2RML mapping is defined as a set of mappings from logical tables to sets of RDF triples. A logical table may be a database table, a view, or a valid SQL query. Each individual mapping, which is called a triples map, is a rule consisting of two main parts: (a) a subject map that generates the subject of the RDF triples that will be generated from each logical table row, and (b) one or more predicate-object maps that in turn consist of predicate and object maps, which specify the predicates and the objects of the RDF triples that will be generated for the respective subject. In the context of ABoxes, subjects, predicates and objects should be IRIs, and the subject, predicate and object maps should provide instructions on how to generate them. An example of a mapping is the following:

1. Use the template http://image.ece.ntua.gr/cinemaOntology/{DirID} to generate the subject IRI from the DirID column of the DIRECTOR-OF table.
2. Use the constant IRI cine:isDirector as predicate.
3. Use the template http://image.ece.ntua.gr/cinemaOntology/{MovID} to generate the object IRI from the MovID column.

Expressed in R2RML the above mapping is the following:

```
@prefix rr: <http://www.w3.org/ns/r2rml#>.
@prefix cine: <http://image.ece.ntua.gr/cinemaOntology/>.

<#TriplesMap1>
  rr:logicalTable [ rr:tableName "DIRECTOR-OF" ];
  rr:subjectMap [
```

```
    rr:template "http://image.ece.ntua.gr/cinemaOntology/{DirID}";
    rr:class cine:Director;
  ];
  rr:predicateObjectMap [
    rr:predicate cine:isDirector;
    rr:objectMap [
    rr:template "http://image.ece.ntua.gr/cinemaOntology/{MovID}";
    ];
  ].
```

The above R2RML document implements the mapping described above, and in addition specifies that for each subject IRI a triple determining the subject as being of type cine:Director should also be created. Another example is the following R2RML mapping, which generates ABox assertions for the concept DirectorOfComedy using an SQL query as logical table.

```
<#TriplesMap2>
  rr:logicalTable [rr:sqlQuery "
         SELECT DIRECTOR-OF.DirID,
         FROM MOVIES, DIRECTOR-OF
         WHERE MOVIES.MovID = DIRECTOR-OF.MovID AND
               MOVIES.Genre ='Comedy';".
  rr:subjectMap [
    rr:template "http://image.ece.ntua.gr/cinemaOntology/{DirID}";
    rr:class cine:DirectorOfComedy;
  ].
```

5.4 SPARQL

The set of RDF triples that are stored in a triple store can be queried using SPARQL [53]. A typical SPARQL query consists of two parts: a SELECT clause that identifies the query answer variables, and a WHERE clause that provides the basic graph pattern to be matched against the underlying RDF graph. The basic graph pattern is a set of triple patterns. Triple patterns are like RDF triples but the subject, the predicate or the object may be variables. Variables are names preceded by a question mark. A simple SPARQL query is the following:

```
PREFIX cine: <http://image.ece.ntua.gr/cinemaOntology/>
SELECT ?s ?o
WHERE { ?s cine:isDirector ?o }
```

which will return the subject and the object of all triples having isDirector as predicate. It corresponds to the conjunctive query $q(x, y) = \{\mathsf{isDirector}(x, y)\}$. This query example consists of a single triple pattern with the variable ?s in the subject position and the variable ?o in the object position.

To express conjunctive queries, a basic graph pattern consisting of more than one triple patterns can be used. E.g. the query

```
PREFIX cine: <http://image.ece.ntua.gr/cinemaOntology/>
PREFIX <rdf: <http://www.w3.org/1999/02/22-rdf-syntax-ns#>
SELECT ?s
WHERE { ?s cine:isDirector ?o .
        ?s rdf:type cine:Actor }
```

will return all directors of some film that are also actors and corresponds to the conjunctive query $q(x) = \{\mathsf{isDirector}(x, y), \mathsf{Actor}(x)\}$.

SPARQL allows also disjunctive queries through the UNION keyword. E.g. the query

```
PREFIX cine: <http://image.ece.ntua.gr/cinemaOntology/>
SELECT ?s
WHERE {{ ?s cine:isDirector ?o } UNION { ?s cine:isProducer ?o } }
```

will return everyone that has directed or produced a movie.

SPARQL includes many more facilities, such as negation, property paths, assignment, aggregation, multiple graphs, federated querying, filtering, sorting and limiting answers. Several of these facilities are used with more general triple stores than ABoxes and more general queries than conjunctive queries we are interested in this paper.

By default, a triple store answers a SPARQL query by matching the query pattern with the RDF graph of the data it holds. If the triple store is a pure ABox $\mathcal{A}$, this is all that is needed. As we have discussed in detail in Sect. 4, however, if the triple store is a knowledge base $\langle \mathcal{T}, \mathcal{A} \rangle$, some answers to the query may not be explicitly present in $\mathcal{A}$, but need to be inferred using the axioms in $\mathcal{T}$. To allow for such inference processes to be performed by triples stores, SPARQL provides the so-called *entailment regimes* [54]. For OWL 2 TBoxes (OWL 2 DL ontologies), the OWL 2 Direct Semantics Entailment Regime is provided.

Due to the computational difficulties in reasoning under the full expressivity of OWL 2, several practical implementation of triple stores usually provide some limited support of the full OWL 2 entailment, limiting themselves to supporting an OWL 2 profile, usually the OWL 2 RL profile, in which, as we have seen in Sect. 4.1, inferences can be computed using materialization rule-based techniques.

6 Conclusions

The paper discusses how ontological descriptions can be used as a basis for semantic data access. Specifically, we saw how we can build efficient user interfaces that provide the user with the ability to express queries in terms of a rich vocabulary relevant to the domain of interest, rather than queries employing the technical terminology of the database schemas.

We started our paper (Sect. 2) by describing technologies used to store semantic data, either by directly using the vocabulary, or by 'semantifying' the information stored in the database, using the vocabulary terminology. Then, in Sect. 3

we saw how the use of ontological knowledge representation languages (description logics), that are supported by automated reasoning, can advance the level of semantic data description, enriching the vocabulary by adding new terms, or by expressing formal restrictions and constraints of the domain of interest. In Sect. 4 we saw that the use of ontology reasoning, specifically the use of ontology-based data access technologies, can support realistic scenarios of concept-based data access systems for pragmatic applications, with a lot of advantages. Finally, in Sect. 5 we described technologies and standards for the representation and use of semantic data in the web.

References

1. Abiteboul, S., Manolescu, I., Rousset, M.-C., Senellart, P.: Web Data Management. Cambridge University Press, New York (2011)
2. Abiteboul, S., Hull, R., Vianu, V.: Foundations of Databases. Addison-Wesley, Chicago (1995)
3. Garcia-Molina, H., Ullman, J.D., Widom, J.: Database Systems - The Complete Book, 2nd edn. Pearson Education, Harlow (2009)
4. Poggi, A., Lembo, D., Calvanese, D., De Giacomo, G., Lenzerini, M., Rosati, R.: Linking data to ontologies. J. Data Semant. **10**, 133–173 (2008)
5. Calvanese, D., De Giacomo, G., Lembo, D., Lenzerini, M., Poggi, A., Rodriguez-Muro, M., Rosati, R., Ruzzi, M., Savo, D.F.: The MASTRO system for ontology-based data access. Semant. Web **2**(1), 43–53 (2011)
6. Jiménez-Ruiz, E., et al.: BootOX: practical mapping of RDBs to OWL 2. In: Arenas, M., et al. (eds.) ISWC 2015. LNCS, vol. 9367, pp. 113–132. Springer, Cham (2015). doi:10.1007/978-3-319-25010-6_7
7. Rudolph, S.: Foundations of description logics. In: Polleres, A., d'Amato, C., Arenas, M., Handschuh, S., Kroner, P., Ossowski, S., Patel-Schneider, P. (eds.) Reasoning Web 2011. LNCS, vol. 6848, pp. 76–136. Springer, Heidelberg (2011). doi:10.1007/978-3-642-23032-5_2
8. Krötzsch, M., Simančík, F., Horrocks, I.: A description logic primer, CoRR abs/1201.4089 (2012)
9. Baader, F., Calvanese, D., McGuinness, D.L., Nardi, D., Patel-Schneider, P.F.: The Description Logic Handbook: Theory, Implementation, and Applications, 2nd edn. Cambridge University Press, Cambridge (2007)
10. van Harmelen, F., Lifschitz, V., Porter, B.: Handbook of Knowledge Representation. Foundations of Artificial Intelligence. Elsevier Science, New York (2008)
11. Hitzler, P., Krötzsch, M., Rudolph, S.: Foundations of Semantic Web Technologies. Chapman and Hall/CRC, Boca Raton (2009)
12. Staab, S., Studer, R.: Handbook on Ontologies. International Handbooks on Information Systems. Springer, Heidelberg (2010)
13. Baader, F., Sattler, U.: An overview of tableau algorithms for description logics. Studia Logica **69**(1), 5–40 (2001)
14. Motik, B., Sattler, U.: A comparison of reasoning techniques for querying large description logic ABoxes. In: Hermann, M., Voronkov, A. (eds.) LPAR 2006. LNCS (LNAI), vol. 4246, pp. 227–241. Springer, Heidelberg (2006). doi:10.1007/11916277_16

15. De Giacomo, G., Lenzerini, M.: TBox and ABox reasoning in expressive description logics. In: Proceedings of the 1996 International Workshop on Description Logics, 2–4 November, 1996, Cambridge, MA, USA, pp. 37–48 (1996)
16. Horrocks, I., Kutz, O., Sattler, U.: The even more irresistible SROIQ. In: Proceedings of the 10th International Conference on Principles of Knowledge Representation and Reasoning (KR 2006), pp. 57–67. AAAI Press (2006)
17. Grosof, B.N., Horrocks, I., Volz, R., Decker, S.: Description logic programs: combining logic programs with description logic. In: Proceedings of the 12th International Conference on World Wide Web (WWW 2003), pp. 48–57 (2003)
18. Glimm, B., Horrocks, I., Motik, B., Stoilos, G., Wang, Z.: HermiT: an OWL 2 reasoner. J. Autom. Reasoning **53**(3), 245–269 (2014)
19. Haarslev, V., Hidde, K., Möller, R., Wessel, M.: The RacerPro knowledge representation and reasoning system. Semant. Web J. **3**(3), 267–277 (2012)
20. Sirin, E., Parsia, B., Cuenca Grau, B., Kalyanpur, A., Katz, Y.: Pellet: a practical OWL-DL reasoner. J. Web Semant. **5**(2), 51–53 (2011)
21. Steigmiller, A., Liebig, T., Glimm, B.: Konclude: system description. Web Semant. Sci. Serv. Agents World Wide Web **27–28**, 78–85 (2014)
22. Volz, R., Staab, S., Motik, B.: Incrementally maintaining materializations of ontologies stored in logic databases. J. Data Semant. **2**, 1–34 (2005)
23. Motik, B., Nenov, Y., Piro, R., Horrocks, I., Olteanu, I.: Parallel OWL 2 RL materialisation in centralised, main-memory RDF systems. In: Bienvenu, M., Ortiz, M., Rosati, R., Simkus, M. (eds.) Informal Proceedings of the 27th International Workshop on Description Logics, Vienna, Austria, 17–20 July, 2014, vol. 1193 of CEUR Workshop Proceedings, pp. 311–323. CEUR-WS.org (2014)
24. Bishop, B., Kiryakov, A., Ognyanoff, D., Peikov, I., Tashov, Z., Velkov, R.: OWLIM: a family of scalable semantic repositories. Semant. Web **2**(1), 33–42 (2011)
25. Calvanese, D., De Giacomo, G., Lembo, D., Lenzerini, M., Rosati, R.: Tractable reasoning and efficient query answering in description logics: the DL-Lite family. J. Autom. Reasoning **39**(3), 385–429 (2007)
26. Rosati, R., Almatelli, A.: Improving query answering over dl-lite ontologies. In: Principles of Knowledge Representation and Reasoning: Proceedings of the Twelfth International Conference, KR 2010, Toronto, Ontario, Canada, 9–13 May, 2010 (2010)
27. Pérez-Urbina, H., Motik, B., Horrocks, I.: Tractable query answering and rewriting under description logic constraints. J. Appl. Logic **8**(2), 186–209 (2010)
28. Rodriguez-Muro, M., Calvanese, D.: High performance query answering over dl-lite ontologies. In: Principles of Knowledge Representation and Reasoning: Proceedings of the Thirteenth International Conference (KR 2012), Rome, Italy, 10–14 June, 2012 (2012)
29. Chortaras, A., Trivela, D., Stamou, G.: Optimized query rewriting for OWL 2 QL. In: Bjørner, N., Sofronie-Stokkermans, V. (eds.) CADE 2011. LNCS (LNAI), vol. 6803, pp. 192–206. Springer, Heidelberg (2011). doi:10.1007/978-3-642-22438-6_16
30. Trivela, D., Stoilos, G., Chortaras, A., Stamou, G.: Optimising resolution-based rewriting algorithms for OWL ontologies. J. Web Semant. **33**, 30–49 (2015)
31. Eiter, T., Ortiz, M., Simkus, M., Tran, T., Xiao, G.: Query rewriting for Horn-SHIQ plus rules. In: Proceedings of the Twenty-Sixth AAAI Conference on Artificial Intelligence, 22–26 July, 2012, Toronto, Ontario, Canada (2012)

32. Lutz, C., Toman, D., Wolter, F.: Conjunctive query answering in the description logic EL using a relational database system. In: Proceedings of the 21st International Joint Conference on Artificial Intelligence (IJCAI 2009), Pasadena, California, USA, 11–17 July, 2009, pp. 2070–2075 (2009)
33. Hustadt, U., Motik, B., Sattler, U.: Reasoning in description logics by a reduction to disjunctive datalog. J. Autom. Reasoning **39**(3), 351–384 (2007)
34. Calvanese, D., Giacomo, G., Lembo, D., Lenzerini, M., Poggi, A., Rodriguez-Muro, M., Rosati, R.: Ontologies and databases: the DL-Lite approach. In: Tessaris, S., Franconi, E., Eiter, T., Gutierrez, C., Handschuh, S., Rousset, M.-C., Schmidt, R.A. (eds.) Reasoning Web 2009. LNCS, vol. 5689, pp. 255–356. Springer, Heidelberg (2009). doi:10.1007/978-3-642-03754-2_7
35. Orsi, G., Pieris, A.: Optimizing query answering under ontological constraints. J. Very Large Database (VLDB) Endow. **11**(4), 1004–1015 (2011)
36. Venetis, T., Stoilos, G., Stamou, G.: Query extensions and incremental query rewriting for OWL 2 QL ontologies. J. Data Semant. **3**(1), 1–23 (2014)
37. Rodriguez-Muro, M., Kontchakov, R., Zakharyaschev, M.: Query rewriting and optimisation with database dependencies in ontop. In: Proceedings of the 26th International Workshop on Description Logics (DL 2013) (2013)
38. Trivela, D., Stoilos, G., Chortaras, A., Stamou, G.: Query rewriting in Horn-SHIQ. In: Proceedings of the 28th International Workshop on Description Logics, Athens, Greece, 7–10 June, 2015 (2015)
39. Kontchakov, R., Lutz, C., Toman, D., Wolter, F., Zakharyaschev, M.: The combined approach to query answering in DL-Lite. In: Principles of Knowledge Representation and Reasoning: Proceedings of the Twelfth International Conference (KR 2010), Toronto, Ontario, Canada, 9–13 May, 2010 (2010)
40. Stefanoni, G., Motik, B., Horrocks, I.: Introducing nominals to the combined query answering approaches for EL. In: Proceedings of the Twenty-Seventh AAAI Conference on Artificial Intelligence, 14–18 July, 2013, Bellevue, Washington, USA (2013)
41. Zhou, Y., Grau, B.C., Nenov, Y., Horrock, I.: PAGOdA: pay-as-you-go ABox reasoning. In: Calvanese, D., Konev, B. (eds.), Proceedings of the 28th International Workshop on Description Logics, Athens, Greece, 7–10 June, 2015, vol. 1350 of CEUR Workshop Proceedings. CEUR-WS.org (2015)
42. Glimm, B., Kazakov, Y., Kollia, I., Stamou, G.: Lower and upper bounds for SPARQL queries over OWL ontologies. In: Proceedings of the 29th AAAI Conference on Artificial Intelligence (AAAI 2015). AAAI Press (2015)
43. Stoilos, G., Stamou, G.: Hybrid query answering over OWL ontologies. In: Proceedings of the 21st European Conference on Artificial Intelligence (ECAI 2014) (2014)
44. Berners-Lee, T., Hendler, J., Lassila, O.: The semantic web. Sci. Am. 96–101(2001)
45. Horrocks, I., Patel-Schneider, P.F.: The Generation of DAML+OIL. In: Proceedings of the 2001 Description Logic Workshop (2001)
46. Fensel, D., van Harmelen, F., Horrocks, I., McGuinness, D., Patel-Schneider, P.F.: OIL: an ontology infrastructure for the semantic web. IEEE Intell. Syst. **16**(2), 38–45 (2001)
47. Horrocks, I.: Ontologies and the semantic web. Commun. ACM **51**(12), 58–67 (2008)
48. Cuenca Grau, B., Horrocks, I., Motik, B., Parsia, B., Patel-Schneider, P., Sattler, U.: OWL 2: the next step for OWL. J. Web Semant. **6**(4), 309–322 (2008)
49. Horrocks, I., Patel-Schneider, P.F., van Harmelen, F.: From SHIQ and RDF to OWL: the making of a web ontology language. J. Web Semant. **1**, 7–26 (2003)

50. RDF 1.1 concepts and abstract syntax. W3C Recommendation (2014). https://www.w3.org/TR/rdf11-concepts/
51. RDF Schema 1.1. W3C Recommendation (2014). https://www.w3.org/TR/2014/PER-rdf-schema-20140109/
52. SPARQL Query Language for RDF. W3C Recommendation (2008). http://www.w3.org/TR/rdf-sparql-query/
53. SPARQL 1.1 Query Language. W3C Recommendation (2013). http://www.w3.org/TR/sparql11-query/
54. SPARQL 1.1 1.1 Entailment Regimes. W3C Recommendation (2013). https://www.w3.org/TR/sparql11-entailment/)
55. OWL Web Ontology Language document overview. W3C Recommendation (2004). http://www.w3.org/TR/owl-features/
56. OWL 2 Web Ontology Language document overview (second edition). W3C Recommendation (2012). http://www.w3.org/TR/owl2-overview/
57. R2RML: RDB to RDF Mapping Language. W3C Recommendation (2012). https://www.w3.org/TR/r2rml/

Ontology Querying: Datalog Strikes Back

Andrea Calì[1,2(✉)]

[1] Department of Computer Science and Information Systems Birkbeck, University of London, London, UK
andrea@dcs.bbk.ac.uk

[2] Oxford-Man Institute of Quantitative Finance, University of Oxford, Oxford, UK

Abstract. In this tutorial we address the problem of ontology querying, that is, the problem of answering queries against a theory constituted by facts (the data) and inference rules (the ontology). A varied landscape of ontology languages exists in the scientific literature, with several degrees of complexity of query processing. We argue that Datalog$^{\pm}$, a family of languages derived from Datalog, is a powerful tool for ontology querying. To illustrate the impact of this comeback of Datalog, we present the basic paradigms behind the main Datalog$^{\pm}$ as well as some recent extensions. We also present some efficient query processing techniques for some cases.

The Datalog language has seen a recent revival with the introduction of Datalog$^{\pm}$ languages for ontology modelling and querying. While the core rules of Datalog$^{\pm}$ languages are the well-known tuple-generating dependencies, several novel languages have been proposed that enjoy good computational properties regarding ontology querying. We argue that Datalog$^{\pm}$ is a powerful formalism for knowledge representation and reasoning, suitable also for the Semantic Web. We illustrate the main languages in the Datalog$^{\pm}$ family as well as several issues arising in ontological query processing in this context.

Datalog. Datalog [1,16,17] is a declarative query language that has been used for many years for expressive query answering on relational databases. The applications of Datalog include source code analysis [20], distributed systems and Web data extraction [7,18]. A Datalog program consists of a set of Horn clauses without function symbols. The predicates appearing in the program are partitioned into *extensional database (EDB) predicates*, whose values reside in an input database, and *intensional database (IDB) predicates*, whose values are computed via the program rules. EDB predicate symbols appear only in rule bodies. The following program[1] computes the transitive closure, represented by the IDB predicate c, of the binary relation e, represented by an EDB predicate.

$$e(X,Y) \rightarrow c(X,Y),$$
$$e(X,Y), c(Y,Z) \rightarrow c(X,Z).$$

[1] Notice that here we deviate from the classic Datalog notation *head* $\leftarrow$ *body* or *head* :- *body*; instead, we use the notation *body* $\rightarrow$ *head*. Notice also that in Datalog the head is composed of a single atom.

G. Ianni et al. (Eds.): Reasoning Web 2017, LNCS 10370, pp. 64–67, 2017.
DOI: 10.1007/978-3-319-61033-7_3

Ontology Querying. Ontological information is information about relationships between objects and classes in a certain domain. The most prominent formalism for representing such information are so-called *description logics (DLs)* [5]. In DLs, sets of objects are represented by *concepts* and binary relations between concepts are called *roles*; in DL languages we can express, for instance, that *(1)* every manager is an employee; this is expressed by the rule $\mathsf{mgr} \sqsubseteq \mathsf{emp}$; *(2)* every manager supervises an employee; this is expressed by the rule $\mathsf{mgr} \sqsubseteq \exists\,\mathsf{supervises.emp}$; *(3)* each employee is supervised by at most one manager, expressed by the rule $(\mathbf{funct}\ \mathsf{supervises}^-)$ (the role $\mathsf{supervises}^-$, that is $\mathsf{supervises}$ with the two arguments inverted, is functional). To express the above rules, Datalog is not sufficient—we need the possibility of existential quantification (e.g. there exists an employee supervised by a certain manager, but such an employee is not known). This motivates the introduction of the Datalog$^\pm$ family of languages [13], whose main rules are in fact the well-known *tuple-generating dependencies (TGDs).* In Datalog$^\pm$, the above rules can be easily expressed:

$$\begin{aligned} mgr(X) &\rightarrow emp(X)\\ mgr(X) &\rightarrow \exists Y\, supervises(X,Y)\\ supervises(X,Y), supervises(Z,Y) &\rightarrow X = Z. \end{aligned}$$

Notice that the last rule is not a TGD, but an *equality-generating dependency (EGD)*, which has as consequence the equality of two values. Given a Datalog$^\pm$ program Σ on a schema $\mathcal{R}$, a database D for $\mathcal{R}$ and a query q on $\mathcal{R}$, a tuple $\mathbf{t}$ is and answer to q under $D \cup \Sigma$ if $\mathbf{t}$ is an answer to q in all models of $D \cup \Sigma$, that is, in all instances that contain D and satisfy all rules in Σ.

Datalog$^\pm$ Variants and Main Underlying Notions. Processing conjunctive queries (select-project-join queries) under TGDs is undecidable [8], even when the schema and the TGDs are fixed [11]. Languages in the Datalog$^\pm$ family adopt syntactic restrictions on rules so as to achieve decidability of (conjunctive) query answering and possibly tractability. Guardedness [3] is a property of first-order logic theories that ensure decidability of the satisfiability problem. Inspired by such notion, *guarded* Datalog$^\pm$ was introduced [11]; in guarded Datalog$^\pm$, each TGD-rule has a body-atom that contains all variables of the rule. Guarded Datalog$^\pm$ and variants are studied in [11], and further extensions in [6]. *Linear* Datalog$^\pm$ [12] is a more tractable variant of guarded Datalog$^\pm$ where each TGD-rule has exactly one atom in the body and one in the head; interestingly, though linear Datalog$^\pm$ TGD-rules are only slightly more expressive than the well known class of inclusion dependencies, linear Datalog$^\pm$ is capable of expressing a wide variety of relevant ontology languages. *Sticky* Datalog$^\pm$ [14], alongside with its extensions, captures a wide class of non-guarded rules, while achieving low data complexity (complexity where only the database is considered as input, while all the rest is fixed) of query answering in some cases. Disjunction in Datalog$^\pm$ is introduced in [9], where the complexity of the language called Datalog$^{\exists,\vee}$ is studied, together with the complexity of the variant *linear* Datalog$^{\exists,\vee}$. Negation in Datalog$^\pm$ poses several challenges; it has been studied under different semantics: stratified negation [4,12], well founded negation [2] and stable-model negation [2,19].

Functional Constraints. In several Datalog$^\pm$ languages, functional constraints in the form of EGDs are considered, often in their elementary form of well-known *key* constraints, as they are a fundamental modelling tool in ontologies. However, their introduction leads very easily to undecidability of query answering (see e.g. [15]); hence, syntactic restrictions that preserve decidability are needed. In the DL literature, such functional constraints have been studied under strong syntactic limitations. In Datalog$^\pm$, the main notion is that of *non-conflicting* EGDs [12], which does not go much beyond the analogous notion studied under more traditional database constraints [15]. Non-conflicting EGDs and TGDs guarantee *separability* of EGDs and TGDs, a semantic notion that expresses the fact that EGDs do not influence the logical inference performed through the TGDs. A more general approach is adopted in [10], where two notions of separability (simple separability and *deep* separability) are studied, depending on how EGDs participate in the logical inference—in the case of deep separability, an immediate application of an EGD in the inference might seem to have influence, but such application is then made irrelevant by an eventual application of some TGD in the inference process. Along the lines of [10], we try to clarify the notion of separability in the literature and to provide a more general syntactic criterion for TGDs and EGDs, that guarantees separability.

Practical Algorithms for Expressive Ontologies. Ontology querying under some expressive Datalog$^\pm$ languages has been studied from the point of view of the computational complexity, often providing nondeterministic algorithms, but much is to be done from the point of view of practical implementations; this is especially important if we consider that the worst case rarely occurs in real-world ontologies. A deterministic algorithm for conjunctive query answering under the expressive class of *weakly-sticky* Datalog$^\pm$ is presented in [21]. We illustrate the main ideas underlying this work, so as to identify the main issues in the problem of efficient query answering in this case.

References

1. Abiteboul, S., Hull, R., Vianu, V.: Foundations of Databases. Addison-Wesley, Reading (1995)
2. Alviano, M., Pieris, A.: Default negation for non-guarded existential rules. In: Proceeding of PODS, pp. 79–90 (2015)
3. Andréka, H., Németi, I., van Benthem, J.: Modal languages and bounded fragments of predicate logic. J. Philos. Logic **27**(3), 217–274 (1998)
4. Arenas, M., Gottlob, G., Pieris, A.: Expressive languages for querying the semantic web. In: Proceeding of PODS, pp. 14–26 (2014)
5. Baader, F., Calvanese, D., McGuinness, D.L., Nardi, D., Patel-Schneider, P.F. (eds.): The Description Logic Handbook: Theory, Implementation, and Applications. Cambridge University Press, Cambridge (2003)

6. Baget, J.-F., Leclère, M., Mugnier, M.-L., Salvat, E.: On rules with existential variables: walking the decidability line. Artif. Intell. **175**(9–10), 1620–1654 (2011)
7. Baumgartner, R., Gatterbauer, W., Gottlob, G.: Monadic datalog and the expressive power of web information extraction languages. In: Liu, L., Tamer Özsu, M. (eds.) Encyclopedia of Database Systems, pp. 3465–3471. Springer, New York (2009)
8. Beeri, C., Vardi, M.Y.: The implication problem for data dependencies. In: Even, S., Kariv, O. (eds.) ICALP 1981. LNCS, vol. 115, pp. 73–85. Springer, Heidelberg (1981). doi:10.1007/3-540-10843-2_7
9. Bourhis, P., Morak, M., Pieris, A.: The impact of disjunction on query answering under guarded-based existential rules. In: Proceeding of IJCAI, pp. 796–802 (2013)
10. Calì, A., Console, M., Frosini, R.: On separability of ontological constraints. In: Proceeding of AMW, pp. 48–61 (2012)
11. Calì, A., Gottlob, G.: Taming the infinite chase: query answering under expressive relational constraints. J. Artif. Intell. Res. (JAIR) **48**, 115–174 (2013)
12. Calì, A., Gottlob, G., Lukasiewicz, T.: A general datalog-based framework for tractable query answering over ontologies. J. Web Sem. **14**, 57–83 (2012)
13. Calì, A., Gottlob, G., Lukasiewicz, T., Marnette, B., Pieris, A.: Datalog$^{\pm}$: a family of logical knowledge representation and query languages for new applications. In: Proceeding of LICS, pp. 228–242 (2010)
14. Calì, A., Gottlob, G., Pieris, A.: Towards more expressive ontology languages: the query answering problem. Artif. Intell. **193**, 87–128 (2012)
15. Calì, A., Lembo, D., Rosati, R.: On the decidability and complexity of query answering over inconsistent and incomplete databases. In: Proceeding of PODS, pp. 260–271 (2003)
16. Ceri, S., Gottlob, G., Tanca, L.: Logic Programming and Databases. Springer, Heidelberg (1990)
17. Dantsin, E., Eiter, T., Georg, G., Voronkov, A.: Complexity and expressive power of logic programming. ACM Comput. Surv. **33**(3), 374–425 (2001)
18. Furche, T., Gottlob, G., Grasso, G., Gunes, O., Guo, X., Kravchenko, A., Orsi, G., Schallhart, C., Sellers, A., Wang, C.: DIADEM: domain-centric, intelligent, automated data extraction methodology. In: Proceeding of WWW (Companion Volume), pp. 267–270 (2012)
19. Gottlob, G., Hernich, A., Kupke, C., Lukasiewicz, T.: Stable model semantics for guarded existential rules and description logics. In: Proceeding of KR (2014)
20. Hajiyev, E., Verbaere, M., Moor, O.: *codeQuest*: scalable source code queries with datalog. In: Thomas, D. (ed.) ECOOP 2006. LNCS, vol. 4067, pp. 2–27. Springer, Heidelberg (2006). doi:10.1007/11785477_2
21. Milani, M., Calì, A., Bertossi, L.E.: A hybrid approach to query answering under expressive Datalog$^{\pm}$. In: Proceeding of RR, pp. 144–158 (2016)

Integrating Relational Databases with the Semantic Web: A Reflection

Juan F. Sequeda(✉)

Capsenta, Austin, USA
juan@capsenta.com

Abstract. From the beginning it was understood that the success of the Semantic Web hinges on integrating the vast amount of data stored in Relational Databases. This manuscript reflects on the last 10 years of our research results to integrate Relational Databases with the Semantic Web. Since 2007, our research has led us to answer the following question: *How and to what extent can Relational Databases be Integrated with the Semantic Web?* The answer comes in two parts. We start by presenting how to get from Relational Databases to the Semantic Web via mappings, such as the W3C Direct Mapping and R2RML standards. Subsequently, we present how the Semantic Web can access Relational Databases. We finalize with how Relational Databases and Semantic Web technologies are being used practice for data integration and discuss open challenges.

1 Introduction

The success of the Semantic Web hinges on integrating the vast amount of data stored in Relational Databases. We have gone a long way in the past 10 years. As of 2017, a successful repeated use case for Relational Databases and the Semantic Web is to address data integration needs. Such systems are now being deployed in industrial applications. So, how did we get here? The goal of this manuscript is to reflect on the last 10 years of our research results to integrate Relational Databases with the Semantic Web [64].

In 2007, we began investigating the relationship between Relational Databases and the Semantic Web. Specifically, the research question was the following: *How and to what extent can Relational Databases be integrated with the Semantic Web?* The thesis is that much of the existing Relational Database infrastructure can be reused to support the Semantic Web.

In the first part, we describe how to get from Relational Databases to the Semantic Web via mappings. Starting with a 2007 workshop, titled "RDF Access to Relational Databases"[1], the W3C sponsored a series of activities to address this issue. At that workshop, the acronym, RDB2RDF, Relational Database to Resource Description Framework, was coined. In September 2012, these activities culminated in the ratification of two W3C standards, colloquially known as Direct Mapping [7] and R2RML [25].

[1] http://www.w3.org/2007/03/RdfRDB/.

G. Ianni et al. (Eds.): Reasoning Web 2017, LNCS 10370, pp. 68–120, 2017.
DOI: 10.1007/978-3-319-61033-7_4

By design, both these standards avoid any content that speaks about implementation, directly or indirectly. The standards concern is syntactic transformation of the contents of rows in relational tables to RDF. The R2RML language includes statements that specify which columns and tables are mapped to properties and classes of a domain ontology. Thus, the language empowers a developer to examine the contents of a relational database and write a mapping specification. Furthermore, we present an extended Direct Mapping which address some shortcomings of the W3C Direct Mapping and study it with respect to two fundamental (information and query preservation) and two desired (monotonicity and semantics preservation) properties.

In the second part, we describe the opposite direction, how the Semantic Web can access Relational Databases. Once a mapping has been defined, let it be a Direct Mapping or a user defined R2RML mappings, the goal is to evaluate SPARQL queries against the Relational Database. These contributions are embodied in our system called Ultrawrap. We identified two existing relational query optimizations in commercial Relational Databases, detection of unsatisfiable conditions and self-join elimination which are used for SPARQL execution. Empirical analysis consistently yield that SPARQL query execution performance on Ultrawrap is comparable to that of SQL queries written directly for the relational representation of the data. Furthermore, we present a method for Relational Databases to support inheritance and transitivity by compiling the ontology as mappings, implementing the mappings as SQL views, using SQL recursion and optimizing by materializing a subset of views. This approach was implemented as an extension of Ultrawrap to support the Ontology-Based Data Access paradigm. Empirical analysis reveals that Relational Databases are able to effectively act as reasoners.

To understand the relationship between Relational Databases and the Semantic Web, we adopt a methodology where we first start small. That is why we first studied a simple mapping which is the Direct Mapping. Subsequently we studied how to accomplish SPARQL to SQL rewriting under the direct mapping. After the direct mapping relationship was understood, we continued our work with customized mappings represented in R2RML and reasoning.

We highlight two on-going challenges when Relational Databases and Semantic Web technologies are combined for data integration in the real world: ontology and mapping engineering. We argue for the need of a pay-as-you-go methodology to create mappings and ontologies. We close with a set of open problems.

2 Preliminaries

This sections presents the notation and definitions used throughout this manuscript. We define the three standards comprising Semantic Web: RDF, the graph data model; OWL, the ontology language; and SPARQL, the query language for RDF. Subsequently, the expressivity of the OWL dialect used in this research is presented. For more detailed preliminaries, we refer the reader to Chap. 2 of [64]

2.1 Running Example

Throughout this manuscript, we use the data illustrated in Fig. 1 as a running example. The precise corresponding SQL statements are:

```
CREATE TABLE order (
  orderid INT PRIMARY KEY,
  date DATE,
  total FLOAT,
  currency VARCHAR(50),
  status INT
)

CREATE TABLE lineitem (
  lineid INT PRIMARY KEY,
  price FLOAT,
  quantity INT,
  product VARCHAR(50),
  orderid INT,
  FOREIGN KEY(orderid) REFERENCES ORDER(orderid)
)
```

orderid	date	total	currency	status
1234	2017-04-15	100	USD	1

lineid	price	quantity	product	orderid
6789	30	2	Foo	1234
6790	20	2	Bar	1234

Fig. 1. SQL used to create the running example

2.2 Relational Databases

A database is a collection of data. A Relational Database is a database founded on the relational model. The relational model represents data in terms of tuples (rows), grouped into relations (tables). Relational Algebra is used as a query language for Relational Databases.

Because nulls appear in practice in RDBMS, it is important to present a formal definition of Relational Databases with respect to null values. Assume, a countably infinite domain $\mathbf{D}$ of constants and a reserved symbol NULL that is not in $\mathbf{D}$. A *database schema* $\mathbf{R}$ is a finite set of relation names, where for each $R \in \mathbf{R}$, $att(R)$ denotes the nonempty finite set of attribute names associated with R. The arity of R, denoted as $arity(R)$, is the number of elements of the set $att(R)$. An instance I of $\mathbf{R}$ assigns to each relation symbol $R \in \mathbf{R}$, a finite set of tuples $R^I = \{t_1, \ldots, t_\ell\}$. Each tuple t_j $(1 \leq j \leq \ell)$ is a function that assigns to each attribute in $att(R)$ a value from $(\mathbf{D} \cup \{\texttt{NULL}\})$, denoted as $t : att(R) \rightarrow (\mathbf{D} \cup \{\texttt{NULL}\})$. The value of an attribute A in a tuple t_j is denoted by $t_j.A$. Moreover, $R(t_j)$ is a fact in I if $t_j \in R^I$. The notation $R(t_j) \in I$ is used in this case. We also view instances as sets of facts.

Relational Algebra consists of operators which take one or two relations as operands and produce one relation as a result. The basic operators of relational algebra are: selection, projection, rename, join, union and difference. Selection selects tuples from a relation satisfying a condition. Projection chooses subset of the attributes of a relation. Rename allows to change the name of an attribute. Join combines two relations into one on the basis of a condition. Union is the relation containing all tuples from both relations. Difference is the relation containing all tuples of the first relation that do not appear in the second relation. Relational Algebra operators can be composed into relational algebraic expressions. These relational algebraic expressions are then used to formulate queries over a Relational Database.

Recall that Relational Databases containing null values are considered. For full details on the syntax and semantics of Relational Algebra where null values play a role, we refer the reader to Chap. 2 of [64].

2.3 Semantic Web

The Semantic Web is an extension to the Web that enables intelligent access to data on the Web. The technologies supporting the Semantic Web consist of a set of standards: RDF as the graph data model, OWL as the ontology language, and SPARQL as the query language.

RDF: RDF stands for Resource Description Framework, which is a framework for representing information about resources in the Web. By resource, we mean anything in the world including physical things, documents, abstract concepts, etc[2]. RDF considers three types of values: resource identifiers (IRIs) to denote resources, literals to denote values such as strings, and blank nodes to denote the existence of unnamed resources which are existentially quantified variables that can be used to make statements about unknown (but existent) resources.

Assume there are pairwise disjoint infinite sets $\mathbf{I}$ (IRIs), $\mathbf{B}$ (blank nodes) and $\mathbf{L}$ (literals). A tuple $(s, p, o) \in (\mathbf{I} \cup \mathbf{B}) \times \mathbf{I} \times (\mathbf{I} \cup \mathbf{B} \cup \mathbf{L})$ is called an RDF triple, where s is the subject, p is the predicate and o is the object. A finite set of RDF triples is called an RDF graph. Assume that `triple` is a ternary predicate that stores RDF graphs in the obvious way: every triple $(a, b, c) \in G$ is stored as $\texttt{triple}(a, b, c)$. Moreover, assume the existence of an infinite set $\mathbf{V}$ of variables disjoint from the above sets, and assume that every element in $\mathbf{V}$ starts with the symbol "?".

[2] The term "entity" can be considered synonymous to resource.

Example 1. Consider representing the statement "There is a person whose name is Juan Sequeda" in RDF. This can be represented with two RDF triples. The first RDF triple

$$\texttt{triple(http://juansequeda.com\#me, type, foaf:Person)}$$

states that the resource identified by http://juansequeda.com#me *is of type Person. The type relationship is represented with* `rdf:type`. *Additionally, the concept Person is identified by the IRI* `foaf:Person`. *Note that* `rdf:` *and* `foaf:` *are being used instead of a full IRI. These are prefixes that replace a part of the IRI*[3]. *The second RDF triple*

$$\texttt{triple(http://juansequeda.com\#me, foaf:name, "Juan Sequeda")}$$

states that http://juansequeda.com#me *has a name which is "Juan Sequeda". The concept of name is identified by the IRI* `foaf:name`.

OWL: OWL stands for Web Ontology Language, which is the language to represent ontologies on the Web. In order to define the notion of ontology, the following set of reserved keywords are defined as **O**: {`subClass`, `subProp`, `dom`, `range`, `type`, `equivClass`, `equivProp`, `inverse`, `symProp`, `transProp`}.

Assume that $\mathbf{O} \subseteq \mathbf{I}$. Two types of RDF triples are distinguished: ontological and assertional. Ontological RDF triples define the ontology. Assertional RDF triples define the facts. The formal definitions are the following:

Definition 1 (Ontological RDF Triple). *Following the definition presented by Weaver and Hendler [75], an RDF triple* (a, b, c) *is ontological if:*

1. $a \in (\mathbf{I} \setminus \mathbf{O})$, *and*
2. *either* $b \in (\mathbf{O} \setminus \{\texttt{type}\})$ *and* $c \in (\mathbf{I} \setminus \mathbf{O})$, *or* $b = \texttt{type}$ *and* c *is either* `symProp` *or* `transProp`.

In other words, an ontological RDF triple will always have as a subject an element in **I** but not in **O**. There are two types of ontological RDF triples. First, the predicate is an element in **O** but not `type` and the object is an element in **I** but not in **O**. Second, if the predicate is `type`, then the object is either `symProp` or `transProp`.

Definition 2 (Assertional RDF Triple). *An RDF triple* (a, b, c) *is assertional if it is not ontological.*

Definition 3 (Ontology). *An ontology* $\mathcal{O}$ *is defined as a finite set of ontological RDF triples.*

[3] The prefix "`rdf:`" represents http://www.w3.org/1999/02/22-rdf-syntax-ns#, hence the full IRI for `rdf:type` is http://www.w3.org/1999/02/22-rdf-syntax-ns#type. Additionally, the prefix "`foaf:`" represents http://xmlns.com/foaf/0.1/, hence the full IRI for `foaf:Person` is http://xmlns.com/foaf/0.1/Person.

The semantics of an ontology $\mathcal{O}$ is usually defined by representing it as a set of description logic axioms, and then relying on the semantics of the logic [10] (which, in turn, is derived from the semantics of first-order logic). It is more convenient to directly define a set of first-order formulae, denoted as $\Sigma_{\mathcal{O}}$, to encode the ontology $\mathcal{O}$. The semantics of each ontological triple of an ontology, $t \in \mathcal{O}$, is defined as a first-order formula φ_t over the predicate `triple`. Definitions 4–12 presents the first-order formula for ontological triples. Finally, the set $\Sigma_{\mathcal{O}}$ of first-order formulae encoding the ontology $\mathcal{O}$ is define as $\{\varphi_t \mid t \in \mathcal{O}\}$.

Definition 4 (Subclass). If a is a subclass of b and x is an instance of a, then x is an instance of b. The first-order formula is:

$$\varphi_{(a,\texttt{subClass},b)} = \forall x\,(\texttt{triple}(x,\texttt{type},a) \rightarrow \texttt{triple}(x,\texttt{type},b))$$

Definition 5 (Subproperty). If a is a subproperty of b, then all pairs of resources (x, y) which are related by a are also related by b. The first-order formula is:

$$\varphi_{(a,\texttt{subProp},b)} = \forall x \forall y\,(\texttt{triple}(x,a,y) \rightarrow \texttt{triple}(x,b,y))$$

Definition 6 (Domain). If a has a domain b then any resource x that is related to a is an instance of b. The first-order formula is:

$$\varphi_{(a,\texttt{dom},b)} = \forall x \forall y\,(\texttt{triple}(x,a,y) \rightarrow \texttt{triple}(x,\texttt{type},b))$$

Definition 7 (Range). If a has a range b then any resource y that is related to a is an instance of b. The first-order formula is:

$$\varphi_{(a,\texttt{range},b)} = \forall x \forall y\,(\texttt{triple}(x,a,y) \rightarrow \texttt{triple}(y,\texttt{type},b))$$

Definition 8 (Equivalent Class). If a has an equivalent class of b and x is an instance of a, then x is an instance of b. Conversely, if x is an instance of b, then x is an instance of a. The first-order formula is:

$$\varphi_{(a,\texttt{equivClass},b)} = \forall x\,(\texttt{triple}(x,\texttt{type},a) \leftrightarrow \texttt{triple}(x,\texttt{type},b))$$

Definition 9 (Equivalent Property). If a has an equivalent property of b, then all pairs of resources (x, y) which are related by a are also related by b. Conversely, all pairs of resources (x, y) which are related by b are also related by a. The first-order formula is:

$$\varphi_{(a,\texttt{equivProp},b)} = \forall x \forall y\,(\texttt{triple}(x,a,y) \leftrightarrow \texttt{triple}(x,b,y))$$

Definition 10 (Inverse Property). If a has an inverse property of b, then all pairs of resources (x, y) which are related by a are also related by b by the pair (y, x). Conversely, all pairs of resources (y, x) which are related by b are also related by a by the pair (x, y) The first-order formula is:

$$\varphi_{(a,\texttt{inverse},b)} = \forall x \forall y\,(\texttt{triple}(x,a,y) \leftrightarrow \texttt{triple}(y,b,x))$$

Definition 11 (Symmetric Property). If a is a symmetric property, then all pairs of resources (x, y) which are related by a are also related as the pair (y, x). The first-order formula is:

$$\varphi_{(a,\texttt{type},\texttt{symProp})} = \forall x \forall y\, (\texttt{triple}(x, a, y) \rightarrow \texttt{triple}(y, a, x))$$

Definition 12 (Transitive Property). If a is a transitive property, and for all pairs of resources (x, y) and (y, z) which are related by a then the pair (x, z) is also related by a. The first-order formula is:

$$\varphi_{(a,\texttt{type},\texttt{transProp})} = \forall x \forall y \forall z\, (\texttt{triple}(x, a, y) \wedge \texttt{triple}(y, a, z) \rightarrow \texttt{triple}(x, a, z))$$

Given that the semantics of an ontology $\mathcal{O}$ has been defined as set of first order logic formulae $\Sigma_{\mathcal{O}}$ and a RDF graph G using the predicate `triple`, then $\Sigma_{\mathcal{O}} \cup G$ is consistent (and inconsistent) in the usual sense of First Order Logic.

Example 2 The following ontology states that an Executive and ITEmployee are both Employees. Additionally that the property hasSuperior is a transitive relationship from an Employee to another Employee.

```
triple(:Executive, subClass, :Employee)
triple(:Programmer, subClass, :ITEmployee)
triple(:SysAdmin, subClass, :ITEmployee)
triple(:ITEmployee, subClass, :Employee)
triple(:hasSuperior, type, transProp)
triple(:hasSuperior, dom, :Employee)
triple(:hasSuperior, range, :Employee)
```

Ontology Profiles. The expressiveness of an ontology language can be specified by profiles. The Semantic Web technology stack specifies four ontology profiles: RDFS, OWL 2 EL, OWL 2 QL and OWL 2 RL [13,50].

RDF Schema (RDFS) extends RDF as a schema language for RDF and a lightweight ontology language [13]. It includes constructs to declare classes, hierarchies between classes and properties and relate the domain and range of a property to a certain class. Ontological triples with `subClass`, `subProp`, `dom`, `range`, `type`, `equivClass`, `equivProp` are in this profile. The following three profiles, OWL 2 EL, QL and RL, extend the expressiveness of RDFS.

OWL 2 EL profile is used to represent ontologies that define very large numbers of classes and/or properties with transitivity. This language has been tailored to model large life science ontologies, while still supporting efficient reasoning. OWL 2 EL is based on the EL++ Description Logic [9]. Ontological triples with `transProp` are in this profile.

OWL 2 QL provides constructs to express conceptual models such as UML class diagrams and ER diagrams. This language was designed so that data that is stored in a standard relational database system can be queried through an ontology via rewriting mechanisms. OWL 2 QL is based on the DL-Lite family of description logics [16]. Ontological triples with `inverse` and `symProp` are in this profile.

OWL 2 RL provides constructs to represent rules in ontologies. This language has been tailored for rule-based reasoning engines. OWL 2 RL is based on Description Logic Programs (DLP) [35]. Ontological triples with `inverse` and `symProp` are also in this profile.

The ontology expressivity considered in this work (as defined in Definitions 4–12) is not specific to a single OWL profile. Thus, we propose a new ontology profile, OWL-SQL, which expresses the types of ontologies considered in this dissertation. Figure 2 denotes the expressivity of OWL-SQL with respect to the OWL 2 EL, QL and RL profiles.

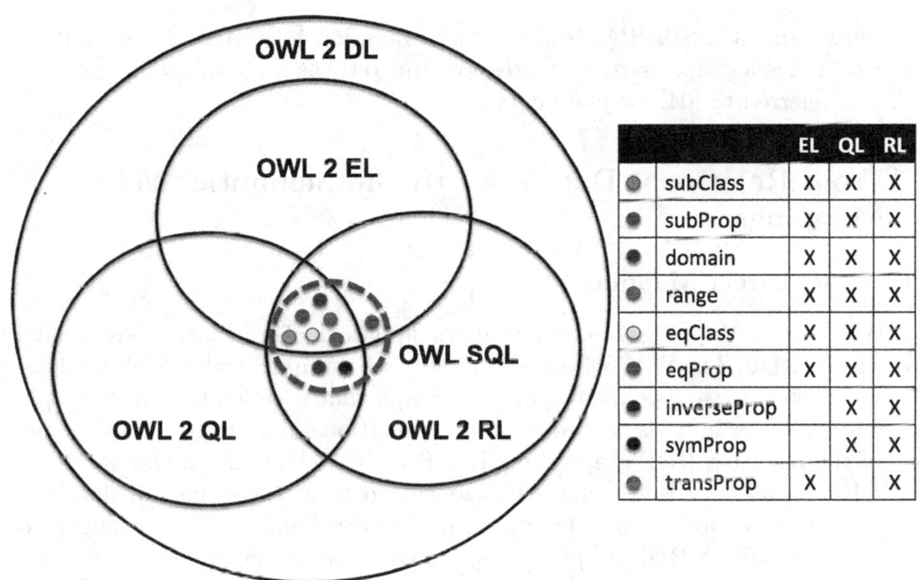

	EL	QL	RL
subClass	X	X	X
subProp	X	X	X
domain	X	X	X
range	X	X	X
eqClass	X	X	X
eqProp	X	X	X
inverseProp		X	X
symProp		X	X
transProp	X		X

Fig. 2. OWL-SQL, proposed OWL profile

The expressivity of OWL-SQL is subsumed by early ontology profile proposals known as RDFS-Plus [4], OWL-LD [32] and RDFS 3.0 [39].

2.4 SPARQL

SPARQL is the standard query language for RDF [38,59]. SPARQL is a graph pattern matching query language and has a syntax similar to SQL. A SPARQL query contains a set of triple patterns called basic graph patterns. Triple patterns are similar to RDF triples with the exception that the subject, predicate or object can be variables (denoted by a leading question mark "?"). The answer of a SPARQL query P over an RDF graph G is a finite set of *mappings*, where a mapping μ is a partial function from the set $\mathbf{V}$ of variables to $(\mathbf{I} \cup \mathbf{L} \cup \mathbf{B})$[4].

[4] Recall that $\mathbf{V}$ is an infinite set of variables disjoint from $\mathbf{I}$, $\mathbf{B}$ and $\mathbf{L}$ and that every element in $\mathbf{V}$ starts with the symbol "?". See Sect. 2.3.

Example 3. Consider the RDF triples in Example 1. *The following SPARQL query asks for all names of people.*

```
SELECT ?n
WHERE {
  ?s rdf:type foaf:Person.
  ?s foaf:name ?n.
}
```

The basic graph pattern consists of two triple patterns. Matching these triple patterns with the RDF triples gives the answer `"Juan Sequeda"`.

The semantics of SPARQL is defined as a function $[\![\cdot]\!]_G$ that, given an RDF graph G, takes a graph pattern expression and returns a set of mappings. The reader is referred to [64] for more detail.

3 From Relational Databases to the Semantic Web: Mappings

3.1 W3C Direct Mapping

The W3C Direct Mapping [7] is an automatic approach of translating a relational database to RDF. The W3C Direct Mapping takes as input a relational database (data and schema), and generates an RDF graph that is called the direct graph. No additional user input is needed to map the relational data to RDF. The structure of the resulting RDF graph directly reflects the structure of the database. The RDF vocabulary is automatically generated from the names of database schema elements. Neither the structure nor the vocabulary can be changed. If needed, the resulting RDF graph can be transformed further by the user using other RDF to RDF mapping approaches such as SPARQL CONSTRUCT.

The W3C Direct Mapping consists of two parts. A specification to generate identifiers for a table, column foreign key and rows and a specification using the identifiers, in order to generate the direct graph.

Generating Identifiers. The W3C Direct Mapping generates an identifier for rows, tables, columns and foreign keys. If a table has a primary key, then the row identifier will be an IRI, otherwise a blank node. The identifiers for tables, columns and foreign keys are IRIs. It is important to note that in this paper we present relative IRIs which must be resolved by appending to a given base IRI. Throughout this document, http://ex.com/rdb2rdf/ is the base IRI. All strings are percent encoded in order to generate a safe IRI[5].

If a table has a primary key, then the row identifier will be an IRI, obtained by concatenating the base IRI, the percent-encoded form of the table name, the '#' character and for each column in the primary key, in order:

[5] For example, a space is replaced with %20 e.g., the percent encoding of "Hello World" is "Hello%20World".

- the percent-encoded form of the column name,
- the '=' character
- the percent-encoded lexical form of the canonical RDF literal representation of the column value
- if it is not the last column in the primary key, the ';' character

For example the IRI for the row of the order table is <http://ex.com/rdb2rdf/order#orderid=1234>. If a table does not have a primary key, then the row identifier is a fresh blank node that is unique to each row

The IRI for a table is obtained by concatenating the base IRI with the percent-encoded form of the table name. For example the table IRI of the order table is <http://ex.com/rdb2rdf/order> The IRI for an attribute is obtained by concatenating the base IRI with the percent-encoded form of the table name, the '#' character and the percent-encoded form of the column name. For example, the Literal Property IRI of the date attribute of the order table is <http://ex.com/rdb2rdf/order#date> Finally the IRI for foreign key is obtained by concatenating the base IRI with the percent-encoded form of the table name, the string '#ref-' and for each column in the foreign key, in order:

- the percent-encoded form of the column name,
- if it is not the last column in the foreign key, a ';' character

For example, the reference Property IRI of the foreign key orderid of the lineitem table is <http://ex.com/rdb2rdf/lineitem#ref-orderid>

Generating the Direct Graph. A Direct Graph is the RDF graph resulting from directly mapping each of the rows of each table and view in a database schema. Each row in a table generates a Row Graph. The row graph is an RDF graph consisting of the following triples: (1) a row type triple, (2) a literal triple for each column in a table where the column value is non-NULL and (3) a reference triple for each foreign key in the table where none of the column values is NULL. A row type triple is an RDF triple with the subject as the row node for the row, the predicate as the RDF IRI `rdf:type` and the object as the table IRI for the table name. A literal triple is an RDF triple with the subject as the row node for the row, the predicate as the literal property IRI for the column and the object as the natural RDF literal representation of the column value. Finally, a reference triple is an RDF triple with the subject as the row node for the row, the predicate as the reference property IRI for the columns and the object as the row node for the referenced row.

Example 4 (W3C Direct Mapping of Running Example). RDF generated by the W3C Direct Mapping of the running example, in Turtle syntax. Recall that the IRIs in the example are relative IRIs which must be resolved by appending to the base IRI http://ex.com/rdb2rdf/.

```
<order#orderid=1234> rdf:type <order> ;
    <order#orderid>"1234" ;
```

```
    <order#date> "2017-04-15";
    <order#total> "100";
    <order#currency> "USD";
    <order#status> "1".
<lineitem#lineid=6789> rdf:type <lineitem>;
    <lineitem#lineid> "6789";
    <lineitem#price> "30";
    <lineitem#quantity> "2";
    <lineitem#product> "Foo";
    <lineitem#orderid> "1234";
    <lineitem#ref-orderid> <order#orderid=1234>.
<lineitem#lineid=6790> rdf:type <lineitem>;
    <lineitem#lineid> "6790";
    <lineitem#price> "20";
    <lineitem#quantity> "2";
    <lineitem#product> "Bar";
    <lineitem#orderid> "1234";
    <lineitem#ref-orderid> <order#orderid=1234>.
```

The formal semantics of the W3C Direct Mapping has been defined in Datalog. We refer the reader to the W3C Direct Mapping standard document for details [7]. The left hand side of each rule is the RDF Triple output. The right hand side of each rule consists of a sequence of predicates from the relational database and built-in predicates.

3.2 $\mathcal{DM}$: Direct Mapping as Ontology

The W3C Direct Mapping standard has two main shortcomings. First, the mapping is only from relational data to RDF data. The relational schema is not taken in account. Second, the semantics of the W3C Direct Mapping is not defined for NULL values as described in the specification: *"The direct mapping does not generate triples for NULL values. Note that it is not known how to relate the behavior of the obtained RDF graph with the standard SQL semantics of the NULL values of the source RDB."* In this section, we first formally introduce the notion of a direct mapping. Subsequently we introduce a new Direct Mapping which addresses the aforementioned shortcomings.

A direct mapping is a default way to translate relational databases into RDF (without any input from the user on how the relational data should be translated). The input of a direct mapping $\mathcal{M}$ is a relational schema $\mathbf{R}$, a set Σ of PKs (Primary Keys) and FKs (Foreign Keys) over $\mathbf{R}$ and an instance I of $\mathbf{R}$. The output is an RDF graph with OWL vocabulary.

Assume $\mathcal{G}$ is the set of all RDF graphs and $\mathcal{RC}$ is the set of all triples of the form $(\mathbf{R}, \Sigma, I)$ such that $\mathbf{R}$ is a relational schema, Σ is a set of PKs and FKs over $\mathbf{R}$ and I is an instance of $\mathbf{R}$.

Definition 13 (Direct Mapping). *A direct mapping $\mathcal{M}$ is a total function from $\mathcal{RC}$ to $\mathcal{G}$.*

We introduce the Direct Mapping as Ontology [65], denoted as $\mathcal{DM}$, which extends the W3C Direct Mapping [7] and combines with a direct mapping of relational database schema to an OWL ontology [69,73]. Additionally, $\mathcal{DM}$ considers the case when the input database has NULL values. $\mathcal{DM}$ is defined as a set of Datalog predicate and rules[6].

1. Five predicates that encode the input relational schema and instance to $\mathcal{DM}$: $\textsc{Rel}(r)$: Indicates that r is a relation name in $\mathbf{R}$, $\textsc{Attr}(a, r)$: Indicates that a is an attribute in the relation r in $\mathbf{R}$, $\text{PK}_n(a_1, \ldots, a_n, r)$: Indicates that $r[a_1, \ldots, a_n]$ is a primary key in Σ, $\text{FK}_n(a_1, \ldots, a_n, r, b_1, \ldots, b_n, s)$: Indicates that $r[a_1, \ldots, a_n] \subseteq_{\text{FK}} s[b_1, \ldots, b_n]$ is a foreign key in Σ, and $\textsc{Value}(v, a, t, r)$ which Indicates that v is the value of an attribute a in a tuple with identifier t in a relation r (that belongs to $\mathbf{R}$).
2. Three predicates that are used to store an ontology: $\textsc{Class}(c)$ indicates that c is a class; $\text{OP}_n(p_1, \ldots, p_n, d, r)$ indicates that $p_1, \ldots, p_n$ $(n \geq 1)$ form an object property with domain d and range r and $\text{DTP}(p, d)$ indicates that p is a data type property with domain d.
3. Twelve Datalog rules that generate a putative ontology from a relational schema. The rules can be summarized as follows: a table is translated to an OWL Class unless the table represents a binary relationship, then it is translated to an OWL Object Property. Foreign Keys are translated to OWL Object Properties while attributes are translated to OWL Datatype Properties.
4. Ten Datalog rules that generate the OWL ontology from the predicates that are used to store an ontology which include rules to generate IRIs and express the ontology as RDF triples.
5. Ten Datalog rules that generate RDF triples from a relational instance based on the putative ontology.

We present example Datalog rules for the generation of classes and datatype properties. We refer the reader to [65] for the detailed list of Datalog rules. A class, defined by the predicate $\textsc{Class}$, is any relation that is not a binary relation. A relation R is a binary relation, defined by the predicate $\textsc{BinRel}$, between two relations S and T if (1) both S and T are different from R, (2) R has exactly two attributes A and B, which form a primary key of R, (3) A is the attribute of a foreign key in R that points to S, (4) B is the attribute of a foreign key in R that points to T, (5) A is not the attribute of two distinct foreign keys in R, (6) B is not the attribute of two distinct foreign keys in R, (7) A and B are not the attributes of a composite foreign key in R, and (8) relation R does not have incoming foreign keys. The formal definition of $\textsc{BinRel}$ can be found in [65]. Therefore, the predicate $\textsc{Class}$ is defined by the following Datalog rules:

$$\textsc{Class}(X) \leftarrow \textsc{Rel}(X), \neg\textsc{IsBinRel}(X)$$
$$\textsc{IsBinRel}(X) \leftarrow \textsc{BinRel}(X, A, B, S, C, T, D)$$

For instance, we have that $\textsc{Class}(\texttt{order})$ holds in our example.

[6] We refer the reader to [2] for the syntax and semantics of Datalog.

Every attribute in a non-binary relation is mapped to a data type property, defined by the predicate DTP, which is defined by the following Datalog rule:

$$\mathrm{DTP}(A, R) \leftarrow \textsc{Attr}(A, R), \neg\textsc{IsBinRel}(R)$$

For instance, we have that DTP(`date`, `order`) holds in our example.

We now briefly define the rules that translates a relational database schema into an OWL vocabulary. We introduce a family of rules that produce IRIs for classes and data type properties identified by the mapping (which are stored in the predicates Class and DTP). Note that the IRIs generated can be later on replaced or mapped to existing IRIs available in the Semantic Web. Assume given a base IRI `base` for the relational database to be translated (for example, "http://ex.com/rdb2rdf/"), and assume a family of built-in predicates $\textsc{Concat}_n$ ($n \geq 2$) is given, such that $\textsc{Concat}_n$ has $n+1$ arguments and $\textsc{Concat}_n(x_1, \ldots, x_n, y)$ holds if y is the concatenation of the strings x_1, ..., x_n. Then by following the approach proposed in [7], $\mathcal{DM}$ uses the following Datalog rules to produce IRIs for classes and data type properties:

$$\begin{aligned} \textsc{Class}\mathrm{IRI}(R, X) &\leftarrow \textsc{Class}(R), \textsc{Concat}_2(\texttt{base}, R, X) \\ \mathrm{DTP\_IRI}(A, R, X) &\leftarrow \mathrm{DTP}(A, R), \textsc{Concat}_4(\texttt{base}, R, \texttt{"\#"}, A, X) \end{aligned}$$

For instance, http://ex.com/rdb2rdf/order is the IRI for the `order` relation in our example, and http://ex.com/rdb2rdf/order#date is the IRI for attribute `date` in the `order` relation.

The following Datalog rules are used to generate the RDF representation of the OWL vocabulary. A rule is used to collect all the classes:

$$\begin{aligned} \textsc{Triple}(U, \texttt{"rdf:type"}, \texttt{"owl:Class"}) \leftarrow& \\ \textsc{Class}(R), \textsc{Class}\mathrm{IRI}(R, U)& \end{aligned}$$

The predicate Triple is used to collect all the triples of the RDF graph generated by the direct mapping $\mathcal{DM}$. The following rule is used to collect all the data type properties:

$$\begin{aligned} \textsc{Triple}(U, \texttt{"rdf:type"}, \texttt{"owl:DatatypeProperty"}) \leftarrow& \\ \mathrm{DTP}(A, R), \mathrm{DTP\_IRI}(A, R, U)& \end{aligned}$$

The following rule is used to collect the domains of the data type properties:

$$\begin{aligned} \textsc{Triple}(U, \texttt{"rdfs:domain"}, W) \leftarrow& \\ \mathrm{DTP}(A, R), \mathrm{DTP\_IRI}(A, R, U), \textsc{Class}\mathrm{IRI}(R, W)& \end{aligned}$$

Example 5 (Direct Mapping as Ontology of Running Example). OWL generated by the Direct Mapping as Ontology of the running example, in Turtle syntax. The RDF triples from the Direct Mapping as Ontology are the same as in Example 4. Recall that the IRIs in the example are relative IRIs which must be resolved by appending to the base IRI http://ex.com/rdb2rdf/.

```
<order> rdf:type owl:Class.
<order#orderid> rdf:type owl:DatatypeProperty ;
   rdfs:domain <order>.
<order#date> rdf:type owl:DatatypeProperty;
   rdfs:domain <order>.
<order#total> rdf:type owl:DatatypeProperty;
   rdfs:domain <order>.
<order#currency> rdf:type owl:DatatypeProperty;
   rdfs:domain <order>.
<order#status> rdf:type owl:DatatypeProperty;
   rdfs:domain <order>.
<lineitem> rdf:type owl:Class.
<lineitem#lineid> rdf:type owl:DatatypeProperty;
   rdfs:domain <lineitem>.
<lineitem#price> rdf:type owl:DatatypeProperty;
   rdfs:domain <lineitem>.
<lineitem#quantity> rdf:type owl:DatatypeProperty;
   rdfs:domain <lineitem>.
<lineitem#product> rdf:type owl:DatatypeProperty;
   rdfs:domain <lineitem>.
<lineitem#orderid> rdf:type owl:DatatypeProperty;
   rdfs:domain <lineitem>.
<lineitem#ref-pid> rdf:type owl:ObjectProperty;
   rdfs:domain <lineitem>;
   rdfs:range <order>.
```

Direct Mapping Properties. We study two properties that are fundamental to a direct mapping: information preservation and query preservation. Additionally we study two desirable properties: monotonicity and semantics preservation.

A direct mapping is information preserving if it does not lose any information about the relational instance being translated, that is, if there exists a way to recover the original database instance from the RDF graph resulting from the translation process. Formally, assuming that $\mathcal{I}$ is the set of all possible relational instances, we have that:

Definition 14 (Information Preservation). *A direct mapping $\mathcal{M}$ is* information preserving *if there is a computable mapping $\mathcal{N} : \mathcal{G} \rightarrow \mathcal{I}$ such that for every relational schema $\mathbf{R}$, set Σ of PKs and FKs over $\mathbf{R}$, and instance I of $\mathbf{R}$ satisfying Σ: $\mathcal{N}(\mathcal{M}(\mathbf{R}, \Sigma, I)) = I$.*

Recall that a mapping $\mathcal{N} : \mathcal{G} \rightarrow \mathcal{I}$ is computable if there exists an algorithm that, given $G \in \mathcal{G}$, computes $\mathcal{N}(G)$.

Theorem 1. *The direct mapping $\mathcal{DM}$ is information preserving.*

The proof of this theorem is straightforward, and it involves providing a computable mapping $\mathcal{N} : \mathcal{G} \rightarrow \mathcal{I}$ that satisfies the condition in Definition 14, that is, a computable mapping $\mathcal{N}$ that can reconstruct the initial relational instance from the generated RDF graph.

A direct mapping is query preserving if every query over a relational database can be translated into an equivalent query over the RDF graph resulting from the mapping. That is, query preservation ensures that every relational query can be evaluated using the mapped RDF data.

I define query preservation, we focus on relational queries Q that can be expressed in relational algebra [2] and RDF queries $Q^\star$ that can be expressed in SPARQL [55,59]. Given the mismatch in the formats of these query languages (null can appear as a result of a relational query while null does not in a SPARQL query), we introduce a function *tr* that converts tuples returned by relational algebra queries into mappings returned by SPARQL. Formally, given a relational schema $\mathbf{R}$, a relation name $R \in \mathbf{R}$, an instance I of $\mathbf{R}$ and a tuple $t \in R^I$, define $tr(t)$ as the mapping μ such that: (1) the domain of μ is $\{?A \mid A \in att(R)$ and $t.A \neq \texttt{NULL}\}$, and (2) $\mu(?A) = t.A$ for every A in the domain of μ.

Definition 15 (Query Preservation). *A direct mapping $\mathcal{M}$ is* query preserving *if for every relational schema $\mathbf{R}$, set Σ of PKs and FKs over $\mathbf{R}$ and relational algebra query Q over $\mathbf{R}$, there exists a SPARQL query $Q^\star$ such that for every instance I of $\mathbf{R}$ satisfying Σ: $tr([\![Q]\!]_I) = [\![Q^\star]\!]_{\mathcal{M}(\mathbf{R},\Sigma,I)}$.*

We show that the way $\mathcal{DM}$ maps relational data into RDF allows one to answer a query over a relational instance by translating it into an equivalent query over the generated RDF graph.

Theorem 2. *The direct mapping $\mathcal{DM}$ is query preserving.*

Angles and Gutierrez proved that SPARQL has the same expressive power as relational algebra [5]. Thus, one may be tempted to think that this result could be used to prove this theorem. However, the version of relational algebra considered in Angles and Gutierrez does not include the value NULL and hence does not apply to $\mathcal{DM}$. The proof is by induction on the structure of a relational query Q. The proof is also constructive and yields a bottom-up algorithm for translating Q into an equivalent SPARQL query.

Before defining monotonicity, consider the following: given two database instances I_1 and I_2 over a relational schema $\mathbf{R}$, instance I_1 is said to be contained in instance I_2, denoted by $I_1 \subseteq I_2$, if for every $R \in \mathbf{R}$, it holds that $R^{I_1} \subseteq R^{I_2}$. A direct mapping $\mathcal{M}$ is considered monotone if for any such pair of instances, the result of mapping I_2 contains the result of mapping I_1. In other words, if we insert new data to the database, then the elements of the mapping that are already computed are unaltered.

Definition 16 (Monotonicity). *A direct mapping $\mathcal{M}$ is monotone if for every relational schema $\mathbf{R}$, set Σ of PKs and FKs over $\mathbf{R}$, and instances I_1, I_2 of $\mathbf{R}$ such that $I_1 \subseteq I_2$: $\mathcal{M}(\mathbf{R},\Sigma,I_1) \subseteq \mathcal{M}(\mathbf{R},\Sigma,I_2)$.*

Theorem 3. *The direct mapping $\mathcal{DM}$ is monotone.*

It is straightforward to see that $\mathcal{DM}$ is monotone, because all the negative atoms in the Datalog rules defining $\mathcal{DM}$ refer to the schema, the PKs and the FKs of the database, and these elements are kept fixed when checking monotonicity.

A direct mapping is semantics preserving if the satisfaction of a set of PKs and FKs by a relational database is encoded in the translation process. More precisely, given a relational schema $\mathbf{R}$, a set Σ of PKs and FKs over $\mathbf{R}$ and an instance I of $\mathbf{R}$, a semantics preserving mapping should generate from I a consistent RDF graph if $I \models \Sigma$, and it should generate an inconsistent RDF graph otherwise.

Definition 17 (Semantics Preservation). *A direct mapping $\mathcal{M}$ is semantics preserving if for every relation schema $\mathbf{R}$, set Σ of PKs and FKs over $\mathbf{R}$ and instance I of $\mathbf{R}$: $I \models \Sigma$ iff $\mathcal{M}(\mathbf{R}, \Sigma, I)$ is consistent under OWL semantics.*

Unfortunately, the situation is completely different for the case of semantics preservation, as the following example shows that the direct mapping $\mathcal{DM}$ does not satisfy this property.

Example 6. Assume that a relational schema contains a relation with name STUDENT *and attributes* SID, NAME, *and assume that the attribute* SID *is the primary key. Moreover, assume that this relation has two tuples, t_1 and t_2 such that* t_1.SID $= 1$, t_1.NAME $=$ *John* and t_2.SID $= 1$, t_2.NAME $=$ *Peter. It is clear that the primary key is violated, therefore the database is inconsistent. However, it is not difficult to see that after applying $\mathcal{DM}$, the resulting RDF graph is consistent.* □

In fact, the result in Example 6 can be generalized as it is possible to show that the direct mapping $\mathcal{DM}$ always generates a consistent RDF graph, hence, it cannot be semantics preserving[7].

Proposition 1. *The direct mapping $\mathcal{DM}$ is not semantics preserving.*

Consider a new direct mapping $\mathcal{DM}_{pk}$ that extends $\mathcal{DM}$ as follows. A Datalog rule is used to determine if the value of a primary key attribute is repeated, and a family of Datalog rules are used to determine if there is a value NULL in a column corresponding to a primary key. If some of these violations are found, then an artificial triple is generated that would produce an inconsistency.

If we apply $\mathcal{DM}_{pk}$ to the database of Example 6, it is straightforward to see that starting from an inconsistent relational database, one obtains an RDF graph that is also inconsistent. In fact, we have that:

Proposition 2. *The direct mapping $\mathcal{DM}_{pk}$ is information preserving, query preserving, monotone, and semantics preserving if one considers only PKs. That is, for every relational schema $\mathbf{R}$, set Σ of (only) PKs over $\mathbf{R}$ and instance I of $\mathbf{R}$: $I \models \Sigma$ iff $\mathcal{DM}_{pk}(\mathbf{R}, \Sigma, I)$ is consistent under OWL semantics.*

---

[7] In practice an RDBMS will not allow a violation of an integrity constraint. However, it may be the case that an RDBMS is not being used and a user may have a dump of data (e.g. in CSV format) and may indicate that a particular column is the primary key when in reality the column violates the constraint.

Information preservation, query preservation and monotonicity of $\mathcal{DM}_{pk}$ are corollaries of the fact that these properties hold for $\mathcal{DM}$, and of the fact that the Datalog rules introduced to handle primary keys are monotone.

The following theorem shows that the desirable condition of being monotone is, unfortunately, an obstacle to obtain a semantics preserving direct mapping.

Theorem 4. *No monotone direct mapping is semantics preserving.*

It is important to understand the reasons why we have not been able to create a semantics preserving direct mapping. The issue is with two characteristics of OWL: (1) it adopts the Open World Assumption (OWA), where a statement cannot be inferred to be false on the basis of failing to prove it, and (2) it does not adopt the Unique Name Assumption (UNA), where two different names can identify the same thing. On the other hand, a relational database adopts the Closed World Assumption (CWA), where a statement is inferred to be false if it is not known to be true. In other words, what causes an inconsistency in a relational database, can cause an inference of new knowledge in OWL.

In order to preserve the semantics of the relational database, we need to ensure that whatever causes an inconsistency in a relational database, is going to cause an inconsistency in OWL. Following this idea, we now present a non-monotone direct mapping, $\mathcal{DM}_{pk+fk}$, which extends $\mathcal{DM}_{pk}$ by introducing rules for verifying beforehand if there is a violation of a foreign key constraint. If such a violation exists, then an artificial RDF triple is created which will generate an inconsistency with respect to the OWL semantics.

It should be noticed that $\mathcal{DM}_{pk+fk}$ is non-monotone because if new data in the database is added which now satisfies the FK constraint, then the artificial RDF triple needs to be retracted.

Theorem 5. *The direct mapping $\mathcal{DM}_{pk+fk}$ is information preserving, query preserving and semantics preserving.*

Information preservation and query preservation of $\mathcal{DM}_{pk+fk}$ are corollaries of the fact that these properties hold for $\mathcal{DM}$ and $\mathcal{DM}_{pk}$.

A direct mapping that satisfies the four properties can be obtained by considering an alternative semantics of OWL that expresses integrity constraints. Because OWL is based on Description Logic, we would need a version of DL that supports integrity constraints, which is not a new idea [17,28,29,34,49,51,72]. Thus, it is possible to extend $\mathcal{DM}_{pk}$ to create an information preserving, query preserving and monotone direct mapping that is also semantics preserving, but it is based on a non-standard version of OWL.

3.3 W3C R2RML: RDB to RDF Mapping Language

R2RML [25] is a language for expressing customized mappings from relational databases to RDF expressed in a graph structure and domain ontology of the user's choice. The R2RML language is also defined as an RDFS schema[8]. An

[8] http://www.w3.org/ns/r2rml.

R2RML mapping is itself represented as an RDF graph. Turtle is the recommended RDF syntax for writing R2RML mappings. The following is an example of an R2RML mapping for the database in Fig. 1. Note that the mapping developer decides which tables and attributes of the database should be exposed as RDF. The Direct Mapping automatically maps all of the tables and attributes of the database.

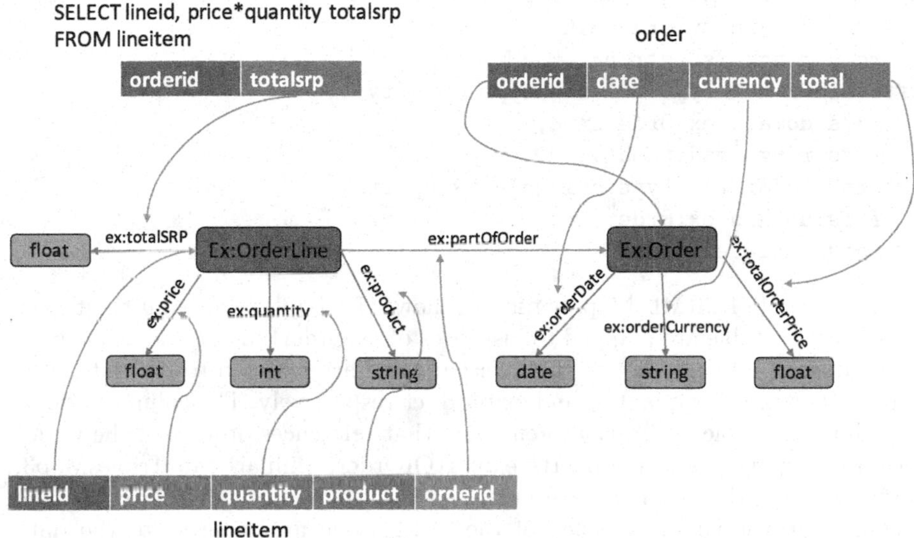

Fig. 3. Example mapping

Example 7 (An R2RML Mapping). Figure 3 represents a mapping from our running example database to an ontology. In this example we will present an R2RML mapping that represents the depiction of Fig. 3.

The target ontology is defined as follows:

```
@prefix ex: <http://ex.com/schema/>.
ex:Order rdf:type owl:Class.
ex:totalOrderPrice rdf:type owl:DatatypeProperty ;
    rdfs:domain ex:Order;
    rdfs:range xsd:float.
ex:orderCurrency rdf:type owl:DatatypeProperty;
    rdfs:domain ex:Order;
    rdfs:range xsd:string.
ex:OrderDate rdf:type owl:DatatypeProperty;
    rdfs:domain ex:Order;
    rdfs:range xsd:date.
```

```
ex:OrderLine rdf:type owl:Class.
ex:price rdf:type owl:DatatypeProperty;
    rdfs:domain ex:OrderLine;
    rdfs:range xsd:float.
ex:quantity rdf:type owl:DatatypeProperty;
    rdfs:domain ex:OrderLine;
    rdfs:range xsd:int.
exproduct rdf:type owl:DatatypeProperty;
    rdfs:domain ex:OrderLine;
    rdfs:range xsd:string.
ex#totalSRP rdf:type owl:DatatypeProperty;
    rdfs:domain ex:OrderLine;
    rdfs:range xsd:float.
ex:partOfOrder rdf:type owl:ObjectProperty;
    rdfs:domain ex:OrderLine;
    rdfs:range ex:Order.
```

The example R2RML Mapping is as follows. In TriplesMap1, all the tuples of the lineitem table are mapped to instances of ex:OrderLine class. The column price, quantity and product of the lineitem table are mapped to the data type properties ex:price ex:quantity and ex:product respectively. The column orderid of the lineitem table which is a foreign key that references orderid of the Order table is mapped to object property ex:partOfOrder. Similarly, in TriplesMap3, all the tuples of the order table are mapped to instances of ex:Order class. The column date, total and currency of the order table are mapped to the data type properties ex:orderDate, ex:totalOrderPrice and ex:orderCurrency respectively. Finally, in TriplesMap2 we have a SQL query that returns a calculation (price*quantity) associated to each lineid. This calculation (the renamed attribute totalsrp) is mapped to the data type property ex:totalSRP.

```
@prefix rr: <http://www.w3.org/ns/r2rml#>.
@prefix ex: <http://ex.com/schema/>.

<#TriplesMap1>
    rr:logicalTable [ rr:tableName "lineitem" ];
    rr:subjectMap [
        rr:template "http://ex.com/data/orderline/{lineid}";
        rr:class ex:OrderLine;
    ];
    rr:predicateObjectMap [
        rr:predicateMap [ rr:constant ex:price ];
        rr:objectMap [ rr:column "price" ];
    ];
    rr:predicateObjectMap [
        rr:predicateMap [ rr:constant ex:quantity ];
        rr:objectMap [ rr:column "quantity" ];
```

```
    ];
    rr:predicateObjectMap [
        rr:predicateMap [ rr:constant ex:product ];
        rr:objectMap [ rr:column "product" ];
    ];
    rr:predicateObjectMap [
        rr:predicate [ rr:constant ex:partOfOrder ];
        rr:objectMap [
            rr:parentTriplesMap <#TriplesMap3>;
            rr:joinCondition [
                rr:child "orderid";
                rr:parent "orderid";
            ];
        ];
    ].

<#TriplesMap2>
    rr:logicalTable [ rr:sqlQuery """
        SELECT lineid, price*quantity totalsrp FROM lineitem
       """ ];
    rr:subjectMap [
        rr:template "http://ex.com/data/orderline/{lineid}";
    ];
   rr:predicateObjectMap [
        rr:predicateMap [ rr:constant ex:totalSRP ];
        rr:objectMap [ rr:column "totalsrp" ];
    ].

<#TriplesMap3>
    rr:logicalTable [ rr:tableName "order" ];
    rr:subjectMap [
        rr:template "http://ex.com/data/order/{orderid}";
        rr:class ex:Order;
    ];
    rr:predicateObjectMap [
        rr:predicateMap [ rr:constant ex:orderDate ];
        rr:objectMap [ rr:column "date" ];
    ];
    rr:predicateObjectMap [
        rr:predicateMap [ rr:constant ex:totalOrderPrice ];
        rr:objectMap [ rr:column "total" ];
    ];
    rr:predicateObjectMap [
        rr:predicateMap [ rr:constant ex:orderCurrency ];
        rr:objectMap [ rr:column "currency" ];
```

```
    ];
.
```

The following is the resulting RDF after the mapping has been applied on the example database:

```
<http://ex.com/data/order/1234> rdf:type ex:Order;
    ex:orderDate "2017-04-15";
    ex:totalOrderPrice "100";
    ex:orderCurrency "USD".

<http://ex.com/data/orderline/6789> rdf:type ex:OrderLine;
    ex:price "30";
    ex:quantity "2";
    ex:totalSRP "60";
    ex:product "Foo";
    ex:partOfOrder <http://ex.com/data/order/1234>.

<http://ex.com/data/orderline/6790> rdf:type ex:OrderLine
    ex:price "20";
    ex:quantity "2";
    ex:totalSRP "40";
    ex:product "Bar";
    ex:partOfOrder <http://ex.com/data/order/1234>.
```

An R2RML processor may include an R2RML default mapping generator. This is a facility that introspects the schema of the input database and generates an R2RML mapping intended for further customization by a user. This default mapping could be the W3C Direct Mapping or the Direct Mapping as Ontology $\mathcal{DM}$.

The R2RML language features can be divided in two parts: features generating RDF terms (IRI, Blank Nodes or Literals) and features for generating RDF triples.

Generating RDF Terms. An RDF term is either an IRI, a Blank node, or a Literal. A term map generates an RDF term for the subjects, predicates and objects of the RDF triples from either a constant, a template or a column value. A constant-valued term map ignores the row and always generates the same RDF term. A column-valued term map generates an RDF term from the value of a column. A template-valued term map generates an RDF term from a string template, which is a format string that can be used to build strings from multiple components, including the values of a column. Template-valued term maps are commonly used to specify how an IRI should be generated.

The R2RML language allows a user to explicitly state the type of RDF term that needs to be generated (IRI, Blank node or Literal). If the RDF term is for a subject, then the term type must be either an IRI or Blank Node. If the

RDF term is for a predicate, then the term type must be an IRI. If the RDF term is for a subject, then the term type can be either an IRI, Blank node or Literal. Additionally, a developer may assert that an RDF term has an assigned language tag or datatype.

Generating RDF Triples. RDF triples are derived from a logical table. A logical table can be either a base table or view in the relational schema, or an R2RML view. An R2RML view is a logical table whose contents are the result of executing a SQL SELECT query against the input database. In an RDB2RDF mapping, it may be required to transform, compute or filter data before generating RDF triples. This can be achieved by defining a SQL view and referring to it as a base view. However, it may be the case that this is not possible due to lack of sufficient database privileges to create views. R2RML views achieve the same effect without requiring any changes to the input database.

A triples map is the heart of an R2RML mapping. It specifies a rule for translating each row of a logical table to zero or more RDF triples. Example 7 contains two triple maps identified by `<#TriplesMap1>` and `<#TriplesMap2>`. The RDF triples generated from one row in the logical table all share the same subject. A triples map is represented by a resource that references the following other resources:

- It must have exactly one logical table. Its value is a logical table that specifies a SQL query result to be mapped to triples. In Example 7, both Triple Map's 1 and 3 have a table name as a logical table, `lineitem` and `order`, respectively. TripleMap2 has a logical table which is a SQL Query.
- It must have exactly one subject map that specifies how to generate a subject for each row of the logical table.
- It may have zero or more predicate-object maps, which specify pairs of predicate maps and object maps that, together with the subject generated by the subject map, may form one or more RDF triples for each row.

Recall that there are three types of term maps that generate RDF terms: constant-valued, column-valued and template-valued. Given that a subject, predicate and object of an RDF triple must be RDF terms, this means that a subject, predicate and object can be any of the three possible term maps, called subject map, predicate map and object map, respectively. A predicateObject map groups predicate-object map pairs.

A subject map is a term map that specifies the subject of the RDF triple. The primary key of a table is usually the basis for creating an IRI. Therefore, it is normally the case that a subject map is a template-valued term map with an IRI template using the value of a column which is usually the primary key. Consider the triple map `<#TriplesMap1>` in Example 7. The subject map is a template-valued term map where the template is `http://ex.com/data/order/{orderid}`. This means that the subject IRI for each row is formed using values of the `orderid` attribute. Optionally, a subject map may have one or more class IRIs. For each RDF term generated by the subject map, RDF triples with predicate `rdf:type` and the class IRI as object will be generated. In this example, the class IRI is `ex:Order`.

A predicate-object map is a function that creates one or more predicate-object pairs for each row of a logical table. It is used in conjunction with a subject map to generate RDF triples in a triples map. A predicate-object map is represented by a resource that references the following other resources: One or more predicate maps and one or more object maps or referencing object maps. In `<#TriplesMap1>`, there are four predicate-object maps while `<#TriplesMap2>` only has one.

A predicate map is a term map. It is common that the predicate of an RDF triple is a constant. Therefore, a predicate map is usually a constant-valued term map. For example, the first predicate-object map of `<#TriplesMap1>` has a predicate map which is a constant-valued term map. The predicate IRI will always be the constant is `ex:price`. An object map is also a term map. Several use cases may arise where the object could be either a constant-valued, template-valued or column-valued term map. The first predicate-object map of `<#TriplesMap1>` has an object map which is a column-valued term map. Therefore, the object will be a literal coming from the value of the `price` attribute.

A referencing object map allows using the subjects of another triples map as the objects generated by a predicate-object map. Since both triples maps may be based on different logical tables, this may require a join between the logical tables. A referencing object map is represented by a resource that has exactly one parent triples maps. Additionally, it may have one or more join conditions. Join conditions are represented by a resource that has exactly one value for each of the following: (1) a child, whose value is known as the join condition's child column and must be a column name that exists in the logical table of the triples map that contains the referencing object map (2) a parent, whose value is known as the join condition's parent column and must be a column name that exists in the logical table of the referencing object map's parent triples map. The last predicate-object map of `<#TriplesMap1>` has a referencing object map. The parent triples map is `<#TriplesMap3>`. A join condition is created between the child attribute `orderid`, which is an column name in the logical table of `<#TriplesMap1>` and the parent attribute `orderid`, which is a column name in the logical table of `<#TriplesMap3>`

3.4 Relational Databases to RDF Mappings

Even though there has been attempts to formalize R2RML [62], to the best of our knowledge, there is no formal public definition of R2RML. Nevertheless, we believe it is important to formalize a notion of a customized mapping from Relation Databases to RDF, which we denote as an RDB2RDF mapping. This alternative approach follows the widely used formalization in the data exchange [6] and data integration areas [46], and which is based on the use of first-order logic and its semantics to define mappings.

Given a relational schema **R** such that triple $\notin$ **R**, a class RDB2RDF-rule ρ over **R** is a first-order formula of the form:

$$\forall s \forall p \forall o \forall \bar{x}\ \alpha(s, \bar{x}) \land p = \texttt{type} \land o = c \rightarrow \texttt{triple}(s, p, o), \qquad (1)$$

where $\alpha(s, \bar{x})$ is a domain-independent first-order formula over **R** and $c \in \mathbf{D}$.

Moreover, a predicate RDB2RDF-rule ρ over **R** is a first-order formula of the form:

$$\forall s \forall p \forall o \forall \bar{x}\ \beta(s, o, \bar{x}) \land p = c \rightarrow \texttt{triple}(s, p, o), \qquad (2)$$

where $\beta(s, o, \bar{x})$ is a domain-independent first-order formula over **R** and $c \in \mathbf{D}$. Finally, an RDB2RDF-rule over **R** is either a class or a predicate RDB2RDF-rule over **R**. In what follows, we omit the universal quantifiers $\forall s \forall p \forall o \forall \bar{x}$ from RDB2RDF rules, and we implicitly assume that these variables are universally quantify.

Example 8. Consider the relational database from our running example (see Example 1). Then the following RDB2RDF rule maps all the instances of the order *table as instances of the* Order *class:* $\texttt{order}(s, x_1, x_2, x_3, x_4, x_5) \land p = \texttt{type} \land o = \texttt{Order} \rightarrow \texttt{triple}(s, p, o)$.

The RDB2RDF mapping in Example 8 can be represented as follows in R2RML:

```
<#TriplesMap>
    rr:logicalTable [ rr:tableName "order" ];
    rr:subjectMap [
        rr:template "http://ex.com/data/order/{orderid}";
        rr:class ex:Order;
    ];
.
```

Additionally, it could also be represented as follows:

```
<#TriplesMap>
    rr:logicalTable [ rr:tableName "order" ];
    rr:subjectMap [
        rr:template "http://ex.com/data/order/{orderid}";
    ];
    rr:predicateObjectMap [
        rr:predicate rdf:type ;
        rr:object ex:Order ;
    ];
.
```

Let **R** be a relational schema. An RDB2RDF mapping $\mathcal{M}$ over **R** is a finite set of RDB2RDF rules over **R**. Given an RDB2RDF mapping $\mathcal{M}$ and an instance

I over $\mathbf{R}$, the result of applying $\mathcal{M}$ over I, denoted by $[\![\mathcal{M}]\!]_I$, is an instance over the schema $\{\texttt{triple}\}$ that is defined as the result of the following process. For every RDB2RDF rule of the form (1) and value $c_1 \in \mathbf{D}$, if there exists a tuple of values $\bar{d}$ from $\mathbf{D}$ such that $I \models \alpha(c_1, \bar{d})$,[9] then $\texttt{triple}(c_1, \texttt{type}, c)$ is included as a fact of $[\![\mathcal{M}]\!]_I$, and likewise for every RDB2RDF rule of the form (2). Notice that this definition coincides with the notion of canonical universal solution in the context of data exchange [6]. Besides, notice that $[\![\mathcal{M}]\!]_I$ represents an RDF graph and, thus, mapping $\mathcal{M}$ can be considered as a mapping from relational databases into RDF graphs.

Example 9. Consider the relational database from our running example, and let $\mathcal{M}$ be an RDB2RDF mapping consisting of the rule in Example 1 *and the following rule:*

$$\texttt{order}(s, x_1, o, x_3, x_4, x_5) \wedge p = \texttt{orderDate} \rightarrow \texttt{triple}(s, p, o) \tag{3}$$

If I is the instance from our running example, then $[\![\mathcal{M}]\!]_I$ consists of the following facts:

$$\texttt{triple}(1234, \texttt{type}, \texttt{Order}),\ \texttt{triple}(1234, \texttt{orderDate}, 2017-04-15).$$

The RDB2RDF mapping in Example 9 can be represented as follows in R2RML:

```
<#TriplesMap>
    rr:logicalTable [ rr:tableName "order" ];
    rr:subjectMap [
        rr:template "http://ex.com/data/order/{orderid}";
        rr:class ex:Order;
    ];
    rr:predicateObjectMap [
        rr:predicate  ex:orderDate ;
        rr:objectMap [ rr:column "date" ];
    ];
.
```

4 From the Semantic Web to Relational Databases: Data Access

The Semantic Web's promise of web-wide data integration requires the inclusion of legacy Relational Databases. In the previous section, we discussed how to go from a Relational Database to the Semantic Web through means of mappings. In this section, we present the other direction: how the Semantic Web can access a Relational Database.

[9] Given that $\alpha(s, \bar{x})$ is domain-independent, there exists a finite number of tuples $(c_1, \bar{d})$ such that $I \models \alpha(c_1, \bar{d})$.

In RDF data management there are efforts that concern Triplestores and those that concern legacy Relational Databases. Triplestores are database management systems whose data model is RDF, and support at least SPARQL execution against the stored contents. Native triplestores are those that are implemented from scratch [14,53,76]. RDBMS-backed Triplestores are built by adding an application layer to an existing relational database management system. Within that literature there is a discourse concerning the best database schema, SPARQL to SQL query translations, indexing methods and even storage managers, (i.e. column stores vs. row stores) [1,21,30,77]. NoSQL Triplestores are also being investigated as possible RDF storage managers [24,31,41,44]. In all three triplestore cases (native, RDBMS-backed and NoSQL), RDF is the primary data model.

The research herein is concerned with the mapping of legacy relational data with the Semantic Web. Within that, the research concerns wrapper systems that present a logical RDF representation of relational data that is physically stored in an RDBMS such that no copy of the relational data is made. It follows that some or all of a SPARQL query evaluation is executed by the SQL engine. An alternative approach is the one in which the relational data is extracted from the relational database, transformed to RDF, and loaded (ETL) into a Triplestore.

Since both RDBMS-backed Triplestores and RDB2RDF Wrapper systems involve relational databases and translation from SPARQL to SQL, there is a potential for confusion. The difference is that RDBMS backed Triplestores translate SPARQL queries to SQL queries that are executed on database schemas that model and store RDF. RDB2RDF Wrapper systems translate SPARQL queries to SQL queries that are executed on legacy database schemas that model and store relational data.

An RDB2RDF ETL approach is recommended when the data in the legacy relational database is stale, or updated infrequently. In an ETL system, at best, updates occur on a regular cycle. Thus semantic web applications querying stale data just prior to an update is a risk. In the common case of legacy relational databases which are continually updated, an ETL approach is not feasible. A solution to this problem is the use of a RDB2RDF wrapper systems which compiles SPARQL to SQL.

4.1 SPARQL to SQL Rewriting with Direct Mapping

In mid to late 2000s, RDB2RDF wrapper systems such as D2RQ, Virtuoso RDF Views and Squirrel RDF, predicated on preprocessing and/or optimizing the SQL query before sending it to the SQL optimizer. Open-source code and forums[10] provide evidence of their architecture. For example, we observed that for some SPARQL queries, D2RQ generates multiple SQL queries and necessarily executed a join among those results outside of the database. In 2011, we postulated that by carefully constructing SQL views to represent a RDB2RDF

[10] https://github.com/d2rq/d2rq/issues/94 As of April 2017, this issue is still open.

mapping, then the existing algorithmic machinery in SQL optimizers were sufficient to effectively execute SPARQL queries on native relational data [67]. Thereby, legacy relational database systems may be made upwardly compatible with the Semantic Web, while simultaneously minimizing the complexity of the wrapping system.

In 2008, Angles and Gutierrez showed that SPARQL is equivalent in expressive power to relational algebra [5]. Thus, one might have expected that the validity of this research's postulate at that time, to be a foregone conclusion. However, in 2009, two independent studies that evaluated three RDB2RDF wrapper systems, D2RQ, Virtuoso RDF Views and Squirrel RDF, came to the opposite conclusion: existing SPARQL to SQL translation systems do not compete with traditional relational databases [11,33].

The March 2009 Berlin SPARQL Benchmark on the 100 million triple dataset reported that SPARQL queries on the evaluated RDB2RDF systems were up to 1000 times slower that the native SQL queries. Bizer and Schultz [11], creators of the Berlin SPARQL Benchmark, concluded that: "*Setting the results of the RDF stores and the SPARQL-to-SQL rewriters in relation to the performance of classical RDBMS unveiled an unedifying picture. Comparing the overall performance (100 M triple, single client, all queries) of the fastest rewriter with the fastest relational database shows an overhead for query rewriting of 106%. This is an indicator that there is still room for improving the rewriting algorithms*".

Gray et al. [33] tested D2RQ and SquirrelRDF on a scientific database. This study concluded that "*... current rdb2rdf systems are not capable of providing the query execution performance required to implement a scientific data integration system based on the rdf model. [...] it is likely that with more work on query translation, suitable mechanisms for translating queries could be developed. These mechanisms should focus on exploiting the underlying database system's capabilities to optimize queries and process large quantities of structured data, e.g. pushing the selection conditions to the underlying database system*".

A motivation for this research, at that time, was to resolve the apparent contradiction among the aforementioned papers. Toward that end we researched and engineered the Ultrawrap system [67].

Ultrawrap Architecture. The first version of Ultrawrap was compliant with the W3C Direct Mapping standard. The goal was to understand if existing commercial relational databases already subsume the algorithms and optimizations needed to support effective SPARQL execution on existing relationally stored data under the simplest mapping possible. This initial version of Ultrawrap was organized as a set of four compilers with the understanding that the SQL optimizer formed one of the compilers.

1. The generation of the Direct Mapping with the translation of a SQL schema, including constraints, to an OWL ontology: the putative ontology (PO).
2. The creation of an intensional triple table in the database by augmenting the relational schema with one or more SQL Views: the Tripleview.

3. Translation of SPARQL queries to equivalent SQL queries operating on the Tripleview.
4. The native SQL query optimizer, which becomes responsible for rewriting triple based queries and effecting their execution on extensional relational data.

These four components can be seen as four different language compilers. As an ensemble, the first three provide for the logical mapping of schema, data and queries between the relational and Semantic Web languages. The fourth component, the SQL optimizer, is responsible for the evaluation of the data mappings and concomitant optimization of the query.

To define the mapping of the relational data to RDF, the system first identifies an ontological representation of the relational schema, which is done by the Direct Mapping and the generation of the putative ontology. The putative ontology is the input to a second compilation step that creates a logical definition of the relational data as RDF and embeds it in a view definition. In a off-line process, Ultrawrap defines a SQL view whose query component is a specification of a mapping from the relational data to an RDF triple representation, the Tripleview. Per the Direct Mapping, concatenating the table name with the primary key value or table name with attribute name creates unique identifiers for subject, predicate and objects. Subsequently, unique identifiers can be appended to a base URI. The SQL Tripleview is comprised of a union of SELECT-FROM-WHERE (SFW) statements. The WHERE clause filters attributes with null values (IS NOT NULL), given that null values are not expressible in RDF.

Due to its simplicity, our starting point is the triple table approach. Even though, studies have shown that storing RDF with the triple table approach in a relational database is easily improved upon [1,48], this issue is not relevant to Ultrawrap because the relational data is not being materialized in a triple table; instead the relational data is virtually represented as a triple table through unmaterialized views.

Even though our goal is to define a virtual triple table, we still have to anticipate the physical characteristics of the database and the capacity of the SQL optimizer to produce optimal physical plans. Toward that end, the Tripleview has the following characteristics.

The Tripleview is of the form: <subject, primary key of subject, predicate, object, primary key of object>. Separating the primary key in the Tripleview allows the query optimizer to exploit them because the joins are done on these values. If the object is a data value, then a NULL is used as the primary key of the object. The subject and object are still kept as the concatenation of the table name with the primary key value because this is used to generate the final URI, which uniquely identifies each tuple in the database. It is possible to augment the number of attributes in the Tripleview to include each separate key value.

Instead of having a single Tripleview to represent the entire mapping, it is beneficial to create a separate Tripleview for each datatype. For varchar, this includes each length declared in the schema. For example, datatypes with varchar(50) and varchar(200) are considered different. Using multiple Tripleviews requires less bookkeeping than one might anticipate. Each attribute is mapped to its corresponding Tripleview and stored in a hashtable. Then, given an attribute, the corresponding Tripleview can be retrieved.

For example, the Tripleviews for the direct mapping of our running example is the following:

```
CREATE VIEW Tripleview_type(s,s_id,p,o,o_id) AS
SELECT "order"+orderid as s, orderid as s_id, "type" as p,
       "order" as o, null as o_id
FROM order
UNION ALL
SELECT "lineitem"+lineid as s, lineid as s_id,"type" as p,
       "lineitem" as o, null as o_id
FROM lineitem

CREATE VIEW Tripleview_int(s,s_id,p,o,o_id) AS
SELECT "order"+orderid as s, orderid as s_id, "orderid" as p,
       orderid as o, null as o_id
FROM order WHERE orderid IS NOT NULL
UNION ALL
SELECT "order"+orderid as s, orderid as s_id, "status" as p,
      status as o, null as o_id
FROM order WHERE status IS NOT NULL
UNION ALL
SELECT "lineitem"+lineid as s, lineid as s_id,"price" as p,
     price as o, null as o_id
FROM lineitem WHERE price IS NOT NULL
UNION ALL
SELECT "lineitem"+lineid as s, lineid as s_id,"quantity" as p,
      quantity as o, null as o_id
FROM lineitem WHERE quantity IS NOT NULL
UNION ALL
SELECT "lineitem"+lineid as s, lineid as s_id,"orderid" as p,
      orderid as o, null as o_id
FROM lineitem WHERE orderid IS NOT NULL

CREATE VIEW Tripleview_varchar50(s,s_id,p,o,o_id) AS
SELECT "order"+orderid as s, orderid as s_id, "currency" as p,
      currency as o, null as o_id
FROM order WHERE currency IS NOT NULL
UNION ALL
SELECT "lineitem"+lineid as s, lineid as s_id,"product" as p,
      product as o, null as o_id
FROM lineitem WHERE product IS NOT NULL

CREATE VIEW Tripleview_float(s,s_id,p,o,o_id) AS
SELECT "order"+orderid as s, orderid as s_id, "total" as p,
       total as o, null as o_id
FROM order WHERE total IS NOT NULL
UNION ALL
```

```
SELECT "lineitem"+lineid as s, lineid as s_id,"price" as p,
       price as o, null as o_id
FROM lineitem WHERE price IS NOT NULL

CREATE VIEW Tripleview_object(s,s_id,p,o,o_id) AS
SELECT "lineitem"+lineid as s, lineid as s_id,
       "lineitem#ref-orderid" as p, "order"+orderid as o, orderid as o_id
FROM lineitem WHERE orderid IS NOT NULL
```

Ultrawrap's runtime phase encompasses the translation of SPARQL queries to SQL queries on the Tripleviews and the maximal use of the SQL infrastructure to do the SPARQL query rewriting and execution. At runtime, a compiler translates an incoming SPARQL query to a SQL query in terms of the Tripleview. The translation of the SPARQL query to a SQL query on the Tripleviews follows a classic compiler structure: a parser converts the SPARQL query string to an Abstract Syntax Tree (AST). The AST is translated into an SPARQL algebra expression tree. The SQL translation is accomplished by traversing the expression tree and replacing each SPARQL operator. Each internal node of the expression tree represents a SPARQL binary algebra operator while the leaves represent a Basic Graph Patterns (BGP), which is a set of triple patterns. A SPARQL BGP is a set of triple patterns where each one maps to a Tripleview. A SPARQL Join maps to a SQL Inner Join, a SPARQL Union maps to the SQL Union, a SPARQL Optional maps to SQL Left-Outer Join. Consequently, the RDBMS must use both the logical mapping represented in the Tripleview and optimize the resulting translated SQL query, forming the final compiler.

Example 10. The following SPARQL query returns all the quantity and products in a line item.

```
SELECT ?quantity ?product
WHERE {
 ?x <lineitem#quantity> ?quantity.
 ?x <lineitem#product>  ?product.
}
```

The Ultrawrap SQL query is the following:

```
SELECT t1.o AS quantity, t2.o AS product
FROM Tripleview_varchar50 t1, Tripleview_int t2
WHERE t1.p = "quantity"AND t2.p ="product"
AND t1.s = t2.s AND t1.s_id = t2.s_id
```

Two Important Optimizations. Upon succeeding in ultrawrapping different RDBMSs and reviewing query plans, two relational optimizations emerged as important for effective execution of SPARQL queries: (1) detection of unsatisfiable conditions and (2) self-join elimination. Perhaps, not by coincidence, these two optimizations are among semantic query optimization (SQO) methods introduced in the 1980's [18,20,70]. In SQO, the objective is to leverage the semantics, represented in integrity constraints, for query optimization. The basic idea is to use integrity constraints to rewrite a query into a semantically equivalent one. These techniques were initially designed for deductive databases and then integrated in commercial relational databases [20].

The idea behind the **detection of unsatisfiable conditions optimization** is to determine that a query result is empty by determining, without executing the query. This happens, for example, when a pair of predicate constants are inconsistent [18]. The application of the following transformations eliminates columns from the plan that are not needed to evaluate the SPARQL query.

Elimination by contradiction: Consider a query `SELECT * FROM R WHERE A=x AND A=y such that x != y`. Then the result of that query is empty. For example, it is clear that the query `SELECT * FROM order WHERE orderid = 1 AND orderid = 2` will never return results.

Unnecessary union sub-tree pruning: Given a query that includes the UNION operator and where it has been determined that an argument of the UNION is empty; then the corresponding argument can be eliminated. For example: `UNION ALL ({}, S, T) = UNION ALL (S, T)` and `UNION ALL ({}, T) = T`

In Ultrawrap's Tripleview, the constant value in the predicate position acts as the integrity constraint. Consider the following Tripleview:

```
CREATE VIEW Tripleview_varchar50(s,s_id,p,o,o_id) AS
SELECT "order"+orderid as s, orderid as s_id, "currency" as p,
       currency as o, null as o_id FROM order
WHERE currency IS NOT NULL
UNION ALL
SELECT "lineitem"+lineid as s, lineid as s_id,"product" as p,
       product as o, null as o_id FROM lineitem
WHERE product IS NOT NULL
```

Now consider the following query "return all product labels":

```
SELECT o FROM Tripleview_varchar50 WHERE p = "product"
```

The first SFW statement from Tripleview_varchar50 defines `p="currency"`. The query contains `p ="product"`. Both predicates cannot be satisfied simultaneously. Given the contradiction, the first SFW statement of Tripleview_varchar50 can be replaced with the empty set. Since the Tripleview's definition includes all possible columns, any specific SPARQL query will only need a subset of the statements defined in the view. Application of elimination by contradiction enables removing, the unnecessary UNION ALL conditions. Thus the combination of the two transformations reduces the Tripleview to precisely the subset of referenced columns.

Example 11. Consider the Ultrawrap SQL query in Example 10, after applying the detection of unsatisfiable condition optimization, the new Ultrawrap SQL query would *logically* be the following

```
SELECT t1.o AS quantity, t2.o AS product
FROM
   (SELECT"lineitem"+lineid as s, lineid as s_id,"quantity"as p,
    quantity as o, null as o_id FROM lineitem WHERE quantity IS NOT NULL) t1,
   (SELECT"lineitem"+lineid as s, lineid as s_id,"product"as p,
    product as o, null as o_id FROM lineitem WHERE product IS NOT NULL) t2
   WHERE t1.p ="quantity"AND t2.p ="product"
   AND t1.s = t2.s AND t1.s_id = t2.s_id
```

Join elimination is one of the several SQO techniques, where integrity constraints are used to eliminate a literal clause in the query. This implies that a join could also be eliminated if the table that is being dropped does not contribute any attributes in the results [18]. The type of join elimination that is desired is the **self-join elimination**, where a join occurs between the same tables. Two different cases are observed: self-join elimination of projection and self-join elimination of selections.

Self-join elimination of projection: This occurs when attributes from the same table are projected individually and then joined together. For example, the following unoptimized query projects the attributes total and currency from the table order where orderid = 1, however each attribute projection is done separately and then joined:

```
SELECT p1.total, p2.currency
FROM order p1, order p2
WHERE p1.orderid = 1 AND p1.orderid = p2.orderid
```

Given a self-join elimination optimization, the previous query may be rewritten as:

```
SELECT total, currency FROM order WHERE orderid = 1
```

Self-join elimination of selection: This occurs when a selection on attributes from the same table are done individually and then joined together. For example, the following unoptimized query selects on price > 100 and quantity > 10 separately and then joined:

```
SELECT p1.lineid
FROM lineitem p1, lineitem p2
WHERE p1.price > 100 AND p2.quantity > 10 AND p1.lineid = p2.lineid
```

Given a self-join elimination optimization, the previous query may be rewritten as:

```
SELECT lineid FROM lineitem WHERE price > 100 AND quantity > 10
```

Example 12. Consider the logical Ultrawrap SQL query in Example 11. After the self join elimination optimization has been applied, the new Ultrawrap SQL query would *logically* be the following

```
SELECT t1.quantity, t1.product
FROM lineitem t1
WHERE t1.quantity IS NOT NULL and t1.product IS NOT NULL
```

Evaluation. Ultrawrap was evaluated using the three leading RDBMS systems and two benchmark suites, Microsoft SQL Server, IBM DB2 and Oracle RDBMS, and the Berlin and Barton SPARQL benchmarks. The SPARQL benchmarks were chosen as a consequence of the fact that they derived their RDF content from a relational source. Both benchmark provide both SPARQL queries and SQL queries, where each query was derived independently from an English language specification. Since wrappers produce SQL from SPARQL we refer to the benchmark's SQL queries as benchmark-provided SQL queries.

By using benchmarks containing independently created SPARQL and SQL queries, and considering the effort and maturity embodied in the leading RDBMS's SQL optimizers, we suppose that the respective benchmark-provided SQL query execution time forms a worthy baseline, and the specific query plans to yield insight into methods for creating wrappers.

By starting with a simple wrapper system and evaluating it with sophisticated SQL query optimizers we are able to identify existing, well understood optimization methods that enable wrappers. We determined that DB2 implements both optimizations. SQL Server implements the detection of unsatisfiable conditions optimization but does not implement the self-join elimination optimization. Oracle does not implement the detection of unsatisfiable conditions optimization. It does implement the self-join elimination optimization, but only if the detection of unsatisfiable conditions optimization is applied separately. MySQL does not implement any of these optimizations.

The following points deserve elaboration:

- Self-join elimination: The number of self-joins and their elimination is not, by itself, an indicator of poor performance. The impact of the self-join elimination optimization is a function of the selectivity and the number of properties in the SPARQL query that are co-located in a single table. The value of optimization is less as selectivity increases.
- Join predicate push-down: The experiments with Oracle revealed that pushing join predicates [3] can be as effective as the detection of unsatisfiable conditions optimization.
- Join ordering: Join order is a major factor for poor query execution time, both on Ultrawrap and benchmark-provided SQL queries.
- Left-outer joins: We found that no commercial optimizer eliminates self left-outer joins and OPTIONALs appear in many of the queries where sub-optimal join orders are determined. We speculate that these types of queries are not common in a relational setting, hence the lack of support in commercial systems.
- Counting NULLs: Each SFW statement of the Tripleview filters null values. Such a filter could produce an overhead, however we speculate that the optimizer has statistics of null values and avoids the overhead.

The results of the Ultrawrap system provided a foundation for identifying minimal requirements for effective SPARQL to SQL wrapper systems. Since then, other research groups have continued this work and developed systems such as Morph [58] and Ontop [61].

4.2 Ontology-Based Data Access

In the previous section, we presented the initial Ultrawrap system, who focus is on supporting a Direct Mapping. In this section, we present how Ultrawrap has been extended for Ontology-Based Data Access, denoted as Ultrawrap^{OBDA}, and thus supports customized mappings in R2RML [66].

Given a source relational database, a target OWL ontology and a mapping from the relational database to the ontology, Ontology-Based Data Access (OBDA) concerns answering queries over the target ontology using these three components. Commonly, researchers have taken two approaches to developing OBDA systems: materialization-based approach (forward chaining) or rewriting-based approach (backward chaining). In the materialization approach, the input relational database D, target ontology $\mathcal{O}$ and mapping $\mathcal{M}$ (from D to $\mathcal{O}$) are used to derive new facts that are stored in a database D_o, which is considered to be the materialization of the data in D given $\mathcal{M}$ and $\mathcal{O}$. Then the answer to a SPARQL query Q over the target ontology over D, $\mathcal{M}$ and $\mathcal{O}$ is computed by directly posing Q over D_o [6]. In the rewriting approach, three steps are executed. First, a new query Q_o is generated from the query Q and the ontology $\mathcal{O}$, which is considered to be the rewriting of Q w.r.t. to $\mathcal{O}$. The majority of the OBDA literature focuses on this step [54]. Second, the mapping $\mathcal{M}$ is used to compile Q_o to a SQL query Q_{sql} over D [56,57]. Finally, Q_{sql} is evaluated on the database D, which gives us the answer to the initial query Q. Therefore, the answer to a query Q over O, D, and M is computed by directly posing Q_{sql} over D.

We develop an OBDA system, Ultrawrap^{OBDA}, which combines materialization and query rewriting. Ultrawrap^{OBDA} is an extension of our previous Ultrawrap system which supports customized mappings in R2RML. In the same spirit of our Ultrawrap work, the objective is to effect optimizations by pushing processing into the Relational Databases Management Systems (RDBMS) and closer to the stored data, hence making maximal use of existing SQL infrastructure. We distinguish two phases: a compile and runtime phase. In the compile phase, we are given as input a relational database D, an ontology $\mathcal{O}$ and a mapping $\mathcal{M}$ from D to $\mathcal{O}$. The mapping $\mathcal{M}$ is given in R2RML. The first step of this phase is to embed in $\mathcal{M}$ the ontological entailments of $\mathcal{O}$, which gives rise to a new mapping $\mathcal{M}^\star$, that is called the *saturation* of $\mathcal{M}$ w.r.t. $\mathcal{O}$. The mapping $\mathcal{M}^\star$ is implemented using SQL views. In order to improve query performance, an important issue is to decide which views should be materialized. This is the last step of the compilation phase. We then study when a view should be materialized in order to improve query performance. In the runtime phase, the input is a query Q over the target ontology $\mathcal{O}$, which is written in the RDF query language SPARQL, and the problem is to answer this query by rewriting it into some SQL queries over the views. A key observation at this point is that some existing SQL optimizers are able to perform rewritings in order to execute queries against materialized views.

To the best of our knowledge, in 2014, we presented the first OBDA system which supported ontologies with transitivity by using SQL recursion. The ontology profile considered in this work is our proposed OWL-SQL. More specifically, our contributions are the following. (1) We present an efficient algorithm to generate saturated mappings. (2) We provide a proof that every SPARQL query over a target ontology can be rewritten into a SQL query in our context, where mappings play a fundamental role. It is important to mention that such a result is a minimal requirement for a query-rewriting OBDA system relying on relational database technology. (3) We present a cost model that help us to determine which views to materialize to attain the fastest execution time. And (4) we present an empirical evaluation using (i) Oracle, (ii) two benchmarks including an extension of the Berlin SPARQL Benchmark, and (iii) six different scenarios. This evaluation includes a comparison against a state-of-the-art OBDA system, and its results validate the cost model and demonstrate favorable execution times for Ultrawrap^{OBDA}.

Related work. This research builds upon the work of Rodriguez-Muro et al. implemented in Ontop [61] and our previous work on Ultrawrap [67]. Rodriguez-Muro et al. uses the tree-witness rewriting algorithm and introduced the idea of compiling ontological entailments as mappings, which they named $\mathcal{T}$-Mappings. There are three key differences between Rodriguez-Muro et al. and our work in this paper: (1) we have extended the work of Rodriguez-Muro et al. to support more than hierarchy of classes and properties, including transitivity; (2) we introduce an efficient algorithm that generates saturated mappings while Rodriguez-Muro et al. has not presented an algorithm before; and (3) we represent the mappings as SQL views and study when the views should be materialized. Ultrawrap is a system that encodes a fix mapping, the direct mapping [7,65], of the database as RDF. These mappings are implemented using unmaterialized SQL views. The approach presented extends Ultrawrap in three important aspects: (1) supports a customized mapping language; (2) supports reasoning through saturated mappings; and (3) considers materializing views for query optimization. Another related work is the combined approach [47], which materializes entailments as data, without considering mappings, and uses a limited form of query rewriting. The main objective of this approach is to deal with the case of infinite materialization, which cannot occur for the type of ontologies considered in this paper.

Saturation of RDB2RDF Mappings. Being able to modify an RDB2RDF mapping to embed a given ontology is a fundamental step in our approach. This process is formalized by means of the notion of saturated mapping.

Definition 18 (Saturated Mapping). *Let $\mathcal{M}$ and $\mathcal{M}^\star$ be RDB2RDF mappings over a relational schema* $\mathbf{R}$ *and* $\mathcal{O}$ *an ontology. Then* $\mathcal{M}^\star$ *is a saturation of* $\mathcal{M}$ *w.r.t.* $\mathcal{O}$ *if for every instance* I *over* $\mathbf{R}$ *and assertional RDF-triple* (a, b, c)*:*

$$[\![\mathcal{M}]\!]_I \cup \Sigma_{\mathcal{O}} \models \texttt{triple}(a, b, c) \quad \textit{iff} \quad \texttt{triple}(a, b, c) \in [\![\mathcal{M}^\star]\!]_I.$$

We study the problem of computing a saturated mapping from a given mapping and ontology. In particular, we focus on the case of ontologies not mentioning any triple of the form $(a, \texttt{type}, \texttt{transProp})$, which we denote by non-transitive ontologies. In the next section, we extend these results to the case of arbitrary ontologies.

In our system, the saturation step is performed by exhaustively applying the inference rules in Table 1, which allow us to infer new RDB2RDF rules from the existing ones and the input ontology. More precisely, given an inference rule $t{:}\frac{\rho_1}{\rho_2}$ from Table 1, where t is a triple and ρ_1, ρ_2 are RDB2RDF rules, and given an RDB2RDF mapping $\mathcal{M}$ and an ontology $\mathcal{O}$, we need to do the following to apply $t{:}\frac{\rho_1}{\rho_2}$ over $\mathcal{M}$ and $\mathcal{O}$. First, we have to replace the letters A and B in t with actual URIs, say $a \in \mathbf{I}$ and $b \in \mathbf{I}$, respectively.[11] Second, we need to check whether the triple obtained from t by replacing A by a and B by b belongs to $\mathcal{O}$, and whether the RDB2RDF rule obtained from ρ_1 by replacing A by a belongs to $\mathcal{M}$. If both conditions hold, then the inference rule can be applied, and the result is an RDB2RDF mapping $\mathcal{M}'$ consisting of the rules in $\mathcal{M}$ and the rule obtained from ρ_2 by replacing A by a and B by b.

Table 1. Inference rules to compute saturated mappings.

$$(\mathtt{A}, \mathtt{subClass}, \mathtt{B}) : \frac{\alpha(s, \bar{x}) \wedge p = \mathtt{type} \wedge o = \mathtt{A} \rightarrow \mathtt{triple}(s, p, o)}{\alpha(s, \bar{x}) \wedge p = \mathtt{type} \wedge o = \mathtt{B} \rightarrow \mathtt{triple}(s, p, o)}$$

$$(\mathtt{A}, \mathtt{subProp}, \mathtt{B}) : \frac{\beta(s, o, \bar{x}) \wedge p = \mathtt{A} \rightarrow \mathtt{triple}(s, p, o)}{\beta(s, o, \bar{x}) \wedge p = \mathtt{B} \rightarrow \mathtt{triple}(s, p, o)}$$

$$(\mathtt{A}, \mathtt{dom}, \mathtt{B}) : \frac{\beta(s, o, \bar{x}) \wedge p = \mathtt{A} \rightarrow \mathtt{triple}(s, p, o)}{\beta(s, y, \bar{x}) \wedge p = \mathtt{type} \wedge o = \mathtt{B} \rightarrow \mathtt{triple}(s, p, o)}$$

$$(\mathtt{A}, \mathtt{range}, \mathtt{B}) : \frac{\beta(s, o, \bar{x}) \wedge p = \mathtt{A} \rightarrow \mathtt{triple}(s, p, o)}{\beta(y, s, \bar{x}) \wedge p = \mathtt{type} \wedge o = \mathtt{B} \rightarrow \mathtt{triple}(s, p, o)}$$

$$\begin{array}{r}(\mathtt{A}, \mathtt{equivClass}, \mathtt{B}) \\ \text{or } (\mathtt{B}, \mathtt{equivClass}, \mathtt{A})\end{array} : \frac{\alpha(s, \bar{x}) \wedge p = \mathtt{type} \wedge o = \mathtt{A} \rightarrow \mathtt{triple}(s, p, o)}{\alpha(s, \bar{x}) \wedge p = \mathtt{type} \wedge o = \mathtt{B} \rightarrow \mathtt{triple}(s, p, o)}$$

$$\begin{array}{r}(\mathtt{A}, \mathtt{equivProp}, \mathtt{B}) \\ \text{or } (\mathtt{B}, \mathtt{equivProp}, \mathtt{A})\end{array} : \frac{\beta(s, o, \bar{x}) \wedge p = \mathtt{A} \rightarrow \mathtt{triple}(s, p, o)}{\beta(s, o, \bar{x}) \wedge p = \mathtt{B} \rightarrow \mathtt{triple}(s, p, o)}$$

$$\begin{array}{r}(\mathtt{A}, \mathtt{inverse}, \mathtt{B}) \\ \text{or } (\mathtt{B}, \mathtt{inverse}, \mathtt{A})\end{array} : \frac{\beta(s, o, \bar{x}) \wedge p = \mathtt{A} \rightarrow \mathtt{triple}(s, p, o)}{\beta(o, s, \bar{x}) \wedge p = \mathtt{B} \rightarrow \mathtt{triple}(s, p, o)}$$

$$(\mathtt{A}, \mathtt{type}, \mathtt{symProp}) : \frac{\beta(s, o, \bar{x}) \wedge p = \mathtt{A} \rightarrow \mathtt{triple}(s, p, o)}{\beta(o, s, \bar{x}) \wedge p = \mathtt{A} \rightarrow \mathtt{triple}(s, p, o)}$$

Example 13. Consider the RDB2RDF rule $\mathtt{order}(s, x_1, x_2, x_3, x_4, 1) \wedge p = \mathtt{type} \wedge o = \mathtt{ShippedOrder} \rightarrow \mathtt{triple}(s, p, o)$., *and assume that we are given an ontology* $\mathcal{O}$ containing the triple $(\mathtt{ShippedOrder}, \mathtt{subClass}, \mathtt{SuccessfulOrder})$. *Then by applying the first inference rule in Table* 1, *we infer the following RDB2RDF rule:* $\mathtt{order}(s, x_1, x_2, x_3, x_4, 1) \wedge p = \mathtt{type} \wedge o = \mathtt{SuccessfulOrder} \rightarrow \mathtt{triple}(s, p, o)$.

[11] If $t = (\mathtt{A}, \mathtt{type}, \mathtt{symProp})$, then we only need to replace A by a.

Given an RDB2RDF mapping $\mathcal{M}$ and an ontology $\mathcal{O}$, we denote by $\text{SAT}(\mathcal{M}, \mathcal{O})$ the RDB2RDF mapping obtained from $\mathcal{M}$ and $\mathcal{O}$ by successively applying the inference rules in Table 1 until the mapping does not change. The following theorem shows that $\text{SAT}(\mathcal{M}, \mathcal{O})$ is a saturation of $\mathcal{M}$ w.r.t. $\mathcal{O}$, which justifies its use in our system.

Theorem 6. *For every RDB2RDF mapping $\mathcal{M}$ and ontology $\mathcal{O}$ in RDFS, it holds that $\text{SAT}(\mathcal{M}, \mathcal{O})$ is a saturation of $\mathcal{M}$ w.r.t. $\mathcal{O}$.*

Theorem 6 is a corollary of the fact that the first six rules in Table 1 encode the rules to infer assertional triples from an inference system for RDFS given in [52].

A natural question at this point is whether $\text{SAT}(\mathcal{M}, \mathcal{O})$ can be computed efficiently. In our setting, the approach based on exhaustively applying the inference rules in Table 1 can be easily transformed into a polynomial time algorithm for this problem. However, if this transformation is done in a naïve way, then the resulting algorithm is not really efficient. In [66], we present an efficient algorithm to compute $\text{SAT}(\mathcal{M}, \mathcal{O})$ that is linear in the size of the input RDB2RDF mapping $\mathcal{M}$ and ontology $\mathcal{O}$, which are denoted by $\|\mathcal{M}\|$ and $\|\mathcal{O}\|$, respectively.

Theorem 7. *There exists an algorithm that, given an RDB2RDF mapping $\mathcal{M}$ and a non-transitive ontology $\mathcal{O}$, computes $\text{SAT}(\mathcal{M}, \mathcal{O})$ in time $O(\|\mathcal{M}\| \cdot \|\mathcal{O}\|)$.*

The main ingredients of the algorithm mentioned in Theorem 7 can be found in [66].

Dealing with Transitive Predicates. We show here how the approach presented in the previous section can be extended with recursive predicates. This functionality is of particular interest as the current work on OBDA under OWL 2 QL does not consider transitivity, mainly because the query language in which the query over the ontology has to be rewritten is SQL without recursion [15].

From now on, given a first-order formula $\varphi(x, y)$, we use $\text{TC}_\varphi(x, y)$ to denote the transitive closure of $\varphi(x, y)$. This formula can be written in many different formalisms. For example, if $\varphi(x, y)$ is a conjunction of relational atoms, then $\text{TC}_\varphi(x, y)$ can be written as follows in Datalog:

$$\varphi(x, y) \rightarrow \text{TC}_\varphi(x, y), \qquad \varphi(x, z), \text{TC}_\varphi(z, y) \rightarrow \text{TC}_\varphi(x, y).$$

In our system, $\text{TC}_\varphi(x, y)$ is written as an SQL query with recursion. Then to deal with an ontology $\mathcal{O}$ containing transitive predicates, the set of inference rules in Table 1 is extended with the following inference rule:

$$(\texttt{A}, \texttt{type}, \texttt{transProp}) : \frac{\{\beta_i(s, o, \bar{x}_i) \wedge p = \texttt{A} \rightarrow \texttt{triple}(s, p, o)\}_{i=1}^{k}}{\text{TC}_{[\bigvee_{i=1}^{k} \exists \bar{x}_i \beta_i]}(s, o) \wedge p = \texttt{A} \rightarrow \texttt{triple}(s, p, o)}.$$

This rule tell us that given a transitive predicate $\texttt{A}$, we can take any number k of RDB2RDF rules $\beta_i(s, o, \bar{x}_i) \wedge p = \texttt{A} \rightarrow \texttt{triple}(s, p, o)$ for this predicate, and we can generate a new RDB2RDF rule for A by putting together the conditions $\beta_i(s, o, \bar{x}_i)$ in a formula $\gamma(s, o) = \bigvee_i \exists \bar{x}_i \beta_i(s, o, \bar{x}_i)$, and then using the transitive closure $\text{TC}_\gamma(s, o)$ of γ in an RDB2RDF rule $\text{TC}_\gamma(s, o) \wedge p = \texttt{A} \rightarrow \texttt{triple}(s, p, o)$. In order for this approach to work, notice that we need to extend the syntax of RDB2RDF rules (1) and (2), so that formulae α and β in them can be arbitrary formulae in a more expressive formalism such as (recursive) Datalog.

Implementing RDB2RDF Mappings as Views. Inspired by our previous work on Ultrawrap [67], every RDB2RDF rule is implemented as a triple-query, that is, as a SQL query which outputs triples. For example, the RDB2RDF rules:

$$\texttt{order}(s, x_1, x_2, x_3, x_4, 1) \wedge p = \texttt{type} \wedge o = \texttt{SuccessfulOrder} \rightarrow \texttt{triple}(s, p, o)$$
$$\texttt{order}(s, x_1, x_2, x_3, x_4, 2) \wedge p = \texttt{type} \wedge o = \texttt{SuccessfulOrder} \rightarrow \texttt{triple}(s, p, o)$$

give rise to the following triple-queries:

```
SELECT orderid as S, “type” as P, “SuccessfulOrder” as O FROM order WHERE status = “1”
SELECT orderid as S, “type” as P, “SuccessfulOrder” as O FROM order WHERE status = “2”
```

In practice, the triple-queries may include additional projections in order to support indexes, URI templates, datatypes and languages. However, for readability, we will consider here this simple version of these queries. Then to implement an RDB2RDF mapping, all the class (resp. predicate) RDB2RDF-rules for the same class (resp. predicate) are grouped together to generate a triple-view, that is, a SQL view comprised of the union of the triple-queries for this class (resp. predicate). For instance, in our previous example the following is the triple-view for the class `SuccessfulOrder`:

```
CREATE VIEW SuccessfulOrderView AS
SELECT orderid as S, “type” as P, “SuccessfulOrder” as O FROM order WHERE status = “1”
UNION ALL
SELECT orderid as S, “type” as P, “SuccessfulOrder” as O FROM order WHERE status = “2”
```

SPARQL to SQL Rewriting with RDB2RDF Mappings. The runtime phase executes SPARQL queries on the RDBMS. We reuse Ultrawrap's approach of translating SPARQL queries to SQL queries in terms of the views defined for every class and property, which are denoted as triple-views. Thus, we make maximal use of existing query optimization tools in commercial RDBMS, such as Oracle, to do the SPARQL query execution and rewriting.

Continuing with the example in Sect. 4.2, consider now a SPARQL query which asks for all the Successful Orders: `SELECT ?x WHERE {?x type SuccessfulOrder}`. It is clear that this query needs to be rewritten to ask for the orders with status 1 and 2. The `SuccessfulOrderView` triple-view in Sect. 4.2 implements the mappings to the SuccessfulOrder class which consists of two triple-queries, one each for status = 1 and status = 2. Therefore, it is sufficient to generate a SQL query in terms of the `SuccessfulOrderView`. Given that a triple-view models a table with three columns, a SPARQL query is syntactically translated to a SQL query in terms of the triple-view. The resulting SQL query is `SELECT t1.s AS x FROM SuccessfulOrderView t1`.

A natural question at this point is whether every SPARQL query has an equivalent SQL query in our context, where RDB2RDF mappings play a fundamental role. In what follows we give a positive answer to this question.

Theorem 8. *Given an RDB2RDF mapping $\mathcal{M}$, every SPARQL query is SQL-rewritable under $\mathcal{M}$.*

The proof that the previous condition holds is by induction on the structure of a SPARQL query P and, thus, it gives us a (naïve) bottom-up algorithm for translating P into an equivalent SQL query Q (given the mapping $\mathcal{M}$). More precisely, in the base case we are given a triple pattern $t = \{$`s p o`$\}$, where each one of its component is either a URI or a literal or a variable. This triple pattern is first translated into a SPARQL query P_t, where each position in t storing a URI or a literal is replaced by a fresh variable, a filter condition is added to ensure that these fresh variables are assigned the corresponding URIs or literals, and a SELECT clause is added to ensure that the output variables of t and P_t are the same. For example, if $t = \{$`?x type SuccessfulOrder`$\}$, then P_t is the following SPARQL query: `SELECT ?x WHERE {?x ?y ?z} FILTER (?y = type && ?z = SuccessfulOrder)`. Then a SQL-rewriting of P_t under $\mathcal{M}$ is computed just by replacing a triple pattern of the form $\{$`?s ?p ?o`$\}$ by a union of all the triple-queries representing the RDB2RDF rules in $\mathcal{M}$, and also replacing the SPARQL filter condition in P_t by a filter condition in SQL.

In the inductive step, we assume that the theorem holds for two SPARQL queries P_1 and P_2.

The proof then continues by presenting rewritings for the SPARQL queries constructed by combining P_1 and P_2 through the operators SELECT, AND (or '.' operator), OPTIONAL, FILTER and UNION, which is done by using existing approaches to translate SPARQL to SQL [5,19].

Cost Model for View Materialization. A common approach for query optimization is to use materialized views [36]. Given that we are implementing RDB2RDF mappings as views, it is a natural to pursue this option. There are three implementation alternatives: (1) Materialize all the views: This approach gives the best query response time. However, it consumes the most space. (2) Materialize nothing: In this approach, every query needs to go to the raw data. However, no extra space is needed. (3) Materialize a subset of the views: Try to find a trade-off between the best query response time and the amount of space required. Note that in the previous Ultrawrap work, only unmaterialized views were considered.

In this section, we present a cost model for these three alternatives. First we must introduce some terminology. We consider ontologies consisting of hierarchy of classes which form a tree with a unique root, where a root class of an ontology is a class that has no superclasses. Then a leaf class of an ontology is a class that has no subclasses, and the depth of a class is the number of subclass relationships from the class to the root class (notice that there is a unique path from a class to the root class). Moreover, the depth of an ontology is the maximum depth of all classes present in the ontology.

First, we consider the cost of answering a query Q is equal to the number of rows present in the relation used to construct Q. For example, if a relation R has 100 rows, then the cost of the query `SELECT * FROM R` is 100. Second, assume we have a single relation R and that mappings are from a query on the relation R with a selection on an attribute A, to a class in the ontology. For example, consider the relation R is `order`, the attribute A is `status` and the mapping is to the class `SuccessfulOrder`. Finally, we consider a query workload of queries asking for the instances of a class in the ontology, i.e. `SELECT ?x WHERE {?x type C}`, which can be translated into the triple-view implementing the mapping to the class `C`.

Our cost model is the following: If all the views implementing mappings are materialized, the query cost is $n \times N_R \times S(A, R)$ where n is the number of leaf classes underneath the class that is being queried for, N_R is the number of tuples of the relation R in the mapping, and $S(A, R)$ is the selectivity of the attribute A of the relation R in the mapping. The space cost is $N_R + (N_R \times d)$ where d is the depth of the ontology. The reason for this cost is because the number of rows in a materialized view depends on the selectivity of the attribute and the number of leaf classes. Additionally, the sum of all the rows of each triple-view representing the mapping to classes in a particular depth d of an ontology, is equivalent at most to the number of rows of the relation. If no views are materialized, then the query cost is $n \times N_R$, assuming there are no indices. The space cost is simply N_R. The reason for this cost is because to answer a query, the entire relation needs to be accessed n times because there are no indices[12].

The question now is: How can we achieve the query cost of materializing all the views while keeping space to a minimum? Our hypothesis is the following: If a RDBMS rewrites queries in terms of materialized views, then by only materializing the views representing mappings to the leaf classes, the query cost would be $n \times N_R \times S(A, R)$, the same as if we materialized all the views, and the space cost would only be $2 \times N_R$. The rationale is the following: A triple-view representing a mapping to a class, can be rewritten into the union of triple-views representing the mapping to the child classes. Subsequently, a triple-view representing the mapping to any class in the ontology can be rewritten into a union of triple-views representing the mappings to leaf classes of an ontology. Finally, given a set of triple-views representing mappings from a relation to each leaf class of an ontology, the sum of all the rows in the set of triple-views is equivalent to the number of rows in the relation.

[12] In the evaluation, we also consider the case when indices are present.

Given the extensive research of answering queries using views [37] and the fact that Oracle implements query rewriting on materialized views[13], we strongly suspect that our hypothesis will hold. The evaluation provides empirical results supporting our hypothesis.

Evaluation. The evaluation requires benchmarks consisting of a relational database schema and data, ontologies, mappings from the database to ontologies and a query workload. Thus, we created a synthetic benchmark, the *Texas Benchmark*, inspired by the Wisconsin Benchmark [27] and extended the Berlin SPARQL Benchmark (BSBM) Explore Use Case [11]. More details about the benchmarks can be found at http://obda-benchmark.org.

The objective of our experiments is to observe the behavior of a commercial relational database, namely Oracle, and its capabilities of supporting subclass and transitivity reasoning under our proposed approach. The evaluation considered six scenarios: (**all-mat**) all the views are materialized; (**union-leaves**) only views representing mappings to the leaf classes are materialized, implemented with UNION; (**or-leaves**) same as in the previous scenario but with the views implemented with OR instead of UNION, (**union-index**) none of the views, implemented with UNION, are materialized, instead an index on the respective attributes have been added, (**or-index**) same as in the previous scenario but with the views implemented with OR; and (**ontop**) we compare against Ontop, a state of the art OBDA system [61].

An initial assessment suggests the following four expected observations: (1) The fastest execution time is *all-mat*; (2) our hypothesis should hold, meaning that the execution time of *union-leaves* should be comparable, if not equal, to the execution time of *all-mat*; (3) given that the Ontop system generates SQL queries with OR instead of UNION [61], the execution time of *ontop* and *or-index* should be comparable if not equal; (4) with transitivity, the fastest execution time is when the views are materialized.

The experimental results suggest the following. The expected observations (1), (2), (3) and (4) hold. The fastest execution time corresponds to *all-mat*. The execution time of *union-leaves* is comparable, if not equal, to the execution time of *all-mat*, because Oracle was able to rewrite queries in terms of the materialized views. The number of rows examined is equivalent to the number of rows in the views where everything was materialized. This result provides evidence supporting our hypothesis and validates our cost model. Finally the execution time of *ontop* and *or-index* are comparable. It is clear that materializing the view outperforms the non-materialized view for the following reasons: when the view is materialized, the size of the view is known beforehand and the optimizer is able to do a range scan with the index. However, when the view is not materialized, the size is not known therefore the optimizer does a full scan of the table.

[13] http://docs.oracle.com/cd/B28359_01/server.111/b28313/qrbasic.htm.

5 Relational Databases and Semantic Web in Practice

A successfully repeated use case for using Semantic Web technologies with Relational Databases is for data integration. In this approach, an ontology serves as a uniform conceptual federating model, which is accessible to both IT developers and business users. We highlight two challenges: ontology and mapping engineering. We postulate the need of a pay-as-you-go methodology that address these challenges and enables agility.

5.1 A Real World Example

Consider the following real-world example. Executives of a large e-commerce company need to know, "*How many orders were placed in a given month and the corresponding net sales*". Depending on whom they ask they get three different answers. The IT department managing the web site records an order when a customer has checked out. The fulfillment department records an order when it has shipped. Yet the accounting department records an order when the funds charged against the credit card are actually transferred to the company's bank account, regardless of the shipping status. Unaware of the source of the problem the executives are vexed by inconsistencies across established business intelligence (BI) reports.

This is precisely where the use of ontologies to intermediate IT development and business users is valuable. Ontologies serve as a uniform conceptual federated model describing the domain of interest. The long standing relationship between Semantic Web technologies and Relational Databases, specifically the Ontology Based Database Access (OBDA) paradigm and its extension as Ontology Based Data Integration is maturing, and yielding successful applications.

Even though OBDA has been widely researched theoretically, there is still need to understand how to effectively implement OBDA systems in practice.

5.2 Where Do Ontologies and Mappings Come From?

The common definition of OBDA states that given a source relational database, a target ontology and a mapping from the relational database to the ontology, the goal is to answer queries over the target ontology using these three components. From a practical point of view, this begs the question: where does the target ontology and the mappings come from?

Ontology Challenges. Ontology engineering is a challenge by itself. In order to create the target ontology, users can follow traditional ontology engineering methodologies [23,74], using competency questions [8,60], test driven development [43], ontology design patterns [40], etc. Additionally, per standard practices, it is recommended to reuse and extend existing ontologies in domains of interest such as Good Relations for e-commerce[14], FIBO for finance[15], Gist

[14] http://www.heppnetz.de/projects/goodrelations/.

[15] http://www.edmcouncil.org/financialbusiness.

for general business concepts[16], Schema.org[17], etc. In OBDA, the challenge increases because the source database schemas can be considered as additional inputs to the ontology engineering process. Common enterprise application's database schema commonly consist of thousands of tables and tens of thousands of attributes. A common approach is to bootstrap ontologies derived from the source database schemas, known as putative ontologies [65,69]. The putative ontologies can gradually be transformed into target ontologies, using existing ontology engineering methodologies.

Mapping Challenges. Once the target ontology has been created, the source databases can be mapped. The W3C Direct Mapping standard can be used to bootstrap mappings [7]. The declarative nature of W3C R2RML mapping language [25] enables users to state which elements from the source database are connected to the target ontology, instead of writing procedural code. Given that source database schemas are very large, the OBDA mapping challenge is suggestive of an ontology matching problem: the putative ontology of the source database and the target ontology. In addition to 1–1 correspondences between classes and properties, mappings can be complex involving calculations and rules that are part of business logic. For example, the notion of net sales of an order is defined as gross sales minus taxes, discounts given, etc. The discount can be different depending on the type of user. Therefore, a business user needs to provide these definitions before hand. That is why it is hard to automate this process. Another challenge is to create tools that can create and manage mappings [68].

Addressing these challenges is crucial for the success of a data integration project using the OBDA paradigm. However, recall that data integration is a means to an end. The engineering of a target ontology and mappings are the means. Answering business questions are the ends. We observe that target ontologies and mappings are developed in a holistic approach. Given how OWL ontologies are flexible and R2RML mappings are declarative, these elements could enable the incremental development of a target ontology and database mappings. Thus, we argue for a pay-as-you-go methodology for OBDA.

A Pay-as-you-go Methodology for OBDA. We present a methodology to create the target ontology and mappings for an OBDA system, driven by a prioritized list of business questions. The data answering the business questions serve as content of the Business Intelligence (BI) reports that business users require. The objective is to create a target ontology and mappings, that enable to answer a list of business questions, in an incremental manner. After a minimal set of business questions have been successfully modeled, mapped, answered and made into dashboards, then the set of business questions can be extended. The new questions, in turn, may extend the target ontology and new mappings

[16] https://semanticarts.com/gist/.
[17] http://schema.org/.

incrementally added. With this methodology, the target ontology and mappings are developed in an iterative pay-as-you-go approach. Thus, providing an agile methodology to integrate data using the OBDA paradigm because the focus is to provide early and continuous delivery of answers to the business users.

We identify three actors involved throughout the process:

- Business User: a subject matter expert who has knowledge of the business and can identify the list of prioritized business questions.
- IT Developer: a person who has knowledge of databases and knows how the data is interconnected.
- Knowledge Engineer: a person who serves as a communication bridge between Business Users and IT Developers and has expertise in modeling data using ontologies.

Our methodology is divided in two phases: knowledge capture and implementation. Figure 4 summarizes the methodology.

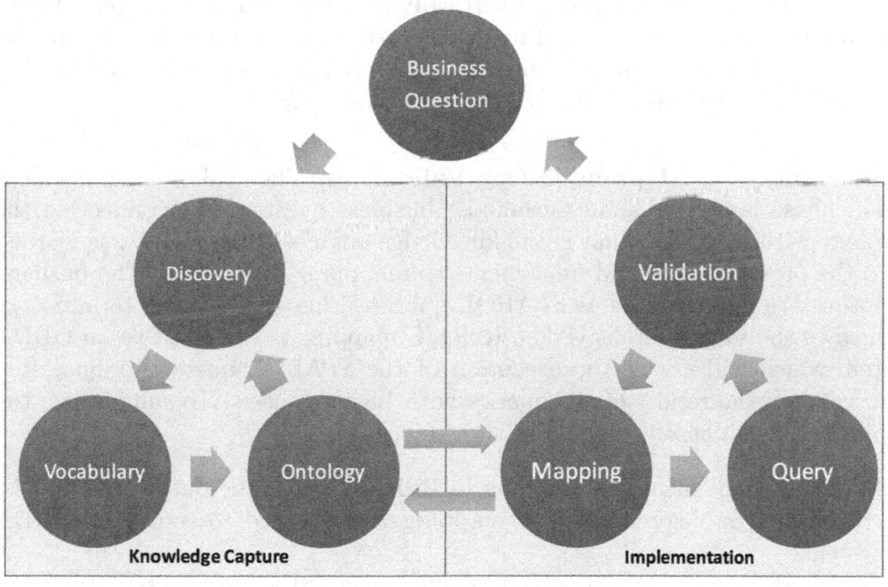

Fig. 4. The pay-as-you-go methodology for OBDA

Knowledge Capture: Discover-Vocabulary-Ontology. The goal of the knowledge capture phase is twofold. The first goal is to extract key concepts and relationships from the set of prioritized business questions. The knowledge engineer works with business users to understand the meaning of extracted concepts and relationships in order to eliminate ambiguity. The second goal is to identify which source database(s) contains data relating to the extracted concepts and relationships. The knowledge engineer takes what has been extracted with the business users and works with IT developers to identify which tables and attributes are required. This knowledge capture phase is divided in three steps:

- Discovery: Discover the concepts and relationships from the input set of prioritized business questions and identify how the concepts and relationships are connected to the database(s).
- Vocabulary: Identify the business terminology such as preferred labels, alternative labels and natural language definitions for the concepts and relationships.
- Ontology: Formalize the ontology in OWL such that it covers the business questions.

Continuing with our initial example; the knowledge engineer works with business users to understand the meaning of the word "Order". Furthermore, working with IT developers, the knowledge engineer may learn that the Order Management System is the authoritative source for all orders. Within that database, the data relating to orders may be vertically partitioned across a several tables totaling hundreds of attributes. Finally, the attributes required for the calculation of the net sales of an order prove to be only a handful of the hundreds of attributes. The next step is to implement the mappings.

Implementation: Mapping-Query-Validation. The goal of the implementation phase is to enable answering the business questions by connecting the ontology with the data. That is the knowledge engineer takes what was learned from the previous steps and implements the mapping in R2RML. The business questions are implemented as SPARQL queries using the business terminology defined in the target ontology. The R2RML mapping is the input to an OBDA system which will enable the execution of the SPARQL queries. A final step is to validate the results of the queries with business users. To summarize, the implementation phase is divided in three steps:

- Mapping: Implement the mapping in R2RML, given the output of the Discover and Ontology steps. The mapping is then used to setup the OBDA system.
- Query: Business questions are implemented as SPARQL queries using the terminology of the target ontology. The answers to the business questions are the SPARQL results.
- Validation: Confirm that the SPARQL queries return the correct answers.

Continuing with our running example; the result from the knowledge capture phase revealed that the business users considered an order, "an order", if it had shipped or the accounts receivable had been received. The knowledge engineer (the R2RML writer) in conversation with the IT developer identified that requirement as all tuples in the MASTERORDER table where order status is equal to 2 or 3. Therefore, an R2RML mapping consists of the following SQL query:

```
SELECT * FROM MASTERORDER WHERE orderstatus IN (2,3)
```

The definition of net sales of an order is a math formula that uses attributes from the order and ordertax table. This can be represented in the following SQL query:

```
SELECT o.orderid, o.ordertotal - ot.finaltax -
  CASE WHEN o.currencyid in ('USD', 'CAD') THEN o.shippingcost
       ELSE o.shippingcost - ot.shippingtax END AS netsales
FROM order o, ordertax ot
WHERE o.orderid = ordertax.orderid
```

At this point, we can go back to the knowledge capture step for two reasons. If the validation was successful, then we can start another iteration of the approach by soliciting a new set of business questions. On the other hand, if the validation was unsuccessful because the queries did not return the expected results, we can revisit the mappings for that specific fragment. Fixing the problem is now in a compartmentalized section of the ontology and corresponding mappings. Progress is made in an incremental and isolated effort. In worst case the original business logic needs to be revisited and we can go back to the discovery step.

Using this pay-as-you-go methodology for applications across multiple industries is yielding agile results. Development cycles of 1–2 weeks yield new dashboards. All stakeholders are concentrated on a specific task, an agreed upon set of business questions. As development issues arise conversations between the knowledge engineers, business users and IT developers are focused on specific, manageably scoped concepts. The knowledge capture and implementation steps can be accomplished independently. Furthermore, by starting small, the target ontology and mappings are created monotonically. This means that new concepts, relationships and mappings are added without disturbing the work that already has been done. In the case when change to past work is required, it is accomplished without much disruption. The declarative aspect of R2RML mappings, enables focus on what needs to be connected between the source and target instead of writing procedural code and scripts which can be complex to maintain.? Finally, success of each iteration is well defined: answer the business questions.

6 Conclusion

The answer to the question: *How and to what extent can Relational Databases be integrated with the Semantic Web?* comes in three parts:

- **Relational Databases can be directly mapped to RDF and OWL**: Relational Databases can be automatically mapped to the Semantic Web. An OWL ontology can be generated from the relational schema and the relational data can be represented as an RDF graph. This mapping does not loose information, preserves queries, is monotone and is positive semantics preserving. Additionally, it is not possible to have a monotone and full semantics preserving direct mapping.

- **Relational Databases can evaluate and optimize SPARQL queries**: Relational Databases are able to efficiently evaluate SPARQL queries. By implementing the direct mapping using SQL views, relational optimizer exploit two important semantic query optimizations: detection of unsatisfiable conditions and self join elimination.
- **Relational Databases can act as reasoners**: Given a Relational Database, an OWL ontology with inheritance and transitivity, and a mapping between the two, Relational Databases are able to act reasoner. This is possible by implementing the mappings as SQL views and including SQL recursion, materializing a subset of the views based on a cost model, and exploiting existing optimizations such as query rewriting using materialized views.

The results of our research is embodied in a system called Ultrawrap.

6.1 Open Problems

The relationship between Relational Databases and the Semantic Web is via **mappings**. Semantic Web technology provides the following features. OWL Ontologies enable reasoning (**reasoning**). SPARQL queries with variables in the predicate position reveal metadata. This is useful because it enables exploration of the data in case the schema is not known beforehand. Additionally, queries of this form are intrinsic to faceted search (**variable predicate**). Given the graph model of RDF, the latest version of SPARQL, SPARQL 1.1, increased the expressivity and now provides constructs to navigate the graph (**graph traversal**). Another virtue of dealing with graphs is that insertion of data is reduced to adding an edge with a node to the graph. There are no physical requirements to conform to a schema (**dynamic schema**). Finally, data can be easily integrated by simply adding edges between nodes of different graphs (**data integration**).

A goal of our research has been to understand *up to what extent* can Relational Databases be integrated with the Semantic Web. The extent of our research has focused on mappings and reasoning. A remaining question is: can that extent be expanded? And up to where? We call this the Tipping Point problem.

Assume the starting point are legacy relational databases and we want to take advantage of these five features of the Semantic Web (reasoning, variable predicate, graph traversal, dynamic schema, data integration). How much can be subsumed by Relational Database technology before the balance is tipped over and we end up using native Semantic Web technology? What is the tipping point (or points)?

- **Mappings**: The engineering of mappings is still open grounds for research. What mappings patterns can be defined and reused in order to solve a commonly occurring problem [63]? Given that R2RML mappings are represented in RDF, these can be stored in a triplestore, queried and reasoned upon. This opens up potential such as mapping analysis, automatically generating mappings, reusing existing mappings during the engineering of new

mappings, consistency checking of mappings in conjunction with the ontology, adding provenance information to the mappings to support data lineage [22,26,42,45,71]. Additionally, there is a need for tools to support users to create mappings [12,68].
- **Reasoning**: Our research proposed to represent ontological entailments as mappings and implement them as views. Subsequently, a subset of these views are materialized. Open questions remain. What is the state of the art of other RDBMS's optimizers in order to support this approach? How does this approach respond to complex query workloads? The model assumed a read-only database, therefore, what is the cost of maintaining views when the underlying data is updated? Evidence is provided that Relational Databases can act as reasoners for RDFS and Transitivity. Can the expressivity be increased while maintaining efficient computation by the RDBMS optimizer? What is the trade-off between reasoning over relational databases with mappings and using native RDF databases which supports reasoning?
- **Variable Predicate**: For queries with variables in the predicate position, the mapping stipulates that the variable may be bound to the name of any column in the database. These queries are a syntactic construct of higher order logic. Ultrawrap translates these queries into a SQL query consisting of a union for each attribute in the database. This query ends up reading the entire database and suffers a performance penalty. What optimizations can be implemented in order to overcome this issue? What hints can be provided in a query?
- **Graph Traversal**: Regular Path Queries and SPARQL 1.1 property path queries enable pattern-based reachability queries. These types of queries enable the traversal and navigation of the graph. A natural question is how much of SQL recursion can be used to implement these types of queries?
- **Dynamic Schema**: Relational Databases have a fixed schema. Insertion of data needs to adhere to the schema. A schema needs to be altered in case new data is inserted which does not adhere to the schema. Can a Relational Database become hybrid graph/relational database? What effect does the sparsity of data have? What is the best storage manager (column vs row store)?
- **Data Integration**: When it comes to integrate disparate databases, one approach is to extract the relational data, transform it physically to RDF and then load it into a RDF database (ETL). Another approach is to federate queries. In other words, legacy data continues to reside in the relational databases and queries are sent to each source (Federation). Which approach is practical? Depending on what? Can hybrid system be efficient?

An overarching theme is the need to create systematic and real-world benchmarks in order to evaluate different solutions for these features.

These open questions provide a roadmap to further expand the extent that Relational Databases can be integrated with the Semantic Web.

References

1. Abadi, D.J., Marcus, A., Madden, S.R., Hollenbach, K.: Scalable semantic web data management using vertical partitioning. In: Proceedings of the 33rd International Conference on Very Large Data Bases, pp. 411–422 (2007)
2. Abiteboul, S., Hull, R., Vianu, V.: Foundations of Databases. Addison-Wesley, Reading (1995)
3. Ahmed, R., Lee, A., Das, D.: Join predicate push-down optimizations. US Patent 7,945,562, May 17 2011
4. Allemang, D., Hendler, J.A.: Semantic Web for the Working Ontologist - Effective Modeling in RDFS and OWL, 2nd edn. Morgan Kaufmann, San Francisco (2011)
5. Angles, R., Gutierrez, C.: The expressive power of SPARQL. In: Sheth, A., Staab, S., Dean, M., Paolucci, M., Maynard, D., Finin, T., Thirunarayan, K. (eds.) ISWC 2008. LNCS, vol. 5318, pp. 114–129. Springer, Heidelberg (2008). doi:10.1007/978-3-540-88564-1_8
6. Arenas, M., Barceló, P., Libkin, L., Murlak, F.: Foundations of Data Exchange. Cambridge University Press, Cambridge (2014)
7. Arenas, M., Bertails, A., Prud'hommeaux, E., Sequeda, J.: Direct mapping of relational data to RDF. W3C Recomendation, 27 September 2012. http://www.w3.org/TR/rdb-direct-mapping/
8. Azzaoui, K.: Scientific competency questions as the basis for semantically enriched open pharmacological space development. Drug Discov. Today **18**, 843–852 (2013)
9. Baader, F., Brandt, S., Lutz, C.: Pushing the el envelope. In: IJCAI (2005)
10. Baader, F., Calvanese, D., McGuinness, D.L., Nardi, D., Patel-Schneider, P.F. (eds.): The Description Logic Handbook: Theory, Implementation, and Applications. Cambridge University Press, Cambridge (2003)
11. Bizer, C., Schultz, A.: The Berlin SPARQL benchmark. Int. J. Semant. Web Inf. Syst. **5**(2), 1–24 (2009)
12. Blinkiewicz, M., Bąk, J.: SQuaRE: a visual approach for ontology-based data access. In: Li, Y.-F., Hu, W., Dong, J.S., Antoniou, G., Wang, Z., Sun, J., Liu, Y. (eds.) JIST 2016. LNCS, vol. 10055, pp. 47–55. Springer, Cham (2016). doi:10.1007/978-3-319-50112-3_4
13. Brickley, D., Guha, R.: RDF vocabulary description language 1.0: RDF schema, W3C recommendation, February 2004
14. Broekstra, J., Kampman, A., Harmelen, F.: Sesame: a generic architecture for storing and querying RDF and RDF schema. In: Horrocks, I., Hendler, J. (eds.) ISWC 2002. LNCS, vol. 2342, pp. 54–68. Springer, Heidelberg (2002). doi:10.1007/3-540-48005-6_7
15. Calvanese, D., De Giacomo, G., Lembo, D., Lenzerini, M., Rosati, R.: Data complexity of query answering in description logics. Artif. Intell. **195**, 335–360 (2013)
16. Calvanese, D., Giacomo, G., Lembo, D., Lenzerini, M., Rosati, R.: Tractable reasoning and efficient query answering in description logics: the DL-Lite family. J. Autom. Reason. **39**(3), 385–429 (2007)
17. Calvanese, D., Giacomo, G.D., Lembo, D., Lenzerini, M., Rosati, R.: EQL-Lite: effective first-order query processing in description logics. In: IJCAI, pp. 274–279 (2007)
18. Chakravarthy, U.S., Grant, J., Minker, J.: Logic-based approach to semantic query optimization. ACM Trans. Database Syst. **15**(2), 162–207 (1990)
19. Chebotko, A., Lu, S., Fotouhi, F.: Semantics preserving SPARQL-to-SQL translation. Data Knowl. Eng. **68**(10), 973–1000 (2009)

20. Cheng, Q., Gryz, J., Koo, F., Leung, T.Y.C., Liu, L., Qian, X., Schiefer, K.B.: Implementation of two semantic query optimization techniques in DB2 universal database. In: VLDB, pp. 687–698 (1999)
21. Chong, E.I., Das, S., Eadon, G., Srinivasan, J.: An efficient SQL-based RDF querying scheme. In: Proceedings of the 31st International Conference on Very Large Data Bases, pp. 1216–1227 (2005)
22. Civili, C., Mora, J., Rosati, R., Ruzzi, M., Santarelli, V.: Semantic analysis of R2RML mappings for ontology-based data access. In: Ortiz, M., Schlobach, S. (eds.) RR 2016. LNCS, vol. 9898, pp. 25–38. Springer, Cham (2016). doi:10.1007/978-3-319-45276-0_3
23. Corcho, Ó., Fernández-López, M., Gómez-Pérez, A.: Methodologies, tools and languages for building ontologies: where is their meeting point? Data Knowl. Eng. **46**(1), 41–64 (2003)
24. Cudré-Mauroux, P., et al.: NoSQL databases for RDF: an empirical evaluation. In: Alani, H., et al. (eds.) ISWC 2013. LNCS, vol. 8219, pp. 310–325. Springer, Heidelberg (2013). doi:10.1007/978-3-642-41338-4_20
25. Das, S., Sundara, S., Cyganiak, R.: R2RML: RDB to RDF mapping language. W3C Recomendation, 27 September 2012. http://www.w3.org/TR/r2rml/
26. Medeiros, L.F., Priyatna, F., Corcho, O.: MIRROR: automatic R2RML mapping generation from relational databases. In: Cimiano, P., Frasincar, F., Houben, G.-J., Schwabe, D. (eds.) ICWE 2015. LNCS, vol. 9114, pp. 326–343. Springer, Cham (2015). doi:10.1007/978-3-319-19890-3_21
27. DeWitt, D.J.: The Wisconsin benchmark: past, present, and future. In: The Benchmark Handbook, pp. 119–165 (1991)
28. Donini, F., Lenzerini, M., Nardi, D., Nutt, W., Schaerf, A.: An epistemic operator for description logics. Artif. Intell. **100**(1–2), 225–274 (1998)
29. Donini, F.M., Nardi, D., Rosati, R.: Description logics of minimal knowledge and negation as failure. ACM Trans. Comput. Log. **3**(2), 177–225 (2002)
30. Elliott, B., Cheng, E., Thomas-Ogbuji, C., Ozsoyoglu, Z.M.: A complete translation from SPARQL into efficient SQL. In: Proceedings of the 2009 International Database Engineering & Applications Symposium, pp. 31–42 (2009)
31. Franke, C., Morin, S., Chebotko, A., Abraham, J., Brazier, P.: Distributed semantic web data management in HBase and MySQL cluster. In: Proceedings of the 2011 IEEE 4th International Conference on Cloud Computing, pp. 105–112 (2011)
32. Glimm, B., Hogan, A., Krotzsch, M., Polleres, A.: OWL-LD. http://semanticweb.org/OWLLD/
33. Gray, A.J., Gray, N., Ounis, I.: Can RDB2RDF tools feasibily expose large science archives for data integration? In: Aroyo, L., et al. (eds.) ESWC 2009. LNCS, vol. 5554, pp. 491–505. Springer, Heidelberg (2009). doi:10.1007/978-3-642-02121-3_37
34. Grimm, S., Motik, B.: Closed world reasoning in the semantic web through epistemic operators. In: OWLED (2005)
35. Grosof, B.N., Horrocks, I., Volz, R., Decker, S.: Description logic programs: combining logic programs with description logic. In: WWW, pp. 48–57 (2003)
36. Gupta, A., Mumick, I.S., Views, M.: Techniques, Implementations, and Applications. MIT Press, Cambridge (1999)
37. Halevy, A.Y.: Answering queries using views: a survey. VLDB J. **10**(4), 270–294 (2001)
38. Harris, S., Seaborne, A.: SPARQL 1.1 query language. W3C Recommendation, 21 March 2013. http://www.w3.org/TR/sparql11-query/
39. Hendler, J.: RDFS 3.0. In: W3C Workshop - RDF Next Steps (2010)

40. Hitzler, P., Gangemi, A., Janowicz, K., Krisnadhi, A., Presutti, V. (eds.): Ontology Engineering with Ontology Design Patterns - Foundations and Applications. Studies on the Semantic Web, vol. 25. IOS Press (2016)
41. Huang, J., Abadi, D.J., Ren, K.: Scalable SPARQL querying of large RDF graphs. PVLDB **4**(11), 1123–1134 (2011)
42. Jiménez-Ruiz, E.: BootOX: practical mapping of RDBs to OWL 2. In: Arenas, M., et al. (eds.) ISWC 2015. LNCS, vol. 9367, pp. 113–132. Springer, Cham (2015). doi:10.1007/978-3-319-25010-6_7
43. Keet, C.M., Lawrynowicz, A.: Test-driven development of ontologies. In: Sack, H., Blomqvist, E., d'Aquin, M., Ghidini, C., Ponzetto, S.P., Lange, C. (eds.) ESWC 2016. LNCS, vol. 9678, pp. 642–657. Springer, Cham (2016). doi:10.1007/978-3-319-34129-3_39
44. Ladwig, G., Harth, A.: CumulusRDF: linked data management on nested key-value stores. In: 7th International Workshop on Scalable Semantic Web Knowledge Base Systems (SSWS 2011) (2011)
45. Lembo, D., Mora, J., Rosati, R., Savo, D.F., Thorstensen, E.: Mapping analysis in ontology-based data access: algorithms and complexity. In: Arenas, M., et al. (eds.) ISWC 2015. LNCS, vol. 9366, pp. 217–234. Springer, Cham (2015). doi:10.1007/978-3-319-25007-6_13
46. Lenzerini, M.: Data integration: a theoretical perspective. In: PODS, pp. 233–246 (2002)
47. Lutz, C., Seylan, İ., Toman, D., Wolter, F.: The combined approach to OBDA: taming role hierarchies using filters. In: Alani, H., et al. (eds.) ISWC 2013. LNCS, vol. 8218, pp. 314–330. Springer, Heidelberg (2013). doi:10.1007/978-3-642-41335-3_20
48. MahmoudiNasab, H., Sakr, S.: An experimental evaluation of relational RDF storage and querying techniques. In: Yoshikawa, M., Meng, X., Yumoto, T., Ma, Q., Sun, L., Watanabe, C. (eds.) DASFAA 2010. LNCS, vol. 6193, pp. 215–226. Springer, Heidelberg (2010). doi:10.1007/978-3-642-14589-6_22
49. Mehdi, A., Rudolph, S., Grimm, S.: Epistemic querying of OWL knowledge bases. In: Antoniou, G., Grobelnik, M., Simperl, E., Parsia, B., Plexousakis, D., Leenheer, P., Pan, J. (eds.) ESWC 2011. LNCS, vol. 6643, pp. 397–409. Springer, Heidelberg (2011). doi:10.1007/978-3-642-21034-1_27
50. Motik, B., Grau, B.C., Horrocks, I., Wu, Z., amd Carsten Lutz, A.F.: Owl 2 web ontology language profiles, 2nd edn., W3C recommendation, December 2012
51. Motik, B., Horrocks, I., Sattler, U.: Bridging the gap between OWL and relational databases. J. Web Semant. **7**(2), 74–89 (2009)
52. Muñoz, S., Pérez, J., Gutierrez, C.: Simple and efficient minimal RDFS. J. Web Semant. **7**(3), 220–234 (2009)
53. Neumann, T., Weikum, G.: The RDF-3x engine for scalable management of RDF data. VLDB J. **19**(1), 91–113 (2010)
54. Ortiz, M., Šimkus, M.: Reasoning and query answering in description logics. In: Eiter, T., Krennwallner, T. (eds.) Reasoning Web 2012. LNCS, vol. 7487, pp. 1–53. Springer, Heidelberg (2012). doi:10.1007/978-3-642-33158-9_1
55. Pérez, J., Arenas, M., Gutierrez, C.: Semantics and complexity of SPARQL. ACM Trans. Database Syst. **34**(3), 16 (2009)
56. Pinto, F.D., Lembo, D., Lenzerini, M., Mancini, R., Poggi, A., Rosati, R., Ruzzi, M., Savo, D.F.: Optimizing query rewriting in ontology-based data access. In: EDBT (2013)
57. Poggi, A., Lembo, D., Calvanese, D., Giacomo, G.D., Lenzerini, M., Rosati, R.: Linking data to ontologies. J. Data Semant. **10**, 133–173 (2008)

58. Priyatna, F., Corcho, Ó, Sequeda, J.: Formalisation and experiences of R2RML-based SPARQL to SQL query translation using Morph. In: 23rd International World Wide Web Conference, WWW 2014, Seoul, 7–11 April 2014, pp. 479–490 (2014)
59. Prud'hommeaux, E., Seaborne, A.: SPARQL query language for RDF. W3C Recommendation 15 January 2008. http://www.w3.org/TR/rdf-sparql-query/
60. Ren, Y., Parvizi, A., Mellish, C., Pan, J.Z., Deemter, K., Stevens, R.: Towards competency question-driven ontology authoring. In: Presutti, V., d'Amato, C., Gandon, F., d'Aquin, M., Staab, S., Tordai, A. (eds.) ESWC 2014. LNCS, vol. 8465, pp. 752–767. Springer, Cham (2014). doi:10.1007/978-3-319-07443-6_50
61. Rodríguez-Muro, M., Kontchakov, R., Zakharyaschev, M.: Ontology-based data access: *Ontop* of databases. In: Alani, H., et al. (eds.) ISWC 2013. LNCS, vol. 8218, pp. 558–573. Springer, Heidelberg (2013). doi:10.1007/978-3-642-41335-3_35
62. Sequeda, J.: On the semantics of R2RML and its relationship with the direct mapping. In: Proceedings of the ISWC 2013 Posters & Demonstrations Track, Sydney, 23 October 2013, pp. 193–196 (2013)
63. Sequeda, J., Priyatna, F., Villazón-Terrazas, B.: Relational database to RDF mapping patterns. In: Proceedings of the 3rd Workshop on Ontology Patterns, Boston, 12 November 2012
64. Sequeda, J.F.: Integrating relational databases with the semantic web. IOS Press (2016). https://repositories.lib.utexas.edu/bitstream/handle/2152/30537/SEQUEDA-DISSERTATION-2015.pdf
65. Sequeda, J.F., Arenas, M., Miranker, D.P.: On directly mapping relational databases to RDF and OWL. In: WWW, pp. 649–658 (2012)
66. Sequeda, J.F., Arenas, M., Miranker, D.P.: OBDA: query rewriting or materialization? In practice, both!. In: Mika, P., et al. (eds.) ISWC 2014. LNCS, vol. 8796, pp. 535–551. Springer, Cham (2014). doi:10.1007/978-3-319-11964-9_34
67. Sequeda, J.F., Miranker, D.P.: Ultrawrap: SPARQL execution on relational data. J. Web Semant. **22**, 19–39 (2013)
68. Sequeda, J.F., Miranker, D.P.: Ultrawrap mapper: a semi-automatic relational database to RDF (RDB2RDF) mapping tool. In: Proceedings of the ISWC 2015 Posters & Demonstrations Track co-located with the 14th International Semantic Web Conference (ISWC-2015), Bethlehem, 11 October 2015
69. Sequeda, J.F., Tirmizi, S.H., Corcho, O., Miranker, D.P.: Survey of directly mapping SQL databases to the semantic web. Knowl. Eng. Review **26**(4), 445–486 (2011)
70. Shenoy, S.T., Ozsoyoglu, Z.M.: A system for semantic query optimization. In: SIGMOD, pp. 181–195 (1987)
71. Sicilia, Á., Nemirovski, G.: AutoMap4OBDA: automated generation of R2RML mappings for OBDA. In: Blomqvist, E., Ciancarini, P., Poggi, F., Vitali, F. (eds.) EKAW 2016. LNCS (LNAI), vol. 10024, pp. 577–592. Springer, Cham (2016). doi:10.1007/978-3-319-49004-5_37
72. Tao, J., Sirin, E., Bao, J., McGuinness, D.L.: Integrity constraints in OWL. In: AAAI (2010)
73. Tirmizi, S.H., Sequeda, J., Miranker, D.: Translating SQL applications to the semantic web. In: Bhowmick, S.S., Küng, J., Wagner, R. (eds.) DEXA 2008. LNCS, vol. 5181, pp. 450–464. Springer, Heidelberg (2008). doi:10.1007/978-3-540-85654-2_40
74. Uschold, M., Gruninger, M.: Ontologies: principles, methods and applications. Knowledge Eng. Review **11**(2), 93–136 (1996)

75. Weaver, J., Hendler, J.A.: Parallel materialization of the finite RDFS closure for hundreds of millions of triples. In: Bernstein, A., Karger, D.R., Heath, T., Feigenbaum, L., Maynard, D., Motta, E., Thirunarayan, K. (eds.) ISWC 2009. LNCS, vol. 5823, pp. 682–697. Springer, Heidelberg (2009). doi:10.1007/978-3-642-04930-9_43
76. Weiss, C., Karras, P., Bernstein, A.: Hexastore: sextuple indexing for semantic web data management. Proc. VLDB Endow. **1**(1), 1008–1019 (2008)
77. Wilkinson, K.: Jena property table implementation. Technical report HPL-2006-140, HP Laboratories (2006)

Datalog Revisited for Reasoning in Linked Data

Marie-Christine Rousset[1,2(✉)], Manuel Atencia[1], Jerome David[1], Fabrice Jouanot[1], Olivier Palombi[3,4], and Federico Ulliana[5]

[1] Université Grenoble Alpes, Grenoble INP, CNRS, Inria, LIG, 38000 Grenoble, France
Marie-Christine.Rousset@imag.fr
[2] Institut universitaire de France, 75005 Paris, France
[3] Université Grenoble Alpes, Grenoble INP, CNRS, Inria, LJK, 38000 Grenoble, France
[4] Université Grenoble Alpes, LADAF, CHU Grenoble, 38000 Grenoble, France
[5] Université de Montpellier, CNRS, Inria, LIRMM, 34000 Montpellier, France

Abstract. Linked Data provides access to huge, continuously growing amounts of open data and ontologies in RDF format that describe entities, links and properties on those entities. Equipping Linked Data with inference paves the way to make the Semantic Web a reality. In this survey, we describe a unifying framework for RDF ontologies and databases that we call deductive RDF triplestores. It consists in equipping RDF triplestores with Datalog inference rules. This rule language allows to capture in a uniform manner OWL constraints that are useful in practice, such as property transitivity or symmetry, but also domain-specific rules with practical relevance for users in many domains of interest. The expressivity and the genericity of this framework is illustrated for modeling Linked Data applications and for developing inference algorithms. In particular, we show how it allows to model the problem of data linkage in Linked Data as a reasoning problem on possibly decentralized data. We also explain how it makes possible to efficiently extract expressive modules from Semantic Web ontologies and databases with formal guarantees, whilst effectively controlling their succinctness. Experiments conducted on real-world datasets have demonstrated the feasibility of this approach and its usefulness in practice for data integration and information extraction.

1 Introduction

Thanks to the RDF data model, the Semantic Web has become a reality with the rapid development of Linked Data. Linked Data provides access to huge, continuously growing amounts of open data in RDF format that describe properties and links on entities referenced by so-called Uniform Resource Identifiers (URIs).

This work has been partially supported by the ANR projects Pagoda (12-JS02-007-01) and Qualinca (12-CORD-012), the joint NSFC-ANR Lindicle project (12-IS01-0002), and LabEx PERSYVAL-Lab (11-LABX-0025-01).

G. Ianni et al. (Eds.): Reasoning Web 2017, LNCS 10370, pp. 121–166, 2017.
DOI: 10.1007/978-3-319-61033-7_5

RDFS and OWL languages [5] allow to express a lot of useful logical constraints on top of RDF datasets, and existing Semantic Web tools implement inference algorithms to exploit them. In particular, the Jena environment[1] includes a rule-based reasoner that implements the RETE algorithm [21]. When the inference mode is launched, the *saturated* dataset is computed, which is the set of RDF facts that can be logically inferred from the input RDF dataset and a given set of rules. The saturation process is guaranteed to terminate if the rules are safe, i.e., if the variables appearing in the conclusion of each rule also appear in its condition part.

Safe rules (also called Datalog rules) on top of RDF facts capture in a uniform way most of the OWL constraints useful in practice, as well as mappings across different datasets, and also domain knowledge provided by experts, while guaranteeing a polynomial data complexity of reasoning and query answering [2].

In the setting of a unifying framework that we have called *deductive RDF triplestores*, we have followed a rule-based approach to address several problems raised by exploiting semantic web knowledge bases. For this, we have extended and adapted forward-chaining and backward-chaining algorithms initially developed for Datalog deductive databases.

This survey is structured as follows. In Sect. 2, we first recall the ingredients of Linked Data and we define what we call a deductive RDF dataset to capture several ontological constraints expressing data semantics. In Sect. 3, we survey the rule-based data linkage approach that we have developed in the context of Linked Data based on reasoning for inferring differentFrom and sameAs facts. In Sect. 4, we summarize our approach for extracting *bounded-level* modules from RDF knowledge bases. Finally, in Sect. 5, we illustrate our methodology for rule-based integration of heterogeneous data and ontologies through several applications related to Medicine. Finally, we conclude in Sect. 6.

2 Datalog Rules on Top of RDF Datasets

We first recall the ingredients of Linked Data and then we define what we call a deductive RDF dataset to capture several ontological constraints expressing data semantics.

2.1 RDF Datasets in Linked Data

An RDF dataset in Linked Data is defined by a URL u and a set F of RDF facts that are accessible as URL through a query endpoint. We will denote by $ds(u)$ the set F of RDF facts that can be queried at the URL u.

An RDF fact is a triple $t = (s, p, o)$ where the subject s is either a URI or a blank node, the predicate p is a URI, and the object o may be either a URI, a blank node or a literal. We will denote the vocabulary used in $ds(u)$ by $voc(u)$, i.e., the names of predicates used to declare triples in the dataset accessible at the URL u.

[1] https://jena.apache.org/documentation/inference/.

2.2 Queries over RDF Datasets in Linked Data

Queries over Linked Data are SPARQL **conjunctive queries** entered through a given query endpoint accessible at a given URL. In this paper, we use a simplified notation for SPARQL queries, and, without loss of generality, we consider that all variables are distinguished.

A query $q(u)$ asked to an RDF dataset identified by (and accessible at) the URL u is a conjunction of **triple patterns** denoted by $TP_1(v_1), \ldots, TP_k(v_k)$ where each triple pattern $TP_i(v_i)$ is a triple (s^v, p^v, o^v) in which the subject s^v, the predicate p^v, or the object o^v can be variables: v_i is the set of variables appearing in the triple pattern. Variables are denoted by strings starting by '?'. $TP_i(v_i)$ is a **ground** triple pattern if its set of variables v_i is empty (denoted by $TP_i()$). A ground triple pattern corresponds to a RDF fact. A **boolean query** is a conjunction of ground triple patterns.

The evaluation of a query $q(u) : TP_1(v_1), \ldots, TP_k(v_k)$ over the dataset $ds(u)$ consists in finding substitutions θ assigning the variables in $\bigcup_{i \in [1..k]} v_i$ to constants (i.e., identifiers or literals) such that $TP_1(\theta.v_1), \ldots, TP_k(\theta.v_k)$ are RDF facts in the dataset.

The corresponding answer is equally defined as the tuple of constants assigned by θ to the variables or as the set of corresponding RDF facts $TP_1(\theta.v_1), \ldots, TP_k(\theta.v_k)$ that will be denoted by $\theta.q(u)$. In the remainder of the paper, we will adopt the latter definition. The answer set of the query $q(u)$ against the dataset $ds(u) = F$ is thus defined as:

$$Answer(q(u), F) = \bigcup_{\{\theta | \theta.q(u) \subseteq F\}} \{\theta.q(u)\}$$

For a boolean query $q(u)$, either the answer set is not empty and we will say that the query is evaluated to **true**, or it is empty and we will say that it evaluated to **false**.

For a query $q(u)$ to have a chance to get an answer when evaluated over the dataset $ds(u)$, it must be **compatible with** the vocabulary used in this dataset, i.e., (a) the predicates appearing in the triple patterns of $q(u)$ must belong to the set $voc(u)$ of predicates known to occur in $ds(u)$, (b) the URIs appearing as constants in the triple patterns of $q(u)$ must have u as prefix.

In accordance with SPARQL queries allowing different FROM operators, a conjunctive query can in fact specify several entry points $u_1, \ldots, u_n$ of datasets over which the query has to be.evaluated. We will denote such a query $q(u_1, \ldots, u_n)$. The above definitions of answers and compatibility can be generalized appropriately by replacing the dataset $ds(u)$ by the union $\bigcup_{i \in [1..n]} ds(u_i)$ of the specified datasets.

2.3 Deductive RDF Datasets

In order to capture in a uniform way semantic constraints that can be declared on top of a given RDF dataset, but also possibly mappings between local predicates and external predicates within the vocabulary of other datasets, and domain knowledge provided by domain experts, we consider that RDF datasets can be enriched with Datalog rules. The Datalog rules that we consider are of the form: $Cond_r \rightarrow Conc_r$, in which the condition $Cond_r$ is a conjunction of triple patterns (i.e., a conjunctive query) and the conclusion $Conc_r$ is a triple pattern. We consider **safe** rules, i.e., rules such that all the variables in the conclusion are also in the condition. Datalog rules on top of RDFS facts capture most of the OWL constraints used in practice, while guaranteeing a polynomial data complexity for reasoning and query answering.

A deductive RDF dataset $dds(u)$ accessible at the URL u is thus a local knowledge base (F, R) made of a set of RDF facts F and a set R of rules. The application of rules allows to infer new facts that are logically entailed from $F \cup R$. A rule r can be applied to F if there exists a substitution θ such that $\theta.Cond_r \subseteq F$ and the result of the rule application is $F \cup \{\theta.Conc_r\}$. These new facts can in turn trigger rules and infer additional facts. This is formalized in the following definition of the standard semantics of a knowledge base $F \cup R$ composed of a finite set of facts F and a finite set of rules R, based on the least fixed point of immediate consequence operator T_R.

Definition 1 (Datalog semantics)

- $(F, R) \vdash_1 f$ *iff there exists a rule* $TP_1(v_1) \wedge \ldots \wedge TP_k(v_k) \rightarrow TP(v)$ *is in* R *and there exists a mapping* θ *from its variables to constants such that* $f = \theta.TP(v)$ *and* $\theta.TP_i(v_i) \in F$ *for every* $i \in [1..k]$.
- $(F, R) \vdash f$ *iff there exists* i *such that* $f \in T_R(F_i)$ *where* $F_0 = F$, *and for every* $i \geq 0$, $F_{i+1} = T_R(F_i) = F_i \cup \{f | F_i, R \vdash_1 f\}$.

For a finite set of facts F and a finite set of safe rules R, there exists a unique least fixed point F_n (denoted by $SAT(F, R)$) such that for every $k \geq n$ $F_k = T_R(F_n)$, i.e., there exists a step in the iterative application of the immediate consequence operator for which no new fact is inferred. Several forward-chaining algorithms exist to compute $SAT(F, R)$, in particular the semi-naive bottom-up evaluation in Datalog [2], and the RETE algorithm [21] that is implemented in many rule-based reasoners, including in Semantic Web tools such as Jena (see Footnote 1).

Query Evaluation over a Deductive Dataset

The evaluation of a query $q(u) : TP_1(v_1), \ldots, TP_k(v_k)$ over a deductive dataset $dds(u)$ consists in finding substitutions θ such that the facts $TP_1(\theta.v_1), \ldots, TP_k(\theta.v_k)$ can be **inferred** from the deductive dataset, or equivalently belong to the result $SAT(F, R)$ of the facts that can be inferred from F and R:

$$Answer(q(u), (F, R)) = Answer(q(u), SAT(F, R))$$

Thus, a boolean query $q(u)$ is evaluated to **true** if and only if $q(u) \in SAT(F, R)$, i.e., if and only if $(F, R) \vdash q(u)$, where $\vdash$ is the standard notation for logical inference.

Within the vocabulary of a deductive dataset, we distinguish the extensional predicates (EDB predicates for short) that appear in the triplets of the dataset F, from the intentional predicates (IDB predicates) that appear in conclusion of some rules in R. Like in deductive databases, and without loss of generality (i.e., by possibly renaming predicates and adding rules), we suppose that these two sets are disjoint. We will denote ODB predicates the *external* predicates (i.e., defined in a different namespace than the considered deductive dataset) that possibly appear in the dataset or in the rules. These predicates are the core of Linked Data in which a good practice is to re-use existing reference vocabularies. We suppose (again, without loss of generality) that the set of ODB predicates is disjoint from the set of IDB predicates (but not necessarily from the set of EDB predicates).

3 Rule-Based Data Linkage

Data linkage consists in deciding whether two URIs refer to the same real-world entity. This is a crucial task in Linked Data. In particular, it is very important to correctly decide whether two URIs refer to the same real-world entity for developing innovative applications on top of Linked Data, that exploit the cross-referencing of data [20,26]. This task is often referred to as data interlinking, and is also known as record linkage and entity resolution, and it has been widely studied for the case of relational data [16]. As regards to Linked Data, data linkage is especially challenging since (1) tools need to scale well with large amounts of data, (2) data is frequently described using heterogeneous vocabularies (ontologies), and (3) tools need to deal with data which is inherently incomplete, and very often noisy.

In the context of Linked Data and RDF data, different approaches to data linkage have been proposed. Most of them are based on numerical methods that use linkage rules to compare property values of resources, using similarity measures to handle noisy data. They conclude weighted sameAs links, from which the links with higher weights are expected (but never guaranteed) to be correct [34,48]. These approaches suffer from two weaknesses. First, rules cannot be chained, as they are thought to be applied only once; and second, weights are combined in a non-formal manner, since there is no formal semantics that captures the combination of weights.

In contrast, like a few other works [31,40], we promote a rule-based approach equipped with full reasoning.

First, we have investigated a logical approach that exploits uniqueness constraints (such as inverse functional properties and keys) and other schema constraints, domain knowledge and alignments between different vocabularies which can be modelled as logical rules. This enables to infer all *certain* sameAs and differentFrom facts that are logically entailed from a given set of domain constraints and input facts. Our main contribution is a novel algorithm, called Import-by-Query, that enables the scalable deployment of such an approach in the decentralized setting of Linked Data. The main challenge is to identify the data, possibly distributed over several datasets, useful for inferring owl:sameAs and owl:differentFrom facts of interest. Compared to the approach reported in [31], relying on a global import obtained by a breadth-first crawl of the Linked Data cloud, we perform a selective import while guaranteeing completeness for the inference of the targeted owl:sameAs and owl:differentFrom facts. For doing so, the Import-by-Query algorithm that we have designed alternates steps of sub-query rewriting and of tailored querying of the Linked Data cloud to import data as specific as possible to infer owl:sameAs and owl:differentFrom facts. It is an extension of the well-known query-subquery algorithm for answering Datalog queries over deductive databases. Experiments conducted on a real-world dataset have demonstrated the feasibility of this approach and its usefulness in practice for data linkage and disambiguation.

We summarize this logical approach in Sect. 3.1.

Logical approaches applying only certain rules over clean and complete data guarantee to provide sound results, i.e., a 100% precision. However, the recall may be low because in Linked Data, data is inherently incomplete and possibly noisy. Input facts may be missing to trigger rules, either because some values for properties involved in rules conditions are absent for some URIs, or because some of these values are noisy with some misspelling that prevents some conditions to be satisfied. In addition, rules may be missing to infer sameAs facts with certainty, although some strong evidence could be obtained from the combination of soft constraints. In order to handle this, we have modeled the general data linkage problem as a reasoning problem with uncertainty. We have introduced a probabilistic framework for modelling and reasoning over uncertain RDF facts and rules that is based on the semantics of probabilistic Datalog, and we have designed an algorithm, ProbFR, based on this framework. This approach is summarized in Sect. 3.2

3.1 Logical Approach for Data Linkage [4]

Illustrative Scenario

We describe here a simplified scenario inspired by the task of disambiguation of named entities in a large real-world RDF documentary catalog produced by the French National Audiovisual Institute (INA), and that we have used in our experiments.

Figure 1 shows an extract of the INA vocabulary and a sample of RDF triples from the INA dataset.[2] Any person entity is an instance of the class ina:PhysicalPerson, which has two subclasses: ina:Person and ina:VideoPerson. The class ina:Person is used for representing French personalities while ina:VideoPerson is used for identifying person entities that play a role in a video. INA experts want to disambiguate individuals within ina:Person, and link these individuals to the ones of ina:VideoPerson.

[2] We have slightly modified the INA vocabulary (e.g. translating French terms into English terms) for the sake of readability.

Three homonymous persons are described in Fig. 1, all named "Jacques Martin": ina:per1, ina:per2 and ina:per3. It is unknown if these entities represent the same or different persons, but some additional information is given: ina:per1 is known to be the presenter of a program recorded in the video ina:vid1 whose title is "Le Petit Rapporteur", whereas ina:per2 and ina:per3 have dates of birth "1933-06-22" and "1921-09-25", respectively.

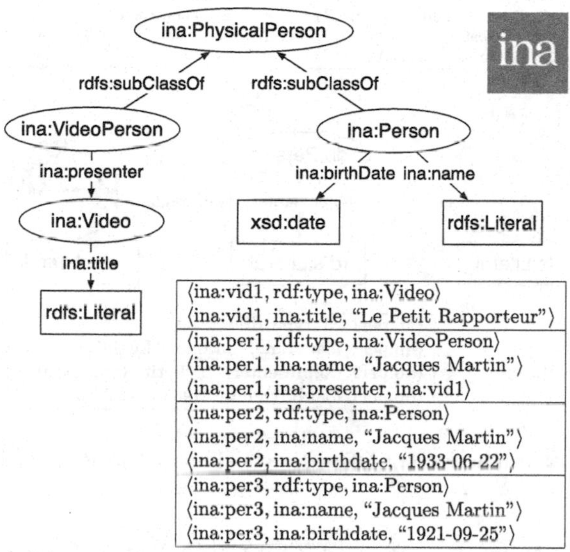

Fig. 1. An extract of INA vocabulary and RDF facts.

Our approach to disambiguating the person entities ina:per1, ina:per2 and ina:per3 consists in exploiting domain knowledge and constraints, as well as general properties of owl:sameAs and owl:different From, all this knowledge being expressed in a uniform way by rules. Table 1 shows rules which, for the purpose of this simplified scenario, we can assume they have been validated by INA experts. R1-R3 are domain-specific rules. R1 expresses that ina:birthdate is functional. This rule can be used to infer that ina:per2 and ina:per3 are different because they have different dates of birth. R2 expresses that ina:name and ina:birthdate form a key (within the INA dataset), and R3 the fact that two persons who have the same name and presented programs recorded in videos with the same title must be the same. R2 and R3 indeed could be useful for deciding if ina:per1 refers to the same person as ina:per2 or ina:per3, but some information is missing: the date of birth of ina:per1 is not known, or whether ina:per2 or ina:per3 are presenters and of which programs.

The above missing information can be completed thanks to external data coming from DBpedia. In Fig. 2, we show DBpedia facts describing the DBpedia person entity db:per1, and an extract of the DBpedia vocabulary. Rules R4

Table 1. Rules in the INA illustrative scenario.

R1 : $(?x1$, ina:birthdate, $?b1)$, $(?x2$, ina:birthdate, $?b2)$, $(?b1$, notEqualTo, $?b2) \rightarrow (?x1$, owl:differentFrom, $?x2)$
R2 : $(?x1$, ina:name, $?n)$, $(?x2$, ina:name, $?n)$, $(?x2$, ina:birthdate, $?b)$, $(?x1$, ina:birthdate, $?b)$ $\rightarrow (?x1$, owl:sameAs, $?x2)$
R3 : $(?x1$, ina:name, $?n)$, $(?x2$, ina:name, $?n)$, $(?x1$, ina:presenter, $?v1)$, $(?x2$, ina:presenter, $?v2)$, $(?v1$, ina:title, $?t)$, $(?v2$, ina:title, $?t) \rightarrow (?x1$, owl:sameAs, $?x2)$
R4 : $(?x1$, ina:name, $?n)$, $(?x2$, foaf:name, $?n)$, $(?x1$, ina:presenter, $?v)$, $(?v$, ina:title, $?t)$, $(?x2$, db:presenter, $?t)$ $\rightarrow (?x1$, owl:sameAs, $?x2)$
R5 : $(?x1$, ina:name, $?n)$, $(?x2$, foaf:name, $?n)$, $(?x1$, ina:birthdate, $?b)$, $(?x2$, foaf:birthdate, $?b)$ $\rightarrow (?x1$, owl:sameAs, $?x2)$
R6 : $(?x1$, owl:sameAs, $?x2)$, $(?x2$, owl:sameAs, $?x3) \rightarrow (?x1$, owl:sameAs, $?x3)$
R7 : $(?x1$, owl:sameAs, $?x2)$, $(?x2$, owl:differentFrom, $?x3) \rightarrow (?x1$, owl:differentFrom, $?x3)$
R8 : $(?x1$, ina:name, $?n1)$, $(?x2$, foaf:name, $?n2)$, $(?n1$, built-in:name-similar, $?n2)$, $(?x1$, ina:birthdate, $?b)$, $(?x2$, foaf:birthdate, $?b) \rightarrow (?x1$, owl:sameAs, $?x2)$

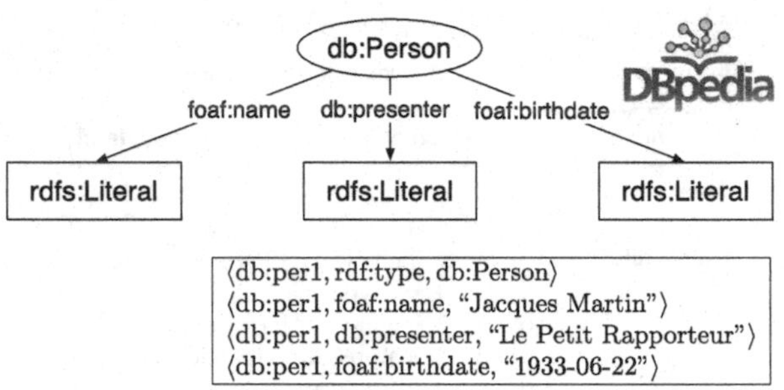

Fig. 2. An extract of DBpedia vocabulary and RDF facts.

and R5 in Table 1 translate mappings from the INA and DBpedia vocabularies. Specifically, these mappings state that ina:name and ina:birthdate are equivalent to foaf:name and foaf:birthdate, respectively, and that the composition of ina:presenter and ina:title is equivalent to db:presenter. Let us assume that rules R4 and R5 have been validated by INA experts too. With these rules it can be inferred that db:per1 is the same as ina:per1 because they have the same name and they have presented a program with the same title; and that db:per1 is the same as ina:per2 since they have the same name and birthdate. Therefore, by transitivity of same-as (rule R6 in Table 1), it can be inferred that ina:per1 is the same as ina:per2, and, since ina:per2 is different from ina:per3 then (due to R7) ina:per1 is different from ina:per3 too.

To avoid downloading the complete DBpedia, and, more generally, the whole Linked Open Data (something that is not practical), our import-by-query approach generates, for each targeted owl:sameAs fact, a sequence of external sub-queries as specific as possible to obtain just the missing facts. The external sub-queries generated by our algorithm for the particular query (ina:per1, owl:sameAs, ina:per2) in our example are shown in Fig. 3.

Problem Statement

Given a deductive dataset $dds(u) = (F, R)$, and a boolean query $q(u)$ the local evaluation of which gives an empty answer set (i.e., $(F, R) \not\vdash q(u)$), we

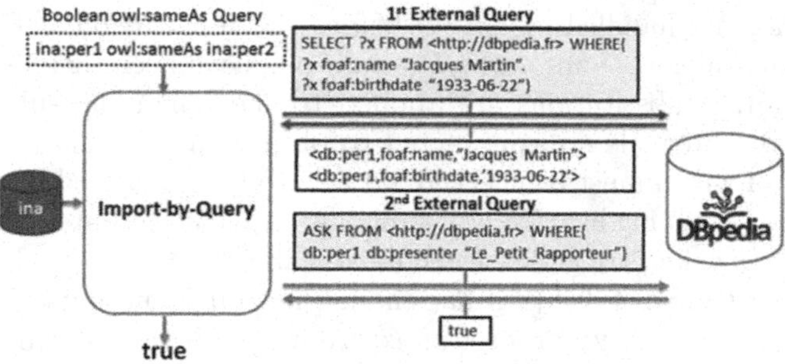

Fig. 3. The resultant external sub-queries submitted to DBpedia and their returned answers.

aim to construct a set of external queries $q_1(u_1), \ldots, q_k(u_k)$ for which we can guarantee that the subsets of external facts resulting from their evaluation over the (possibly huge) external datasets are sufficient to answer the initial query. More formally:

$$(F \cup \bigcup_{i \in [1..k]} Answer(q_i(u_i), ds(u_i)), R) \vdash q(u)$$

$$\text{iff } (F \cup \bigcup_{i \in [1..k]} ds(u_i), R) \vdash q(u)$$

The more specific the external queries are, the less external facts have to be added and stored to the local dataset and therefore the more interesting a proposed approach is to solve this problem.

The Iterative Import-by-Query Algorithm

We now describe the algorithm that we have designed and implemented for solving the problem stated above.

Given an input boolean same-as query q, a deductive dataset (F, R), and a set $\bar{u}$ of query entry points to external datasets, Import-by-Query iteratively alternates steps of sub-query rewriting based on backward chaining and of external query evaluation.

Each sub-query rewriting step is realized by an adaptation of the *Query-Subquery* algorithm [2,47] that is a set-oriented memoing backward chaining method [29] used in deductive databases for evaluating Datalog programs. This results in the *Query-External-Subquery* (*QESQ* for short) algorithm. For space limitation, here we just explain its main principles, compared to *Query-Subquery*, when applied to a list *SG* of subgoals. QESQ handles the subgoals built on EDB or IDB predicates exactly like *Query-Subquery*, i.e., iteratively removes subgoals built on EDB predicates if they can be matched with local facts, propagates the corresponding substitutions to the remaining subgoals, replaces a subgoal g built on an IDB predicate by the list of partially instantiated conditions of a rule whose conclusion can be matched to g. As for the subgoals on ODB predicates, they are handled by QESQ before the subgoals on IDB predicates, and once all the subgoals built on EDB predicates have been removed, and after the corresponding substitutions are applied to the remaining subgoals in the list. These ODB subgoals are conjuncted to obtain an external query q_{ext}, the compatibility of which must be checked w.r.t. $\bar{u}$ to be considered further. QESQ then treats the remaining list SG_{idb} of subgoals on IDB predicates just as *Query-External-Subquery*, i.e., triggers the recursive call $QESQ(SG_{idb})$. It will return as output either **true** or **false** (if it has enough local information to infer a result to the input boolean query), or a set of external queries that, if compatible with the vocabulary of the given external datasets, are then conjuncted with q_{ext} to constitute the output returned by QESQ(SG). As a result QESQ ($\{q\}$) succeeds in handling locally the goal q using F and R just like *Query-Subquery* and then the process is stopped and the result returned by Import-by-Query is **true** or **false** accordingly, or it produces a set $\{q_1(\bar{u}_1), \ldots, q_k(\bar{u}_k)\}$ of external queries the evaluation of which is likely to bring missing facts to F for proving the goal q using R. If this set is empty, the process is stopped and the result returned by Import-by-Query is **false**.

Each evaluation step simply consists in choosing one of the external query $q_i(\bar{u}_i)$ produced by the sub-query rewriting step and to submit it to Linked Data through the specified query entry points. The result is either an empty set (negative result) or a set of external facts (positive result) that can be added to the current local dataset. In both cases, the result is memorized in an associated answer table for the sub-query $q_i(\bar{u}_i)$ that will be thus marked as an already processed subgoal for which the (positive or negative) result is known and can be directly exploited later on. If the result is positive, a new iteration of Import-by-Query is started on the same input except for the set of facts F that is enriched with the facts obtained as the result of the evaluation of the external query $q_i(\bar{u}_i)$. If the result is negative, another external query $q_j(\bar{u}_j)$ in the set produced by the current call to QESQ is evaluated. If the evaluation of all the external queries in the set returns 'false', then the process is stopped and the result returned by Import-by-Query on q is **false**.

The termination of the Import-by-Query algorithm relies on the termination of QESQ, which is guaranteed by the same memoing technique as *Query-Subquery* (i.e., by handling goal and answer tables for each ODB and IDB predicate). The soundness and completeness of the Import-by-Query algorithm results from the soundness and completeness of *Query-Subquery* [47] and from the observation that the result produced by *Query-Subquery*, if applied to the same input in which the ODB predicates are just considered as additional EDB predicates, would be the same as the one produced by Import-by-Query. The reason is that the only difference of Import-by-Query is to replace successive matching of atomic goals against the facts by matching *all at once* the atomic goals composing the external queries produced by QESQ. This does not impact the global boolean result of the sequence of goal matching.

Combining Forward and Backward Chaining

Like any backward chaining method, Import-by-Query (and its main component QESQ) re-starts from scratch for each new goal it tries to solve, even if the facts and the rules remain unchanged. The intermediate subgoals generated and handled by QESQ can be simplified if the input rules are replaced by their (partial) instantiations obtained by the propagation of the facts into (the conditions of) the rules.

Fact propagation is a forward chaining method used in inference engines such as RETE [21] for rule-based systems. It avoids redundant evaluation of same conditions appearing in several rules by memorizing, for each fact f, which condition it satisfies in which rule (possibly already partially instantiated by facts previously propagated), and the corresponding variable substitution that is then applied to all the remaining conditions of the rules.

In our setting, we perform fact propagation as a pre-processing step of the Import-by-Query algorithm, by computing at the same time the set $SAT(F,R)$ of facts that can be inferred locally, and the set $PI(F,R)$ of partial instantiations of the rules in R. This forward reasoning step can be summarized as follows, where $SAT(F,R)$ is initialized as F and $PI(F,R)$ is initialized as R:

- **for** each f in $SAT(F,R)$
  for each rule $Cond_r \rightarrow Conc_r$ in $PI(F,R)$ having a condition c that can be matched with f, i.e., there exists θ such that $\theta.c = f$
  * **IF** c is the only condition in $Cond_r$ **THEN** add $\theta.Conc_r$ to $SAT(F,R)$
  * **ELSE** add to $PI(F,R)$ the rule obtained from $\theta.Cond_r \rightarrow \theta.Conc_r$ by removing the condition $\theta.c$ (that is satisfied by the fact f).
- Remove from $PI(F,R)$ those rules whose condition contains EDB predicates that are not ODB predicates (and thus cannot be satisfied by local facts).
- **RETURN** $(SAT(F,R), PI(F,R))$

Each partially instantiated rule r_i returned in $PI(F,R)$ is issued from an input rule r in which some conditions have been matched to facts f_1, ..., f_k that have been inferred before (and added to $SAT(F,R)$), and thus allows us to infer the same conclusion as the input rule r on any set of facts including f_1, ..., f_k. The result $SAT(F,R) \cup PI(F,R)$ is then logically equivalent to the input deductive dataset $F \cup R$ for inferring facts on IDB predicates from the union of F and a set OF of external facts (with ODB predicates), i.e. for every fact f an external set of facts OF:

$$(F \cup OF, R) \vdash f \text{ iff } (SAT(F,R) \cup OF, PI(F,R)) \vdash f$$

Therefore, it can be equivalently used for proving goals by checking whether they belong to $SAT(F,R)$, or for rewriting goals by applying $QESQ$ to the $PI(F,R)$ (instead of the original R).

Experiments

We have conducted experiments on a real deductive dataset composed of 35 rules and about 6 million RDF facts from INA dataset. Most of the 35 rules capture local knowledge in the domain (functional properties and keys declared as schema constraints, and rules provided by INA experts), mappings between INA and DBpedia vocabularies, and general properties of owl:sameAs and owl:differentFrom. Some of the rules of our experiments involve a built-in predicate (called built-in:name-similar) to allow slight differences when comparing literal values corresponding to person names (e.g. R8 in Table 1). This predicate depends on a built-in function which checks if the similarity of the two name strings is above a given threshold. In all our experiments we used edit distance and 0.99 as a threshold. Other built-in predicates involved in the rules are not-equal, less-or-equal, sum, etc. It is worth noting that the 35 rules can be extended or modified without the need of changing the algorithmic machinery of our approach.

Experimental Goals and Set-Up. The goal of our experiments was threefold: (1) to show that external information available in Linked Open Data is useful to infer owl:sameAs and owl:differentFrom facts within INA referenced persons, and, thus, to disambiguate local homonyms; (2) to assess the gain in reduced imported facts of our Import-by-Query approach compared to approaches based on forward reasoning only; and (3) to evaluate the runtime of our Import-by-Query algorithm and the possible amortized gain if fact propagation is performed beforehand.

The external datasets from Linked Open Data with which the INA vocabulary shares terms are DBpedia.org and DBpedia.fr. The baseline for evaluating our two first goals is a set of 0.5 million external facts obtained by downloading from DBpedia.org and DBpedia.fr (using their SPARQL endpoints) all the facts about entities having the same name as one of the homonyms in the INA dataset. We applied a preprocessing step on the original INA dataset to keep only the facts on predicates appearing in the rules conditions. The resulting dataset contains almost 1.15 million of RDF facts and will be the INA dataset referred to henceforth.

Our algorithms have been implemented in SWI-Prolog. All the evaluations were done on a machine with an Intel i7 Quad-core processor and 6 GB of memory.

Experimental Results. For evaluating our first goal, we applied (using our forward reasoner) the set of 35 rules to (a) the INA dataset only and (b) the union of the INA dataset with the baseline external facts, and then we compared the number of owl:sameAs and owl:differentFrom facts on INA homonyms we obtained. The rules applied to the INA dataset only allowed to infer 2 owl:sameAs facts and 108 owl:differentFrom facts, compared to the 4,884 owl:sameAs and 9,764 owl:differentFrom facts inferred when the external facts were added to the process. This clearly demonstrates the benefit of using external information from Linked Open Data for local disambiguation. These resulting 14,648 facts are guaranteed to be correct under the assumption that both rules and data are correct. However, since this is not ensured for DBpedia data, we asked INA experts to evaluate a random sample of 500 of such facts, and all of them were assessed to be true.

The rule expressing sameAs transitivity is crucial for inferring all the owl:sameAs facts that cannot be inferred locally. More generally, full reasoning is very important to discover owl:sameAs and owl:differentFrom facts. In order to show this, we applied Silk to the same two datasets (the INA dataset only, and the union of the INA dataset with the baseline external facts). For doing so, we first had to translate our rules into the Silk specification language. It is not possible, however, to translate into Silk our rules concluding on owl:differentFrom atoms. Thus, we focused on the rules leading to owl:sameAs inference. Among the 4,884 owl:sameAs facts discovered by our full forward reasoner, Silk (which does not perform full reasoning) only discovered 88, i.e. less than 2% of the total. This shows that inference is important for data linkage.

For evaluating our second experimental goal, we took as reference boolean queries the above sample of 500 owl:sameAs and owl:differentFrom facts, and we applied our Import-by-Query algorithm to each of these boolean queries. The number of external facts imported by our algorithm for all boolean queries was 6,417, which makes, on average, 13 imported facts per boolean query. In contrast, the total number of baseline external facts needed to conclude the boolean queries with the forward reasoner was much higher (~500,000). This shows that our Import-by-Query algorithm reduces drastically the number of imported facts needed for disambiguating local data.

Concerning the runtime evaluation, the import-by-query algorithm requires 3 iterations on average — it successively outputs and evaluates 3 external subqueries (each of them being produced by calling QESQ) — before termination. It takes on average 186 s per boolean query when applied to the initial set of rules and the local dataset. This drops to 7 s when it is applied to the partially instantiated rules obtained by fact propagation beforehand, which means a gain in time of 179 s (~96%). With respect to the fact propagation, we propagated all facts involving properties of class ina:Person. This took 191 s but it is done only once for all queries, and its cost is amortized very fast, as shown by the above numbers.

Discussion

We have proposed a novel approach for data linkage based on reasoning and adapted to the decentralized nature of the Linked Data cloud. This approach builds on the formal and algorithmic background of answering Datalog queries over deductive databases, that we have extended to handle external rewriting when local answers cannot be obtained. In contrast with existing rule-based approaches for data linkage [31,40] based on forward reasoning to infer same-as facts, Import-by-Query is a backward chaining algorithm that imports *on demand* only external facts useful to infer target same-as facts handled as boolean queries. Our experiments have shown that this approach is feasible and reduces the number of facts needed to be imported. Compared to the depth-first approach sketched in [1] for distributed Query-Subquery, our QESQ algorithm generates external rewriting in a breadth-first way.

Performing fact propagation beforehand in order to apply Import-by-Query to a set of more specific rules than the original ones is an optimization close to the ones proposed in QueryPIE [46] for efficient backward reasoning on very large deductive datasets. One important difference, though, is that in the QueryPIE setting, the problem of handling recursive rules can be fully delegated to forward reasoning because all the facts are given and the recursive rules concern a well identified subset of them (so called terminological facts). Another major difference is that Import-by-Query performs query rewriting if no local answer is obtained from the input deductive dataset.

The Import-by-Query approach in [25] is limited to ABox satisfiability queries used as oracles in Tableau-based reasoning. Compared to the many recent works on ontology-based data access initiated by [14], in which query rewriting is done independently of the data, we have designed a *hybrid* approach that alternates (external) query rewriting and (local) query answering. We plan to look into this hybrid approach further, in particular to deal with ontological constraints expressible in Datalog$^{+}_{-}$ [13].

The interest of our rule-based approach is that it is generic and declarative: new rules can be added without changing the algorithmic machinery. At the moment the rules that we consider are certain. As a result, the same-as facts that they allow to infer are guaranteed to be correct (under the assumption that the input data does not contain erroneous facts). This is crucial to get automatically same-as facts that are certain, in particular when the goal of discovering same-as links is data fusion, i.e. replacement of two URIs by a single one in all relevant facts. Another added-value to get certain same-as and different-from facts is to find noisy data thanks to contradictions. However, in many cases, domain knowledge is not 100% sure such as pseudo-keys [11] and probabilistic mappings [45]. Data itself may be uncertain due to trust and reputation judgements towards data sources [9]. Handling uncertain domain knowledge should enable to discover more same-as facts that may be true even if inferred with some uncertainty. This is addressed in the next section.

3.2 Reasoning over Uncertain RDF Facts and Rules [3]

We have designed a probabilistic framework to model and reason on uncertain RDF facts and rules, based on the semantics of probabilistic Datalog [23]. Probabilistic Datalog extends (deterministic) Datalog [2] by associating each ground fact and each instantiated rule with a basic probabilistic *event* that the corresponding fact or rule is true. Each derived fact is then inferred with its *provenance* in the form of an event expression made of a boolean combination of the basic events of the ground facts and rules involved in its derivation. It can be put in disjunctive normal form, in which a conjunction of events represents a derivation branch, and disjunctions represent the different derivation branches. Some simplifications can be performed before the computation of the resulting probabilities: a conjunction containing disjoint events can be suppressed; basic events known to be certain can be removed from the conjunctions where they are involved thus leading to conjunctions with only uncertain events. An extreme case is when a conjunction is made of certain events only, which represent a way to derive a fact with certainty. In this case the whole event expression can be simplified to $\top$ which denotes certain events. The logical semantics of the (simplified) event expression is then the basis for computing the probability of the corresponding derived fact in function of the probabilities assigned to the events identifying the input facts and rules participating to its derivation. In the general case, computing the probability of the disjunction of conjunctions of events requires to know the probabilities of all the combinations of events in the expression. In practice, in particular in applications dealing with large amounts of data, only the probabilities of single events will be known. We will then make the same default assumptions of independence or disjointness of single events, as usually done in most Information Retrieval models [22]. To fit with such assumptions, we have to impose some constraints on the rules, that will be explained below.

Probabilistic RDF facts extends the standard data model of Linked Data used to state properties on entities referenced by so-called Uniform Resource Identifiers (URIs). Properties are themselves identified by URIs. So-called data properties relate entities with literals (e.g., numbers, strings or dates), while object properties relate two entities.

A **probabilistic RDF fact** is an RDF triple $t = (s, p, o)$ (in which the subject s is a URI, the predicate p is a URI, and the object o may be either a URI or a literal) associated with an event key e denoting the probabilistic event that t is true. A **probabilistic RDF rule** is a safe rule with variables, associated with an event key denoting the probability that any of its instantiations is true.

Each probabilistic RDF fact and rule are assigned a distinct event key, except the certain facts and rules that are assigned the special event key $\top$ denoting events that are certain. For a probabilistic fact f (respectively rule r), we will denote $e(f)$ (respectively $e(r)$) the probabilistic event e associated with the fact f (respectively the rule r).

In the rules, we also allow conditions $B(\bar{x}, \bar{a})$ where B is a built-in predicate (i.e., a function call), $\bar{x}$ a vector of variables appearing in the triple conditions of the same rule, and $\bar{a}$ may be a non empty set of values of parameters for calling B. The following rule is an example of a rule with a built-in predicate:$Similar(?s_1, ?s_2, levenshtein, 0.2)$: r_0 : $(?x\ hasName\ ?s_1) \wedge$ $(?y\ hasName\ ?s_2) \wedge$ $Similar(?s_1,\ ?s_2,\ levenshtein,\ 0.2) \rightarrow (?x\ sameName\ ?y)$ For each pair of strings $(s_1,\ s_2)$ for which the two triple conditions are satisfied by facts $(i_1\ hasName\ s_1)$ and $(i_2\ hasName\ s_2)$, $Similar(s_1,\ s_2,\ levenshtein,\ 0.2)$ applies the normalized Levenshstein distance $levenshtein(s_1, s_2)$ on the two strings s_1 and s_2, and if this distance is less than 0.2 returns the corresponding probablistic fact $Similar(s_1,\ s_2,\ levenshtein,\ 0.2)$ with $1 - levenshtein(s_1, s_2)$ as probability.

The semantics of inferred probabilistic facts is defined by extending the definition of $SAT(F, R)$ (see Definition 1) with their *provenance* defined as boolean combinations of all the events associated with the input facts and rules involved in their inference.

Definition 2 (Provenance-based semantics of probabilistic inferred facts). *For every fact f in $SAT(F, R)$, its provenance (denoted $Prov_{R,F}(f)$) is defined as follows:*

- *if $f \in F$: $Prov_{R,F}(f) = e(f)$*
- *else: $Prov_{R,F}(f) = \bigvee_{(r,\theta)\in R(f)} e(r) \wedge \bigwedge_{i\in[1..k]} Prov_{R,F}(\theta.TP_i(v_i))$ where $R(f)$ is the set of instantiated rules (r, θ) having f as conclusion (i.e., rules r of the form $TP_1(v_1)\wedge \ldots \wedge TP_k(v_k) \rightarrow TP(v)$ for which θ is a mapping such that $\theta.TP(v) = f$ and $\theta.TP_(v_i) \in SAT(F, R)$ for every $i \in [1..k]$).*

For every fact f in $SAT(F, R)$, its probability (denoted $P(f)$) is defined as the probability of its provenance: $P(f) = P(Prov_{R,F}(f))$

Illustrative Example

Let us consider the following probabilistic RDF facts and rules (for which we omit to display the event keys) composed of 5 input facts and of 4 rules expressing different ways to infer sameAs facts between individuals (to have the same name, to have the same name and the same birthdate, to be married to the same individual, or by transitivity of the sameAs relation):

f_1: $(i_1\, sameName\, i_2)$
f_2: $(i_1\, sameBirthDate\, i_2)$
f_3: $(i_1\, marriedTo\, i_3)$
f_4: $(i_2\, marriedTo\, i_3)$
f_5: $(i_2\, sameName\, i_4)$
r_1: $(?x\, sameName\, ?y) \rightarrow (?x\, sameAs\, ?y)$
r_2: $(?x\, sameName\, ?y), (?x\, sameBirthDate\, ?y) \rightarrow (?x\, sameAs\, ?y)$
r_3: $(?x\, marriedTo\, ?z), (?y\, marriedTo\, ?z) \rightarrow (?x\, sameAs\, ?y)$
r_4: $(?x\, sameAs\, ?z), (?z\, sameAs\, ?y) \rightarrow (?x\, sameAs\, ?y)$

Three derived facts are obtained with their provenance:

$$Prov_{R,F}((i_1\, sameAs\, i_2)) = (e(r_1) \wedge e(f_1)) \vee (e(r_2) \wedge e(f_1) \wedge e(f_2)) \vee (e(r_3) \wedge e(f_3) \wedge e(f_4))$$
$$Prov_{R,F}((i_2\, sameAs\, i_4)) = (e(r_1) \wedge e(f_5))$$
$$Prov_{R,F}((i_1\, sameAs\, i_4)) = e(r_4) \wedge Prov_{R,F}((i_1\, sameAs\, i_2)) \wedge Prov_{R,F}((i_2\, sameAs\, i_4))$$

The first one captures that the fact $(i_1\, sameAs\, i_2)$ can be inferred as a result of 3 different derivation branches (one using the rule r_1 and the input fact f_1, another one using the rule r_2 and the input facts f_1 and f_2, and the third one using the rule r_3 and the input facts f_3 and f_4). The second one captures that $(i_2\, sameAs\, i_4)$ results from a single derivation branch, using the rule r_1 and the fact f_5. The last one illustrates how the provenances can be built iteratively during the saturation process: the last derivation step leading to the inference of $(i_1\, sameAs\, i_4)$ involves the rule r_4 and two facts inferred at a previous iteration (namely, $(i_1\, sameAs\, i_2)$

and (i_2 *sameAs* i_4)) for which the event expressions computed beforehand as their provenance can be combined with the event key of r_4.

These event expressions can be simplified by exploiting facts and rules that are certain. For instance, if we know that the two facts f_2 and f_3 are certain as well as the rule r_4, we can suppress $e(f_2)$, $e(f_3)$ and $e(r_4)$ in the conjuncts of the above expressions because they are all equal to the event $\top$ always true. We now obtain for $Prov_{R,F}((i_1\ sameAs\ i_2))$: $(e(r_1) \wedge e(f_1)) \vee (e(r_2) \wedge e(f_1)) \vee (e(r_3) \wedge e(f_4))$

When many facts and several rules are certain, such simplifications lead to a drastic reduction of the size of event expressions, which is important for the feasibility and the scalability of the approach in practice.

This example illustrates how the construction and the simplification of the provenance can be incorporated into the saturation process and thus how a given forward-reasoning algorithm can be easily extended to compute the provenance during the inference of the corresponding facts.

The ProbFR Algorithm

Algorithm 1 describes the ProbFR algorithm that we have implemented and used in our experiments.

Algorithm 1. The *ProbFR* algorithm

Input: A set F of input (probabilistic) facts and a set R of (probabilistic) rules

Output: The set F_{sat} of inferred (probabilistic) facts with for each inferred fact f its event expression $x(f)$

for each $f \in F$: $x(f) \leftarrow e(f)$
$F_{sat} \leftarrow F$
$\Delta \leftarrow F$
repeat
  $\Delta_1 \leftarrow \emptyset$
  foreach rule r: $c_1 \wedge \ldots \wedge c_k \rightarrow c$ for which there exists a substitution θ and facts $f_1, \ldots, f_k \in F_{sat}$ (among which atleast one of them belongs to Δ) such that $f_i = \theta.c_i$ for every $i \in [1..k]$:
   let $f = \theta.c$:
   if $f \notin F_{sat}$
    add f to Δ_1
    $x(f) \leftarrow \mathcal{N}_\vee(e(r) \wedge \bigwedge_{i\in[1..k]} x(f_i))$
   else $x(f) \leftarrow x(f) \vee$
        $\mathcal{N}_\vee(e(r) \wedge \bigwedge_{i\in[1..k]} x(f_i))$
  $F_{sat} \leftarrow F_{sat} \cup \Delta_1$
  $\Delta \leftarrow \Delta_1$
until $\Delta_1 = \emptyset$
return F_{sat}

It starts with the set of initial facts and rules and repeats inference steps until saturation. Each inference step (Line (4) to (15)) triggers all the rules whose conditions can be matched with known facts (i.e., input facts or facts inferred at previous steps). At each iteration, the set Δ contains the facts that have been inferred at the previous iteration. The constraint (expressed in Line (6)) that rules are only triggered if atleast one of their conditions can be matched with facts in Δ guarantees that instantiated rules are not triggered twice during the inference process. The algorithm stops as soon as no new fact has been inferred during a given iteration (i.e., Δ_1 remains empty over this iteration). The algorithm returns the set F_{sat} of inferred facts, and computes for each of them an event expression $x(f)$ (Lines (10) and (11)). The function $\mathcal{N}_\vee$ denotes the transformation of a conjunction into its disjunctive normal form. It consists in applying iteratively the distributivity of the conjunction connector ($\wedge$) over the disjunction connector ($\vee$), and in simplifying when possible the (intermediate) results as follows: (1) remove the duplicate events and the certain events $\top$ from each conjunction of events, (2) if a conjunction within a disjunction becomes empty (i.e., if all its events are certain), replace the whole disjunction by $\top$. Each event expression $x(f)$ is thus either $\top$ or of the form $Conj_1 \vee ... \vee Conj_l$ where each $Conj_i$ is a conjunction of event keys tracing the uncertain input facts and rules involved into one of the l branches of uncertain derivation of f.

The termination of the ProbFR algorithm is guaranteed by the fact that the rules are safe. The only facts that can be inferred from safe rules and a set F of ground atoms are instantiations of conclusion atoms by constants appearing in F. Their number is finite. More precisely, since the input facts and conclusion atoms are built on are binary predicates, the number of constants appearing in the input facts is less than $2 \times |F|$ (at most two distinct constants per input fact), and the number of inferred facts is then less than $4 \times |R| \times |F|^2$ (atmost as many predicates in conclusion as rules, and for each of them, atmost as many instantiations as pairs of constants).

The following theorem states the soundness and completeness of the algorithm.

Theorem 1. *Let F_{sat} be the result returned by ProbFR(F, R):*
$F_{sat} = SAT(F, R)$.
For each $f \in F_{sat}$, let $x(f)$ be the event expression $x(f)$ computed by ProbFR(F, R):
$x(f) \equiv Prov_{F,R}(f)$

For the first point, we prove by induction on i that each iteration $i \geq 1$ of the algorithm computes the set of facts $F_i = T_R(F_{i-1})$ (as defined in Definition 1), and thus $SAT(F, R)$ at the last iteration where the least fixed point reached. For the second point, for a derived fact f, we prove, by induction on the number n of iterations of *ProbFR* after which no new instantiation of rules can infer f, that $x(f)$ is a disjunctive normal form of $Prov_{F,R}(f)$, and therefore is logically equivalent to it.

As a result of Definition 2 and Theorem 1, it worths to emphasize that the probabilities values of inferred facts is independent of the order in which the rules are triggered to derive them.

Data Complexity Analysis

We are interested in estimating how the worst-case time complexity of the algorithm depends on the size $|F|$ of the input data, which is the most critical parameter in the setting of Linked Data. The number of iterations of ProbFR is atmost $|F_{sat}|$, which is less than $4 \times |R| \times |F|^2$ as shown just above. At each iteration, in the worst case, the condition part of each rule must be evaluated against the facts, and the event expressions for the provenance of the inferred facts must be computed. Let c the maximum number of conditions per rule. The evaluation of each condition part of each rule can be performed in polynomial time (in fact, in at most $|R| \times |F_{sat}|^c$ elementary steps).

For the computation of the event expressions, the most costly operation is the transformation $\mathcal{N}_\vee$ into disjunctive normal form of conjunctions $e(r) \wedge \bigwedge_{i\in[1..k]} x(f_i)$. The number k of conjunctions is less than the bound c of conditions per rule, and each $x(f_i)$ is a disjunction of at most l conjunctions of event keys, where l is the maximum number of uncertain derivation branches for inferred facts. This parameter l is bounded by b^d where d is the maximal depth of reasoning to infer a fact from F and R, and b is the maximal branching factor of $ground(F, R)$ (which denotes the set of rules triggered during the execution of $ProbFR(F, R)$). Therefore, each call of $\mathcal{N}_\vee$ performs at most $b^{d\times c}$ distributivity operations on conjunctions of at most $|F| + |R|$ event keys. Since the maximal depth of reasoning is the number of iterations of $ProbFR(F, R)$, d can be equal to $|F_{sat}|$. Then, the data complexity of the provenance computation may be exponential in the worst-case. This meets known results on query evaluation in probabilistic databases [43]. Different solutions are possible to circumvent this worst-case complexity, like restricting the form of rules/queries like in [17] or imposing some constraints on the input facts (such as a bounded treewidth in [6]). In practice, in particular if most of the input facts are certain, the size of the event expressions remains small. If all the input facts are certain, the only event keys that can be involved in the event expressions are the ones attached to the uncertain rules. The complexity of the algorithm can be controlled by imposing a practical bound in the number l of conjunctions produced in Line (11). This solution is justified in our setting since the computed probabilities are used to keep only the most probable inferred facts, i.e., the facts that are inferred with a probability greater than a given high threshold. For our experiments, we have limited this number l to be 8.

Effective Computation of Probabilities of Inferred Facts from Their Provenance

For each inferred fact, given its provenance as an event expression in disjunctive normal form, the following formula is the basic theoretical tool to compute its probability:

$$P(A \vee B) = P(A) + P(B) - P(A \wedge B). \tag{1}$$

The recursive application of the above formula for computing the probability of a disjunction of l conjunctions of events $E_1 \vee \ldots \vee E_l$ leads to alternate the subtractions and additions of the probabilities of all the possible conjunctions $E_{j_1} \wedge \ldots \wedge E_{j_i}$. This raises two major issues: first, their number is exponential in l; second the exact values of all these probabilities is usually not available.

An usual way to circumvent the latter is to make the assumption of independence between events, as it is done in probabilistic databases [43] or in most Information Retrieval models [22]. In our case however, two rules such that the condition part of one rule is contained in the condition part of the second (like the rules r_1 and r_2 of the example) are obviously not independent. For such rules, we enforce pairwise disjointness by imposing that the more general rule applies only if the more specific rules do not apply. In this way, we are sure that the corresponding dependent events do not appear in any event expression computed during the saturation process. To be consistent with the probabilistic setting, we also impose that the probability assigned to the event corresponding to the more specific rule (r_2 in our example) is higher than the one assigned to the event of more general rule (r_1 in our example).

For each pair r, r' with same conclusion (up to variables names), let us denote $r \preceq r'$ if $Cond_r$ is contained into $Cond_{r'}$. Checking whether $r \preceq r'$ can be done by using any conjunctive query containment algorithm [15] with a complexity independent of the data.

To summarize, we make the assumptions of:

- pairwise *disjointness* between events associated with pairs of rules r, r' such that $r \preceq r'$
- *independence* of the events that are not disjoint.

  For the effective computation of the probability of an inferred fact f,
- first, the provenance expressions $x(f) = E_1 \vee \ldots \vee E_l$ computed by the $ProbFR$ algorithm are simplified by removing each conjunction of events E_i in which an event $e(r)$ appears if there is a conjunction of events E_j ($j \neq i$) such that $e(r')$ appears in E_j and $r \preceq r'$.
- second, the probability of f is computed by iteratively applying the formula (1) on the resulting event expression.

In our example, the rules r_2 and r_1 are such that $r_1 \preceq r_2$. We can thus remove the conjuncts containing $e(r_1)$ and we obtain for $x((i_1\, sameAs\, i_2))$:

$$(e(r_2) \wedge e(f_1)) \vee (e(r_3) \wedge e(f_4)).$$

Now, considering the remaining events as independent, we can compute the effective probability $P((i_1\, sameAs\, i_2))$ as follows:

$$\begin{aligned} &P((i_1\, sameAs\, i_2)) = \\ &\quad (P(e(r_2)) \times P(e(f_1))) + (P(e(r_3)) \times P(e(f_4))) \\ &\quad - (P(e(r_2)) \times P(e(f_1)) \times P(e(r_3)) \times P(e(f_4))) \end{aligned}$$

Note that the above simplification can be incorporated into the $ProbFR$ algorithm at each update of event expression (Line (11)) and that determining the possible pairs of rules r, r'such that $r \preceq r'$ can be done in advance before launching $ProbFR$ as it is independent of the set of facts F.

This simplification has an impact on the practical complexity of the effective computation of the probabilities, even if, in theory and in the worst-case, it remains exponential in the number l of conjunctions within provenance expressions. As we have explained it before, this number l can be bounded in practice.

The assumption of disjointness between events associated with rules r, r' such that $r \preceq r'$ is important for the feasability of the approach but it also fits well with the open-world assumption that holds in Linked Data. In fact, it captures a restricted form of negation since, under this disjointness assumption, the event $e(r)$ models worlds where the condition of r is satisfied and the additional conditions of r' are not satisfied.

Setting Up of the Input Probabilities

The above approach for probabilistic inference is agnostic with respect to the way the input probabilities are obtained, either given by experts, returned by built-in predicates or tools, or learned by supervised methods. This said, it is important to note that training sets (required by supervised machine learning techniques) that would be big enough to scale to the setting of Linked Data do not exist and are almost impossible to build manually. On the other hand, it is quite easy for domain experts to decide whether a given rule is uncertain, but setting up its probability is tricky. The two-steps computation of a provenance-based approach as ours has the big advantage to possibly re-compute the numerical values of probabilities for the inferred facts from the provenance expressions computed once for all. This enables to start with a rough setting of rules probabilities chosen from a small set of values just for distinguishing rules on a simple scale of uncertainty (for instance set at 0.9 the rules a priori considered as almost always certain, 0.8 the rules judged as highly probable but less than the previous ones, and so on), and to adjust these values a posteriori based on a feedback on a sample of results. The provenance of wrong sameAs links inferred with a high probability provides explicitly the rules involved in the different reasoning branches leading to their derivation. It is a useful information for a domain expert to choose the rules to penalize by decreasing their numerical probabilities.

3.3 Rule-Based Data Linkage with Uncertainty

When used for data interlinking, rules typically translate varied knowledge that combines schema constraints, alignments between different ontologies and general properties on OWL relations such as owl:sameAs. This knowledge may be certain, but, very often, it has some degree of uncertainty. It is the case when a correspondence in an ontology alignment is attached a confidence value lower than 1, or when domain experts provide knowledge they are not 100% sure about, or the case of pseudo-keys that are automatically computed by pseudo-key

Table 2. Certain rules for interlinking person entities in DBpedia and MusicBrainz.

ID	Conditions	Conclusion
musicalArtist	(?w dbo:musicalArtist ?x)	(?w dbo:artist ?x)
enrich_dboBand1	(?x rdf:type schema:MusicGroup)	(?x rdf:type dbo:Band)
sameAsVIAF	(?x dbp:viaf ?id), (?y mb:ViafID ?id)	(?x :sameAsPerson ?y)
sameAsIsPerson1	(?x :sameAsPerson ?y), (?z mb:is_person ?y)	(?x :sameAsPerson ?z)
similarNamesPerson	(?x rdf:type dbo:Person), (?x rdfs:label ?l), MBsolrsimilar(?l,0.8,?z, 'persons_mb')	(?x :solrPSimilarName ?z)

Table 3. Uncertain rules for interlinking person entities in DBpedia and MusicBrainz.

ID	Conditions	Conclusion	Weight
sameAsBirthDate	(?x :solrPSimilarName ?l), (?y skos:myLabel ?l), (?x dbo:birthDate ?$date$), (?y mb:beginDateC ?$date$)	(?x :sameAsPerson ?y)	w_1
sameAsPersonArtistWr	(?$w1$ dbo:artist ?x), (?$w1$:solrWrSimilarName ?lw), (?y mb:writer ?$w2$), (?$w2$ skos:myLabel ?lw), (?x :solrPSimilarName ?lp), (?y skos:myLabel ?lp)	(?x :sameAsPerson ?y)	w_2
sameAsMemberOfBand	(?x :solrPSimilarName ?l), (?y skos:myLabel ?l), (?y mb:member_of_band ?$gr2$), (?$gr2$ skos:myLabel ?lg), (?$gr1$ dbp:members ?x), (?$gr1$:solrGrSimilarName ?lg)	(?x :sameAsPerson ?y)	w_3

discovery tools [11,44]. This uncertain knowledge can be translated by means of probabilistic rules.

Tables 2 and 3 show rules translating, respectively, certain and uncertain knowledge for the task of interlinking person entities in DBpedia and MusicBrainz datasets. These rules are actually part of the rules that we used in our experiments (reported in Sect. 3.4). Rule musicalArtist in Table 2, for example, is a certain rule that translates the DBpedia knowledge that the class dbo:musicalArtist is subsumed by dbo:Artist. Rule enrich_dboBand1 translates a certain correspondence in an alignment between Schema.org vocabulary and DBpedia ontology stating that the class schema:Person is subsumed by dbo:Person. The rule sameAsVIAF is a certain rule that translates the assertion that the VIAF id is a key for persons and, therefore, allows to infer sameAs links between person entities from DBpedia and MusicBrainz. Notice that this rule actually involves the two equivalent properties dbp:viaf and mb:ViafID of DBpedia and MusicBrainz vocabularies. This means that the condition (?x dbp:viaf ?id) in the rule will be instantiated by a DBpedia entity, and (?y mb:ViafID ?id) by a MusicBrainz entity. This kind of "key across different datasets" is called a link key in the literature [10]. Note also that, instead of using owl:sameAs, we use our own customized sameAs predicates (:sameAsPerson) which allowed us to easily identify the type of the inferred sameAs links in our experiments. Rule sameAsIsPerson1 is a certain rule that translates transitivity of sameAs.

Rule similarNamesPerson deserves special attention because it contains a built-in predicate (namely MBsolrsimilar) that encapsulates the call to a full-text search tool (namely Solr[3]) to extract strings from MusicBrainz similar to labels of person entities in DBpedia. More precisely, for each string instantiation s of the variable $?l$, obtained by mapping with DBpedia facts the two first conditions ($?x$ rdf:type dbo:Person) and ($?x$ rdfs:label $?l$) of the rule, MBsolrsimilar(s, 0.8, $?z$, 'person_mb') is a procedure call returning as many probabilistic facts MBsolrsimilar(s, 0.8, s', 'person_mb') as labels s' of person entities in MusicBrainz detected by Solr as similar to s with a similarity greater than 0.8. The probability attached to each probabilistic fact MBsolrsimilar(s, 0.8, s', 'person_mb') is the calculated string similarity. Thus similarNamesPerson is a certain rule that will infer uncertain facts of the form ($?x$:solrPSimilarName $?z$) due to condition MBsolrsimilar($?l$,0.8,$?z$, 'persons_mb'), which will be instantiated with built-in uncertain facts. Built-in predicates such as MBsolrsimilar enable to embed standard similarity functions into our rule-based approach to overcome the problem of misspelling errors in names of persons, groups and songs that may occur in DBpedia and MusicBrainz datasets.

Table 3 shows three additional rules allowing to infer sameAs links between person entities from DBpedia and MusicBrainz datasets, but, in contrast with the sameAsVIAF rule explained above, they are not 100% certain. Rule sameAsBirthDate, for example, says that if two persons have similar names and the same birthdate then they are *likely* to be the same person. This rule must be considered uncertain for two reasons. First, it relaxes the strict condition of having exactly the same name by the soft constraint of having similar names as it is specified by ($?x$:solrPSimilarName $?l$). Second, strictly speaking the properties "name" and "birthdate" do not constitute a key, even if it is likely that two named entities representing persons that are well-known enough to be described in datasets like DBpedia and MusicBrainz will refer to the same person if they share the same name and birthdate. In fact, sameAsBirthDate translate a *soft* link key, as it combines the equivalent properties dbo:birthDate and mb:beginDateC that are used in DBpedia and MusicBrainz vocabularies to relate a person with her date of birth. The rules sameAsPersonArtistWr and sameAsMemberOfBand are uncertain too. The first one says that, if two persons have similar names and they are artists of songs with similar names, they are the same person, and the second rule says that if two persons have similar names and are members of musical bands with similar names, they are the same person. Again, this may not be always true, but in most cases. The weights in Table 3 correspond to the probabilistic events associated with each of these uncertain rules.

An important point to emphasize is that the (certain or uncertain) rules allowed in our rule-based modeling express pieces of knowledge that can be assembled and combined through several reasoning steps. For instance, the

[3] http://lucene.apache.org/solr/.

condition (?w_1 dbo:artist ?x) of the sameAsPersonArtistWr rule may be triggered by facts inferred by the musicalArtist rule. The chaining between rules is not known in advance and is determined by the input datasets which they apply to. In addition, due to recursive rules (such as sameAsIsPerson rule), even if the termination of the saturation process is guaranteed, the number of reasoning steps cannot be known in advance and also depends on the input datasets. It is worthwhile to note that recursive rules add an expressive power that is required for data linkage in particular to express sameAs transitivity.

The translation into rules can be semi-automatic, for instance for translating into certain rules schema constraints that have been declared in OWL such as the functionality or transitivity of some relations, or for translating into (certain or uncertain) rules alignments discovered by ontology mapping tools [19]. A certain number of uncertain rules useful for data interlinking must however be provided by domain experts to express fine-grained knowledge that may be specific to the datasets concerned by the linkage task. While it is quite easy for domain experts to decide whether a given rule is uncertain, setting up its probability is tricky. The two-steps computation has the big advantage to possibly re-compute the numerical values of probabilities for the inferred facts, starting from the event expressions built once for all in the first step that is a symbolic computation independent of the numerical values of rules probabilities. This enables to start with a rough setting of rules probabilities chosen from a small set of values just for distinguishing rules on a simple scale of uncertainty (for instance set at 0.9 the rules a priori considered as almost always certain, 0.8 the rules judged as highly probable but less than the previous ones, and so on), and to adjust these values a posteriori based on a feedback on a sample of results. The event expressions of wrong sameAs links inferred with a high probability provide explicitly the rules involved in the different reasoning branches leading to their derivation. It is a useful information for a domain expert to choose the rules to penalize by decreasing their numerical probabilities.

In our experiments, such an incremental adjustment for the probabilities of the three uncertain rules of Table 3 resulted into: $w_1 = 0.9$, $w_2 = 0.4$ and $w_3 = 0.6$.

It is worth emphasizing that rules with quite low probabilities (such as 0.4 for the sameAsPersonArtistWr rule) can yet significantly contribute to the final probability of a fact inferred by different reasoning branches.

3.4 Experimental Evaluation

We have conducted experiments to evaluate the performance of our method on real datasets. Our main goal was to measure the effectiveness of our method to discover links at large scale, and to assess the expected gain in terms of recall and the loss in precision when using uncertain rules instead of certain rules only. We also wanted to show how the probabilistic weights attached to the links allow to filter out incorrect links. Finally, we aimed at comparing our tool to a state-of-the-art interlinking tool, namely Silk [48].

Experimental Setting. We used three datasets in our experiments: DBpedia, INA and MusicBrainz. The objective was to find sameAs links between named entities of person, musical band, song and album included in the datasets. Our choice of these datasets was based upon the fact that these are all large datasets (tens of millions of triples), and of a very different nature: DBpedia was built from Wikipedia infoboxes, INA from catalog records mainly containing plain text, and MusicBrainz from more structured data coming from a relational database.

The DBpedia version we used was DBpedia 2015-04,[4] the latest version at the time the experiments were conducted. From all available (sub) datasets, we only used the ones including RDF triples with properties appearing in the rules that we used in the experiments (below we give more details about the rules), which make together one single dataset of around 73 million RDF triples. The INA dataset contains around 33 million RDF triples, while the MusicBrainz dataset around 112 million RDF triples. The INA dataset was built from all the records (plain text) in a catalog of French TV musical programs using an specialised RDF extractor. Some RDF facts in the INA dataset have numerical weights between 0 and 1 since their accuracy could not be 100% assessed during the extraction process. The MusicBrainz dataset was built from the original postgreSQL table dumps available at the MusicBrainz web site using an RDF converter. This version is richer than the one of the LinkedBrainz project.[5]

Table 4 shows the number of person, musical band, song and album entities in each of the considered datasets, where Person, e.g. symbolises the class union of all the classes that represent persons in each dataset. No bands or albums are declared in INA, written NA (not applicable) in Table 4.

Table 4. Number of person, musical band, song and album entities in DBpedia, MusicBrainz and INA.

Class	DBpedia	MusicBrainz	INA
Person	1,445,773	385,662	186,704
Band	75,661	197,744	NA
Song	52,565	448,835	67,943
Album	123,374	1,230,731	NA

We have designed two sets of rules that we used as inputs for our algorithm to interlink DBpedia and MusicBrainz first and then MusicBrainz and INA. We came up with 86 rules for interlinking DBpedia and MusicBrainz, from which 50 of them are certain and 36 are uncertain, and 147 rules for interlinking MusicBrainz and INA, 97 of them certain and 50 uncertain. By a way of example, Tables 2 and 3 of Sect. 3.3 include some of the certain and uncertain rules that we used for interlinking DBpedia and MusicBrainz.

[4] http://wiki.dbpedia.org/Downloads2015-04.

[5] http://linkedbrainz.org/.

ProbFR has been implemented on top of Jena RETE and uses SWI-Prolog v6 to compute the disjunctive normal forms for the event expressions during RETE inference. Prolog is also used to implement the second step of ProbFR, i.e. to compute effective probabilities given event expressions. In order to avoid potential combinatorial explosion, the current parameter of ProbFR is tuned to a maximum of 8 derivation branches for each event expression. All ProbFR experiments were run on a Bi-processor intel Xeon 32 × 2.1 GHz, 256 GB of RAM, with Linux CentOS 6 as operating system.

Experimental Results. We ran our algorithm to interlink DBpedia and MusicBrainz first, and then MusicBrainz and INA, using in each case the corresponding rules. Our algorithm discovered 144,467 sameAs links between entities of DBpedia and MusicBrainz and 28,910 sameAs links between entities of MusicBrainz and INA. Additionally, our algorithm found 132,166 sameAs links internal to the INA dataset.

In order to evaluate the quality of the found links, and since no gold standard was available, we estimated precision, recall and F-measure by sampling and manual checking. In order to compute precision, for each of the classes considered we took a sample of 50 links from the links found by our algorithm (i.e. 200 links in total for DBpedia and MusicBrainz, and 100 links for MusicBrainz and INA), and we manually checked whether these links were correct. For computing recall, we randomly selected 50 instances of each of the classes, and we found links manually. Then, we calculated recall based on this make-do gold standard. F-measure was based on the estimations of precision and recall.

In order to assess the gain of using uncertain rules, we also ran our algorithm only with certain rules, and then we compared the results obtained using only certain rules with the ones obtained using all rules (both certain and uncertain rules). This concerned the experiments between DBpedia and MusicBrainz only, as no other certain rule than sameAs transitivity was used for MusicBrainz and INA.

Table 5. Precision (P), recall (R) and F-measure (F) for the task of interlinking DBpedia and MusicBrainz datasets, and MusicBrainz and INA datasets, using certain rules only, and certain and uncertain rules together.

	DBpedia and MusicBrainz						MusicBrainz and INA					
	Only certain rules			All rules			Only certain rules			All rules		
	P	R	F	P	R	F	P	R	F	P	R	F
Person	1.00	0.08	0.15	1.00	0.80	0.89	NA	NA	NA	1.00	0.34	0.51
Band	1.00	0.12	0.21	0.94	0.84	0.89	NA	NA	NA	NA	NA	NA
Song	NA	NA	NA	0.96	0.74	0.84	NA	NA	NA	1.00	0.40	0.57
Album	NA	NA	NA	1.00	0.53	0.69	NA	NA	NA	NA	NA	NA

Table 5 shows all the results. Let us focus on the results concerning DBpedia and MusicBrainz. As expected, when certain rules were used only, precision was 100%. This only concerns Person and Band classes because the initial set of rules did not include any certain rule concluding links for Song and Album (written NA in Table 5). However, recall was very low: 0.08 for Person and 0.12 for Band. When both certain and uncertain rules were used, a 100% precision was achieved for Person and Album classes only, since for Band and Song, precision was 0.94 and 0.96, respectively. However, recall increased significantly for Person and Band: 0.80 and 0.84. This shows the gain of using uncertain rules for data linkage. Now, when looking at the samples of Band and Song classes, we realised that all wrong links had a probability value lower than 0.9 and 0.6, respectively. This means that, when limited to those links having a probability value higher or equal to 0.9 and 0.6, the estimated precision for the classes Band and Song was 100% (Table 6). The estimated recall was 0.80 and 0.54. This shows the gain of using weights for interlinking.

Table 6. Gain of using weights for interlinking DBpedia and MusicBrainz.

	P	R	F
$\text{Band}_{\geqslant 0.90}$	1.00	0.80	0.89
$\text{Song}_{\geqslant 0.60}$	1.00	0.54	0.72

Table 7 shows the number of links that are discovered when n sameAs rules[6] are implied in the derivation. For instance, 28,614 links are discovered using two sameAs rules, and among these links 27,692 are new links, i.e. they were not discovered using only one rule. With tools like Silk and LIMES, using the same set of rules, we can expect to find around 115,609 links only.

Table 7. Number of links discovered when n rules are implied in the derivation. Results given for interlinking DBpedia and MusicBrainz.

# rules	# links	# new links
1	115,609	115,609
2	28,614	27,692
3	1,790	1,152
4	59	14

[6] We only consider rules that conclude to sameAs statements because other rules can be handled with preprocessing by tools like Silk or LIMES.

Comparison with Silk. Since Silk cannot handle rule chaining, we divided the rules used by ProbFR into sameAs rules (i.e. rules with sameAs in the conclusion), and intermediate rules that are used to trigger antecedents of other rules (including the sameAs rules). We manually translated these intermediate rules into SPARQL Update queries and these updates were performed before the Silk execution. Some sameAs rules could not be translated into Silk because they are recursive (sameAs appears in their antecedent and conclusion). To be able to compare methods on the same basis, we employed the levenshtein normalised distance with a threshold of 0.2, which corresponds to the similarity parameter set up to 0.8 in Solr. The aggregation of different comparisons within a rule was performed using maximum distance to be compliant with the conjunction used in rules. We executed Silk for interlinking DBpedia and MusicBrainz. Silk found 101,778 sameAs links, from which 100,544 were common to the ones found by ProbFR. ProbFR found 43,923 links that were not discovered by Silk and Silk found 1,234 links not discovered by ProbFR. In theory all the links discovered by Silk should have been discovered by ProbFR and Silk should have found up to 115,609 links. These differences can be explained by the way levenshtein distance are implemented in each tools and by a normalisation of URL that is performed by ProbFR and not available in Silk. As a conclusion, ProbFR outperformed Silk because of rule chaining (more links are discovered). Dealing with uncertainty allows to enhance precision without losing much recall.

In terms of time performance, Silk took more than 53 h (with 16 threads, blocking activated, on a Bi-processor Intel Xeon, 24×1.9 GHz) while ProbFR achieved the task in 18 h (on a Bi-processor Intel Xeon, 32×2.1 GHz). Even if the difference could be partially explained by the difference in hardware, the main reason comes from implementation design. Silk mainly relies on disk indexing and uses few RAM (around 1–2 GB) while ProbFR runs into main memory and uses around 250 GB of RAM for this experiment.

3.5 Discussion

Dedupalog [7] is a Datalog-like language that has been specially designed for handling constraints useful for record linkage. It handles both hard and soft rules that define respectively valid clusterings and their costs. The associated algorithm computes a valid clustering with a minimal cost. Whereas the general problem is NP-complete, they provide a practical algorithm that scales to the ACM database that contains 436,000 records. Even if the algorithmic techniques are very different from ours, the scalability is obtained by similar restrictions on the rule language. However, the goal is to compute a valid clustering and not to compute probabilities of inferred facts.

Probabilistic logical frameworks such as Markov logic [41] and Probabilistic Soft Logic (PSL) [12] have been used for entity resolution. Markov Logic allows for full probabilistic reasoning. The weights attached to formulas are learned either from data or from probabilities arbitrarily given. This learning phase is made under closed-world assumption. Once a Markov Logic Network is learned, the weighted satisfiability of any candidate link has to be computed. This is not scalable in practice. Then, candidate pairs are filtered using a cheap similarity such as TF.IDF: non matching pairs are added as false atoms. Experiments have been conducted on Cora dataset (1295 instances) and a sample of Bibserv (10,000 instances). PSL allows probabilistic inference based on similarities functions. As Markov Logic, formulas' weights are learned making closed world assumption. Furthermore, it allows to assign weights to facts using the similarity of sets of property values (which assumes that sets are fully known). Like Datalog, it is restricted to conjunctive rules. Experiments have been performed on the task of Wikipedia article classification and ontology matching.

Contrary to aforementioned approaches, in ProbFR, probability computation and inference are separated. All rules are iteratively applied to compute the saturation and the provenances of every deduced facts. Probabilities are then computed from the provenances. This allows to change the probabilities assigned to rules and reevaluated quickly the probabilities of inferred facts without recomputing the saturation. Another difference is that probabilities attached to formulas can be given or learned from data. No further learning is required.

Decoupling the symbolic computation of provenances from the numerical computation of probabilities makes probabilistic reasoning more modular and more transparent for users. This provides explanations on probabilistic inference for end-users, and useful traces for experts to set up the input probabilistic weights.

Currently, the threshold for filtering the probabilistic sameAs facts that will be retained as being true must be set up and adjusted manually. As future work, we plan to design a method to set up this threshold automatically by, besides inferring sameAs facts, inferring differentFrom facts too, and then exploiting the sameAs and differentFrom facts (and their probabilities) that are inferred for the same pairs of entities. We also plan to design a backward-reasoning algorithm able to deal with probabilistic rules, that could be combined with the ProbFR probabilistic forward-reasoner for importing on demand useful data from external sources.

4 Extraction of Modules from RDF Knowledge Bases [39]

The Semantic Web consolidated a legacy of ontologies and databases today seen as *reference systems* for building new Semantic Web applications. To illustrate, consider a medical application for anatomy, whose goal is to showcase the structure of the human body, the most common pathologies and diseases, and the scientists that contributed to their study. A structural description of human anatomy can be drawn from FMA[7] or My Corporis Fabrica (MyCF).[8] A taxonomy of clinical terms about diseases can be extracted from SNOMED,[9] while biographical informations about scientists implied in studies can be taken from DBPedia.[10] These reference system contain knowledge that can be *reused* to

[7] fma.biostr.washington.edu.

[8] www.mycorporisfabrica.org.

[9] www.ihtsdo.org/snomed-ct.

[10] www.dbpedia.org.

minimize the introduction of errors in the application. However, it is inconvenient to integrate in the application the whole datasets, as they contain complementary data and ontology axioms that are logically redundant. It is thus preferable to extract lightweight fragments of these reference systems - the *modules* - that are relevant for the application, and then to build on top of them.

While extracting modules from ontologies has been largely investigated for Description Logics (DL) [24,32], module extraction from RDF triplestores has received little attention. Yet, more and more huge RDF datasets are flourishing in the Linked Data and some of them, like DBPedia or YAGO [42], are increasingly reused in other more specialized datasets. RDF is a graph data model based on triples accepted as the W3C standard for Semantic Web data, with a simple ontology language, RDF Schema (RDFS). The W3C proposed OWL for writing expressive ontologies based on DL constructors. Whereas OWL is often seen as an extension of RDFS, this is not exactly the case. Both RDFS and the RDF query language (SPARQL) feature the possibility of accessing *at the same time* the ontology data and schema, by making variables ranging over classes or properties. This *domain meta-modeling* goes beyond the first-order setting typically considered in DL [18]. As a consequence, DL modularization frameworks are not applicable to popular RDF datasets like DBpedia or YAGO. Also, the clear separation between the ABox and the TBox made in DL to define the semantics of modules is not appropriate for RDF where facts and schema statements can be combined within a single RDF triplestore to accommodate heterogeneous knowledge from the Web. Another limit of the current approaches is that the existing semantics do not allow to limit the *size* of the extracted modules. As discussed in [24], the risk in practice is to output large portions of the initial ontologies, thus jeopardizing the gains of modularization.

The RDF knowledge bases that we consider are deductive RDF datasets as defined in Sect. 2.3: an RDF knowledge base is a pair $\langle D, R\rangle$ where D is an RDF dataset and R is a finite set of (possibly recursive) rules.

Figure 4 presents an RDF dataset, together with its graph version. The example is inspired by the MyCF ontology [36], which classifies digital representation of human body parts, acquired by IRMs or tomographies, according to anatomical knowledge. For instance, the type edge connecting irm_{42} with knee, corresponds to the triplestore atom $(\mathsf{irm}_{42}, \mathsf{type}, \mathsf{knee})$, which is the standard RDF syntax for class membership.

A path $p_{(u_0,u_n)} = (u_0, v_1, u_1), (u_1, v_2, u_2), \ldots, (u_{n-1}, v_n, u_n)$ is a sequence of atoms where each u_i, v_i are terms. The *length* of a path is the number of its atoms, here $|p_{(u_0,u_n)}| = n$.

We denote a rule by r and a set of rules by R. To illustrate, the rules for class subsumption
$r_1 : (x, \mathsf{type}, y), (y, \mathsf{subClassOf}, z) \rightarrow (x, \mathsf{type}, z)$
$r_2 : (x, \mathsf{subClassOf}, y), (y, \mathsf{subClassOf}, z) \rightarrow (x, \mathsf{subClassOf}, z)$
on D_1 entail that irm_{42} has type anatomical_structure, and that a subclass of this last one is tendon_gastr._muscle.

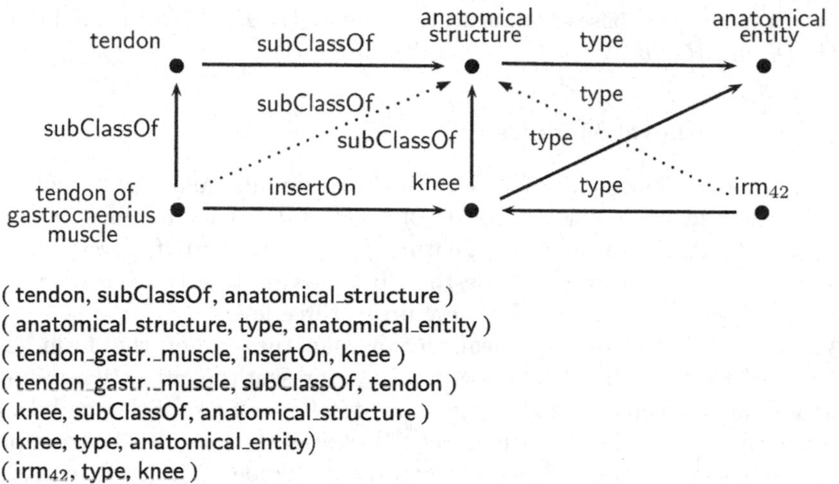

Fig. 4. Triplestore D_1

Datalog supports recursion by design. A rule r is said to be recursive if its conclusion unifies with one of its premises. In this work, we consider sets of rules where recursion is limited to recursive rules, like

$$r_1 : (x, \mathsf{hasPart}, y) \rightarrow (y, \mathsf{partOf}, x)$$
$$r_2 : (x, \mathsf{insertOn}, y), (y, \mathsf{partOf}, z) \rightarrow (x, \mathsf{insertOn}, z)$$
$$r_3 : (x, \mathsf{partOf}, y), (y, \mathsf{partOf}, z) \rightarrow (x, \mathsf{partOf}, z)$$

and, we exclude the presence of *indirect* recursion, in all cases where this involves *non-recursive rules*, like

$$r_4 : (x, \mathsf{contains}, y) \rightarrow (x, \mathsf{partOf}, y)$$
$$r_5 : (x, \mathsf{partOf}, y), (y, \mathsf{partOf}, z) \rightarrow (z, \mathsf{contains}, x)$$

This mild restriction on recursion is of practical relevance, as it is enjoyed by the most relevant RDFS rules, like the mutually recursive ones for domain and range.

$r_{\mathsf{dom}} : (x, \mathsf{domain}, z), (y, x, y') \rightarrow (y, \mathsf{type}, z)$
$r_{\mathsf{ran}} : (x, \mathsf{range}, z'), (y, x, y') \rightarrow (y', \mathsf{type}, z')$

Following Definition 1, the saturated RDF dataset obtained from D and the set of rules R, is defined as $\textsc{Sat}(D, R) = \{\mathrm{t} \in D' \mid D, R \vdash D'\}$.

We write $D, R \vdash p_{(u_0,u_n)}$ for the entailment of a path that holds if all path atoms are in $\textsc{Sat}(D, R)$.

Rule entailment, also referred as the immediate consequence operator for rules defines, by means of *semantic conditions*, when a Datalog rule r is entailed by a set R.

Definition 3 (Rule Entailment). *A rule r is entailed by a set R, denoted by $R \vdash r$, if for all triplestore D it holds that $\textsc{Sat}(D, r) \subseteq \textsc{Sat}(D, R)$. A set R' is entailed from R, denoted by $R \vdash R'$ when $R \vdash r$ for all $r \in R'$.*

Finally, knowledge base entailment, denoted by $\langle D, R\rangle \vdash \langle D', R'\rangle$, holds when $D, R \vdash D'$ and $R \vdash R'$.

4.1 Bounded-Level Modules

We propose a novel semantics for bounded-level modules allowing to effectively control their size. We employ a notion of *level of detail* for modules in such a *deductive* setting. For example, a signature $(\mathsf{subClassOf}, \mathsf{partOf})^3[\mathsf{eye}]$ limits the module-data extracted from a triplestore, by allowing to retrieve a description of all subclasses and subparts of the eye up to three levels.

A module is declared by means of a signature Σ of the form $\Sigma = (\mathsf{p}_1, \ldots, \mathsf{p}_n)^k[\mathsf{a}]$ where the constants $\mathsf{p}_1, \ldots, \mathsf{p}_n$ represent the *properties of interest* of the module, the constant a represents an *object of interest* of the module, and k is a positive integer denoting the *level of detail* of the module. An example of module signature is $(\mathsf{partOf})^3[\mathsf{eye}]$. Intuitively, a module M induced by a signature Σ on a reference system $\langle D, R\rangle$ is a deductive triplestore $M = \langle D_M, R_M\rangle$ which is logically entailed by $\langle D, R\rangle$ and conforming to Σ, in the sense that all data and rule atoms employ the properties $\mathsf{p}_1, \ldots, \mathsf{p}_n$ *only*. Furthermore, to control the module size, the facts in M are restricted to the *paths* rooted at the object of interest a, of length bounded by k.

We say that an atom conforms to Σ, denoted by $(v_1, u, v_2) \mathrel{\substack{\circ\\\circ}} \Sigma$, if u is a property of Σ or $u \in \textsc{Vars}$. A set of atoms Δ conforms to Σ if all of its atoms do. Then, $\langle D, R\rangle$ conforms to Σ if so do D and R.

In Fig. 5(c) it holds that $D_3 \mathrel{\substack{\circ\\\circ}} (\mathsf{partOf}, \mathsf{subClassOf})^2[\mathsf{knee}]$. However, it does not hold that $D_3 \mathrel{\substack{\circ\\\circ}} (\mathsf{subClassOf})^1[\mathsf{knee}]$.

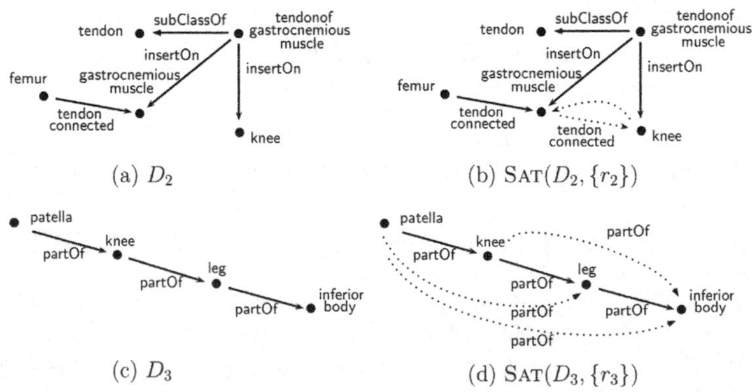

Fig. 5. Triplestore examples

Restricting the module paths is a way to effectively control the module size. Nevertheless, for the completeness of the module data, it is essential to guarantee that the module entails *all* of such bounded paths entailed by $\langle D, R\rangle$. In a deductive setting, adding new paths in the graph, defining properly D_M becomes challenging.

First, we observe that to avoid incomplete modules, the paths of D_M have to be drawn from $\text{SAT}(D, R)$. To see this, consider D_2 in Fig. 5(a) and a rule inferring pairs of organs (y, z) physically connected by a tendon

$r_2 : (x, \mathsf{insertOn}, y), (x, \mathsf{insertOn}, z), (x, \mathsf{subClassOf}, \mathsf{tendon}) \Rightarrow (y, \mathsf{tendonConnected}, z)$

A user interested in the organs directly and indirectly connected to the femur of this triplestore can declare the module signature $\Sigma_2 = (\mathsf{tendonConnected})^2[\mathsf{femur}]$. By restricting the module data D_M to the paths in D_2 of length bounded by 2 that are rooted at femur and that use the property tendonConnected only, we get:

$D_M = \{(\mathsf{femur}, \mathsf{tendonConnected}, \mathsf{gastroc.Muscle})\}$.

This dataset has however to be considered incomplete. As shown in Fig. 5(b), the rule r_2 entails on D_2 also the fact

(gastroc.Muscle, tendonConnected, knee).

This forms a path of length two together with the original triple

(femur, tendonConnected, gastroc.Muscle),

that should be included in D_M. The example illustrates clearly that D_M depends from the rules in R.

However, taking into account *all* paths in $\text{SAT}(D, R)$ is not desirable for defining modules of bounded size. In some cases, the triples entailed by *recursive* rules may produce new edges in the data graph that behave like shortcuts between resources, thereby wasting the module parametricity. Consider D_3 in Fig. 5(c) and the recursive rule r_3 defining the transitivity of partOf

$r_3 : (x, \mathsf{partOf}, y), (y, \mathsf{partOf}, z) \rightarrow (x, \mathsf{partOf}, z)$

The saturated triplestore $\text{SAT}(D_3, r_3)$ is depicted in Fig. 5(d).

It contains (patella, partOf, knee) but also

(patella, partOf, leg)

and (patella, partOf, inferiorBody).

More generally, it contains all triples of the form $\mathsf{t_b} = (\mathsf{patella}, \mathsf{partOf}, \mathsf{b})$ entailed by the transitivity of partOf. This means that if we take into account the recursive rule r_3 for defining the module paths, then all triples $\mathsf{t_b}$ are likely to be part of the module induced by signature $(\mathsf{partOf})^1[\mathsf{knee}]$. This undermines the module parametricity because it retrieves all resources connected with knee regardless of the level of detail k.

Our solution to both keep into account implicit triples and make parametricity effective, is to define the module data as a subgraph of a *partially-saturated* triplestore obtained by applying non-recursive rules only, while fully *delegating* the recursive rules to the module rules. This leads to the following novel definition of module.

Definition 4 (Module). *Let* $\langle D, R \rangle$ *be a deductive triplestore and* $\Sigma = (\mathsf{p}_1, \ldots, \mathsf{p}_n)^k[\mathsf{a}]$ *a signature. Then,* $M = \langle D_M, R_M \rangle$ *is a module for* Σ *on* $\langle D, R \rangle$ *if*

1. $\langle D_M, R_M \rangle \;\mathring{\circ}\; \Sigma$
2. $\langle D, R \rangle \vdash \langle D_M, R_M \rangle$

3. if $p_{(\mathsf{a},\mathsf{b})} \circ\!\!\circ \Sigma$ *and* $|p_{(\mathsf{a},\mathsf{b})}| \leq k$ *then*
(a) $D, R^{\mathsf{NonRec}} \vdash p_{(\mathsf{a},\mathsf{b})}$ *implies* $D_M, R_M \vdash p_{(\mathsf{a},\mathsf{b})}$
(b) $D_M, R \vdash p_{(\mathsf{a},\mathsf{b})}$ *implies* $D_M, R_M \vdash p_{(\mathsf{a},\mathsf{b})}$

Point 1 and 2 of the definition state the well-formedness and the logical entailment of the modules, respectively. Point 3 is the crux of the definition. Property 3(a) says that every path rooted at a of k-bounded length and conforming to Σ, that is entailed by the *non-recursive* rules of the reference system R^{NonRec}, must also be inferable by M. Property 3(b) enforces that the module rules R_M infer the same paths conforming to Σ as the *whole set of rules R*, but only when applied to the module data D_M. In contrast with the spirit of previous approaches (e.g., [24]), our definition does not enforce that *every* fact in the signature entailed by the reference triplestore also belongs to the module. Relaxing the module conditions in this way allows to control the module size, and cope with recursive rules.

To illustrate the definition, consider the triplestore D_4 of Fig. 6(a) equipped with the rules below.

$r_4 : (x, \mathsf{hasFunction}, y) \rightarrow (x, \mathsf{participatesTo}, y)$
$r_4' : (x, \mathsf{participatesTo}, y), (y, \mathsf{subClassOf}, z) \rightarrow (x, \mathsf{participatesTo}, z)$

Fig. 6(b) depicts $\mathrm{SAT}(D_4, \{r_4, r_4'\})$. Consider now:
$\Sigma_4 = (\mathsf{participatesTo}, \mathsf{subClassOf})^2[\mathsf{knee}]$.

A module M_4 for Σ_4 contains all paths rooted at knee of length at most 2, employing participatesTo and subClassOf only. Note that if the recursive rule r_4' is considered, then the triple t_1 = (knee, participatesTo, bodyPosture) is included in the module dataset, which is not desirable. In contrast, t_2 = (knee, participatesTo, kneePosture) is expected to be in a module for the signature Σ_4. A structure satisfying Definition 4 is $M_4 = \langle D_{M_4}, R_{M_4} \rangle$ with D_{M_4} depicted in Fig. 6(c) and $R_{M_4} = \{r_4'\}$. Note that t_2 is not explicitly in the module dataset D_{M_4} but can be inferred by r_4' as shown in Fig. 6(d).

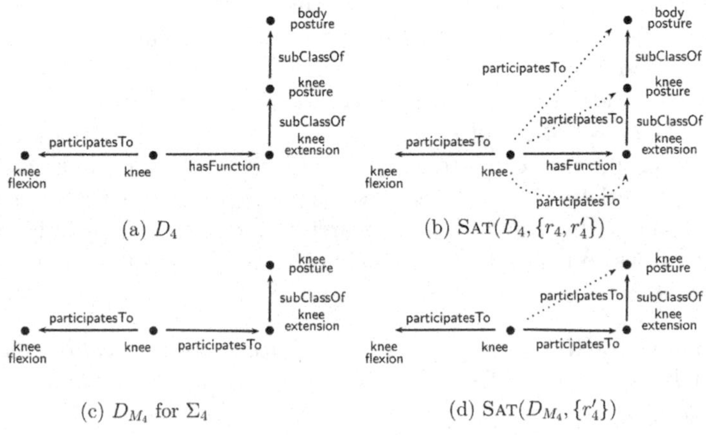

Fig. 6. Triplestore and module examples

Next, we present two algorithms for extracting module data and rules compliant with this novel semantics.

4.2 Extracting Module Data

The extraction of the module dataset can be done by leveraging on the evaluation of Datalog queries and implemented on top of existing engines. Given a module signature $\Sigma = (\mathsf{p}_1, \ldots, \mathsf{p}_n)^k[\mathsf{a}]$, the Datalog program Π_Σ below computes all paths rooted at a, of length bounded by k, and built on the properties of interest of Σ. It does so, in the extension of the relation m, starting from a triplestore modeled with a single relation t.

$$\Pi_\Sigma = \begin{cases} t(\mathsf{a}, \mathsf{p}_i, x) & \rightarrow m^1(\mathsf{a}, \mathsf{p}_i, x) \\ m^j(x_1, y_1, x)\,, t(x, \mathsf{p}_i, y) & \rightarrow m^{j+1}(x, \mathsf{p}_i, y) \\ m^j(x, y, z) & \rightarrow m(x, y, z) \end{cases}$$

An instance of the rules is included for each $i = 1..n$ and $j = 1..k$. Π_Σ is a non-recursive set of rules of size $O(nk)$ that can always be evaluated in at most k steps. Then, to infer all paths of bounded length entailed by non-recursive rules of a reference system, the set Π_Σ is evaluated together with R^{NonRec}. As a result, the union $\Pi_\Sigma \cup R^{\mathsf{NonRec}}$ gives a non-recursive set of rules that can be evaluated in LOGSPACE data-complexity. The completeness of module data extraction follows from the completeness of Datalog query evaluation. Below, we write $Q_m(D, \Pi_\Sigma \cup R^{\mathsf{NonRec}})$ for the answer set of the evaluation of the Datalog program $\Pi_\Sigma \cup R^{\mathsf{NonRec}}$ defining the relation m, on top of the dataset D. This constitutes the module data D_M.

Theorem 2 (Module Data Extraction). *For all path $p_{(\mathsf{a},\mathsf{b})} \mathbin{\mathring{\circ}} \Sigma$ with $|p_{(\mathsf{a},\mathsf{b})}| \leq k$ we have $D, R^{\mathsf{NonRec}} \vdash p_{(\mathsf{a},\mathsf{b})}$ if and only if $p_{(\mathsf{a},\mathsf{b})} \in Q_m(D, \Pi_\Sigma \cup R^{\mathsf{NonRec}})$.*

4.3 Extracting Module Rules

We now present an algorithm for module rule extraction that, together with the dataset extracted in the previous section, yields a module compliant with our semantics.

By Definition 4, a module is constituted of rules *entailed* by that of the reference system, and built on the properties of interest *only*. As the properties of interest of a module may restrict those employed by a reference system, the module rules cannot be just a subset of the original ones. Rule extraction is thus performed by an *unfolding* algorithm, that proceeds by replacing the premises of a rule with that of another one, until obtaining a set conforming to the signature. To illustrate, consider $\Sigma = (\mathsf{p}, \mathsf{q})^k[\mathsf{a}]$ and the rules below.

$r_1 : (x, \mathsf{q}, y), (y, \mathsf{partOf}, x) \rightarrow (x, \mathsf{q}, y)$
$r_2 : (x, \mathsf{p}, y) \rightarrow (x, \mathsf{partOf}, y)$

Although the rule r_1 does not conform to Σ, it can be unfolded with r_2 so as to obtain a module rule. As the atom (y, partOf, x) in the body of r_1 unifies with the conclusion of r_2, it can be replaced by (y, p, x), so as to get the rule $\bar{r} = (x, \mathsf{q}, y), (y, \mathsf{p}, x) \rightarrow (x, \mathsf{q}, y)$. Rule $\bar{r}$ is called an *unfolding* of r_1 with r_2.

In the above example, one unfolding step is enough to have a rule $\bar{r}$ that is conform to the module signature and that, by construction, is entailed by $\{r_1, r_2\}$. It is easy to see that this can be generalized, and that rules belonging to unfoldings of a set of rules R are entailed by R. However, in presence of recursive rules the set of unfoldings of a rule may be infinite, as illustrated below.

Example 2. *Consider* $\Sigma = (\mathsf{p}, \mathsf{q})^3[\mathsf{a}_1]$ *and* R *with*
$r_1 : (x, \mathsf{partOf}, y) \rightarrow (x, \mathsf{q}, y)$
$r_2 : (x, \mathsf{partOf}, y), (y, \mathsf{partOf}, z) \rightarrow (x, \mathsf{partOf}, z)$
$r_3 : (x, \mathsf{p}, y) \rightarrow (x, \mathsf{partOf}, y)$

Here, r_1 can be unfolded with r_2 and r_3, thus obtaining
$\bar{r} : (x_1, \mathsf{p}, x_2), (x_2, \mathsf{p}, x_3) \longrightarrow (x_1, \mathsf{q}, x_3)$
However, there exist infinitely many unfoldings of rule r_2 with itself that yield expressions of the form $(x_1, \mathsf{p}, x_2), (x_2, \mathsf{p}, x_3), (x_3, \mathsf{p}, x_4) \longrightarrow (x_1, \mathsf{q}, x_4)$ that use any finite sequence of variables $x_1, \ldots, x_n$. This set of unfoldings cannot be strictly speaking a set of triplestore or module rules, because it is *infinite*.

Algorithm 2. MRE($N_{ToUnfold}, R_{ToApply}, \Sigma$)

    for all $r_1 \in N_{ToUnfold}$
        if $r_1 \mathrel{\substack{\circ\\\circ}} \Sigma$ **then:**
            $R_M \leftarrow r_1$
            remove r_1 from $R_{ToApply}$
        else:
            for all $r_2 \in R_{ToApply}$ s.t. $r_1 \neq r_2$
                for all $r \in$ RuleUnfolding(r_1, r_2)
                    if $r \mathrel{\substack{\circ\\\circ}} \Sigma$ **then:** $R_M \leftarrow r$
                    $R_M \leftarrow$ MRE($\{r\}, R_{ToApply} \backslash \{r, r_2\}, \Sigma$)
    return R_M

To avoid ending up with infinite sets of module rules, we devised an unfolding algorithm based on a *breadth-first* strategy. Algorithm MRE (Algorithm 2) performs Module Rules Extraction. It takes as input a set of rules to be unfolded $N_{ToUnfold}$, a set of rules to be used for the unfolding $R_{ToApply}$, and a signature Σ. Given a deductive triplestore $\langle D, R \rangle$ the first call to the algorithm is MRE($N_{ToUnfold}, R, \Sigma$). The set $N_{ToUnfold} \subseteq R$ is constituted of all rules $r \in R$ that conclude on a property of interest, that is *head*$(r) \mathrel{\substack{\circ\\\circ}} \Sigma$. Any rule belonging to $N_{ToUnfold}$ (whose premises use properties that are not in Σ) is unfolded in a breadth-first fashion until no rule in $R_{ToApply}$ can be applied. All rules in R are considered for unfolding ($R_{ToApply} = R$). Procedure *RuleUnfolding*(r_1, r_2) progressively unfolds each *subset* of atoms in the body of r_1 that unify with the conclusion of r_2. For example, the three breadth-first unfoldings of $r_1 : (x, \mathsf{p}, y), (x, \mathsf{p}, z) \rightarrow (x, \mathsf{p}, y)$ with $r_2 : (x, \mathsf{partOf}, y) \rightarrow (x, \mathsf{p}, y)$ are

$\bar{r}_3 : (x, \mathsf{p}, y), (x, \mathsf{partOf}, z) \rightarrow (x, \mathsf{p}, y)$
$\bar{r}_4 : (x, \mathsf{partOf}, y), (x, \mathsf{p}, z) \rightarrow (x, \mathsf{p}, y)$
$\bar{r}_5 : (x, \mathsf{partOf}, y), (x, \mathsf{partOf}, z) \rightarrow (x, \mathsf{p}, y)$

Note that a rule is never unfolded with itself by the algorithm (thus avoiding a depth-first fashion). The fact that r_2 used for the unfolding is discarded from $R_{ToApply}$ (line 10) ensures the termination of the extraction procedure, even in the presence of recursive rules.

Theorem 3 (Rule Extraction Algorithm). *Let R be a set of rules and Σ a module signature. Algorithm MRE always terminates in $O(2^{|R|\times|r|})$ and produces a set of rules R_M conforming to Σ such that for all $r \between \Sigma$ it holds*

$$R_M \vdash r \quad \textit{implies} \quad R \vdash r \quad (\text{SOUNDNESS})$$

Furthermore, when $R^{\mathsf{Rec}} \between \Sigma$ we also have

$$R \vdash r \quad \textit{implies} \quad R_M \vdash r \quad (\text{COMPLETENESS})$$

Algorithm MRE is sound, in the sense that it computes a set of rules entailed by R. Furthermore, for the case where all recursive rules in R conform to Σ, the algorithm is also complete, in the sense that it produces a set of rules R_M that entails all rules R can entail on the properties of Σ. As a consequence, any dataset D_M (computed as for Theorem 2) paired with R_M constitutes a module meeting Definition 4, and in particular the point 3(b). If this condition does not hold, module extraction may be incomplete. To see this, consider again $\langle D, R\rangle$ of Example 2 with $D = \{(\mathsf{a}_1, \mathsf{p}, \mathsf{a}_2), (\mathsf{a}_2, \mathsf{p}, \mathsf{a}_3), (\mathsf{a}_3, \mathsf{p}, \mathsf{a}_4)\}$. Recall that $\Sigma = (\mathsf{p}, \mathsf{q})^3[\mathsf{a}_1]$, and then notice that the recursive rule $r_2 \not\between \Sigma$. Here, module data extraction yields $D_M = D$. Observe now that the atom $(\mathsf{a}_1, \mathsf{q}, \mathsf{a}_4)$ belongs to $\mathrm{SAT}(D_M, R)$. As MRE outputs the set $R_M = \{(x, \mathsf{p}, y), (y, \mathsf{p}, z) \rightarrow (x, \mathsf{q}, z)\}$, the triple $(\mathsf{a}_1, \mathsf{q}, \mathsf{a}_4)$ does not belong to $\mathrm{SAT}(D_M, R_M)$, while it should. Hence, $\langle D_M, R_M\rangle$ does not satisfy Definition 4.

Surprisingly enough, this case of incompleteness *is independent of algorithm MRE*. In fact, when R includes recursive rules that do not conform to Σ, it does not exist an algorithm that outputs a finite set of rules R_M such that $R \vdash r$ implies $R_M \vdash r$, for all $r \between \Sigma$. As Example 2 illustrates, the extracted R_M must mimic an *infinite* set of rules of the form $(x_1, \mathsf{p}, x_2), (x_2, \mathsf{p}, x_3) \ldots (x_{n-1}, \mathsf{p}, x_n) \rightarrow (x_1, \mathsf{q}, x_n)$. One may think of capturing this infinite set by adding a recursive rule $r_{\mathsf{p}} : (x, \mathsf{p}, y), (y, \mathsf{p}, z) \rightarrow (x, \mathsf{p}, z)$ together with $\bar{r} : (x_1, \mathsf{p}, x_2), (x_2, \mathsf{p}, x_3) \rightarrow (x_1, \mathsf{q}, x_3)$. However, adding this recursive rule makes infer triples using p that are not entailed by the reference system, thereby violating point 2 of Definition 4. We can also ask whether this infinite set of rules can be reduced to a finite set that directly depends on k. Unfortunately, the answer is negative. Furthermore, it is unpractical for real systems to consider a specific module data D_M and bound by $O(|D_M|)$ the number of self-unfolding of a recursive rule during extraction, as this can output an unmanageable set of rules, that are (still) not robust to updates. Therefore, understanding when algorithm MRE is complete is key for module extraction.

This kind of unfolding issues have also been recognized and studied by earlier works on the optimization of recursive Datalog [28].

Finally, note that Theorem 3 is actually stronger than what required by Definition 4, because (*i*) it is based on *semantic* conditions and therefore it holds for any rule r entailed by R (unfoldings are just a particular case) and (*ii*) it is independent from the module data, and thus suitable for other module semantics.

A characterization of the whole module extraction task follows as a corollary of Theorems 2 and 3.

4.4 Experiments

We implemented bounded-level module extraction on top of Jena 2.11.2 TDB, and compared it against two related approaches to show its benefits in terms of flexibility and succinctness of the extracted modules. We considered the following three Semantic Web datasets.

MyCF	0.5M triples	11 domain-specific rules
GO	1M triples	15 domain-specific rules
Yago2*	14M triples	6 RDFS rules

Yago2* is the union of Yago2Taxonomy, Yago2Types and Yago2Facts datasets. We sampled classes and properties from these ontologies, and combined them to obtain a set of signatures used to run module extraction. We considered 2500 MyCF ontology classes combined with 20 subsets of its properties, of size 1–4. For the GO ontology (www.geneontology.org), we sampled 350 classes and 12 property sets (size 1–4). Since Yago knowledge is more diverse than a domain-specific ontology, to avoid empty modules we first selected three groups of properties that are frequently used together, and then subset them (size 2, 4, 6). We tested 100 Yago resources for each group. Finally, we made k ranging over $\{1, 2, 3, 5, 10\}$.

Closest Competitor Approaches. Relevant methods to our work are Traversal Views [35] and Locality-based modules [24]. Traversal Views (TV) compute a bounded-level view of an RDF database, in the same spirit as our approach. This method does not support inference rules, and it does not give any guarantee about extracted modules. In practice, in the presence of rules, a traversal view may miss relevant triples. Locality-Based (LB) module extraction computes a conservative extension of an ontology by checking logical conditions on its schema. In contrast with our method, it cannot modularize untyped RDF data and, because it enforces strong logical guarantees on a module, it cannot control a priori its size.

Results of Module Data Extraction. Figures 7 and 8 report on the size of bounded-level modules, compared with those of TV and LB. The graphs show the average number of triples, for modules grouped by the same number of properties and k value, in logarithmic scale. In Fig. 9 we report the test on Yago2 with our approach, since LB does not support this RDF dataset.

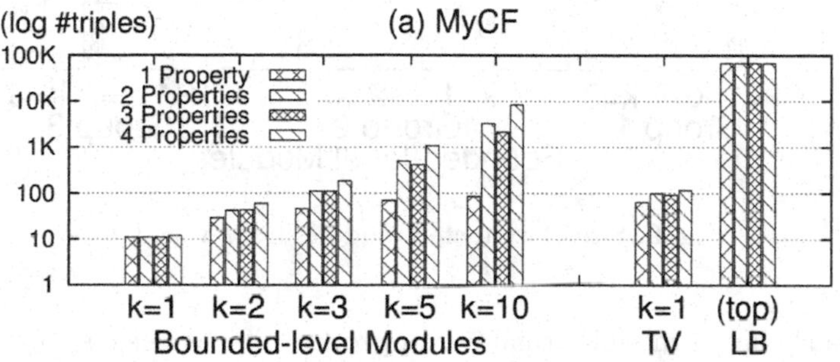

Fig. 7. Size of extracted modules from MyCF

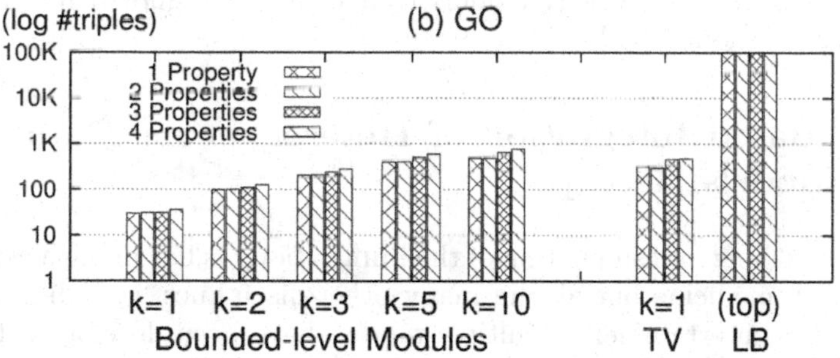

Fig. 8. Size of extracted modules from GO

As expected, the succinctness of bounded-level modules depends on k. The transitivity of the properties declared in the signature also has an impact. This is evident with Yago2 in Fig. 9. Group 2 has properties inherently transitive (isLocatedIn, isConnectedWith) dominating for example (created, owns) in group 1 and (hasGender, isAffiliatedTo) in group 3. Hence, bounded-level modules can be very helpful to control the data succinctness with transitive properties.

Being TV unaware of rules, it may miss relevant data when implicit triples are not considered. We tested this claim, over the *non-saturated* MyCF ontology. Indeed, 42% (15072/35740) of the (non-empty) modules extracted by TV were missing relevant triples wrt our approach, as some subproperty rules were not evaluated. To overcome this limitation, we tested TV over the *saturated* MyCF. For concision, in Fig. 7 we report only the minimal level of detail ($k = 1$). This already outlines a lower bound for the module size. As we can see, $k = 1$ already

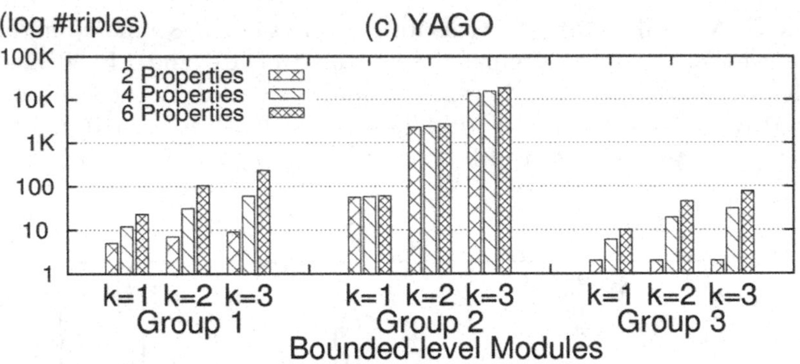

Fig. 9. Size of extracted modules from Yago2

produces fairly larger modules than our approach. This is because of the MyCF rules for transitivity and property-chains. Increasing k gives modules of size in the order of the saturated triplestore. The same discussion holds for GO in Fig. 8. LB extraction for *top-locality* modules has been tested thanks to the available prototype[11]. For MyCF and GO, it outputs almost the whole ontology (Figs. 7 and 8). This is due to ontology axioms that cannot be ignored for the logical completeness of the method.

5 Rule-Based Integration of Heterogeneous Data and Models [36,37]

Computer modeling and simulation of the human body is becoming a critical and central tool in medicine but also in many other disciplines, including engineering, education, entertainment. Multiple models have been developed, for applications ranging from medical simulation to video games, through biomechanics, ergonomics, robotics and CAD, to name only a few. However, currently available anatomical models are either limited to very specific areas or too simplistic for most of the applications.

For anatomy, the reference domain ontology is the Foundational Model of Anatomy (FMA [38]) which is a comprehensive description of the structural organization of the body. Its main component is a taxonomy with more then 83000 classes of anatomical structures from the macromolecular to the macroscopic levels. The FMA symbolically represents the structural organization of the human body. One important limitation of the state-of-the-art available ontologies is the lack of explicit relation between anatomical structures and their functions. Yet, human body modeling relies on morphological components on the one hand and functional and process descriptions on the other hand. The need for a formal description of anatomical functions has been outlined in [30], with some guidelines for getting a separate ontology of anatomical functions based on an

[11] www.cs.ox.ac.uk/isg/tools/ModuleExtractor/.

ontological analysis of functions in general formal ontologies such as GFO [27] or Dolce [33]. Complex 3D graphic models are present in more and more application software but they are not explicitly related to the (anatomical) entities that they represent making difficult the interactive management of these complex objects.

Our approach for supporting efficient navigation and selection of objects in 3D scenes of human body anatomy is to make explicit the anatomic and functional semantics of 3D objects composing a complex 3D scene through a symbolic and formal representation that can be queried on demand. It has been implemented in *My Corporis Fabrica* (MyCF), which realizes a rule-based integration of three types of models of anatomy: structural, functional model and 3D models. The added-value of such a declarative approach for interactive simulation and visualization as well as for teaching applications is to provide new visualization/selection capabilities to manage and browse 3D anatomical entities based on the querying capabilities incorporated in MyCF.

The core of MyCF is a comprehensive anatomical ontology, the novelty of which is to make explicit the links between anatomical entities, human body functions, and 3D graphic models of patient-specific body parts. It is equipped with inference-based query answering capabilities that are particularly interesting for different purposes such as:

- automatic verification of the anatomical validity of 3D models. Indeed, it is important to select the correct set of anatomical entities that participates to a simulation, e.g. a simulation of movements where the correct bones, muscles, ligaments, ..., are required to set up all the 3D and mechanical simulation parameters. These requirements are very close to the selection requirements described in the 'Background' section. They can be regarded as equivalent to a selection operator;
- automatic selection and display of anatomical entities within a 3D scene. Anatomical entities can vary largely in size, can be very close to each other or even hidden by other anatomical entities. The use of geometric means to select useful sets of entities is not suited whereas inference-based queries using human body functions can provide much more suited means. Such selection capabilities are particular relevant for diagnosis for instance;
- training students on anatomical entities participating to a certain body function. Here again, this purpose is close to that of selection functions where the connection between function and anatomical entities provides new means to browse and highlight features of anatomical structures accessible in 3D.

The current version of the ontology contains almost 74000 classes and relations as well as 11 rules stored in a deductive RDF triple store using a Sesame server, and that can be queried with a remote-access facility via a web server[12]. The ontology can be easily updated, just by entering or deleting triples and/or by modifying the set of rules, without having to change the reasoning algorithmic machinery used for answering queries. It is the strength of a declarative approach

[12] http://mycorporisfabrica.org/mycf/.

that allows a fine-grained domain-specific modeling and the exploitation of the result by a generic (domain-independent) reasoning algorithm.

MyCF features three distinct taxonomies linked by relations and rules:

- Anatomical entities, such as *knee*, *shoulder*, and *hand*, denote parts of the human body, and give a formal description of canonical anatomy;
- Functional entities, such as *gait*, *breath*, and *stability*, denote the functions of the human body, and are the fundamental knowledge to explain the role of each anatomical entity;
- Finally, 3D scenes with entities such as *3D-object*, *3D-scene* define the content required to get 3D views of patient-specific anatomical entities described by 3D graphical models related to anatomical entities.

Figure 10 shows an extract of this integrated ontology, in which the green classes refer to the 3D models, the pink classes to the structural model and blue classes to the functional entities.

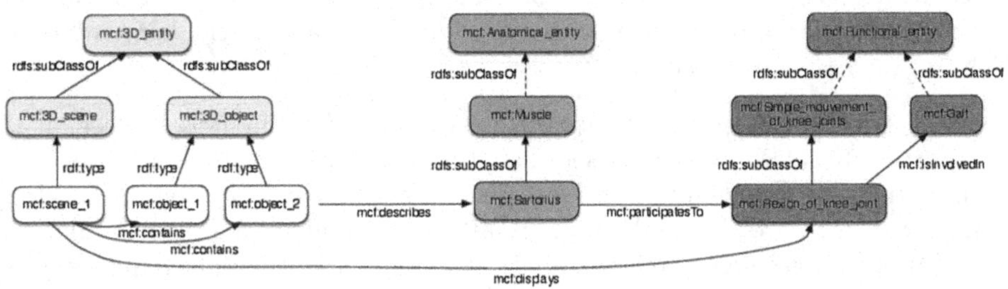

Fig. 10. The general structure of MyCF integrated ontology (extract) (Color figure online)

The inference rules of MyCF express complex connections between relations, within or across the three taxonomies. For instance, the following rules express connections that hold in anatomy between the relations rdfs:subClassOf and mcf:InsertOn, but also between rdfs:subClassOf and mcf:IsInvolvedIn, rdfs:subClassOf and mcf:participatesTo, mcf:participatesTo and mcf:IsInvolvedIn, mcf:PartOf and mcf:InsertOn respectively. The first rule says that if a given class representing an anatomical entity ?a (e.g., Sartorius) is a subclass of an anatomical entity ?c (e.g., Muscle) that is known to be inserted on an anatomical entity ?b (e.g., Bone), then ?a is inserted on ?b (Sartorius inserts on a Bone).

(?a rdfs:subClassOf ?c), (?c mcf:InsertOn ?b) → (?a mcf:InsertOn ?b)
(?a mcf:IsInvolvedIn ?c), (?c rdfs:subClassOf ?b) → (?a mcf:IsInvolvedIn ?b)

(?a mcf:participatesTo ?c), (?c rdfs:subClassOf ?b) → (?a mcf:participatesTo ?b)

(?a mcf:participatesTo ?c), (?c mcf:IsInvolvedIn ?b) → (?a mcf:participatesTo ?b)

(?a mcf:InsertOn ?c), (?c mcf:PartOf ?b) → (?a mcf:InsertOn ?b)

The following rule crosses the anatomy domain and the 3D domain and expresses that the conventional color for visualizing bones in anatomy is yellow:

(?x rdf:type 3D-object), (?x mcf:Describes ?y), (?y rdfs:subClassOf Bone)
→ (?x mcf:hasColour yellow)

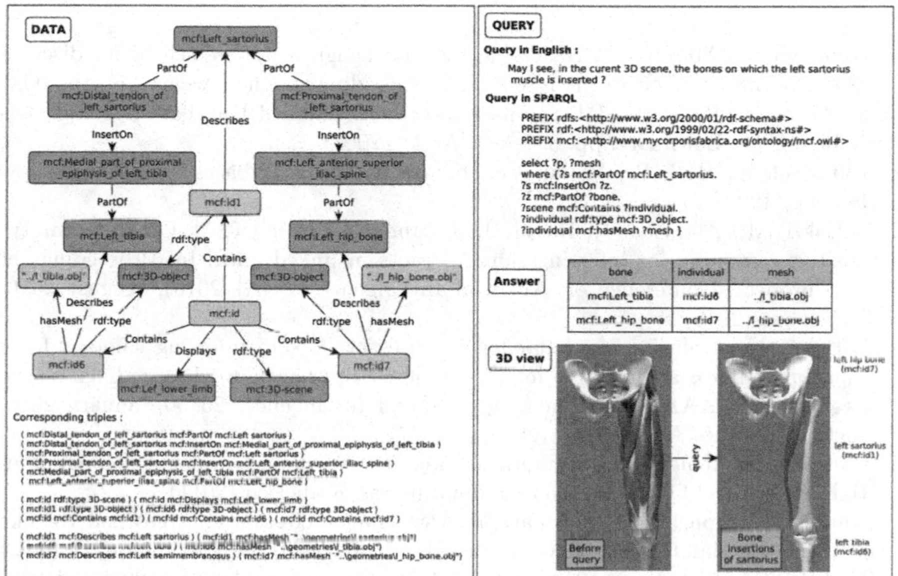

Fig. 11. Illustration of ontology-based querying and visualization using MyCF (Color figure online)

Figure 11 illustrates a complete example from query to 3D visualization. Data are presented as a graph with corresponding RDF triples on the bottom. The query is explained in English and translated in SPARQL. The answers are used to select and highlight corresponding 3D models in the 3D scene.

We have extended this rule-based approach for 3D spatio-temporal modeling of human embryo development in [37]. It results in a unified description of both the knowledge of the organs evolution and their 3D representations enabling to visualize dynamically the embryo evolution.

In an ongoing work, following a similar methodology for ontology-based integration of data extracted from several heterogeneous sources, we are developing OntoSIDES to offer personalized and interactive services for student progress monitoring on top of the national e-learning and evaluation platform of French medical schools.

6 Conclusion

We have shown that Datalog rules on top of RDF triples provides a good trade-off between expressivity and scalability for reasoning in the setting of Linked

Data. It would be worthwhile to investigate the usefulness in practice and the scalability of the Datalog extension proposed in [8] allowing for value invention and stratified negation.

References

1. Abiteboul, S., Abrams, Z., Haar, S., Milo, T.: Diagnosis of asynchronous discrete event systems: datalog to the rescue! In: Proceedings of the Twenty-Fourth ACM SIGACT-SIGMOD-SIGART Symposium on Principles of Database Systems, 13–15 June 2005, Baltimore, pp. 358–367. ACM (2005)
2. Abiteboul, S., Hull, R., Vianu, V.: Foundations of Databases. Addison-Wesley, Reading (1995)
3. Al-Bakri, M., Atencia, M., David, J., Lalande, S., Rousset, M.-C.: Uncertainty-sensitive reasoning for inferring sameAS facts in linked data. In: Proceedings of the European Conference on Artificial Intelligence (ECAI 2016), August 2016, The Hague (2016)
4. Al-Bakri, M., Atencia, M., Lalande, S., Rousset, M.-C.: Inferring same-as facts from linked data: an iterative import-by-query approach. In: Proceedings of the Twenty-Ninth AAAI Conference on Artificial Intelligence, 25–30 January 2015, Austin, pp. 9–15. AAAI Press (2015)
5. Allemang, D., Hendler, J.: Semantic Web for the Working Ontologist: Modeling in RDF, RDFS and OWL. Morgan Kaufmann, San Francisco (2011)
6. Amarilli, A., Bourhis, P., Senellart, P.: Provenance circuits for trees and treelike instances. In: Halldórsson, M.M., Iwama, K., Kobayashi, N., Speckmann, B. (eds.) ICALP 2015. LNCS, vol. 9135, pp. 56–68. Springer, Heidelberg (2015). doi:10.1007/978-3-662-47666-6_5
7. Arasu, A., Ré, C., Suciu, D.: Large-scale deduplication with constraints using dedupalog. In: Proceedings of the 25th International Conference on Data Engineering, ICDE 2009, 29 March 2009–2 April 2009, Shanghai, pp. 952–963. IEEE Computer Society (2009)
8. Arenas, M., Gottlob, G., Pieris, A.: Expressive languages for querying the semantic web. In: Proceedings of the International Conference on Principles of Database Systems (PODS 2014) (2014)
9. Atencia, M., Al-Bakri, M., Rousset, M.-C.: Trust in networks of ontologies and alignments. J. Knowl. Inf. Syst. (2013). doi:10.1007/s10115-013-0708-9
10. Atencia, M., David, J., Euzenat, J.: Data interlinking through robust linkkey extraction. In: ECAI 2014 - 21st European Conference on Artificial Intelligence, 18–22 August 2014, Prague, - Including Prestigious Applications of Intelligent Systems (PAIS 2014). Frontiers in Artificial Intelligence and Applications, vol. 263, pp. 15–20. IOS Press (2014)
11. Atencia, M., David, J., Scharffe, F.: Keys and pseudo-keys detection for web datasets cleansing and interlinking. In: Teije, A., et al. (eds.) EKAW 2012. LNCS (LNAI), vol. 7603, pp. 144–153. Springer, Heidelberg (2012). doi:10.1007/978-3-642-33876-2_14
12. Bröcheler, M., Mihalkova, L., Getoor, L.: Probabilistic similarity logic. In: Proceedings of the Twenty-Sixth Conference on Uncertainty in Artificial Intelligence, UAI 2010, Catalina Island, 8–11 July 2010, pp. 73–82. AUAI Press (2010)
13. Calì, A., Gottlob, G., Lukasiewicz, T.: A general datalog-based framework for tractable query answering over ontologies. J. Web Semant. **14**, 57–83 (2012)

14. Calvanese, D., De Giacomo, G., Lembo, D., Lenzerini, M., Rosati, R.: Tractable reasoning and efficient query answering in description logics: the DL-Lite family. J. Autom. Reason. **39**(3), 385–429 (2007)
15. Chandra, A.K., Merlin, P.M.: Optimal implementation of conjunctive queries in relational databases. In: Proceedings of the 9th ACM Symposium on Theory of Computing, pp. 77–90 (1975)
16. Christen, P.: Data Matching - Concepts and Techniques for Record Linkage, Entity Resolution, and Duplicate Detection. Data-Centric Systems and Applications. Springer, Heidelberg (2012)
17. Dalvi, N., Suciu, D.: The dichotomy of probabilistic inference for unions of conjunctive queries. J. ACM **59**(6), 17–37 (2012)
18. De Giacomo, G., Lenzerini, M., Rosati, R.: Higher-order description logics for domain metamodeling. In: Proceedings of the Twenty-Fifth AAAI Conference on Artificial Intelligence (AAAI-11) (2011)
19. Euzenat, J., Shvaiko, P.: Ontology Matching, 2nd edn. Springer, Heidelberg (2013)
20. Ferrara, A., Nikolov, A., Scharffe, F.: Data linking for the semantic web. Int. J. Semant. Web Inf. Syst. **7**(3), 46–76 (2011)
21. Forgy, C.: Rete: a fast algorithm for the many patterns/many objects match problem. Artif. Intell. **19**(1), 17–37 (1982)
22. Fuhr, N.: Probabilistic models in information retrieval. Comput. J. **3**(35), 243–255 (1992)
23. Fuhr, N.: Probabilistic datalog: implementing logical information retrieval for advanced applications. J. Am. Soc. Inf. Sci. **51**(2), 95–110 (2000)
24. Cuenca Grau, B., Horrocks, I., Kazakov, Y., Sattler, U.: Modular reuse of ontologies: theory and practice. J. Artif. Intell. Res. (JAIR-08) **31**, 273–318 (2008)
25. Grau, B.C., Motik, B.: Reasoning over ontologies with hidden content: the import-by-query approach. J. Artif. Intell. Res. (JAIR) **45**, 197–255 (2012)
26. Heath, T., Bizer, C.: Linked Data: Evolving the Web into a Global Data Space. Morgan and Claypool, Palo Alto (2011)
27. Herre, H.: General formal ontology (GFO): a foundational ontology for conceptual modelling. In: Poli, R., Healy, M., Healy, A. (eds.) Theory and Applications of Ontology, vol. 2, pp. 297–345. Springer, Berlin (2010)
28. Hillebrand, G.G., Kanellakis, P.C., Mairson, H.G., Vardi, M.Y.: Undecidable boundedness problems for datalog programs. J. Log. Program. (JLP-95) **25**, 163–190 (1995)
29. Hinkelmann, K., Hintze, H.: Computing cost estimates for proof strategies. In: Dyckhoff, R. (ed.) ELP 1993. LNCS, vol. 798, pp. 152–170. Springer, Heidelberg (1994). doi:10.1007/3-540-58025-5_54
30. Hoehndorf, R., Ngonga Ngomo, A.-C., Kelso, J.: Applying the functional abnormality ontology pattern to anatomical functions. J. Biomed. Semant. **1**(4), 1–15 (2010)
31. Hogan, A., Zimmermann, A., Umbrich, J., Polleres, A., Decker, S.: Scalable and distributed methods for entity matching, consolidation and disambiguation over linked data corpora. J. Web Semant. **10**, 76–110 (2012)
32. Konev, B., Lutz, C., Walther, D., Wolter, F.: Semantic modularity and module extraction in description logics. In: Proceedings of the European Conference on Artificial Intelligence (ECAI-08) (2008)
33. Masolo, C., Borgo, S., Gangemi, A., Guarino, N., Oltramari, A., Schneider, L.: Wonder-web deliverable D17. The WonderWeb library of foundational ontologies and the DOLCE ontology. Technical report, ISTC-CNR (2002)

34. Ngonga Ngomo, A.-C., Auer, S.: LIMES - a time-efficient approach for large-scale link discovery on the web of data. In: Proceedings of the 22nd International Joint Conference on Artificial Intelligence, IJCAI 2011, Barcelona, 16–22 July 2011, pp. 2312–2317. IJCAI/AAAI (2011)
35. Noy, N.F., Musen, M.A.: Specifying ontology views by traversal. In: McIlraith, S.A., Plexousakis, D., Harmelen, F. (eds.) ISWC 2004. LNCS, vol. 3298, pp. 713–725. Springer, Heidelberg (2004). doi:10.1007/978-3-540-30475-3_49
36. Palombi, O., Ulliana, F., Favier, V., Rousset, M.-C.: My Corporis Fabrica: an ontology-based tool for reasoning and querying on complex anatomical models. J. Biomed. Semant. (JOBS 2014) **5**, 20 (2014)
37. Rabattu, P.-Y., Masse, B., Ulliana, F., Rousset, M.-C., Rohmer, D., Leon, J.-C., Palombi, O.: My Corporis Fabrica embryo: an ontology-based 3D spatio-temporal modeling of human embryo development. J. Biomed. Semant. (JOBS 2015) **6**, 36 (2015)
38. Rosse, C., Mejino, J.L.V.: A reference ontology for biomedical informatics: the foundational model of anatomy. J. Biomed. Inform. **36**, 500 (2003)
39. Rousset, M.-C., Ulliana, F.: Extractiong bounded-level modules from deductive triplestores. In: Proceedings of the Twenty-Ninth AAAI Conference on Artificial Intelligence, 25–30 January 2015, Austin. AAAI Press (2015)
40. Saïs, F., Pernelle, N., Rousset, M.-C.: Combining a logical and a numerical method for data reconciliation. J. Data Semant. **12**, 66–94 (2009)
41. Singla, P., Domingos, P.M.: Entity resolution with Markov logic. In: Proceedings of the 6th IEEE International Conference on Data Mining (ICDM 2006), 18–22 December 2006, Hong Kong, pp. 572–582. IEEE Computer Society (2006)
42. Suchanek, F.M., Kasneci, G., Weikum, G.: Yago: a core of semantic knowledge. In: Proceedings of the World Wide Web Conference (WWW-07) (2007)
43. Suciu, D., Olteanu, D., Ré, C., Koch, C.: Probabilistic Databases. Morgan & Claypool, San Francisco (1995)
44. Symeonidou, D., Armant, V., Pernelle, N., Saïs, F.: SAKey: scalable almost key discovery in RDF data. In: Mika, P., et al. (eds.) ISWC 2014. LNCS, vol. 8796, pp. 33–49. Springer, Cham (2014). doi:10.1007/978-3-319-11964-9_3
45. Tournaire, R., Petit, J.-M., Rousset, M.-C., Termier, A.: Discovery of probabilistic mappings between taxonomies: principles and experiments. J. Data Semant. **15**, 66–101 (2011)
46. Urbani, J., Harmelen, F., Schlobach, S., Bal, H.: QueryPIE: backward reasoning for OWL horst over very large knowledge bases. In: Aroyo, L., et al. (eds.) ISWC 2011. LNCS, vol. 7031, pp. 730–745. Springer, Heidelberg (2011). doi:10.1007/978-3-642-25073-6_46
47. Vieille, L.: Recursive axioms in deductive databases: the query/subquery approach. In: Expert Database Conference, pp. 253–267 (1986)
48. Volz, J., Bizer, C., Gaedke, M., Kobilarov, G.: Silk - a link discovery framework for the web of data. In: Proceedings of the WWW 2009 Workshop on Linked Data on the Web, LDOW 2009, Madrid, 20 April 2009, vol. 538. CEUR Workshop Proceedings. CEUR-WS.org (2009)

A Tutorial on Hybrid Answer Set Solving with *clingo*

Roland Kaminski[1], Torsten Schaub[1,2](✉), and Philipp Wanko[1]

[1] University of Potsdam, Potsdam, Germany
torsten@uni-potsdam.de

[2] Inria, Bretagne Atlantique, Rennes, France

Abstract. Answer Set Programming (ASP) has become an established paradigm for Knowledge Representation and Reasoning, in particular, when it comes to solving knowledge-intense combinatorial (optimization) problems. ASP's unique pairing of a simple yet rich modeling language with highly performant solving technology has led to an increasing interest in ASP in academia as well as industry. To further boost this development and make ASP fit for real world applications it is indispensable to equip it with means for an easy integration into software environments and for adding complementary forms of reasoning.

In this tutorial, we describe how both issues are addressed in the ASP system *clingo*. At first, we outline features of *clingo*'s application programming interface (API) that are essential for multi-shot ASP solving, a technique for dealing with continuously changing logic programs. This is illustrated by realizing two exemplary reasoning modes, namely branch-and-bound-based optimization and incremental ASP solving. We then switch to the design of the API for integrating complementary forms of reasoning and detail this in an extensive case study dealing with the integration of difference constraints. We show how the syntax of these constraints is added to the modeling language and seamlessly merged into the grounding process. We then develop in detail a corresponding theory propagator for difference constraints and present how it is integrated into *clingo*'s solving process.

1 Introduction

Answer Set Programming (ASP [4]) has established itself among the popular paradigms for Knowledge Representation and Reasoning (KRR), in particular, when it comes to solving knowledge-intense combinatorial (optimization) problems. ASP's unique combination of a simple yet rich modeling language with highly performant solving technology has led to an increasing interest in ASP in academia as well as industry. Another primary asset of ASP is its versatility, arguably elicited by its roots in KRR. On the one hand, ASP's first-order

T. Schaub—Affiliated with the School of Computing Science at Simon Fraser University, Burnaby, Canada, and the Institute for Integrated and Intelligent Systems at Griffith University, Brisbane, Australia.

G. Ianni et al. (Eds.): Reasoning Web 2017, LNCS 10370, pp. 167–203, 2017.
DOI: 10.1007/978-3-319-61033-7_6

modeling language offers, for instance, cardinality and weight constraints as well as means to express multi-objective optimization functions. This allows ASP to readily express problems in neighboring fields such as Satisfiability Testing (SAT [7]) and Pseudo-Boolean Solving (PB [37]), as well as Maximum Satisfiability Testing (MaxSAT [28]) and even more general constraint satisfaction problems possibly involving optimization. On the other hand, these constructs must be supported by the corresponding solvers, leading to dedicated treatments of cardinality and weight constraints along with sophisticated optimization algorithms. Moreover, mere satisfiability testing is often insufficient for addressing KRR problems. That is why ASP solvers offer additional reasoning modes involving enumerating, intersecting, or unioning solutions, as well as combinations thereof, e.g., intersecting all optimal solutions.

In a sense, the discussed versatility of modern ASP can be regarded as the result of hybridizing the original approach [24] in several ways. So far, however, most hybridization was accomplished within the solvers and is thus inaccessible to the user. For instance, the dedicated treatment of aggregates like cardinality and weight constraints is fully opaque. The same applies to the control of successive solver calls happening during optimization. Although a highly optimized implementation of such prominent concepts makes perfect sense, the increasing range and resulting diversification of applications of ASP calls for easy and generic means to enrich ASP with dedicated forms of reasoning. This involves the extension of ASP's solving capacities with means for handling constraints foreign to ASP as well as means for customizing solving processes to define complex forms of reasoning. The former extension is usually called *theory reasoning* (or *theory solving*) and the resulting conglomerate of ASP extensions is subsumed under the umbrella term *ASP modulo theories*. The other extension addresses the customization of ASP solving processes by *multi-shot ASP solving*, providing operative solving processes that deal with continuously changing logic programs.

Let us motivate both techniques by means of two exemplary ASP extensions, aggregate constraints and optimization. With this end in view, keep in mind that ASP is a model, ground, and solve paradigm. Hence such extensions are rarely limited to a single component but often spread throughout the whole workflow. This begins with the addition of new language constructs to the input language, requiring in turn amendments to the grounder as well as syntactic means for passing the ground constructs to a downstream system. In case they are to be dealt with by an ASP solver, it must be enabled to treat the specific input and incorporate corresponding solving capacities. Finally, each such extension is theory-specific and requires different means at all ends.

So first of all, consider what is needed to extend an ASP system like *clingo* with a new type of aggregate constraint? The first step consists in defining the syntax of the aggregate type. Afterwards, the ASP grounder has to be extended to be able to parse and instantiate the corresponding constructs. Then, there are two options, either the ground aggregates are translated into existing ASP language constructs (and we are done),[1] or they are passed along to a

[1] Alternatively, this could also be done before instantiation.

downstream ASP solver. The first alternative is also referred to as *eager*, the latter as *lazy theory solving*. The next step in the lazy approach is to define an intermediate format (or data structure) to pass instances of the aggregate constraints from the grounder to the solver, not to forget respective extensions to the back- and front-ends of the two ASP components. Now, that the solver can internalize the new constructs, it must be equipped with corresponding processing capacities. They are usually referred to as *theory propagators* and inserted into the solver's infrastructure for propagation. When solving, the idea is to leave the Boolean solving machinery intact by associating with each theory constraint an auxiliary Boolean variable. During propagation, the truth values of the auxiliary variables are passed to the corresponding theory propagators that then try to satisfy or falsify the respective theory constraints, respectively. Finally, when an overall solution is found, the theory propagators are in charge of outputting their part (if applicable). One can imagine that each such extension involves a quite intricate engineering effort since it requires working with the ASP system's low level API. *clingo* allows us to overcome this problem by providing easy and generic means for adding theory solving capacities. On the one side, it offers theory grammars for expressing theory languages whose expressions are seamlessly integrated in its grounding process. On the other side, a simple interface consisting of four methods offers an easy integration of theory propagators into the solver, either in C, C++, Lua, or Python.

Let us now turn to (branch-and-bound-based) optimization and see what infrastructure is needed to extend a basic ASP solver. In fact, for the setup, we face a similar situation as above and all steps from syntax definition to internalization are analogous for capturing objective functions. The first step in optimization is to find an initial solution. If none exists, we are done. Otherwise the system enters a simple loop. The objective value of the previous solution is determined and a constraint is added to the problem specification requiring that a solution must have a strictly better objective value than the one just obtained. Then, the solver is launched again to compute a better solution. If none is found, the last solution is optimal. Otherwise, the system re-enters the loop in order to find an even better solution. This solving process faces a succession of solver invocations dealing with slightly changing problem specifications. The direct way to implement this is to use a script that repeatedly calls an ASP solver after each problem expansion. However, such an approach bears great redundancies due to repeated grounding and solving efforts from scratch. Unlike this, *clingo* offers evolving grounding and solving processes. Such processes lead to operative ASP systems that possess an internal state that can be manipulated by certain operations. Such operations allow for adding, grounding, and solving logic programs as well as setting truth values of (external) atoms. The latter does not only provide a simple means for incorporating external input but also for enabling or disabling parts of the current logic program. These functionalities allow for dealing with changing logic programs in a seamless way. As above, corresponding application programming interfaces (APIs) are available in C, C++, Lua, or Python.

The remainder of this tutorial is structured as follows. Section 2 provides some formal underpinnings for the following sections without any claim to completeness. Rather we refer the reader to the literature for comprehensive introductions to ASP and its computing machinery, among others [4,14,19,23,30]. As a result, this tutorial is not self-contained and rather aims at a hands-on introduction to using *clingo*'s API for multi-shot and theory solving. Both approaches are described in Sects. 3 and 4 by drawing on material from [20,21] and [18], respectively. Section 5 is dedicated to a case-study detailing how *clingo* can be extended with difference constraints over integers, or more precisely Quantifier-free Integer Difference Logic (QF-IDL).

2 Answer Set Programming

As usual, a logic program consists of rules of the form

$$\texttt{a}_1\texttt{;}\ldots\texttt{;a}_m \texttt{ :- } \texttt{a}_{m+1}\texttt{,}\ldots\texttt{,a}_n\texttt{,not a}_{n+1}\texttt{,}\ldots\texttt{,not a}_o$$

where each $\texttt{a}_i$ is an atom of form $\texttt{p(t}_1\texttt{,}\ldots\texttt{,t}_k\texttt{)}$ and all $\texttt{t}_i$ are terms, composed of function symbols and variables. Atoms $\texttt{a}_1$ to $\texttt{a}_m$ are often called head atoms, while $\texttt{a}_{m+1}$ to $\texttt{a}_n$ and $\texttt{not a}_{n+1}$ to $\texttt{not a}_o$ are also referred to as positive and negative body literals, respectively. An expression is said to be ground, if it contains no variables. As usual, `not` denotes (default) negation. A rule is called a fact if $m = o = 1$, normal if $m = 1$, and an integrity constraint if $m = 0$. Semantically, a logic program induces a set of stable models, being distinguished models of the program determined by the stable models semantics; see [25] for details.

To ease the use of ASP in practice, several extensions have been developed. First of all, rules with variables are viewed as shorthands for the set of their ground instances. Further language constructs include conditional literals and cardinality constraints [38]. The former are of the form $\texttt{a:b}_1\texttt{,}\ldots\texttt{,b}_m$, the latter can be written as[2] $\texttt{s}\{\texttt{d}_1\texttt{;}\ldots\texttt{;d}_n\}\texttt{t}$, where `a` and $\texttt{b}_i$ are possibly default-negated (regular) literals and each $\texttt{d}_j$ is a conditional literal; `s` and `t` provide optional lower and upper bounds on the number of satisfied literals in the cardinality constraint. We refer to $\texttt{b}_1\texttt{,}\ldots\texttt{,b}_m$ as a condition. The practical value of both constructs becomes apparent when used with variables. For instance, a conditional literal like `a(X):b(X)` in a rule's antecedent expands to the conjunction of all instances of `a(X)` for which the corresponding instance of `b(X)` holds. Similarly, `2{a(X):b(X)}4` is true whenever at least two and at most four instances of `a(X)` (subject to `b(X)`) are true. Finally, objective functions minimizing the sum of a set of weighted tuples $(w_i, \boldsymbol{t}_i)$ subject to condition c_i are expressed as $\texttt{\#minimize}\{w_1\texttt{@}l_1\texttt{,}\boldsymbol{t}_1\texttt{:}c_1\texttt{;}\ldots\texttt{;}w_n\texttt{@}l_n\texttt{,}\boldsymbol{t}_n\texttt{:}c_n\}$ Lexicographically ordered objective functions are (optionally) distinguished via levels indicated by l_i. An omitted level defaults to 0.

As an example, consider the rule in Line 9 of Listing 1.1:

[2] More elaborate forms of aggregates can be obtained by explicitly using function (eg. `#count`) and relation symbols (eg. <=).

```
1 { move(D,P,T) : disk(D), peg(P) } 1 :- ngoal(T-1), T<=n.
```

This rule has a single head atom consisting of a cardinality constraint; it comprises all instances of `move(D,P,T)` where `T` is fixed by the two body literals and `D` and `P` vary over all instantiations of predicates `disk` and `peg`, respectively. Given 3 pegs and 4 disks as in Listing 1.2, this results in 12 instances of `move(D,P,T)` for each valid replacement of `T`, among which exactly one must be chosen according to the above rule.

Full details on the input language of *clingo* along with various examples can be found in [16].

3 Multi-shot ASP Solving

Let us begin with an informal overview of the central features and language constructs of *clingo*'s multi-shot solving capacities. We illustrate them in the two following sections by implementing two exemplary reasoning modes, namely branch-and-bound-based optimization and incremental ASP solving. The material in Sects. 3.1 and 3.3 is borrowed from [20,21], respectively, where more detailed accounts can be found.

3.1 A Gentle Introduction

A key feature, distinguishing *clingo* from its predecessors, is the possibility to structure (non-ground) input rules into subprograms. To this end, a program can be partitioned into several subprograms by means of the directive `#program`; it comes with a name and an optional list of parameters. Once given in the input, the directive gathers all rules up to the next such directive (or the end of file) within a subprogram identified by the supplied name and parameter list. As an example, two subprograms `base` and `acid(k)` can be specified as follows:

```
1 a(1).
2 #program acid(k).
3  b(k).
4 c(X,k) :- a(X).
5 #program base.
6 a(2).
```

Note that `base` is a dedicated subprogram (with an empty parameter list): in addition to the rules in its scope, it gathers all rules not preceded by any `#program` directive. Hence, in the above example, the `base` subprogram includes the facts `a(1)` and `a(2)`, although, only the latter is in the actual scope of the directive in line 5. Without further control instructions (see below), *clingo* grounds and solves the `base` subprogram only, essentially, yielding the standard behavior of ASP systems. The processing of other subprograms such as `acid(k)` is subject to scripting control.

For customized control over grounding and solving, a main routine (taking a control object representing the state of *clingo* as argument) can be supplied. For illustration, let us consider two Python main routines:[3]

```
 7 #script(python)
 8 def main(prg):
 9     prg.ground([("base",[])])
10     prg.solve()
11 #end.
```

While the above control program matches the default behavior of *clingo*, the one below ignores all rules in the base program but rather contains a ground instruction for acid(k) in line 8, where the parameter k is to be instantiated with the term 42.

```
 7 #script(python)
 8 def main(prg):
 9     prg.ground([("acid",[42])])
10     prg.solve()
11 #end.
```

Accordingly, the schematic fact b(k) is turned into b(42), no ground rule is obtained from 'c(X,k) :- a(X)' due to lacking instances of a(X), and the solve command in line 10 yields a stable model consisting of b(42) only. Note that ground instructions apply to the subprograms given as arguments, while solve triggers reasoning w.r.t. all accumulated ground rules.

In order to accomplish more elaborate reasoning processes, like those of *iclingo* [17] and *oclingo* [15] or other customized ones, it is indispensable to activate or deactivate ground rules on demand. For instance, former initial or goal state conditions need to be relaxed or completely replaced when modifying a planning problem, e.g., by extending its horizon.[4] While the two mentioned predecessors of *clingo* relied on the #volatile directive to provide a rigid mechanism for the expiration of transient rules, *clingo* captures the respective functionalities and customizations thereof in terms of the #external directive. This directive goes back to *lparse* [39] and was also supported by *clingo*'s predecessors to exempt (input) atoms from simplifications (and fixing them to false). As detailed in the following, the #external directive of *clingo* provides a generalization that, in particular, allows for a flexible handling of yet undefined atoms.

For continuously assembling ground rules evolving at different stages of a reasoning process, #external directives declare atoms that may still be defined by rules added later on. In terms of module theory [35], such atoms correspond to inputs, which (unlike undefined output atoms) must not be simplified.

[3] The ground routine takes a list of pairs as argument. Each such pair consists of a subprogram name (e.g. base or acid) and a list of actual parameters (e.g. [] or [42]).

[4] The planning horizon is the maximum number of steps a planner takes into account when searching for a plan.

For declaring input atoms, *clingo* supports schematic `#external` directives that are instantiated along with the rules of their respective subprograms. To this end, a directive like

```
#external p(X,Y) : q(X,Z), r(Z,Y).
```

is treated similar to a rule '`p(X,Y) :- q(X,Z), r(Z,Y)`' during grounding. However, the head atoms of the resulting ground instances are merely collected as inputs, whereas the ground rules as such are discarded.

Once grounded, the truth value of external atoms can be changed via the *clingo* API (until the atoms become defined by corresponding rules). By default, the initial truth value of external atoms is set to false. Then, for example, with *clingo*'s Python API, `assign_external(self,p(a,b),True)`[5] can be used to set the truth value of the external atom `p(a,b)` to true. Among others, this can be used to activate and deactivate rules in logic programs. For instance, the integrity constraint '`:- q(a,c), r(c,b), p(a,b)`' is ineffective whenever `p(a,b)` is false.

A full specification of *clingo*'s Python API can be found at https://potassco.org/clingo/python-api/current/clingo.html.

3.2 Branch-and-Bound-Based Optimization

We illustrate *clingo*'s multi-shot solving machinery in this as well as the next section via a simple Towers of Hanoi puzzle. The complete source code of this example is available at https://github.com/potassco/clingo/tree/master/examples/clingo/opt. Our example consists of three pegs and four disks of different size; it is shown in Fig. 1. The goal is to move all disks from the left peg to the right one. Only the topmost disk of a peg can be moved at a time. Furthermore, a disk cannot be moved to a peg already containing a disk of smaller size. Although there is an efficient algorithm to solve our simple puzzle, we do not exploit it and below merely specify conditions for sequences of moves being solutions. More generally, the Towers of Hanoi puzzle is a typical planning problem, in which the aim is to find a plan, that is, a sequence of actions, that leads from an initial state to a state satisfying a goal.

To illustrate how multi-shot solving can be used for realizing branch-and-bound-based optimization, we consider the problem of finding the shortest plan solving our puzzle within a given horizon. To this end, we adapt the Towers of Hanoi encoding from [19] in Listing 1.1. Here, the length of the horizon is given by parameter `n`. The problem instance in Listing 1.2 together with line 2 in Listing 1.1 gives the initial configuration of disks in Fig. 1. Similarly, the goal is checked in lines 5–6 of Listing 1.1 (by drawing on the problem instance in Listing 1.2). Because the overall objective is to solve the problem in the minimum number of steps within a given bound, it is successively tested in line 5. Once the goal is established, it persists in the following steps. This allows us to

[5] In order to construct atoms, symbolic terms, or function terms, respectively, the *clingo* API function `Function` has to be used. Hence, the expression `p(a,b)` actually stands for `Function("p", [Function("a"), Function("b")])`.

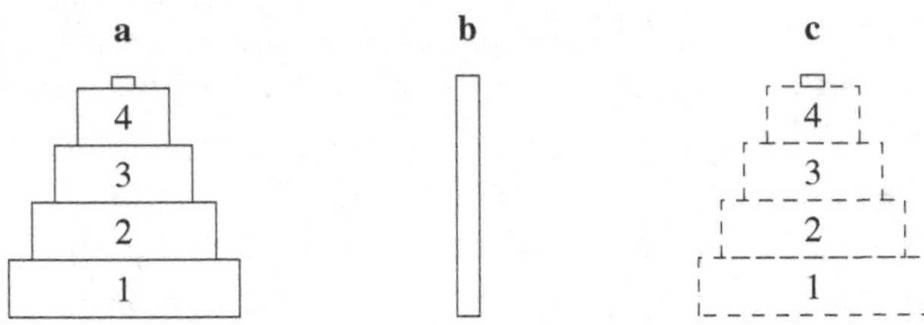

Fig. 1. Towers of Hanoi: initial and goal situation

read off whether the goal was reached at the planning horizon (in line 6). The state transition function along with state constraints are described in lines 9–19. Since the encoding of the Towers of Hanoi problem is fairly standard, we refer the interested reader to [19] and devote ourselves in the sequel to implementing branch-and-bound-based minimization. In view of this, note that line 9 ensures that moves are only permitted if the goal is not yet achieved in the previous state. This ensures that the following states do not change anymore and allows for expressing the optimization function in line 23 as: minimize the number of states where the goal is not reached.

Listing 1.3 contains a logic program for bounding the next solution and the actual optimization algorithm. The logic program expects a bound `b` as parameter and adds an integrity constraint in line 3 ensuring that the next stable model yields a better bound than the given one. The minimization algorithm starts by grounding the `base` program in line 10 before it enters the loop in lines 11–26. This loop implements the branch-and-bound-based search for the minimum by searching for stable models while updating the bound until the problem is unsatisfiable. Note the use of the `with` clause in line 13 that is used to acquire and release a solve handle. With it, the nested loop in lines 14–21 iterates over the found stable models. If there is a stable model, lines 15–20 iterate over the atoms of the stable model while summing up the current bound by extracting the weight of atoms over predicates `_minimize`/n with $n > 0$.[6] We check that the first argument of the atom is an integer and ignore atoms where this is not the case; just as is the case of the `#sum` aggregate in line 3. The loop over the stable models is exited in line 21. Note that this bypasses the `else` clause in line 22 and the algorithm continues in line 25 with printing the bound and adding an integrity constraint in line 26 making sure that the next stable model is strictly better than the current one. Furthermore, note that grounding happens after the `with` clause because it must not interfere with an active search for stable models. Finally, if the program becomes unsatisfiable, the branch and bound loop in lines 11–26 is exhausted. Hence, control continues in the `else` clause in lines 22–24 printing that the previously found stable model (if any) is the optimal solution and exiting the outermost while loop in line 24 terminating the algorithm.

[6] In our case, $n = 2$ would be sufficient.

```
% initial situation
on(D,P,0) :- init_on(D,P).

% check goal situation
ngoal(T) :- on(D,P,T), not goal_on(D,P).
:- ngoal(n).

% state transition and state constraints
1 { move(D,P,T) : disk(D), peg(P) } 1 :- ngoal(T-1), T<=n.

move(D,T)          :- move(D,P,T).
on(D,P,T)          :- move(D,P,T).
on(D,P,T)          :- on(D,P,T-1), not move(D,T), T<=n.
blocked(D-1,P,T) :- on(D,P,T-1).
blocked(D-1,P,T) :- blocked(D,P,T), disk(D).

:- move(D,P,T), blocked(D-1,P,T).
:- move(D,T), on(D,P,T-1), blocked(D,P,T).
:- disk(D), not 1 { on(D,P,T) } 1, T=1..n.

#show move/3.

_minimize(1,T) :- ngoal(T).
```

Listing 1.1. Bounded towers of hanoi encoding (tohB.lp)

```
peg(a;b;c).
disk(1..4).
init_on(1..4,a).
goal_on(1..4,c).
```

Listing 1.2. Towers of hanoi instance (tohI.lp)

When running the augmented logic program in Listings 1.1, 1.2, and 1.3 with a horizon of 17, the solver finds plans of length 17, 16, and 15 and shows that no plan of length 14 exists. This is reflected by *clingo*'s output indicating 4 solver calls and 3 found stable models:

```
$ clingo tohB.lp tohI.lp opt.lp -c n=17
clingo version 5.2.0
Reading from tohB.lp ...
Solving...
[...]
Solving...
Answer: 1
move(3,c,2)  move(4,b,1)  move(4,c,3)  move(2,b,4)  \
move(4,a,5)  move(3,b,6)  move(4,b,7)  move(1,c,8)  \
move(4,c,9)  move(3,a,10) move(4,a,11) move(2,c,12) \
move(4,b,13) move(3,c,14) move(4,c,15)
```

```
#program bound(b).

:- #sum { V,I: _minimize(V,I) } >= b.

#script (python)

import clingo

def main(prg):
    prg.ground([("base", [])])
    while True:
        bound = 0
        with prg.solve(yield_=True) as h:
            for m in h:
                for atom in m.symbols(atoms=True):
                    if (atom.name == "_minimize"
                    and len(atom.arguments) > 0
                    and atom.arguments[0].type
                    is  clingo.SymbolType.Number):
                        bound += atom.arguments[0].number
                break
            else:
                print "Optimum found"
                break
        print "Found new bound: {}".format(bound)
        prg.ground([("bound", [bound])])

#end.
```

Listing 1.3. Branch and bound optimization (opt.lp)

```
Found new bound: 15
Solving...
Optimum found
UNSATISFIABLE

Models       : 3
Calls        : 4
Time         : 0.048s (Solving: 0.01s [...])
CPU Time     : 0.040s
```

Last but not least, note that the implemented above functionality is equivalent to using *clingo*'s inbuilt optimization mode by replacing line 23 in Listing 1.1 with

```
23 #minimize { 1,T : ngoal(T) }.
```

3.3 Incremental ASP Solving

As mentioned, *clingo* fully supersedes its special-purpose predecessor *iclingo* aiming at incremental ASP solving. To illustrate this, we give below in Listing 1.5 a Python implementation of *iclingo*'s control loop, corresponding to the one shipped with *clingo*.[7,8] Roughly speaking, *iclingo* offers a step-oriented, incremental approach to ASP that avoids redundancies by gradually processing the extensions to a problem rather than repeatedly re-processing the entire extended problem (as in iterative deepening search). To this end, a program is partitioned into a base part, describing static knowledge independent of the step parameter `t`, a cumulative part, capturing knowledge accumulating with increasing `t`, and a volatile part specific for each value of `t`. In *clingo*, all three parts are captured by `#program` declarations along with `#external` atoms for handling volatile rules. More precisely, the implementation in Listing 1.5 relies upon subprograms named `base`, `step`, and `check` along with external atoms of form `query(t)`.[9]

We illustrate this approach by adapting the Towers of Hanoi encoding from Listing 1.1 in Sect. 3.2 to an incremental version in Listing 1.4. To this end, we arrange the original encoding in program parts `base`, `check(t)`, and `step(t)`, use `t` instead of `T` as time parameter, and simplify checking the goal. Checking the goal is easier here because the iterative deepening approach guarantees a shortest plan and, hence, does not require additional minimization.

At first, we observe that the problem instance in Listing 1.2 as well as line 2 in Listing 1.4 constitute static knowledge and thus belong to the `base` program. More interestingly, the query is expressed in line 5 of Listing 1.4. Its volatility is realized by making it subject to the truth assignment to the external atom `query(t)`. For convenience, this atom is predefined in line 33 in Listing 1.5 as part of the `check` program (cf. line 32). Hence, subprogram `check` consists of a user- and predefined part. Finally, the transition function along with state constraints are described in the subprogram `step` in lines 8–19.

The idea is now to control the successive grounding and solving of the program parts in Listings 1.2 and 1.4 by the Python script in Listing 1.5. Lines 5–11 fix the values of the constants `imin`, `imax`, and `istop`. In fact, the setting in line 9 and 11 relieves us from adding '`-c imin=0 -c istop="SAT"`' when calling *clingo*. All three constants mimic command line options in *iclingo*. `imin` and `imax` prescribe a least and largest number of iterations, respectively; `istop` gives a termination criterion. The initial values of variables `step` and `ret` are set in line 13. The value of `step` is used to instantiate the parametrized subprograms and `ret` comprises the solving result. Together, the previous five variables control the loop in lines 14–29.

---

[7] Alternatively, this can be invoked by `#include<incmode>`

[8] The Python as well as a Lua implementation can be found in `examples/clingo/iclingo` in the *clingo* distribution.

[9] These names have no general, predefined meaning; their meaning emerges from their usage in the associated script (see below).

```
3  #program base.
4  on(D,P,0) :- init_on(D,P).

6  #program check(t).
7  :- goal_on(D,P), not on(D,P,t), query(t).


10 #program step(t).
11 1 { move(D,P,t) : disk(D), peg(P) } 1.

13 move(D,t)          :- move(D,P,t).
14 on(D,P,t)          :- move(D,P,t).
15 on(D,P,t)          :- on(D,P,t-1), not move(D,t).
16 blocked(D-1,P,t) :- on(D,P,t-1).
17 blocked(D-1,P,t) :- blocked(D,P,t), disk(D).

19 :- move(D,P,t), blocked(D-1,P,t).
20 :- move(D,t), on(D,P,t-1), blocked(D,P,t).
21 :- disk(D), not 1 { on(D,P,t) } 1.

23 #show move/3.
```

Listing 1.4. Towers of Hanoi incremental encoding (`tohE.lp`)

The subprograms grounded at each iteration are accumulated in the list `parts`. Each of its entries is a pair consisting of a subprogram name along with its list of actual parameters. In the very first iteration, the subprograms `base` and `check(0)` are grounded. Note that this involves the declaration of the external atom `query(0)` and the assignment of its default value false. The latter is changed in line 28 to true in order to activate the actual query. The `solve` call in line 29 then amounts to checking whether the goal situation is already satisfied in the initial state. As well, the value of `step` is incremented to `1`.

As long as the termination condition remains unfulfilled, each following iteration takes the respective value of variable `step` to replace the parameter in subprograms `step` and `check` during grounding. In addition, the current external atom `query(t)` is set to true, while the previous one is permanently set to false. This disables the corresponding instance of the integrity constraint in line 5 of Listing 1.4 before it is replaced in the next iteration. In this way, the query condition only applies to the current horizon.

An interesting feature is given in line 24. As its name suggests, this function cleans up domains used during grounding. That is, whenever the truth value of an atom is ultimately determined by the solver, it is communicated to the grounder where it can be used for simplifications.

The result of each call to `solve` is printed by *clingo*. In our example, the solver is called 16 times before a plan of length 15 is found:

```
#script (python)

from clingo import Function

def get(val, default):
    return val if val != None else default

def main(prg):
    imin   = get(prg.get_const("imin"), 1)
    imax   = prg.get_const("imax")
    istop  = get(prg.get_const("istop"), "SAT")

    step, ret = 0, None
    while ((imax is None or step < imax) and
           (step == 0   or step < imin or (
              (istop == "SAT"     and not ret.satisfiable) or
              (istop == "UNSAT"   and not ret.unsatisfiable) or
              (istop == "UNKNOWN" and not ret.unknown)))):
        parts = []
        parts.append(("check", [step]))
        if step > 0:
            prg.release_external(Function("query", [step-1]))
            parts.append(("step", [step]))
            prg.cleanup()
        else:
            parts.append(("base", []))
        prg.ground(parts)
        prg.assign_external(Function("query", [step]), True)
        ret, step = prg.solve(), step+1
#end.

#program check(t).
#external query(t).
```

Listing 1.5. Python script implementing *iclingo* functionality in *clingo* (`inc.lp`)

```
$ clingo tohE.lp tohI.lp inc.lp 0
clingo version 5.2.0
Reading from tohE.lp ...
Solving...
[...]
Solving...
Answer: 1
move(4,b,1)  move(3,c,2)  move(4,c,3)  move(2,b,4)  \
move(4,a,5)  move(3,b,6)  move(4,b,7)  move(1,c,8)  \
move(4,c,9)  move(3,a,10) move(4,a,11) move(2,c,12) \
move(4,b,13) move(3,c,14) move(4,c,15)
SATISFIABLE

Models      : 1
Calls       : 16
Time        : 0.020s (Solving: 0.00s [...])
CPU Time    : 0.020s
```

4 Theory-Enhanced ASP Solving

This section provides the fundamental concepts for extending *clingo* with theory-specific reasoning. We begin by showing how its input language can be customized with theory-specific constructs. We then sketch *clingo*'s algorithmic approach to ASP solving with theory propagation in order to put the following description of *clingo*'s theory reasoning interface on firm grounds. The below material is an abridged version of [18].

4.1 Input Language

This section introduces the theory-related features of *clingo*'s input language. All of them are situated in the underlying grounder *gringo* and can thus also be used independently of *clingo*. We start with a detailed description of *gringo*'s generic means for defining theories and complement this in Appendix A with an overview of the corresponding intermediate language.

Our generic approach to theory specification rests upon two languages: the one defining theory languages and the theory language itself. Both borrow elements from the underlying ASP language, foremost an aggregate-like syntax for formulating variable length expressions. To illustrate this, consider Listing 1.6, where a logic program is extended by constructs for handling difference and linear constraints. While the former are binary constraints of the form[10] $x_1 - x_2 \leq k$, the latter have a variable size and are of form $a_1 x_1 + \cdots + a_n x_n \circ k$, where x_i are integer variables, a_i and k are integers, and $\circ \in \{\leq, \geq, <, >, =\}$ for $1 \leq i \leq n$. Note that solving difference constraints is polynomial, while solving linear equations (over integers) is NP-complete. The theory language for expressing both types of constraints is defined in lines 1–15 and preceded by the directive `#theory`. The elements of the resulting theory language are preceded by `&` and used as regular atoms in the logic program in lines 17–27.

To be more precise, a *theory definition* has the form

#theory T `{`D_1`;...;`D_n`}.`

where T is the theory name and each D_i is a definition for a theory term or a theory atom for $1 \leq i \leq n$. The language induced by a theory definition is the set of all theory atoms constructible from its theory atom definitions.

A *theory atom definition* has form

`&`p`/`k `:` t`,`o or `&`p`/`k `:` t`,{`$\diamond_1$`,...,`$\diamond_m$`},`t'`,`o

where p is a predicate name and k its arity, t, t' are names of theory term definitions, each $\diamond_i$ is a theory operator for $m \geq 1$, and $o \in$ {`head`, `body`, `any`, `directive`} determines where theory atoms may occur in a rule. Examples of theory atom definitions are given in lines 11–14 of Listing 1.6. The language of a theory atom definition as above contains all *theory atoms* of form

[10] For simplicity, we consider normalized difference constraints rather than general ones of form $x_1 - x_2 \circ k$.

```
1  #theory lc {

3    constant    { - : 0, unary };
4    diff_term   { - : 0, binary, left };
5    linear_term { + : 2, unary; - : 2, unary;
6                  * : 1, binary, left;
7                  + : 0, binary, left; - : 0, binary, left };
8    domain_term { .. : 1, binary, left };
9    show_term   { / : 1, binary, left };

11   &dom/0 : domain_term, {=}, linear_term, any;
12   &sum/0 : linear_term, {<=,=,>=,<,>,!=}, linear_term, any;
13   &diff/0 : diff_term, {<=}, constant, any;
14   &show/0 : show_term, directive
15 }.

17 #const n=2.  #const m=1000.

19 task(1..n).
20 duration(T,200*T) :- task(T).

22 &dom  { 1..m } = start(T) :- task(T).
23 &dom  { 1..m } = end(T)   :- task(T).
24 &diff { end(T)-start(T) } <= D :- duration(T,D).
25 &sum  { end(T) : task(T); -start(T) : task(T) } <= m.

27 &show { start/1; end/1 }.
```

Listing 1.6. Logic program enhanced with difference and linear constraints (`lc.lp`)

$$\&a \ \{C_1 : L_1; \ldots; C_n : L_n\} \quad \text{or} \quad \&a \ \{C_1 : L_1; \ldots; C_n : L_n\} \ \diamond \ c$$

where a is an atom over predicate p of arity k, each C_i is a tuple of theory terms in the language for t, c is a theory term in the language for t', $\diamond$ is a theory operator among $\{\diamond_1, \ldots, \diamond_m\}$, and each L_i is a regular condition (i.e., a tuple of regular literals) for $1 \leq i \leq n$. Whether the last part '$\diamond\, c$' is included depends on the form of a theory atom definition. Further, observe that theory atoms with occurrence type `any` can be used both in the head and body of a rule; with occurrence types `head` and `body`, their usage can be restricted to rule heads and bodies only. Occurrence type `directive` is similar to type `head` but additionally requires that the rule body must be completely evaluated during grounding. Five occurrences of theory atoms can be found in lines 22–27 of Listing 1.6.

A *theory term definition* has form

$$t \ \{D_1; \ldots; D_n\}$$

where t is a name for the defined terms and each D_i is a theory operator definition for $1 \leq i \leq n$. A respective definition specifies the language of all theory terms that can be constructed via its operators. Examples of theory term definitions are given in lines 3–9 of Listing 1.6. Each resulting *theory term* is one of the following:

- a constant term: c
- a variable term: v
- a binary theory term: $t_1 \diamond t_2$
- a unary theory term: $\diamond t_1$
- a function theory term: $f(t_1, \ldots, t_k)$
- a tuple theory term: $(t_1, \ldots, t_l,)$
- a set theory term: $\{t_1, \ldots, t_l\}$
- a list theory term: $[t_1, \ldots, t_l]$

where each t_i is a theory term, $\diamond$ is a theory operator defined by some D_i, c and f are symbolic constants, v is a first-order variable, $k \geq 1$, and $l \geq 0$. (The trailing comma in tuple theory terms is optional if $l \neq 1$.) Parentheses can be used to specify operator precedence.

A *theory operator definition* has form

$\diamond$: p,unary or $\diamond$: p,binary,a

where $\diamond$ is a unary or binary theory operator with precedence $p \geq 0$ (determining implicit parentheses). Binary theory operators are additionally characterized by an associativity $a \in$ {right, left}. As an example, consider lines 5–6 of Listing 1.6, where the left associative binary operators + and * are defined with precedence 2 and 1. Hence, parentheses in terms like '(X+(2*Y))+Z' can be omitted. In total, lines 3–9 of Listing 1.6 include nine theory operator definitions. Specific *theory operators* can be assembled (written consecutively without spaces) from the symbols '!', '<', '=', '>', '+', '-', '*', '/', '\', '?', '&', '|', '.', ':', ';', '~', and '^'. For instance, in line 8 of Listing 1.6, the operator '..' is defined as the concatenation of two periods. The tokens '.', ':', ';', and ':-' must be combined with other symbols due to their dedicated usage. Instead, one may write '..', '::', ';;', '::-', etc.

While theory terms are formed similar to regular ones, theory atoms rely upon an aggregate-like construction for forming variable-length theory expressions. In this way, standard grounding techniques can be used for gathering theory terms. (However, the actual atom &a within a theory atom comprises regular terms only.) The treatment of theory terms still differs from their regular counterparts in that the grounder skips simplifications like, e.g., arithmetic evaluation. This can be nicely seen on the different results in Listing 1.7 of grounding terms formed with the regular and theory-specific variants of operator '..'. Observe that the fact task(1..n) in line 19 of Listing 1.6 results in n ground facts, viz. task(1) and task(2) because of n=2. Unlike this, the theory expression 1..m stays structurally intact and is only transformed into 1..1000 in view of m=1000. That is, the grounder does not evaluate the theory term 1..1000 and leaves its interpretation to a downstream theory solver. A similar situation is encountered when comparing the treatment of the regular term '200*T' in line 20 of Listing 1.6 to the theory term 'end(T)-start(T)' in line 24. While each instance of '200*T' is evaluated during grounding, instances of the theory term 'end(T)-start(T)' are left intact in lines 11 and 12 of Listing 1.7. In fact, if '200*T' had been a theory term as well, it would have resulted in the unevaluated instances '200*1' and '200*2'.

4.2 Semantic Underpinnings

Given the hands-on nature of this tutorial, we only give an informal idea of the semantic principles underlying theory solving in ASP.

```
1  task(1).
2  task(2).
3  duration(1,200).
4  duration(2,400).

6  &dom { 1..1000 } = start(1).
7  &dom { 1..1000 } = start(2).
8  &dom {1..1000 } = end(1).
9  &dom { 1..1000 } = end(2).

11 &diff { end(1)-start(1) } <= 200.
12 &diff { end(2)-start(2) } <= 400.

14 &sum { end(1); end(2); -start(1); -start(2) } <= 1000.

16 &show { start/1; end/1 }.
```

Listing 1.7. Human-readable result of grounding Listing 1.6 via '`gringo -text lc.lp`'

As mentioned in Sect. 2, a logic program induces a set of stable models. To extend this concept to logic programs with theory expressions, we follow the approach of lazy theory solving [5]. We abstract from the specific semantics of a theory by considering the theory atoms representing the underlying theory constraints. The idea is that a regular stable model of a program over regular and theory atoms is only valid with respect to a theory, if the constraints induced by the truth assignment to the theory atoms are satisfiable in the theory.

In the above example, this amounts to finding a numeric assignment to all theory variables satisfying all difference and linear constraints associated with theory atoms. The ground program in 1.7 has a single stable model consisting of all regular and theory atoms in lines 1–16. Here, we easily find assignments satisfying the induced constraints, e.g. `start(1)` $\mapsto$ 1, `end(1)` $\mapsto$ 2, `start(2)` $\mapsto$ 2, and `end(1)` $\mapsto$ 3.

In fact, there are alternative semantic options for capturing theory atoms, as detailed in [18]. First of all, we may distinguish whether imposed constraints are only determined outside or additionally inside a logic program. This leads to the distinction between *defined* and *external* theory atoms.[11] While external theory atoms must only be satisfied by the respective theory, defined ones must additionally be derivable through rules in the program. The second distinction concerns the interplay of ASP with theories. More precisely, it is about the logical correspondence between theory atoms and theory constraints. This leads us to the distinction between *strict* and *non-strict* theory atoms. The strict correspondence requires a constraint to be satisfied *iff* the associated theory atom is true. A weaker since only implicative condition is imposed in the non-strict case. Here, a constraint must hold *only if* the associated theory atom is true. In other

[11] This distinction is analogous to that between head and input atoms, defined via rules or `#external` directives [20], respectively.

words, only non-strict theory atoms assigned true impose requirements, while constraints associated with falsified non-strict theory atoms are free to hold or not. However, by contraposition, a violated constraint leads to a false non-strict theory atom.

4.3 Algorithmic Aspects

The algorithmic approach to ASP solving modulo theories of *clingo*, or more precisely that of its underlying ASP solver *clasp*, follows the lazy approach to solving in Satisfiability Modulo Theories (SMT [5]). We give below an abstract overview that serves as light algorithmic underpinning for the description of *clingo*'s implementation given in the next section.

As detailed in [22], a ground program P induces *completion* and *loop nogoods*, called Δ_P or Λ_P, respectively, that can be used for computing stable models of P. Nogoods represent invalid partial assignments and can be thought of as negative Boolean constraints. We represent (partial) assignments as consistent sets of literals. An assignment is total if it contains either the positive or negative literal of each atom. We say that a nogood is violated by an assignment if the former is contained in the latter; a nogood is unit if all but one of its literals are in the assignment. Each total assignment not violating any nogood in $\Delta_P \cup \Lambda_P$ yields a regular stable model of P, and such an assignment is called a solution (for $\Delta_P \cup \Lambda_P$). To accommodate theories, we identify a theory T with a set Δ_T of *theory nogoods*,[12] and extend the concept of a solution in the straightforward way.

The nogoods in $\Delta_P \cup \Lambda_P \cup \Delta_T$ provide the logical fundament for the Conflict-Driven Constraint Learning (CDCL) procedure (cf. [22,32]) outlined in Fig. 2. While the completion nogoods in Δ_P are usually made explicit and subject to unit propagation,[13] the loop nogoods in Λ_P as well as theory nogoods in Δ_T are typically handled by dedicated propagators and particular members are selectively recorded.

While a dedicated propagator for loop nogoods is built-in in systems like *clingo*, those for theories are provided via the interface **Propagator** in Fig. 3. To utilize custom propagators, the algorithm in Fig. 2 includes an *initialization* step in line (I). In addition to the "registration" of a propagator for a theory as an extension of the basic CDCL procedure, common tasks performed in this step include setting up internal data structures and so-called watches for (a subset of) the theory atoms, so that the propagator will be invoked (only) when some watched literal gets assigned.

As usual, the main CDCL loop starts with unit propagation on completion and loop nogoods, the latter handled by the respective built-in propagator, as well as any nogoods already recorded. If this results in a non-total assignment without conflict, theory propagators for which some of their watched literals

[12] See [18] for different ways of associating theories with nogoods.

[13] Unit propagation extends an assignment with literals complementary to the ones missing in unit nogoods.

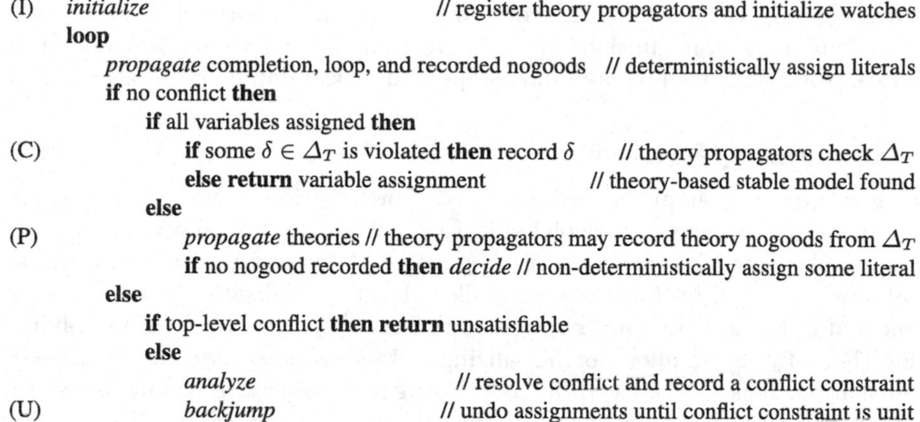

(I) initialize // register theory propagators and initialize watches
loop
propagate completion, loop, and recorded nogoods // deterministically assign literals
if no conflict then
if all variables assigned then
(C) if some $\delta \in \Delta_T$ is violated then record δ // theory propagators check Δ_T
else return variable assignment // theory-based stable model found
else
(P) propagate theories // theory propagators may record theory nogoods from Δ_T
if no nogood recorded then decide // non-deterministically assign some literal
else
if top-level conflict then return unsatisfiable
else
analyze // resolve conflict and record a conflict constraint
(U) backjump // undo assignments until conflict constraint is unit

Fig. 2. Basic algorithm for Conflict-Driven Constraint Learning (CDCL) modulo theories

have been assigned are invoked in line (P). A propagator for a theory T can then inspect the current assignment, update its data structures accordingly, and most importantly, perform *theory propagation* determining theory nogoods $\delta \in \Delta_T$ to record. Usually, any such nogood δ is unit in order to trigger a conflict or unit propagation, although this is not a necessary condition. The interplay of unit and theory propagation continues until a conflict or total assignment arises, or no (further) watched literals of theory propagators get assigned by unit propagation. In the latter case, some non-deterministic decision is made to extend the partial assignment at hand and then to proceed with unit and theory propagation.

If no conflict arises and an assignment is total, in line (C), theory propagators are called, one by one, for a final *check*. The idea is that, e.g., a "lazy" propagator for a theory T that does not exhaustively test violations of its theory nogoods by partial assignments can make sure that the assignment is indeed a solution for Δ_T, or record some violated nogood(s) from Δ_T otherwise. Even in case theory propagation on partial assignments is exhaustive and a final check is not needed to detect conflicts, the information that search led to a total assignment can be useful in practice, e.g., to store values for integer variables like `start(1)`, `start(2)`, `end(1)`, and `end(2)` in Listing 1.7 that witness the existence of a solution for T.

Finally, in case of a conflict, i.e., some completion or recorded nogood is violated by the current assignment, provided that some non-deterministic decision is involved in the conflict, a new conflict constraint is recorded and utilized to guide backjumping in line (U), as usual with CDCL. In a similar fashion as the assignment of watched literals serves as trigger for theory propagation, theory propagators are informed when they become unassigned upon backjumping. This allows the propagators to *undo* earlier operations, e.g., internal data structures can be reset to return to a state taken prior to the assignment of watches.

In summary, the basic CDCL procedure is extended in four places to account for custom propagators: initialization, propagation of (partial) assignments, final check of total assignments, and undo steps upon backjumping.

4.4 Propagator Interface

We now turn to the implementation of theory propagation in *clingo* 5 and detail the structure of its interface depicted in Fig. 3. The interface `Propagator` has to be implemented by each custom propagator. After registering such a propagator with *clingo*, its functions are called during initialization and search as indicated in Fig. 2. Function `Propagator.init`[14] is called once before solving (line (I) in Fig. 2) to allow for initializing data structures used during theory propagation. It is invoked with a `PropagateInit` object providing access to symbolic (`SymbolicAtom`) as well as theory (`TheoryAtom`) atoms. Both kinds of atoms are associated with program literals,[15] which are in turn associated with solver literals.[16] Program as well as solver literals are identified by non-zero integers, where positive and negative numbers represent positive or negative literals, respectively. In order to get notified about assignment changes, a propagator can set up watches on solver literals during initialization.

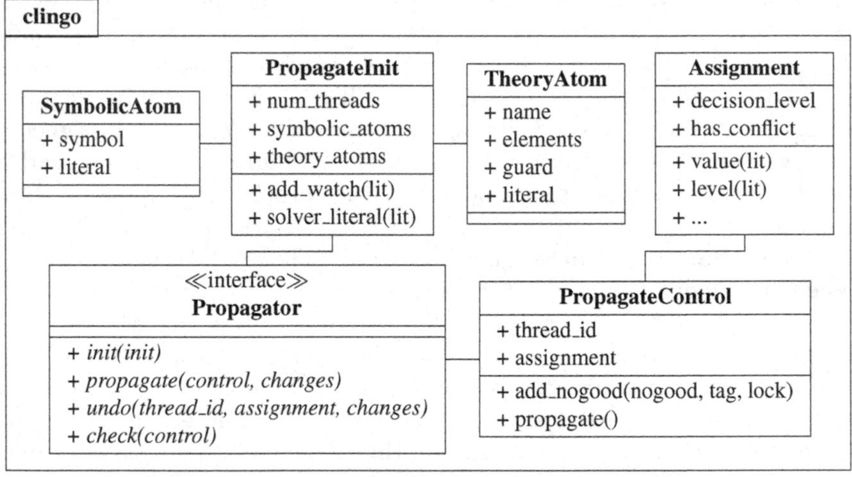

Fig. 3. Class diagram of *clingo*'s (theory) propagator interface

During search, function `propagate` is called with a `PropagateControl` object and a (non-empty) list of watched literals that got assigned in the recent

---

[14] For brevity, we below drop the qualification `Propagator` and use its function names unqualified.

[15] Program literals are also used in the *aspif* format (see Appendix A).

[16] Note that *clasp*'s preprocessor might associate a positive or even negative solver literal with multiple atoms.

round of unit propagation (line (P) in Fig. 2). The `PropagateControl` object can be used to inspect the current assignment, record nogoods, and trigger unit propagation. Furthermore, to support multi-threaded solving, its `thread_id` property identifies the currently active thread, each of which can be viewed as an independent instance of the CDCL algorithm in Fig. 2.[17] Function `undo` is the counterpart of `propagate` and called whenever the solver retracts assignments to watched literals (line (U) in Fig. 2). In addition to the list of watched literals that have been retracted (in chronological order), it receives the identifier and the assignment of the active thread. Finally, function `check` is similar to `propagate`, yet invoked without a list of changes. Instead, it is (only) called on total assignments (line (C) in Fig. 2), independently of watches. Overriding the empty default implementations of propagator methods is optional. For brevity, we below focus on implementations of the methods in Python, while C, C++, or Lua could be used as well.

5 A Case-Study on ASP Modulo Difference Logic

In this section, we develop a propagator to extend ASP with *quantifier free integer difference logic* (*IDL*). The complete source code of this propagator is available in the github repository at https://github.com/potassco/clingo/tree/master/examples/clingo/dl.

In addition to the rules introduced in Sect. 2, we now also support rules of form

$$\texttt{\&diff\{}u\texttt{-}v\texttt{\} <= } d \texttt{ :- } a_1\texttt{,...,}a_n\texttt{,not } a_{n+1}\texttt{,...,not } a_o$$

where u and v are (regular) terms, d is an integer constant, each a_i is an atom, and $0 \leq n \leq o$. For simplicity, we restrict the occurrence of theory atoms to rule heads.[18] Hence, stable models may now also include theory atoms of form '`&diff`$\{u - v\}$ <= d'. More precisely, for a stable model X, let C_X be the set of *difference constraints* such as $u - v \leq d$ associated with theory atoms '`&diff`$\{u{-}v\}$ <= d' in X and V_X be the set of all (integer) variables occurring in the difference constraints in C_X. In our case, a stable model X is then *IDL-stable*, if there is a mapping from V_X to the set of integers satisfying all constraints in C_X.

To allow for writing difference constraints in rule heads, we define theory `dl` in lines 1–5 in Listing 1.8, a subset of the theory `lc` presented in Listing 1.6 in Sect. 4.1. The following lines 16–20 implement a customized main function. The difference to *clingo*'s regular main function is that a propagator for difference constraints is registered at the beginning; grounding and solving then follow as usual. Note that the solve function in line 20 takes a model callback as argument.

[17] Depending on the configuration of *clasp*, threads can communicate with each other. For example, some of the recorded nogoods can be shared. This is transparent from the perspective of theory propagators.

[18] More general settings are discussed in [26] and made available at https://potassco.org/clingo.

```
#theory dl {
    constant  { - : 1, unary };
    diff_term { - : 1, binary, left };
    &diff/0 : diff_term, {<=}, constant, head
}.

#script (python)

import clingo, dl

def print_assignment(p, m):
    a = p.get_assignment(m.thread_id)
    print "Valid assignment for constraints found:"
    print "".join(["{}={}".format(n, v) for n, v in a])

def main(prg):
    p = dl.Propagator()
    prg.register_propagator(p)
    prg.ground([("base", [])])
    prg.solve(on_model = lambda m: print_assignment(p, m))

#end.
```

Listing 1.8. Theory language and main loop for difference constraints (dl.lp)

Whenever an *IDL*-stable model X is found, this callback prints the mapping satisfying the corresponding difference constraints C_X. The model X (excluding theory atoms) is printed as part of *clingo*'s default output.

Our exemplary propagator implements the algorithm presented in [10]. The idea is that deciding whether a set of difference constraints is satisfiable can be mapped to a graph problem. Given a set of difference constraints, let (V, E) be the weighted directed graph where V is the set of variables occurring in the constraints, and E the set of edges (u, v, d) for each constraint $u - v \leq d$. The set of difference constraints is satisfiable if the corresponding graph does not contain a negative cycle. The `Graph` class whose interface is given in Fig. 4 is

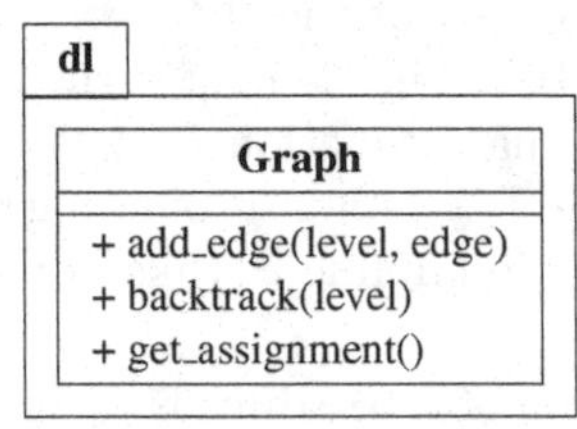

Fig. 4. Class diagram for the graph class

in charge of cycle detection. We refrain from giving the code of the `Graph` class and rather concentrate on describing its interface:

- Function `add_edge` adds an edge of form `(u,v,d)` to the graph. If after adding the edge to the graph there is a negative cycle, the function returns the cycle in form of a list of edges; otherwise, it returns `None`. Furthermore, each edge added to the graph is associated with a decision level[19]. This additional information is used to backtrack to a previous state of the graph, whenever the solver has to backtrack to recover from a conflict.
- Function `backtrack` takes a decision level as argument. It removes all edges added on that level from the graph. For this to work, decision levels have to be backtracked in chronological order. Note that the CDCL algorithm in Fig. 2 calling our propagator also backtracks decision levels in chronological order.
- As a side effect, the `Graph` class internally maintains an assignment of integers to nodes. This assignment can be turned into an assignment to the variables such that the difference constraints corresponding to the edges of the graph are satisfied. Function `get_assignment` returns this assignment in form of a list of pairs of variables and integers.

We give our exemplary propagator for difference constraints in Listing 1.9. It implements the `Propagator` interface (except for `check`) in Fig. 3 in lines 105–133, while featuring aspects like incremental propagation and backtracking, solving with multiple threads, and multi-shot solving. Whenever the set of edges associated with the current partial assignment of a solver induces a negative cycle and, hence, the corresponding difference constraints are unsatisfiable, it adds a nogood forbidding the negative cycle. To this end, it maintains data structures for, given newly added edges, detecting whether there is a conflict. More precisely, the propagator has three data members:

1. The `self.__l2e` dictionary in line 101 maps solver literals for difference constraint theory atoms to their corresponding edges[20],
2. the `self.__e2l` dictionary in line 102 maps edges back to solver literals,[21]
3. and the `self.__state` list in line 103 stores for each solver thread its current graph with the edges assigned so far.

Function `init` in lines 105–119 sets up watches as well as the dictionaries in `self.__l2e` and `self.__e2l`. To this end, it traverses the theory atoms over `diff/0` in lines 106–119. Note that the loop simply ignores all other theory

[19] The assignment maintains the decision level; it is incremented for each decision made and decremented for each decision undone while backjumping; initially, the decision level is zero.

[20] A solver literal might be associated with multiple edges (see Footnote 16).

[21] In one solving step, the *clingo* API guarantees that a (grounded) theory atom is associated with exactly one solver literal. Theory grounded in later solving steps can be associated with fresh solver literals though.

```
class Propagator:
    def __init__(self):
        self.__l2e = {}    # {literal: [(node, node, weight)]}
        self.__e2l = {}    # {(node, node, weight): [literal]}
        self.__states = [] # [Graph]

    def init(self, init):
        for atom in init.theory_atoms:
            term = atom.term
            if term.name == "diff" and len(term.arguments) == 0:
                if len(atom.guard[1].arguments) > 0:
                    weight = -atom.guard[1].arguments[0].number
                else:
                    weight = atom.guard[1].number
                u = str(atom.elements[0].terms[0].arguments[0])
                v = str(atom.elements[0].terms[0].arguments[1])
                edge = (u, v, weight)
                lit = init.solver_literal(atom.literal)
                self.__l2e.setdefault(lit, []).append(edge)
                self.__e2l.setdefault(edge, []).append(lit)
                init.add_watch(lit)

    def propagate(self, control, changes):
        state = self.__state(control.thread_id)
        level = control.assignment.decision_level
        for lit in changes:
            for edge in self.__l2e[lit]:
                cycle = state.add_edge(level, edge)
                if cycle is not None:
                    c = [self.__literal(control, e) for e in cycle]
                    control.add_nogood(c) and control.propagate()
                    return

    def undo(self, thread_id, assign, changes):
        self.__state(thread_id).backtrack(assign.decision_level)

    def get_assignment(self, thread_id):
        return self.__state(thread_id).get_assignment()

    def __state(self, thread_id):
        while len(self.__states) <= thread_id:
            self.__states.append(Graph())
        return self.__states[thread_id]

    def __literal(self, control, edge):
        for lit in self.__e2l[edge]:
            if control.assignment.is_true(lit):
                return lit
```

Listing 1.9. Propagator for difference constraints (dl.py) atoms making it possible to also add propagators for other theories. In lines 109–115 we extract the edge from the theory atom.[22] Each such atom is associated with a solver literal, obtained in line 116. The mappings between solver literals and corresponding edges are then stored in the `self.__l2e` and `self.__e2l` dictionaries in lines 117 and 118.[23] In the last line of the loop, a watch is added for each solver literal at hand, so that the solver calls `propagate` whenever the edge has to be added to the graph.

Function `propagate`, given in lines 121–130, accesses `control.thread_id` in line 122 to obtain the graph associated with the active thread. The loops in lines 124–130 then iterate over the list of changes and associated edges. In line 126 each such edge is added to the graph. If adding the edge produced a negative cycle, a nogood is added in line 129. Because an edge can be associated with multiple solver literals, we use function `__literal`_literal retrieving the first solver literal associated with an edge that is true, to construct the nogood forbidding the cycle. Given that the solver has to resolve the conflict and backjump, the call to `add_nogood` always yields false, so that propagation is stopped without processing the remaining changes any further.[24]

Given that each edge added to the graph in line 126 is associated with the current decision level, the implementation of function `undo` is quite simple. It calls function `backtrack` on the solver's graph to remove all edges added on the current decision level.

task	duration on machine
a	
b	
c	

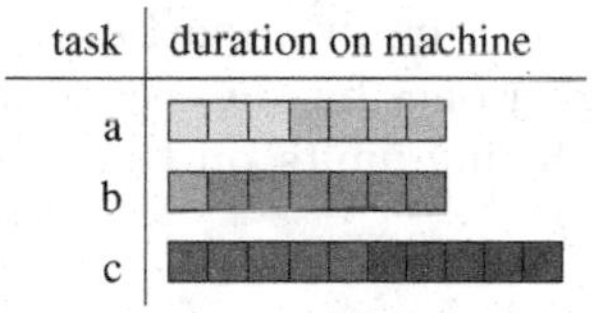

Fig. 5. Flow shop: instance with three tasks and two machines

To see our propagator in action, we consider the flow shop problem, dealing with a set of tasks T that have to be consecutively executed on m machines. Each task has to be processed on each machine from 1 to m. Different parts of one task are completed on each machine resulting in the completion of the task after execution on all machines is finished. Before a task can be processed on machine i, it has to be finished on machine $i-1$. The duration of different tasks

[22] Here we assume that the user supplied a valid theory atom. A propagator for production should check validity and provide proper error messages.

[23] Python's `setdefault` function is used to update the mappings. Depending on whether the given key already appears in the dictionary, the function either retrieves the associated value or inserts and returns the second argument.

[24] The optional arguments `tag` and `lock` of `add_nogood` can be used to control the scope and lifetime of recorded nogoods. Furthermore, if a propagator adds nogoods that are not necessarily violated, function `control.propagate` can be invoked to trigger unit propagation.

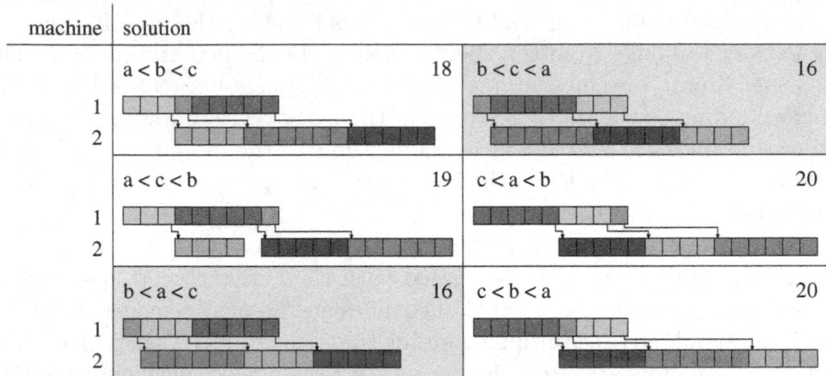

Fig. 6. Flow shop: solutions for all possible permutations with the total execution length in the top right corner and optimal solutions with a blue background (Color figure online)

on the same machine may vary. A task can only be executed on one machine at a time and a machine must not be occupied by more than one task at a time. An (optimal) solution to the problem is a permutation of tasks so that all tasks are finished as early as possible.

Figure 5 depicts a possible instance for the flow shop problem. The three tasks `a`, `b`, and `c` have to be scheduled on two machines. The colored boxes indicate how long a task has to run on a machine. Lighter shades of the same color are for the first and darker ones for the second machine. For example, task `a` needs to be processed for 3 time units on the first and 4 time units on the second machine.

```
                machine(1).         machine(2).
task(a). duration(a,1,3). duration(a,2,4).
task(b). duration(b,1,1). duration(b,2,6).
task(c). duration(c,1,5). duration(c,2,5).
```

Listing 1.10. Flow shop instance (fsI.lp)

Next we encode this problem using difference constraints. We give in Listing 1.10a straightforward encoding of the instance in Fig. 5. Listing 1.11 depicts the encoding of the flow shop problem. Following the generate, define, and test methodology of ASP, we first generate in lines 1–14 all possible permutations of tasks, where atoms of form `permutation(T,U)` encode that task T has to be executed before task U. Then, in the following lines 16–21, we use difference constraints to calculate the duration of the generated permutation. The difference constraint in line 20 guarantees that the tasks are executed in the right order. For example, `(a,1)` $-$ `(a,2)` $\leq -d$ ensures that task `a` can only be executed on machine 2 if it has finished on machine `1`. Hence, variable `(a,2)` has to be assigned so that it is greater or equal to `(a,2)` $- d$ where d is the duration of

```
1  % select a cycle
2  1 { cycle(T,U) : task(U), U != T } 1 :- task(T).
3  1 { cycle(T,U) : task(T), U != T } 1 :- task(U).

5  % make sure the cycle is connected
6  reach(M) :- M = #min { T : task(T) }.
7  reach(U) :- reach(T), cycle(T,U).
8  :- task(T), not reach(T).

10 % select a start point
11 1 { start(T) : task(T) } 1.

13 % obtain an order
14 permutation(T,U) :- cycle(T,U), not start(U).

16 % place tasks sequentially on machines
17 seq((T,M),(T,M+1),D) :- task(T), duration(T,M,D), machine(M+1).
18 seq((T1,M),(T2,M),D) :- permutation(T1,T2), duration(T1,M,D).

20 &diff { T1-T2 } <= -D :- seq(T1,T2,D).
21 &diff { 0-(T,M) } <= 0 :- duration(T,M,D).

24 #show permutation/2.
```

Listing 1.11. Encoding of flow shop using difference constraints (fsE.lp)

task a on machine 1. Similarly, (a,1) − (b,1) $\leq -d$ makes sure that task b can only be executed on machine 1 if task a has finished on machine 1. While the first constraint is a fact (see line 17), the latter is subject to the generated permutation of tasks (see line 18). The difference constraint in line 21 ensures that all time points at which a task is started are greater than zero. Note that this constraint is in principle redundant but since sets of difference constraints always have infinitely many solutions it is good practice to encode relative to a starting point. Furthermore, note that 0 is actually a variable. In fact, the Graph class takes care of subtracting the value of variable 0 from all other variables when returning an assignment to get easier interpretable solutions.

Running encoding and instance with the dl propagator results in the following 6 solutions corresponding to the solutions in Fig. 6.[25] One for each possible permutation of tasks:

```
$ clingo dl.lp fsE.lp fsI.lp 0
clingo version 5.2.0
Reading from dl.lp ...
Solving...
Answer: 1
permutation(b,a) permutation(c,b)
Valid assignment for constraints found:
(b,2)=10 (a,2)=16 (c,1)=0 (a,1)=6 (c,2)=5 (b,1)=5
```

[25] Note that in each solution all tasks are executed as early as possible. This is no coincidence and actually guaranteed by the algorithm implemented in the Graph class.

```
Answer: 2
permutation(c,b) permutation(a,c)
Valid assignment for constraints found:
(b,2)=13 (a,2)=3 (c,1)=3 (a,1)=0 (c,2)=8 (b,1)=8
Answer: 3
permutation(b,a) permutation(a,c)
Valid assignment for constraints found:
 (b,2)=1 (a,2)=7 (c,1)=4 (a,1)=1 (c,2)=11 (b,1)=0
Answer: 4
permutation(c,a) permutation(a,b)
Valid assignment for constraints found:
(b,2)=14 (a,2)=10 (c,1)=0 (a,1)=5 (c,2)=5 (b,1)=8
Answer: 5
permutation(b,c) permutation(c,a)
Valid assignment for constraints found:
(b,2)=1 (a,2)=12 (c,1)=1 (a,1)=6 (c,2)=7 (b,1)=0
Answer: 6
permutation(b,c) permutation(a,b)
Valid assignment for constraints found:
(b,2)=7 (a,2)=3 (c,1)=4 (a,1)=0 (c,2)=13 (b,1)=3
SATISFIABLE

Models        : 6
Calls         : 1
Time          : 0.032s (Solving: 0.00s [...])
CPU Time      : 0.020s
```

Finally, to find optimal solutions, we combine the algorithms in Listings 1.3 and 1.8 to minimize the total execution time of the tasks. The adapted algorithm is given in Listing 1.12. As with algorithm in 1.8, a propagator is registered before solving. And the control flow is similar to the branch-and-bound-based optimization algorithm in Listing 1.3 except that we now minimize the variable bound; or better the difference between variable 0 and bound by adding the difference constraint $0 - \mathtt{bound} \leq b$ to the program in line 9 where b is the best known execution time of the tasks as obtained from the assignment in line 23 minus 1. To bound maximum execution time of the task, we have to add one more line to the encoding in Listing 1.11:

```
    &diff { (T,M)-bound } <= -D :- duration(T,M,D).
```

This makes sure that each task ends within the given bound. Running encoding and instance with the `dl` propagator results in the optimum bound 16 where the obtained solution corresponds to the left of the two optimal solutions indicated by a light blue background in Fig. 6:

```
$ clingo dlO.lp fsE.lp fsI.lp 0
clingo version 5.2.0
Reading from
dlO.lp ...
Solving...
[...]
Solving...
```

```
#theory dl {
    constant {- : 1, unary};
    diff_term {- : 1, binary, left};
    &diff/0 : diff_term, {<=}, constant, any
}.

#program bound(b).

&diff { bound-0 } <= b.

#script (python)

import clingo, dl

def main(prg):
    p = dl.Propagator()
    prg.register_propagator(p)
    prg.ground([("base", [])])
    while True:
        bound = 0
        with prg.solve(yield_=True) as h:
            for m in h:
                a = p.get_assignment(m.thread_id)
                for n, v in a:
                    if n == "bound":
                        bound = v
                        break
                print "Valid␣assignment␣for␣constraints␣found:"
                print "".join(["{}={}".format(n, v) for n, v in a])
                break
            else:
                print "Optimum␣found"
                break
        print "Found␣new␣bound:␣{}".format(bound)
        prg.ground([("bound", [bound-1])])
#end.
```

Listing 1.12. Main loop for difference constraints with optimization (dlO.lp)

```
Answer: 1
permutation(b,a) permutation(a,c)
Valid assignment for constraints
found: (b,2)=1 (a,2)=7 bound=16 (c,1)=4 (a,1)=1 (c,2)=11 (b,1)=0
Found new bound: 16
Solving...
Optimum found
UNSATISFIABLE

Models       : 4
Calls        : 5
Time         : 0.017s (Solving: 0.00s [...])
CPU Time     : 0.010s
```

6 Discussion

We described two essential techniques, viz. multi-shot and theory solving, for enhancing ASP solving by different forms of hybridization. While multi-shot solving allows for fine-grained control of ASP reasoning processes, theory solving allows for refining basic ASP solving by incorporating foreign types of constraints. Since ASP follows a model, ground, and solve methodology both techniques pervade the whole work-flow of ASP, starting with extensions to the input language, over means for incremental and theory-enhanced grounding, to stateful and theory-enhanced solving. Multi-shot solving even adds a fourth dimension to control ASP reasoning processes.

Our focus on *clingo* should not conceal other approaches to hybrid ASP solving. Foremost, *dlvhex* [36] builds upon *clingo*'s infrastructure to provide a higher level of hybridization via higher-order logic programs. As well, *clingcon* [3] and *lc2casp* [8] rely on *clingo* for extending ASP with linear constraints over integers. Similar yet customized approaches include *adsolver* [33], *inca* [13], and *ezcsp* [1]. Another category of ASP systems, such us *ezsmt* [29], *dingo* [27], and *aspmt* [6] translate ASP with constraints to SAT Modulo Theories (SMT [34]) and use appropriate back-ends. Similarly, *mingo* [31] translates to Mixed Integer Linear Programming (MILP) and *aspartame* [2] back to ASP using the order encoding [11,40].

Theory propagators have recently also been added to the ASP solver *wasp* [12]; these can be made accessible via the theory language of Sect. 4.1 along with the intermediate format described in Appendix A.

A Intermediate Language

To accommodate the richer input language, a more general grounder-solver interface is needed. Although this could be left internal to *clingo* 5, it is good practice to explicate such interfaces via an intermediate language. This also allows for using alternative downstream solvers or transformations.

Unlike the block-oriented *smodels* format, the *aspif*[26] format is line-based. Notably, it abolishes the need of using symbol tables in *smodels*' format[27] for passing along meta-expressions and rather allows *gringo*5 to output information as soon as it is grounded. An *aspif* file starts with a header, beginning with the keyword asp along with version information and optional tags:

$$\texttt{asp}\sqcup v_m \sqcup v_n \sqcup v_r \sqcup t_1 \sqcup \dots \sqcup t_k$$

where v_m, v_n, v_r are non-negative integers representing the version in terms of *major*, *minor*, and *revision* numbers, and each t_i is a tag for $k \geq 0$. Currently, the only tag is incremental, meant to set up the underlying solver for multi-shot solving. An example header is given in line 1 of Listings 1.13a and 1.14. The

[26] ASP Intermediate Format.

[27] http://www.tcs.hut.fi/Software/smodels.

rest of the file is comprised of one or more logic programs. Each logic program is a sequence of lines of *aspif* statements followed by a `0`, one statement or `0` per line, respectively. Positive and negative integers are used to represent positive or negative literals, respectively. Hence, `0` is not a valid literal.

Let us now briefly describe the format of *aspif* statements and illustrate them with a simple logic program in Listing 1.13 as well as the result of grounding a subset of Listing 1.6 in Listing 1.14.

```
{a}.
b :- a.
c :- not a.
```

(a) Logic program

```
asp 1 0 0
1 1 1 1 0 0
1 0 1 2 0 1 1
1 0 1 3 0 1 -1
4 1 a 1 1
4 1 b 1 2
4 1 c 1 3
0
```

(b) *aspif* representation label

Listing 1.13. Representing a simple logic program in *aspif* format

Rule statements have form

$$\texttt{1}\text{\textvisiblespace}H\text{\textvisiblespace}B$$

in which head H has form

$$h\text{\textvisiblespace}m\text{\textvisiblespace}a_1\text{\textvisiblespace}\ldots\text{\textvisiblespace}a_m$$

where $h \in \{\texttt{0}, \texttt{1}\}$ determines whether the head is a disjunction or choice, $m \geq 0$ is the number of head elements, and each a_i is a positive literal.

Body B has one of two forms:

- Normal bodies have form

$$\texttt{0}\text{\textvisiblespace}n\text{\textvisiblespace}l_1\text{\textvisiblespace}\ldots\text{\textvisiblespace}l_n$$

  where $n \geq 0$ is the length of the rule body, and each l_i is a literal.
- Weight bodies have form

$$\texttt{1}\text{\textvisiblespace}l\text{\textvisiblespace}n\text{\textvisiblespace}l_1\text{\textvisiblespace}w_1\text{\textvisiblespace}\ldots\text{\textvisiblespace}l_n\text{\textvisiblespace}w_n$$

  where l is a positive integer to denote the lower bound, $n \geq 0$ is the number of literals in the rule body, and each l_i and w_i are a literal and a positive integer.

All types of ASP rules are included in the above rule format. Heads are disjunctions or choices, including the special case of singular disjunctions for representing normal rules. As in the *smodels* format, aggregates are restricted to a singular body, just that in *aspif* cardinality constraints are taken as special weight constraints. Otherwise, a body is simply a conjunction of literals.

The three rules in Listing 1.13a are represented by the statements in lines 2–4 of Listing 1.13b. For instance, the four occurrences of `1` in line 2 capture a rule with a choice in the head, having one element, identified by `1`. The two remaining zeros capture a normal body with no element. For another example, lines 2–7 of Listing 1.14 represent the four facts in lines 1 and 2 of Listing 1.7 along with the ones (comprising theory atoms) in line 6 of Listing 1.7.

Minimize statements have form

$$\mathtt{2}\textvisiblespace p\textvisiblespace n\textvisiblespace l_1\textvisiblespace w_1\textvisiblespace\dots\textvisiblespace l_n\textvisiblespace w_n$$

where p is an integer priority, $n \geq 0$ is the number of weighted literals, each l_i is a literal, and each w_i is an integer weight. Each of the above expressions gathers weighted literals sharing the same priority p from all `#minimize` directives and weak constraints in a logic program. As before, maximize statements are translated into minimize statements.

Projection statements result from `#project` directives and have form

$$\mathtt{3}\textvisiblespace n\textvisiblespace a_1\textvisiblespace\dots\textvisiblespace a_n$$

where $n \geq 0$ is the number of atoms, and each a_i is a positive literal.

Output statements result from `#show` directives and have form

$$\mathtt{4}\textvisiblespace m\textvisiblespace s\textvisiblespace n\textvisiblespace l_1\textvisiblespace\dots\textvisiblespace l_n$$

where $n \geq 0$ is the length of the condition, each l_i is a literal, and $m \geq 0$ is an integer indicating the length in bytes of string s (where s excludes byte '\0' and newline). The output statements in lines 5–7 of Listing 1.13b print the symbolic representation of atom `a`, `b`, or `c`, whenever the corresponding atom is true. For instance, the string '`a`' is printed if atom '`1`' holds. Unlike this, the statements in lines 8–11 of Listing 1.14 unconditionally print the symbolic representation of the atoms stemming from the four facts in lines 1 and 2 of Listing 1.7.

External statements result from `#external` directives and have form

$$\mathtt{5}\textvisiblespace a\textvisiblespace v$$

where a is a positive literal, and $v \in \{0, 1, 2, 3\}$ indicates free, true, false, and release.

Assumption statements have form

$$\mathtt{6}\textvisiblespace n\textvisiblespace l_1\textvisiblespace\dots\textvisiblespace l_n$$

where $n \geq 0$ is the number of literals, and each l_i is a literal. Assumptions instruct a solver to compute stable models such that $l_1, \ldots, l_n$ hold. They are only valid for a single solver call.

Heuristic statements result from `#heuristic` directives and have form

$$7␣m␣a␣k␣p␣n␣l_1␣\ldots␣l_n$$

where $m \in \{0, \ldots, 5\}$ stands for the $(m+1)$th heuristic modifier among `level`, `sign`, `factor`, `init`, `true`, and `false`, a is a positive literal, k is an integer, p is a non-negative integer priority, $n \geq 0$ is the number of literals in the condition, and the literals l_i are the condition under which the heuristic modification should be applied.

Edge statements result from `#edge` directives and have form

$$8␣u␣v␣n␣l_1␣\ldots␣l_n$$

where u and v are integers representing an edge from node u to node v, $n \geq 0$ is the length of the condition, and the literals l_i are the condition for the edge to be present.

Let us now turn to the theory specific part of *aspif*. Once a theory expression is grounded, *gringo* 5 outputs a serial representation of its syntax tree. To illustrate this, we give in Listing 1.14 the (sorted) result of grounding all lines of Listing 1.6 related to difference constraints, viz. lines 2/3, 11, 15/16, and 19, as well as lines 1 and 13.

Theory terms are represented using the following statements:

$$9␣0␣u␣w \tag{1}$$

$$9␣1␣u␣n␣s \tag{2}$$

$$9␣2␣u␣t␣n␣u_1␣\ldots␣u_n \tag{3}$$

where $n \geq 0$ is a length, index u is a non-negative integer, integer w represents a numeric term, string s of length n represents a symbolic term (including functions) or an operator, integer t is either `-1`, `-2`, or `-3` for tuple terms in parentheses, braces, or brackets, respectively, or an index of a symbolic term or operator, and each u_i is an integer for a theory term. Statements (1), (2), and (3) capture numeric terms, symbolic terms, as well as compound terms (tuples, sets, lists, and terms over theory operators).

Fifteen theory terms are given in lines 12–26 of Listing 1.14. Each of them is identified by a unique index in the third spot of each statement. While lines 12–20 stand for primitive entities of type (1) or (2), the ones beginning with represent compound terms. For instance, line 21 and 22 represent `end(1)` or `start(1)`, respectively, and line 23 corresponds to `end(1)-start(1)`.

```
1  asp 1 0 0
```

```
2  1 0 1 1 0 0
3  1 0 1 2 0 0
4  1 0 1 3 0 0
5  1 0 1 4 0 0
6  10 1 5 0 0
7  1 0 1 6 0 0
8  4 7 task(1) 0
9  4 7 task(2) 0
10 4 15 duration(1,200) 0
11 4 15 duration(2,400) 0
12 9 0 1 200
13 9 0 3 400
14 9 0 6 1
15 9 0 11 2
16 9 1 0 4 diff
17 9 1 2 2 <=
18 9 1 4 1 -
19 9 1 5 3 end
20 9 1 8 5 start
21 9 2 7 5 1 6
22 9 2 9 8 1 6
23 9 2 10 4 2 7 9
24 9 2 12 5 1 11
25 9 2 13 8 1 11 9
26 2 14 4 2 12 13
27 9 4 0 1 10 0
28 9 4 1 1 14 0
29 9 6 5 0 1 0 2 1
30 9 6 6 0 1 1 2 3
31 0
```

Listing 1.14. *aspif* format

Theory atoms are represented using the following

$$9\textvisiblespace 4\textvisiblespace v\textvisiblespace n\textvisiblespace u_1\textvisiblespace \dots\textvisiblespace u_n\textvisiblespace m\textvisiblespace l_1\textvisiblespace \dots\textvisiblespace l_m \quad (4)$$

$$9\textvisiblespace 5\textvisiblespace a\textvisiblespace p\textvisiblespace n\textvisiblespace v_1\textvisiblespace \dots\textvisiblespace v_n \quad (5)$$

$$9\textvisiblespace 6\textvisiblespace a\textvisiblespace p\textvisiblespace n\textvisiblespace v_1\textvisiblespace \dots\textvisiblespace v_n\textvisiblespace g\textvisiblespace u_1 \quad (6)$$

where $n \geq 0$ and $m \geq 0$ are lengths, index v is a non-negative integer, a is a positive literal or `0` for directives, each u_i is an integer for a theory term, each l_i is an integer for a literal, integer p refers to a symbolic term, each v_i is an integer for a theory atom element, and integer g refers to a theory operator. Statement (4) captures elements of theory atoms and directives, and statements (5) and (6) refer to the latter.

For instance, line 27 captures the (single) theory element in '{ `end(1)-start(1)` }', and line 29 represents the theory atom '**`&diff`** { `end(1)-start(1)` } `<=200`'.

Comments have form

$$\texttt{10}\sqcup s$$

where s is a string not containing a newline.

The *aspif* format constitutes the default output of *gringo* 5. With *clasp* 3.2, ground logic programs can be read in both *smodels* and *aspif* format.

References

1. Balduccini, M., Lierler, Y.: Constraint answer set solver EZCSP and why integration schemas matter. CoRR, abs/1702.04047 (2017)
2. Banbara, M., Gebser, M., Inoue, K., Ostrowski, M., Peano, A., Schaub, T., Soh, T., Tamura, N., Weise, M.: *aspartame*: solving constraint satisfaction problems with answer set programming. In: Calimeri, F., Ianni, G., Truszczyński, M. (eds.) LPNMR 2015. LNCS (LNAI), vol. 9345, pp. 112–126. Springer, Cham (2015). doi:10.1007/978-3-319-23264-5_10
3. Banbara, M., Kaufmann, B., Ostrowski, M., Schaub, T.: Clingcon: the next generation. Theory and Practice of Logic Programming (2017, To appear)
4. Baral, C.: Knowledge Representation, Reasoning and Declarative Problem Solving. Cambridge University Press, New York (2003)
5. Barrett, C., Sebastiani, R., Seshia, S., Tinelli, C.: Satisfiability modulo theories. In: Biere et al. [7], Chap. 26, pp. 825–885
6. Bartholomew, M., Lee, J.: System ASPMT2SMT: computing ASPMT theories by SMT solvers. In: Fermé, E., Leite, J. (eds.) JELIA 2014. LNCS (LNAI), vol. 8761, pp. 529–542. Springer, Cham (2014). doi:10.1007/978-3-319-11558-0_37
7. Biere, A., Heule, M., van Maaren, H., Walsh, T. (eds.) Handbook of Satisfiability. Frontiers in Artificial Intelligence and Applications, vol. 185. IOS Press (2009)
8. Cabalar, P., Kaminski, R., Ostrowski, M., Schaub, T.: An ASP semantics for default reasoning with constraints. In: Kambhampati, R. (ed.) Proceedings of the Twenty-Fifth International Joint Conference on Artificial Intelligence (IJCAI 2016), pp. 1015–1021. IJCAI/AAAI Press (2016)
9. Carro, M., King, A. (eds.): Technical Communications of the Thirty-second International Conference on Logic Programming (ICLP 2016). Open Access Series in Informatics (OASIcs), vol. 52 (2016)
10. Cotton, S., Maler, O.: Fast and flexible difference constraint propagation for DPLL(T). In: Biere, A., Gomes, C.P. (eds.) SAT 2006. LNCS, vol. 4121, pp. 170–183. Springer, Heidelberg (2006). doi:10.1007/11814948_19
11. Crawford, J., Baker, A.: Experimental results on the application of satisfiability algorithms to scheduling problems. In: Hayes-Roth, B., Korf, R. (eds.) Proceedings of the Twelfth National Conference on Artificial Intelligence (AAAI 1994), pp. 1092–1097. AAAI Press (1994)
12. Dodaro, C., Ricca, F., Schüler, P.: External propagators in wasp: preliminary report. In: Proceedings of the Twenty-Third International Workshop on Experimental Evaluation of Algorithms for Solving Problems with Combinatorial Explosion (RCRA 2016), vol. 1745, pp. 1–9. CEUR Workshop Proceedings (2016)
13. Drescher, C., Walsh, T.: A translational approach to constraint answer set solving. Theory Pract. Logic Program. **10**(4–6), 465–480 (2010)

14. Eiter, T., Ianni, G., Krennwallner, T.: Answer set programming: a primer. In: Tessaris, S., Franconi, E., Eiter, T., Gutierrez, C., Handschuh, S., Rousset, M.-C., Schmidt, R.A. (eds.) Reasoning Web 2009. LNCS, vol. 5689, pp. 40–110. Springer, Heidelberg (2009). doi:10.1007/978-3-642-03754-2_2
15. Gebser, M., Grote, T., Kaminski, R., Schaub, T.: Reactive answer set programming. In: Delgrande, J.P., Faber, W. (eds.) LPNMR 2011. LNCS (LNAI), vol. 6645, pp. 54–66. Springer, Heidelberg (2011). doi:10.1007/978-3-642-20895-9_7
16. Gebser, M., Kaminski, R., Kaufmann, B., Lindauer, M., Ostrowski, M., Romero, J., Schaub, T., Thiele, S.: Potassco User Guide, 2nd edn. University of Potsdam (2015)
17. Gebser, M., Kaminski, R., Kaufmann, B., Ostrowski, M., Schaub, T., Thiele, S.: Engineering an incremental ASP solver. In: Garcia de la Banda, M., Pontelli, E. (eds.) ICLP 2008. LNCS, vol. 5366, pp. 190–205. Springer, Heidelberg (2008). doi:10.1007/978-3-540-89982-2_23
18. Gebser, M., Kaminski, R., Kaufmann, B., Ostrowski, M., Schaub, T., Wanko, P.: Theory solving made easy with clingo 5. In: Carro and King [9], pp. 2:1–2:15
19. Gebser, M., Kaminski, R., Kaufmann, B., Schaub, T.: Answer Set Solving in Practice, Synthesis Lectures on Artificial Intelligence and Machine Learning. Morgan and Claypool Publishers (2012)
20. Gebser, M., Kaminski, R., Kaufmann, B., Schaub, T.: Clingo = ASP + control: Preliminary report. In: Leuschel, M., Schrijvers, T. (eds.) Technical Communications of the Thirtieth International Conference on Logic Programming (ICLP 2014). Theory and Practice of Logic Programming, arXiv:1405.3694v1, Online Supplement (2014). http://arxiv.org/abs/1405.3694v1
21. Gebser, M., Kaminski, R., Obermeier, P., Schaub, T.: Ricochet robots reloaded: a case-study in multi-shot ASP solving. In: Eiter, T., Strass, H., Truszczyński, M., Woltran, S. (eds.) Advances in Knowledge Representation, Logic Programming, and Abstract Argumentation. LNCS (LNAI), vol. 9060, pp. 17–32. Springer, Cham (2015). doi:10.1007/978-3-319-14726-0_2
22. Gebser, M., Kaufmann, B., Schaub, T.: Conflict-driven answer set solving: from theory to practice. Artif. Intell. **187–188**, 52–89 (2012)
23. Gelfond, M., Kahl, Y.: Knowledge Representation, Reasoning, and the Design of Intelligent Agents: The Answer-Set Programming Approach. Cambridge University Press (2014)
24. Gelfond, M., Lifschitz, V.: The stable model semantics for logic programming. In: Kowalski, R., Bowen, K. (eds.) Proceedings of the Fifth International Conference and Symposium of Logic Programming (ICLP 1988), pp. 1070–1080. MIT Press (1988)
25. Gelfond, M., Lifschitz, V.: Classical negation in logic programs and disjunctive databases. New Gener. Comput. **9**, 365–385 (1991)
26. Janhunen, T., Kaminski, R., Ostrowski, M., Schaub, T., Schellhorn, S., Wanko, P.: Clingo goes linear constraints over reals and integers: A preliminary study (2017, In preparation)
27. Janhunen, T., Liu, G., Niemelä, I.: Tight integration of non-ground answer set programming and satisfiability modulo theories. In: Cabalar, P., Mitchell, D., Pearce, D., Ternovska, E. (eds.) Proceedings of the First Workshop on Grounding and Transformation for Theories with Variables (GTTV 2011), pp. 1–13 (2011)
28. Li, C., Manyà, F.: MaxSAT. In: Biere et al. [7], Chap. 19, pp. 613–631
29. Lierler, Y., Susman, B.: SMT-based constraint answer set solver EZSMT (system description). In: Carro and King [9], pp. 1:1–1:15

30. Lifschitz, V.: Introduction to answer set programming. Unpublished draft (2004)
31. Liu, G., Janhunen, T., Niemelä, I.: Answer set programming via mixed integer programming. In: Brewka, G., Eiter, T., McIlraith, S. (eds.) Proceedings of the Thirteenth International Conference on Principles of Knowledge Representation and Reasoning (KR 2012), pp. 32–42. AAAI Press (2012)
32. Marques-Silva, J., Lynce, I., Malik, S.: Conflict-driven clause learning SAT solvers. In: Biere et al. [7], Chap. 4, pp. 131–153
33. Mellarkod, V., Gelfond, M., Zhang, Y.: Integrating answer set programming and constraint logic programming. Ann. Math. Artif. Intell. **53**(1–4), 251–287 (2008)
34. Nieuwenhuis, R., Oliveras, A., Tinelli, C.: Solving SAT and SAT modulo theories: from an abstract Davis-Putnam-Logemann-Loveland procedure to DPLL(T). J. ACM **53**(6), 937–977 (2006)
35. Oikarinen, E., Janhunen, T.: Modular equivalence for normal logic programs. In: Brewka, G., Coradeschi, S., Perini, A., Traverso, P. (eds.) Proceedings of the Seventeenth European Conference on Artificial Intelligence (ECAI 2006), pp. 412–416. IOS Press (2006)
36. Redl, C.: The dlvhex system for knowledge representation: recent advances (system description). Theory Pract. Logic Program. **16**(5–6), 866–883 (2016)
37. Roussel, O., Manquinho, V.: Pseudo-Boolean and cardinality constraints. In: Biere et al. [7], Chap. 22, pp. 695–733
38. Simons, P., Niemel, I., Soininen, T.: Extending and implementing the stable model semantics. Artif. Intell. **138**(1–2), 181–234 (2002)
39. Syrjänen, T.: Lparse 1.0 user's manual (2001)
40. Tamura, N., Taga, A., Kitagawa, S., Banbara, M.: Compiling finite linear CSP into SAT. Constraints **14**(2), 254–272 (2009)

Answer Set Programming with External Source Access

Thomas Eiter[1(✉)], Tobias Kaminski[1], Christoph Redl[1], Peter Schüller[2], and Antonius Weinzierl[1]

[1] Institut für Informationssysteme, Knowledge Based Systems Group, Technische Universität Wien, Vienna, Austria
{eiter,kaminski,redl,weinzierl}@kr.tuwien.ac.at

[2] Department of Computer Engineering, Faculty of Engineering, Marmara University, Istanbul, Turkey
peter.schuller@marmara.edu.tr

Abstract. Access to external information is an important need for Answer Set Programming (ASP), which is a booming declarative problem solving approach these days. External access not only includes data in different formats, but more general also the results of computations, and possibly in a two-way information exchange. Providing such access is a major challenge, and in particular if it should be supported at a generic level, both regarding the semantics and efficient computation. In this article, we consider problem solving with ASP under external information access using the DLVHEX system. The latter facilitates this access through special external atoms, which are two-way API style interfaces between the rules of the program and an external source. The DLVHEX system has a flexible plugin architecture that allows one to use multiple predefined and user-defined external atoms which can be implemented, e.g., in Python or C++. We consider how to solve problems using the ASP paradigm, and specifically discuss how to use external atoms in this context, illustrated by examples. As a showcase, we demonstrate the development of a HEX program for a concrete real-world problem using Semantic Web technologies, and discuss specifics of the implementation process.

1 Introduction

The rise of the World Wide Web and a growing trend towards computation in distributed systems has increased the need for accessing external information sources in logic programs. More and more also multiple sources must be accessed, which moreover may be of different kind and provide their information in heterogeneous formats. There is a broad range from light-weight data access (e.g., based on XML, RDF, or relational data repositories) to knowledge-intensive access (e.g., OWL resp. description logic knowledge bases), and from

This research has been supported by the Austrian Science Fund (FWF) projects P27730 and W1255-N23, and by the Scientific and Technological Research Council of Turkey (TUBITAK) Grant 114E777.

G. Ianni et al. (Eds.): Reasoning Web 2017, LNCS 10370, pp. 204–275, 2017.
DOI: 10.1007/978-3-319-61033-7_7

access to information sources that merely provide data (as, e.g., in dictionaries or thesauri), to sources providing computation services that are instantaneously executed (as, e.g., route planning to get from A to B) or may return a result at a later stage of a computation.

The variety of source access with its dynamic aspects poses a challenge for proper modelling and efficient evaluation in the context of declarative programming, where desired computation results are semantically described rather than obtained after running through a prescribed sequence of computation commands. This is in particular true for Answer Set Programming (ASP) [73,77,84], which is a declarative problem solving approach in which a problem is described by the rules of a nonmonotonic logic program such that the answer sets [59] (i.e., specific models) of the program correspond to the solutions of the problem. After computing the answer sets using an ASP solver, the solutions can be extracted from them. Due to the availability of increasingly efficient and expressive such solvers (e.g., smodels [96], dlv [70], ASSAT [75], GRINGO plus CLASP [56,57]), and WASP [1], the ASP approach has been successfully used for applications in different areas and disciplines, cf. [14,48]. However, these solvers provide no or only limited support for external information access.[1]

The need for external information access in ASP has been recognized early on and led to theoretical formalisms such as logic programs with generalized quantifiers [38], and later to DLV-EX programs [18] and the more expressive HEX programs [42]. The latter pick up notions in [18,38] and provide a bidirectional interface between a nonmonotonic logic program and other sources, via designated *external atoms*. These atoms abstractly define external predicates whose valuation is determined by external computation. For example, a rule

$$pointsTo(X, Y) \leftarrow \&hasHyperlink[X](Y), url(X)$$

may informally determine pairs (X, Y) of URLs, where X actually links Y on the Web. Here, $\&hasHyperlink$ is an *external predicate* that is associated with an external source; X is the input for the latter and Y is a result returned, which is determined in whatever (computable) way. Notably, the input of external atoms can also comprise predicate names, not only constants; e.g.,

$$pointsTo(X, Y) \leftarrow \&hasAdmissbleHyperlink[X, black\_list](Y), url(X)$$

would be a variant of the previous rule, where $black\_list$ is a predicate that contains URLs which should be excluded from retrieval.

The abstract concept of an external atom has been realized in the open-source software DLVHEX[2] as an API, which provides a suite of external atoms and, by means of a plugin mechanism, allows the user to tailor external atoms for her needs using Python or C++. This makes the system very powerful; depending on the external evaluation cost, HEX programs offer a range of problem solving capacity, from Σ_2^p for polynomial-time external atoms in the ground case to

[1] For more information, see the related work section.
[2] www.kr.tuwien.ac.at/research/systems/dlvhex.

Turing-completeness in general. Moreover, external atoms may return values that do not occur in the program itself (this is known as *value invention*), which by recursion may in principle lead to an infinite domain; this is in analogy to the infinite universes of existential rules or description logic ontologies, which result from skolemization.

The generic nature of external atoms, which are blackboxes in general, combined with possible predicate input and/or value invention poses a big challenge for the development of an efficient solver for HEX programs. In the last years, a number of advanced methods and techniques have been researched which have led to significant improvements [29–31,34,35]. Furthermore, an open software architecture that supports a flexible plugin mechanism and is easy to use also for non-experts poses a further challenge, which has been addressed in parallel [90].

In this paper, we present in a tutorial style fashion the HEX formalism as well as the DLVHEX system, which constitutes the state-of-the-art solver for HEX programs. At this, we take a user-centric view, where we omit many technical details. Particular attention is payed to the use of HEX programs and DLVHEX for interoperability on the Semantic Web – and indeed the original development of HEX programs was driven by this issue, as a generalization of a concrete combination of rules and ontologies, a topic that emerged as necessary in the Semantic Web Layer cake proposed by Tim Berners-Lee and has led to a stream of works and a plethora of different approaches [26,83]. While HEX programs support problem solving at different levels of abstraction, we focus here on the basic end-user level where external atoms can be utilized in different ways in order to enrich the problem solving capacity of ASP.

More specifically, the presentation is structured along the following sections:

- In the next section, we give an introduction to the syntax and semantics of answer set programs and HEX programs. The part on ordinary answer set programs is kept deliberately short and compact, as a number of texts exist that provide an ample introduction to the subject, e.g. [5,13,14,39]; see also Sect. 7 for further pointers. Furthermore, we do not consider the full repertoire of language constructs that is available in ASP, but concentrate on a core part that is sufficient from a conceptual perspective.
- In Sect. 3 then, we turn to the issue of using HEX programs. We provide a basic methodology to this end, which enhances the methodology of ordinary ASP programs with the use of external atoms; different such uses, for information outsourcing and computation outsourcing, respectively, will be discussed following [47], as well as typical kinds of external sources. Furthermore, we will go over example encodings of two quite diverse HEX application scenarios, viz. RDF graph exploration in the Semantic Web and the AngryHEX agent for playing Angry Birds, which has been suggested as a low-cost AI challenge for developing programs that outperform human capabilities.[3]
- In Sect. 4, based on [90] we introduce the DLVHEX system, which is an elaborated software platform for designing and evaluating HEX programs. We will

[3] https://aibirds.org/.

present the system architecture, the Python programming interface for developing external atom implementations, and specific annotations of external source properties that are important for deciding whether a finite portion of the instantiated rules is sufficient for evaluation and moreover, for evaluation efficiency.
- In Sect. 5 we go over a full-fledged case study in the area of semantic route planning, that is route planning under further semantic constraints. The application program will be developed stepwise, where in each step additional aspects are addressed; code examples show the implementation of simple external sources, and access to an ontology in a lightweight Description Logic through an external atom is illustrated.
- In the subsequent Sect. 6, we provide an overview of further HEX applications and HEX extensions. Furthermore, we discuss related work, where in particular we compare DLVHEX to the CLINGO system[4] [56,57], its closest relative.
- We conclude the paper in Sect. 7 with a brief summary and outlook; pointers to further material and resources can be found in the appendix.

2 ASP and HEX Programs

In this section, we formally introduce the syntax and semantics of HEX programs; for more details and background, see e.g. [29,42,43,94].

2.1 ASP

In this section we briefly introduce ASP and its underlying concepts. For a more detailed introduction see [39].

From Procedural Programming to Logic Programming. In computer science, all students are taught programming in procedural programming languages like Java, C/C++, Python, and many others. The basic building blocks of procedural programming differ a lot from logic programming and providing a full introduction is beyond the scope of this article. The following paragraphs, however, may help bridging the gap. A procedural programming language is about the contents of the machines memory, i.e., bits organized in basic data types of bytes, integers, characters, arrays, and potentially structures as well as objects. Procedural programs modify data using instructions that are executed one after another, i.e., instructions like addition, subtraction for basic bit manipulation; if, else, and switch for conditional checks; various loops for repeating instructions, and functions or methods to organize sequences of instructions.

In contrast to that, logic programming is about a statement being either true or false. A statement itself may be structured or not: a statement can be

[4] A tutorial covering hybrid answer set solving with the CLINGO system can also be found in this volume [67].

unstructured like *jaguar_is_an_animal* or structured like *is_bigger_than*(*45*, *42*). A logic program expresses whether a statement is true or false by rules, basically just if-then expressions. In principle, a logic program can only influence whether a statement is true or false, it cannot otherwise modify statements. Data in logic programs is represented by structured statements, called atoms. An atom is composed of a predicate name (e.g., *is_bigger_than*) and a sequence of terms, e.g., (*42*, *45*). Terms can be simple constants, or again be structured using function symbols. For readability, however, we will ignore function symbols in the most of what follows. Terms and atoms originate from formal logic, specifically from first-order logic, the most prominent logic formalism that is widely used in mathematics.

An alternative view on atoms is based on relational data bases (e.g. SQL): every predicate can be considered the name of a table while its terms are the values of attributes in the table. In that view, a true atom $at(t_1, \ldots, t_n)$ is a tuple $(t_1, \ldots, t_n)$ that is in the table *at* while a false atom is simply not in the table. Hence, logic programming may be seen as a (powerful) form of database querying. Formally, statements are expressions in a relational language or first-order language.

Syntax. Statements of the form $relation\_name(t_1, \ldots, t_n)$ where each t_i is a constant or a variable, are formalized as relational languages. A relational language is the set of all statements that can be expressed over a relational signature.

Definition 1 (Relational signature). *A* relational signature *is a tuple* $S = (\mathcal{C}, \mathcal{P}, \mathcal{X})$ *of pair-wise disjoint sets of* constants, predicate symbols, *and* variables, *respectively. We assume that predicate symbols* $p \in \mathcal{P}$ *come with an associated* arity $n \in \mathbb{N}$, *denoted by* $p/n \in \mathcal{P}$.

Intuitively, a constant denotes something the logic program speaks about, i.e., it denotes an entity like the number 43 or *tomatoes*. Predicate symbols are used to denote relations, e.g., the $\leq$ relation or *is_edible*. Variables may denote any element out of a set of possible candidates. Variables may occur in any place where a constant may occur.

Usually constants in $\mathcal{C}$ are denoted with first letter in lower case while variables in $\mathcal{X}$ are denoted with first letter in upper case.

Definition 2 (Terms, Atoms). *Given a relational signature* $S = (\mathcal{C}, \mathcal{P}, \mathcal{X})$, *an element of* $\mathcal{C} \cup \mathcal{X}$ *is called a* term. *Furthermore, if* $p/n \in \mathcal{P}$ *is a* n*-ary predicate symbol and* $t_1, \ldots, t_n$ *are terms, then* $p(t_1, \ldots, t_n)$ *is an* atom. *The set of all atoms is denoted by* $\mathcal{A}_S$.

If the signature S is clear from the context, one also writes simply $\mathcal{A}$ for $\mathcal{A}_S$.

Given the *is_edible* relation and the constant *tomatoes*, one can form the atom *is_edible*(*tomatoes*) to denote that tomatoes are edible. Atoms may contain variables as, e.g., in *is_edible*(X). An atom that contains no variables is called *ground*. Hence, *is_edible*(*tomatoes*) is ground while *is_edible*(X) is not. We likewise say a term is *ground*, if it contains no variable; that is, if it is from $\mathcal{C}$.

Note that *is_edible*(43) also forms an atom, which intuitively is a false statement while *is_edible*(*tomatoes*) intuitively is a true statement. On the other hand, however, a rotten tomato should not be considered edible and we may even think of a fantasy story where a mythical creature is eating numbers. Statements therefore may be true or false depending on their interpretation.

Formally, an interpretation for logic formulas (an ASP program is a set of a certain kind of formulas) interprets all constants of the logic formula with entities or individuals, which are called the universe of discourse. For classical logic, the universe may be any set, e.g. the set of natural numbers, and an interpretation is then free to interpret the constant *tomatoes* with the number 51.[5] Since this kind of freedom is not always intuitive and not needed, logic programs consider interpretations where the universe is from the set of symbols of the relational signature and each symbol is interpreted by itself, i.e., *tomatoes* is interpreted as *tomatoes* and 43 is interpreted as 43.

Definition 3 (Herbrand Universe, Herbrand Base, Interpretation). *Given a relational signature* $S = (\mathcal{C}, \mathcal{P}, \mathcal{X})$, *the* Herbrand universe HU *is the set of all ground terms wrt.* S *and the* Herbrand base HB *is the set of all ground atoms wrt.* S. *An (Herbrand)* interpretation *is any set* $I \subseteq HB$. *Here* $a \in I$ *is read as* a *is true under* I, *and false otherwise.*

In the following, we will assume the relational signature to be given implicitly by the program at hand. Readers knowledgeable in formal logic may observe that the given notion of an interpretation is very simplified compared to the usual notion, yet an interpretation in our terms can be easily extended to a first-order logic interpretation I on the universe HU.

Observe that Herbrand interpretations cannot interpret two different constants by the same entity, they implicitly assume that different constants denote different entities. They follow the so-called unique-name-assumption (UNA).

Logic Programs. Logic programs are comprised of rules. A rule expresses that if something holds, other things have to hold, i.e., a rule is simply an if-then expression. The if-part may contain several conditions, some possibly containing negation, which all have to hold while the then-part may also contain several conditions of which at least one has to hold whenever the if-part holds.

Definition 4 (Rule). *A (disjunctive) rule* r *is of the form*

$$A_1 \vee \ldots \vee A_m \leftarrow L_1 \ldots, L_n, \quad m, n \geq 0 \tag{1}$$

where $A_1, \ldots, A_m$ *are atoms and* $L_1, \ldots, L_n$ *are literals, i.e., an atom or a negated atom, written as* **not** b, *where* b *is an atom. A rule is* ground, *if all atoms occurring in it are ground.*

---

[5] As the elements of $\mathcal{C}$ need to be interpreted they are thus called *constant symbols* in classical logic.

The intuition of a rule is that: *if* L_1 to L_n all hold, *then* one of A_1 to A_m must also hold. Given an interpretation I, an atom a holds if $a \in I$ while a negated atom **not** a holds if $a \notin I$. The atoms occurring left of the $\leftarrow$ are called the head atoms while the literals occurring right of it are the body atoms. Formally, for a rule r of the form (1), the *head* is the set $head(r) = \{A_1, \ldots, A_m\}$ while the *body* is the set $body(r) = \{L_1, \ldots, L_n\}$. Rules then can be read as "if the whole body holds, some element of the head must hold".

A rule r with empty body, i.e., $body(r) = \emptyset$, is called a *fact* and a rule with empty head, i.e., $head(r) = \emptyset$, is called a *constraint*.

Example 1. Consider the following three rules:

$$day \vee night.$$
$$\leftarrow sunshine, raining.$$
$$sunshine \leftarrow day, \mathbf{not}\ raining.$$

The first rule is a fact which expresses that it is day or night. The second rule is a constraint and expresses that it cannot be the case that both the sun shines and it is raining. The third rule is neither a fact nor a constraint, and it expresses that whenever it is day and not raining, then the sun shines. Observe that all rules are ground.

The **not** in rule bodies is called *default negation* in ASP since atomic pieces of information that are not known to be true are presumed to be false by default. In this way, ASP implements reasoning under the *Closed World Assumption* (*CWA*), where complete knowledge about atomic facts is assumed. For instance, in Example 1, the atom *raining* is not stated as a fact and cannot be derived by any of those rules, therefore *raining* is false by default. Subsequently, the body of the last rule is satisfied if *day* is true.

Rules that contain variables have to be *safe*, i.e., all variables that occur in the rule must also occur in some positive literal of the rule. Effectively, this allows an implementation to ensure that the relevant range of variables is finite whenever the set of constants $\mathcal{C}$ is finite.

Example 2. Consider the following rules:

$$r_1: \quad p(X) \leftarrow q(X,Y), at, \mathbf{not}\ r(X).$$
$$r_2: \quad p(X) \leftarrow \mathbf{not}\ t(Z).$$

Rule r_1 is safe because every variable (X and Y) occurring in it occurs in its positive body, specifically, in $q(X,Y)$. Rule r_2 on the other hand is not safe for two reasons: X occurs not in its positive body and neither does Z. Intuitively, it is not clear which value for X should be chosen once the body of r_2 is true. Letting $p(X)$ hold for all possible values of X, i.e., for the whole universe HU, seems far too much. Likewise, for Z in the negative body. If one lets it range over HU, it expresses that the rule fires unless for every $u \in HU$ it holds that $t(u)$ is true. Intuitively, it thus makes sense to exclude rules that are not safe.

From a computational perspective, not-safe rules are also hard to deal with since the universe may be infinite and hence it is impossible to treat each atom individually within finite time.

In the following we consider only safe rules.

Example 3. The following rule expresses that whenever some X is reachable from Y and Y is reachable from Z, then Z is reachable from X.

$$\mathit{reachable}(X, Z) \leftarrow \mathit{reachable}(X, Y), \mathit{reachable}(Y, Z).$$

This rule is not ground as it contains the variables X, Y, and Z. They are variables, because their initial letters are in upper case. Variables occurring in a rule can be seen as implicitly universally quantified, i.e., the if-then statement expressed by the rule has to hold for all X, Y, and Z. Note that the rule is safe, because all variables X, Y, and Z occur in the positive body.

Logic programs are simply sets of rules, formally:

Definition 5 (Logic Program). *A* logic program *is a finite set of rules.*

A program P is ground, if all rules $r \in P$ are ground.

Example 4. The following is a logic program consisting of three rules:

$$\begin{aligned} \mathit{reachable}(X, Y) &\leftarrow \mathit{connection}(X, Y). \\ \mathit{reachable}(X, Z) &\leftarrow \mathit{reachable}(X, Y), \mathit{reachable}(Y, Z). \\ \mathit{not\_reachable}(X, Y) &\leftarrow \mathit{location}(X), \mathit{location}(Y), \mathbf{not}\ \mathit{reachable}(X, Y). \end{aligned}$$

The program can be used to compute all pairs of locations (e.g. in a city) which are not reachable from each other by taking connections in the public transport system alone. For this, facts such as $\mathit{connection}(a, b)$ and $\mathit{location}(a)$ need to be added, representing a concrete problem instance, i.e., a public transport network in a city.

The first rule states that one location is reachable from another one if it is possible to take a direct connection. The second rule computes the transitive closure of the *connection* relation as described in Example 3. In the third rule, default negation is used to obtain all pairs of locations that are not in the transitive closure. Note that for this rule to be safe, the variables X and Y must be bound by the positive atoms $\mathit{location}(X)$ and $\mathit{location}(Y)$. Otherwise, not all variables would occur in a positive body atom. Further note that variables having the same name but occurring in different rules are treated like distinct variables.

Semantics. In order to define the semantics of rules and programs, we first need to define when an interpretation satisfies a rule; this in turn depends on the satisfaction of its components. Based on this, answer sets of a program can be defined as special interpretations that satisfy all rules in a program. We first consider the ground case, which can then be naturally lifted to programs with variables.

Satisfaction for Ground Programs. For ground rules, satisfaction for rules is as in classical logic.

Definition 6 (Satisfaction, Model). *An interpretation I* satisfies

- *a ground atom a, denoted $I \models a$, if $a \in I$,*
- *a negated ground atom* **not** *a, denoted $I \models$* **not** *a if $I \not\models a$,*
- *a conjunction $L_1, \ldots, L_n$ of ground literals, denoted $I \models L, \ldots, L_n$, if for each $i \in \{1, \ldots, n\}$ it holds that $I \models L_i$,*
- *a disjunction $A_1 \vee \ldots \vee A_m$ of ground atoms, denoted $I \models A_1 \vee \ldots \vee A_m$, if there exists $k \in \{1, \ldots, m\}$ with $I \models A_k$, and*
- *a ground rule r, denoted $I \models r$, if $I \models body(r)$ implies that $I \models head(r)$, i.e., if all literals in the body hold at least one atom in the head is true.*

An interpretation I is a model *of a ground program P, if $I \models r$ for each rule $r \in P$. A model I is* minimal *if there is no other model $I' \subset I$.*

Given a rule r and an interpretation I, if the body of r holds under I, i.e., if $I \models body(r)$, then the rule r is said to *fire* under I.

The correct semantics of ground rules containing negation was heavily discussed in the past and multiple approaches have been introduced. For programs without negation, however, there was early consensus that the minimal models are most fitting. It best captures the intuition that a rule's head should only hold, if the body of the rule holds.

Example 5. Consider the following program:

$$P = \{\, b. \quad a \leftarrow b. \quad c \leftarrow d. \,\}$$

The interpretation $I = \{a, b, c\}$ is a model of P, i.e., $I \models P$, because I satisfies each rule of P. Note that $I \models c \leftarrow d$, which may not seem intuitive, because the head of the rule is true although its body is not true. The notion of a model is therefore not sufficient to capture the intuitive meaning of this program. The (unique) minimal model $I' = \{a, b\}$ also satisfies all rules of P and for this program, it is close to our intuitive understanding of a rule, namely that its head atom is only there if the body is satisfied. Note that $a \leftarrow b$ fires under I' while $c \leftarrow d$ does not fire under I'.

Example 6. Consider the program $P = \{a \vee b\}$. Clearly, this program has three models, viz. $I_1 = \{a\}$, $I_2 = \{b\}$ and $I_3 = \{a, b\}$, of which intuitively I_1 and I_2 are preferable to I_3 because that model contains an unnecessary atom; however, by the perfect symmetry between a and b in the program, it is not justified to prefer I_1 over I_2 or vice versa. If we add the rule $b \leftarrow a$, for the resulting program

$$P' = \{a \vee b. \quad b \leftarrow a.\}$$

I_1 is no longer a model; in this case, $\{b\}$ is the only intended model.

Answer Sets. ASP adopts a multiple models approach, i.e., a given program P can have multiple models that are considered to be correct and these models can be disjoint from each other; this may even be the case if the program does not contain disjunctive rules. Intuitively, an answer set is a model of the program that can be (re-)constructed by rule application. Once a rule is applicable and fires, it has to stay applicable throughout the whole construction and also in the final model.

Example 7. Consider a program with negation as follows:

$$P = \{\, a \leftarrow \textbf{not}\, b. \quad b \leftarrow \textbf{not}\, a. \,\}$$

This program has two minimal models, $I = \{a\}$ and $I' = \{b\}$. Under I the first rule fires while the second does not, while under I' it is the other way round. Answer-set semantics now declares both models to be correct, because each captures the intuitive meaning of the rules: in I the atom a is true and b is false, so the first rule does fire, deriving a and the second rule does not fire, hence not deriving b. Intuitively, I can be reconstructed from P by letting the first rule fire to obtain a, ensuring that it will fire later on fixes b to be false, hence the second rule is not applicable and I is successfully reconstructed. Thus I is an answer set. Considering I', the same holds vice versa, i.e., both I and I' capture the meaning of the rules in P.

In order to define answer sets formally, the notion of a reduct is important. Intuitively, the reduct with respect to an interpretation I and a program P is obtained by removing all rules from P which cannot fire under I.

Definition 7 (FLP-Reduct). *Given a program P and an interpretation I, the* FLP-reduct P^I *of P wrt. I is obtained as follows: delete from P all rules r with $I \not\models r$, i.e., $P^I = \{r \in P \mid I \models r\}$.*

Answer sets of a program P are then defined as follows:

Definition 8 (Answer-Set). *An interpretation I is an* answer set *of P if I is a minimal model of P^I.*

Intuitively, an answer set is such an interpretation which is (re-)constructable under the rules that fire in the interpretation. Due to this, answer sets are also called stable models.

Example 8. Consider the following program P containing a fact and two rules using default negation:

$$
\begin{aligned}
&restaurant(osteria).\\
&indoor(osteria) \leftarrow restaurant(osteria), \textbf{not}\ outdoor(osteria).\\
&outdoor(osteria) \leftarrow restaurant(osteria), \textbf{not}\ indoor(osteria).
\end{aligned}
$$

Intuitively, the program states that *osteria* is a *restaurant*, and that it is either an *outdoor* or an *indoor* restaurant. Now, we consider all interpretations that satisfy the rules in P, and start with:

$$I_1 = \{restaurant(osteria), indoor(osteria)\}.$$

Since I_1 does not satisfy the last rule, the corresponding FLP-reduct P^{I_1} is the following:

$$restaurant(osteria).$$
$$indoor(osteria) \leftarrow restaurant(osteria), \mathbf{not}\ outdoor(osteria).$$

As the atom $outdoor(osteria)$ is not contained in I_1, the body of the remaining rule is satisfied under I_1, and $indoor(osteria)$ needs to be true in every model of P^{I_1}. Hence, we can verify that I_1 is a minimal model of P^{I_1}, such that I_1 qualifies as an answer set of P. Analogously, we derive that

$$I_2 = \{restaurant(osteria), outdoor(osteria)\}$$

is an answer set as well. Because $restaurant(osteria)$ must be true in any model of P due to the fact in the program, there is only one remaining interpretation to consider, which is:

$$I_3 = \{restaurant(osteria), indoor(osteria), outdoor(osteria)\}.$$

The FLP-reduct P^{I_3} only contains the fact $restaurant(osteria)$. as none of the two rule bodies in P are satisfied by I_3. Because both $indoor(osteria)$ and $outdoor(osteria)$ could be removed from I_3 while the interpretation would still satisfy P^{I_3}, I_3 is not a minimal model of the FLP-reduct, and thus, not an answer set of P.

Example 9. Next, we consider the following program P, which, in addition to default negation in rule bodies, also employs disjunction in the head of a rule:

$$restaurant(osteria).$$
$$indoor(osteria) \vee outdoor(osteria) \leftarrow restaurant(osteria).$$
$$eat(osteria) \leftarrow indoor(osteria), raining.$$
$$eat(osteria) \leftarrow outdoor(osteria), \mathbf{not}\ raining.$$

Accordingly, P encodes that *osteria* is an *indoor* or an *outdoor restaurant* (now, by using a disjunctive head), and that we *eat* there if it is an *indoor restaurant* and it is *raining*, or if it is an an *outdoor restaurant* and it is not *raining*. Again, we check for different interpretations if they are answer sets by constructing the respective FLP-reducts. First, consider the interpretation

$$I_1 = \{restaurant(osteria), indoor(osteria)\}.$$

In the FLP-reduct P^{I_1}, the last two rules are both removed since *osteria* is not an *outdoor restaurant* and I_1 does not contain the atom *raining*, resulting in the reduct:

$$restaurant(osteria).$$
$$indoor(osteria) \vee outdoor(osteria) \leftarrow restaurant(osteria).$$

It is easy to see that I_1 is indeed an answer set because it is not a model of P^{I_1} anymore if one of the two atoms is removed from the interpretation. When checking the interpretation

$$I_2 = \{restaurant(osteria), outdoor(osteria), eat(osteria)\}$$

we obtain a reduct P^{I_2} that still contains the last rule as *osteria* is now assumed to be an *outdoor restaurant*:

$$restaurant(osteria).$$
$$indoor(osteria) \vee outdoor(osteria) \leftarrow restaurant(osteria).$$
$$eat(osteria) \leftarrow outdoor(osteria), \mathbf{not}\ raining.$$

By checking minimality we find that I_2 is another answer set for P. Finally, consider the following interpretation, which also contains the atom *raining*:

$$I_3 = \{restaurant(osteria), indoor(osteria), raining\}.$$

The corresponding FLP-reduct P^{I_3} is identical to P^{I_1}, but now assumes that it is *raining*, which is not supported by any rule or fact, such that I_3 does not represent an answer set. In fact, there are no further answer sets for P. Note that any interpretation containing both *indoor*(*osteria*) and *outdoor*(*osteria*) cannot be a minimal model of the respective reduct because the head of the first rule is already satisfied when only one of them is true.

Historically, there are several slightly different notions of a reduct (e.g. the seminal GL-reduct [58,59], which removes negative literals from rules), but for ASP programs as introduced above, they are equivalent. In fact, there are many quite diverse definitions of answer set, cf. [74], which indicates some intrinsic interest of this notion.

Answer Sets of Nonground Programs. The semantics for ground programs can be extended to programs with variables by transforming the latter into an equivalent ground program. This is achieved by substituting each occurring variable with all possible constants. For this, let a *substitution* $\sigma : \mathcal{X} \cup \mathcal{C} \rightarrow \mathcal{C}$ be a mapping from terms to constants such that σ is the identity function on constants, i.e., $\sigma(c) = c$ for any $c \in \mathcal{C}$. Given an atom $a = p(t_1, \ldots, t_n)$ the ground atom obtain from applying σ to a, denoted by $a\sigma$ is $p(t_1\sigma, \ldots, t_n\sigma)$. Given a rule r of the form (1), the ground rule obtained from applying σ to r, denoted by $r\sigma$ is $A_1\sigma \vee \ldots \vee A_m\sigma \leftarrow L_1\sigma \ldots, L_n\sigma$.

Definition 9 (Grounding). *The grounding of a rule r, denoted by $grnd(r)$ is the set of all possible substitutions applied to r, i.e., $grnd(r) = \{r\sigma \mid \sigma \text{ is a substitution}\}$. The grounding of a program P is the grounding of each rule, i.e., $grnd(P) = \bigcup_{r \in P} grnd(r)$.*

The answer-sets of a non-ground program P are then simply the answer-sets of $grnd(P)$.

Example 10. Reconsider two of the non-ground rules from Example 4 forming the following program P:

$$reachable(X,Y) \leftarrow connection(X,Y).$$
$$reachable(X,Z) \leftarrow reachable(X,Y), reachable(Y,Z).$$

Since P does not contain any constants, we obtain $grnd(P) = \emptyset$. Intuitively, this makes sense because there are no locations for which reachability could be derived. Hence, the only answer set of P is the empty set. We introduce constants into the encoding by extending P in the following way:

$$P' = P \cup \{\, connection(a,b). \quad connection(b,c).\, \}$$

We obtain the grounding of P' by replacing all variables by constants in all possible ways and aggregating the resulting ground rules. The ground program $grnd(P')$ is represented by the following rules:

$$reachable(a,b) \leftarrow connection(a,b). \qquad reachable(c,b) \leftarrow connection(c,b).$$
$$reachable(b,a) \leftarrow connection(b,a). \qquad reachable(c,a) \leftarrow connection(c,a).$$
$$reachable(b,c) \leftarrow connection(b,c). \qquad reachable(a,c) \leftarrow connection(a,c).$$

$$reachable(a,b) \leftarrow reachable(a,b), reachable(a,b).$$
$$reachable(b,a) \leftarrow reachable(b,a), reachable(b,a).$$
$$reachable(b,c) \leftarrow reachable(b,c), reachable(b,c).$$
$$reachable(c,b) \leftarrow reachable(c,b), reachable(c,b).$$
$$reachable(c,a) \leftarrow reachable(c,a), reachable(c,a).$$
$$reachable(a,c) \leftarrow reachable(a,c), reachable(a,c).$$

The resulting program $grnd(P')$ has the single answer set $\{connection(a,b), connection(b,a), reachable(a,b), reachable(b,c), reachable(a,c)\}$, because informally speaking, b can be reached from a, and c from b, with a single connection, and c can be reached from a via b.

Note that the grounding contains many rules that do not fire w.r.t. the mentioned answer set. However, the essential point is that the set of ground rules which is needed for deriving the correct answer set is over-approximated by the grounding step, such that $grnd(P')$ has the same answer set(s) as P'.

Properties of Answer Sets. All answer sets satisfy certain properties, of which we present some in the following. First, it holds that each answer set is a minimal model.

Proposition 1. *Given a program P and an answer set A of P, then $A \models P$ and there exists no answer set $A' \neq A$ of P with $A' \subseteq A$.*

From minimality follows that answer sets are incomparable wrt. $\subseteq$. Formally:

Corollary 1. *Given two different answer sets A, A' of a program P, then $A \not\subseteq A'$ and $A' \not\subseteq A$ both hold.*

Given a program P, an interpretation I, and an atom a occurring in P, then a is said to be *supported* in I, if there is a ground rule $r \in \mathit{grnd}(P)$ such that $I \models \mathit{body}(r)$ and $a \in \mathit{head}(r)$. Intuitively, an atom is supported in I, if its presence is supported by the rules that fire in I, i.e., a is contained in the head of a firing rule. A model I is supported, if each atom $a \in I$ is supported in I.

Proposition 2. *Let A be an answer set of a program P, then A is a supported model.*

In Example 7, we have already illustrated that atoms which are not supported should not be derived because there is no necessity for them to appear in a model. However, not all supported models are also answer sets. In fact, answer sets adhere to a stronger property called foundedness, which intuitively excludes positive cycles supporting itself.

Example 11. Consider the program

$$P = \{a \leftarrow b. \quad b \leftarrow a.\},$$

where there is a cyclic dependency involving the atoms a and b. This program has two models, namely $I = \{a, b\}$ and $I' = \emptyset$. According to our previous observation, only I' should be the intended model as it represents a subset of I, i.e. it is the minimal model. Intuitively, this makes sense because, even though both atoms are supported by a positive rule body under I now, this support is cyclic and hence, not founded by a positive rule body depending on neither a nor b. In other words, we have no reason independent from a and b to believe either of them.

Example 12. Although every answer set is a minimal supported model, the converse does not hold. Consider the following program:

$$P = \{a \leftarrow a. \quad a \leftarrow \mathbf{not}\ a.\}$$

The interpretation $I_1 = \emptyset$ satisfies the body of the second rule, but not its head, therefore I_1 is not a model of P, i.e., $I \not\models P$. The interpretation $I_2 = \{a\}$ on the other hand satisfies the heads of both rules, therefore $I_2 \models P$. Furthermore, each atom in I_2 is supported by some rule, namely the first one. Thus, I_2 is a supported model and since I_1 is not a model, I_2 is the minimal supported model of P.

Considering answer sets now, we observe that I_1 is not an answer set because it is not an model of P. The reduct wrt. I_2 is $P^{I_2} = \{a \leftarrow a.\}$ and the minimal model of this program is $I' = \emptyset$. Therefore I_2 is not a minimal model of P^{I_2} and hence I_2 is not an answer set of P. In fact, P has no answer sets. Intuitively, the first rule of P is only deriving a from the presence of a while the second rule is contradictory in itself and can only be satisfied if a is true. Together P requires a to hold but gives only a self-cyclic reason for a to hold, which is not enough. Therefore it makes sense for P to have no answer sets.

In conclusion, the notion of answer set is different from the notion of minimal supported model and answer sets have to satisfy more conditions than minimal supported models even. In some sense, answer sets are minimal derivable models, specifically excluding positive self-support.

The computational complexity of finding answer sets that contain no disjunction in any rule heads is **NP**, i.e., under common assumptions, there is no feasible algorithm to construct answer sets. The best known algorithms for constructing answer sets have an exponential run time in the worst case.

Proposition 3 (Computational Complexity: Non-disjunctive Programs [78]**).** *Given a ground program P without disjunction, deciding whether P has an answer set is* **NP***-complete.*

If the input program contains disjunction, the complexity rises even further. Formally, the complexity is at the second level of the polynomial hierarchy. This means that an algorithm to construct answer sets of a disjunctive logic program following an **NP**-style guess and check approach would need to solve subproblems that are by themselves **NP**-complete.

Proposition 4 (Computational Complexity: Disjunctive Programs [28]**).** *Let P be a ground program including disjunction, then deciding whether P has an answer set is Σ_2^P-complete in the worst case.*

Luckily, despite these results, ASP solving works quite well in practice; this is because the worst case is often not encountered in practical problems. For further background and results on the complexity of logic programs, we refer to [23].

Further ASP Constructs. The rules presented so far already allow to express many problems, but some conditions are cumbersome to express using rules only. Therefore ASP allows more constructs, mainly for more convenience. One of those constructs are *aggregates* in rule bodies to count or sum over some values. Briefly, an aggregate atom starts with # followed by the name of the aggregate function, e.g., *count*, *sum*, *min*, *max*, *avg*, a collection of aggregate elements $\{t_1, \ldots, t_m : l_1, \ldots, l_n\}$ followed by a relation symbol, e.g., $\leq$, $<$, or$=$ and a term. The aggregate elements $t_1, \ldots, t_m : l_1, \ldots, l_n$ are comprised of terms $t_1, \ldots, t_m$ and literals $l_1, \ldots, l_n$.

Example 13. Assume one wants to count the number of stations in a train network where each station is given by the predicate $station(Name)$. This is possible using rules alone but very inconvenient. An aggregate allows counting directly as follows:

$$num\_stations(C) \leftarrow \#count\{X : station(X)\} = C.$$

Intuitively, the aggregate $\#count\{X : station(X)\} = C$ counts all X which are station names and assigns the number of such to the variable C.

In order to find optimal answer sets, *weak constraints* may be used. Intuitively, a weak constraint is like an ordinary constraint but an answer set may violate the weak constraint incurring a penalty of some specified cost. In the presence of weak constraints, answer sets with lowest cost are considered optimal. A weak constraint is of the form

$$\leftharpoondown Body.\ [C@L, t_1, \ldots, t_n] \tag{2}$$

where additional cost C at level L is added to the answer sets if *Body* is satisfied, and $t_1, \ldots, t_n$ are terms. Cost C can be incurred on different priority levels L: cost on higher levels is minimized before cost on lower levels is minimized. The terms $t_1, \ldots, t_n$ serve to count multiple times those same cost, e.g., 3@0, that appear in different rules.

Example 14. Consider some route planner where the duration of a trip should be minimized with highest priority and the number of stops should be minimal, but is less important than the duration.

$$\leftharpoondown trip\_duration(T).[T@2]$$
$$\leftharpoondown trip\_stop(X).[1@1, X]$$

For a duration T of a trip, the first rule incurs cost T at level 2. The second rule incurs a cost of 1 at level 1, and in order to count the cost of every stop, the term X is used in $[1@1, X]$. For illustration, assume that the above weak constraints are part of a larger program with three answer sets,

$$A_1 = \{trip\_duration(5), trip\_stop(a)\},$$
$$A_2 = \{trip\_duration(3), trip\_stop(a), trip\_stop(c), trip\_stop(d)\}, \text{and}$$
$$A_3 = \{trip\_duration(3), trip\_stop(e), trip\_stop(d)\}.$$

Then the cost of A_1 are 5@2 and 1@1, the cost of A_2 are 3@2 and 3@1 while the cost of A_3 are 3@2 and 2@1. Higher levels have higher minimization priority, so A_1 is less optimal than A_2 and A_3. Both A_2 and A_3 have the same cost on level 2, so the lower level 1 is used for comparison and here the answer set A_3 has smaller cost. Therefore A_3 is the optimal answer set given the above weak constraints.

Example 15. To illustrate the usage of the terms in weak constraints consider the following programs:

$$P_1 = \{a. \quad \leftharpoondown a.[3@0, t] \quad \leftharpoondown a.[4@0, t]\}$$
$$P_2 = \{a. \quad \leftharpoondown a.[3@0, t] \quad \leftharpoondown a.[3@0, t]\}$$
$$P_3 = \{a. \quad \leftharpoondown a.[3@0, t] \quad \leftharpoondown a.[3@0, o]\}$$

P_1 has one answer set $A = \{a\}$ with cost 7@0. P_2 has the same answer set A with cost 3@0 although both weak constraints are violated. P_3 has the answer set A with cost 6@0, because the different terms lead to 3@0 being present twice, once with t and once with o as term.

For interoperability of different ASP implementations, the ASP language has been standardized in the *ASP-Core-2 input language format* [19] which allows several more constructs like choice rules (e.g. a rule $2 \leq \{a, b, c\} \leq 2 \leftarrow d.$ which expresses that whenever d holds exactly two of a, b, and c have to hold), conditional literals, and queries.

2.2 Important Classes of Logic Programs

Often one can formulate a specific problem without making use of all constructs available in logic programming and it turns out that restricted programs are often easier and faster to evaluate.

Recall that the computational complexity of programs with disjunction is significantly higher than the complexity of programs without it. In some cases, however, the disjunction can be removed by *shifting* it from the head into the body using negation. Consider a rule $a \vee b \leftarrow c, \mathbf{not}\, d.$ and observe that this rule has the same answer sets as the two rules

$$a \leftarrow c, \mathbf{not}\, d, \mathbf{not}\, b.$$
$$b \leftarrow c, \mathbf{not}\, d, \mathbf{not}\, a.$$

where the disjunction has been shifted into the rule bodies. The intuition behind this shifting is that whenever the original rule fires, one of a or b becomes true, but not both. The latter two rules express this directly making use of negation to avoid that both become true at the same time. Of course, this is only correct, if no other rule has a and b in the head, because otherwise both might be true. Shifting can be done if the program is *head-cycle free* (cf. [7,70] for a formal definition).

Furthermore, a program P is called *normal*, if each rule $r \in P$ is normal, that is $|head(r)| \leq 1$; thus P is normal if it contains no disjunction at all. The semantics of normal programs is easier to evaluate (cf. Proposition 3) and the minimal models of such programs can be operationally computed. The *immediate consequences operator* $T_P : HB \rightarrow HB$ for a normal program P is an operator on interpretations such that $T_P(I) \mapsto I'$ where $I' = \{head(r) \mid r \in P, I \models body(r)\}$. Intuitively, the operator takes an interpretation and returns the heads of all rules that fire in the given interpretation. Answer sets of a normal logic program P can be characterized as the least fixpoint of the operator applied to the corresponding reduct, formally: I is an answer set if $I = lfp(T_{P^I}(\emptyset))$. The least fixpoint is obtained simply by applying the operator recursively until its result no longer changes.

Example 16. Consider the program

$$P = \{\, a \leftarrow \mathbf{not}\, b. \quad b \leftarrow \mathbf{not}\, a. \quad c \leftarrow a. \,\}$$

and note that it is a normal program. Consider the interpretation $I = \{a, c\}$ which yields the reduct $P^I = \{ a \leftarrow \textbf{not}\ b. \quad c \leftarrow a. \}$. Applying the immediate consequences operator yields

$$I' = T_{P^I}(\emptyset) = \{a\}; \qquad I'' = T_{P^I}(I') = \{a, b\}; \qquad I'' = T_{P^I}(I'') = \{a, b\}$$

thus $I'' = I$ is the least fixpoint, i.e., $lfp(T_{P^I}) = I$ and consequently I is an answer set of P.

Another important class of logic programs is the class of Horn programs. A logic program is *Horn*, if it is normal and each rule of the form (1) contains in its body only positive literals, i.e., the body is a conjunction of atoms. The complexity of Horn programs is in **P** and thus Horn programs are far easier to evaluate than normal programs. In fact, every Horn program that has a model has a unique minimal model and this model is its (single) answer set.

2.3 HEX Program Syntax

HEX extends ASP by external atoms, that are special atoms to access external information sources. As such, external atoms may only occur in the body of a rule, since the external source can only be queried for information. To distinguish external atoms from ordinary atoms, the names of external atoms start with the & symbol. The set of *external predicate names* is denoted by $\mathcal{G}$, which is disjoint from the set of terms and variables. A relational signature for a HEX program therefore is a quadruple $S = (\mathcal{C}, \mathcal{P}, \mathcal{X}, \mathcal{G})$.

External atoms may receive as input ordinary terms as well as the extensions of predicates. To specify that an external atom shall receive as input the whole extension of a predicate, the predicate name, i.e., an element from $\mathcal{P}$, is provided as input.

Definition 10 (External Atom). *An* external atom *over a relational signature $S = (\mathcal{C}, \mathcal{P}, \mathcal{X}, \mathcal{G})$ is of the form*

$$\&g[Y_1, \ldots, Y_n](X_1, \ldots, X_m) \tag{3}$$

where $Y_1, \ldots, Y_n$ is a list (called input *list) of terms and predicate names from $\mathcal{C} \cup \mathcal{X} \cup \mathcal{P}$ and $X_1, \ldots, X_m$ is a list of terms from $\mathcal{C} \cup \mathcal{X}$ (called* output *list), and $\&g \in \mathcal{G}$ is an external predicate name. We assume that $\&g$ has fixed lengths $in(\&g) = n$ and $out(\&g) = m$ for input and output lists, respectively.*

In the ground case, the input terms $Y_1, \ldots, Y_n$ intuitively consist of individual constants (e.g. *tomatoes*) and predicate names (e.g. *edge*). An external atom provides a way for deciding the truth value of an output tuple depending on the input tuple and a given interpretation.

Example 17. Consider an external atom $\&concat[X, Y](Z)$ that takes two input constants and returns an output constant representing the string obtained from concatenating the string representations of the two input constants. This external atom depends only on constants from the program with which the external atom is instantiated during grounding. For instance, in the following rule the external atom is called with a first name and a last name, and the full name is retrieved.

$$\mathit{fullname}(Z) \leftarrow \&\mathit{concat}[X,Y](Z), \mathit{firstname}(X), \mathit{lastname}(Y).$$

When grounding the HEX program containing the previous rule as well as the two facts $\mathit{firstname}(\mathit{bob})$ and $\mathit{lastname}(\mathit{dylan})$, we obtain a rule that contains the ground instance $\&\mathit{concat}[\mathit{bob}, \mathit{dylan}](\mathit{bobdylan})$ of $\&\mathit{concat}[X,Y](Z)$. The atom $\&\mathit{concat}[\mathit{bob}, \mathit{dylan}](\mathit{bobdylan})$ evaluates to true, and $\mathit{fullname}(\mathit{bobdylan})$ can be derived.

Often terms alone do not suffice as input to an external atom. This is the case whenever the output of an external atom (respectively the truth value of a ground external atom), depends on the extension of one or more predicates in a given HEX program.

Example 18. For instance, suppose we want to retrieve reachability information w.r.t. the transport network from Example 4 via an external atom instead of computing it by means of program rules, e.g. in order to apply a dedicated algorithm.

The external atom $\&\mathit{reachable}[\mathit{connection}, a](X)$ may be devised for computing the nodes which are reachable from node a in a graph represented by atoms of form $\mathit{connection}(u,v)$. In this case, the external atom has a predicate name as well as a constant term as input parameters.

Intuitively, given an interpretation I, $\&\mathit{reachable}[\mathit{connection}, a](X)$ will be true for all ground substitutions $X \mapsto b$ such that b is a node in the graph whose set of edges is $\{(u,v) \mid \mathit{connection}(u,v) \in I\}$, and there is a path from a to b in that graph.

An external atom of the form (3) for which it holds that $n = 0$ is an atom that only imports external information, while an external atom with $m = 0$ imports no information but can be either true or false. Hence, the latter behaves like a Boolean predicate and may be used as an external checker, e.g., to run a specific checking algorithm.

Example 19. Consider an external atom $\&\mathit{importConnections}[](X,Y)$ which returns all connections of some public transport network. Here, we have that $n = 0$ and thus, the evaluation of the external atom does not depend on information derived from the HEX program in which it is used. However, a rule of the form

$$\mathit{connection}(X,Y) \leftarrow \&\mathit{importConnections}[](X,Y), \mathit{location}(X), \mathit{location}(Y).$$

could be used to, e.g., import all connections between locations from a given set into the program from Example 4.

Alternatively, consider the atom $\&\mathit{distanceLessThan}[\mathit{connection}, X, Y, N]()$, which does not have any output parameters, i.e. $m = 0$. Suppose it constitutes a Boolean predicate that evaluates to true if and only if location X has distance less than N from location Y in the transport network represented by the extension of the predicate *connection*. Then, it could be used in a HEX program in a constraint such as

$$\leftarrow \textbf{not } \&distanceLessThan[connection, X, Y, 5](), location(X), location(Y).$$

to ensure that no two locations have distance greater or equal 5 from each other in the network induced by the predicate *connection*.

A *HEX-literal* is either an ordinary literal, an external atom, or a default-negated external atom. Rules in HEX then are exactly like ordinary rules in ASP except that the literals in the body may contain external atoms.

Definition 11 (HEX rule). *A* HEX rule r *is of the form*

$$A_1 \vee \ldots \vee A_m \leftarrow L_1 \ldots, L_n. \tag{4}$$

where all A_i *are atoms, and all* L_j *are either literals or HEX-literals, for* $1 \leq i \leq m$, $1 \leq j \leq n$, $m, n \geq 0$.

In the following, we call HEX-rules just rules.

Example 20. Consider an external atom to query a web-based weather report which receives as input a set of pairs of dates and locations one is interested and reports the set of all weather conditions that occur at some of the locations on the specified date as output. Such an external atom might be

$$\&weatherreport[dateLocationPredicate](WeatherConditions).$$

Let *goto* be a predicate containing pairs of days and cities to be visited. Then, the following constraint excludes extensions of the predicate *goto* where bad weather occurs in some city on the day of visit:

$$\leftarrow \&weatherreport[goto](W), badweather(W).$$

Definition 12 (HEX program). *A HEX* program *is a set* P *of (HEX) rules.*

A rule is *ordinary* if no external atom occurs in it, and a program is ordinary if all its rules are ordinary. The notions of constraint and fact carry over from ordinary rules. In practice, we shall be interested in finite programs only, while theoretically, programs may be infinite.

Example 21 (continued). Consider the following program Π_{goto} to decide on what day to go to which city for planning a city trip, but exclude trips where the (external) weather report indicates that bad weather occurs during the trip.

$$\begin{array}{l} badweather(rain). \qquad badweather(snow). \\ goto(1, paris) \vee goto(1, london). \\ goto(2, paris) \vee goto(2, london). \\ \leftarrow \&weatherreport[goto](W), badweather(W). \end{array}$$

The facts in the first row state that snow and rain are bad weather, the rules in the second and third line choose a destination for the first and second day, respectively, which can be Paris or London (and possibly the same city for both days), and the constraint excludes extensions of the predicate *goto* such that bad weather is expected on the chosen trip.

2.4 HEX Program Semantics

The semantics of HEX programs generalizes the answer-set semantics of ordinary programs. The notion of a *Herbrand base HB* for HEX is analogous to ordinary ASP, i.e., *HB* is the set containing all ground ordinary atoms and all ground external atoms. The grounding of a rule r, $grnd(r)$, is defined accordingly, and the grounding of P is given by $grnd(P) = \bigcup_{r \in P} grnd(r)$. Unless specified otherwise, the relational signature $S = (\mathcal{C}, \mathcal{P}, \mathcal{X}, \mathcal{G})$ is implicitly given by P, but different from the 'usual' ASP setting, the set $\mathcal{C}$ of constants used for grounding a program is only partially given by the program itself; in HEX, external computations may introduce new constants that are relevant for semantics of the program.

The notion of interpretation for ordinary logic programs naturally extends to HEX programs, where the valuation of external predicates depends only on (i) the valuation of the ordinary predicates and (ii) some external semantics. Formally, we define interpretations of HEX programs as follows.

Definition 13 (HEX interpretation). *An* interpretation relative to *a HEX program P is any subset $I \subseteq HB$ that contains no external atoms.*

Satisfaction of ordinary atoms with respect to an interpretation I is then as usual; for external atoms, we use the notion of an oracle function.

Definition 14 (Oracle Function). *Every external predicate name $\&g \in \mathcal{G}$, has an associated decidable $(n+m+1)$-ary Boolean function $f_{\&g}$, called* oracle function, *which maps each tuple $(I, \vec{y}, \vec{x})$ to either* **T** *or* **F**, *where $I \subseteq HB$ is an interpretation, $\vec{y} = y_1, \ldots, y_n$, $n = in(\&g)$, $\vec{x} = x_1, \ldots, x_m$, $m = out(\&g)$, $x_i \in \mathcal{C}$, $y_j \in \mathcal{C} \cup \mathcal{P}$, and $m, n \geq 0$.*

In the following we make the restriction that for any oracle function $f_{\&g}$, interpretation I and input vector $\vec{y}$, there are only finitely many vectors $\vec{x}$ such that $f_{\&g}(I, \vec{y}, \vec{x}) = \mathbf{T}$.

This definition of external atom semantics is very general; indeed an external atom may depend on every part of the interpretation. For practical reasons, external atom semantics is usually restricted so that it depends only on the extension of those predicates in I that are given in the input list.

Example 22 (continued). Suppose that the weather report for *paris* is *sun* on day 1 and day 2 of the trip, and for *london* the forecast indicates *rain* for both days. The oracle function $f_{\&weatherreport}(I, goto, W)$ corresponding to this information evaluates to $\mathbf{T}$ if and only if:

$\{goto(1, london), goto(2, london)\} \subseteq I$ and $W = rain$,
$\{goto(1, london), goto(2, paris)\} \subseteq I$ and $W = sun$ or $W = rain$,
$\{goto(1, paris), goto(2, london)\} \subseteq I$ and $W = sun$ or $W = rain$, or
$\{goto(1, paris), goto(2, paris)\} \subseteq I$ and $W = sun$.

In all other cases, $f_{\&weatherreport}(I, goto, W)$ evaluates to $\mathbf{F}$.

Definition 15 (Satisfaction of External Atom). *An interpretation* $I \subseteq HB$ *is a* model *of a ground external atom* $a = \&g[\vec{y}](\vec{x})$, *denoted* $I \models a$, *if* $f_{\&g}(I, \vec{y}, \vec{x}) = \mathbf{T}$.

The notion of satisfaction for ordinary atoms, literals, rules, and programs carries over directly from disjunctive logic programs.

Given a HEX program P, the *FLP-reduct* P^I of P with respect to $I \subseteq HB$ is the same as for ordinary programs, i.e., P^I is the set of all $r \in grnd(P)$ such that $I \models body(r)$.

Definition 16 (Answer Set of a HEX Program). *An interpretation* $I \subseteq HB$ *is an* answer set *of a HEX program* P *if,* I *is a minimal model of* P^I. *We denote by* $\mathcal{AS}(P)$ *the set of all answer sets of* P.

Observe that if P has no external atoms, then the answer sets according to the above definition are exactly the answer sets for ordinary ASP programs. In other words, HEX programs are a conservative extension of disjunctive [59] (resp., normal [58]) logic programs under the answer set semantics.

Example 23 (continued). Suppose that the weather report for *paris* is *sun* on day 1 and day 2 of the trip, and for *london* the forecast indicates *rain* for both days, i.e., $f_{\&weatherreport}(I, goto, W)$ from Example 22 is employed. In this case, $I \models \&weatherreport[goto](sun)$ holds if $I \models goto(1, paris)$ or if $I \models goto(2, paris)$. Moreover, it holds that $I \models \&weatherreport[goto](rain)$ if $I \models goto(1, london)$ or if $I \models goto(2, london)$, and Π_{goto} has one answer set:

$$\{goto(1, paris), goto(2, paris), badweather(snow), badweather(rain)\}$$

If weather reports of both cities are sunny for the two days, i.e., if another oracle function is employed, we obtain three further answer sets where London is visited on the first, the second, or on both days, respectively. Finally if the weather report for both cities is *snow* for days 1 and 2, there is no answer set.

3 Methodology

We next present basic methodology for using HEX to solve declarative problems. At this, applying the methodology presented in this section not only helps in formulating a HEX encoding for a problem at hand, but also has a potential impact on the efficiency of the solving process. In practice, when computing the answer sets of a HEX program, the evaluation of external sources for determining the truth values of external atoms is interleaved with ordinary answer set search. In this way, it is ensured that all answer sets computed for a given HEX program comply with the formal semantics based on oracle functions (which abstract external sources). More details on the evaluation of HEX programs can be found in Sect. 4.

In Sect. 3.1 we provide methodology specifically for using external atoms and distinguish typical kinds of external sources. They can be classified as

1. outsourcing of computation,
2. outsourcing of information, or
3. combination thereof.

A primary use case of HEX is the direct usage as a formalism for modeling user applications. Section 3.2 describes several application scenarios with examples.

In each of these scenarios, all types of external sources can be used.

Basic Methodology. HEX is an extension of ASP, therefore all modeling techniques from ASP may also be used in HEX programs. One of the most important examples is the *guess and check paradigm*, where default negation or disjunctive rules are used to generate a superset of the intended solutions (*guessing part*), and constraints are used to eliminate spurious candidates (*checking part*). For instance, if we assume that facts over predicates *node* and *edge* define a graph, then the well-known graph 3-colorability problem can be solved by guessing all possible colorings of the nodes of a graph using the disjunctive rule

$$g\colon\ \mathit{color}(\mathit{red}, X) \vee \mathit{color}(\mathit{green}, X) \vee \mathit{color}(\mathit{blue}, X) \leftarrow \mathit{node}(X), \tag{5}$$

and eliminating all colorings which assign the same color to adjacent nodes using the constraint

$$c\colon\ \leftarrow \mathit{color}(C, X), \mathit{color}(C, Y), \mathit{edge}(X, Y). \tag{6}$$

However, unlike in ASP, HEX programs allow for using external atoms in addition. They can occur both in the guessing and in the checking part. In the former case, they may be used to import individuals over which guessing is performed. For instance, one may replace the atom $\mathit{node}(X)$ in the body of rule (5) by $\&\mathit{node}[\,](X)$ to import the nodes of the graph. In the latter case, external atoms can be used in the body of constraints to check given conditions. For instance, rule c may be replaced by

$$c'\colon\ \leftarrow \mathbf{not}\ \&\mathit{check}[\mathit{color}, \mathit{edge}](), \tag{7}$$

where $\&\mathit{check}[\mathit{color}, \mathit{edge}]()$ is true if *color* is a valid 3-coloring wrt. *edge* and false otherwise. Here, the external atom $\&\mathit{check}[\mathit{color}, \mathit{edge}]()$ implements a Boolean check, such that no output terms are required. This type of usage is common when external atoms are utilized for external checks.

The *saturation technique* [37] is an advanced modeling technique for solving problems up to Σ_2^P-completeness, by exploiting the subset-minimality of answer sets for checking whether a property holds *for all* guesses in a search space [39]. A typical example is the check if a graph is *not* 3-colorable, i.e., all possible colorings are invalid. Also here, the checking part may employ external atoms.

For more details about ASP modeling techniques we refer to [39,53].

3.1 Methodology for Using External Atoms

In general, one can roughly distinguish between two main usages of external sources that we call *computation outsourcing* and *information outsourcing*, respectively, and combinations thereof. We stress that this distinction concerns the usage in applications, as both usages are based on the same language constructs. For each of them we will describe some typical use cases that serve as usage patterns for external atoms when writing HEX programs.

Computation Outsourcing means to send the definition of a subproblem to an external source and retrieve its result. The input to the external source uses predicate extensions and constants to define the problem at hand and the output terms are used to retrieve the result, which can in simple cases also be a Boolean decision.

On-demand constraints are of the form $\leftarrow \&forbidden[p_1, \ldots, p_n]()$. They eliminate certain extensions of predicates $p_1, \ldots, p_n$ and are a special case of computation outsourcing, see also the 3-colorability example above. The external evaluation of such a constraint can return reasons for conflicts to the reasoner in order to restrict the search space and avoid reconstruction of the same conflict [30]. This technique avoids explicitly grounding a set of ordinary ASP constraints representing the forbidden combinations and by this, reduces the size of the ground program. On-demand constraints have been used for efficient planning in robotics where external atoms verify the feasibility of a 3D motion [49,63].

Computations that Cannot (Easily) be Expressed by Rules. Outsourcing computations also allows for including algorithms which cannot (easily or efficiently) be expressed by rules. As a concrete example, an artificial intelligence agent for the skills and tactics game *AngryBirds* needs to perform physics simulations [21]. This requires floating point computations which cannot be done by rules in a practical way (this would either come at the costs of very limited precision or a blow-up of the grounding). Therefore, the physics simulations are integrated with game playing rules as external atoms in a HEX program.

Complexity Lifting. This is another kind of computation outsourcing that allows for realizing computations with a complexity higher than the complexity of ordinary ASP programs. The external atom serves then as an 'oracle' for deciding subprograms. While for the purpose of complexity analysis of the formalism, it is often assumed that external atoms can be evaluated in polynomial time[6] [50], as long as external sources are decidable, there is no practical reason for limiting their complexity. External sources can also be other ASP or HEX programs, which allows for encoding other formalisms of higher complexity in HEX programs, e.g., *abstract argumentation frameworks* [27].

Information Outsourcing refers, in contrast to computational outsourcing, to external sources which import information, while reasoning itself is done in the logic program.

[6] Under this assumption, deciding the existence of an answer set of a propositional HEX program is Σ_2^P-complete.

A typical example can be found in Web resources which provide information for import, e.g., *RDF triple stores* [68] or *geographic data* [82]. More advanced use cases are *multi-context systems*, which are systems of knowledge-bases (*contexts*) that are abstracted to acceptable belief sets (roughly speaking, sets of atoms) and interlinked by *bridge rules* that range across knowledge bases [12] (see also Sect. 6.1); access to individual contexts has been provided through external atoms [9]. Also sensor data, as often used when planning and executing actions in an environment, is a form of information outsourcing (cf. ACTHEX [6]).

Combinations. It is also possible to outsource computation and information at the same time. A typical example are logic programs with access to Description Logic knowledge bases (DL KB), called *DL-programs* [41]. A DL KB not only stores information, but also provides reasoning services. This allows for interleaving reasoning within the DL KB and the logic program with information that flows across the external atom API in both directions.

3.2 Concrete Application Scenarios

The HEX language can be directly used for modeling a problem at hand and computing its solutions. Note that the problem instance formally consists both of the HEX program and the external sources, but external sources may be reused for different applications if suitable.

The typical procedure when modeling an end user application starts with identifying and realizing the required external sources, followed by writing a HEX program which makes use of these external sources. The two steps may be repeated in order to refine the encoding, i.e., while writing the HEX program, the need for further or modified external sources may arise. In some cases, external atoms of other applications can be reused. Some existing plugins are generic and useful for different applications, e.g., string manipulation functions and an interface to RDF triple stores.

We next give concrete application scenarios including HEX example code.

Semantic Web Applications. In the context of the Semantic Web, HEX was applied to connect SPARQL and RDF querying with logic programming rules [87]. Moreover, HEX was used for archaeological research in order to combine geographical and cultural knowledge from various ontologies [82], and for adapting user interfaces targeted at elderly and disabled people by combining ontologies about user profiles with rules about potential user interface styles [100].

The following example uses the FOAF (Friend-of-a-friend) RDF schema to return all pairs of nicknames that know each other, as stored in a FOAF RDF datasource such as can be obtained from www.livejournal.com.

$$explore(\text{"http://}\langle Nick\rangle\text{.livejournal.com/data/foaf"}). \quad (8)$$

$$triple(S,P,O) \leftarrow \&rdf[What](S,P,O),\ explore(What). \quad (9)$$

$$knows(Nick_1, Nick_2) \leftarrow triple(Id_1, \text{"http://xmlns.com/foaf/0.1/knows"}, Id_2),$$
$$triple(Id_1, \text{"http://xmlns.com/foaf/0.1/nick"}, Nick_1),\ Nick_1 < Nick_2,$$
$$triple(Id_2, \text{"http://xmlns.com/foaf/0.1/nick"}, Nick_2). \quad (10)$$

$$knows(A,C) \leftarrow knows(A,B),\ knows(B,C). \quad (11)$$

We start with a fact (8) that represents FOAF-URLs of users that we want to explore, where we substitute the nickname for $\langle Nick\rangle$. Rule (9) uses the external atom *&rdf* to retrieve all RDF-triples from the URL instantiated as input argument *What*, i.e., all URLs that we specified in predicate *explore*. The external atom *&rdf* is true for all RDF-triples found in the resource, therefore they are represented in the predicate *triple*. Rule (10) uses the FOAF relations 'knows' and 'nick' to build all pairs of nicknames of people that know each other, and define the predicate *knows* as result. Finally, we obtain the transitive closure of *knows* using rule (11). As a result, we represent all pairs of nicknames who know each other directly or indirectly.

In the above example, the set of URLs to retrieve was given explicitly in the predicate *explore*.

In the following example, a FOAF RDF-graph is explored implicitly by following URLs retrieved via RDF.

$$explore\_to(What, 3) \leftarrow explore(What). \quad (12)$$

$$triple\_at(S,P,O,D) \leftarrow \&rdf[Uri](S,P,O),\ explore\_to(Uri,D),\ D > 1. \quad (13)$$

$$explore\_to(U, D_2) \leftarrow D_2 = D_1 - 1,$$
$$triple\_at(Id, \text{"http://www.w3.org/2000/01/rdf-schema\#seeAlso"}, U, D_1),$$
$$triple\_at(Id, \text{"http://xmlns.com/foaf/0.1/nick"}, Nick, D_1). \quad (14)$$

$$found(Nick) \leftarrow triple\_at(S, \text{"http://xmlns.com/foaf/0.1/nick"}, Nick, D). \quad (15)$$

To avoid excessive exploration, we limit following URLs in RDF up to a fixed depth. Resources of interest are again assumed to be given as facts of the predicate *explore*. Rule (12) defines *explore_to* for these resources of interest with a fixed exploration depth of 3. In (13) we retrieve RDF triples for resources where the exploration depth is above zero and represent triples together with their exploration depth. To follow links, in (14) we define *explore_to* also for all RDF links that are associated with nicknames in the RDF graph. This indirection decreases exploration depth by one. Finally (15) defines predicate *found* to represent all nicknames found during exploration, independent from the depth.

The RDF examples are available in the repository of the dlvhex manual.[7]

[7] https://github.com/hexhex/manual/RW2017/rdf/.

AngryHEX. The annual *AIBirds Competition*[8] is a competition for AI agents based on the popular *Angry Birds*[9] game, which is about using a slingshot to shoot birds of different types at pigs placed on a scene in order to destroy them. The pigs are usually protected by obstacles of different types. The game uses a realistic physics simulation, including gravity and statics. In the competition, agents are given the positions and dimensions of the objects in the scene and need to return the angle and velocity for shooting the next bird.

The *AngryHEX* agent [20] is implemented on top of HEX programs. The basic strategy is to maximize the estimated damage to obstacles and pigs for all possible targets. Plain ASP is ill-suited for this application as the computation involves physics simulation and floating point numbers. Therefore, a HEX program was used to realize the basic strategy including the optimal selection of the target, while low-level numeric computations have been outsourced. The agent participated in the competition since 2012 and ranked second in 2015.

$$\begin{aligned}
\mathit{shootable}(O, \mathit{Type}, \mathit{Tr}) \leftarrow\ & \&\mathit{shootable}[O, \mathit{Tr}, V, \mathit{Sx}, \mathit{Sy}, \mathit{Sw}, \mathit{Sh}, B, \mathit{bb}](O),\\
& \mathit{birdType}(B),\ \mathit{velocity}(V),\ \mathit{objectType}(O, \mathit{Type}),\\
& \mathit{slingshot}(\mathit{Sx}, \mathit{Sy}, \mathit{Sw}, \mathit{Sh}),\ \mathit{trajectory}(\mathit{Tr}). && (16)\\
\mathit{tgt}(O, \mathit{Tr}) \vee \mathit{ntgt}(O, \mathit{Tr}) \leftarrow\ & \mathit{shootable}(O, \mathit{Type}, \mathit{Tr}). && (17)\\
\leftarrow\ & \mathit{target}(X, _),\ \mathit{target}(Y, _), X \neq Y. && (18)\\
\leftarrow\ & \mathit{target}(_, T_1),\ \mathit{target}(_, T_2),\ T_1 \neq T_2. && (19)\\
\mathit{target_ex} \leftarrow\ & \mathit{target}(_, _). && (20)\\
\leftarrow\ & \mathbf{not}\ \mathit{target_ex}. && (21)\\
\mathit{directDmg}(O, P, E) \leftarrow\ & \mathit{target}(O, \mathit{Tr}),\ \mathit{objectType}(O, T),\ \mathit{birdType}(\mathit{Bird}),\\
& \mathit{dmgProbability}(\mathit{Bird}, T, P),\\
& \mathit{energyLoss}(\mathit{Bird}, T, E). && (22)\\
\mathit{exDirectDmg}(O) \leftarrow\ & \mathit{directDmg}(O, _, _). && (23)\\
\mathit{nexDirectDmg}(O) \leftarrow\ & \mathbf{not}\ \mathit{exDirectDmg}(O),\ \mathit{objectType}(O, _). && (24)\\
\mathit{goodObject}(O) \leftarrow\ & \mathit{objectType}(O, \mathit{pig}). && (25)\\
\mathit{goodObject}(O) \leftarrow\ & \mathit{objectType}(O, \mathit{tnt}). && (26)\\
\leftsquigarrow\ & \mathit{nexDirectDmg}(O), \mathit{goodObject}(O).\quad [1@4, O, \mathit{nexDirectDmg}] && (27)\\
\leftsquigarrow\ & \mathit{nexDirectDmg}(O).\quad [1@1, O, \mathit{nexDirectDmg}] && (28)
\end{aligned}$$

Fig. 1. AngryHex tactics layer (simplified)

A very simplified example of the tactics layer of AngryHex, which is evaluated for each shot, is shown in Fig. 1 Intuitively, (16) uses external atom *&shootable* to determine which objects O in the scene can be hit by shooting with trajectory Tr, velocity V, and bird type B, given that the slingshot (which ejects the bird) is located at coordinates Sx, Sy and has width

[8] https://aibirds.org.

[9] https://www.angrybirds.com.

Sw and height Sh, and given that bb represents bounding boxes of all objects in the scene. The vision module of the AngryHex client represents the scene in facts of form $birdType(Type)$, $objectType(O, Type)$, $slingshot(Sx, Sy, Sw, Sh)$, and $bb(O, Type, X, Y, Width, Height, Angle)$ where O is a unique object ID. Moreover, possible velocities (a set of integers) and trajectories (either *low* or *high*) are present as facts. External atom $\&shootable$ extracts the extension of the bb argument, builds a 2D representation of the world in the Box2D library,[10] and simulates the shot specified in arguments $O, \ldots, B$. If the shot hits the object, the atom is true for that object.

Rule (17) guesses whether a shootable object shall be the target of the next shot, and (18)–(21) ensure that a single target is chosen. Rule (22) represents direct damage to objects that are hit by the shot, using background knowledge about damage probability and energy loss (disadvantage) of the bird type with respect to the object type. Presence and absence of direct damage is represented in (23)–(24).

Objects that are of type *pig* or *tnt* (explosive blocks) are defined as 'good' objects to hit in (25)–(26), and weak constraint (27) incurs a cost of 1 with priority level 4 for each good object that does not obtain direct damage. Moreover weak constraint (28) incurs a cost of 1 for each object that does not obtain direct damage, however with a lower priority (1) than for good objects.

Recall from (2) that weak constraints are of form $\leftsquigarrow Body.\ [C@L, \ldots]$ and add cost C at level L to answer sets that satisfy $Body$. Answer sets with lowest cost are considered optimal and minimizing cost on higher levels has priority.

The full encoding of AngryHex uses several more external atoms, for example $\&next[O, Tr, Sx, Sy, Sw, Sh, bb](Idx, O')$ is true for a set of pairs $\langle Idx, O' \rangle$ that represent the sequence of objects that a bird shot at object O with parameters $Tr, \ldots, Sh$ would pass through: O' is the Idx'th object hit in the trajectory. Another external atom is $\&firstbelow[O, bb](O')$, which yields true for pairs of objects O, O' such that O would hit O' before hitting any other object when falling down. These and further external atoms are used to select the target and trajectory that will inflict the most useful direct and indirect damage to all objects of the scene. The AngryHex project is publicly available.[11]

Route Planning. While many commercial and free route planning applications exist (Google Maps is currently perhaps the most popular), the supported query types are usually limited. In contrast, an implementation in HEX programs allows for an easy addition of side constraints and thus tailoring to very specific settings. As a concrete use-case, [32] considered tours with multiple stops (e.g. at shops, a pharmacy, kindergarden, etc.) using an external source that supports only point-to-point queries. Side constraints may include restrictions on the order of stops, the tour length, or opening hours at the stops.

Related to route planning is a trip planning scenario. When planning a holiday trip with multiple stops, the order of the stops is often irrelevant, but one

[10] http://box2d.org/.

[11] https://github.com/DeMaCS-UNICAL/Angry-HEX.

wants to spend a certain number of days at each location. However, due to shifts of the dates, the overall price often differs significantly with different sequences. In addition to the sequence of the locations, also other considerations affect the price. E.g. instead of a multi-stop flight through all locations, one may book a return flight to one of them plus local flights from there to the others; sometimes special offers for two-way-tickets make this more attractive. A logic program can automatically generate flight plans according to the constraints and enquire their ticket prices by an external atom that internally uses an online flight booking service. An additional weak constraint can select the cheapest.

Our case study in Sect. 5 provides details for route planning with HEX.

Description Logic Programs. *Description logics (DLs)* provide a logical formalism for ontologies that are well-suited for the Semantic Web [64] or in medical applications [65]. Ontologies represent classes of objects, referred to as *concepts*, and the relations between objects, called *roles*. Concepts and roles correspond to unary and binary predicates in first-order logic, respectively. A *description logic knowledge base* consists of a *Tbox* (*the terminology*) that defines concepts and roles and represents relations between them, and an *Abox* (*assertions*), that contains specific information on membership of individuals in concepts resp. of pairs of individuals in roles.

Example 24. Suppose *PhDStudent*, *Student* and *Professor* are concepts and *isAssistantOf* is a role. The Tbox may contain the *concept inclusion axiom* $\mathit{PhDStudent} \sqsubseteq \mathit{Student}$, which states that the class of PhD students is a subclass of all students. The Abox contains concept membership assertions like *Professor*(*smith*) and *PhDStudent*(*johnson*), representing that *smith* is a professor and *johnson* a PhD student. An assertion *isAssistantOf*(*johnson*, *smith*) states that *johnson* is an assistant of professor *smith*. □

Typical reasoning tasks over description logic knowledge bases include concept and role retrieval, i.e., listing all individuals or pairs of individuals which are members of a given concept or role, respectively. In the example above one may ask for all members of *Student* and expects as answer *johnson* as he is a *PhDStudent* and thus, by the terminological knowledge, also a *Student*.

Combining ontologies and answer set programming is especially valuable as existing domain knowledge can be accessed from logic programs. To this end, *DL-programs* have been developed by [40,41] which have been implemented on top of HEX programs with dedicated external atoms; where the external source features external atoms for concept and role queries. Prior to query evaluation, concepts and/or roles are enriched by the contents designated unary resp. binray predicates that occur in the ASP program. This allows for advanced reasoning tasks such as terminological default reasoning or closed world reasoning on description logic knowledge bases [24].

As description logics are monotonic, default reasoning can only be realized by the (cyclic) interaction of rules and the DL knowledge base. To this end, appropriate encodings and an implementation were developed [24]. DL-programs have, e.g., been applied in complaint management for e-government [101].

Our case study in Sect. 5 contains a code example and a walkthrough for integrating DL reasoning with logic programming using the HEX formalism.

4 The DLVHEX System

In this section we present the DLVHEX system[12] for evaluating HEX programs. The system is implemented in C++ and available as open-source software for all major platforms (Linux, OS X, Windows). Pre-compiled binaries are also provided. External sources are implemented using a plugin interface, which is currently available for C++ and Python.

At the beginning of the DLVHEX project, the system focused on applications for the Semantic Web. Early versions of the system were based on dlv[13] and extended it with higher-order and external atoms. Higher-order atoms allow for using variables in place of a predicate symbol, such as in the rule $C(X) \leftarrow \mathit{subClassOf}(D, C), D(X)$ to model a general subclass relation; while they are still supported, they were less emphasized in later versions as they can be compiled away. External atoms were introduced for accessing arbitrary external sources and are a generalization of DL-atoms, which allow only for interfacing a description logic reasoner.

The first evaluation algorithms used dlv as a blackbox backend for single-shot evaluation of ordinary ASP programs. In a nutshell, the traditional HEX-algorithm translates the HEX-program into an ordinary ASP program which guesses the values of external atoms (disregarding the actual semantics), evaluates this ASP program using the backend, and performs for each answer set a post-check to ensure that the guesses were correct and that minimality wrt. the FLP-reduct is given. As this approach did not scale to real applications, the evaluation algorithms were improved over time, which required a tighter integration with the backend (such as separate access to the grounding and the solving component of the backend, a callback interface, etc.). In context of these improvements, the default backend was replaced by GRINGO and CLASP from the Potassco suite[14]; the original system name DLVHEX was kept and should now be read as *Datalog with disjunctions, higher-order and external atoms.* However, our interface allows for the integration of further solver backends. For instance, in order to make the system self-contained and for testing purposes, we further provide as another alternative an internal grounder and solver, which do not rely on any third-party components. Also dlv is still supported as an alternative to GRINGO and CLASP (used with the traditional algorithms).

We will first discuss the basic evaluation approach and the system architecture, before we switch to the user perspective and point out system features which distinguish DLVHEX from ordinary ASP solvers and also from previous versions. However, since this paper focuses on the usage of HEX-programs rather than evaluation algorithms, we refer to [89] for details.

[12] http://www.kr.tuwien.ac.at/research/systems/dlvhex.
[13] http://www.dlvsystem.com.
[14] https://potassco.org.

4.1 Evaluation Approach and System Architecture

In practice, external sources are evaluated wrt. truth assignments computed by the employed ASP solver. Hereby, the information that can be gained from external evaluations depends on the semantic properties of external sources and the extent of the solver assignment at the point of evaluation. Because a solver only assigns truth values to a subset of the Herbrand base during model search, we explicitly represent truth valuations of ground atoms by means of assignments $\mathbf{A}$. An *assignment* $\mathbf{A}$ is a consistent set of literals of form $\mathbf{T}a$ or $\mathbf{F}a$, where a is an atom which is said to be *true* in $\mathbf{A}$ if $\mathbf{T}a \in \mathbf{A}$, *false* if $\mathbf{F}a \in \mathbf{A}$, and *undefined* otherwise. We say that $\mathbf{A}$ is *complete* over a program P if for all atoms a in $grnd(P)$ either $\mathbf{T}a \in \mathbf{A}$ or $\mathbf{F}a \in \mathbf{A}$ holds. The interpretation I corresponding to a complete assignment $\mathbf{A}$ is $I = \{a \mid \mathbf{T}a \in \mathbf{A}\}$.

Traditionally, ground HEX programs have been evaluated by replacing each external atom $\&e[\vec{p}](\vec{c})$ by an ordinary atom $e_{\&e[\vec{p}]}(\vec{c})$ and introducing a rule $e_{\&e[\vec{p}]}(\vec{c}) \vee ne_{\&e[\vec{p}]}(\vec{c}) \leftarrow$ to guess its truth value; the resulting program is evaluated by an ordinary ASP solver (such as GRINGO and CLASP) to produce model candidates. Since the ordinary ASP solver is not aware of the actual semantics of external atoms, each candidate $\mathbf{A}$ is subsequently checked by testing (i) if the external atom guesses are correct, i.e., if $\mathbf{A} \models e_{\&e[\vec{p}]}(\vec{c})$ iff $\mathbf{A} \models \&e[\vec{p}](\vec{c})$ for all external atoms $\&e[\vec{p}](\vec{c})$, and (ii) if assignment $\mathbf{A}$ is a *subset-minimal* model of $f\Pi^{\mathbf{A}}$. If both conditions are satisfied, an answer set has been found. However, this approach did not scale well because there are exponentially many independent guesses in the number of external atoms in the ground program.

To overcome the problem, novel evaluation algorithms based on *conflict-driven* techniques have been introduced [30]. As in ordinary ASP solving, the input program is translated to a set of *nogoods*, i.e., a set of literals which must not be true at the same time. Given this representation, techniques from SAT solving are applied to find an assignment which satisfies all nogoods [57]. Notably, as the encoding as a set of nogoods is of exponential size due to *loop nogoods* which avoid cyclic justifications of atoms, those parts are generated only on-the-fly. Moreover, additional nogoods are learned from conflict situations, i.e., violated nogoods which cause the solver to backtrack; this is called *conflict-driven nogood learning*.

The extension of this algorithm towards the integration of external sources into the learning component works as follows. Whenever an external atom $\&e[\vec{p}](\vec{c})$ is evaluated under an assignment $\mathbf{A}$ in the checking part (i), the actual truth value under the assignment becomes evident. Then, regardless of whether the guessed value was correct or not, one can add a nogood which represents that $e_{\&e[\vec{p}]}(\vec{c})$ must be true under $\mathbf{A}$ if $\mathbf{A} \models \&e[\vec{p}](\vec{c})$ or that $e_{\&e[\vec{p}]}(\vec{c})$ must be false under $\mathbf{A}$ if $\mathbf{A} \not\models \&e[\vec{p}](\vec{c})$. If the guess was incorrect, the newly learned nogood will trigger backtracking, if the guess was correct, the learned nogood will prevent future wrong guesses.

Example 25. Suppose $\&\mathit{diff}[p,q](X)$ computes the set difference between the extensions of predicates p and q and that it is evaluated under $\mathbf{A} = \{\mathbf{T}p(a), \mathbf{T}p(b), \mathbf{F}q(a), \mathbf{T}q(b)\}$ with Herbrand universe $\mathcal{C} = \{a, b\}$. Then one can add the nogood $\{\mathbf{T}p(a), \mathbf{T}p(b), \mathbf{F}q(a), \mathbf{T}q(b), \mathbf{F}e_{\&\mathit{diff}[p,q]}(a)\}$ in order to learn that $\mathbf{A} \models e_{\&\mathit{diff}[p,q]}(a)$, i.e., whenever $p(a), p(b), q(b)$ are true and $q(a)$ is false, then $\&\mathit{diff}[p,q](a)$ must not be false. Conversely, one can learn that $\mathbf{A} \not\models \&\mathit{diff}[p,q](b)$ by adding nogood $\{\mathbf{T}p(a), \mathbf{T}p(b), \mathbf{F}q(a), \mathbf{T}q(b), \mathbf{T}e_{\&\mathit{diff}[p,q]}(b)\}$.

Experimental results show a significant, up to exponential speedup [35]. This is explained by the exclusion of up to exponentially many guesses by the learned nogoods.

The system architecture is shown in Fig. 2. The arcs model both control and data flow within the system. The evaluation of a HEX program works as follows. First, the input program is read from the file system or from standard input and passed to an *evaluation framework* ①, which may partition the input program depending on the chosen evaluation heuristics. This results in a number of acyclically interconnected *evaluation units*, which can be evaluated independently and interplay only by their input and output interpretations. While this interplay of the units is managed by the evaluation framework, the individual units are handled by *model generators* of different kinds depending on the different program classes. Each instance of a model generator takes care of a single evaluation unit, receives *input interpretations* from the framework (which are either output by predecessor units or come from the input facts for leaf units), and sends output interpretations back to the framework ②, which manages the integration of these interpretations to final answer sets.

Internally, the model generators make use of a *grounder* and a *solver* for ordinary ASP programs. The architecture of our system is flexible and supports multiple concrete backends which can be plugged in. Currently it supports GRINGO and CLASP, dlv, and an (unoptimized) internal grounder and solver, which serve mainly as a fallback option and for testing purposes. The reasoner backends GRINGO and CLASP are statically linked to our system, thus no interprocess communication is necessary. The model generator within the DLVHEX core sends a non-ground program to the HEX-grounder, and receives a ground program ③. The HEX-grounder in turn uses an (intelligent) ordinary ASP grounder (e.g. GRINGO, dlv's grounder, etc.) as submodule ④ and accesses external sources to handle value invention, i.e., values returned by external sources that do not occur in the input program ⑤. The ground-program is then sent to the solver and answer sets of the ground program (i.e. candidate compatible sets) are returned ⑥. Note that the grounder and the solver are separated and communicate only through the model generator, which is in contrast to previous implementations of DLVHEX where the external grounder and solver were used as a single unit (i.e., the non-ground program was sent and the answer sets were retrieved). Separating the two units became necessary because the DLVHEX core needs access to the ground-program in order to obtain important structural information (e.g. cyclicity) for optimization purposes.

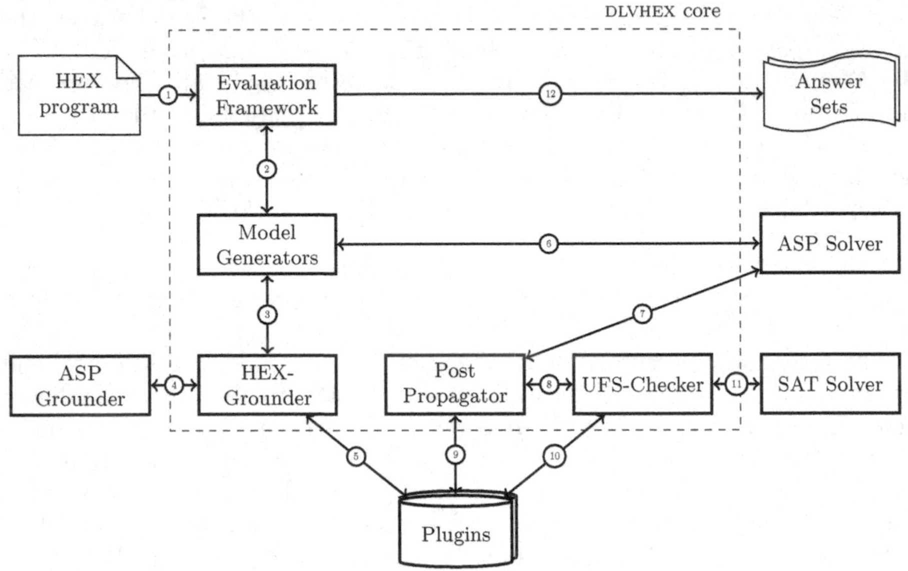

Fig. 2. Architecture of DLVHEX

The solver backend makes callbacks to the *post propagator* in the DLVHEX core once a model has been found or after deterministic propagation has been finished. During the callback, a complete or partial model is sent from the solver backend to the post propagator, and learned nogoods are sent back to the external solver ⑦. In case of CLASP as backend, we exploit its SMT interface, which was previously used for the special case of constraint answer set solving. The post propagator performs checks to eliminate spurious answer set candidates, which requires calls to the *plugins*, which implement the external sources. The input list is sent to the external source and the truth values and possibly user-defined learnt nogoods are returned to the post propagator ⑨. Moreover, the post propagator also sends the (complete or partial) model to the *unfounded set checker (UFS checker)*. UFS checking is one possible realization of minimality checking wrt. the reduct. While foundedness (cf. Sect. 2) means that each true atom is supported by some rule, this additional step is necessary to exclude self-justified atoms due to cyclic dependencies. While the ordinary ASP solver already performs such a check, it does not know the semantics of external sources and thus cannot detect all unfounded sets, which makes an additional check necessary. For this, the UFS checker employs a SAT solver ⑪, which can either be CLASP or the internal solver. More precisely, a specific SAT instance depending on the current answer set candidate and the semantics of the external atoms wrt. this candidate is constructed, such that the models of this instance correspond to unfounded sets. In order to consider the semantics of external atoms during UFS detection for constructing the SAT instance, it needs to call the external sources ⑩. The UFS checker possibly returns nogoods learned from unfounded sets to the post propagator ⑧. The post propagator sends all learned nogoods back to the ASP solver. This makes sure that eventually only valid answer sets arrive at the model generator ⑥.

Finally, after the evaluation framework has built the final answer sets from the output interpretations of the individual evaluation units, they are output to the user ⑫.

For more details we refer to [89].

4.2 Using the DLVHEX System

The system is provided as a command-line tool called `dlvhex2` which expects as only mandatory parameter the filename of the HEX program to evaluate (or `--` to read from standard input). Plugins are loaded from a global plugin directory where they need to be installed before. Thus, the simplest possible call is of form `dlvhex2 prog.hex` where `prog.hex` refers to a program.

However, the system provides numerous command-line options to customize the reasoning process. They include technical options such as the possibility to load plugins from custom locations (e.g. `--plugindir=$HOME/myplugin`), options for customizing the output such as to project answer sets to certain predicates (e.g. `--filter=p`) or restrictions of the maximum number of answer sets to compute (e.g. `-n=7`), and options for tuning the reasoning algorithms; the latter may be used to select heuristics and reasoning techniques based on the problem to be solved. For an exhaustive overview of the usage of the system and its command-line options, we refer to its manual [46]. The system also provides online help, which can be retrieved by calling `dlvhex2 -h`.

In the following we focus on recently added features which distinguish the DLVHEX system from other similar systems and from earlier versions.

While previous releases were mainly prototypes for empirically evaluating algorithms and research results, recent releases also aim at practical applicability of the system for implementing real applications. To this end, important system features have been added to improve the overall user's convenience by simplifying its usage, to speed up the evaluation, and in order to reduce syntactic restrictions. The enhancements can be organized in two main groups: (i) **usability and system features**, including a novel convenient programming interface for providers of external sources and the integration of support for popular ASP extensions and interoperability, and (ii) enhancements based on **exploiting external source properties** towards *scalability boosts* and increased *language flexibility* based on *liberal safety*, which is a safety criterion that is less restrictive than previous notions of safety. We describe these features in the following.

4.3 Usability and System Features

In this section we present recent work on the system side to improve the user's convenience. We start with general remarks on the DLVHEX software and its dissemination. DLVHEX was previously only available in source format (released under GNU LGPL) and only for Linux platforms. This deployment method turned out to be inconvenient for ASP programmers who want to use the system as is without custom modifications, We thus now provide pre-built binaries for all major platforms (Linux-based, OS X and Windows) in addition. We further created an online demo of the system under http://www.kr.tuwien.ac.at/research/systems/dlvhex/demo.php which allows for evaluating HEX programs directly in the browser (the user may specify both the logic program and custom Python-implemented external atoms in two input fields). The demo comes with a small set of examples to demonstrate the main features of the KR formalism. We further provide a manual to support new users of the system [46].

Next, the following two subsections give an overview of the new Python programming interface and interoperability of the system.

Python Programming Interface. With earlier versions of the system, users who wanted to integrate custom external sources had to write plugins in C++. While this was natural as the reasoner itself is implemented in C++, it was cumbersome and introduced development overhead even for experienced developers. This is because multiple configuration, source and header files need to be created even when realizing only a small and simple plugin. Also the compilation and linking overhead during development and debugging was considered inconvenient.

As a user-friendly alternative, DLVHEX 2.5.0 introduces a plugin API for Python-implemented external sources. A plugin consists of a single file (unless the user explicitly wants to use multiple files), which imports a dedicated `dlvhex` package and specifies a single method for each external atom. Thanks to higher-level features of Python and modern packages, this usually results in much shorter and simpler code than with C++-implemented plugins. A central `register` method exports the available external atoms and (optionally) their properties to DLVHEX.

Example 26. The following snippet implements $\&diff[p,q](X)$ for computing the values X which are in the extension of p but not in that of q.

```
import dlvhex

def diff(p,q):
  for x in dlvhex.getTrueInputAtoms():     # for all true input atoms
    if x.tuple()[0] == p:                   # is it of form p(c)?
      if dlvhex.isFalse(dlvhex.storeAtom(# is q(c) false?
        (q, x.tuple()[1]))):
        dlvhex.output((x.tuple()[1], )); # then c is in the output

def register():
  dlvhex.addAtom("diff", (dlvhex.PREDICATE, dlvhex.PREDICATE),
    1, prop)
```

The following example illustrates the usage of an external atom in a HEX program, for which the corresponding Python plugin is created subsequently.

Example 27. Consider the program

$$\Pi = \left\{ \begin{array}{l} r_1\colon start(s). \\ r_2\colon scc(X) \leftarrow start(X). \quad r_3\colon scc(Y) \leftarrow scc(X), \&edge[X](Y). \end{array} \right\}$$

where r_1 selects a node s from an externally defined (finite) graph, and r_2 and r_3 recursively compute the strongly connected component of s. To this end, the external atom $\&edge[X](Y)$ is used, which is true if Y is directly reachable from X (and false otherwise).

The implementation of $\&edge[X](Y)$ may look as follows:

```
def edge(x):
  graph=((1,2),(1,3),(2,3))          # simplified example implementation
  for edge in graph:                 # search for outgoing edges
    if edge[0]==x.intValue():        # of node x
      dlvhex.output((edge[1],))      # output edge target
```

On the command-line, the call

```
dlvhex2 --python-plugin=plugin.py prog.hex
```

loads the external atoms defined in `plugin.py` and then evaluates HEX program `prog.hex`.

In the system, the Python programming interface is realized as a wrapper of the generic C++ interface as shown in Fig. 3, where arcs model both control and data flow. That is, the Python interface uses only the C++ interface but does not communicate with the core reasoning components otherwise. This turns the Python interface in fact into a special C++ plugin. The performance gap between C++ and Python plugins is normally negligible (the update of the Python data structures is in the worst case linear in the number of input atoms), unless the plugin is itself computationally expensive. Wrappers for other languages such as Java or C# can be added similarly and can also be implemented externally, i.e., they do not necessarily need to be part of the DLVHEX solver.

For a complete API description we refer to the system website.

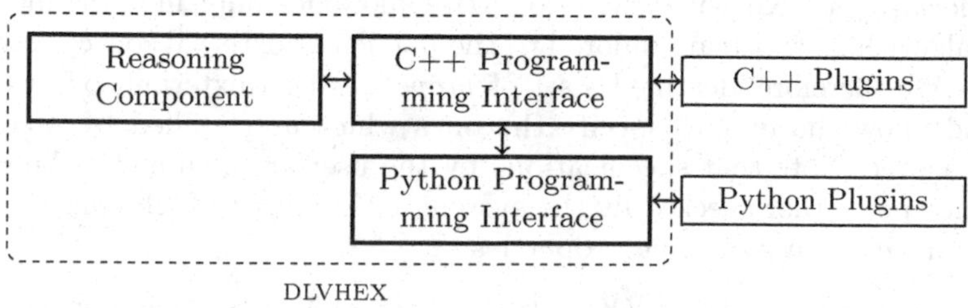

Fig. 3. Architecture of the python programming interface

ASP-Core-2 Standard, Extensions and Interoperability. In the course of the organization of the fourth ASP competition, the input language of ASP systems was standardized in the *ASP-Core-2 input language format* [19].[15] The DLVHEX system in its current version supports all features defined in the standard, including function symbols, choice rules, conditional literals, aggregates, and weak constraints. The supported language is therefore a strict superset of the standard.

The system further supports input and output in CSV format to improve interoperability with other systems such as Unix commands or spreadsheet applications. That is, facts may be read from the lines of a CSV file, where the different values are mapped to the arguments of a predicate. After the computation, the extension of a specified predicate may be written in CSV format to allow a seamless further processing by other applications. For instance, consider `salary.csv`:

```
joe,smith,2000
sue,johnson,2200
```

It can be read as facts $emp(1, joe, smith, 2000)$ and $emp(2, sue, johnson, 2200)$ (where the first element is the original line number if relevant) using the DLVHEX command-line option `--csvinput=emp,salary.csv`. Conversely, results can be output in CSV format.

4.4 Exploiting External Source Properties

External sources were seen as black boxes in earlier versions of DLVHEX. It was assumed that the system does not have any information about them, except that there is an oracle function which decides satisfaction of an external atom under a complete assignment. As a consequence, the room for optimizations in the algorithms was limited because the value of an external atom under one assignment did not allow for drawing any conclusions about its behavior under other assignments.

However, in many practical applications the provider of an external source and/or the HEX programmer have additional knowledge about the behavior of the source, for instance, that the source is monotonic, functional, has a limited domain, returns only elements which are smaller than the input (according to some ordering), etc. Knowing such properties allows for implementing more specialized algorithms which are tailored to the particular external sources used in a program. We therefore identified a set of *properties* that external sources might have, and allow the user to specify the ones which are fulfilled by a concrete external source. Note that specifications by the user are assumed to be correct and cannot be further checked by the system, either due to high computational costs or undecidability of some properties.

Example 28. Suppose $\&tail[X](Y)$ is true whenever Y is the string which results from string X if the first character is dropped. Then the output is always smaller than the input wrt. string length.

[15] https://www.mat.unical.it/aspcomp2013/files/ASP-CORE-2.01c.pdf.

The system exploits these properties automatically, mainly for two purposes: in the *learning algorithms for scalability enhancements* and in the *grounding component for more flexibility of the language* due to reduced syntactic limitations. In addition, there are several other system components which exploit the properties to further speed up the evaluation, such as skipping various checks if their result is definite due to known behavior of external sources, partitioning a reasoning task into smaller independent tasks, avoiding unnecessary evaluations of external atoms, and drawing deterministic conclusions rather than guessing.

However, as this section presents the system from a user's perspective, we focus on *which* properties can be specified, *how* the user can do that, and give a rough idea of how the system makes use of this information, but we refrain from discussing the involved algorithms in detail. This is in line with the goal of these properties: the user can benefit from the advantages when specifying them, but without the need to care about how the system is going to exploit this information. Instead, the user can generally expect that the more information is available to the system, the more efficient evaluation will be; if the added information does not yield a speedup, it does at least no harm.[16] Some of the properties, such as monotonicity, do even lead to a drop of complexity from Σ_2^P to *NP* for answer set existence checking over ground disjunction-free programs, provided that external sources are polynomial [51].

Furthermore, properties also serve as *assertions*: if the reasoner observes a behavior of external sources which contradicts the declared properties, appropriate error messages are printed. However, a systematic check of asserted properties is not performed because of high computational costs or even undecidability of some properties.

Specifying Properties. The specification of properties is supported in two ways. The first option is to declare them as part of the external source implementation via the *external source interface.* The second option is to specify them as part of the HEX program using so-called *property tags.*

Specification via the External Source Interface. Properties are mostly specified via the (C++ or Python) programming interface for external sources. To this end, the procedural code which implements external atoms calls specific *setter methods* provided by the programming interface to inform the system that the source has certain properties.

Example 29. The implementation of $\&md5[X](Y)$ which computes for a string X its MD5 hash value Y might call `prop.setFunctionality(true)` to let DLVHEX know that for each X there is exactly one Y. This allows the system, for instance, to conclude that $\&md5[x](y_2)$ is false without evaluating the external source, if it has already found a value $y_1 \neq y_2$ such that $\&md5[x](y_1)$ is true.

[16] The only property related to potential performance decrease is provision of a *three-valued semantics* as additional calls of the external source are sometimes counterproductive [44]. However, even then the property itself does not harm since it is only exploited by certain (non-default) evaluation heuristics selected via command-line options.

If a property is declared in this way, the source is meant to *always* provide a certain behavior, independent of its usage in a HEX program, like in case of the computation of a hash value. Another example is $\&\mathit{diff}[p,q](X)$ from Example 26, which computes all values X in the extension of p but not in that of q wrt. assignment $\mathbf{A}$ (formally, these are all values x s.t. $f_{\&\mathit{diff}}(\mathbf{A}, p, q, x) = \mathbf{T}$). This external atom is always monotone/antimonotone in the first/second parameter, which can be specified by calling `prop.addMonotonicInputPredicate(0)` and `prop.addAntimonotonicInputPredicate(1)`.

Example 30. Reconsider the external atom $\&\mathit{diff}[p,q](X)$ from Example 26. It is monotonic in p and antimonotonic in q. We adopt the implementation of the external source as follows in order to inform the reasoner about the properties, which typically leads to efficiency improvements.

```
import dlvhex

def diff(p,q):
  for x in dlvhex.getTrueInputAtoms():    # for all true input atoms
    if x.tuple()[0] == p:                  # is it of form p(c)?
      if dlvhex.isFalse(dlvhex.storeAtom(# is q(c) false?
        (q, x.tuple()[1]))):
        dlvhex.output((x.tuple()[1], )); # then c is in the output

def register():
  prop = dlvhex.ExtSourceProperties()    # inform dlvhex about
  prop.addMonotonicInputPredicate(0)     # monotonicity/antimon.
  prop.addAntimonotonicInputPredicate(1)# in first/second parameter
  dlvhex.addAtom("diff", (dlvhex.PREDICATE, dlvhex.PREDICATE),
    1, prop)
```

Specification via Property Tags. However, it might also be the case that only a specific usage of an external source in a concrete program has a property. Then the implementer of the external source cannot declare it yet; instead, only the implementer of the HEX program has sufficient knowledge and can declare the property as part of an external atom in the program.

Example 31. Suppose $\&\mathit{greaterThan}[p, 10]()$ checks if the sum of integer values c s.t. $p(c)$ is true is greater than 10. It is not monotone in general if negative integers are allowed, but it is monotone if a program uses only positive integers. While the provider of the external source cannot assert the property, the user of the external source in a concrete program, who knows the context, can.

To this end, the HEX language and implementation were extended such that external atoms can be followed by *property tags* of form $\langle$*list of properties*$\rangle$, where the list of properties is comma-separated. Each property is a whitespace-separated list of constants, consisting of a *property type* (first element in the list), and a number of *property parameters* (remaining elements in the list), whose number depends on the property type and may also have default values. For example, $\&\mathit{diff}[p,q](X)\langle \mathit{monotonic}\ p, \mathit{antimonotonic}\ q\rangle$ specifies two properties which declare that the external atom is monotonic in p and antimonotonic in q wrt. their extension in the input assignment. Here, the first property *monotonic p* uses the property type *monotonic* and the property parameter p, while the second property *antimonotonic q* uses the property type *antimonotonic* and the property parameter q. Another example is the external atom $\&greaterThan[p, 10]()\langle monotonic\rangle$, which declares that the external source is monotonic in all parameters (because it is monotonic in p and it is trivially monotonic in constant input parameters because they are independent of the input assignment); the property type is *monotonic* and no property parameters are explicitly specified, which indicates by default that the source is monotonic in all inputs. Properties declared by tags are understood to hold *in addition* to those declared via the external source interface (stating conflicting properties is not possible with the currently available ones).

Supported properties. The following list gives an overview about the currently available properties and how to specify them if the property tag language is used (but all of them can be specified both via the external source interface or in property tags). Each property is explained with an example in order to show the property type and the expected property parameters.

- **Functionality:** $\&add[X, Y](Z)\langle functional\rangle$
  The external atom adds integers X and Y and is true for their sum Z. The source provides exactly one output value for a given input. There are no property parameters.
- **Monotonicity in a parameter** $\&diff[p, q](X)\langle monotonic\ p\rangle$
  The external atom computes the difference of the extensions of p and q. The source is monotonic in predicate parameter p (i.e., if the extension of p increases, the output does not shrink), as indicated by the property parameter.
- **Global monotonicity:** $\&union[p, q](X)\langle monotonic\rangle$
  The source computes the set union of the extensions of p and q. It is monotonic in all parameters (indicated by the default value of the missing property parameter). Another example are queries over DL ontologies and RDF queries as mentioned in Sect. 3.2.
- **Antimonotonicity in a parameter:** $\&diff[p, q](X)\langle antimonotonic\ q\rangle$
  The source is antimonotonic in predicate parameter q (i.e., if the extension of q shrinks, the output does not shrink).
- **Global antimonotonicity:** $\&complement[p](X)\langle antimonotonic\rangle$
  The source computes the complement of the extension of p wrt. a fixed domain. It is antimonotonic in all parameters.
- **Linearity on atoms:** $\&union[p, q](X)\langle atomlevellinear\rangle$
  We have domain independence on the level of atoms, i.e., the source can be separately evaluated for each input atom s.t. the final result is the union of the results of all evaluations. For instance, the evaluation under assignment $\mathbf{A} = \{\mathbf{T}p(a), \mathbf{T}p(b), \mathbf{T}q(c)\}$, which yields $\{a, b, c\}$, can be split up into three evaluations under $\mathbf{A}_1 = \{\mathbf{T}p(a)\}$, $\mathbf{A}_2 = \{\mathbf{T}p(b)\}$ and $\mathbf{A}_3 = \{\mathbf{T}q(c)\}$, which yield $\{a\}$, $\{b\}$ and $\{c\}$, respectively, and their union the result of the evaluation under $\mathbf{A}$. There are no property parameters.

- **Linearity on tuples:** $\&\mathit{diff}[p,q](X)\langle \mathit{tuplelevellinear}\rangle$
  We have domain independence on the level of tuples in the extensions of predicate input parameters, i.e., the source can be separately evaluated for each pair of atoms $p(\vec{c})$ and $q(\vec{c})$ for all vectors of terms $\vec{c}$ s.t. the final result is the union of the results of all evaluations. For instance, the evaluation under $\mathbf{A} = \{\mathbf{T}p(a), \mathbf{T}p(b), \mathbf{F}q(a), \mathbf{T}q(b)\}$, which yields $\{a\}$, can be split up into two evaluations under $\mathbf{A}_1 = \{\mathbf{T}p(a), \mathbf{F}q(a)\}$ and $\mathbf{A}_2 = \{\mathbf{T}p(b), \mathbf{T}q(b)\}$, which yield $\{a\}$ and $\emptyset$, respectively, and their union in the result of the evaluation under $\mathbf{A}$. However, it would not be correct to split $\mathbf{A}_2$ further up into $\mathbf{A}_{2.1} = \{\mathbf{T}p(b)\}$ and $\mathbf{A}_{2.2} = \{\mathbf{T}q(b)\}$ as they would yield the results $\{b\}$ and $\emptyset$, which would put b into the final result, which differs from the evaluation under $\mathbf{A}$. There are no property parameters.
- **Finite domain:** $\&\mathit{edges}[\mathit{graph.dot}](X,Y)\langle \mathit{finitedomain}\ 0, \mathit{finitedomain}\ 1\rangle$
  Imports the edges of a predefined graph. Both output values can have only finitely many different values. To this end, we specify two properties with type *finitedomain* with property parameters that identify the output terms X and Y by index (0 and 1, respectively).
  In the route planning application mentioned in Sect. 3.2, and shown in more detail below, accesses to external maps fulfill this property since real-world maps are always finite.
- **Finite domain wrt. the input:** $\&\mathit{diff}[p,q](X)\langle \mathit{relativefinitedomain}\ 0\ 0\rangle$
  Only constants which already appear in the 0-th input (indicated by the first property parameter 0; points in this case to the predicate p) may occur as first output term (indicated by the second property parameter 0). Informally, the difference between sets represented by predicates p and q can only contain elements which appear in the set represented by p.
- **Finite fiber:** $\&\mathit{sqrt}[X](Z)\langle \mathit{finitefiber}\rangle$
  The source computes the square root of X. Each element in the output is only produced by finitely many different inputs (in this case, in fact, only by a single input value). There are no property parameters.
- **Well-ordering wrt. string lengths:** $\&\mathit{tail}[X](Z)\langle \mathit{wellorderingstrlen}\ 0\ 0\rangle$
  The source drops the first character of string X and returns the result in Z. The 0-th output (indicated by the second property parameter 0) is no longer than the longest string in the 0-th input (indicated by the first property parameter 0).
- **General well-ordering:** $\&\mathit{decrement}[X](Z)\langle \mathit{wellordering}\ 0\ 0\rangle$
  The external atom decrements a given integer. There is an ordering of all constants such that the 0-th output (second parameter) is no greater than the 0-th input (first parameter) wrt. this ordering.
- **Three-valued semantics:** $\&g[\vec{X}](\vec{Y})\langle \mathit{providespartialanswer}\rangle$
  The external source can be evaluated under partial assignments, i.e., it can handle assignments which do not define all atoms, but may evaluate to *undefined* ($\mathbf{U}$) in this case (can be used with any external source if implemented).

Note that properties are only useful if they are exploited by at least one solving technique or algorithm implemented in the reasoner. It is therefore *not* intended that typical users introduce custom properties, but only tag external atoms with existing ones from the above list. However, for advanced users who contribute to or customize the reasoner itself, the framework supports easy extension of the parser and data structures. Exploiting such a new property in the algorithms might be more sophisticated depending on the particular property and the envisaged goal.

Scalability Boost. Recall that the current evaluation algorithm for HEX-programs employs a conflict-driven approach, which learns nogoods from external sources to exclude incorrect guesses. This basic approach can be further improved by keeping the learned nogoods small by exploiting external source properties or external source evaluation under partial assignments.

Exploiting External Source Properties. In Example 25, atoms $p(a)$ and $q(a)$ in the assignment are in fact irrelevant when deciding whether $\&\mathit{diff}[p,q](b)$ is true because constants a and b are independent (similarly for $p(b)$ and $q(b)$ when deciding $\&\mathit{diff}[p,q](a)$). If this information is available to the system, it can be exploited to shrink nogoods to the relevant part such that the search space is pruned more effectively.

One way to gain the required information is to make use of external source properties. In particular, the independence of a and b in the previous example can be derived from the property 'linearity on tuples'. Then we can reduce the nogood $\{\mathbf{T}p(a), \mathbf{T}p(b), \mathbf{F}q(a), \mathbf{T}q(b), \mathbf{F}e_{\&\mathit{diff}[p,q]}(a)\}$ to $\{\mathbf{T}p(a), \mathbf{F}q(a), \mathbf{F}e_{\&\mathit{diff}[p,q]}(a)\}$ and nogood $\{\mathbf{T}p(a), \mathbf{T}p(b), \mathbf{F}q(a), \mathbf{T}q(b), \mathbf{T}e_{\&\mathit{diff}[p,q]}(b)\}$ to the smaller nogood $\{\mathbf{T}p(b), \mathbf{T}q(b), \mathbf{T}e_{\&\mathit{diff}[p,q]}(b)\}$. If monotonicity in p is known in addition, then nogood $\{\mathbf{T}p(b), \mathbf{T}q(b), \mathbf{T}e_{\&\mathit{diff}[p,q]}(b)\}$ can be further simplified to $\{\mathbf{T}q(b), \mathbf{T}e_{\&\mathit{diff}[p,q]}(b)\}$ by dropping $\mathbf{T}q(a)$ because $\&\mathit{diff}[p,q](b)$ will remain false even if $q(a)$ becomes false.

Exploiting Three-Valued Oracle Functions. Alternatively or in addition to external source properties, also three-valued oracle functions can be exploited for shrinking learned nogoods to the essential part [44]. If the truth value is already known and will not change when the assignment becomes more complete, then the set of yet unassigned atoms is irrelevant for the output of the external source. This is exploited for nogood minimization as follows. Whenever a nogood is learned, the system iteratively tries to remove one of the input atoms and evaluate again in order to check if the truth value is still defined. If so, the according atom is not necessary and can be removed from the nogood.

For instance, a proper three-valued oracle function in the previous example allows for reducing the nogood $\{\mathbf{T}p(a), \mathbf{T}p(b), \mathbf{F}q(a), \mathbf{T}q(b), \mathbf{T}e_{\&\mathit{diff}[p,q]}(b)\}$ from above to $\{\mathbf{T}q(b), \mathbf{T}e_{\&\mathit{diff}[p,q]}(b)\}$, because whenever $\mathbf{T}q(b)$ is in the assignment, it is already definite that $\&\mathit{diff}[p,q](b)$ is false.

Discussion and Extensions. Whether to exploit external source properties, three-valued oracle functions, or both, largely depends on the use case. Depending on the type of external source to be realized, the implementation of a three-valued oracle function might be more challenging than that of a Boolean one (implementing an algorithm which decides over partial assignments is in general more difficult than if all information is known). However, it allows for exploiting application-specific knowledge in an optimal way [44]. In contrast, tagging external sources with properties from a list is easy and can still lead to good efficiency.

Language Flexibility Based on Liberal Safety. As already discussed, external atoms may introduce constants which do not appear in the program (*value invention*). Obviously, this can in general lead to programs Π where no finite subset of the full, possibly infinite grounding $grnd(\Pi)$ of the program has the same answer sets as Π. Since this inhibits grounding in general, it is crucial to identify classes of programs for which the existence of such a finite grounding is guaranteed; we call this property *finite groundability.* Traditionally, *strong safety* was used, which basically forbids value invention by recursive external atoms (i.e., external atoms whose input possibly depends on its own output wrt. the predicate dependency graph, for a formal definition cf. [43]). If only non-recursive external atoms introduce new values, termination is guaranteed. However, it turns out that this is only a sufficient but not a necessary criterion, i.e., strong safety is overly restrictive.

Example 32. The program Π from Example 27 is *not* strongly safe because $\&edge[X](Y)$ is recursive (output Y may be input to the same external atom by another application of r_3) but may introduce values for Y which do not appear in Π. However, if one knows that the graph is finite, one can conclude that the recursive addition of new values will end at some point.

In the example, the criterion may be circumvented by importing the full domain a priori and adding *domain predicates*, i.e., adding $node(Y)$ to the body of r_3 and another rule $node(X) \leftarrow \&node[](X)$ to import all nodes. Then $\&edge[X](Y)$ does no longer invent values because all possible values for Y are determined in a non-recursive fashion using $\&node[](X)$. However, this comes at the price of importing the whole graph although only a small set of nodes might be in the strongly connected component of s.

Therefore, new safety criteria have been introduced which allow for exploiting both syntactic and semantic conditions to derive finite groundability, where the latter are based on external source properties. For instance, if it is known that the input to an external atom can have only finitely many different values, then (due to the restrictions for oracle functions introduced in Sect. 2.4) also the set of possible output values will be finite. Furthermore, if an external atom is acyclic, then the set of relevant output values will also be finite. Such considerations have been formalized by the notion of *liberally safe* HEX programs, which are guaranteed to have a finite grounding that can be computed using a novel algorithm [34]. Formally, the notion is based on *attribute positions* of external atoms; however, since the technical details are more elaborated, we give only an intuitive overview here.

Example 33. Let $\&tail[X](Y)$ drop the first character of string X and return it as Y. Then Y is no longer than X and – even if used recursively – it is guaranteed that it can generate only finitely many strings because there are only finitely many strings with a length up to the one of X.

In addition to the declaration of predefined properties, the generic framework is also extensible in such a way that custom knowledge about external sources can be exploited. To this end, providers may implement additional safety criteria, which are integrated into the safety check. The safety check itself is fast (at most quadratic in the size of the non-ground program).

The system combines the available information, given by syntactic conditions, specified semantic properties, and safety plugins in order to check safety of the program. This does not only allow for writing programs with fewer syntactic restrictions, but the implementation of some applications may become possible in the first place. For instance, in *route planning applications*, importing the whole map material a priori is practically impossible due to the large amount of data, while a selective import using liberal safety makes the application possible [34], as is the case for the route planning application described in the next section.

In case a program is not safe, the system prints hints such as the rule and the variable for which finiteness during instantiation could not be proven. This information is intended to guide the user when providing more information in order to make the program safe, e.g., by adding properties which constrain the values of this variable further. Alternatively, a command-line option allows to disable the safety check altogether, in which case there is no guarantee that the reasoner terminates.

5 Case Study

In this section, a case study is presented, where we describe the practical treatment of a realistic problem by employing DLVHEX, following the methodology introduced in Sect. 3. This section also serves as a tutorial covering the basic usage of DLVHEX, as well as some advanced features. For this purpose, we develop a HEX-encoding step by step, which is more elaborated than the example programs considered in the previous section, and discuss possible efficiency improvements that can be achieved by exploiting facilities provided by the DLVHEX-system. More details on implementing HEX applications can be found in the DLVHEX user guide [46]. The code snippets presented in this section are fragments of the complete implementation for this case study available at https://github.com/hexhex/manual/tree/master/RW2017/.

The problem of our case study is from the *route planning* domain, which has already been considered for HEX before, e.g. in [34,46,47,90]. Suppose one wants to plan a trip through the city of Vienna, where a number of places should be visited on the way. For planning the trip, we rely on data about metro, tram and bus stations, which can be obtained from data.wien.gv.at. It contains tuples of the form (l, l', c, t), where l and l' are locations in Vienna, for

```
1 Museumsquartier                Karlsplatz       1  U2
2 Floetzersteigbruecke           Matschgasse      3  51A
3 WaehringerStrasseVolksoper     Kutschkergasse   2  40
4 ...
```

Fig. 4. vienna_transport.graph

example 'Karlsplatz' or 'Wien Mitte', t is a means of transport that connects both locations, e.g. 'Bus 65A' or 'Metro U4', and c is an integer representing the associated costs, e.g. the amount of time required to travel from l to l' by using t. For our implementation, the data is contained in a file which is structured as shown in Fig. 4.

For instance, line 1 states that 'Karlsplatz' can be reached from 'Museumsquartier' taking 'U2' at cost 1.

5.1 Sequence Generation

Given a subset of all possible locations contained in the data set, the general goal is to compute a sequence of locations that satisfies a number of criteria, which we are going to introduce in several stages. We start developing our encoding by generating all possible sequences in which a number of destinations could be visited, by means of the HEX program shown in Fig. 5 (which will be extended in the sequel of this section). This corresponds to the *guessing part* of the encoding as described in the basic methodology in Sect. 3.

```
1  sequence(I,L) v nsequence(I,L) :- destination(L),
2          #int(I), #int(C), C = #count{N : destination(N)}, I < C.
3
4  :- sequence(I1,L), sequence(I2,L), I1 != I2.
5  :- sequence(I,L1), sequence(I,L2), L1 != L2.
6
7  inSequence(L) :- sequence(I,L)}.
8  :- destination(L), not inSequence(L).
9
10 haveLocation(I) :- sequence(I,L).
11 :- sequence(I,L), I1 < I, #int(I1), not haveLocation(I1).
```

Fig. 5. route_planning.hex

The first rule generates a guess for each combination of locations that should be visited and possible position in the resulting sequence. Here, the locations that should be visited are assumed to be all locations contained in the extension of the predicate `destination`, and `C` is the number of such locations obtained by using the `#count`-aggregate. The constraints in lines 4 and 5 state that each location should only appear once in the sequence, and that two locations cannot be visited at the same time, respectively. The rules in lines 7 to 11 ensure that every destination appears in the sequence and that there are no gaps in the sequence.

If we add two destinations via the facts `destination("Stephansplatz")` and `destination("Karlsplatz")`, and execute the program by making the command-line call:

```
$ dlvhex2 route_planning.hex --filter=sequence --maxint=10
```

the DLVHEX-system returns the following two answer sets:

```
{sequence(1,"Stephansplatz"),sequence(0,"Karlsplatz")}
{sequence(0,"Stephansplatz"),sequence(1,"Karlsplatz")}
```

By using the command line option `--filter`, we can limit the output to a specific predicate, and `--maxint` sets an upper limit for the integers that occur in the grounding of the program. The latter value needs to be chosen large enough depending on the program. The returned answer sets correspond to all possible sequences in which the given destinations can be visited.

5.2 Trip Planning

Next, we want to exploit the information we have in our data set about connections between locations (via metro, tram or bus) in order to retrieve which means of transport we can use regarding a particular visit sequence. In addition, based on the associated costs for each trip via a certain means of transport, we are interested in the fastest connections between destinations in the sequence. For this reason, the next step in the development of our encoding consists in creating an external source that computes the shortest path between two locations in Vienna, by employing a dedicated algorithm. The plugin should retrieve the fastest connection together with the required costs and the traffic lines that need to be taken. At this, the corresponding plugin method needs access to our data set file.

Our goal is to implement an external source that can be interfaced by means of an external atom of the following form:

```
&route[File,Location1,Location2](Station1,Station2,Costs,Line)
```

Given the name of a file containing the transport data ('vienna_transport.graph' in our case) and two location names, the external source should yield all tuples representing direct connections between stations that need to be visited in order to travel from `Location1` to `Location2` with minimal costs, together with the costs for each connection and the transport line used. Thus, the shortest path from one location to another needs to be computed externally by the corresponding plugin. This corresponds to *computation outsourcing* as described in Sect. 3.

Here, we utilize the *Python* interface of DLVHEX to implement the plugin, which allows faster prototyping than the alternative *C++* interface, on which the *Python* interface is based. By outsourcing the computation of the optimal connection between two locations, we can access an off-the-shelf implementation

```
1  import dlvhex
2  import networkx as nx

   ...

6  def route(graph, start, end):
7    G = nx.read_edgelist(graph.value()[1:-1], nodetype=str,
8      data=[('weight', float),('label', str)],
9      create_using=nx.MultiDiGraph())
10   shortestPath = nx.shortest_path(G, source=start.value()[1:-1],
11     target=end.value()[1:-1], weight='weight')
12
13   for i in range(0, len(shortestPath)-1):
14     costs = 10
15
16     for edge in G.edges(data=True):
17       if edge[0] == shortestPath[i] and
18         edge[1] == shortestPath[i+1] and
19         edge[2]['weight'] < costs:
20         costs = edge[2]['weight']
21         transport = edge[2]['label']
22
23     dlvhex.output(('"' + shortestPath[i] + '"',
24       '"' + shortestPath[i+1] + '"',
25       int(costs), '"' + transport + '"'))

   ...

56 def register():
57   prop = dlvhex.ExtSourceProperties()
58   prop.addFiniteOutputDomain(0)
59   prop.addFiniteOutputDomain(1)
60   prop.addFiniteOutputDomain(2)
61   prop.addFiniteOutputDomain(3)
62   dlvhex.addAtom("route", (dlvhex.CONSTANT, dlvhex.CONSTANT,
63     dlvhex.CONSTANT), 4, prop)
```

Fig. 6. route_plugin.py

contained in a *Python* library for this task. The plugin implementation is realized as shown in Fig. 6.

First, we need to import the *Python* library `dlvhex`, and the `networkx` package for performing graph computations. The implementation of the external source mirrors the input-output structure of external atoms, in that a plugin is constituted by a *Python* method with arguments corresponding to the input parameters of the external atom; and output tuples of an external atom are added via the interface method `dlvhex.output()`, representing the results of the plugin method. In this respect, it is essential that the plugin method implements a stateless behavior where the same set of output tuples is returned for a specific input each time the method is called, as the semantics of HEX and the DLVHEX-algorithm rely on this property.

Inside the plugin method starting at line 6, we first import the transport network using the file name provided in the call of the external source. The respective input constant can be retrieved by calling the method `value()` on the first argument of the plugin method. As the transport network does not change between calls of the external source, the graph could additionally be cached in the implementation, so that it would not need to be reloaded each time the source is evaluated. However, we omit the caching here to keep the code listing succinct. Afterwards, we compute and store the shortest path between the locations provided as input constants by means of the library function `nx.shortest_path`, in line 10. Finally, in lines 13 to 25, we build the output tuples representing separate connections on the way from the start to the end location, together with the traffic line taken in each step and the associated costs; and we return them via the method `dlvhex.output()`.

For DLVHEX to be able to call the plugin method for evaluating the truth value of an external atom, we need to register all plugins in a designated method called `register` (line 56). This is done via the method `dlvhex.addAtom` in line 62, which takes the method name corresponding to the external atom name, a tuple defining the input parameter types, the output arity, and a properties-object as arguments. For the external atom at hand, all input parameters are declared to be constants. If the evaluation of an external atom depends on the extension of some input predicate in the given interpretation, the type `dlvhex.PREDICATE` is used instead (as will be demonstrated below). A properties-object is obtained via the method `dlvhex.ExtSourceProperties()` and stored in the variable `prop` in line 57. It can be used to declare the external source properties described in Sect. 4. Here, we just define that each element of the output tuple can take only finitely many different values since our transport network is finite.

Now, we can extend our encoding by further rules that utilize the external atom named `&route` as shown in Fig. 7.

```
11 ...
12
13 connection(L1,L2,X,Y,C,T) :- sequence(N,L1), sequence(Next,L2),
14         Next = N + 1,
15         &route["vienna_transport.graph",L1,L2](X,Y,C,T).
16
17 pathLength(L) :- L = #count{L1,L2,X,Y : connection(L1,L2,X,Y,C,T)}.
18
19 tripTmp(0, X, L2, X, Y, C, T) :- sequence(0, X),
20         connection(X, L2, X, Y, C, T).
21 tripTmp(S, L1, L2, Y, Z, C2, T2) :- tripTmp(P, L1, L2, X, Y, C, T),
22         connection(L1, L2, Y, Z, C2, T2), S = P + 1, #int(S),
23         pathLength(L), S <= L.
24 tripTmp(S, Y, L3, Y, Z, C2, T2) :- tripTmp(P, L1, Y, X, Y, C, T),
25         connection(Y, L3, Y, Z, C2, T2), S = P + 1, #int(S),
26         pathLength(L), S <= L.
27
28 trip(S, X, Y, C, T) :- tripTmp(S, L1, L2, X, Y, C, T).
```

Fig. 7. route_planning.hex - second part

We extend the file *route_planning.hex* by a rule that retrieves all connections we have to take regarding a given visit sequence from the external source, in line 13. Note that, besides the locations in the extension of the predicate `destination` which we add to the program, the encoding does not contain any other locations. Thus, these need to be introduced by *value invention* by the external atom, restricted to the relevant stations. Moreover, we want to obtain the connections we are taking during the trip in sequential order. For this, we reference the overall length of the computed trip via the predicate `pathLength`, in line 17. In lines 19 to 26, we aggregate the connections between stations in form of a new sequence containing the whole trip in `tripTmp`, where we take connections between two destinations in line 21, and transitions between destinations from the initial sequence in line 24. For this, we use the variables `L1` and `L2` to associate sub-paths with trips between destinations, which we project away in line 28 to obtain the relevant trip information.

Now, assume we indicate a starting position by means of the fact `sequence (0,"Volkstheater")`, and add the facts `destination("Taubstummengasse")`, `destination("Stephansplatz")` and `destination("Volkstheater")` to the encoding. If DLVHEX is called by

```
$ dlvhex2 route_planning.hex --python-plugin=route_plugin.py
  --maxint=10 --filter=trip
```

the following possible trips are returned:

```
{trip(0,"Volkstheater","Museumsquartier",1,"U2"),
 trip(1,"Museumsquartier","Karlsplatz",1,"U2"),
 trip(2,"Karlsplatz","Taubstummengasse",1,"U1"),
 trip(3,"Taubstummengasse","Karlsplatz",1,"U1"),
 trip(4,"Karlsplatz","Stephansplatz",1,"U1")}

{trip(0,"Volkstheater","Herrengasse",1,"U3"),
 trip(1,"Herrengasse","Stephansplatz",1,"U3"),
 trip(2,"Stephansplatz","Karlsplatz",1,"U1"),
 trip(3,"Karlsplatz","Taubstummengasse",1,"U1")}
```

When calling DLVHEX with a program containing an external atom for which the corresponding plugin is implemented in a *Python* file, the path to the file needs to be provided via the option `--python-plugin`.

Consequently, there are two different options we can choose from, where the second trip is shorter. In order to only obtain the shortest trip, we could make use of weak constraints as introduced in Sect. 2, by adding the following to our encoding:: ∼ `trip(S, X, Y, C, T). [C@1,S,X,Y,C,T]`. As a consequence, by minimizing overall costs, DLVHEX only returns the answer set where the sum of costs of `trip`-atoms in the answer set is minimal. Computing shortest trips is related to the traveling salesperson problem.

5.3 Cyclic Dependencies

Next, suppose we want to refine our encoding further by also taking the requirement into account that if the whole trip is longer than a certain value, we want to include a destination that has a restaurant for having lunch in our trip. For this, we can introduce another external atom that checks whether we need a

```
25  ...
26
27  def needRestaurant(trip, limit):
28    tripLength = 0
29
30    for x in dlvhex.getInputAtoms():
31      if x.tuple()[0] == trip and x.isTrue():
32        tripLength += int(x.tuple()[4].value())
33
34    if tripLength > int(limit.value()):
35      dlvhex.output(())

    ...

56  def register():

    ...

65    prop = dlvhex.ExtSourceProperties()
66    prop.addMonotonicInputPredicate(0)
67    dlvhex.addAtom("needRestaurant",
68                   (dlvhex.PREDICATE, dlvhex.CONSTANT), 0, prop)
```

Fig. 8. route_plugin.py - second part

restaurant, by making use of the fact that it is easy to combine several external sources in a program with DLVHEX. We create the *Python* implementation for an external atom of the form `&needRestaurant[trip,Limit]()`. It should simply evaluate to true if the sum of the costs of the connections contained in the true extension of `trip` (relative to the current solver assignment) exceeds the constant value `Limit`. In contrast to `&route`, this external atom does not provide any output values, which is often the case when external atoms are used for checks or constraints in a HEX program. We extend our plugin file as shown in Fig. 8.

In the plugin method, we iterate over all input atoms and filter those that have the predicate name which has been passed to the external source, and which are true in the current solver assignment, in lines 30 and 31. Then, we add up all according costs by accessing the fourth argument of the respective atom. Finally, we define that the external atom evaluates to true if the provided limit is exceeded, by returning an empty output tuple, in line 35. If the output method of a Boolean external atom is not called at all, DLVHEX interprets this as an evaluation to false.

Here, we can declare that the external atom behaves monotonically on the first input parameter because once the costs associated to some trip exceed the limit, the external atom cannot be false when further connections are added to the trip. Defining such properties often has a large impact on the efficiency of the solving process. For instance, if we call the plugin method for a trip containing only one connection, the costs of which already exceed the limit, the truth value of the external atom is implied for any other trip as soon as it contains that connection, due to monotonicity of the external source. However, this cannot be detected by DLVHEX if the corresponding property declaration is missing.

Also, in contrast to the first plugin, we now declare the external atom to have a predicate input parameter, which causes DLVHEX to pass the complete extension of the predicate occurring in the ground HEX program (and, in the standard configuration, to postpone the external evaluation until the truth values of all its instances are decided during solving).

The additional external atom is used in the extension of our HEX-encoding shown in Fig. 9 in order to decide whether a location having a restaurant needs to be included in the trip.

```
27  ...
28
29  needRestaurant v notNeedRestaurant.
30  needRestaurant :- &needRestaurant[trip, 3]().
31  notNeedRestaurant :- not &needRestaurant[trip, 3]().
32
33  chooseRestaurant(R,L) v nchooseRestaurant(R,L) :- needRestaurant,
34          restaurant(R,L).
35  :- needRestaurant, chooseRestaurant(R1,L1),
36          chooseRestaurant(R2,L2), R1 != R2.
37  chosen :- needRestaurant, chooseRestaurant(R,L).
38  :- needRestaurant, not chosen.
39
40  destination(L) :- needRestaurant, chooseRestaurant(R,L).
```

Fig. 9. route_planning.hex - third part

Here, we apply the external atom `&needRestaurant` to decide if we need a restaurant or not, in lines 29 to 31. Then, we choose exactly one location that has a restaurant from all locations that are declared to have a restaurant by the predicate `restaurant`, in lines 33 to 38. Finally, we add the chosen restaurant location to our destinations.

We test the extended HEX program with the same destinations and starting location as before, and state that the location 'Museumsquartier' has a restaurant by adding the fact `restaurant("Museumsquartier")`. We use the following command:

```
$ dlvhex2 route_planning.hex --python-plugin=route_plugin.py
  --maxint=10 --filter=trip --aggregate-mode=ext
```

where the additional option `--aggregate-mode=ext` activates the internal aggregates implementation of DLVHEX. This is necessary whenever there is a cycle in a HEX program that contains aggregates as well as external atoms. Overall, the call yields six answer sets as both of the two trips from before have costs greater than 3 and an additional restaurant location needs to be added to the respective sequences. The shortest trip from before is not viable anymore since it does not include a restaurant location, but a detour to 'Museumsquartier' can be inserted, so that the following answer set is a solution regarding our new encoding:

```
{trip(0,"Volkstheater","Herrengasse",1,"U3"),
 trip(1,"Herrengasse","Stephansplatz",1,"U3"),
 trip(2,"Stephansplatz","Karlsplatz",1,"U1"),
 trip(3,"Karlsplatz","Museumsquartier",1,"U2"),
 trip(4,"Museumsquartier","Karlsplatz",1,"U2"),
 trip(5,"Karlsplatz","Taubstummengasse",1,"U1")}
```

Note that now the information retrieved from the external atom named `&route` influences the input of the same atom since the extension of the predicate `destination`, and in turn of the predicate `sequence`, depends on the costs for the retrieved connections. Such loops over external atoms potentially make the grounding of a HEX program infinite, even when only finitely many values are introduced by each separate call of an external source. In general, this can be avoided by imposing the *strong safety* condition [34], which, informally speaking, forbids cyclic dependencies over external atoms that introduce new values.

However, the strong safety condition is overly restrictive, and we observe that our encoding can be handled without problems by DLVHEX, even though value invention is employed. This is because the *liberal safety* condition is used by DLVHEX by default, which has been introduced in Sect. 4 and ensures that programs that are not strongly safe still have a finite grounding. This is the case for our program as the traffic network is finite. Using the command line option `--strongsafety` would yield a warning. To make our program strongly safe, we could add a domain predicate to the rule in line 12 of the encoding containing all possible connections in the transport network. However, this is infeasible in our case due to the large size of the network, of which only a small fraction is relevant for planning the trip.

5.4 Partial Evaluation

During solving, DLVHEX incrementally extends the set of truth assignments for ground atoms such as `trip(0,"Volkstheater","Herrengasse",1,"U3")` and `destination("Museumsquartier")`. The external source for the atom `&needRestaurant[trip,3]()` is invoked as soon as all ground atoms with predicate name `trip` have a truth value because the truth value of the external atom could still change before the complete true/false extension of `trip` is known.

When calling the plugin method `needRestaurant(trip,limit)`, DLVHEX provides information concerning all ground instances of atoms with predicate name `trip` via the interface method `getInputAtoms()`, as demonstrated in Fig. 8. Their respective truth values can be queried in *Python* by means of the methods `isTrue()` and `isFalse()`. Based on the truth values of atoms in its input extension, the plugin declares the corresponding output tuples. Accordingly, all ground external atoms that instantiate one of these output tuples need to evaluate to true under the given assignment, and the remaining ground instances are assumed to be false. The according input-output relations obtained from an external call are then added as nogoods to the solver, so that the correct truth values for the respective ground external atoms are implied.

For instance, when the method `needRestaurant(trip,limit)` is called under an assignment that assigns true to six ground atoms with predicate `trip`, each associated with a cost of 1, and false to all other `trip`-atoms, a nogood is generated that implies that `&needRestaurant[trip,3]()` is true whenever the respective six atoms are true in an assignment. However, note that the truth value of `&needRestaurant[trip,3]()` is already fixed as soon as just four `trip`-atoms have been assigned the value true (assuming costs of 1 for each connection), even though all other atoms might still be unassigned. On the other side, if the plugin method in Fig. 8 would be called by DLVHEX under an assignment only containing three true `trip`-atoms (while all others are not assigned), `&needRestaurant[trip,3]()` would be inferred to be false whenever the three `trip`-atoms are true, which does not hold in general. Hence, external sources cannot directly be called under partial assignments without taking care of the latter issue.

For this reason, DLVHEX enables partial evaluation of external atoms by providing the additional output method `outputUnknown()` for declaring that the correctness of some output tuple cannot be determined without information about further truth assignments. This corresponds to the three-valued oracle functions from Sect. 4. We exploit this feature in a variant of the method from Fig. 8, as shown in Fig. 10.

```
...

def needRestaurant(trip, limit):
  tripLength = 0
  maxTripLength = 0

  for x in dlvhex.getInputAtoms():
    if x.tuple()[0] == trip and x.isTrue():
      tripLength += int(x.tuple()[4].value())

  for x in dlvhex.getInputAtoms():
    if x.tuple()[0] == trip and not x.isFalse():
      maxTripLength += int(x.tuple()[4].value())

  if tripLength > int(limit.value()):
    dlvhex.output(())
  elif maxTripLength > int(limit.value()):
    dlvhex.outputUnknown(())

...

def register():

...

  prop = dlvhex.ExtSourceProperties()
  prop.addMonotonicInputPredicate(0)
  prop.setProvidesPartialAnswer(True)
  dlvhex.addAtom("needRestaurant", (dlvhex.PREDICATE,
    dlvhex.CONSTANT), 0, prop)
```

Fig. 10. route_plugin.py - partial evaluation

An external source is only called under partial input assignments by DLVHEX if the property `setProvidesPartialAnswer(True)` is set. In this case, it is the responsibility of the source developer to make sure that all outputs that may potentially be derived when the assignment is extended are declared via the method `outputUnknown()`. The additional implementation effort for allowing partial evaluations often pays off, since partial external sources allow DLVHEX to evaluate external atoms earlier during search. This leads to an earlier detection of wrong guesses and smaller (thus, more general) input-output nogoods, resulting in efficiency improvements. Moreover, external sources allowing partial evaluations can also be used by DLVHEX for minimizing nogoods to find the "essential" part of an input assignment on which a given output depends, as described in Sect. 4.

Regarding our `needRestaurant`-plugin, in addition to counting the costs of `trip`-atoms that are true in the given assignment, we now also need to keep track of the maximal costs that may result from extending the assignment. For this purpose, in lines 35 to 37, we count the costs for all atoms that are true or not assigned, i.e. those which are not known to be false. Furthermore we state that the truth value of the external atom is not known if the limit has not been exceeded, but may be exceeded during future evaluation steps, in line 42.

To enable partial evaluation when starting DLVHEX, the command line option `--eaevalheuristics=always` needs to be set, so that all external sources allowing partial evaluations are queried whenever the solver assignment is extended. If the option `--eaevalheuristics=periodic` is used, DLVHEX waits ten iterations before a source is evaluated again, mitigating potential runtime overheads when the computation inside the external source requires more runtime. Nogood minimization is activated with the option `--ngminimization=always`.

5.5 Interfacing a Description Logic Reasoner

While the two external sources discussed so far in this section are tailored to our specific problem, existing plugins often accomplish more generic tasks. For instance, *Semantic Web* technologies can be leveraged in HEX programs by interfacing a *Description Logic* (*DL*) reasoner for taxonomical reasoning, as introduced in Sect. 3. Moreover, it is often a useful strategy to implement new plugins that are created for a specific purpose in a generic manner, so that they can be easily reused in other HEX programs. In the last part of our case study, we provide examples for both of these use cases.

Before, we simply declared one location as a restaurant location by adding the corresponding fact to our encoding. Now suppose we have a DL ontology available, containing information about restaurants in Vienna and their corresponding locations, which we want to use for inferring suitable lunch locations. To illustrate this, we use a small sample ontology formalized in *RDF* syntax in the file 'lunch.owl'. The definitions in our ontology file correspond to the axioms and assertions shown in Fig. 11.

In the ontology, for instance the concepts `BeerGarden` and `IndoorRestaurant` are disjoint, every `Restaurant` is close to some `Location`, and `bg1` is a

$$
\begin{array}{rll}
BeerGarden & \sqsubseteq Restaurant & Location(Karlsplatz) \\
BeerGarden & \sqsubseteq \neg IndoorRestaurant & Location(Museumsquartier) \\
IndoorRestaurant & \sqsubseteq Restaurant & Location(Praterstern) \\
IndoorRestaurant & \sqsubseteq \neg BeerGarden & BeerGarden(bg1) \\
IndoorRestaurant & \sqsubseteq \neg WurstStand & closeTo(bg1, Praterstern) \\
Restaurant & \sqsubseteq \exists closeTo.Location & IndoorRestaurant(ir1) \\
WurstStand & \sqsubseteq Restaurant & closeTo(ir1, Museumsquartier) \\
WurstStand & \sqsubseteq \neg IndoorRestaurant & WurstStand(ws1) \\
 & & closeTo(ws1, Karlsplatz)
\end{array}
$$

Fig. 11. DL-Lite axioms and assertions defined in lunch.owl

`BeerGarden` close to the `Location Praterstern`. For reasoning with ontologies expressed in lightweight DLs [22], the *DL-Lite* plugin for DLVHEX has been developed which is publicly available at https://github.com/hexhex/dlliteplugin. The plugin can be installed and used off the shelf by an end-user of DLVHEX, without the need for understanding the details of its implementation or for additional configurations. The plugin provides external sources for several external atoms that can be used for role and concept queries, as well as consistency checking, and uses a dedicated DL reasoner in the back-end.

For example, by adding the rule

```
restaurant(R,L) :- &rDL["lunch.owl",cp,cm,rp,rm,"closeTo"](R,L).
```

we can retrieve all restaurants with their close-by locations. The external atom for retrieving the extensions of roles has the name `&rDL`, while `&cDL` is used for concept queries. At this, the name of a file containing the ontology encoding and a role name need to be provided as arguments to the external atom. The input predicates `cp`, `cm`, `rp`, `rm` can be used to declare additions to the extensions of concepts and roles as well as to their complements, which are performed before the according query is executed. Consequently, a bidirectional information exchange between the HEX program and the DL reasoner is possible, but we are not exploiting this feature here.[17]

5.6 Accessing Remote Data

As a final refinement of our HEX-encoding, we consider a situation where we need to dynamically integrate some remote data into the evaluation of a HEX program. This represents another common use case for DLVHEX, since remote data that is subject to changes cannot be incorporated into an encoding during construction time, even though no external reasoning is required in this case.

[17] For more details, refer to the documentation of the *DL-Lite* plugin at http://www.kr.tuwien.ac.at/research/systems/dlvhex/dlliteplugin.html.

Hence, this usage of external sources constitutes a typical case of information outsourcing.

Nowadays, many web services provide access to their data resources via APIs. These often return data in the now ubiquitous *JSON* format, which expresses data objects by means of (nested) key-value pairs. For example, weather data can be retrieved from http://openweathermap.org/, and the following represents part of the data which is returned as JSON string when a request for the current weather in a given location is sent:


```
{"weather":[{"id":803,"main":"Clouds","description":"clouds",
            "icon":"04d"}], ...}.
```


Our aim is to exploit this data in our program and to decide based on the current weather if we should have lunch outside or inside. At the same time, the external source we create for querying the JSON data should be generic, so that it can be used for querying arbitrary JSON providers that are reachable via an URL. Here, the external atom should enable accessing a specified data field of a JSON object. For instance, in order to retrieve the string representing the current weather inside the JSON object from above, we need to access the array stored under the key 'weather', and retrieve the value for the key 'main' of the object contained in this array. A corresponding plugin method can be realized as shown in Fig. 12.

```
...
import urllib as ul
import json

...

def getJSON(url, fields):
  jsonurl = ul.urlopen(url.value()[1:-1])
  data = json.loads(jsonurl.read())

  for field in fields:
    if field.value()[1:-1].isdigit():
      data = data[int(field.value()[1:-1])]
    else:
      data = data[field.value()[1:-1]]

  dlvhex.output(('"' + str(data) + '"', ))

def register():

...

  prop = dlvhex.ExtSourceProperties()
  prop.setFunctional(True)
  dlvhex.addAtom("getJSON", (dlvhex.CONSTANT, dlvhex.TUPLE), 1,
    prop)
```

Fig. 12. route_plugin.py - third part

For retrieving data from a URL and parsing JSON strings, we import the libraries `urllib` and `json`, respectively. The plugin method is provided with a URL and information about the keys that need to be used to obtain the data chunk that should be returned. At this, the input parameter `fields` is declared to be of the type `dlvhex.TUPLE`, allowing an arbitrary number of input constants to be provided. Here, these constants represent the sequence of keys that need to be used to access the data field containing the respective value of interest. After loading the JSON data from the provided URL in lines 45 and 46, we iterate through the keys of the input tuple provided as second argument, following the path to the target value, in lines 48 to 52. If an entry constitutes an array, an integer needs to be used as key to access the respective entry, in line 50. Otherwise, we can simply use the respective string as key. Once the complete sequence has been processed, the target value is declared as output value of the external source. Note that here we can declare functionality of the external atom as only one value is returned for a given input.

Now, we can utilize the DL-Lite plugin and our new JSON plugin in combination to choose a lunch location depending on the current weather. For this purpose, we extend our HEX-encoding by the rules shown in Fig. 13.

```
39  ...
40
41  weather(X) :- &getJSON["http://api.openweathermap.org/data/2.5/
42          weather?q=Vienna&apikey=APIKEY","weather","0","main"](X).
43
44  restaurant(R,L) :- &rDL["lunch.owl",cp,cm,rp,rm,"closeTo"](R,L),
45          &cDL["lunch.owl",cp,cm,rp,rm,"IndoorRestaurant"](R),
46          weather("Rain").
47
48  restaurant(R,L) :- &rDL["lunch.owl",cp,cm,rp,rm,"closeTo"](R,L),
49          &cDL["lunch.owl",cp,cm,rp,rm,"-IndoorRestaurant"](R),
50          not weather("Rain").
```

Fig. 13. route_planning.hex - fourth part

In the first rule in line 41, we retrieve the current weather from the *Open Weather Map* service. For this to work, the string `APIKEY` needs to be replaced by a valid API key, which can be obtained from http://openweathermap.org/. All of the constants we provide after the URL are contained in the tuple `fields` when the external source is called. They denote that we first want to lookup the array that is mapped to the key `"weather"`. Then, we select the element with index 0 in the retrieved array and obtain the value associated with the key `"main"`, which is a string describing the current weather. Finally, we retrieve all indoor restaurants from the ontology if it is raining. Otherwise, we pose a query for all restaurants that can be derived to be not an indoor restaurant, in line 48. In our case, these are all restaurants that can be derived to be a beer garden or a wurst stand, due to the disjointness axioms in Fig. 11.

5.7 Summary of the Case Study

We started by generating all permutations of a set of locations in Vienna, representing different visit sequences, and ended up with an elaborate encoding for planning trips through the city of Vienna, satisfying a number of heterogeneous constraints. The final encoding makes use of four different types of external atoms, which are used for computation outsourcing (computing shortest paths by means of a dedicated algorithm), information outsourcing (retrieving remote data from an URL), combined information and computation outsourcing (concept and role queries to an external ontology), and external checks. We discussed the implementation of three plugin methods in detail, and we demonstrated how the corresponding external atoms can be used in combination with already available plugin implementations for DLVHEX, such as the DL-Lite plugin. For this usage, it is important to adhere to the conditions imposed by the formal semantics of oracle functions, by ensuring a stateless behavior of external sources, and by declaring all potential outputs under partial evaluations. The result is a working HEX implementation, which is available at https://github.com/hexhex/manual/tree/master/RW2017/ and can be executed by using the DLVHEX-system.

6 Further HEX Usage and Related Work

In Sects. 3 and 5, we have already considered concrete application scenarios where external atoms are used in a problem encoding. The specific external atoms considered were mostly tailored to the given problem and similar plugins can be developed by a user on demand. However, there are also other types of usage scenarios for HEX, where either new language features are implemented based on the HEX formalism, or other formalisms are translated into HEX programs. In this section, we give an overview over further applications falling into these classes, and consider related work.

6.1 Further HEX Use Scenarios and HEX Extensions

Some advanced HEX applications call for additional language features, which cannot be realized easily in pure HEX programs. However, often such extensions can be realized by compiling them to pure HEX programs. HEX programs can also be used as a backend for realizing formalisms that do not resemble HEX, by using an appropriate translation.

HEX$^{\exists}$ Programs. As already mentioned earlier, an important feature of HEX programs is that they are capable of value invention, i.e., that new constants are introduced into a program. This can be used to realize existential quantification in the head of rules in a formalism called HEX$^{\exists}$ [33]. The approach is related to Datalog$^{\pm}$ [17], which also allows existential quantification in heads, but HEX$^{\exists}$ offers *domain-specific existential quantification* such that the structure of introduced values can be controlled via external atoms.

For example the following rule, intuitively 'every employee has an office',

$$r_1: \qquad \exists X\colon \mathit{office}(Y,X) \leftarrow \mathit{employee}(Y).$$

is not interpretable in standard ASP due to the existential quantification in the head. The rule, which is also called an *existential rule*, can be rewritten into the following HEX$^{\exists}$ rule:

$$r_1': \qquad \mathit{office}(Y,X) \leftarrow \mathit{employee}(Y), \&\mathit{exists}^{1,1}[r_1, Y](X).$$

The external atom introduces novel constant terms into the program, based on the rule identifier (here r_1) and universally quantified variables in the rule body (here Y). Superscripts '$1,1$' on the external atom indicate that we need to invent one value from values of one universally quantified variable.

HEX Programs with Function Symbols. Uninterpreted function symbols, for example $do(a,s)$ to represent the follow up of a situation s after executing an action a, can be realized in HEX using external atoms. To this end, composition and decomposition of function terms with external atoms are simulated as in [18].

As a simple example, the program

$$q(f(X)) \leftarrow p(X).$$
$$r(Y) \leftarrow q(f(Y)).$$

would be rewritten into the HEX program

$$q(A) \leftarrow p(X), \&comp_1[f,X](A).$$
$$r(Y) \leftarrow q(B), \&decomp_1[B](f,Y).$$

where the external atom $\&comp_1[f,x](a)$ is true for a constant a that represents the function term $f(x)$. Moreover, $\&decomp_1[b](f,y)$ analyzes and decomposes the term b: if b contains a representation of a function term of form $f(y)$, then the external atom is true for output term y. While being formally defined on ground terms x, y, a, and b, the program contains variables X, Y, A, and B, respectively.

This way function terms can be emulated via HEX programs, moreover we obtain an increased control over issues like maximum nesting depth of terms in the external atoms.

ACTHEX: HEX Programs with Action Atoms. ACTHEX [6,52] is an extension of HEX: an ACTHEX-program is repeatedly executed in an *environment*, can obtain (sense) information from the environment using external atoms, and can declaratively schedule actions to be executed in the environment using *action atoms* in the head of rules. The environment is an abstraction of the world outside the logic program. External atoms are generalized such that the environment may influence their truth values.

Example 34 (simplified from [52]). The following ACTHEX-program controls a robot capable of executing a parameterized action *#robot*, where an external *&sensor* predicate enables to access sensor data.

$$\begin{aligned}
\#robot[clean, kitchen]\{c, 2\} &\leftarrow night \\
\#robot[clean, bedroom]\{c, 2\} &\leftarrow day \\
\#robot[goto, charger]\{b, 1\} &\leftarrow \&sensor[bat](low) \\
night \vee day &\leftarrow
\end{aligned}$$

Informally, in the night the kitchen should be cleaned, and during daytime the bedroom; if the battery is low, the robot needs to go to the charger. The option b (brave) makes charging mandatory, while other actions with option c (cautious) are only executed if they occur in every answer set. By the disjunctive fact, this is not the case. Precedence 1 of the charging action makes the robot recharge (if needed) before any cleaning. □

Constraint HEX Programs. *Constraint Answer Set Programming (CASP)* (see e.g. [71, 81]) combines ASP with constraint programming [3]. A well-known implementation is the clingcon system [86], which integrates GRINGO, CLASP and the constraint solver GECODE. Constraints can be encoded in plain ASP using builtin predicates, but this quickly produces groundings of unmanageable size; hence, a genuine support of constraints in ASP is reasonable, which can hide instances of constraint variables in the constraint solver. Dedicated CASP do not allow to integrate background theories other than constraints, which motivated an integration of CASP with HEX programs to *constraint HEX programs* [93]. Constraint HEX programs are strictly more general than CASP programs, as in addition to constraint atoms also external atoms can be used. Informally, a constraint HEX program may contain besides ordinary and external atoms also *constraint atoms.* The latter are comparisons of arithmetic expressions such as $x + y < 10$, where x and y are constraint variables which range over a certain domain. Different from ASP variables, constraint variables are global, i.e., each occurrence in a program is bound to the same value; thus, the atoms $x < 10$ and $x > 20$ can never be jointly true, even if they occur in different rules. For evaluating constraint HEX programs, constraint atoms are rewritten to auxiliary atoms in rule heads and bodies, e.g., $con(x, +, y, <, 10)$ for the above expression. Additionally, a constraint

$$\leftarrow \textbf{not}\ \&check[con, sum]()$$

eliminates answer sets where the extension of predicate *con* contains an inconsistent set of conditions over the constraint variable theory.

HEX Programs with Nested Program Calls. Notably, DLVHEX can be used to 'call' HEX programs from other HEX programs (called *host programs*). Specifically, one can process the collection of answer sets of a different program and can for instance reason on top of it. To this end, dedicated external atoms for evaluating subprograms and inspecting their answer sets are available [45, 91].

When a subprogram call (corresponding to the evaluation of a special external atom) is encountered in the host program, the external atom internally creates another instance of DLVHEX to evaluate the subprogram. The result is then stored in an *answer cache* and gets a unique *handle* that can be later used to reference the result and access its components (e.g., predicate names, literals, arguments) via other external atoms. The subprogram can either be *directly embedded* in the host program, or *stored in a separate file.* In the latter case, code reuse is easy and libraries for solving re-occurring subproblems in ASP applications, e.g., graph problems or combinatorial optimization problems, can be built, where code updates are automatically reflected in the call program.

The MELD Belief Merging System deals with merging *collections of belief sets* [88,91], which are roughly sets of classical ground literals. A merging strategy is defined by tree-shaped *merging plans*, whose leaves are the collections of belief sets to be merged, and whose inner nodes are *merging operators* (provided by the user). The structure is akin to syntax trees of terms. The automatic evaluation of tree-shaped merging plans is based on nested HEX programs; it proceeds bottom-up, where every step requires inspection of the subresults, i.e., accessing the answer sets of subprograms. In fact, the need for such processing has led to develop nested HEX program.

Interactive ASP. Interactive applications based on ASP can be realized with the Answer Set Application Programming (ASAP) framework [95] where incoming events (e.g., keyboard inputs) are processed by ASP and the application state is managed using state variables (as in planning, where these are called fluents). An ASAP program is rewritten to a HEX program where each evaluation obtains fluent values and event information via HEX external atoms. This is a *hybrid* HEX use scenario: an ASAP program is rewritten into a HEX program, transforming fluent atoms into regular atoms and adding rules containing external atoms. At the same time an ASAP program can use arbitrary external atoms, e.g., for string processing. This use scenario combines computation outsourcing (string processing) with information outsourcing (events and fluents) and moreover applies HEX for interfacing with the real world.

Multi-context Systems. Heterogeneous nonmonotonic multi-context systems (MCSs) [12] are a formalism for interlinking multiple knowledge based systems called *contexts.* This formalism is on an evolution line of multi-context systems that goes back to seminal work of John McCarthy [80] and which has been further developed by the Trento school [15,61,62]. The MCS formalism abstracts from the knowledge representation language and models context semantics in terms of accepted *belief sets.* The latter are abstractly modeled as naked sets whose elements (i.e., the beliefs) need not bear logical structure. The contexts are interlinked by so called *bridge rules* which add formulas to the knowledge base of a context depending on the presence and/or absence of beliefs from the belief sets of other contexts. The MCS formalism is suitable for modeling many Semantic Web scenarios where distributed knowledge repositories interact, e.g., [10,11,79], and MCSs have been adapted for the Ambient Intelligence domain [8] and for modularly combining nonmonotonic rules bases in the MWeb approach [2].

The semantics of an MCS is given in terms of *equilibria*, which are global states that consist of acceptable belief sets for each context, such that all bridge rules are satisfied. Equilibria computation has been realized in a tool based on a HEX program [9], in which external atoms *outsource contextual reasoning* and check whether a context accepts a certain belief set. This application hides HEX within a tool that realizes MCS semantics and inconsistency analysis [36].

6.2 Related Work

Because there are many scenarios where it is more natural, and often more efficient, to outsource some information or computation in the context of declarative problem solving, a number of approaches have been developed for this purpose, realizing different degrees of integration.

Motivated by the need for integration of data in commercial relational databases, extensions of dlv have been developed that allow to access external data. The dlv^{DB} system [98,99] offers via an ODBC interface access to dispersed relational databases, where both direct (remote) execution of possibly recursive queries on databases and main memory execution (after loading the databases) are supported. The ontodlv system [92], allows the user to retrieve information from OWL ontologies, which can be utilized in a genuine ontology representation language that extends ASP with features such as classes, inheritance, relations and axioms.

DLV-EX programs [18] represent an early generic integration approach, which enables bidirectional communication with an external source, and allows the introduction of new terms by value invention into an answer set program. However, the interaction is more restricted than in the case of HEX since only terms can be used as inputs to external sources and thus, e.g., nonmonotonic aggregates cannot be expressed in this formalism.

The CLINGO system also provides a mechanism for importing the extension of user-defined predicates [55] similar to DLV-EX, but they are different from external atoms in HEX in that their evaluation is not interleaved with the solving process. For this, GRINGO supports custom functions (implemented in the scripting languages Lua or Python) which are evaluated during the program grounding and thus compiled away prior to the solving step. They are intended to be used as customizable built-in atoms, but no cyclic dependencies are possible.

Recently, CLINGO 5 has been released [54], which provides generic interfaces for integrating theory solving into ASP. A main difference between ASP modulo theories solving in CLINGO 5 and the HEX-framework consists in the fact that unfounded support over theory atoms is allowed by the semantics defined for CLINGO, which would violate the minimality criterion w.r.t. the FLP-reduct in HEX. This can be illustrated by the following example.

Example 35 Consider the program $\Pi = \{p \leftarrow \&id[p]()\}$, where $\&id[p]()$ is true iff p is true. Then Π has the answer set $\mathbf{A}_1 = \emptyset$; but $\mathbf{A}_2 = \{p\}$ is not an answer set because the support for p is not founded and thus, it is not a minimal model of the FLP-reduct.

Consequently, a more sophisticated minimality check has to be applied in DLVHEX, lifting the computational complexity of the formalism.[18]

Moreover, even though the CLINGO system moves into a similar direction as DLVHEX by facilitating the integration of external reasoners, the perspectives taken by the two systems are different, and their roles can be viewed as somewhat orthogonal.

While theory atoms are interrelated via an external theory in CLINGO, where the consistency of their truth assignments is usually checked during theory propagation, the truth value of external atoms in HEX depends on the evaluation of ordinary atoms representing their input. Thus, the focus of the HEX-approach is more on input-output relations over external atoms, which are easy to understand from a user's perspective and can be used to call external sources in an API-like fashion.

As a result, external atoms have a number of distinguishing features, which are tailored to their specific role in the HEX-framework. For instance, external source properties as described in Sect. 4 constitute a user-friendly high-level interface for steering the external evaluation process, which has to be implemented manually for each theory in CLINGO's propagation methods.

The input-output structure of external atoms facilitates the introduction of constants by value invention relying on the liberal safety condition for HEX programs, which is of special interest for applications in the area of the Semantic Web. There is no comparable mechanism for value invention in CLINGO 5 as new values cannot be imported based on the respective answer set, and theory solving is performed w.r.t. the pre-grounded program.

On the other side, CLINGO 5 is well-suited for system development and powerful solver building, by providing a comprehensive and rich infrastructure at the low technical levels for integrating theory reasoning into CLINGO, which is accessible through an interface. This novel interface will be exploited in future versions of DLVHEX, which benefits a lot from the CLINGO advances.

Besides CLINGO, the WASP solver was recently extended with support for general external Python propagators [25]. Furthermore there are extensions of ASP towards the integration of specific external sources. Examples are constraint ASP as an integration of ASP with constraint programming as realized e.g. in clingcon [86] lc2casp [16], ezcsp [4], and EZSMT [97]. The latter is like mingo [76] an SMT-based solver for constraint ASP; other formalisms that extend ASP with SMT are dingo [66], which uses difference logic, and ASPMT [69]. For an overview of systems that combine ASP with constraint solving and other theories, we refer to [72].

Similar to SMT [85], where usually only specific theories are considered, the mentioned approaches rely on a tailored integration of an external solver and

[18] Deciding the existence of an answer set of a ground HEX program in the presence of nonmonotonic external atoms that are decidable in polynomial time is Σ_2^p-complete already for Horn programs [35].

hence, can easily leverage the propagation capabilities of the respective solver. The aim of the HEX formalism differs in that its goal is to enable a broad range of users to implement custom external sources and to harness efficient solving techniques for HEX programs. Moreover, clingcon and approaches in SMT usually only consider monotonic external theories, which facilitates the integration of their evaluation into the respective solving algorithm. In contrast, HEX allows for the integration of arbitrary external sources through a general interface and their flexible combination; the other use cases correspond to special cases thereof.

7 Conclusion

Arriving at the end, we give a summary and discuss ongoing work. Pointers to further resources regarding DLVHEX and ASP can be found in the appendix.

Summary. The HEX formalism extends ASP with access to external sources through an API-style interface, which has been implemented in the DLVHEX-system and has been fruitfully deployed to various applications. In this paper, we introduced the formalism and focused on its application to practical problems in KR and Semantic Web.

To this end, we first introduced HEX programs as a generalization of answer set programs, which constitute logic programs interpreted under the stable model semantics. In ASP, a problem can be solved by modeling it as an answer set program using variables, grounding the program to obtain a variable-free program, and using an answer set solver to compute (possibly multiple) answer sets of the program. Then, each answer set corresponds to a solution of the initial problem. By extending ASP with external atoms, HEX enables a bidirectional interaction between an answer set program and external sources of computation.

For modeling problems utilizing external atoms, we first presented the general methodology as a strict generalization of the common methodology for designing an ASP encoding. In particular, the prominent guess and check paradigm can be seamlessly combined with external sources, both in the guessing and in the checking part. Also other ASP techniques, such as saturation, can be used with external sources. We then discussed two typical types of external sources for computation outsourcing and for information outsourcing, respectively, and for combinations thereof. We further demonstrated the usage of external sources in existing applications in the areas of the Semantic Web and planning.

Subsequently, we presented the DLVHEX system, which implements a feature-rich solver for HEX programs. There, we described the architecture of DLVHEX and its practical usage. In DLVHEX, external sources that are used by the system for the evaluation of external atoms can be implemented via a user-friendly interface in C++ and Python. We also discussed how properties of external sources can be exploited for solving and demonstrated the configuration of DLVHEX for use cases with specific properties, e.g. with the need for introducing new values.

Finally, we integrated insights from previous sections by showcasing the development of a HEX encoding for a realistic application scenario, by following the methodology for designing HEX programs and using different features of the

DLVHEX system. In addition, we reviewed related formalisms and applications where HEX is used for implementing language extensions and backends for other formalisms, in the last section.

Outlook. Current developments regarding the HEX formalism and DLVHEX comprise the design and implementation of new solving techniques for improving the efficiency of the formalism in general, as well as for specific classes of programs. At the same time, the goal is to relieve the user from the burden to configure the system manually for each type of problem, while still profiting from performance gains. For instance, different static heuristics for partial evaluation of external atoms and minimization of nogoods have been introduced [44], and future work in this direction concerns the development of dynamic evaluation heuristics that adjust the frequency of external evaluations based on the amount of information gained from previous external calls.

Moreover, recently a lazy grounding solver has been integrated into the DLVHEX system, which exhibits promising results for classes of programs where the grounding bottleneck of ASP is an issue. This issue is even more challenging to tackle within the framework of HEX due to the need for grounding external atoms, which are largely black boxes from the viewpoint of the solver. Lazy grounding avoids an exponential blowup of the grounding by interleaving grounding and solving, whereby rules are grounded on-the-fly depending on the satisfaction of their bodies.

Furthermore, since HEX has already been applied to many different problems from the area of KR, another focus of ongoing work is on exploring new application areas for HEX to combine approaches that are different in nature, for solving concrete problems. For instance, external atoms could be utilized to integrate probabilistic methods into ASP for tackling problems from the area of *Statistical Relational Learning* [60], where complex relational as well as uncertain information is required simultaneously.

Acknowledgments. We appreciate the review feedback and are thankful for the detailed suggestions in it to improve the presentation of the material in this article. We also thank Roland Kaminski and Torsten Schaub for comments regarding CLINGO.

A Further Resources

The following list contains some further links to web resources regarding practical aspects of ASP, HEX programs and the DLVHEX system, and summarizes those already given in the paper.

- All executable examples from this paper are available under:
  ⇒ https://github.com/hexhex/manual/tree/master/RW2017/
- Slides of a tutorial considering the topic "ASP for the Semantic Web" and many executable ASP/HEX-examples related to Semantic Web applications can be found at:
  ⇒ http://asptut.gibbi.com/

- A tutorial paper providing a gentle introduction to ASP and an overview over programming techniques (also considering Semantic Web applications) is available at:
  ⇒ http://www.kr.tuwien.ac.at/staff/tkren/pub/2009/rw2009-asp.pdf
- The main website of DLVHEX contains all relevant information about the system and existing plugins, and many further references to the relevant literature and related work:
  ⇒ http://www.kr.tuwien.ac.at/research/systems/dlvhex/
- An online demo of the DLVHEX system can be found at:
  ⇒ http://www.kr.tuwien.ac.at/research/systems/dlvhex/demo.php
- The easiest way to use DLVHEX is by downloading the pre-built binaries, which are available for Linus, OS X and Windows under:
  ⇒ http://www.kr.tuwien.ac.at/research/systems/dlvhex/downloadb.html
- The source code of DLVHEX and corresponding plugins is available on Github, which is also the best place for filing bug reports:
  ⇒ https://github.com/hexhex/
- The website of the *Potsdam Answer Set Solving Collection* (*Potassco*) is the main portal for CLINGO and related systems and tools, and contains a lot of additional information on them:
  ⇒ https://potassco.org/
- Material of the Potsdam ASP course can be found under:
  ⇒ https://potassco.org/teaching/
- The source code of CLINGO, clingcon, and related systems is publicly available at:
  ⇒ https://github.com/potassco/
- *ASPIDE* is an integrated development environment for ASP with a wide range of features facilitating the implementation of answer set programs:
  ⇒ http://www.mat.unical.it/ricca/aspide
- Slides of a tutorial covering ASPIDE and the development of answer set programs can be found at:
  ⇒ https://www.mat.unical.it/ricca/downloads/rr2013-tutorial.pdf
- A special issue of the *AI Magazine* has been dedicated to ASP, covering many different perspectives on the topic:
  ⇒ http://aaai.org/ojs/index.php/aimagazine/issue/view/215/

References

1. Alviano, M., Dodaro, C., Faber, W., Leone, N., Ricca, F.: WASP: a native ASP solver based on constraint learning. In: Cabalar, P., Son, T.C. (eds.) LPNMR 2013. LNCS, vol. 8148, pp. 54–66. Springer, Heidelberg (2013). doi:10.1007/978-3-642-40564-8_6
2. Analyti, A., Antoniou, G., Damásio, C.V.: MWeb: a principled framework for modular web rule bases and its semantics. ACM Trans. Comput. Log. **12**(2), 17 (2011)
3. Apt, K.: Principles of Constraint Programming. Cambridge University Press, New York (2003)

4. Balduccini, M.: Representing constraint satisfaction problems in answer set programming. In: Workshop on Answer Set Programming and Other Computing Paradigms (ASPOCP) at ICLP (2009)
5. Baral, C.: Knowledge Representation, Reasoning and Declarative Problem Solving. Cambridge University Press, Cambridge (2003)
6. Basol, S., Erdem, O., Fink, M., Ianni, G.: HEX programs with action atoms. In: Technical Communications of the International Conference on Logic Programming (ICLP), pp. 24–33 (2010)
7. Ben-Eliyahu, R., Dechter, R.: Propositional semantics for disjunctive logic programs. Ann. Math. Artif. Intell. **12**, 53–87 (1994)
8. Bikakis, A., Antoniou, G.: Defeasible contextual reasoning with arguments in ambient intelligence. IEEE Trans. Knowl. Data Eng. **22**(11), 1492–1506 (2010)
9. Bögl, M., Eiter, T., Fink, M., Schüller, P.: The MCS-IE system for explaining inconsistency in multi-context systems. In: Janhunen, T., Niemelä, I. (eds.) JELIA 2010. LNCS (LNAI), vol. 6341, pp. 356–359. Springer, Heidelberg (2010). doi:10.1007/978-3-642-15675-5_31
10. Bouquet, P., Giunchiglia, F., van Harmelen, F., Serafini, L., Stuckenschmidt, H.: Contextualizing ontologies. Web Semant. Sci. Serv. Agents World Wide Web **1**(4), 325–343 (2004)
11. Bozzato, L., Serafini, L.: Materialization calculus for contexts in the semantic web. In: Eiter, T., Glimm, B., Kazakov, Y., Krötzsch, M. (eds.) DL 2013, vol. 1014. CEUR-WP, pp. 552–572 (2013). CEUR-WS.org
12. Brewka, G., Eiter, T.: Equilibria in heterogeneous nonmonotonic multi-context systems. In: AAAI Conference on Artificial Intelligence, pp. 385–390. AAAI Press (2007)
13. Brewka, G., Eiter, T., Truszczyński, M. (eds.): AI Magazine **37**(3), 5–6 (2016). Special issue on Answer Set Programming. AAAI Press
14. Brewka, G., Eiter, T., Truszczynski, M.: Answer set programming at a glance. Commun. ACM **54**(12), 92–103 (2011)
15. Brewka, G., Roelofsen, F., Serafini, L.: Contextual default reasoning. In: Veloso, M.M. (ed.) IJCAI 2007, Proceedings of the 20th International Joint Conference on Artificial Intelligence, Hyderabad, India, 6–12 January 2007, pp. 268–273 (2007)
16. Cabalar, P., Kaminski, R., Ostrowski, M., Schaub, T.: An ASP semantics for default reasoning with constraints. In: Kambhampati, S. (ed.) Proceedings of the Twenty-Fifth International Joint Conference on Artificial Intelligence, IJCAI 2016, New York, 9–15 July 2016, pp. 1015–1021. IJCAI/AAAI Press (2016)
17. Calì, A., Gottlob, G., Pieris, A.: Towards more expressive ontology languages: the query answering problem. Artif. Intell. **193**, 87–128 (2012)
18. Calimeri, F., Cozza, S., Ianni, G.: External sources of knowledge and value invention in logic programming. Ann. Math. Artif. Intell. **50**(3–4), 333–361 (2007)
19. Calimeri, F., Faber, W., Gebser, M., Ianni, G., Kaminski, R., Krennwallner, T., Leone, N., Ricca, F., Schaub, T.: ASP-Core-2 Input Language Format (2013)
20. Calimeri, F., Fink, M., Germano, S., Humenberger, A., Ianni, G., Redl, C., Stepanova, D., Tucci, A., Wimmer, A.: Angry-HEX: an artificial player for angry birds based on declarative knowledge bases. IEEE Trans. Comput. Intell. AI Games **8**(2), 128–139 (2016)
21. Calimeri, F., Fink, M., Germano, S., Ianni, G., Redl, C., Wimmer, A.: Angry-HEX: an artificial player for angry birds based on declarative knowledge bases. In: National Workshop and Prize on Popularize, Artificial Intelligence, pp. 29–35 (2013)

22. Calvanese, D., De Giacomo, G., Lembo, D., Lenzerini, M., Rosati, R.: Tractable reasoning and efficient query answering in description logics: the DL-Lite family. J. Autom. Reasoning **39**(3), 385–429 (2007)
23. Dantsin, E., Eiter, T., Gottlob, G., Voronkov, A.: Complexity and expressive power of logic programming. ACM Comput. Surv. **33**(3), 374–425 (2001)
24. Dao-Tran, M., Eiter, T., Krennwallner, T.: Realizing default logic over description logic knowledge bases. In: Sossai, C., Chemello, G. (eds.) ECSQARU 2009. LNCS, vol. 5590, pp. 602–613. Springer, Heidelberg (2009). doi:10.1007/978-3-642-02906-6_52
25. Dodaro, C., Ricca, F., Schüller,P.: External propagators in WASP: preliminary report. In: Bistarelli, S., Formisano, A., Maratea, M. (eds.) International Workshop on Experimental Evaluation of Algorithms for Solving Problems with Combinatorial Explosion (RCRA), vol. 1745. CEUR Workshop Proceedings, pp. 1–9, November 2016. CEUR-WS.org
26. Drabent, W., Eiter, T., Ianni, G., Krennwallner, T., Lukasiewicz, T., Małuszyński, J.: Hybrid reasoning with rules and ontologies. In: Bry, F., Małuszyński, J. (eds.) Semantic Techniques for the Web. LNCS, vol. 5500, pp. 1–49. Springer, Heidelberg (2009). doi:10.1007/978-3-642-04581-3_1
27. Dung, P.M.: On the acceptability of arguments and its fundamental role in nonmonotonic reasoning, logic programming and n-person games. Artif. Intell. **77**(2), 321–357 (1995)
28. Eiter, T., Gottlob, G.: On the computational cost of disjunctive logic programming: propositional case. Ann. Math. Artif. Intell. **15**(3/4), 289–323 (1995)
29. Eiter, T., Fink, M., Ianni, G., Krennwallner, T., Redl, C., Schüller, P.: A model building framework for answer set programming with external computations. In: Theory and Practice of Logic Programming (2015). http://arxiv.org/abs/1507.01451, doi:10.1017/S1471068415000113
30. Eiter, T., Fink, M., Krennwallner, T., Redl, C.: Conflict-driven ASP solving with external sources. Theory Pract. Logic Program. **12**(4–5), 659–679 (2012)
31. Eiter, T., Fink, M., Krennwallner, T., Redl, C.: Liberal safety criteria for HEX-programs. In: des Jardins, M., Littman, M. (eds.) AAAI Conference on Artificial Intelligence (AAAI). AAAI Press (2013)
32. Eiter, T., Fink, M., Krennwallner, T., Redl, C.: Domain expansion for ASP-programs with external sources. Technical report INFSYS RR-1843-14-02, Institut für Informationssysteme, Technische Universität Wien, A-1040 Vienna, Austria, September 2014
33. Eiter, T., Fink, M., Krennwallner, T., Redl, C.: HEX-programs with existential quantification. In: International Conference on Applications of Declarative Programming and Knowledge Management (INAP) (2014)
34. Eiter, T., Fink, M., Krennwallner, T., Redl, C.: Domain expansion for ASP-programs with external sources. Artif. Intell. **233**, 84–121 (2016)
35. Eiter, T., Fink, M., Krennwallner, T., Redl, C., Schüller, P.: Efficient HEX-program evaluation based on unfounded sets. J. Artif. Intell. Res. **49**, 269–321 (2014)
36. Eiter, T., Fink, M., Schüller, P., Weinzierl, A.: Finding explanations of inconsistency in multi-context systems. Artif. Intell. **216**, 233–274 (2014)
37. Eiter, T., Gottlob, G.: On the computational cost of disjunctive logic programming: propositional case. Ann. Math. Artif. Intell. **15**(3–4), 289–323 (1995)
38. Eiter, T., Gottlob, G., Veith, H.: Generalized quantifiers in logic programs. In: Väänänen, J. (ed.) ESSLLI 1997. LNCS, vol. 1754, pp. 72–98. Springer, Heidelberg (1999). doi:10.1007/3-540-46583-9_4

39. Eiter, T., Ianni, G., Krennwallner, T.: Answer set programming: a primer. In: Reasoning Web Summer School, pp. 40–110 (2009)
40. Eiter, T., Ianni, G., Krennwallner, T., Schindlauer, R.: Exploiting conjunctive queries in description logic programs. Ann. Math. Artif. Intell. **53**(1–4), 115–152 (2008)
41. Eiter, T., Ianni, G., Lukasiewicz, T., Schindlauer, R., Tompits, H.: Combining answer set programming with description logics for the semantic web. Artif. Intell. **172**(12–13), 1495–1539 (2008)
42. Eiter, T., Ianni, G., Schindlauer, R., Tompits, H.: A uniform integration of higher-order reasoning and external evaluations in answer-set programming. In: International Joint Conference on Artificial Intelligence (IJCAI), pp. 90–96. Professional Book Center (2005)
43. Eiter, T., Ianni, G., Schindlauer, R., Tompits, H.: Effective integration of declarative rules with external evaluations for semantic-web reasoning. In: Sure, Y., Domingue, J. (eds.) ESWC 2006. LNCS, vol. 4011, pp. 273–287. Springer, Heidelberg (2006). doi:10.1007/11762256_22
44. Eiter, T., Kaminski, T., Redl, C., Weinzierl, A.: Exploiting partial assignments for efficient evaluation of answer set programs with external source access. In: IJCAI, pp. 1058–1065. IJCAI/AAAI Press (2016)
45. Eiter, T., Krennwallner, T., Redl, C.: HEX-programs with nested program calls. In: Tompits, H., Abreu, S., Oetsch, J., Pührer, J., Seipel, D., Umeda, M., Wolf, A. (eds.) INAP/WLP -2011. LNCS (LNAI), vol. 7773, pp. 269–278. Springer, Heidelberg (2013). doi:10.1007/978-3-642-41524-1_15
46. Eiter, T., Mehuljic, M., Redl, C., Schüller, P.: User guide: dlvhex 2.x. Technical report INFSYS RR-1843-15-05, Vienna University of Technology, Institute for Information Systems (2015)
47. Eiter, T., Redl, C., Schüller, P.: Problem solving using the HEX family. In: Beierle, C., Brewka, G., Thimm, M. (eds.) Computational Models of Rationality - Essays Dedicated to Gabriele Kern-Isberner on the Occasion of her 60th Birthday, Tributes, pp. 150–174. College Publications, January 2016
48. Erdem, E., Gelfond, M., Leone, N.: Applications of answer set programming. AI Mag. **37**(3), 53–68 (2016)
49. Erdem, E., Patoglu, V., Schüller, P.: A systematic analysis of levels of integration between low-level reasoning and task planning. AI Commun. **29**(2), 319–349 (2016)
50. Faber, W., Leone, N., Pfeifer, G.: Recursive aggregates in disjunctive logic programs: semantics and complexity. In: Alferes, J.J., Leite, J. (eds.) JELIA 2004. LNCS (LNAI), vol. 3229, pp. 200–212. Springer, Heidelberg (2004). doi:10.1007/978-3-540-30227-8_19
51. Faber, W., Leone, N., Pfeifer, G.: Semantics and complexity of recursive aggregates in answer set programming. Artif. Intell. **175**(1), 278–298 (2011)
52. Fink, M., Germano, S., Ianni, G., Redl, C., Schüller, P.: ActHEX: implementing HEX programs with action atoms. In: Cabalar, P., Son, T.C. (eds.) LPNMR 2013. LNCS (LNAI), vol. 8148, pp. 317–322. Springer, Heidelberg (2013). doi:10.1007/978-3-642-40564-8_31
53. Gebser, M., Kaminski, R., Kaufmann, B., Schaub, T.: Answer Set Solving in Practice. Synthesis Lectures on Artificial Intelligence and Machine Learning. Morgan and Claypool Publishers (2012)

54. Gebser, M., Kaminski, R., Kaufmann, B., Ostrowski, M., Schaub, T., Wanko, P.: Theory solving made easy with clingo 5. In: ICLP (Technical Communications), vol. 52. OASICS, pp. 2:1–2:15. Schloss Dagstuhl - Leibniz-Zentrum fuer Informatik (2016)
55. Gebser, M., Kaminski, R., Kaufmann, B., Schaub, T.: Clingo = ASP + control: Preliminary report. CoRR, abs/1405.3694 (2014)
56. Gebser, M., Kaufmann, B., Kaminski, R., Ostrowski, M., Schaub, T., Schneider, M.T.: Potassco: the potsdam answer set solving collection. AI Commun. **24**(2), 107–124 (2011)
57. Gebser, M., Kaufmann, B., Schaub, T.: Conflict-driven answer set solving: from theory to practice. Artif. Intell. **187–188**, 52–89 (2012)
58. Gelfond, M., Lifschitz, V.: The stable model semantics for logic programming. In: Kowalski, R., Bowen, K. (eds.) Logic Programming: Proceedings of the 5th International Conference and Symposium, pp. 1070–1080. MIT Press (1988)
59. Gelfond, M., Lifschitz, V.: Classical negation in logic programs and disjunctive databases. Next Gener. Comput. **9**(3–4), 365–386 (1991)
60. Getoor, L.: Introduction to Statistical Relational Learning. MIT Press, Cambridge (2007)
61. Ghidini, C., Giunchiglia, F.: Local models semantics, or contextual reasoning = locality + compatibility. Artif. Intell. **127**(2), 221–259 (2001)
62. Giunchiglia, F., Serafini, L.: Multilanguage hierarchical logics or: how we can do without modal logics. Artif. Intell. **65**(1), 29–70 (1994)
63. Havur, G., Ozbilgin, G., Erdem, E., Patoglu, V.: Geometric rearrangement of multiple movable objects on cluttered surfaces: a hybrid reasoning approach. In: International Conference on Robotics and Automation (ICRA), pp. 445–452 (2014)
64. Heflin, J., Munoz-Avila, H.: LCW-based agent planning for the semantic web. In: Pease, A. (ed.) Ontologies and the Semantic Web. number WS-02-11 in AAAI Technical report, pp. 63–70. AAAI Press, Menlo Park, CA (2002)
65. Hoehndorf, R., Loebe, F., Kelso, J., Herre, H.: Representing default knowledge in biomedical ontologies: application to the integration of anatomy and phenotype ontologies. BMC Bioinformatics **8**(1), 377 (2007)
66. Janhunen, T., Liu, G., Niemelä, I.: Tight integration of non-ground answer set programming and satisfiability modulo theories. In: Cabalar, P., Mitchell, D., Pearce, D., Ternovska, E. (eds.) Informal Proceedings of the 1st Workshop on Grounding and Transformations for Theories with Variables (GTTV 2011), LPNMR, Vancouver, BC, Canada, 16 May 2011, pp. 1–14 (2013)Online available athttp://www.dc.fi.udc.es/GTTV11/GTTV-Proc.pdf
67. Kaminski, R., Schaub, T., Wanko, P.: A tutorial on hybrid answer set solving with clingo. In: Reasoning Web Summer School (2017, to appear)
68. Lassila, O., Swick, R.R.: Resource Description Framework (RDF) model and syntax specification (1999). www.w3.org/TR/1999/REC-rdf-syntax-19990222
69. Lee, J., Meng, Y.: Answer set programming modulo theories and reasoning about continuous changes. In: Rossi, F. (ed.) IJCAI 2013, Proceedings of the 23rd International Joint Conference on Artificial Intelligence, Beijing, China, 3–9 August 2013, pp. 990–996. IJCAI/AAAI (2013)
70. Leone, N., Pfeifer, G., Faber, W., Eiter, T., Gottlob, G., Perri, S., Scarcello, F.: The DLV system for knowledge representation and reasoning. ACM Trans. Comput. Logic (TOCL) **7**(3), 499–562 (2006)
71. Lierler, Y.: Relating constraint answer set programming languages and algorithms. Artif. Intell. **207**, 1–22 (2014)

72. Lierler, Y., Maratea, M., Ricca, F.: Systems, engineering environments, and competitions. AI Mag. **37**(3), 45–52 (2016)
73. Lifschitz, V.: Answer set programming and plan generation. Artif. Intell. **138**, 39–54 (2002)
74. Lifschitz, V.: Thirteen definitions of a stable model. In: Blass, A., Dershowitz, N., Reisig, W. (eds.) Fields of Logic and Computation. LNCS, vol. 6300, pp. 488–503. Springer, Heidelberg (2010). doi:10.1007/978-3-642-15025-8_24
75. Lin, F., Zhao, Y.: ASSAT: computing answer sets of a logic program by SAT solvers. Artif. Intell. **157**(1–2), 115–137 (2004)
76. Liu, G., Janhunen, T., Niemelä, I.: Answer set programming via mixed integer programming. In: Brewka, G., Eiter, T., McIlraith, S.A. (eds.) Principles of Knowledge Representation and Reasoning: Proceedings of the Thirteenth International Conference, KR 2012, Rome, Italy, 10–14 June 2012. AAAI Press (2012)
77. Marek, V.W., Truszczyński, M.: Stable models and an alternative logic programming paradigm. In: Apt, K.R., Marek, V.W., Truszczynski, M., Warren, D.S. (eds.) The Logic Programming Paradigm - A 25-Year Perspective, pp. 375–398. Springer, Heidelberg (1999)
78. Marek, W., Truszczyński, M.: Autoepistemic logic. J. ACM **38**(3), 588–619 (1991)
79. May, W., Alferes, J.J., Amador, R.: Active rules in the semantic web: dealing with language heterogeneity. In: Adi, A., Stoutenburg, S., Tabet, S. (eds.) RuleML 2005. LNCS, vol. 3791, pp. 30–44. Springer, Heidelberg (2005). doi:10.1007/11580072_4
80. McCarthy, J.: Notes on formalizing context. In: Bajcsy, R. (ed.) Proceedings of the 13th International Joint Conference on Artificial Intelligence, Chambéry, France, 28 August - 3 September 1993, pp. 555–562. Morgan Kaufmann (1993)
81. Mellarkod, V.S., Gelfond, M., Zhang, Y.: Integrating answer set programming and constraint logic programming. Ann. Math. Artif. Intell. **53**(1–4), 251–287 (2008)
82. Mosca, A., Bernini, D.: Ontology-driven geographic information system and dlvhex reasoning for material culture analysis. In: Italian Workshop RiCeRcA at ICLP (2008)
83. Boris Motik and Riccardo Rosati. Reconciling description logics and rules. J. ACM, 57(5):30:1–30:62, 2010
84. Niemelä, I.: Logic programming with stable model semantics as constraint programming paradigm. Annals of Mathematics and Artificial Intelligenc **25**(3–4), 241–273 (1999)
85. Nieuwenhuis, R., Oliveras, A., Tinelli, C.: Solving SAT and SAT modulo theories: From an abstract Davis-Putnam-Logemann-Loveland procedure to DPLL(T). J. ACM **53**(6), 937–977 (2006)
86. Ostrowski, M., Schaub, T.: ASP modulo CSP: the clingcon system. Theory Pract. Logic Program. (TPLP) **12**(4–5), 485–503 (2012)
87. Polleres, A.: From SPARQL to rules (and back). In: International Conference on World Wide Web (WWW), pp. 787–796. ACM (2007)
88. Redl, C.: Development of a belief merging framewerk for dlvhex. Master's thesis, Vienna University of Technology, A-1040 Vienna, Karlsplatz 13 (2010)
89. Redl, C.: Answer set programming with external sources: algorithms and efficient evaluation. PhD thesis, Vienna University of Technology (2014)
90. Redl, C.: The dlvhex system for knowledge representation: recent advances (system description). TPLP **16**(5–6), 866–883 (2016)
91. Redl, C., Eiter, T., Krennwallner, T.: Declarative belief set merging using merging plans. In: Rocha, R., Launchbury, J. (eds.) PADL 2011. LNCS, vol. 6539, pp. 99–114. Springer, Heidelberg (2011). doi:10.1007/978-3-642-18378-2_10

92. Ricca, F., Gallucci, L., Schindlauer, R., Dell'Armi, T., Grasso, G., Leone, N.: OntoDLV: an ASP-based system for enterprise ontologies. J. Log. Comput. **19**(4), 643–670 (2009)
93. De Rosis, A.F., Eiter, T., Redl, C., Ricca, F.: Constraint answer set programming based on HEX-programs. In: Eighth Workshop on Answer Set Programming and Other Computing Paradigms (ASPOCP 2015), 31 August 2015, Cork, Ireland, August 2015. Accepted for publication
94. Schindlauer, R.: Answer set programming for the semantic web. PhD thesis, Vienna University of Technology, Vienna, Austria (2006)
95. Schüller, P., Weinzierl, A.: Answer set application programming: a case study on Tetris. In: De Vos, M., Eiter, T., Lierler, Y., Toni, F. (eds.) International Conference on Logic Programming (ICLP), Technical Communications, vol. 1433 (2015). CEUR-WS.org
96. Simons, P., Niemelä, I., Soininen, T.: Extending and implementing the stable model semantics. Artif. Intell. **138**(1–2), 181–234 (2002)
97. Susman, B., Lierler, Y.: SMT-based constraint answer set solver EZSMT (system description). In: Carro, M., King, A., Saeedloei, N., De Vos, M. (eds.) Technical Communications of the 32nd International Conference on Logic Programming, ICLP 2016 TCs, 16–21 October 2016, New York City, USA, vol. 52. OASICS, pp. 1:1–1:15. Schloss Dagstuhl - Leibniz-Zentrum fuer Informatik (2016)
98. Terracina, G., Francesco, E., Panetta, C., Leone, N.: Enhancing a DLP system for advanced database applications. In: Calvanese, D., Lausen, G. (eds.) RR 2008. LNCS, vol. 5341, pp. 119–134. Springer, Heidelberg (2008). doi:10.1007/978-3-540-88737-9_10
99. Terracina, G., Leone, N., Lio, V., Panetta, C.: Experimenting with recursive queries in database and logic programming systems. TPLP **8**(2), 129–165 (2008)
100. Zakraoui, J., Zagler, W.: A method for generating CSS to improve web accessibility for old users. In: Miesenberger, K., Karshmer, A., Penaz, P., Zagler, W. (eds.) ICCHP 2012. LNCS, vol. 7382, pp. 329–336. Springer, Heidelberg (2012). doi:10.1007/978-3-642-31522-0_50
101. Zirtiloğlu, H., Yolum, P.: Ranking semantic information for e-government: complaints management. In: International Workshop on Ontology-supported business intelligence (OBI). ACM (2008)

Uncertainty Reasoning for the Semantic Web

Thomas Lukasiewicz(✉)

Department of Computer Science, University of Oxford, Oxford, UK
thomas.lukasiewicz@cs.ox.ac.uk

Abstract. The Semantic Web has attracted much attention, both from academia and industry. An important role in research towards the Semantic Web is played by formalisms and technologies for handling uncertainty and/or vagueness. In this paper, I first provide some motivating examples for handling uncertainty and/or vagueness in the Semantic Web. I then give an overview of some own formalisms for handling uncertainty and/or vagueness in the Semantic Web.

1 Introduction

The *Semantic Web* [1–4] aims at an extension of the current Web by standards and technologies that help machines to understand the information on the Web so that they can support richer discovery, data integration, navigation, and automation of tasks. The main ideas behind it are to add a machine-understandable "meaning" to Web pages, to use ontologies for a precise definition of shared terms in Web resources, to use KR technology for automated reasoning from Web resources, and to apply cooperative agent technology for processing the information of the Web.

The Semantic Web is divided into several hierarchical layers (see Fig. 1), which include in particular the Ontology, Rules, Logic, and Proof layers. In detail, the *Ontology* layer, in the form of the *OWL Web Ontology Language* [5], consists of three increasingly expressive sublanguages, namely, *OWL Lite*, *OWL DL*, and *OWL Full*. OWL Lite and OWL DL are essentially very expressive description logics (DLs) with an RDF syntax. As shown in [6], ontology entailment in OWL Lite (resp., OWL DL) reduces to knowledge base (un)satisfiability in the description logic $\mathcal{SHIF}(\mathbf{D})$ (resp., $\mathcal{SHOIN}(\mathbf{D})$). The DL $\mathcal{SROIQ}$ [7] is one of the most expressive DLs, which is underlying OWL 2 [8], a new version of OWL. Reasoning in $\mathcal{SROIQ}$ is computationally expensive, and several more tractable languages have been proposed in the Semantic Web community. Among such languages, there are the *DL-Lite* family [9,10], $\mathcal{EL}^{++}$ [11], and DLP [12], which are underlying the OWL 2 profiles QL, EL, and RL [13], respectively. Beside and on top of the Ontology layer, there are sophisticated representation and reasoning capabilities for the *Rules*, *Logic*, and *Proof* layers of the Semantic Web.

A key requirement of the layered architecture of the Semantic Web is in particular to integrate the Rules and the Ontology layer. Here, it is crucial to allow for building rules on top of ontologies, i.e., for rule-based systems that use

G. Ianni et al. (Eds.): Reasoning Web 2017, LNCS 10370, pp. 276–291, 2017.
DOI: 10.1007/978-3-319-61033-7_8

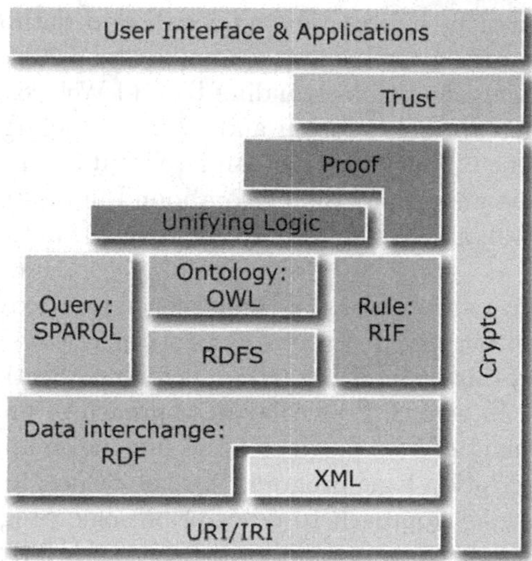

Fig. 1. Layered architecture of the Semantic Web.

vocabulary from ontological knowledge bases. Another type of combination is to build ontologies on top of rules, where ontological definitions are supplemented by rules or imported from rules. Both types of integration have been realized in recent hybrid integrations of rules and ontologies, called *description logic programs* (or *dl-programs*), which are of the form $KB = (L, P)$, where L is a description logic knowledge base, and P is a finite set of rules involving either queries to L in a loose integration (see, e.g., [14,15]) or concepts and roles from L as unary resp. binary predicates in a tight integration (see, e.g., [16]).

However, classical ontology languages and description logics as well as formalisms integrating rules and ontologies are less suitable in all those domains where the information to be represented comes along with (*quantitative*) *uncertainty* and/or *vagueness* (or *imprecision*). For this reason, during the recent years, handling uncertainty and vagueness has started to play an important role in research towards the Semantic Web. A recent forum for approaches to uncertainty reasoning in the Semantic Web is the annual *International Workshop on Uncertainty Reasoning for the Semantic Web (URSW)* at the *International Semantic Web Conference (ISWC)*. There has also been a W3C Incubator Group on *Uncertainty Reasoning for the World Wide Web*. The research focuses especially on probabilistic and fuzzy extensions of description logics, ontology languages, and formalisms integrating rules and ontologies. Note that probabilistic formalisms allow to encode ambiguous information, such as "John is a student with the probability 0.7 and a teacher with the probability 0.3" (roughly, John is either a teacher or a student, but more likely a student), while fuzzy approaches allow to encode vague or imprecise information, such as "John is tall with the degree of truth 0.7" (roughly, John is quite tall). Formalisms for dealing with uncertainty and vagueness are especially applied in ontology mapping, data integration, information retrieval, and database querying. For example, some of the most prominent technologies for dealing with uncertainty are probably the ranking algorithms standing behind Web search engines. Other important applications are belief fusion and opinion pooling, recommendation systems, user preference modeling, trust and reputation modeling, and shopping agents. Vagueness and imprecision also abound in multimedia information processing and retrieval, and are an important aspect of natural language interfaces to the Web.

In this paper, I give an overview of some own recent extensions of description logics and description logic programs by probabilistic uncertainty and fuzzy vagueness. The rest of this paper is organized as follows. Section 2 provides some motivating examples. In Sect. 3, I describe an approach to probabilistic description logics for the Semantic Web. Sections 4 and 5 focus on approaches to probabilistic and fuzzy description logic programs for the Semantic Web, respectively, while Sect. 6 describes an approach to description logic programs for handling both uncertainty and vagueness in a uniform framework for the Semantic Web. For a more detailed overview of extensions of description logics for handling uncertainty and vagueness in the Semantic Web, I also refer the reader to the survey [17].

2 Motivating Examples

We now provide some examples for the use of probabilistic ontologies and of probabilistic and vague extensions of formalisms integrating rules and ontologies.

In order to illustrate probabilistic ontologies, consider some medical knowledge about patients. In such knowledge, we often encounter terminological probabilistic and terminological default knowledge about classes of individuals, as well as assertional probabilistic knowledge about individuals. It is often advantageous to share such medical knowledge between hospitals and/or medical centers, for example, to follow up patients, to track medical history, for case studies research, and to get information on rare diseases and/or rare cures to diseases. The need for sharing medical knowledge is also at the core of the *W3C Semantic Web Health Care and Life Sciences Interest Group*, who state that the "key to the success of Life Science Research and Health Care is the implementation of new informatics models that will unite many forms of biological and medical information across all institutions" (see http://www.w3.org/2001/sw/hcls/).

Example 2.1 (Medical Example [18]). Consider patient records related to cardiological illnesses. We distinguish between heart patients (who have any kind of cardiological illness), pacemaker patients, male pacemaker patients, and female pacemaker patients, who all are associated with illnesses, illness statuses, symptoms of illnesses, and health insurances. Furthermore, we have the patients Tom, John, and Mary, where Tom is a heart patient, while John and Mary are male and female pacemaker patients, respectively, and John has the symptoms arrhythmia (abnormal heart beat), chest pain, and breathing difficulties, and the illness status advanced.

Then, *terminological default knowledge* is of the form "generally (or typically/in nearly all cases), heart patients suffer from high blood pressure" and "generally, pacemaker patients do not suffer from high blood pressure", while *terminological probabilistic knowledge* has the form "generally, pacemaker patients are male with a probability of at least 0.4" (i.e., "generally, a randomly chosen pacemaker patient is male with a probability of at least 0.4"), "generally, heart patients have a private insurance with a probability of at least 0.9", and "generally, pacemaker patients have the symptoms arrhythmia, chest pain, and breathing difficulties with probabilities of at least 0.98, 0.9, and 0.6, respectively". Finally, *assertional probabilistic knowledge* is of the form "Tom is a pacemaker patient with a probability of at least 0.8", "Mary has the symptom breathing difficulties with a probability of at least 0.6", "Mary has the symptom chest pain with a probability of at least 0.9", and "Mary's illness status is final with a probability between 0.2 and 0.8".

Uncertain medical knowledge may also be collected by a medical company from own databases and public sources (e.g., client data, web pages, web inquiries, blogs, and mailing lists) and be used in an advertising campaign for a new product.

Example 2.2 (Medical Example cont'd [18]). Suppose that a medical company wants to carry out a targeted advertising campaign about a new pacemaker product. The company may then first collect all potential addressees of such a campaign (e.g., pharmacies, hospitals, doctors, and heart patients) by probabilistic data integration from different data and web sources (e.g., own databases with data of clients and their shopping histories; and web listings of pharmacies, hospitals, and doctors along with their product portfolio resp. fields of expertise). The result of this process is a collection of individuals with probabilistic memberships to a collection of concepts in a medical ontology as the one above. The terminological probabilistic and terminological default knowledge of this ontology can then be used to derive probabilistic concept memberships that are relevant for a potential addressee of the advertising campaign. For example, for persons that are known to be heart patients with certain probabilities, we may derive the probabilities with which they are also pacemaker patients.

The next example illustrates the use of probabilistic ontologies in information retrieval for an increased recall (which has especially been explored in [19,20]).

Example 2.3 (Literature Search [18]). Suppose that we want to obtain a list of research papers in the area of "logic programming". Then, we should not only collect those papers that are classified as "logic programming" papers, but we should also search for papers in closely related areas, such as "rule-based systems" or "deductive databases", as well as in more general areas, such as "knowledge representation and reasoning" or "artificial intelligence" (since a paper may very well belong to the area of "logic programming", but is classified only with a closely related or a more general area). This expansion of the search can be done automatically using a probabilistic ontology, which has the papers as individuals, the areas as concepts, and the explicit paper classifications as concept memberships. The probabilistic degrees of overlap between the concepts in such a probabilistic ontology then provide a means of deriving a probabilistic membership to the concept "logic programming" and so a probabilistic estimation for the relevance to our search query.

We finally describe a shopping agent example, where we encounter both probabilistic uncertainty (in resource selection, ontology mapping/query transformation, and data integration) and fuzzy vagueness (in query matching with vague concepts).

Example 2.4 (Shopping Agent [44,45]). Suppose a person would like to buy "a sports car that costs at most about 22 000 € and that has a power of around 150 HP".

In todays Web, the buyer has to manually (i) search for car selling sites, e.g., using Google, (ii) select the most promising sites (e.g., http://www.autos.com), (iii) browse through them, query them to see the cars that they sell, and match the cars with our requirements, (iv) select the offers in each web site that match our requirements, and (v) eventually merge all the best offers from each site and select the best ones.

It is obvious that the whole process is rather tedious and time consuming, since, e.g., (i) the buyer has to visit many sites, (ii) the browsing in each site is very time consuming, (iii) finding the right information in a site (which has to match the requirements) is not simple, and (iv) the way of browsing and querying may differ from site to site.

A shopping agent may now support us as follows, automatizing the whole selection process once it receives the request/query q from the buyer:

- *Probabilistic Resource Selection.* The agent selects some sites/resources S that it considers as promising for the buyer's request. The agent has to select a subset of some relevant resources, since it is not reasonable to assume that it will access and query all the resources known to him. The relevance of a resource S to a query is usually (automatically) estimated as the probability $Pr(q|S)$ (the probability that the information need represented by the query q is satisfied by the searching resource S; see, e.g., [21,22]). It is not difficult to see that such probabilities can be represented by probabilistic rules.
- *Probabilistic Ontology Mapping/Query Reformulation.* For the top-k selected sites, the agent has to reformulate the buyer's query using the terminology/ontology of the specific car selling site. For this task, the agent relies on so-called transformation rules, which say how to translate a concept or property of the agent's ontology into the ontology of the information resource (which is called ontology mapping in the Semantic Web). To relate a concept B of the buyer's ontology to a concept S of the seller's ontology, one often automatically estimates the probability $P(B|S)$ that an instance of S is also an instance of B, which can then be represented as a probabilistic rule [23,24].

- *Vague Query Matching.* Once the agent has translated the buyer's request for the specific site's terminology, the agent submits the query. But the buyer's request often contains many so-called vague/fuzzy concepts such as "the price is around 22 000 € or less", rather than strict conditions, and thus a car may match the buyer's condition to a degree. As a consequence, a site/resource/web service may return a ranked list of cars, where the ranks depend on the degrees to which the sold items match the buyer's requests q.
- *Probabilistic Data Integration.* Eventually, the agent has to combine the ranked lists by considering the involved matching (or truth) degrees (vagueness) and probability degrees (uncertainty) and show the top-n items to the buyer.

3 Probabilistic Description Logics

In this section, we briefly describe the probabilistic description logic P-$\mathcal{SHOIN}(\mathbf{D})$, which is a probabilistic generalization of the description logic $\mathcal{SHOIN}(\mathbf{D})$ (behind OWL DL), directed towards sophisticated formalisms for reasoning under probabilistic uncertainty in the Semantic Web [18]. Closely related probabilistic generalizations of the *DL-Lite* family of tractable description logics (which lies between the Semantic Web languages RDFS and OWL Lite) and the description logics $\mathcal{SHIF}(\mathbf{D})$ and $\mathcal{SHOQ}(\mathbf{D})$ (which stand behind OWL Lite and DAML+OIL, respectively) have been introduced in [18,25]. A closely related paper [26] combines *DL-Lite* with Bayesian networks.

Probabilistic description logics allow for representing probabilistic ontologies and for reasoning about them. There is a plethora of applications with an urgent need for handling probabilistic knowledge in ontologies, especially in areas like medicine, biology, defense, and astronomy. Moreover, probabilistic ontologies allow for quantifying the degrees of overlap between the ontological concepts in the Semantic Web, reasoning about them, and using them in Semantic Web applications and systems, such as information retrieval, personalization tasks, and recommender systems. Furthermore, probabilistic ontologies can be used to align the concepts of different ontologies (called ontology mapping) and for handling inconsistencies in Semantic Web data.

The syntax of P-$\mathcal{SHOIN}(\mathbf{D})$ uses the notion of a conditional constraint from [27] to express probabilistic knowledge in addition to the axioms of $\mathcal{SHOIN}(\mathbf{D})$. Its semantics is based on the notion of lexicographic entailment in probabilistic default reasoning [28,29], which is a probabilistic generalization of the sophisticated notion of lexicographic entailment by Lehmann [30] in default reasoning from conditional knowledge bases. Due to this semantics, P-$\mathcal{SHOIN}(\mathbf{D})$ allows for expressing both terminological probabilistic knowledge about concepts and roles, and also assertional probabilistic knowledge about instances of concepts and roles. It naturally interprets terminological and assertional probabilistic knowledge as statistical knowledge about concepts and roles, and as degrees of belief about instances of concepts and roles, respectively, and allows for deriving both statistical knowledge and degrees of belief. As an important additional feature, it also allows for expressing default knowledge about concepts (as a special case of terminological probabilistic knowledge), which is semantically interpreted as in Lehmann's lexicographic default entailment [30].

Example 3.1. Suppose a classical description logic knowledge base T is used to encode knowledge about cars and their properties (e.g., that sports cars and roadsters are cars). A probabilistic knowledge base $KB = (T, P, (P_o)_{o \in \mathbf{I}_P})$ in P-$\mathcal{SHOIN}(\mathbf{D})$ then extends T by terminological default and terminological probabilistic knowledge in P as well as by assertional probabilistic knowledge in P_o for certain objects $o \in \mathbf{I}_P$. For example, the terminological default knowledge (1) "generally, cars do not have a red color" and (2) "generally, sports cars have a red color", and the terminological probabilistic knowledge (3) "cars have four wheels with a probability of at least 0.9", can be expressed by the following conditional constraints in P:

$$\begin{array}{ll} (1) & (\neg\exists\, \mathit{HasColor}.\{\mathit{red}\} \mid \mathit{Car})[1,1], \\ (2) & (\exists\, \mathit{HasColor}.\{\mathit{red}\} \mid \mathit{SportsCar})[1,1], \\ (3) & (\mathit{HasFourWheels} \mid \mathit{Car})[0.9,1]\,. \end{array}$$

Suppose we want to encode some probabilistic information about John's car (which we have not seen so far). Then, the set of probabilistic individuals $\mathbf{I}_P$ contains the individual *John's car*, and the assertional probabilistic knowledge (4) "John's car is a sports car with a probability of at least 0.8" (we know that John likes sports cars) can be expressed by the following conditional constraint in $P_{John's\,car}$:

$$(4) \quad (\mathit{SportsCar} \mid \top)[0.8,1]\,.$$

Then, the following are some (terminological default and terminological probabilistic) tight lexicographic consequences of $PT = (T, P)$:

$$\begin{array}{l} (\neg\exists\, \mathit{HasColor}.\{\mathit{red}\} \mid \mathit{Car})[1,1], \\ (\exists\, \mathit{HasColor}.\{\mathit{red}\} \mid \mathit{SportsCar})[1,1], \\ (\mathit{HasFourWheels} \mid \mathit{Car})[0.9,1], \\ (\neg\exists\, \mathit{HasColor}.\{\mathit{red}\} \mid \mathit{Roadster})[1,1], \\ (\mathit{HasFourWheels} \mid \mathit{SportsCar})[0.9,1], \\ (\mathit{HasFourWheels} \mid \mathit{Roadster})[0.9,1]\,. \end{array}$$

Hence, in addition to the sentences (1) to (3) directly encoded in P, we also conclude "generally, roadsters do not have a red color", "sports cars have four wheels with a probability of at least 0.9", and "roadsters have four wheels with a probability of at least 0.9". Observe here that the default property of not having a red color and the probabilistic property of having four wheels with a probability of at least 0.9 are inherited from cars down to roadsters. Roughly, the tight lexicographic consequences of $PT = (T, P)$ are given by all those conditional constraints that (a) are either in P, or (b) can be constructed by inheritance along subconcept relationships from the ones in P and are not overridden by more specific pieces of knowledge in P.

The following conditional constraints for the probabilistic individual *John's car* are some (assertional probabilistic) tight lexicographic consequences of *KB*, which informally say that John's car is a sports car, has a red color, and has four wheels with probabilities of at least 0.8, 0.8, and 0.72, respectively:

$$(\mathit{SportsCar} \mid \top)[0.8, 1],$$
$$(\exists\, \mathit{HasColor}.\{\mathit{red}\} \mid \top)[0.8, 1],$$
$$(\mathit{HasFourWheels} \mid \top)[0.72, 1]\,.$$

4 Probabilistic Description Logic Programs

We now summarize the main ideas behind loosely and tightly coupled probabilistic dl-programs, introduced in [31–34] and [35–39], respectively. For further details on the syntax and semantics of these programs, their background, and their semantic and computational properties, we refer to the above works.

Loosely coupled probabilistic dl-programs [31–33] are a combination of loosely coupled dl-programs under the answer set and the well-founded semantics with probabilistic uncertainty as in Bayesian networks. Roughly, they consist of a loosely coupled dl-program (L, P) under different "total choices" B (they are the full joint instantiations of a set of random variables, and they serve as pairwise exclusive and exhaustive possible worlds), and a probability distribution μ over the set of total choices B. One then obtains a probability distribution over Herbrand models, since every total choice B along with the loosely coupled dl-program produces a set of Herbrand models of which the probabilities sum up to $\mu(B)$. As in the classical case, the answer set semantics of loosely coupled probabilistic dl-programs is a refinement of the well-founded semantics of loosely coupled probabilistic dl-programs. Consistency checking and tight query processing (i.e., computing the entailed tight interval for the probability of a conditional or unconditional event) in such probabilistic dl-programs under the answer set semantics can be reduced to consistency checking and query processing in loosely coupled dl-programs under the answer set semantics, while tight query processing under the well-founded semantics can be done in an anytime fashion by reduction to loosely coupled dl-programs under the well-founded semantics. For suitably restricted description logic components, the latter can be done in polynomial time in the data complexity. Query processing for stratified loosely coupled probabilistic dl-programs can be reduced to computing the canonical model of stratified loosely coupled dl-programs. Loosely coupled probabilistic dl-programs can especially be used for (database-oriented) probabilistic data integration in the Semantic Web, where probabilistic uncertainty is used to handle inconsistencies between different data sources [34].

Example 4.1. A university database may use a loosely coupled dl-program (L, P) to encode ontological and rule-based knowledge about students and exams. A probabilistic dl-program $KB = (L, P', C, \mu)$ then additionally allows for encoding probabilistic knowledge. For example, the following two probabilistic rules in P' along with a probability distribution on a set of random variables may express that if two master (resp., bachelor) students have given the same exam, then there is a probability of 0.9 (resp., 0.7) that they are friends:

$$\begin{aligned} \mathit{friends}(X,Y) &\leftarrow \mathit{given\_same\_exam}(X,Y), \mathit{DL}[\mathit{master\_student}(X)], \\ &\quad\; \mathit{DL}[\mathit{master\_student}(Y)],\ \mathit{choice}_m\,; \\ \mathit{friends}(X,Y) &\leftarrow \mathit{given\_same\_exam}(X,Y), \mathit{DL}[\mathit{bachelor\_student}(X)], \\ &\quad\; \mathit{DL}[\mathit{bachelor\_student}(Y)],\ \mathit{choice}_b\,. \end{aligned}$$

Here, we assume the set $C = \{V_m, V_b\}$ of value sets $V_m = \{\mathit{choice}_m, \mathit{not\_choice}_m\}$ and $V_b = \{\mathit{choice}_b, \mathit{not\_choice}_b\}$ of two random variables X_m resp. X_b and the probability distribution μ on all their joint instantiations, given by μ: $\mathit{choice}_m, \mathit{not\_choice}_m,\ \mathit{choice}_b, \mathit{not\_choice}_b \mapsto 0.9, 0.1,\ 0.7, 0.3$ under probabilistic independence. For example, the joint instantiation $\mathit{choice}_m, \mathit{choice}_b$ is associated with the probability $0.9 \times 0.7 = 0.63$. Asking about the entailed tight interval for the probability that *john* and *bill* are friends can then be expressed by a probabilistic query $\exists(\mathit{friends}(\mathit{john}, \mathit{bill}))[R, S]$, whose answer depends on the available concrete knowledge about *john* and *bill* (namely, whether they have given the same exams, and are both master or bachelor students).

Tightly coupled probabilistic dl-programs [35,36] are a tight combination of disjunctive logic programs under the answer set semantics with description logics and Bayesian probabilities. They are a logic-based representation formalism that naturally fits into the landscape of Semantic Web languages. Tightly coupled probabilistic dl-programs can especially be used for representing mappings between ontologies [37,38], which are a common way of approaching the semantic heterogeneity problem on the Semantic Web. Here, they allow in particular for resolving inconsistencies and for merging mappings from different matchers based on the level of confidence assigned to different rules (see below). Furthermore, tightly coupled probabilistic description logic programs also provide a natural integration of ontologies, action languages, and Bayesian probabilities towards Web Services. Consistency checking and query processing in tightly coupled probabilistic dl-programs can be reduced to consistency checking and cautious/brave reasoning, respectively, in tightly coupled disjunctive dl-programs. Under certain restrictions, these problems have a polynomial data complexity.

Example 4.2. The two correspondences between two ontologies O_1 and O_2 that (i) an element of *Collection* in O_1 is an element of *Book* in O_2 with the probability 0.62, and (ii) an element of *Proceedings* in O_1 is an element of *Proceedings* in O_2 with the probability 0.73 (found by the matching system hmatch) can be expressed by the following two probabilistic rules:

$$\begin{aligned} &O_2 : \mathit{Book}(X) \leftarrow O_1 : \mathit{Collection}(X) \wedge \mathit{hmatch}_1; \\ &O_2 : \mathit{Proceedings}(X) \leftarrow O_1 : \mathit{Proceedings}(X) \wedge \mathit{hmatch}_2. \end{aligned}$$

Here, we assume the set $C = \{\{\mathit{hmatch}_i, \mathit{not\_hmatch}_i\} \mid i \in \{1, 2\}\}$ of values of two random variables and the probability distribution μ on all joint instantiations of these variables, given by μ: $hmatch_1, not\_hmatch_1, hmatch_2, not\_hmatch_2 \mapsto$ 0.62, 0.38, 0.73, 0.27 under probabilistic independence.

Similarly, two other correspondences between O_1 and O_2 (found by the matching system falcon) are expressed by the following two probabilistic rules:

$$O_2: InCollection(X) \leftarrow O_1: Collection(X) \wedge falcon_1;$$
$$O_2: Proceedings(X) \leftarrow O_1: Proceedings(X) \wedge falcon_2,$$

where we assume the set $\mathcal{C}' = \{\{falcon_i, not\_falcon_i\} \mid i \in \{1,2\}\}$ of values of two random variables and the probability distribution μ' on all joint instantiations of these variables, given by μ': $falcon_1, not\_falcon_1, falcon_2, not\_falcon_2 \mapsto$ 0.94, 0.06, 0.96, 0.04 under probabilistic independence.

Using the trust probabilities 0.55 and 0.45 for hmatch and falcon, respectively, for resolving inconsistencies between rules, we can now define a merged mapping set that consists of the following probabilistic rules:

$$O_2: Book(X) \leftarrow O_1: Collection(X) \wedge hmatch_1 \wedge sel\_hmatch_1;$$
$$O_2: InCollection(X) \leftarrow O_1: Collection(X) \wedge falcon_1 \wedge sel\_falcon_1;$$
$$O_2: Proceedings(X) \leftarrow O_1: Proceedings(X) \wedge hmatch_2;$$
$$O_2: Proceedings(X) \leftarrow O_1: Proceedings(X) \wedge falcon_2.$$

Here, we assume the set $\mathcal{C}''$ of values of random variables and the probability distribution μ'' on all joint instantiations of these variables, which are obtained from $\mathcal{C} \cup \mathcal{C}'$ and $\mu \cdot \mu'$ (defined as $(\mu \cdot \mu')(B\,B') = \mu(B) \cdot \mu'(B')$, for all joint instantiations B of $\mathcal{C}$ and B' of $\mathcal{C}'$), respectively, by adding the values $\{sel\_hmatch_1,\ sel\_falcon_1\}$ of a new random variable, with the probabilities $sel\_hmatch_1, sel\_falcon_1 \mapsto$ 0.55, 0.45 under probabilistic independence, for resolving the inconsistency between the first two rules.

A companion approach to probabilistic description logic programs [39] combines probabilistic logic programs, probabilistic default theories, and the description logics behind OWL Lite and OWL DL. It is based on new notions of entailment for reasoning with conditional constraints, which realize the principle of inheritance with overriding for both classical and purely probabilistic knowledge. They are obtained by generalizing previous formalisms for probabilistic default reasoning with conditional constraints (similarly as for P-$\mathcal{SHOIN}$(**D**) in Sect. 3). In addition to dealing with probabilistic knowledge, these notions of entailment thus also allow for handling default knowledge.

5 Fuzzy Description Logic Programs

We next briefly describe loosely and tightly coupled fuzzy dl-programs, which have been introduced in [40,41] and [42,43], respectively, and extended by a top-k retrieval technique in [46]. All these fuzzy dl-programs have natural special cases where query processing can be done in polynomial time in the data complexity. For further details on their syntax and semantics, background, and properties, we refer to the above works.

Towards dealing with vagueness and imprecision in the reasoning layers of the Semantic Web, loosely coupled (normal) fuzzy dl-programs under the answer set semantics [40,41] generalize normal dl-programs under the answer set semantics by fuzzy vagueness and imprecision in both the description logic and the logic program component. This is the first approach to fuzzy dl-programs that may contain default negations in rule bodies. Query processing in such fuzzy dl-programs can be done by reduction to normal dl-programs under the answer set semantics. In the special cases of positive and stratified loosely coupled fuzzy dl-programs, the answer set semantics coincides with a canonical least model and an iterative least model semantics, respectively, and has a characterization in terms of a fixpoint and an iterative fixpoint semantics, respectively.

Example 5.1. Consider the fuzzy description logic knowledge base L of a car shopping Web site, which defines especially (i) the fuzzy concepts of sports cars (*SportsCar*), "at most 22 000 €" (*LeqAbout22000*), and "around 150 horse power" (*Around150HP*), (ii) the attributes of the price and of the horse power of a car (*hasInvoice* resp. *hasHP*), and (iii) the properties of some concrete cars (such as a *MazdaMX5Miata* and a *MitsubishiES*). Then, a loosely coupled fuzzy dl-program $KB = (L, P)$ is given by the set of fuzzy dl-rules P, which contains only the following fuzzy dl-rule encoding the request of a buyer (asking for a sports car costing at most 22 000 € and having around 150 horse power), where $\otimes$ may be the conjunction strategy of, e.g., Gödel Logic (i.e., $x \otimes y = \min(x, y)$, for all $x, y \in [0, 1]$, is used to evaluate $\wedge$ and $\leftarrow$ on truth values):

$$\begin{aligned} query(x) \leftarrow_{\otimes} &\ DL[SportsCar](x) \wedge_{\otimes} DL[\exists hasInvoice.LeqAbout22000](x) \wedge_{\otimes} \\ &\ DL[\exists hasHP.Around150HP](x) \geqslant 1\,. \end{aligned}$$

The above fuzzy dl-program $KB = (L, P)$ is positive (i.e., without default negation), and has a minimal model M_{KB}, which defines the degree to which some concrete cars in the description logic knowledge base L match the buyer's request, for example,

$$M_{KB}(query(MazdaMX5Miata)) = 0.36, \quad M_{KB}(query(MitsubishiES)) = 0.32\,.$$

That is, the car *MazdaMX5Miata* is ranked top with the degree 0.36, while the car *MitsubishiES* is ranked second with the degree 0.32.

Tightly coupled fuzzy dl-programs under the answer set semantics [42,43] are a tight integration of fuzzy disjunctive logic programs under the answer set semantics with fuzzy description logics. They are also a generalization of tightly coupled disjunctive dl-programs by fuzzy vagueness in both the description logic and the logic program component. This is the first approach to fuzzy dl-programs that may contain disjunctions in rule heads. Query processing in such programs can essentially be done by a reduction to tightly coupled disjunctive dl-programs. A closely related work [46] explores the evaluation of ranked top-k queries. It shows in particular how to compute the top-k answers in data-complexity tractable tightly coupled fuzzy dl-programs.

Example 5.2. A tightly coupled fuzzy dl-program $KB = (L, P)$ is given by a suitable fuzzy description logic knowledge base L and the set of fuzzy rules P, which contains only the following fuzzy rule (where $x \otimes y = \min(x, y)$):

$$\begin{aligned} \mathit{query}(x) \leftarrow_{\otimes} & \mathit{SportyCar}(x) \wedge_{\otimes} \mathit{hasInvoice}(x, y_1) \wedge_{\otimes} \mathit{hasHorsePower}(x, y_2) \wedge_{\otimes} \\ & \mathit{LeqAbout22000}(y_1) \wedge_{\otimes} \mathit{Around150}(y_2) \geqslant 1 \,. \end{aligned}$$

Informally, *query* collects all sports cars, and ranks them according to whether they cost at most around 22 000 € and have around 150 HP. Another fuzzy rule involving also a negation in its body and a disjunction in its head is given as follows (where $\ominus x = 1 - x$ and $x \oplus y = \max(x, y)$):

$$\begin{aligned} \mathit{Small}(x) \vee_{\oplus} \mathit{Old}(x) \leftarrow_{\otimes} & \mathit{Car}(x) \wedge_{\otimes} \mathit{hasInvoice}(x, y) \wedge_{\otimes} \\ & \mathit{not}_{\ominus}\, \mathit{GeqAbout15000}(y) \geqslant 0.7 \,. \end{aligned}$$

This rule says that a car costing at most around 15 000 € is either small or old. Notice here that *Small* and *Old* may be two concepts in the fuzzy description logic knowledge base L. That is, the tightly coupled approach to fuzzy dl-programs under the answer set semantics also allows for using the rules in P to express relationships between the concepts and roles in L. This is not possible in the loosely coupled approach to fuzzy dl-programs under the answer set semantics in [40,41], since the dl-queries there can only occur in rule bodies, but not in rule heads.

6 Probabilistic Fuzzy Description Logic Programs

We finally describe (loosely coupled) probabilistic fuzzy dl-programs [44,45], which combine fuzzy description logics, fuzzy logic programs (with stratified default-negation), and probabilistic uncertainty in a uniform framework for the Semantic Web. Intuitively, they allow for defining several rankings on ground atoms using fuzzy vagueness, and then for merging these rankings using probabilistic uncertainty (by associating with each ranking a probabilistic weight and building the weighted sum of all rankings). Such programs also give rise to important concepts dealing with both probabilistic uncertainty and fuzzy vagueness, such as the expected truth value of a crisp sentence and the probability of a vague sentence. Probabilistic fuzzy dl-programs can be used to model a shopping agent as described in Example 2.4.

Example 6.1. A (loosely coupled) probabilistic fuzzy dl-program is given by a suitable fuzzy description logic knowledge base L and the following set of fuzzy dl-rules P, modeling some query reformulation/retrieval steps using ontology mapping rules:

$$\begin{aligned} \mathit{query}(x) \leftarrow_{\otimes} & \mathit{SportyCar}(x) \wedge_{\otimes} \mathit{hasPrice}(x, y_1) \wedge_{\otimes} \mathit{hasPower}(x, y_2) \wedge_{\otimes} \\ & \mathit{DL}[\mathit{LeqAbout22000}](y_1) \wedge_{\otimes} \mathit{DL}[\mathit{Around150HP}](y_2) \geqslant 1 \,, && (1) \\ \mathit{SportyCar}(x) \leftarrow_{\otimes} & \mathit{DL}[\mathit{SportsCar}](x) \wedge_{\otimes} \mathit{sc}_{pos} \geqslant 0.9 \,, && (2) \\ \mathit{hasPrice}(x, y) \leftarrow_{\otimes} & \mathit{DL}[\mathit{hasInvoice}](x, y) \wedge_{\otimes} \mathit{hi}_{pos} \geqslant 0.8 \,, && (3) \\ \mathit{hasPower}(x, y) \leftarrow_{\otimes} & \mathit{DL}[\mathit{hasHP}](x, y) \wedge_{\otimes} \mathit{hhp}_{pos} \geqslant 0.8 \,, && (4) \end{aligned}$$

where we assume the set $C = \{\{sc_{pos}, sc_{neg}\}, \{hi_{pos}, hi_{neg}\}, \{hhp_{pos}, hhp_{neg}\}\}$ of values of random variables and the probability distribution μ on all joint instantiations of these variables, given by μ: $sc_{pos}, sc_{neg}, hi_{pos}, hi_{neg}, hhp_{pos}, hhp_{neg} \mapsto 0.91, 0.09, 0.78, 0.22, 0.83, 0.17$ under probabilistic independence. Here, rule (1) is the buyer's request, but in a "different" terminology than the one of the car selling site. Rules (2)–(4) are so-called ontology alignment mapping rules. For example, rule (2) states that the predicate "SportyCar" of the buyer's terminology refers to the concept "SportsCar" of the selected site with probability 0.91.

The following are some tight consequences of the above probabilistic fuzzy dl-program (where for ground atoms q, we use $(\mathbf{E}[q])[L, U]$ to denote that the expected truth value of q lies in the interval $[L, U]$):

$$(\mathbf{E}[query(MazdaMX5Miata)])[0.21, 0.21],\ (\mathbf{E}[query(MitsubishiES)])[0.19, 0.19]\,.$$

That is, the car *MazdaMX5Miata* is ranked first with the degree 0.21, while the car *MitsubishiES* is ranked second with the degree 0.19.

Acknowledgments. This work was supported the UK EPSRC grants EP/J008346/1, EP/L012138/1, EP/M025268/1, and EP/N510129/1.

References

1. Berners-Lee, T.: Weaving the Web. Harper, San Francisco (1999)
2. Berners-Lee, T., Hendler, J., Lassila, O.: The Semantic Web. Sci. Amer. **284**(5), 34–43 (2001)
3. Fensel, D., Wahlster, W., Lieberman, H., Hendler, J. (eds.): Spinning the Semantic Web: Bringing the World Wide Web to Its Full Potential. MIT Press, Cambridge (2002)
4. Horrocks, I., Patel-Schneider, P.F., van Harmelen, F.: From $\mathcal{SHIQ}$ and RDF to OWL: the making of a web ontology language. J. Web Sem. **1**(1), 7–26 (2003)
5. W3C: OWL Web Ontology Language Overview (2004) W3C Recommendation, 10 February 2004. http://www.w3.org/TR/2004/REC-owl-features-20040210/
6. Horrocks, I., Patel-Schneider, P.F.: Reducing OWL entailment to description logic satisfiability. In: Fensel, D., Sycara, K., Mylopoulos, J. (eds.) ISWC 2003. LNCS, vol. 2870, pp. 17–29. Springer, Heidelberg (2003). doi:10.1007/978-3-540-39718-2_2
7. Horrocks, I., Kutz, O., Sattler, U.: The even more irresistible $\mathcal{SROIQ}$. In: Proceedings KR-2006, pp. 57–67 (2006)
8. W3C: OWL 2 Web Ontology Language Document Overview (2009) W3C Recommendation, 27 October 2009. http://www.w3.org/TR/owl2-overview/
9. Calvanese, D., De Giacomo, G., Lembo, D., Lenzerini, M., Rosati, R.: Tractable reasoning and efficient query answering in description logics: the DL-Lite family. J. Autom. Reasoning **39**(3), 385–429 (2007)
10. Poggi, A., Lembo, D., Calvanese, D., Giacomo, G., Lenzerini, M., Rosati, R.: Linking data to ontologies. In: Spaccapietra, S. (ed.) Journal on Data Semantics X. LNCS, vol. 4900, pp. 133–173. Springer, Heidelberg (2008). doi:10.1007/978-3-540-77688-8_5

11. Baader, F., Brandt, S., Lutz, C.: Pushing the $\mathcal{EL}$ envelope. In: Proceedings IJCAI-2005, pp. 364–369 (2005)
12. Grosof, B.N., Horrocks, I., Volz, R., Decker, S.: Description logic programs: combining logic programs with description logic. In: Proceedings WWW-2003, pp. 48–57 (2003)
13. W3C: OWL 2 Web Ontology Language Profiles (2009) W3C Recommendation, 27 October 2009. http://www.w3.org/TR/owl2-profiles/
14. Eiter, T., Ianni, G., Lukasiewicz, T., Schindlauer, R., Tompits, H.: Combining answer set programming with description logics for the Semantic Web. Artif. Intell. **172**(12/13), 1495–1539 (2008)
15. Eiter, T., Lukasiewicz, T., Schindlauer, R., Tompits, H.: Well-founded semantics for description logic programs in the semantic web. In: Antoniou, G., Boley, H. (eds.) RuleML 2004. LNCS, vol. 3323, pp. 81–97. Springer, Heidelberg (2004). doi:10.1007/978-3-540-30504-0_7
16. Lukasiewicz, T.: A novel combination of answer set programming with description logics for the semantic web. In: Franconi, E., Kifer, M., May, W. (eds.) ESWC 2007. LNCS, vol. 4519, pp. 384–398. Springer, Heidelberg (2007). doi:10.1007/978-3-540-72667-8_28
17. Lukasiewicz, T., Straccia, U.: Managing uncertainty and vagueness in description logics for the Semantic Web. J. Web Sem. **6**(4), 291–308 (2008)
18. Lukasiewicz, T.: Expressive probabilistic description logics. Artif. Intell. **172**(6/7), 852–883 (2008)
19. Udrea, O., Yu, D., Hung, E., Subrahmanian, V.S.: Probabilistic ontologies and relational databases. In: Meersman, R., Tari, Z. (eds.) OTM 2005. LNCS, vol. 3760, pp. 1–17. Springer, Heidelberg (2005). doi:10.1007/11575771_1
20. Hung, E., Deng, Y., Subrahmanian, V.S.: TOSS: an extension of TAX with ontologies and similarity queries. In: Proceedings ACM SIGMOD 2004. ACM Press, pp. 719–730 (2004)
21. Callan, J.: Distributed information retrieval. In: Croft, W.B. (ed.) Advances in Information Retrieval, pp. 127–150. Kluwer (2000)
22. Fuhr, N.: A decision-theoretic approach to database selection in networked IR. ACM Trans. Inf. Syst. **3**(17), 229–249 (1999)
23. Straccia, U., Troncy, R.: Towards distributed information retrieval in the semantic web: query reformulation using the oMAP framework. In: Sure, Y., Domingue, J. (eds.) ESWC 2006. LNCS, vol. 4011, pp. 378–392. Springer, Heidelberg (2006). doi:10.1007/11762256_29
24. Nottelmann, H., Straccia, U.: Information retrieval and machine learning for probabilistic schema matching. Inf. Process. Manage. **43**(3), 552–576 (2007)
25. Giugno, R., Lukasiewicz, T.: P-$\mathcal{SHOQ}$(D): a probabilistic extension of $\mathcal{SHOQ}$(D) for probabilistic ontologies in the Semantic Web. In: Flesca, S., Greco, S., Ianni, G., Leone, N. (eds.) JELIA 2002. LNCS, vol. 2424, pp. 86–97. Springer, Heidelberg (2002). doi:10.1007/3-540-45757-7_8
26. d'Amato, C., Fanizzi, N., Lukasiewicz, T.: Tractable reasoning with Bayesian description logics. In: Greco, S., Lukasiewicz, T. (eds.) SUM 2008. LNCS (LNAI), vol. 5291, pp. 146–159. Springer, Heidelberg (2008). doi:10.1007/978-3-540-87993-0_13
27. Lukasiewicz, T.: Probabilistic deduction with conditional constraints over basic events. J. Artif. Intell. Res. **10**, 199–241 (1999)
28. Lukasiewicz, T.: Probabilistic logic programming under inheritance with overriding. In: Proceedings UAI-2001, pp. 329–336. Morgan Kaufmann (2001)

29. Lukasiewicz, T.: Probabilistic default reasoning with conditional constraints. Ann. Math. Artif. Intell. **34**(1–3), 35–88 (2002)
30. Lehmann, D.: Another perspective on default reasoning. Ann. Math. Artif. Intell. **15**(1), 61–82 (1995)
31. Lukasiewicz, T.: Probabilistic description logic programs. In: Godo, L. (ed.) ECSQARU 2005. LNCS (LNAI), vol. 3571, pp. 737–749. Springer, Heidelberg (2005). doi:10.1007/11518655_62
32. Lukasiewicz, T.: Probabilistic description logic programs. Int. J. Approx. Reasoning **45**(2), 288–307 (2007)
33. Lukasiewicz, T.: Tractable probabilistic description logic programs. In: Prade, H., Subrahmanian, V.S. (eds.) SUM 2007. LNCS (LNAI), vol. 4772, pp. 143–156. Springer, Heidelberg (2007). doi:10.1007/978-3-540-75410-7_11
34. Calì, A., Lukasiewicz, T.: An approach to probabilistic data integration for the semantic web. In: Costa, P.C.G., d'Amato, C., Fanizzi, N., Laskey, K.B., Laskey, K.J., Lukasiewicz, T., Nickles, M., Pool, M. (eds.) URSW 2005-2007. LNCS (LNAI), vol. 5327, pp. 52–65. Springer, Heidelberg (2008). doi:10.1007/978-3-540-89765-1_4
35. Calì, A., Lukasiewicz, T.: Tightly integrated probabilistic description logic programs for the Semantic Web. In: Dahl, V., Niemelä, I. (eds.) ICLP 2007. LNCS, vol. 4670, pp. 428–429. Springer, Heidelberg (2007). doi:10.1007/978-3-540-74610-2_30
36. Calì, A., Lukasiewicz, T., Predoiu, L., Stuckenschmidt, H.: Tightly coupled probabilistic description logic programs for the Semantic Web. J. Data Sem. **12**, 95–130 (2009)
37. Calì, A., Lukasiewicz, T., Predoiu, L., Stuckenschmidt, H.: Rule-based approaches for representing probabilistic ontology mappings. In: Costa, P.C.G., d'Amato, C., Fanizzi, N., Laskey, K.B., Laskey, K.J., Lukasiewicz, T., Nickles, M., Pool, M. (eds.) URSW 2005-2007. LNCS (LNAI), vol. 5327, pp. 66–87. Springer, Heidelberg (2008). doi:10.1007/978-3-540-89765-1_5
38. Calì, A., Lukasiewicz, T., Predoiu, L., Stuckenschmidt, H.: Tightly integrated probabilistic description logic programs for representing ontology mappings. In: Hartmann, S., Kern-Isberner, G. (eds.) FoIKS 2008. LNCS, vol. 4932, pp. 178–198. Springer, Heidelberg (2008). doi:10.1007/978-3-540-77684-0_14
39. Lukasiewicz, T.: Probabilistic description logic programs under inheritance with overriding for the Semantic Web. Int. J. Approx. Reasoning **49**(1), 18–34 (2008)
40. Lukasiewicz, T.: Fuzzy description logic programs under the answer set semantics for the Semantic Web. In: Proceedings RuleML-2006, pp. 89–96. IEEE Computer Society (2006)
41. Lukasiewicz, T.: Fuzzy description logic programs under the answer set semantics for the Semantic Web. Fundam. Inform. **82**(3), 289–310 (2008)
42. Lukasiewicz, T., Straccia, U.: Tightly Integrated fuzzy description logic programs under the answer set semantics for the Semantic Web. In: Marchiori, M., Pan, J.Z., Marie, C.S. (eds.) RR 2007. LNCS, vol. 4524, pp. 289–298. Springer, Heidelberg (2007). doi:10.1007/978-3-540-72982-2_23
43. Lukasiewicz, T., Straccia, U.: Tightly coupled fuzzy description logic programs under the answer set semantics for the Semantic Web. Int. J. Semant. Web Inf. Syst. **4**(3), 68–89 (2008)
44. Lukasiewicz, T., Straccia, U.: Description logic programs under probabilistic uncertainty and fuzzy vagueness. In: Mellouli, K. (ed.) ECSQARU 2007. LNCS (LNAI), vol. 4724, pp. 187–198. Springer, Heidelberg (2007). doi:10.1007/978-3-540-75256-1_19

45. Lukasiewicz, T., Straccia, U.: Description logic programs under probabilistic uncertainty and fuzzy vagueness. Int. J. Approx. Reasoning **50**(6), 837–853 (2009)
46. Lukasiewicz, T., Straccia, U.: Top-k retrieval in description logic programs under vagueness for the Semantic Web. In: Prade, H., Subrahmanian, V.S. (eds.) SUM 2007. LNCS (LNAI), vol. 4772, pp. 16–30. Springer, Heidelberg (2007). doi:10.1007/978-3-540-75410-7_2

OBDA for Log Extraction in Process Mining

Diego Calvanese, Tahir Emre Kalayci, Marco Montali(✉), and Ario Santoso

KRDB Research Centre for Knowledge and Data,
Free University of Bozen-Bolzano, Bolzano, Italy
{calvanese,tkalayci,montali,santoso}@inf.unibz.it

Abstract. Process mining is an emerging area that synergically combines model-based and data-oriented analysis techniques to obtain useful insights on how business processes are executed within an organization. Through process mining, decision makers can discover process models from data, compare expected and actual behaviors, and enrich models with key information about their actual execution. To be applicable, process mining techniques require the input data to be explicitly structured in the form of an event log, which lists when and by whom different case objects (i.e., process instances) have been subject to the execution of tasks. Unfortunately, in many real world set-ups, such event logs are not explicitly given, but are instead implicitly represented in legacy information systems. To apply process mining in this widespread setting, there is a pressing need for techniques able to support various process stakeholders in data preparation and log extraction from legacy information systems. The purpose of this paper is to single out this challenging, open issue, and didactically introduce how techniques from intelligent data management, and in particular ontology-based data access, provide a viable solution with a solid theoretical basis.

Keywords: Process mining · Ontology-based data access · Event log extraction · Relational database management systems

1 Introduction

SMEs[1] and large enterprises are increasingly adopting business process management to continuously optimise internal work, achieve its strategic business objectives, and guarantee quality of service to their customers. Business process management provides methods, techniques, and tools to comprehensively support managers and domain experts in the design, administration, configuration, execution, monitoring, and analysis of operational business processes [1]. As pointed out in [2], a *business process* consists of a set of activities that are performed in coordination in an organisational and technical environment, and that jointly realise a business goal. At execution time, the process is instantiated multiple times, leading to different sequences of activity executions performed by different resources, where each sequence refers to the evolution of a main,

[1] Small and medium-sized enterprises.

G. Ianni et al. (Eds.): Reasoning Web 2017, LNCS 10370, pp. 292–345, 2017.
DOI: 10.1007/978-3-319-61033-7_9

so-called *case object*. The instantiation of each activity on a case, in turn, gives raise to multiple events, indicating the evolution of each activity instance from its start to its completion or cancellation, according to a so-called *activity transactional lifecycle*.

The notion of case depends on the nature of the process, and on the perspective taken to understand the process. For example, in an order-to-cash scenario, the case typically corresponds to the order first issued by a customer, then manipulated within the enterprise, paid by the customer, and finally shipped to her. Different orders give raise to different process instances and corresponding execution traces. While using the order as a case object to understand the process is the most natural choice in this scenario, alternative case objects may be useful to understand the same process from different viewpoints. For example, suppose that the enterprise managing orders relies on an external shipping company to handle the order deliveries. Such a shipping company may prefer to consider its couriers as cases, and consequently focus its attention to the flow of operations performed by each courier, possibly involving multiple orders at once.

Classical BPM is purely model-driven: processes are elicited using human ingenuity through interviews with the involved stakeholders, and then used in a prescriptive manner to orchestrate the process execution, and to indicate to such stakeholders how they are expected to behave. This has been increasingly considered as the main limiting factor towards large-scale adoption of BPM. On the one hand, people tend to consider processes not as a support, but as a form of control over their behaviour. This is especially true in so-called knowledge-intensive settings, where it is not possible to foresee all potential state of affairs in advance, nor to enumerate all possible courses of execution, which have in fact to be adaptively and incrementally devised at runtime by the involved stakeholders, leveraging their own knowledge. On the other hand, there is an intrinsic mismatch between processes as reflected in models, and process executions resulting from the actual progression of cases in a real organisational setting. Even when processes are executed in line with the elicited process models, considering execution data is crucial to understand how work is effectively carried out inside the enterprise, and consequently obtain useful insights related to key performance indicators (such as average completion time for cases), the detection of bottlenecks and of working relationships among persons, and the identification of frequent and infrequent behaviours, to name a few.

To resolve this mismatch between process models and process executions, the emerging area of *process mining* [3,4] has become increasingly popular both in the academia and the industry. Process mining is a collection of techniques that combine, in a synergic way, model-based and data-oriented analysis to obtain useful insights on how business processes are executed in a real organisational environment. Through process mining, decision makers can *discover* process models from data, *compare* expected and actual behaviours, and *enrich* models with information obtained from their execution. The process mining manifesto [3] provides a thorough introduction to process mining. The book by van der Aalst [4] is the main reference material for students, researchers and professionals interested in this field. In addition, a list of successful stories related to the application of process mining to concrete case studies can be found at the web page of IEEE CIS Task Force on Process Mining[2].

The applicability of process mining depends on two crucial factors:

- the availability of high-quality event data, and of event logs containing correct and complete event data about which cases have been executed, which events occurred for each case, and when they did occur;
- the representation of such data in a format that is understandable by process mining algorithms, such as the XML-based, IEEE standard eXtensible Event Stream (XES) [5].

Event data structured in this form are only readily available if the enterprise under analysis adopts a business process management system, providing direct support for orchestrating the execution of cases according to a given process model, and at the same time providing logging capabilities for cases, events, and corresponding attributes. In this setting, the extraction of an event log for process mining is quite direct. Unfortunately, in many real world settings, the enterprise exploits functionalities offered by more general enterprise systems such as ERP[3], CRM[4], SCM[5], and other business suites. In addition, such systems are typically configured for the specific needs of the company, and connected to domain-specific and other legacy information systems. Within such complex systems, event logs are not explicitly present, but have instead to be reconstructed by extracting and integrating information present in all such different, possibly heterogeneous data sources.

To apply process mining in this widespread setting, there is a pressing need for techniques that are able to support data and process analysts in the data preparation phase [3], and in particular in the extraction of event data from legacy information systems. The purpose of this paper is to single out this challenging, open issue, and didactically introduce how techniques from intelligent data management, and in particular ontology-based data access (OBDA) [6–8], provide a viable solution with a solid theoretical basis. The resulting approach, called onprom [9], comes with a methodology supporting data and process analysts in the conceptual identification of event data, answering questions like: *(i)* Which are relevant concepts and relations? *(ii)* How do such concepts/relations map to the underlying information system? *(iii)* Which concepts/relations relate to the notion of case, event, and event attributes? The methodology is backed up by a toolchain that, once the aforementioned questions are answered, automatically extracts an event log conforming to the chosen perspective, and obtained by inspecting the data *where they are*, thanks to the OBDA paradigm and tools.

---

[2] http://tinyurl.com/ovedwx4.
[3] Enterprise Resource Planning.
[4] Customer Relationship Management.
[5] Supply Chain Management.

2 Process Mining: A Gentle Introduction

In this section, we give broad introduction to process mining, starting with the reference framework for process mining, the main process mining techniques, and an excursus of some contemporary process mining tools. In the second part of the section, we focus on the data preparation phase for process mining, recalling the notion of event log and of the event log format expected by process mining algorithms.

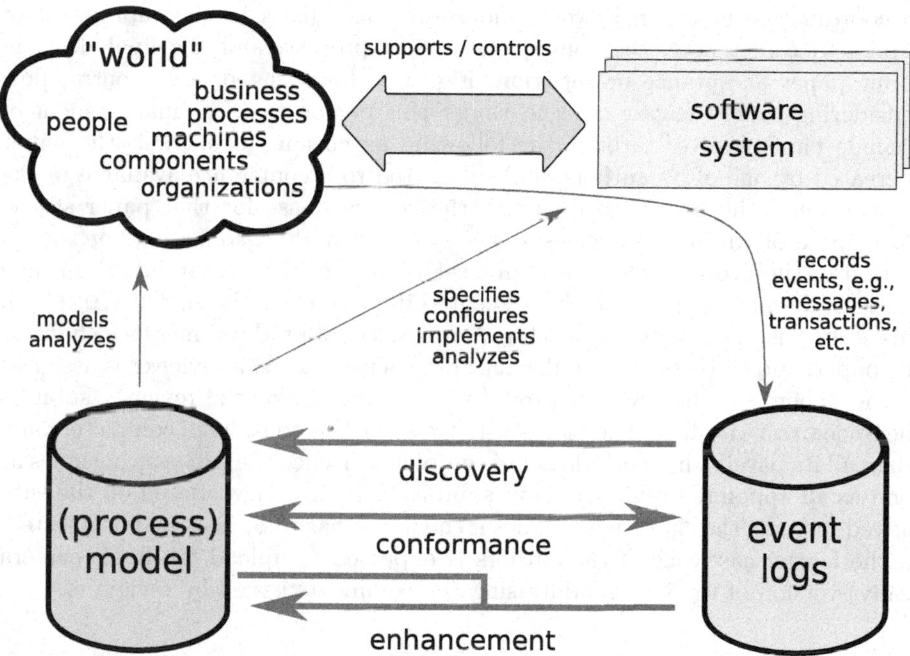

Fig. 1. The reference framework for process mining, and the three types of process mining techniques: discovery, conformance, and enhancement [3]

2.1 The Process Mining Framework

The reference framework for process mining is depicted in Fig. 1. On the one hand, process mining considers conceptual models describing processes, organisational structures, and the corresponding relevant data. On the other hand, it focuses on the real execution of processes, as reflected by the footprint of reality logged and stored by the software systems in use within the enterprise. For process mining to be applicable, such information has to be structured in the form of explicit *event logs*. In fact, all process mining techniques assume that it is possible to record the sequencing of relevant events occurred within the enterprise, such that each event refers to an activity (i.e., a well-defined step in some process) and is related to a particular case [3]. Events may have additional information stored in event logs. In fact, whenever possible, process mining techniques use extra information such as the exact timestamp at which the event has been recorded, the resource (i.e., person or device) that generated the event, the event type in the context of the activity transactional lifecycle (e.g., whether the activity has been started, cancelled, or completed), the timestamp of the event, or data elements recorded with the event (e.g., the size of an order).

Example 1. As a running example, we consider a simplified conference submission system, which we call ConfSys. The main purpose of ConfSys is to coordinate authors, reviewers, and conference chairs in the submission of papers to conferences, the consequent review process, and the final decision about paper acceptance or rejection. Figure 2 shows the process control flow considering papers as case objects. Under this perspective, the management of a single paper evolves through the following execution steps. First, the paper is created by one of its authors, and submitted to a conference available in the system. Once the paper is submitted, the review phase for that paper starts. This phase of the process consists of a so-called *multi-instance section*, i.e., a section of the process where the same set of activities is instantiated multiple times on the same paper, and then executed in parallel. In the case of ConfSys, this section is instantiated for each reviewer selected by the conference chair for the paper, and consists of the following three activities: *(i)* a reviewer is assigned to the paper; *(ii)* the reviewer produces the review; *(iii)* the reviewer submits the review to ConfSys. The multi-instance section is considered completed only when all its parallel instantiations are completed. Hence the process continues as soon as all appointed reviewers have submitted their review. Based on the submitted reviews, the chair then decides if the paper has to be accepted or rejected. In the former case, one of the authors is expected to upload the final (camera ready) version of the paper, addressing the comments issued by reviewers.

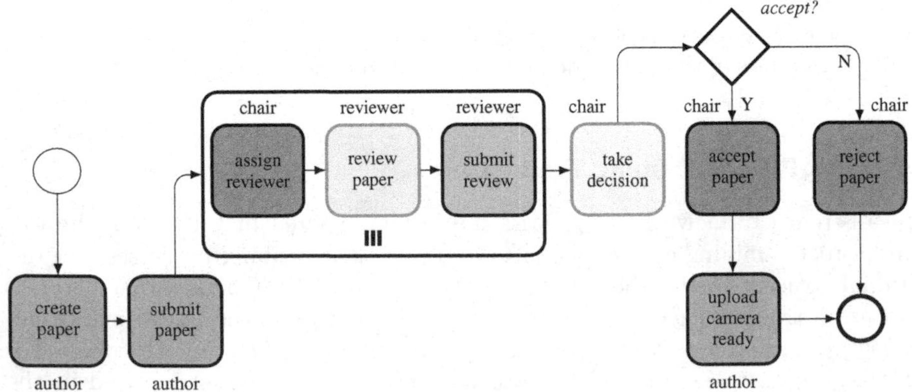

Fig. 2. The process for managing papers in a simplified conference submission system; gray tasks are external to the conference information system and cannot be logged.

It is important to notice, again, that the process model shown in Fig. 2 is only one of the several representations of the process, reflecting the perspective of papers as process cases. A completely different model would emerge from the same process, when focusing on the evolution of reviews instead of that of papers.

A fragment of a sample event log tracking the evolution of papers within ConfSys is shown in Table 1. The logged activities corresponds to those activities in Fig. 2 that actually comprise interaction with the software system of ConfSys, together with those activities that are autonomously executed by the system itself. From the point of view of the software system, the former activities are called *human-interaction activities*, and the latter are called *system activities*. These two types of activity contrast with purely *human activities*, which are executed by humans in the concrete world without software support, and can be indirectly logged only if accompanied by corresponding human-interaction activities. An example of this can be seen in Fig. 2, where *review paper* is a purely human activity carried out by a reviewer without the intervention of the software system, and is in fact coupled with *submit review*, a human-interaction activity executed by a reviewer to communicate to ConfSys the outcome of *review paper*. As we can see from the table there are two different cases (i.e., papers), with various events, each involving different responsible actors. Both cases regard papers that have been subject only to a single review, but in the first case the paper is accepted, while in the second one it is rejected. ■

How do process mining techniques exploit models and/or event logs to extract useful insights, and what do they offer concretely? The three main types of

Table 1. An event log fragment tracking the evolution of two papers within ConfSys. Every paper is a case, which in turn corresponds to a trace of events logging the execution of (human-interaction and system) activities instantiated on that paper.

Case ID	Event data				
	ID	Timestamp	Activity	User	...
1	35654423	30-12-2010:11.02	create paper	Pete	...
	35654424	31-12-2010:10.06	submit paper	Pete	...
	35654425	05-01-2011:15.12	assign review	Mike	...
	35654426	06-01-2011:11.18	submit review	Sara	...
	35654428	07-01-2011:14.24	accept paper	Mike	...
	35654429	06-01-2011:11.18	upload CR	Pete	...
2	35654483	30-12-2010:11.32	create paper	George	...
	35654485	30-12-2010:12.12	submit paper	John	...
	35654487	30-12-2010:14.16	assign review	Mike	...
	35654489	16-01-2011:10.30	submit review	Ellen	...
	35654490	18-01-2011:12.05	reject paper	Mike	...

process mining techniques are marked by the three, thick red arrows in the bottom part of Fig. 1. We briefly discuss them next.

Discovery starts from an event log and *automatically produces a process model that explains the different behaviours observed in the log*, without assuming any prior knowledge on the process. The vast majority of process discovery algorithms focus on the discovery of the process control-flow, towards generating a model that indicates what are the allowed sequences of activities according to the log. One of the first algorithms in this line is the α algorithm [10], which produces a Petri net that compactly explains the sequences of activities present in a given event log. Contemporary control-flow discovery algorithms are much more sophisticated and richer in terms of the produced results, and differ from each other along several dimensions, such as the concrete language they use for the discovered model, the ability of enriching control-flow with additional elements (such as decision and data logic), and the ability of incorporating multiple abstraction levels (i.e., to hide/show details about infrequent or outlier behaviours). In addition, their quality depends on how they trade between the four crucial factors of:

1. *fitness* - to what extent the produced model correctly reconstructs the behaviours present in the log;
2. *simplicity* - how much is the produced model understandable to humans;
3. *precision* - how much is the produced model adherent to the behaviours contained in the log;
4. *generalisation* - what is the extent of behaviours not contained in the log, but supported by the model.

In addition to the control-flow perspective, many other aspects are addressed by process discovery techniques (cf. Sect. 2.2). For example, a class of discovery algorithms focuses on process resources, producing a social network that explains the *hand-over of work* among the stakeholders involved in the process. This is only possible if the input event log contains resource-related information (this is, e.g., the case of the log shown in Table 1).

Conformance Checking *compares an existing process model and an event log* for the same process, with the aim of understanding the presence and nature of *deviations*. Conformance checking techniques take as input an event log and a (possibly discovered) process model, and return indications related to the adherence of the behaviours contained in the log to the prescriptions contained in the model. Detected deviations provide on the one hand the basis to take countermeasures on non-conforming behaviours, and on the other hand to act on the considered model and suitable re-engineer it so as to incorporate also the unaligned behaviours. In this light, conformance checking ranges from the detection and localisation of sources of non-conformance, to the estimation of their severity, the computation of conformance metrics summarising them, and possibly even their explanation and diagnosis.

Enhancement *improves an existing process model using information recorded inside an event log for that process.* The input of enhancement techniques is a process model and an event log, and the output is a new process model that incorporates and reflects new information extracted from the data. The first important class of enhancement techniques is that of *extension*, where the input process model is not altered in its structure, but is extended with additional perspectives, using information present in the log. Examples of extension techniques are those that incorporate frequency- and time-related information into the process model, using the timestamps and the frequencies about activity executions present in the log. The extended process model provides an immediate feedback about which parts of the process are most exploited and which contain outlier behaviours, as well as where bottlenecks are located. A second important class of enhancement techniques is that of *repair*, where deviations detected by checking the conformance of the input event log to the input process model are resolved by suitably modifying the process model. For example, if two activities are sequentially ordered in the given process model, but according to the log they may appear in any order, then the process model may be evolved by relaxing the sequence, and allowing for their concurrent execution.

Example 2. Figure 3 shows the result of a control-flow discovery algorithm, applied to an event log from ConfSys whose structure obeys to what reported in Table 1. Notably, the algorithm does not only discover the control-flow of a process model explaining the behaviours contained in the log, but also extends such a model with frequency information, colouring activities and setting the width of sequence flow connectors depending on how frequent they are. ■

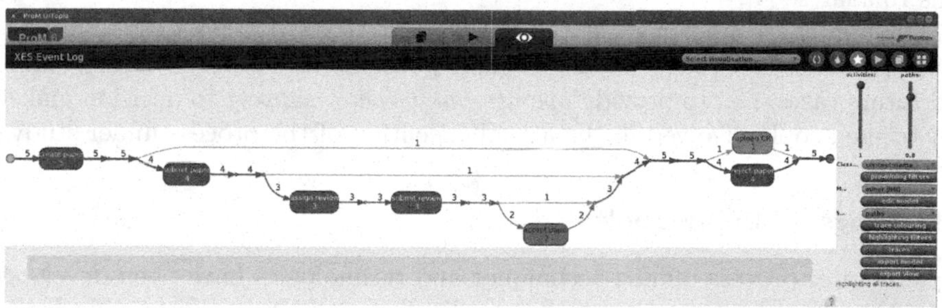

Fig. 3. Result of a process discovery and enhancement technique on a ConfSys event log. The algorithm is called *Inductive Visual Miner* [11], and runs as a plug-in of the ProM process mining platform (cf. Sect. 2.3).

2.2 Application of Process Mining

Since process mining is a relatively new field, methodologies supporting data and process analysts in the application of process mining techniques are still in their infancy [12]. In general, five main stages are foreseen for process mining projects. The *first phase* concerns planning and justification of the project, formulating which research questions shall be answered through process mining, and defining the boundaries of the analysis. This includes the definition of which perspective has to be taken for the analysis, including which notion(s) of case object to consider.

The *second phase* substantiates the first one by handling the extraction of the relevant event data from the software systems of he enterprise. As argued in the introduction, this phase is in general extremely challenging, and for the most part still based on manual, ad-hoc extraction procedures.

The *third phase* exploits control-flow process discovery techniques towards the construction of a first, process model explaining the behaviours reflected in the extracted data, and deriving which are the allowed orderings of activities. The resulting model is usually represented using formal languages such as variants of Petri nets, or concrete control-flow modelling notations such as BPMN, EPCs, or UML activity diagrams. The so-obtained model can be enhanced with information present in the log.

The *fourth phase* consists in the incorporation of additional dimensions, so as to obtain integrated models simultaneously accounting for multiple perspectives, like the *organisational perspective* (i.e., the actors, roles, groups/departments are involved in the process execution), the *case perspective* (i.e., relevant data elements that are attached to cases), and the *time perspective* (i.e., execution times, durations, latencies, and frequencies information about the execution of activities and/or the execution of a certain route within the process). Even though these different perspectives are non-exhaustive and partly overlapping, they provide a quite comprehensive overview of the aspects that process mining aims to analyse [4].

The *fifth phase* aims at exploiting the results obtained so far so as to produce insightful indications, suggestions, recommendations, and predictions on running and future cases, i.e., to provide *operational decision support* to decision makers and to the people involved in the actual execution of the process under study.

2.3 Process Mining Tools

A plethora of process mining techniques and technologies have been developed and successfully employed in several application domains[6]. We provide here a non-exhaustive list of contemporary process mining solutions.

- *ProM* (Process Mining framework)[7] is an Open Source framework for process mining algorithms [13], based on JAVA. It provides a plug-in based, integration platform [14] that users and developers of process mining can exploit to deploy and run their techniques. This pluggable architecture currently hosts a huge amount of plug-ins covering all the different aspects of process mining,

[6] http://tinyurl.com/ovedwx4.
[7] http://www.processmining.org/prom/.

from data import to discovery, conformance checking, enhancement along different perspectives [4]. Hence, it enable users to apply the latest developments in process mining research on their own data. Finally, RapidProM[8] [15] is an extension of RapidMiner based on ProM that supports users in pipelining different ProM plug-ins based on the paradigm of scientific workflows.

- *Celonis*[9] is a commercial, widely adopted process mining software that support various file formats and database management systems to load event data. Its distinctive feature is the possibility of applying process mining natively on top of enterprise systems like SAP. In addition, it exploits well-assessed data warehousing (OLAP) techniques to store and process event data [4].
- *Disco*[10] is a commercial, stand-alone and lightweight process mining tool. It supports various file formats as input, in particular providing native support for importing CSV files, which can be annotated with case and event information prior to the import. Disco has usability, fidelity, and performance as design priorities, and makes process mining easy and fast [16].
- *ARIS PPM*[11] is a tool that can be used to automatically assess business processes and their execution data in terms of speed, cost, quality and quantity, at the same time identifying optimisation opportunities. It ranges from analysis of historical data to process discovery, and notably provides dedicated techniques for the analysis of the organisational structure and improving collaboration.

Beside the aforementioned solutions, worth mentioning are non-commercial tools such as PMLAB[12] and CoBeFra[13], as well as commercial tools such as Enterprise Discovery Suite[14], Interstage Business Process Manager Analytics[15], Minit[16], myInvenio[17], Rialto[18], Perceptive Process Mining[19], QPR ProcessAnalyzer[20], and SNP Business Process Analysis[21].

---

[8] http://www.promtools.org/doku.php?id=rapidprom:home.
[9] http://www.celonis.de.
[10] https://fluxicon.com/disco/.
[11] http://www.softwareag.com/nl/products/aris_platform/aris_controlling/aris_process_performance/overview/default.asp.
[12] https://www.cs.upc.edu/~jcarmona/PMLAB/.
[13] http://www.processmining.be/cobefra.
[14] http://www.stereologic.com.
[15] http://www.fujitsu.com/global/products/software/middleware/application-infrastructure/interstage/solutions/bpmgt/bpm/.
[16] http://www.minitlabs.com.
[17] http://www.my-invenio.com.
[18] http://www.exeura.eu.
[19] http://www.lexmark.com/en_us/products/software/workflow-and-case-management/process-mining.html.
[20] https://www.qpr.com/products/qpr-processanalyzer.
[21] http://www.snp-bpa.com.

2.4 The XES Standard

As extensively argued before, the application of process mining techniques requires the input data to be structured in a format where key notions like case objects and events are explicitly represented, and where their corresponding data are structured in a way that lends itself to be automatically processed. This fundamental requirements led to the development of standard formats for the representation and storage of event data for process mining. In recent years, the *XES (eXtensible Event Stream)* format emerged as the main reference format for the storage, interchange, and analysis of event logs. XES appeared for the first time in 2009 [17], as the successor of the MXML format [18]. It quickly became the de-facto standard in this area, adopted by the IEEE Task Force on Process Mining[22], eventually becoming an official IEEE standard in 2016 [5].

XES is based on XML, and adopts an extensible paradigm that only fixes a minimal structure for event data, allowing one to enrich it with domain-specific

```
<log xes.version="1.0"
     xes.features="nested-attributes"
     openxes.version="1.0RC7">
   <extension name="Time"
              prefix="time"
              uri="http://www.xes-standard.org/time.xesext"/>
   <classifier name="Event Name" keys="concept:name"/>
   <string key="concept:name" value="XES Event Log"/>
   ...
   <trace>
      <string key="concept:name" value="1"/>
      <event>
         <string key="User" value="Pete"/>
         <string key="concept:name" value="create paper"/>
         <int key="Event ID" value="35654424"/>
         ...
      </event>
      <event>
         ...
         <string key="concept:name" value="submit paper"/>
         ...
      </event>
         ...
   </trace>
   <trace>
      ...
   </trace>
   ...
</log>
```

Fig. 4. An example of XES event log

[22] http://www.win.tue.nl/ieeetfpm/doku.php.

attributes and features. More specifically, an *XES event log document* is an XML document formed by the following core components: *(i)* log, *(ii)* trace, *(iii)* event, *(iv)* attribute, *(v)* global attribute, *(vi)* classifier, and *(vii)* extension. We briefly review each such components in the remainder of this section, referring the interested reader to the official IEEE XES standard for further details. Figure 4 encodes in XES a portion of the event log from Table 1.

Log is the root component in XES. It aggregates information about the logged evolution of multiple cases for a process. In the XML serialisation of XES, it is encoded using the XML element `<log>`, which comes with two mandatory attributes:

- `xes.version`, indicating which version of the standard is used;
- `xes.features`, declaring which features of the standard are employed (if none, then it has an empty string as value).

Example 3. The following code

```
<log xes.version="2.0" xes.features="nested-attributes">
   ...
</log>
```

is an example of XES log declaration, which indicates that the version 2.0 of the standard is used, relying on nested attributes. ■

Trace corresponds to the execution log of a single case, in turn comprising a sequence of events that occurred for that case. In our ConfSys running example, a trace may consist of all logged events for a paper, a review, or a user, depending on the adopted notion of case. In the XML representation of XES, a trace is encoded using the XML element `<trace>`, and does not have any attribute. A trace element is directly contained within the log root element, and consequently each trace belongs to a log, whereas each log contains possibly many traces.

Event represents the occurrence of a relevant atomic execution step for a specific case. Usually, this corresponds to the (completion of) execution of an activity instance, or to the progression of an activity instance within its transactional lifecycle, but this is not mandatorily prescribed by the standard.

In the XML serialisation of XES, this component is encoded using the XML tag `<event>`, and does not have any attribute. An event element is contained within the trace element corresponding to its target case, and consequently each event belongs to a trace, whereas each trace contains in general many events.

Attributes represent relevant information items associated to a log, trace, or event. Each attribute element is then child of one of such elements, which in turn may contain in general many attributes. The concrete representation of an attribute follows the typical key-value patterns, where the key describes the type of information slot, while the value is the information stored inside such a slot. The value, in turn, may be primitive, a collection, or a complex structure containing other attributes, consequently giving raise to *elementary*, *composite*, and *nested attributes*.

An *elementary attribute* is an attribute that has an single value. The XES standard supports several types of elementary attributes, namely: *(i) string*, *(ii) datetime*, *(iii) integer*, *(iv) real number*, *(v) boolean*, and *(vi) ID*. In the XML serialisation of XES, an elementary attribute is encoded using the XML tag `<string>` encodes an elementary attribute of type "string". This XML element also mandatorily comes with two XML attributes `key` and `value`, respectively capturing the name of the key and the value carried by the attribute.

Example 4. The following XML element

```
<string key="concept:name" value="upload"/>
```

declares an attribute of type string in XES, indicating its key and value. ■

A *composite attribute* is an attribute that may contain several values. In XES 2.0 [19], there are two kinds of composite attributes, namely *list* and *container*, respectively addressing ordered and unordered collections. However, in the official IEEE XES standard [5], only lists are provided. Based on [5], the list attribute is represented as an XML element `<list>`, with `key` as mandatory attribute. The values belonging to the list are in turn represented as attributes element enclosed within a `<values>` element, direct child of the `<list>` element.

Example 5. The XML element

```
<list key="addresses">
   <values>
      <string key="mainAddress"
              value="P.zza Universita 1"/>
      <string key="deliveryAddress"
              value="P.zza Domenicani 3"/>
   </values>
</list>
```

represents a XES composite attribute containing two elementary attributes, respectively representing the main and delivery address for an expedition. ■

Global attributes are used to define a "template" for attributes to be attached to each element of a certain kind within the given XES document. This makes it possible to declare recurrent attributes that will be consistently attached to each trace or event contained in the log. According to the official IEEE XES Standard [5], global attributes are declared within the root, `<log>` element, as elements called `<global>` coming with a `scope` XML attribute that defines the selected target element kind (trace, or event). Inside such an element, a set of (global) attributes are defined using the standard structure, with the key semantical difference that the value represents, in this context, the default value taken by the attribute once it is attached to a target element.

Example 6. The following excerpt of an XES document

```
<log xes.version="2.0" xes.features="nested-attributes">
   ...
   <global scope="trace">
      <string key="concept:name" value="MyTrace"/>
   </global>
   <global scope="event">
      <date key="time:timestamp"
            value="1970-01-01T01:00:00.000+01:00"/>
      <string key="lifecycle:transition"
              value="complete"/>
      <string key="concept:name" value="MyTask"/>
   </global>
   ...
</log>
```

declares different global attributes. The first <global> element declares that each trace contained in the log will come with a string attribute with key concept:name having a value that, unless specified, will be the string MyTrace. The second <global> element targets instead events, and declares that each event element contained in the log will come with three attributes respectively representing the event execution time, the type of event within the activity transactional lifecycle, and the name of the corresponding activity (with their respective default values). ■

Classifiers are used to provide identification schemes for the elements in a log, based on a combination of attributes associated to them. Similarly to the case of global attributes, each classifier comes with a scope defining whether the classifier is applied to traces or events, and with a combination of strings that represent keys of global attributes attached to the same scope. An event (resp., trace) classifier mentioning strings $k_1, \ldots, k_n$, which are keys of global attributes with scope "event" (resp., "trace"), states that the identity of events (resp., traces) is defined by the values associated to such keys, i.e., that two events (resp., traces) are identical if and only if they assign the same values to the attributes characterised by those keys.

The declaration of a classifier is done in the XML serialisation of XES by inserting a <classifier> element as child of <log>, providing an attribute called scope whose value denotes whether the scope is that of event or trace, and an attribute called keys whose value is a comma-separated set of strings pointing to keys of global attributes defined over the same scope.

Example 7. Consider the following excerpt of an XES document:

```
<log xes.version="2.0" xes.features="nested-attributes">
   ...
   <classifier name="Event Name ID" scope="event"
                                    keys="concept:name"/>
   ...
</log>
```

It indicates that the global attribute with key `concept:name` provides an identification scheme for events. ■

Extensions capture pre-defined sets of global attributes with a clear semantics. In fact, the XES standard allows the modeller to introduce arbitrary domain-specific attributes, whose meaning may be ambiguous and difficult to interpret by other humans or third-party algorithms. The notion of extension fixes this issue by providing a mechanism to define a set of pre-defined attribute keys together with a reference to documentation that describes their meaning. Specifically, each extension must have a *name*, a *prefix* and a Uniform Resource Identifier (*URI*). The prefix is used to unambiguously contextualise the attribute keys and avoid name clashes, whereas the URI to the definition of the extension. An XES event log making use of a particular extension must declare it at the level of its `<log>` element. Notably, the official IEEE XES standard comes with a set of common extensions defining attributes to capture domain-independent important aspects such as: 1. (name of the) activity to which an event refers; 2. timestamp information about the actual time at which the event has been recorded; 3. resource information describing the resource that generated the event; 4. information about the type of event in terms of a corresponding transition within a standard transactional lifecycle for activities, also described in the standard itself.

Example 8. The following excerpt of an XES event log

```
<log xes.version="2.0" xes.features="nested-attributes">
   ...
   <extension name="Time"
              prefix="time"
              uri="http://www.xes-standard.org/
              time.xesext"/>
   ...
   <trace>
      <event>
         <date key="time:timestamp"
               value="2017-03-26T10:45:36.000+01:00"/>
         ...
      </event>
      ...
   </trace>
   ...
</log>
```

declares that the time extension is employed in the log, and that the definition for such an extension may be found at the provided URI. The `timestamp` attribute, defined in the time extension, is then used in the definition of an event, so as to indicate when such an event has been recorded. ■

2.5 The Data Preparation Phase

Thanks to the IEEE XES standard (cf. Sect. 2.4), the challenging phase of data preparation for process mining (i.e., the second phase in the description provided in Sect. 2.2) now has a clear target: it amounts to analyse the event data as natively stored by an enterprise, and to consequently devise suitable mechanisms to extract those data and encode them in the form of an XES log. This phase is extremely delicate because insightful process mining results cannot be obtained if the starting data miss important information or do not reflect the boundaries and research questions and defined in during the first phase of any process mining project. The complexity, and the availability of tool support, to extract event logs from the native enterprise logs depends on several factors, related to the quality, comprehensiveness, and structure of such data. The process mining manifesto provides an intuitive set of criteria to assess the *maturity* of enterprise logs, which in turn characterise the difficulty of extracting event logs. Specifically, five maturity levels are introduced:

★ enterprise logs are low-quality logs that are usually filled in manually, and that include false positives and false negatives, i.e., contain events that do not correspond to reality, while miss events that occurred.

★★ enterprise logs are automatically recorded by generic software systems that can be circumvented by their users, and that are consequently incomplete, at the same time possibly containing improperly recorded events.

★★★ enterprise logs are trustworthy, but possibly incomplete logs automatically recorded through reliable software systems but without following a systematic approach.

★★★★ enterprise logs are high-quality, trustworthy and complete logs, recorded systematically by software systems where the key notions of cases and activities are represented explicitly;

★★★★★ enterprise logs are top-quality logs, where events are recorded in a systematic, comprehensive, and reliable manner, and where all event data have a shared, well-defined unambiguous semantics.

The literature abounds of techniques and tools to handle the extraction of event logs from ★★★★ and ★★★★★ enterprise logs, which are typically generated by BPM/workflow management systems. For example, academic efforts such as ProMimport [20] and XESame [13] provides support in the extraction of MXML/XES event logs from relational databases that contain explicit information about cases, activities, events, and their timestamps. Commercial tools like Disco, Celonis, and Minit, allows users to import CSV files, and guide them in annotating the columns contained therein with such key notions.

However, much less support is provided to users interested in the application of process mining starting from ★★★ enterprise logs. Such logs are widespread in reality, as they correspond to data stored by widely adopted enterprise systems such as ERP, CRM, and SCM solutions, as well as data generated by trustworthy, domain-specific legacy information systems. This is why the typical approach followed in this case is to devise ad-hoc, *Extract, Transform, and Load (ETL) procedures*. Such procedures need to be manually instrumented, assuming a fixed perspective on the data, and covering the following three steps [4]:

1. extraction of data from the native enterprise systems, according to the chosen perspective;
2. transformation of the extracted data, dealing with syntactical and semantical issues, towards fitting the operational needs;
3. load of data into a target system (such as a data warehouse or a dedicated relational database), from which a corresponding XES log can be extracted directly.

This procedure is not only inherently difficult and error prone, but does not lend itself to incrementally and iteratively analyse the enterprise data according to different perspectives (e.g., different boundaries for the analysis, and/or multiple notions of case). In fact, every time the perspective and/or the scope of the analysis changes, an entirely new ETL-like set up has to be instrumented [9]. After having introduced the paradigm of Ontology-Based Data Access in Sect. 3, we show how in Sect. 4 how such a paradigm can be exploited to better support data and process analysts in the extraction of event logs from ★★★ enterprise data.

3 Ontology-Based Data Access

Ontologies are used to provide the conceptualization of a domain of interest, and mechanisms for reasoning about it. The standard language for representing ontologies is the Web Ontology Language (OWL 2), which has been standardized (in its second edition) by the W3C [21]. The formal foundations for ontologies, and in particular for OWL 2, are provided by Description Logics (DLs) [22], which are logics specifically designed to represent structured knowledge and to reason upon it.

In DLs, the domain to represent is structured into classes of objects of interest that have properties in common, and these properties are explicitly represented through relevant relationships that hold among the classes. *Concepts* denote classes of objects, and *roles* denote (typically binary) relations between objects. Both are constructed, starting from atomic concepts and roles, by making use of various constructs, and the set of allowed constructs characterizes a specific DL. The knowledge about the domain is then represented by means of a DL *ontology*, where a separation is made between general structural knowledge and specific extensional knowledge about individual objects. The structural knowledge is provided in a so-called *TBox* (for "Terminological Box"), which consists of a set of universally quantified assertions that state general properties about concepts and roles. The extensional knowledge is represented in an *ABox* (for "Assertional Box"), consisting of assertions on individual objects that state the membership of an individual in a concept, or the fact that two individuals are related by a role.

The setting we are interested in here, however, is the one in which the extensional information, i.e., the data, is not maintained as an ABox, but is stored in an information system, represented as a relational data source[23], and the TBox of the ontology is used not only to capture relevant structural properties of the domain, but also acts as a conceptual data schema that provides a high-level view over the data in the information system. In other words, users formulate their information requests in terms of the conceptual schema provided by the TBox of the ontology, and use it to access the underlying data source. The connection between the conceptual schema/TBox and the information system is provided by a declarative *mapping specification*. Such specification is used to translate the user requests, i.e., the queries the user poses over the conceptual schema, into queries to the information system, which can then directly be answered by the corresponding relational database engine. This setting is known as *ontology-based data access* (OBDA) [6,7], and we are describing it more in detail below.

3.1 Lightweight Ontology Languages

An important aspect to note in the OBDA setting outlined above, is that the data source is in general a full-fledged relational database, and therefore it might be very large (especially when compared to the size of the TBox). On the other hand, the user queries formulated over the TBox, have to be answered while fully taking into account the domain semantics encoded in the TBox itself, i.e., in general under incomplete information. This means that query answering does not correspond to query *evaluation*, but amounts to a form of logical inference, which in general is inherently more complex than query evaluation [23]. More specifically, the complexity of query evaluation strongly depends on the form of the TBox (according to the usual tradeoff between expressive power and efficiency of inference). Therefore we need to carefully choose the language in which the TBox is expressed, so as to guarantee that query answering can be done efficiently, in particular in *data complexity*, i.e., when the complexity is measured with respect to the size of the data only [24]. Ideally, we would like to fully take into account the constraints encoded in the TBox, and at the same time delegate query evaluation over the data source to the relational DBMS in which the data is stored, so as to leverage the more than 30 years of experience gained with commercial relational technology.

We present now a so-called *lightweight ontology language*, specifically, *DL-Lite*$_{\mathcal{A}}$ of the *DL-Lite* family, which is a family of DLs that have been carefully designed so as to allow for efficient query answering over the TBox by

[23] We consider here the case of an information system consisting of a single relational data source. Multiple data sources can be wrapped by a federation tool and presented as a single source.

relying on standard SQL query evaluation done by a relational DBMS [6,25,26]. The logics of the *DL-Lite* family (and specifically, the *DL-Lite*$_\mathcal{R}$ sub-language of *DL-Lite*$_\mathcal{A}$) provide the basis for OWL 2 QL, one of the three standard profiles (i.e., sub-languages) of OWL 2 [21,27], which has been specifically designed to capture the essential features of conceptual modeling formalisms (see also Sect. 3.2). In line with what available in OWL 2 and OWL 2 QL, *DL-Lite*$_\mathcal{A}$ distinguishes concepts, which denote sets of abstract objects, from *value-domains*, which denote sets of (data) values, and roles, which denote binary relations between objects, from *features*[24], which denote binary relations between objects and values. We now define formally syntax and semantics of expressions in our logic.

Syntax. *DL-Lite*$_\mathcal{A}$ expressions are built over an alphabet that comprises symbols for atomic roles, atomic concepts, atomic features, value-domains, and constants. As value-domains we consider the traditional data types, such as *String*, *Integer*, etc., and also the data type *ts* to represent timestamps (considering that timestamps play a crucial role in event logs). Intuitively, these types represent sets of values such that their pairwise intersections are either empty or infinite. In the following, we denote such value-domains by $T_1, \ldots, T_n$, and we consider additionally the *universal value-domain* $\top_d$. Furthermore, we denote with Γ the alphabet for constants, which we assume partitioned into two sets, namely, Γ_O (the set of constant symbols for *objects*), and Γ_V (the set of constant symbols for *values*). In turn, Γ_V is partitioned into n sets $\Gamma_{V_1}, \ldots, \Gamma_{V_n}$, where each Γ_{V_i} is the set of constants for the values in the value-domain T_i.

The syntax of *DL-Lite*$_\mathcal{A}$ expressions is defined as follows:

- *Basic roles*, denoted by R, are built according to the syntax

$$R \longrightarrow P \mid P^-$$

  where P denotes an *atomic role*, and P^- an *inverse role*. In the following, R^- stands for P^- when $R = P$, and for P when $R = P^-$.
- *Basic concepts*, denoted by B, are built according to the syntax

$$B \longrightarrow A \mid \exists R \mid \delta(F)$$

  where A denotes an *atomic concept*, and F an *(atomic) feature*. The concept $\exists R$, called *unqualified existential restriction*, denotes the *domain* of role R, i.e., the set of objects that R relates to some object. Similarly, $\delta(F)$ denotes the *domain* of feature F, i.e., the set of objects that F relates to some value.

In *DL-Lite*$_\mathcal{A}$, the TBox may contain assertions of three types:

[24] In *DL-Lite*$_\mathcal{A}$, features are actually called *attributes*. Here we use the term "feature" to avoid confusion with attributes of UML (see later).

- An *inclusion assertion* has one the forms

$$R_1 \sqsubseteq R_2, \qquad B_1 \sqsubseteq B_2, \qquad F_1 \sqsubseteq F_2, \qquad \rho(F) \sqsubseteq D,$$

denoting respectively, from left to right, inclusions between basic roles, basic concepts, features, and value-domains. For the latter, $\rho(F)$ denotes the range of feature F (i.e., the set of values to which F relates some object), and D a value domain (i.e., either a T_i or $\top_d$.)
Intuitively, an inclusion assertion states that, in every model of $\mathcal{T}$, each instance of the left-hand side expression is also an instance of the right-hand side expression. When convenient, we use $E_1 \equiv E_2$ as an abbreviation for the pair of inclusion assertions $E_1 \sqsubseteq E_2$ and $E_2 \sqsubseteq E_1$.
- A *disjointness assertion* has one the forms

$$R_1 \sqsubseteq \neg R_2, \qquad B_1 \sqsubseteq \neg B_2, \qquad F_1 \sqsubseteq \neg F_2.$$

- A *functionality assertion* has one of the forms

$$(\mathsf{funct}\ R), \qquad (\mathsf{funct}\ F),$$

denoting functionality of a (direct or inverse) role and of a feature, respectively. Intuitively, a functionality assertion states that the binary relation represented by a role (resp., a feature) is a function.

Then, a *DL-Lite*$_\mathcal{A}$ TBox, $\mathcal{T}$, is a finite sets of intensional assertions of the forms above, where in addition a limitation on the interaction between role/feature inclusions and functionality assertions is imposed. Specifically, whenever a role or feature U appears (possibly as U^-) in the right-hand side of an inclusion assertion in $\mathcal{T}$, then neither $(\mathsf{funct}\ U)$ nor $(\mathsf{funct}\ U^-)$ might appear in $\mathcal{T}$.

Intuitively, the condition says that, in *DL-Lite*$_\mathcal{A}$ TBoxes, roles and features occurring in functionality assertions cannot be specialized.

A *DL-Lite*$_\mathcal{A}$ ABox consists of a set of *membership assertions*, which are used to state the instances of concepts, roles, and features. Such assertions have the form

$$A(a), \qquad P(a_1, a_2), \qquad F(a, c),$$

where a, a_1, a_2 are constants in Γ_O, and c is a constant in Γ_V.

A *DL-Lite*$_\mathcal{A}$ ontology $\mathcal{O}$ is a pair $\langle \mathcal{T}, \mathcal{A} \rangle$, where $\mathcal{T}$ is a *DL-Lite*$_\mathcal{A}$ TBox, and $\mathcal{A}$ is a *DL-Lite*$_\mathcal{A}$ ABox all of whose atomic concepts, roles, and features occur in $\mathcal{T}$.

Semantics. Following the standard approach in DLs, the semantics of *DL-Lite*$_\mathcal{A}$ is given in terms of (First-Order) interpretations. All such interpretations agree on the semantics assigned to each value-domain T_i and to each constant in Γ_V. In particular, each value-domain T_i is interpreted as the set $val(T_i)$ of values of the corresponding data type, and each constant $c_i \in \Gamma_V$ is interpreted as one specific value, denoted $val(c_i)$, in $val(T_i)$. Then, an *interpretation* is a pair $\mathcal{I} = (\Delta^\mathcal{I}, \cdot^\mathcal{I})$, where

$$
\begin{array}{rcl}
A^{\mathcal{I}} & \subseteq & \Delta_O^{\mathcal{I}} \\
(\exists R)^{\mathcal{I}} & = & \{\, o \mid \exists o'. (o,o') \in R^{\mathcal{I}} \,\} \\
(\delta(F))^{\mathcal{I}} & = & \{\, o \mid \exists v. (o,v) \in F^{\mathcal{I}} \,\} \\
(\rho(F))^{\mathcal{I}} & = & \{\, v \mid \exists o. (o,v) \in F^{\mathcal{I}} \,\}
\end{array}
\qquad
\begin{array}{rcl}
\top_d^{\mathcal{I}} & = & \Delta_V^{\mathcal{I}} \\
T_i^{\mathcal{I}} & = & val(T_i) \\
P^{\mathcal{I}} & \subseteq & \Delta_O^{\mathcal{I}} \times \Delta_O^{\mathcal{I}} \\
(P^-)^{\mathcal{I}} & = & \{\, (o,o') \mid (o',o) \in P^{\mathcal{I}} \,\} \\
F^{\mathcal{I}} & \subseteq & \Delta_O^{\mathcal{I}} \times \Delta_V^{\mathcal{I}}
\end{array}
$$

Fig. 5. Semantics of *DL-Lite*$_{\mathcal{A}}$ expressions

- $\Delta^{\mathcal{I}}$ is the interpretation domain, which is the disjoint union of two non-empty sets: $\Delta_O^{\mathcal{I}}$, called the *domain of objects*, and $\Delta_V^{\mathcal{I}}$, called the *domain of values*. In turn, $\Delta_V^{\mathcal{I}}$ is the union of $val(T_1), \dots, val(T_n)$.
- $\cdot^{\mathcal{I}}$ is the *interpretation function*, which assigns an element of $\Delta^{\mathcal{I}}$ to each constant in Γ, a subset of $\Delta^{\mathcal{I}}$ to each concept and value-domain, and a subset of $\Delta^{\mathcal{I}} \times \Delta^{\mathcal{I}}$ to each role and feature, in such a way that the following holds:
  - for each $c \in \Gamma_V$, $c^{\mathcal{I}} = val(c)$,
  - for each $d \in \Gamma_O$, $d^{\mathcal{I}} \in \Delta_O^{\mathcal{I}}$,
  - for each $a_1, a_2 \in \Gamma$, $a_1 \neq a_2$ implies $a_1^{\mathcal{I}} \neq a_2^{\mathcal{I}}$, and
  - the conditions shown in Fig. 5 are satisfied.

Note that the above definition implies that different constants are interpreted differently in the domain, i.e., *DL-Lite*$_{\mathcal{A}}$ adopts the so-called *unique name assumption* (UNA).

To specify the semantics of an ontology, we define when an interpretation $\mathcal{I}$ *satisfies* and assertion α, denoted $\mathcal{I} \models \alpha$.

- $\mathcal{I}$ satisfies a role, concept, feature, or value-domain inclusion assertion $E_1 \sqsubseteq E_2$ if $E_1^{\mathcal{I}} \subseteq E_2^{\mathcal{I}}$.
- $\mathcal{I}$ satisfies a role, concept, or feature disjointness assertion $E_1 \sqsubseteq \neg E_2$ if $E_1^{\mathcal{I}} \cap E_2^{\mathcal{I}} = \emptyset$.
- $\mathcal{I}$ satisfies a role functionality assertion (funct R), if for each $o_1, o_2, o_3 \in \Delta_O^{\mathcal{I}}$

$$(o_1, o_2) \in R^{\mathcal{I}} \text{ and } (o_1, o_3) \in R^{\mathcal{I}} \quad \text{implies} \quad o_2 = o_3.$$

- $\mathcal{I}$ satisfies a feature functionality assertion (funct F), if for each $o \in \Delta_O^{\mathcal{I}}$ and $v_1, v_2 \in \Delta_V^{\mathcal{I}}$

$$(o, v_1) \in F^{\mathcal{I}} \text{ and } (o, v_2) \in F^{\mathcal{I}} \quad \text{implies} \quad v_1 = v_2.$$

- $\mathcal{I}$ satisfies a membership assertion

$$
\begin{array}{lll}
A(a), & \text{if} & a^{\mathcal{I}} \in A^{\mathcal{I}}; \\
P(a_1, a_2), & \text{if} & (a_1^{\mathcal{I}}, a_2^{\mathcal{I}}) \in P^{\mathcal{I}}; \\
F(a, c), & \text{if} & (a^{\mathcal{I}}, c^{\mathcal{I}}) \in F^{\mathcal{I}}.
\end{array}
$$

An interpretation $\mathcal{I}$ is a *model* of a *DL-Lite*$_{\mathcal{A}}$ ontology $\mathcal{O}$ (resp., TBox $\mathcal{T}$, ABox $\mathcal{A}$), or, equivalently, $\mathcal{I}$ *satisfies* $\mathcal{O}$ (resp., $\mathcal{T}$, $\mathcal{A}$), written $\mathcal{I} \models \mathcal{O}$ (resp., $\mathcal{I} \models \mathcal{T}$, $\mathcal{I} \models \mathcal{A}$) if and only if $\mathcal{I}$ satisfies all assertions in $\mathcal{O}$ (resp., $\mathcal{T}$, $\mathcal{A}$). The semantics of a *DL-Lite*$_{\mathcal{A}}$ ontology $\mathcal{O} = \langle \mathcal{T}, \mathcal{A} \rangle$ is the set of all *models* of $\mathcal{O}$. Also, we say that a concept, association, or feature E is *satisfiable* with respect to an ontology $\mathcal{O}$ (resp., TBox $\mathcal{T}$), if $\mathcal{O}$ (resp., $\mathcal{T}$) admits a model $\mathcal{I}$ such that $E^{\mathcal{I}} \neq \emptyset$.

3.2 Conceptual Data Models and Relationship to Ontology Languages

We remind the reader that our aim is to use ontologies specified in a lightweight language as conceptual views of the relational data sources that maintain the data from which to extract XES logs. Moreover, the information about how to extract the log information should be provided as easily interpretable annotations of the ontology elements. To simplify the annotation activity, we exploit the well investigated correspondence between (lightweight) ontology languages and conceptual data modeling formalisms [7,28,29], and we specify the TBox of the ontology in terms of a UML class diagram. The *Unified Modeling Language* (UML)[25] is a standardized formalism for capturing at the conceptual level various aspects of information systems, and the UML standard provides also a well established graphical notation which we can leverage. Specifically, we make use of *UML class diagrams*, which are equipped with a formal semantics, provided, e.g., in terms of first-order logic [29], and we show how they can be encoded as *DL-Lite*$_\mathcal{A}$ ontologies. Since we use UML class diagrams as conceptual modeling formalisms, we abstract away those features that are only relevant in a software engineering context (such as operations associated to classes, or public, protected, and private qualifiers for attributes), and we also make some simplifying assumptions. In particular, considering that roles in ontology languages denote binary relations, we consider only associations of arity 2; also, we deal only with those multiplicities of associations that convey meaningful semantic aspects in modeling, namely functional and mandatory participation to associations.

Classes and Data Types. A *class* in a UML class diagram denotes a *set of objects* with common features. The specification of a class contains its *name* and its *attributes*, each denoted by a name (possibly followed by the *multiplicity*, between square brackets) and with an associated *type*, which indicates the domain of the attribute values.

A UML class is represented by a DL concept. This follows naturally from the fact that both UML classes and DL concepts denote *sets of objects*. Similarly, a UML data type is formalized in *DL-Lite*$_\mathcal{A}$ by a value domain.

Attributes. A UML *attribute* a of type T for a class C associates to each instance of C, zero, one, or more instances of a data type T. An optional *multiplicity* $[i..j]$ for a specifies that a associates to each instance of C, at least i and most j instances of T. When the multiplicity for an attribute is missing, [1..1] is assumed, i.e., the attribute is considered *mandatory* and *single-valued*.

To formalize attributes, we have to think of an attribute a of type T for a class C as a binary relation between instances of C and instances of T. We capture such a binary relation by means of a *DL-Lite*$_\mathcal{A}$ feature a_C. To specify

[25] See http://www.omg.org/spec/UML/2.5/ for the latest version of UML at the moment of writing.

the type of the UML attribute we use the *DL-Lite*$_\mathcal{A}$ assertions

$$\delta(a_C) \sqsubseteq C \qquad \text{and} \qquad \rho(a_C) \sqsubseteq T.$$

Such assertions specify precisely that, for each instance (c, v) of the feature a_C, the object c is an instance of concept C, and the value v is an instance of the value domain T. Note that the attribute name a is not necessarily unique in the whole diagram, and hence two different classes, say C_1 and C_2 could both have attribute a, possibly of different types. This situation is correctly captured by our DL formalization, where the attribute is contextualized to each class with a distinct feature, i.e., a_{C_1} and a_{C_2}.

To specify that the attribute is *mandatory*, i.e., has minimum multiplicity 1, we add the assertion

$$C \sqsubseteq \delta(a_C),$$

which specifies that each instance of C participates necessarily at least once to the feature a_C. To specify that the attribute is *single-valued*, i.e., has maximum multiplicity 1, we add the assertion

$$(\mathsf{funct}\ a_C).$$

Finally, if the attribute is both mandatory and single-valued, i.e., has multiplicity [1..1], we use both assertions together, i.e., we add

$$C \sqsubseteq \delta(a_C) \qquad \text{and} \qquad (\mathsf{funct}\ a_C).$$

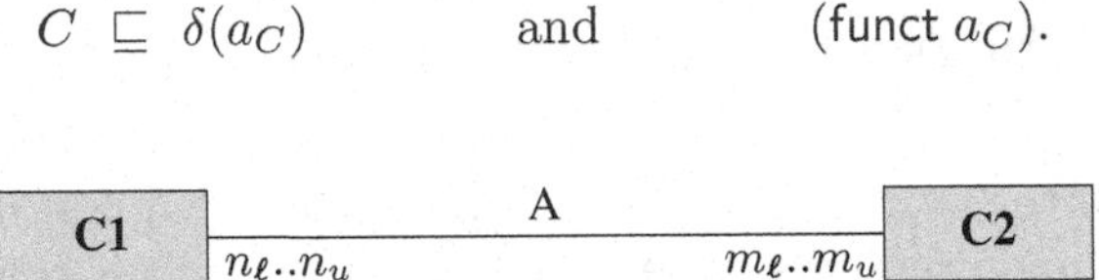

Fig. 6. UML association without association class

Associations. An *association* in UML is a relation between the instances of two (or more) classes. An association often has a related *association class*, which describes properties of the association, such as attributes, operations, etc. A binary association A between the instances of two classes C_1 and C_2 is graphically rendered as in Fig. 6, where the *multiplicity* $m_\ell..m_u$ specifies that each instance of class C_1 can participate at least m_ℓ times and at most m_u times to association A. The multiplicity $n_\ell..n_u$ has an analogous meaning for class C_2. We consider here only the most commonly used forms of multiplicities, namely those where 0 and 1 are the only involved numbers: 0..* (unconstrained, also abbreviated as *), 0..1 (functional participation), 1..* (mandatory participation), and 1..1 (one-to-one correspondence, also abbreviated as 1).

An association A between classes C_1 and C_2 is formalized in *DL-Lite*$_\mathcal{A}$ by means of a role A on which we enforce the assertions

$$\exists A \sqsubseteq C_1 \qquad \text{and} \qquad \exists A^- \sqsubseteq C_2.$$

To express the multiplicity $m_\ell..m_u$ on the participation of instances of C_2 for each given instance of C_1, we use the assertions

$$\begin{array}{ll} C_1 \sqsubseteq \exists A, & \text{if } m_\ell = 1, \text{ and} \\ (\mathsf{funct}\ A), & \text{if } m_u = 1. \end{array}$$

We can use similar assertions for the multiplicity $n_\ell..n_u$ on the participation of instances of C_1 for each given instance of C_2, i.e.,

$$\begin{array}{ll} C_1 \sqsubseteq \exists A^-, & \text{if } n_\ell = 1, \text{ and} \\ (\mathsf{funct}\ A^-), & \text{if } n_u = 1. \end{array}$$

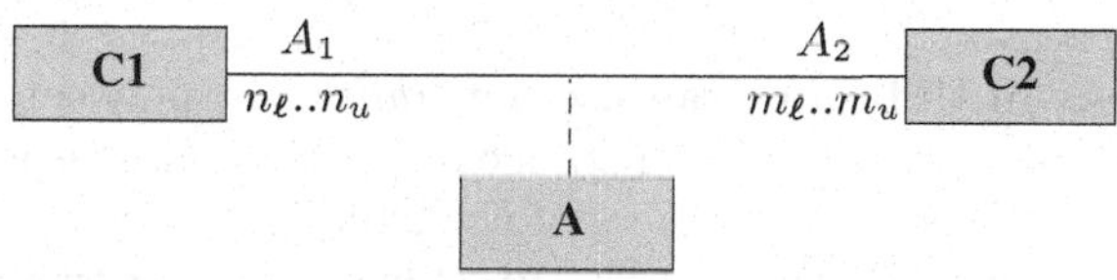

Fig. 7. UML association with association class

Next we focus on an *association* with a related *association class*, as shown in Fig. 7, where the class A is the association class related to the association, and A_1 and A_2, if present, are the *role names* of C_1 and C_2 respectively, i.e., they specify the role that each class plays within the association A.

We formalize in *DL-Lite*$_\mathcal{A}$ an association A with an association class, by using *reification*: we represent the association by means of a DL concept A, and we introduce two DL roles, A_1, A_2, one for each role of A, which intuitively connect an object representing an instance of the association to the instances of C_1 and C_2, respectively, that participate to the association[26]. Then, we enforce that each instance of A participates exactly once both to A_1 and to A_2, by means of the assertions

$$A \sqsubseteq \exists A_1, \qquad (\mathsf{funct}\ A_1), \qquad A \sqsubseteq \exists A_2, \qquad (\mathsf{funct}\ A_2).$$

To represent that the association A is between classes C_1 and C_2, we use the assertions

$$\exists A_1 \sqsubseteq A, \qquad \exists A_1^- \sqsubseteq C_1, \qquad \exists A_2 \sqsubseteq A, \qquad \exists A_2^- \sqsubseteq C_2.$$

We observe that the above formalization does not guarantee that in every interpretation $\mathcal{I}$ of the *DL-Lite*$_\mathcal{A}$ TBox encoding the UML class diagram, each instance of $A^\mathcal{I}$ represents a *distinct* tuple in $C_1^\mathcal{I} \times C_2^\mathcal{I}$. However, this is not really

[26] If the roles of the association are not specified in the UML class diagram, we may use arbitrary fresh DL role names, each of which is identified by the name of the association and the component.

needed for the encoding to preserve satisfiability and answers to queries; we refer to [7,29] for more details. We also observe that the encoding we have proposed for binary associations with association class can immediately be extended to represent also associations of any arity (with or without association class): it suffices to introduce one role A_i for each component i of the association, and add the respective assertions for every component.

We can easily represent in *DL-Lite*$_{\mathcal{A}}$ also multiplicities on an association with association class, by imposing suitable assertions on the inverses of the DL roles modeling the roles of the association. For example, to express that there is a one-to-one participation of instances of C_1 in the association (with related association class) A, we assert

$$C_1 \sqsubseteq \exists A_1^- \qquad \text{and} \qquad (\mathsf{funct}\ A_1^-).$$

Generalizations. In UML, one can use *generalization* between a parent class and a child class to specify that each instance of the child class is also an instance of the parent class. Hence, the instances of the child class inherits the properties of the parent class, but typically they satisfy additional properties that in general do not hold for the parent class.

Generalization is naturally supported in DLs. If a UML class C_2 generalizes a class C_1, we can express this by the *DL-Lite*$_{\mathcal{A}}$ assertion

$$C_1 \sqsubseteq C_2.$$

Inheritance between DL concepts works exactly as inheritance between UML classes. This is an obvious consequence of the semantics of '$\sqsubseteq$', which is based on subsetting. As a consequence, in the formalization, each attribute of C_2 and each association involving C_2 is correctly inherited by C_1. Observe that the formalization in *DL-Lite*$_{\mathcal{A}}$ also captures directly multiple inheritance between classes.

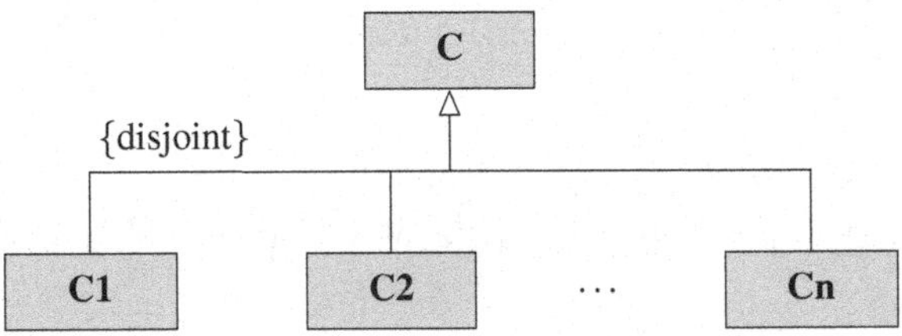

Fig. 8. A class hierarchy in UML

Moreover in UML, one can group several generalizations into a class hierarchy, as shown in Fig. 8. Such a hierarchy is captured in DL by a set of inclusion assertions, one between each child class and the parent class, i.e.,

$$C_i \sqsubseteq C, \qquad \text{for each } i \in \{1, \ldots, n\}.$$

Often, when defining generalizations between classes, we need to add additional assertions among the involved classes. For example, for the class hierarchy in Fig. 8, an assertion may express that $C_1, \ldots, C_n$ are *pairwise disjoint*. In *DL-Lite*$_\mathcal{A}$, such a relationship can be expressed by the assertions

$$C_i \sqsubseteq \neg C_j, \qquad \text{for each } i, j \in \{1, \ldots, n\} \text{ with } i < j.$$

In UML we may also want to express that a generalization hierarchy is *complete*, i.e., that the subclasses $C_1, \ldots, C_n$ are a *covering* of the superclass C. In order to represent such a situation in DLs, one would need to express *disjunctive information*, which however is ruled out in *DL-Lite*$_\mathcal{A}$. Hence, completeness of generalization hierarchies cannot be captured in *DL-Lite*$_\mathcal{A}$.

Similarly to generalization between classes, UML allows one to state *subset assertions* between associations. A subset assertion between two associations A and A' can be modeled in *DL-Lite*$_\mathcal{A}$ by means of the role inclusion assertion $A \sqsubseteq A'$, involving the two DL roles A and A' representing the associations. When the two associations A and A' are represented by means of association classes, we would need to use the concept inclusion assertion $A \sqsubseteq A'$, together with the role inclusion assertions between the DL roles corresponding to the components of A and A'. However, since the roles representing the components of reified associations are functional, they cannot appear in (the right-hand side of) a role inclusion assertion. Therefore, in *DL-Lite*$_\mathcal{A}$, we are able to capture subset assertions between association classes only when (the association class for) the child association connects the same concepts as the parent association, so that we can use the same DL roles to represent the components of the child and parent associations.

Correctness of the Encoding. The encoding we have provided is faithful, in the sense that it fully preserves in the *DL-Lite*$_\mathcal{A}$ ontology the semantics of the UML class diagram. Obviously, since, due to reification, the ontology alphabet may contain additional symbols with respect to those used in the UML class diagram, the two specifications cannot have the same logical models. However, it is possible to show that the logical models of a UML class diagram and those of the *DL-Lite*$_\mathcal{A}$ ontology derived from it correspond to each other, and hence that satisfiability of a class or association in the UML diagram corresponds to satisfiability of the corresponding concept or role [7,29].

Example 9. We illustrate the encoding of UML class diagrams in *DL-Lite*$_\mathcal{A}$ on the UML class diagram shown in Fig. 9, which depicts (a simplified version of) the information model of the ConfSys conference submission system used for our running example. We assume that the components of associations are given from left to right and from top to bottom. Papers are represented through the *Paper* class, with attributes *title* and *type*, both of type *string*. The subclass *DecidedPaper* of *Paper* represents those papers for which an acceptance decision has already been taken, and such a decision is characterized by the *decTime* and *accepted* attributes, and by the unique person who has notified the decision. The

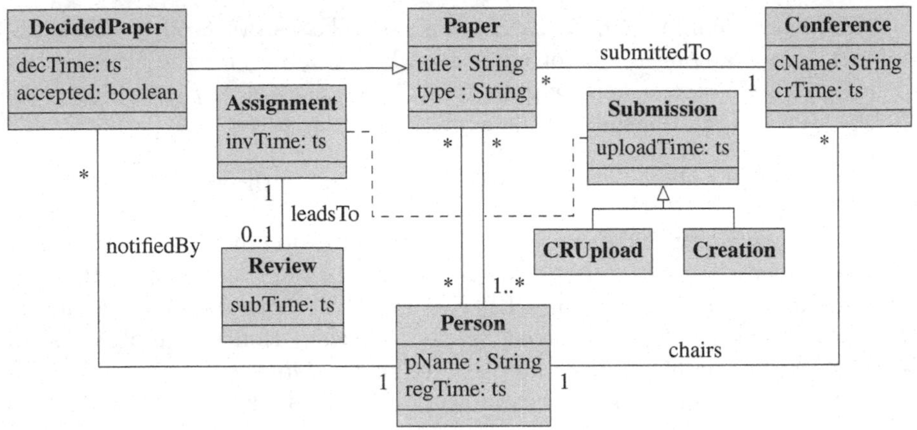

Fig. 9. Data model of our ConfSys running example

type of *decTime* is *ts*, which is the data type we use to represent timestamps. Persons, characterized through their name and the time they have been registered in the system, are related to papers via the *Assignment* and the *Submission* associations, which are both represented through association classes with corresponding timestamps. Among the submissions, we distinguish those that are a *Creation* and those that are a *CRUpload* (i.e., a camera-ready upload). Instead, each assignment possibly *leadsTo* a *Review*, which has its submission time as timestamp. Finally, each paper is submitted to exactly one conference, which is represented through the association *submittedTo* with the class *Conference* and the corresponding multiplicity, and each conference has a unique person who *chairs* it.

We represent such a UML class diagrams through the $DL\text{-}Lite_{\mathcal{A}}$ ontology depicted in Fig. 10. ■

3.3 Queries over $DL\text{-}Lite_{\mathcal{A}}$ Ontologies

We are interested in queries over $DL\text{-}Lite_{\mathcal{A}}$ ontologies (and hence, over the UML class diagrams corresponding to such ontologies), and specifically in unions of conjunctive queries, which correspond to unions of select-project-join queries in relational algebra or SQL.

A First-Order Logic (FOL) *query* q over a $DL\text{-}Lite_{\mathcal{A}}$ ontology $\mathcal{O}$ (resp., TBox $\mathcal{T}$) is a, possibly open, FOL formula whose predicate symbols are atomic concepts, value-domains, roles, or features of $\mathcal{O}$ (resp., $\mathcal{T}$). The *arity* of q is the number of free variables in the formula. A query of arity 0 is called a *boolean query*. When we want to make the free variables of q explicit, we denote the query as $q(\vec{x})$.

A *conjunctive query* (CQ) $q(\vec{x})$ over a $DL\text{-}Lite_{\mathcal{A}}$ ontology is a FOL query of the form

$$\exists \vec{y}.\, conj(\vec{x}, \vec{y}),$$

$$
\begin{array}{rlcrl}
\delta(\mathit{title}) & \equiv \mathit{Paper} & & & \\
\rho(\mathit{title}) & \sqsubseteq \mathit{string} & & & \\
\multicolumn{2}{c}{(\mathsf{funct}\ \mathit{title})} & & \mathit{DecidedPaper} & \sqsubseteq \mathit{Paper} \\
\delta(\mathit{type}) & \equiv \mathit{Paper} & & \mathit{Creation} & \sqsubseteq \mathit{Submission} \\
\rho(\mathit{type}) & \sqsubseteq \mathit{string} & & \mathit{CRUpload} & \sqsubseteq \mathit{Submission} \\
\multicolumn{2}{c}{(\mathsf{funct}\ \mathit{type})} & & & \\
\delta(\mathit{decTime}) & \equiv \mathit{DecidedPaper} & & \exists \mathit{Submission}_1 & \equiv \mathit{Submission} \\
\rho(\mathit{decTime}) & \sqsubseteq \mathit{ts} & & \exists \mathit{Submission}_1^- & \equiv \mathit{Paper} \\
\multicolumn{2}{c}{(\mathsf{funct}\ \mathit{decTime})} & & \multicolumn{2}{c}{(\mathsf{funct}\ \mathit{Submission}_1)} \\
\delta(\mathit{accepted}) & \equiv \mathit{DecidedPaper} & & \exists \mathit{Submission}_2 & \equiv \mathit{Submission} \\
\rho(\mathit{accepted}) & \sqsubseteq \mathit{boolean} & & \exists \mathit{Submission}_2^- & \sqsubseteq \mathit{Person} \\
\multicolumn{2}{c}{(\mathsf{funct}\ \mathit{accepted})} & & \multicolumn{2}{c}{(\mathsf{funct}\ \mathit{Submission}_2)} \\
\delta(\mathit{pName}) & \equiv \mathit{Person} & & \exists \mathit{Assignment}_1 & \equiv \mathit{Assignment} \\
\rho(\mathit{pName}) & \sqsubseteq \mathit{string} & & \exists \mathit{Assignment}_1^- & \sqsubseteq \mathit{Paper} \\
\multicolumn{2}{c}{(\mathsf{funct}\ \mathit{pName})} & & \multicolumn{2}{c}{(\mathsf{funct}\ \mathit{Assignment}_1)} \\
\delta(\mathit{regTime}) & \equiv \mathit{Person} & & \exists \mathit{Assignment}_2 & \equiv \mathit{Assignment} \\
\rho(\mathit{regTime}) & \sqsubseteq \mathit{ts} & & \exists \mathit{Assignment}_2^- & \sqsubseteq \mathit{Person} \\
\multicolumn{2}{c}{(\mathsf{funct}\ \mathit{regTime})} & & \multicolumn{2}{c}{(\mathsf{funct}\ \mathit{Assignment}_2)} \\
\delta(\mathit{cName}) & \equiv \mathit{Conference} & & \exists \mathit{leadsTo} & \sqsubseteq \mathit{Assignment} \\
\rho(\mathit{cName}) & \sqsubseteq \mathit{string} & & \exists \mathit{leadsTo}^- & \equiv \mathit{Review} \\
\multicolumn{2}{c}{(\mathsf{funct}\ \mathit{cName})} & & \multicolumn{2}{c}{(\mathsf{funct}\ \mathit{leadsTo})} \\
\delta(\mathit{crTime}) & \equiv \mathit{Conference} & & \multicolumn{2}{c}{(\mathsf{funct}\ \mathit{leadsTo}^-)} \\
\rho(\mathit{crTime}) & \sqsubseteq \mathit{ts} & & \exists \mathit{submittedTo} & \equiv \mathit{Paper} \\
\multicolumn{2}{c}{(\mathsf{funct}\ \mathit{crTime})} & & \exists \mathit{submittedTo}^- & \sqsubseteq \mathit{Conference} \\
\delta(\mathit{uploadTime}) & \equiv \mathit{Submission} & & \multicolumn{2}{c}{(\mathsf{funct}\ \mathit{submittedTo})} \\
\rho(\mathit{uploadTime}) & \sqsubseteq \mathit{ts} & & \exists \mathit{notifiedBy} & \equiv \mathit{DecidedPaper} \\
\multicolumn{2}{c}{(\mathsf{funct}\ \mathit{uploadTime})} & & \exists \mathit{notifiedBy}^- & \sqsubseteq \mathit{Person} \\
\delta(\mathit{invTime}) & \equiv \mathit{Assignment} & & \multicolumn{2}{c}{(\mathsf{funct}\ \mathit{notifiedBy})} \\
\rho(\mathit{invTime}) & \sqsubseteq \mathit{ts} & & \exists \mathit{chairs} & \sqsubseteq \mathit{Person} \\
\multicolumn{2}{c}{(\mathsf{funct}\ \mathit{invTime})} & & \exists \mathit{chairs}^- & \equiv \mathit{Conference} \\
\delta(\mathit{subTime}) & \equiv \mathit{Review} & & \multicolumn{2}{c}{(\mathsf{funct}\ \mathit{chairs}^-)} \\
\rho(\mathit{subTime}) & \sqsubseteq \mathit{ts} & & & \\
\multicolumn{2}{c}{(\mathsf{funct}\ \mathit{subTime})} & & &
\end{array}
$$

Fig. 10. Encoding in *DL-Lite*$_{\mathcal{A}}$ of the UML class diagram shown in Fig. 9

where $\vec{y}$ is a tuple of pairwise distinct variables not occurring among the free variables $\vec{x}$, and where $conj(\vec{x}, \vec{y})$ is a *conjunction* of atoms (whose predicates are as specified above for FOL queries), possibly involving constants. The variables $\vec{x}$ are also called *distinguished* and the (existentially quantified) variables $\vec{y}$ are called *non-distinguished*.

A *union of conjunctive queries* (UCQ) is a FOL query that is the disjunction of a set of CQs of the same arity, i.e., it is a FOL formula of the form:

$$\exists \vec{y}_1.\, conj_1(\vec{x}, \vec{y}_1) \vee \cdots \vee \exists \vec{y}_n.\, conj_n(\vec{x}, \vec{y}_n).$$

When convenient, we also use the *Datalog* notation for (U)CQs, i.e.,

$$\begin{array}{c} q(\vec{x}) \leftarrow conj'_1(\vec{x}, \vec{y}_1) \\ \vdots \\ q(\vec{x}) \leftarrow conj'_n(\vec{x}, \vec{y}_n) \end{array}$$

where each $conj'_i(\vec{x}, \vec{y}_i)$ in a CQ is considered simply as a set of atoms. In this case, we say that $q(\vec{x})$ is the *head* of the query, and that each $conj'_i(\vec{x}, \vec{y}_i)$ is the *body* of the corresponding CQ.

Semantics of Queries. Given an interpretation $\mathcal{I} = (\Delta^{\mathcal{I}}, \cdot^{\mathcal{I}})$, the *answer* $q^{\mathcal{I}}$ to a FOL query $q = \varphi(\vec{x})$ of arity n is the set of tuples $\vec{o} \in (\Delta^{\mathcal{I}})^n$ such that φ evaluates to true in $\mathcal{I}$ under the assignment that assigns each object in $\vec{o}$ to the corresponding variable in $\vec{x}$ [30]. Notice that the answer to a boolean query is either the empty tuple, "()", considered as true, or the empty set, considered as false.

We remark that a relational database (over the atomic concepts, roles, and features) corresponds to a finite interpretation. Hence the notion of answer to a query introduced here is the standard notion of answer to a query evaluated over a relational database.

The notion of answer to a query is not sufficient to capture the situation where a query is posed over an ontology, since in general an ontology will have many models, and we cannot single out a unique interpretation (or database) over which to answer the query. Given a query, we are interested in those answers that are obtained for *all* possible databases (including infinite ones) that are models of the ontology. This corresponds to the fact that the ontology conveys only incomplete information about the domain of interest, and we want to guarantee that the answers to a query that we obtain are *certain*, independently of how we complete this incomplete information. This leads us to the following definition of *certain answers* to a query over an ontology.

Let $\mathcal{O}$ be a *DL-Lite*$_{\mathcal{A}}$ ontology and q a UCQ over $\mathcal{O}$. The *certain answer* to q over $\mathcal{O}$, denoted $cert(q, \mathcal{O})$, consist of all tuples $\vec{c}$ of constants appearing in $\mathcal{O}$ such that $\vec{c}^{\mathcal{I}} \in q^{\mathcal{I}}$, for every model $\mathcal{I}$ of $\mathcal{O}$.

Remarks on Notation. In the following, as a concrete syntax for specifying CQs and UCQs, we use SPARQL, which is the standard query language defined by the W3C to access RDF data[27]. In SPARQL notation, atoms over unary and binary predicates are given in terms of RDF triples, and a conjunction of atoms

[27] https://www.w3.org/TR/sparql11-overview/.

constitutes a so-called *basic graph pattern*. Specifically, a concept atom $A(t)$, where t is a variable or constant, is specified as the triple t `rdf:type` A, which involves the pre-defined predicate `rdf:type` (intuitively standing for "is instance of"). Instead, a binary atom $U(t_1, t_2)$, where U is either a role or a feature and t_1, t_2 are variables or constants, is specified as the triple t_1 U t_2. Note that, in SPARQL notation, variables names have to start with '`?`', and each triple terminates with '`.`'.

We observe that in the example UML class diagram in Fig. 9 and in its $DL\text{-}Lite_{\mathcal{A}}$ encoding in Fig. 10, we have used abstract names for classes/concepts, associations/roles, attributes/features, and data types, and we have represented them using a *slanted* font. Later, when we describe how these elements are implemented in our prototype system, we introduce also a concrete syntax, for which we use a `typewriter` font. Data types in the abstract syntax are specified using simple intuitive names, such as *String*, *Integer*, and *ts* (for time stamps), while in the concrete syntax we refer to the standard data types of the ontology languages of the OWL 2 family, such as `xsd:string`. We view identifiers written in the abstract and in the concrete syntax as identifical, despite the difference in the used fonts. In the concrete syntax, where appropriate, we also make use of RDF namespaces, which are used as a prefix to identifier names for the purpose of disambiguation. A namespace is separated from the identifier it applies to by '`:`'. It is common to precede an identifier just by '`:`' to denote that the default namespace applies to it, and we will also adopt this convention, even when we do not explicitly introduce or name the default namespace.

3.4 Linking Ontologies to Data

We describe now how to provide the declarative *mapping specification* $\mathcal{M}$, which establishes the connection between the conceptual data schema (or TBox) $\mathcal{T}$ and the underlying information system $\mathcal{I}$. Such a mapping specification actually serves two purposes:

1. It specifies how to extract data from the database $\mathcal{D}$ of $\mathcal{I}$.
2. It specifies how to use the extracted data to (virtually) populate the elements of $\mathcal{T}$.

In populating the elements of $\mathcal{T}$, also the so-called *impedance mismatch* problem is taken into account, i.e., the mismatch between the way in which data is represented in $\mathcal{D}$, and the way in which the corresponding information is rendered through the conceptual data schema $\mathcal{T}$. Indeed, the mapping specification keeps data value constants separate from object identifiers (i.e., URIs), and constructs identifiers as (logic) terms over data values. More precisely, object identifiers are *terms* of the form $t(d_1, \ldots, d_n)$, called *object terms*, where t is a function symbol of arity $n > 0$, and $d_1, \ldots, d_n$ are data values from the data source. Concretely, such function symbols are realized through suitable *templates* containing placeholders for the data values, which result in a valid URI when the placeholders are substituted with actual values.

Specifically, the mapping specification consists of a set of *mapping assertions*, each of the form

$$\Phi(\vec{x}) \rightsquigarrow G(\vec{t}(\vec{y}))$$

where

- $\Phi(\vec{x})$, called the *source part* of the mapping assertion, is an SQL query[28] over the db schema $\mathcal{R}$, with answer variables $\vec{x}$, and
- $G(\vec{t}(\vec{y}))$, called the *target part* of the mapping, is a conjunction of atoms whose predicate symbols are atomic concepts, roles, and features of the conceptual data schema $\mathcal{T}$, and where $\vec{t}(\vec{y})$ represents the arguments of the predicates in the atoms. Specifically, the variables $\vec{y}$ are among the answer variables $\vec{x}$ of the query in the source part, and $\vec{t}(\vec{y})$ represents terms that are either variables in $\vec{y}$, constants, or are obtained by applying URI templates to variables in $\vec{y}$ and constants.

We distinguish three different types of atoms that may appear in the target part $G(\vec{t}(\vec{y}))$ of the mapping assertion, and we specify them as SPARQL triple patterns:

- *concept atoms*, which are unary atoms of the form $t(\vec{y}')$ `rdf:type` A, where A is an atomic concept, t is a URI template with m placeholders, and $\vec{y}'$ is a sequence of m variables among $\vec{y}$ or constants;
- *role atoms*, which are binary atoms of the form $t_1(\vec{y}_1)\ P\ t_2(\vec{y}_2)$, where P is an atomic role, t_1 is a URI template with $m_1 > 0$ placeholders, and $\vec{y}_1$ is a sequence of m_1 variables appearing in $\vec{y}$ or constants; similarly for t_2, m_2, and $\vec{y}_2$;
- *feature atoms*, which are binary atoms of the form $t(\vec{y}_1)\ F\ v_2$, where F is an atomic feature, t is a URI templage with $m_1 > 0$ placeholders, $\vec{y}_1$ is a sequence of m_1 variables appearing in $\vec{y}$ or constants, and v_2 is a variable appearing in $\vec{y}$ or a constant.

Intuitively, mapping assertions involving such atoms are used to map source relations (and the tuples they store), to concepts, roles, and features of the ontology (and the objects and the values that constitute their instances), respectively. Note that for a feature atom, the type of values retrieved from the source database is not specified, and needs to be determined based on the data type of the variable v_2 in the source query $\Phi(\vec{x})$.

Example 10. Consider the ConfSys running example, and an information system whose db schema $\mathcal{R}$ consists of the eight relational tables shown in Fig. 11. We give some examples of mapping assertions:

- The following mapping assertion explicitly populates the concept *Creation*. The term `:submission/{oid}` in the target part represents a URI template with one placeholder, `{oid}`, which gets replaced with the values for `oid`

[28] The formal counterpart of such an SQL query is a first-order logic (FOL) query with distinguished variables $\vec{x}$.

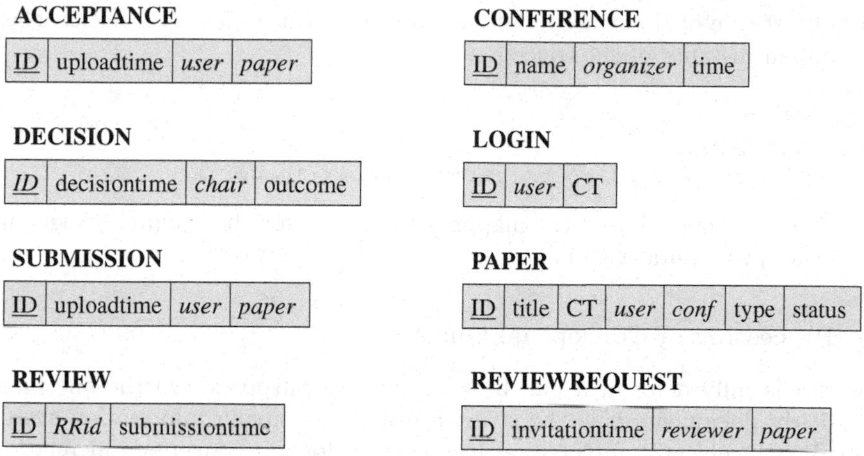

ACCEPTANCE

ID	uploadtime	*user*	*paper*

CONFERENCE

ID	name	*organizer*	time

DECISION

ID	decisiontime	*chair*	outcome

LOGIN

ID	*user*	CT

SUBMISSION

ID	uploadtime	*user*	*paper*

PAPER

ID	title	CT	*user*	*conf*	type	status

REVIEW

ID	*RRid*	submissiontime

REVIEWREQUEST

ID	invitationtime	*reviewer*	*paper*

Fig. 11. DB schema for the information system of the conference submission system. Primary keys are underlined and foreign keys are shown in *italic*

retrieved through the source query. This mapping expresses that each value in SUBMISSION identified by *oid* and such that its upload time equals the corresponding paper's creation time, is mapped to an object :submission/*oid*, which becomes an instance of concept *Creation* in $\mathcal{T}$.

```
SELECT DISTINCT SUBMISSION.ID AS oid
FROM SUBMISSION, PAPER
WHERE SUBMISSION.PAPER = PAPER.ID
  AND SUBMISSION.UPLOADTIME = PAPER.CT
⇝ :submission/{oid} rdf:type :Creation .
```

- The following mapping assertion retrieves from the PAPER table instances of the concept *Paper*, and instantiates also their features *title* and *type* with values of type *String*.

```
SELECT ID, title, type
FROM PAPER
⇝ :paper/{ID} rdf:type :Paper .
   :paper/{ID} :title {title}^^xsd:string .
   :paper/{ID} :type {type}^^xsd:string .
```

- The following mapping assertion retrieves from the SUBMISSION table instances of the concept *Submission*, together with their upload time.

```
SELECT ID, uploadtime
FROM SUBMISSION
⇝ :submission/{ID} rdf:type :Submission .
   :submission/{ID} :uploadTime {uploadtime}^^xsd:dateTime .
```

- Finally, the following mapping assertion retrieves instances of the first component of the reified association *Submission*, which are pairs of URIs consisting of an instance of the concept *Submission*, representing the association class, and of an instance of the concept *Paper*.

```
SELECT ID, paper
FROM SUBMISSION
⇝ :submission/{ID} :Submission1 :paper/{paper} .
```

We omit the specification of the mapping assertions for the remaining elements of the conceptual data schema. ■

3.5 Processing of Conceptual Queries

When $\mathcal{M}$ is fully defined, it can be used for two purposes. On the one hand, it explicitly documents how the structure of the company information system has to be conceptually understood in terms of domain concepts and relations specified in the conceptual data schema $\mathcal{T}$, and thus constitutes an asset for the company that itself might be worth an investment [31]. On the other hand, $\mathcal{S} = \langle \mathcal{R}, \mathcal{T}, \mathcal{M} \rangle$ constitutes what we call an *OBDA schema*, which completely decouples end users from the details of the information system (cf. Fig. 15). Adding to the OBDA schema a database $\mathcal{D}$ that conforms to the database schema $\mathcal{R}$, i.e., replacing $\mathcal{R}$ with an information system $\mathcal{I}$, we obtain what we call an *OBDA model* $\mathcal{B} = \langle \mathcal{I}, \mathcal{T}, \mathcal{M} \rangle$. Whenever a user poses a conceptual query q (e.g., expressed in SPARQL) over $\mathcal{T}$, an OBDA system exploits the OBDA model to answer such query in terms of the data stored in the underlying database $\mathcal{D}$. We sketch now the technique for answering queries in such an OBDA setting [6,7].

We start with the following observation. Suppose we evaluate (over $\mathcal{D}$) the queries in the source part of the mapping assertions of $\mathcal{M}$, and we materialize accordingly the corresponding facts in the target part. This would lead to a set of ground facts, denoted by $\mathcal{A}_{\mathcal{M},\mathcal{D}}$, that can be considered as a *DL-Lite*$_{\mathcal{A}}$ ABox. It can be shown that query answering over $\mathcal{B}$ can be reduced to computing the certain answers over the *DL-Lite*$_{\mathcal{A}}$ ontology $\mathcal{O} = \langle \mathcal{T}, \mathcal{A}_{\mathcal{M},\mathcal{D}} \rangle$ constituted by the TBox $\mathcal{T}$ and the ABox $\mathcal{A}_{\mathcal{M},\mathcal{D}}$. However, the query answering algorithm resulting from this approach would need to perform a materialization of $\mathcal{A}_{\mathcal{M},\mathcal{D}}$, which in general is polynomial in the size of the potentially very large database $\mathcal{D}$, and this might not be practically feasible. However, we can avoid any materialization of the ABox, and rather answer a query q over $\mathcal{T}$ by reformulating it into a new query that can then be evaluated directly over the database $\mathcal{D}$. The resulting query answering algorithm is in general much more efficient than the one based on materialization, and is conceptually divided into three phases, namely *rewriting*, *unfolding*, and *evaluation*, which we briefly describe below.

Rewriting. Given a UCQ q formulated over the conceptual data schema $\mathcal{T}$ of an OBDA schema $\mathcal{S} = \langle \mathcal{R}, \mathcal{T}, \mathcal{M} \rangle$, and a database $\mathcal{D}$ for $\mathcal{R}$, the rewriting step computes a new UCQ q_1, still over $\mathcal{T}$, in which the logical assertions of $\mathcal{T}$ are compiled in. In computing the rewriting, only inclusion assertions of the form $E_1 \sqsubseteq E_2$ are taken into account, while disjointness assertions $E_1 \sqsubseteq \neg E_2$

and functionality assertions (funct Q) are not considered. Intuitively, the query q is rewritten, according to the knowledge specified in $\mathcal{T}$ that is relevant for answering q, into a query q_1 such that $cert(q, \langle \mathcal{T}, \mathcal{A} \rangle) = q_1^{\mathcal{A}}$ for every ABox $\mathcal{A}$ for $\mathcal{T}$, where $q_1^{\mathcal{A}}$ denotes the evaluation of q_1 over $\mathcal{A}$, carried out as if $\mathcal{A}$ was a relational database (i.e., under complete knowledge). Hence, the rewriting allows us to get rid of $\mathcal{T}$.

Different query rewriting algorithms have been proposed in the literature, since the first variants that have been presented in [6,25], to which we refer for more details. We only notice that the rewriting procedure does not depend on the source database $\mathcal{D}$, runs in polynomial time in the size of $\mathcal{T}$, and returns a query q_1 whose size is at most exponential in the size of q (which is also worst-case optimal [32]).

Unfolding. Given the UCQ q_1 over $\mathcal{T}$ computed by the rewriting step, the unfolding step computes, by exploiting the mapping specification $\mathcal{M}$ and using techniques based on partial evaluation of logic programs, an SQL query q_2 that can be directly evaluated over the db schema $\mathcal{R}$. Such a query might return, in addition to values retrieved from $\mathcal{D}$, also URIs constructed according to the URI templates in $\mathcal{M}$. Specifically, the query q_2 is constructed in such a way that $q_2^{\mathcal{D}} = q_1^{\mathcal{A}_{\mathcal{M},\mathcal{D}}}$. Hence, the unfolding allows us to get rid of $\mathcal{M}$. Moreover, also the unfolding procedure does not depend on $\mathcal{D}$, runs in polynomial time in the size of $\mathcal{M}$, and returns a query whose size is at most exponential in the size of q_1.

Evaluation. The evaluation step consists in simply delegating the evaluation of the SQL query q_2, produced by applying first the rewriting step and then the unfolding step, to the RDBMS underlying the information system of the OBDA model. This evaluation step returns $q_2^{\mathcal{D}}$, which is simply the set of tuples resulting from the evaluation of q_2 over $\mathcal{D}$.

Correctness and Complexity of Query Answering. The procedure for processing queries formulated over the conceptual data schema of an OBDA model described above correctly computes the certain answers to UCQs, and it does so by reducing the problem to one of evaluating an SQL query over a relational database. Indeed, we have that $q_2^{\mathcal{D}} = q_1^{\mathcal{A}_{\mathcal{M},\mathcal{D}}} = cert(q, \langle \mathcal{T}, \mathcal{A}_{\mathcal{M},\mathcal{D}} \rangle)$, and the latter expression corresponds to the answers of Q over $\mathcal{B}$. This means that the problem of computing certain answers to UCQs over an OBDA model is First-Order (FO) rewritable.

We have (implicitly) assumed that, given the database $\mathcal{D}$, the OBDA model $\mathcal{B}$ is consistent, i.e., that the ontology $\langle \mathcal{T}, \mathcal{A}_{\mathcal{M},\mathcal{D}} \rangle$ admits at least one model. Notably, it can be shown that the machinery developed for query answering can also be used for checking consistency of $\mathcal{B}$. Therefore, checking consistency can also be reduced to evaluating appropriate SQL queries over the underlying relational database $\mathcal{D}$ [6,25].

Although the presented query answering technique is computationally worst-case optimal, the increase in size of the queries produced by the rewriting and unfolding steps poses a significant practical challenge. Therefore, a lot of effort has been spent recently in studying the problem of query answering in OBDA and in devising optimization techniques and alternative query transformation approaches that allow for efficient query processing. Discussing these aspects in detail is beyond the scope of the present work, and we refer to the extensive literature on the topic, e.g., [8,33–35]. We remark, however, that many of the optimized techniques for query answering in OBDA have been implemented, both in freely available and in commercial systems. Notable examples are *D2RQ*[29], *Mastro*[30], *Ultrawrap*[31], *Morph-RDB*[32], and ontop[33].

For the implementation of the prototype tools for the preparation phase of process mining based on OBDA that we are discussing in this paper, we rely on the ontop system, which is a state-of-the-art OBDA system available under the very liberal Apache 2 licence. ontop implements the query rewriting and unfolding algorithms discussed above, together with an extensive set of optimization techniques, which are aimed on the one hand at reducing the size of the SQL queries generated by the system, and on the other hand at producing queries that are efficiently executable by relational database engines. We refer to [8] for an in depth discussion of ontop.

4 OBDA for Log Extraction: The onprom Approach

We are now in the position of illustrating how OBDA can be effectively applied to the data preparation phase of process mining. The resulting framework, called onprom, is based on the seminal results in [9,36]. We start by recalling the methodological steps that are foreseen by onprom, and move then to the formal model and the corresponding toolchain.

4.1 Methodology

The onprom methodology, sketched in Fig. 12, aims at the semi-automatic extraction of event logs from a legacy information system, reflecting different process-related views on the same data, and consequently supporting analysts in the application of process mining along multiple perspectives.

The methodology comprises four main phases. The first phase is about *understanding* the meaning of the data stored in the information system at hand. Concretely, it consists of the definition of an *OBDA model* (cf. Sect. 3), on the one hand providing a conceptual data schema to semantically describe the domain of interest, and on the other hand linking such a data schema to the underlying information system. While this is in general a labor-intensive, purely human

[29] http://d2rq.org.
[30] http://www.dis.uniroma1.it/~mastro.
[31] http://capsenta.com.
[32] https://github.com/oeg-upm/morph-rdb.
[33] http://ontop.inf.unibz.it.

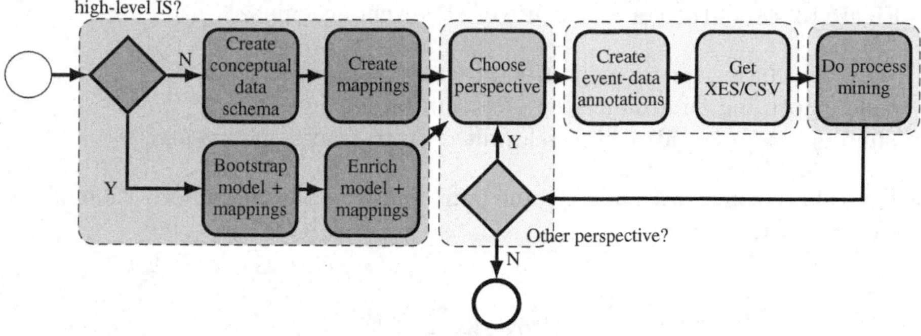

Fig. 12. The onprom methodology and its four phases

activity, if the information system has a "high-level" structure that is understandable by domain experts, such an activity can be partially automatized through *bootstrapping* techniques [37]. These techniques mirror the schema of the information system into a corresponding conceptual data schema, at the same time generating (identity) mappings to link the two specifications. The result of bootstrapping can then be manually refined.

Once the first phase is completed, process analysts and the other involved stakeholders do not need anymore to consider the structure of the legacy information system, but directly focus on the conceptual data schema. Remember, in fact, that the OBDA paradigm allows one to formulate queries over the conceptual data schema, getting back answers expressed over such a schema but computed over the underlying legacy data.

The goal of the second phase is then to decide which perspective on the data has to be considered for the analysis, singling out, among all possible alternatives, which entities and relationships define the desired notion of *case object*, and which other conditions have to be defined so as to properly confine the analysis. Recall that a case object represents the main object that is evolved by an instance of the process of interest. E.g., by considering our ConfSys running example, one may decide to focus on the flow of papers submitted to a given conference, or instead tailor the analysis to the flow of operations performed by persons who registered to the conference management system between 2012 and 2015.

4.2 Event Ontology

Since the final goal of data extraction is the generation of a XES event log, the necessary basis for the application of the onprom methodology is to conceptually clarify which key concepts and relations are part of the XES standard. To this end, a *(conceptual) event schema* is introduced. We denote such an event schema by $\mathcal{E}$. We will see later how such a schema is used to support the semi-automated extraction of an event log from legacy data.

Figure 13 shows the core elements of the event schema:

- *trace*, accounting for the evolution of a case through events;
- *event*, capturing an atomic step of execution for a case;
- (simple) *attributes*, attaching relevant data to traces and events.

Each attribute comes with a key-value pair, and with the characterization of the type taken by the value.

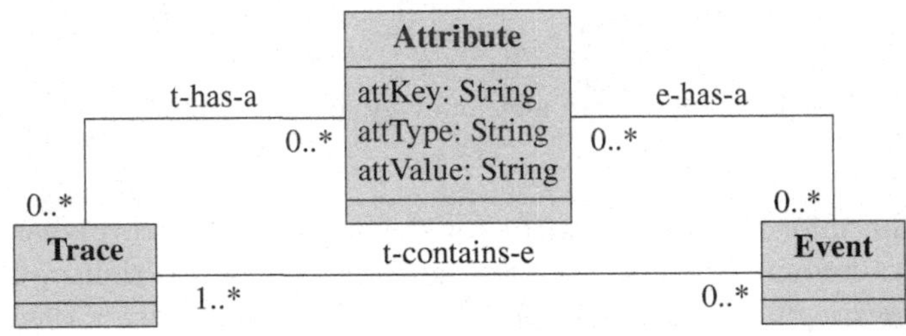

Fig. 13. Core event schema

We show now how such a simple schema can be suitably encoded in $DL\text{-}Lite_{\mathcal{A}}$. To encode the core event schema of Fig. 13, the three concept names *Trace*, *Event*, and *Attribute* are used. In addition, the role names *e-has-a*, *t-has-a*, and *t-contains-e* are used to capture the binary relations among such concepts. To restrict the usage of those role names, the following domain/range axioms are imposed:

$$\begin{array}{rlrl} \exists e\text{-}has\text{-}a \sqsubseteq & Event & \exists e\text{-}has\text{-}a^- \sqsubseteq & Attribute \\ \exists t\text{-}has\text{-}a \sqsubseteq & Trace & \exists t\text{-}has\text{-}a^- \sqsubseteq & Attribute \\ \exists t\text{-}contains\text{-}e \sqsubseteq & Trace & \exists t\text{-}contains\text{-}e^- \sqsubseteq & Event \end{array}$$

Additionally, the following axiom captures that no dangling event may exist, i.e., that each event is assigned to at least one trace:

$$Event \sqsubseteq \exists t\text{-}contains\text{-}e^-$$

The typing axioms of the three DL features of the *Attribute* concept are:

$$\begin{array}{rlrl} \delta(attKey) \sqsubseteq & Attribute & \rho(attKey) \sqsubseteq & String \\ \delta(attType) \sqsubseteq & Attribute & \rho(attType) \sqsubseteq & String \\ \delta(attValue) \sqsubseteq & Attribute & \rho(attValue) \sqsubseteq & String \end{array}$$

Recall, in fact, that XES attribute values are always stored as strings, while the type information indicates how such string may be parsed into more specific data types.

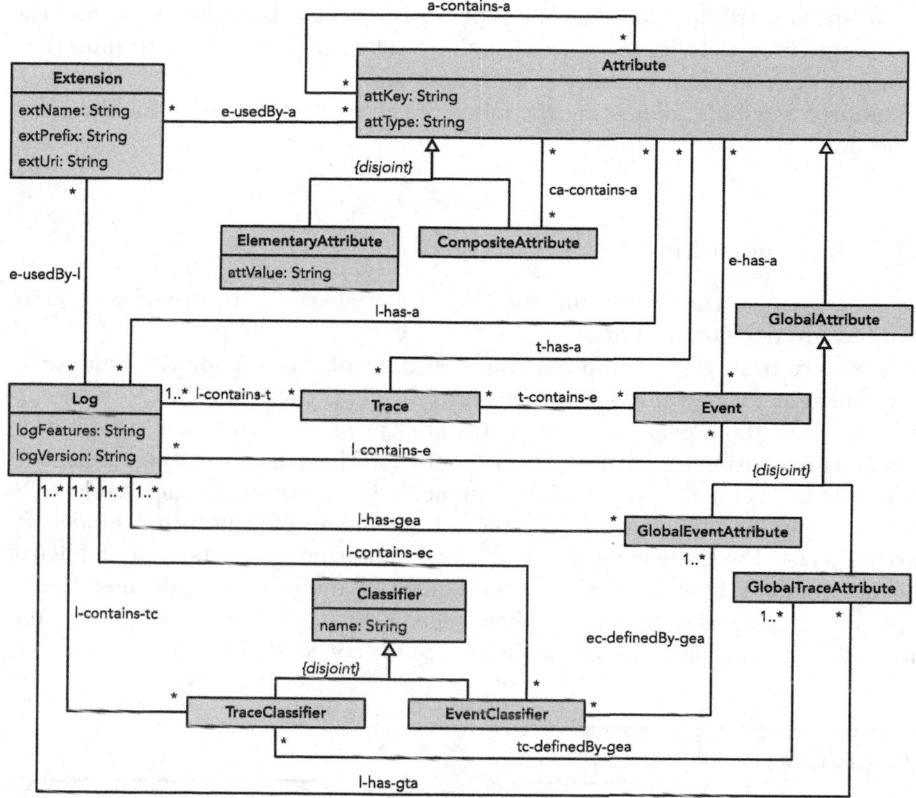

Fig. 14. A more comprehensive event schema, capturing all main abstractions of the XES standard

Finally, by recalling that, in UML, the default multiplicity for an attribute of a class is 1..1, the linkage between the *Attribute* concept and its three features is captured by the following axioms:

$$\begin{array}{ll} \mathit{Attribute} \sqsubseteq \delta(\mathit{attKey}) & (\mathsf{funct}\ \mathit{attKey}) \\ \mathit{Attribute} \sqsubseteq \delta(\mathit{attType}) & (\mathsf{funct}\ \mathit{attType}) \\ \mathit{Attribute} \sqsubseteq \delta(\mathit{attValue}) & (\mathsf{funct}\ \mathit{attValue}) \end{array}$$

Figure 14 shows a richer event schema that more comprehensively captures the XES standard, including classifiers, global and composite attributes, as well as extensions. However, in the remainder of the paper we will just employ the concepts, relations, and features of the core event schema, making use of the following recurrent attributes to capture key event data, which are encapsulated by XES into specific extensions:

- *timestamp* attribute, keeping track of when the event occurred;
- *activity* attribute, indicating to which activity the event refers;

- *transition* attribute, denoting the type of the event within the lifecycle of the corresponding activity (e.g., whether the event refers to the start, termination, or cancellation of an instance of that activity);
- *resource* attribute, indicating the name of the agent responsible for the event occurrence.

4.3 The onprom Model

We describe now the onprom model, whose key elements and their respective relations are depicted in Fig. 15.

We start from the assumption that the data of interest for the analysis is maintained in a legacy information system $\mathcal{I} = \langle \mathcal{R}, \mathcal{D} \rangle$, with schema $\mathcal{R}$ and set $\mathcal{D}$ of facts about the domain of interest. In the typical case where the information system is a relational database, $\mathcal{R}$ accounts for the schema of the tables and their columns, and $\mathcal{D}$ is a set of data structured according to such tables. On top of $\mathcal{I}$, our methodology is centered on the usage of conceptual models in two respects. First, they are used as documentation artifacts that explicitly capture not only knowledge about the domain of interest, but also how legacy information systems relate to that knowledge. This facilitates understanding and interaction among human stakeholders. Second, conceptual models are used as

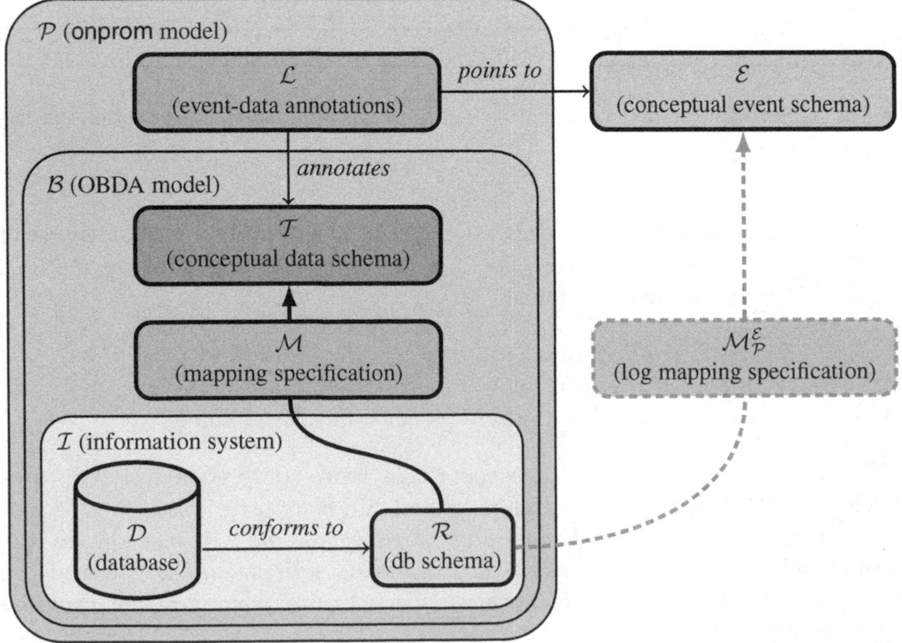

Fig. 15. Sketch of the onprom model. The dashed mapping specification is automatically generated

computational artifacts, that is, to automatize the extraction process as much as possible.

The first phase of the methodology consists in the creation of two conceptual models. The first one is the *conceptual data schema* $\mathcal{T}$, which accounts for the structural knowledge of the domain of interest, i.e., relevant concepts and relations, consequently providing a high-level view of $\mathcal{I}$ that is closer to domain experts. More specifically, we employ UML class diagrams as a concrete language for conceptual data modeling, and we provide their logic-based, formal encoding in terms of the OWL 2 QL ontology language, as illustrated in Sect. 3.2. In the following, depending on the context, we refer to $\mathcal{T}$ as a UML class diagram or as the corresponding OWL 2 QL ontology.

The second conceptual model, the *mapping specification* $\mathcal{M}$, is a distinctive feature introduced by our approach, borrowed from the area of OBDA. As illustrated in Sect. 3.4, $\mathcal{M}$, which explicitly links $\mathcal{I}$ to $\mathcal{T}$, consists of a set of logical assertions that map patterns of data over schema $\mathcal{R}$ to high-level facts over $\mathcal{T}$.

Once the OBDA system is in place, onprom allows one to abstract away the information system. In this way, the analyst responsible for the data extraction can directly focus on $\mathcal{T}$, using the concepts and relations contained therein so as to concretely formulate which perspective has to be taken towards process mining. More specifically, this amounts to enrich $\mathcal{T}$ with annotations $\mathcal{L}$, each creating an implicit link between $\mathcal{T}$ and the core portion of the event schema $\mathcal{E}$ captured in Fig. 13. In this light, each annotation expresses one of the following aspects:

- *definition of a case*, indicating which class provides the basis to identify case objects, and which conditions have to be satisfied by instances of the selected class so as to classify them as case objects;
- *definition of an event*, indicating which class provides the basis to identify occurrences of such an event;
- *definition of an event attribute*, indicating which navigational route has to be followed within the diagram so as to fetch the value for such an attribute given an instance of the corresponding event.

We consider each type of annotation next.

Case Annotation specifies which class constitutes the main entry point for the analysis, and which additional conditions have to be considered when identifying cases. Each object instantiating this so-called *case class*, and satisfying the additional conditions, is a case object. Each case object, in turn, is used to correlate the event of interest, grouping into a single trace all the events that refer to the same case object.

Event Annotations pinpoint which events of interest characterise the evolution of the selected case objects, and to which classes of $\mathcal{T}$ they are attached. Only classes that obey to the following two conditions are eligible to be target for an event annotation, i.e., to be marked as *event classes*. First, the class has to be navigationally connected to the case class. A navigational connection consists of the concatenation of multiple links (i.e., associations or IS-A generalisations), each time imposing that the target class of the current link becomes the source of the next link. Second, the class has to be navigationally connected to a timestamp attribute, through functional associations only.

The first condition is used to establish a relationship between case objects and their related events. The second condition is used to unambiguously identify the execution times associated to those events. It is important to notice that, for both navigations, the concatenated associations may be optional. In this light, only those objects falling under the scope of the annotation, and corresponding to an actual timestamp and to at least one case object, are considered as events. This is used to account for the fact that cases may be still running (i.e., with events that did not occur yet, but that will occur in the future), and that different cases may very well contain different events.

Attribute Annotations capture how to connect events to corresponding values for their characteristic attributes. Each annotation of this form comes with a key that defines the type of targeted attribute, and the specification of a navigational connection to fetch its corresponding value(s). Each event annotation comes with three mandatory attribute annotations, respectively used to capture the relationship between the event and its corresponding case(s), timestamp, and activity. As pointed out before, the timestamp annotation needs to have a functional navigation. This also applies to the activity annotation, with the only difference that, instead of providing a functional navigation, the activity annotation may also be filled with a constant string that independently fixes the name of activity. Beside such three mandatory attributes, additional optional attribute annotations may be provided, so as to cover the various standard extensions provided XES, including the link to a transition within the activity transactional lifecycle, as well as resource information, in turn constituted by the resource name and/or role.

Example 11. Consider again our ConfSys case study, and in particular the data model shown in Fig. 9, under the assumption that the focus of process mining is to analyse the flow of papers within ConfSys, from their creation and submission to their final judgement. An informal account of the different annotations reflecting this perspective on the data is given in Fig. 16. In particular, the case annotation clearly depicts that each *Paper* is a case object. On top of this choice for cases, four types of events are identified:

- Each instance of *DecidedPaper* may determine a Decision event occurring for that paper instance at the given decision time (attribute *decTime*). Notice that, in this case, the case class is directly reached from *DecidedPaper* through its *IS-A* relationship.

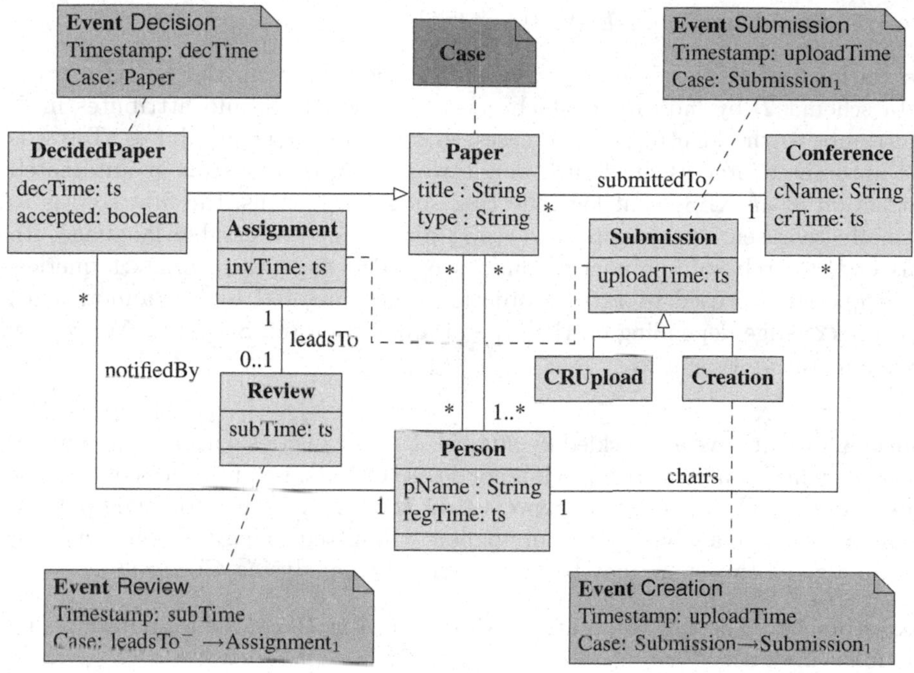

Fig. 16. Annotated data model of our ConfSys running example

- Each instance of *Creation* may determine a Creation event for the paper that is reached by concatenating the *IS-A* relationship pointing to *Submission*, together with the *Submission* association (class), navigating it towards *Paper*. The event occurs at the upload time attached to the *Submission* parent class (attribute *uploadTime* in *Submission*).
- Each instance of *Submission* may determine a Submission for the paper that is obtained by simply navigating the association class *Submission* towards *Paper*. Similar to the previous annotation, also events of this type occur at the upload time (attribute *uploadTime*) for the submission.
- Finally, each instance of *Review* may determine a Review event for the paper that is obtained by navigating backward the *leadsTo* association, in turn navigating the *Assignment* association (class) towards *Paper*. The event comes with the timestamp of submission for that review (attribute *subTime*). ■

Example 12. A completely different set of annotations would be devised on top of the ConfSys data model in Fig. 9, when considering a class different than *Paper* to identify cases. For example, one may focus on the flow of operations performed by users of ConfSys, by declaring *Person* to be the case class. Alternatively, one may consider the flow of review invitations and submissions, by declaring *Assignment* to be the case class. All such different choices would in turn result in different relevant events and corresponding event/attribute annotations. ■

4.4 Formalising Event-Data Annotations

As we have seen, the different event-data annotations enrich the conceptual data schema $\mathcal{T}$ by indicating which classes, associations, and attributes in $\mathcal{T}$ contribute to the identification of cases, events, and event attributes. Towards the automated processing of such annotations, and the consequent automated extraction of an XES event log reflecting such annotations, the first step is to formally represent the annotations using a machine-processable language. To this end, we rely on conjunctive queries encoded as SPARQL SELECT queries. Such queries are used to extract objects/values targeted by the annotations, and thus change depending on the type of annotation (cf. Sect. 4.3). We review each annotation type next.

Case Annotations are tackled by SPARQL SELECT queries with a single answer variable, which matches with the intended case objects, i.e., instances of the case class. Additional filters can be expressed in the WHERE clause to single out the boundaries of the analysis (e.g., only papers submitted to a given conference, or within a given timespan, may be considered when analysing ConfSys).

Example 13. The case annotation captured in Fig. 16 can be formalised using the following query:

```
PREFIX : <http://www.example.com/>
SELECT DISTINCT ?case
WHERE {
   ?case rdf:type :Paper .
}
```

which retrieves all instances of the *Paper* class. ■

Event Annotations are also tackled using SPARQL SELECT queries with a single answer variable, this time matching with actual event identifiers, i.e., objects denoting occurrences of events.

Example 14. Consider the event annotation for creation, as shown in Fig. 16. The actual events for this annotation are retrieved using the following query:

```
PREFIX : <http://www.example.com/>
SELECT DISTINCT ?creationEvent
WHERE {
  ?creationEvent rdf:type :Creation .
}
```

which in fact returns all instances of the *Creation* class. ■

Attribute Annotations are formalised using SPARQL SELECT queries with two answer variables, establishing a relation between events and their corresponding attribute values. In this light, for *timestamp and activity attribute annotations*, the second answer variable will be substituted by corresponding values for timestamps/activity names. For *case attribute annotations*, instead, the second answer variable will be substituted by case objects, thus establishing a relationship between events and the case(s) they belong to.

Example 15. Consider again the annotation for creation events, as shown in Fig. 16. The relationship between creation events and their corresponding timestamps is established by the following query:

```
PREFIX : <http://www.example.com/>
SELECT DISTINCT ?creationEvent ?creationTime
WHERE {
   ?creationEvent rdf:type :Creation .
   ?creationEvent :Submission1  ?Paper .
   ?creationEvent :uploadTime  ?creationTime .
}
```

which indeed retrieves all instances of *Creation*, together with the corresponding values taken by the *uploadTime* attribute. ■

In the remainder of the paper, a SPARQL query q formalising an annotation l is called the *annotation query* for l. Given a set $\mathcal{L}$ of annotations, we denote by $\mathcal{L}_q$ the set of annotation queries formalising the different annotations in $\mathcal{L}$.

4.5 Automated Processing of Annotations

Once the data-annotation step is concluded, the conceptual data schema $\mathcal{T}$ of the input OBDA system $\langle \mathcal{I}, \mathcal{T}, \mathcal{M} \rangle$ is enriched with annotations $\mathcal{L}$ that implicitly link such a system to the event schema $\mathcal{E}$ that conceptually accounts for the main concepts and relations of the XES standard (cf. Sect. 4.2). We now show how such event-data annotations can be automatically processed, so as to synthesise a new OBDA system that directly maps the data in $\mathcal{I}$ to the event schema $\mathcal{E}$ (cf. the dashed part of Fig. 15). This OBDA system, in turn, can be exploited to query the data in $\mathcal{I}$ as they were structured as a XES event log, and also to actually materialise such an event log.

Technically, onprom takes as input an onprom model $\mathcal{P} = \langle \mathcal{I}, \mathcal{T}, \mathcal{M}, \mathcal{L} \rangle$ and the event schema $\mathcal{E}$, and produces new OBDA system $\langle \mathcal{I}, \mathcal{M}_{\mathcal{P}}^{\mathcal{E}}, \mathcal{E} \rangle$, where the annotations in $\mathcal{L}$ are automatically reformulated as OBDA mappings $\mathcal{M}_{\mathcal{P}}^{\mathcal{E}}$ that directly link $\mathcal{I}$ to $\mathcal{E}$. Such mappings are synthesised using the three-step approach described next.

In the first step, the SPARQL queries formalising the annotations in $\mathcal{L}$ are reformulated into corresponding SQL queries posed directly over $\mathcal{I}$. This is done by relying on standard query rewriting and unfolding, where each SPARQL query $q \in \mathcal{L}_q$ is rewritten considering the contribution of the conceptual data schema $\mathcal{T}$, and then unfolded using the mappings in $\mathcal{M}$. The resulting query q_{sql} can then be posed directly over $\mathcal{I}$ so as to retrieve the data associated to the corresponding annotation. In the following, we denote the set of all so-obtained SQL queries as $\mathcal{L}_{\text{sql}}$.

Example 16. Consider the SPARQL query in Example 13, formalising the event annotation that accounts for the creation of papers. A possible reformulation of the rewriting and unfolding of such a query respectively using the conceptual data schema in Fig. 9, and the mappings from Example 10, is the following SQL query:

```
SELECT DISTINCT
CONCAT('http://www.example.com/submission/
',Submission."ID")
AS "creationEvent"
FROM Submission, Paper
WHERE Submission."Paper" = Paper."ID" AND
      Submission."UploadTime" = Paper."CT" AND
      Submission."ID" IS NOT NULL
```

This query is generated by the ontop OBDA system, which applies various optimisations so as to obtain a final SQL query that is not only correct, but also possibly compact and fast to process by a standard DBMS. One such optimisations is the application of conjunctive query containment techniques to remove parts of the query that are subsumed by others. ■

The second step towards the synthesis of $\mathcal{M}_{\mathcal{P}}^{\mathcal{E}}$ amounts to the creation of the actual, direct mappings from $\mathcal{I}$ to $\mathcal{E}$. Each mapping, in turn, is obtained by considering one of the reformulated annotation queries in $\mathcal{L}_{\text{sql}}$, and constructed depending on the corresponding annotation type. In the obtained mapping, the SQL query constitutes the source part of the mapping, while the annotation type indicates which concepts/roles/features have to be considered to form its target part.

More specifically, $\mathcal{M}_{\mathcal{P}}^{\mathcal{E}}$ is obtained from $\mathcal{L}_{\text{sql}}$ as follows:

1. For each SQL query `q(c)` $\in \mathcal{L}_{\text{sql}}$ obtained from a *case annotation*, we insert into $\mathcal{M}_{\mathcal{P}}^{\mathcal{E}}$ the following OBDA mapping:

   ```
   q(c)
   ⇝ :trace/{c} rdf:type :Trace .
   ```

   Intuitively, such a mapping populates the concept *Trace* in $\mathcal{E}$ with the case objects that are created from the answers returned by query `q(c)`.
2. For each SQL query `q(e)` $\in \mathcal{L}_{\text{sql}}$ that is obtained from an *event annotation*, we insert into $\mathcal{M}_{\mathcal{P}}^{\mathcal{E}}$ the following OBDA mapping:

   ```
   q(e)
   ⇝ :event/{e} rdf:type :Event .
   ```

   Intuitively, such a mapping populates the concept *Event* in $\mathcal{E}$ with the event objects that are created from the answers returned by query `q(e)`.

3. For each SQL query `q(e,y)` $\in \mathcal{L}_{\text{sql}}$ that is obtained from an *attribute annotation*, we insert into $\mathcal{M}_{\mathcal{P}}^{\mathcal{E}}$ a mapping that depends on the type of attribute:
   (a) If `q(e,y)` is the query obtained from a *case attribute annotation* (i.e., `e` is bound to events, and `y` to their corresponding cases), then the mapping has the following form:

   ```
   q(e,y)
   ⇝ :trace/{y :t-contains-e :event/{e} .
   ```

   Intuitively, such a mapping populates the the relation that links traces and events in $\mathcal{E}$ (i.e., the role *t-contains-e*) with the answers returned by query `q(e,y)`.
   (b) If `q(e,y)` is the query obtained from a *timestamp attribute annotation* (i.e., `e` is bound to events, and `y` to their corresponding execution times), then the mapping has the following form:

   ```
   q(e,y)
   ⇝ :event/{e} :e-has-a :att/eventTS/{e}/{y};
     :att/eventTS/{e}/{y} :attType "date"^^xsd:string;
     :attKey "time:timestamp"^^xsd:string;
     :attVal "{y}"^^xsd:string .
   ```

   Intuitively, such a mapping populates the concept *Attribute* with the objects representing timestamp attributes. at the same time, it also suitably reconstruct the event-timestamp relationship at the level of $\mathcal{E}$, using the answers returned by query `q(e,y)`.
   (c) If `q(e,n)` is the query obtained from an *activity attribute annotation* (i.e., `e` is bound to events, and `n` to their corresponding activity names), then the mapping has the following form:

   ```
   q(e,n)
   ⇝ :event/{e} :e-has-a :att/aName/{e}/{n};
     :att/aName/{e}/{n} :attType "string"^^xsd:string;
     :attKey "concept:name"^^xsd:string;
     :attVal "{n}"^^xsd:string .
   ```

It is worth noting that the presented approach can be straightforwardly generalised to cover additional types of annotations (e.g., dealing with the activity transactional lifecycle, or the involved resources).

The third, final step consists in leveraging the synthesised OBDA system $\langle\mathcal{I},\mathcal{E},\mathcal{M}_{\mathcal{P}}^{\mathcal{E}}\rangle$ so as to extract the event data of interest. The extraction can be declaratively guided by formulating SPARQL queries over the vocabulary of $\mathcal{E}$ and, if needed, serialising the obtained answers in the form of an XES event log. We provide, in the following, a list of SPARQL queries serving this purpose.

The SPARQL query below retrieves events and their attributes, considering only those events that do actually have a reference trace, timestamp, and activity name:

```
PREFIX : <http://onprom.inf.unibz.it>
SELECT DISTINCT ?event ?att
WHERE {
  ?trace :t-contain-e ?event.
  ?event :e-has-a ?att.
  ?event :e-has-a ?timestamp. ?timestamp :attKey "time:timestamp"^^xsd:string.
  ?event :e-has-a ?name. ?name :attKey "concept:name"^^xsd:string.
}
```

The WHERE clause is used to filter away dangling events (i.e., events for which the corresponding case is not known), or events with missing timestamp or missing activity name.

The following query is instead meant to retrieve (elementary) attributes, considering in particular their key, type, and value.

```
PREFIX : <http://www.example.org/>
SELECT DISTINCT ?att ?attType ?attKey ?attValue
WHERE {
   ?att rdf:type :Attribute;
                 :attType ?attType;
                 :attKey ?attKey;
                 :attVal ?attValue.
}
```

The following query handles the retrieval of empty and nonempty traces, simultaneously obtaining, for nonempty traces, their constitutive events:

```
PREFIX : <http://www.example.org/>
SELECT DISTINCT ?trace ?event
WHERE {
   ?trace a :Trace .
   OPTIONAL {
      ?trace :t-contain-e ?event .
      ?event :e-contain-a ?timestamp .
         ?timestamp :attKey "time:timestamp"^^xsd:string .
      ?event :e-contain-a ?name .
         ?name :attKey "concept:name"^^xsd:string .
   }
}
```

4.6 The onprom Toolchain

onprom comes with a toolchain that supports the various phases of the methodology shown in Fig. 12, and in particular implements the automated processing technique for annotations discussed in Sect. 4.5. The toolchain is open source and can be downloaded from http://onprom.inf.unibz.it. The toolchain is available as a stand-alone software, or as a set of plugins running inside the ProM process mining framework. Specifically, the onprom toolchain consists of the following components:

- a *UML Editor* to model the conceptual data schema (cf. Sect. 4.1);
- an *Annotation Editor* to enrich the conceptual data schema with event-data annotations (cf. Sect. 4.3);
- a *Log Extractor* component that automatically processes the event-data annotations, and extracts an XES event log from a given relational information system (cf. Sect. 4.5).

Notice that the definition of a suitable mapping specification to link a conceptual data schema to an underlying information system is not natively covered within onprom, and we assume that it is realised manually or by exploiting third-party tools, such as the ontop mapping editor for Protégé[34].

We now briefly describe each component, using ConfSys as running example.

UML Editor. The UML editor provides two main functionalities: modelling of a UML class diagram, and import/export from/to OWL 2 QL, leveraging the correspondence described in Sect. 3.2. The editor makes some simplifying assumptions, in line with this correspondence with OWL 2 QL:

- we do not support *completeness* of UML generalisation hierarchies, since the presence of such construct would fundamentally undermine the virtual OBDA approach based on query reformulation [7];

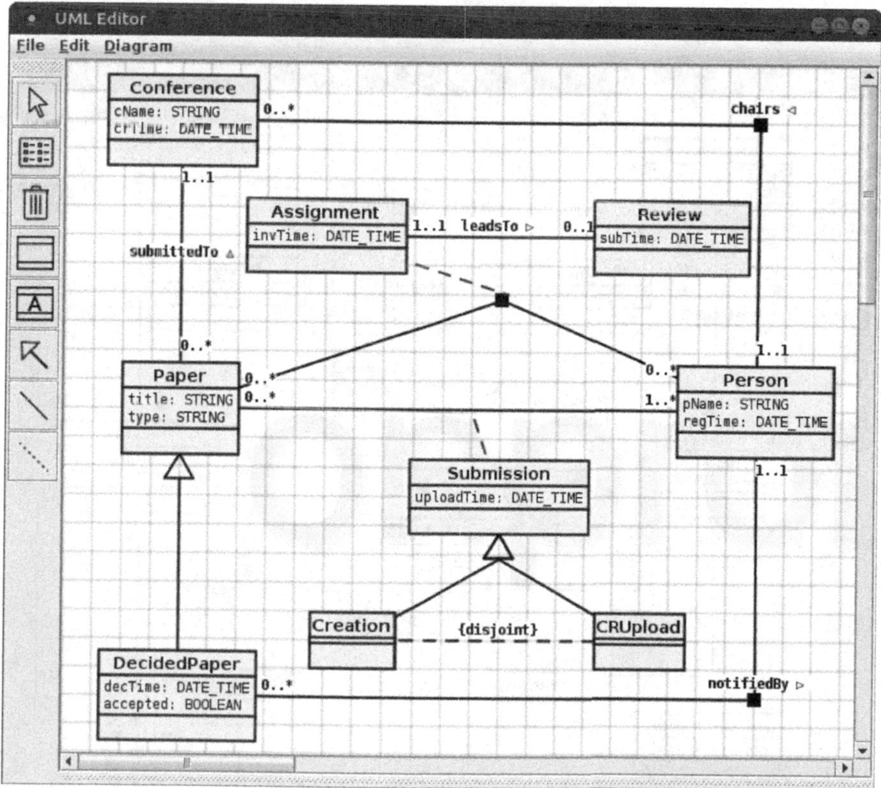

Fig. 17. The onprom UML Editor, showing the conceptual data schema used in our ConfSys running example

[34] http://protege.stanford.edu/.

- in line with Semantic Web languages, we explicitly support binary associations only;
- multiplicities in associations (resp., features) are restricted to be either 0 or 1. Hence, we can express functionality and mandatory participation;
- we do not support *IS-A* between associations;
- we ignore all those features that are not directly related to conceptual modelling, but instrumental to software design, such as stereotypes and methods.

A screenshot of the UML Editor showing the conceptual data schema of ConfSys is shown in Fig. 17.

Annotation Editor. This editor supports data and process analysts in the specification of event-data annotations on top of a UML class diagram developed using the UML editor described above.

A screenshot of the Annotation Editor, showing annotations for our ConfSys conceptual data schema, is shown Fig. 18. Specifically, the screenshot shows that *Paper* has been annotated as case class, and that four events annotations

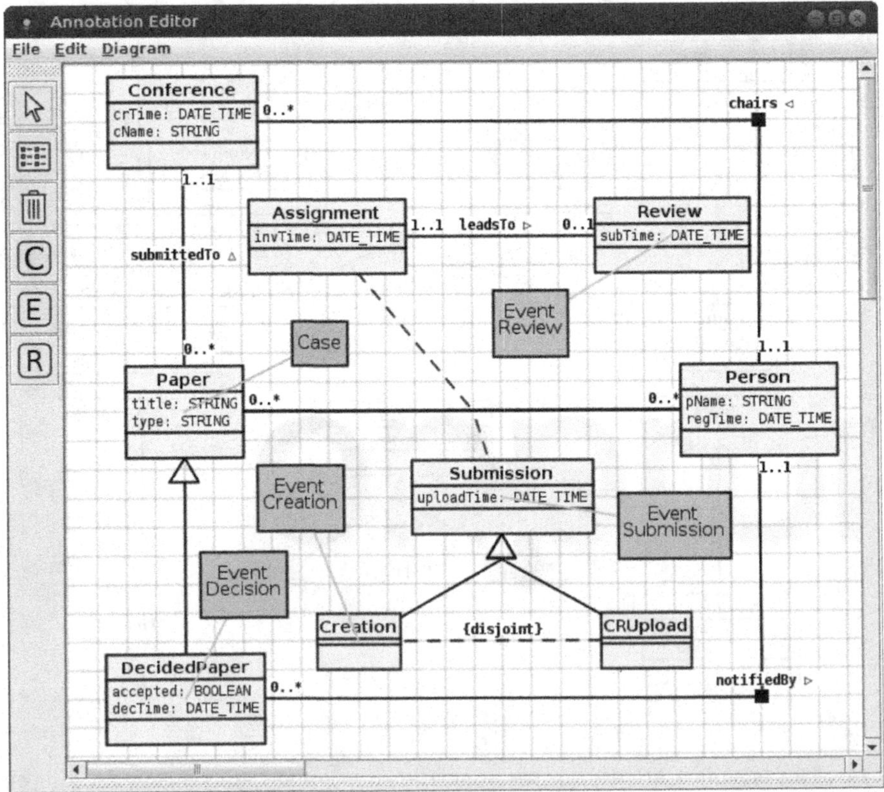

Fig. 18. The Annotation Editor showing annotations for the ConfSys use case

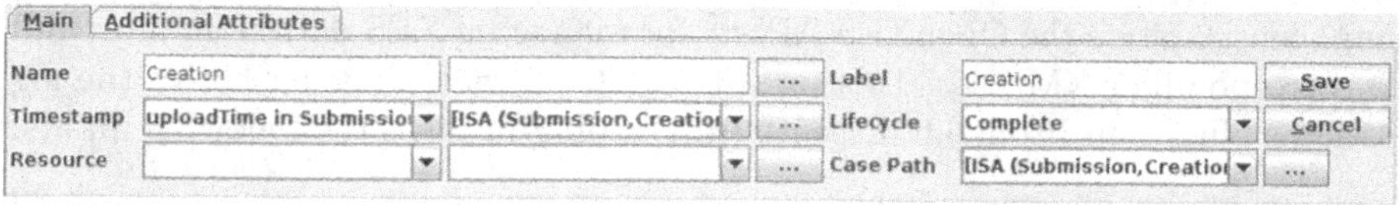

(a) The Creation event

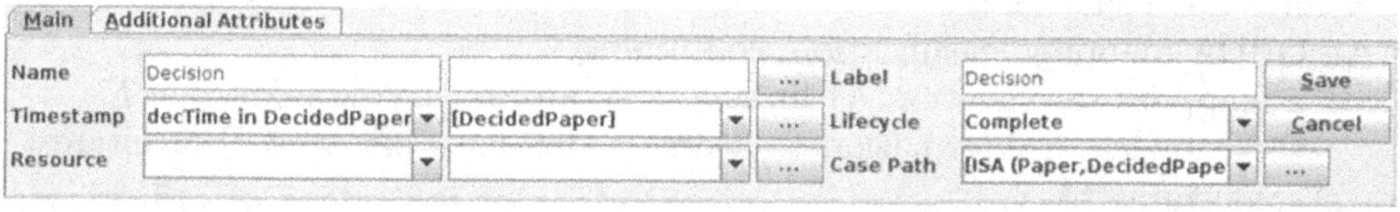

(b) The Decision event

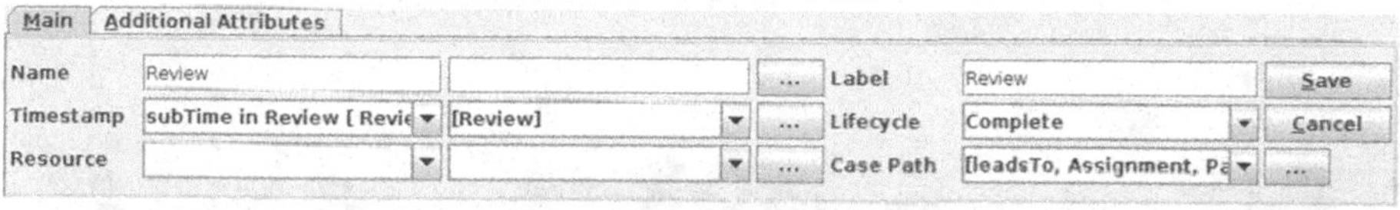

(c) The Review event

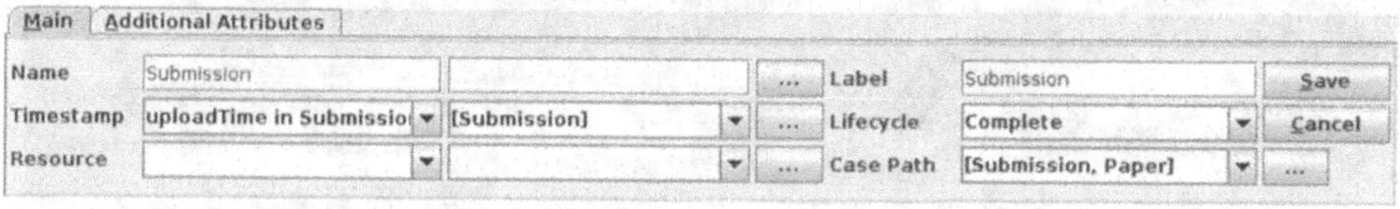

(d) The Submission event

Fig. 19. The properties of event annotations defined for the ConfSys use case

are defined, implementing what is reported in Fig. 16 (together with additional attribute definitions). The input forms for the configurations of such annotations are depicted in Fig. 19.

To simplify the annotation task, the editor supports some advanced operations:

- Properties and paths can be chosen using navigational selections over the diagram via mouse-click operations.
- The editor takes into account multiplicities on associations and attributes; when the user is selecting properties of the case and of events (in particular the timestamp), the editor enables only navigation paths that are functional.

The annotations are automatically translated into corresponding SPARQL queries by the editor.

Log Extraction Plug-in. The last component of the toolchain implements the mapping synthesis technique described in Sect. 4.5 towards log extraction, leveraging the state-of-the-art ontop framework to handle several important tasks such as *(i)* management of OBDA mappings, *(ii)* rewriting and unfolding of SPARQL queries, and *(iii)* query answering. In addition, the log extraction component exploits the OpenXES APIs[35] for managing XES data structures and the corresponding XML serialisation. Figure 20 shows the screenshot of the log extractor plug-in in Prom 6.6. Essentially, the plug-in takes the following inputs:

1. A conceptual data schema $\mathcal{T}$, generated via the UML Editor or represented as an OWL 2 QL file;
2. An OBDA mapping specification, containing
   - a mapping specification $\mathcal{M}$ linking $\mathcal{T}$ to an underlying relational $\mathcal{R}$
   - the connection information to access a database instance $\mathcal{D}$ of interest, conforming to $\mathcal{R}$.
3. Event-data annotations $\mathcal{L}$, which can be created using the Annotation Editor.

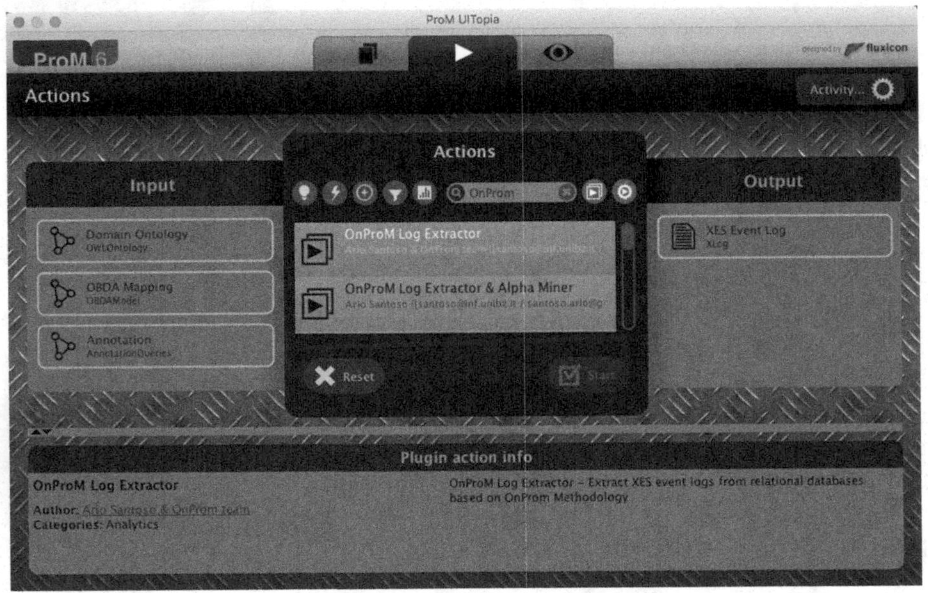

Fig. 20. Screenshot of Log Extractor Plug-in in Prom 6.6.

As output, the plugin produces a XES event log obtained as the result of the processing of the database instance $\mathcal{D}$ through the provided mappings and annotations. The event log is offered as a standard ProM resource within the ProM framework.

5 Conclusions

In this paper, we have presented the onprom framework, which leverages techniques from intelligent data management to tackle the challenging phase of data

[35] http://www.xes-standard.org.

preparation for process mining, enabling the possibility to apply process mining techniques on top of legacy information systems. Instead of forcing data and process analysts to set up ad-hoc, manual extraction procedures, onprom provides support to handle this problem at a higher level of abstraction. Specifically, users focus on modelling the data of interest conceptually, on the one hand linking the resulting conceptual schema to legacy data via declarative mappings, and on the other hand equipping the schema with declarative annotations that indicate where cases, events, and their attributes are "located" within such a schema. onprom then automatises the extraction of event logs, manipulating and reasoning over mappings and annotations by exploiting well-established techniques from knowledge representation and ontology-based data access.

We believe that the synergic integration of techniques coming from data and process management is the key to enable decision makers, analysts and domain experts in improving the way work is conducted within small, medium and large enterprises. At the same time, it provides interesting, open research challenges for computer scientists, covering both foundational and applied aspects. In particular, different interesting lines of research can be developed starting from onprom, ranging from the optimisation of ontology-based data access in the specific context of event log extraction, to the investigation of techniques and methodologies for event modelling and recognition typically studied within formal ontology, to the definition of alternative mechanisms for linking conceptual data schemas to reference, event log models.

Acknowledgements. This research has been partially supported by the Euregio IPN12 *"KAOS: Knowledge-Aware Operational Support"* project, which is funded by the "European Region Tyrol-South Tyrol-Trentino" (EGTC) under the first call for basic research projects, and by the UNIBZ internal project *"OnProm (ONtology-driven PROcess Mining)"*. We thank Wil van der Aalst for the interesting discussions and insights on the problem of extracting event logs from legacy information systems.

References

1. Dumas, M., Rosa, M.L., Mendling, J., Reijers, H.A.: Fundamentals of Business Process Management. Springer, Heidelberg (2013)
2. Weske, M.: Business Process Management - Concepts, Languages, Architectures, 2nd edn. Springer, Heidelberg (2012)
3. van der Aalst, W., et al.: Process mining manifesto. In: Daniel, F., Barkaoui, K., Dustdar, S. (eds.) BPM 2011. LNBIP, vol. 99, pp. 169–194. Springer, Heidelberg (2012). doi:10.1007/978-3-642-28108-2_19
4. van der Aalst, W.M.P.: Process Mining - Data Science in Action, 2nd edn. Springer, Heidelberg (2016)
5. IEEE Computational Intelligence Society: IEEE Standard for eXtensible Event Stream (XES) for Achieving Interoperability in Event Logs and Event Streams. IEEE Std 1849–2016 (2016). i–50
6. Poggi, A., Lembo, D., Calvanese, D., Giacomo, G., Lenzerini, M., Rosati, R.: Linking data to ontologies. In: Spaccapietra, S. (ed.) Journal on Data Semantics X. LNCS, vol. 4900, pp. 133–173. Springer, Heidelberg (2008). doi:10.1007/978-3-540-77688-8_5

7. Calvanese, D., Giacomo, G., Lembo, D., Lenzerini, M., Poggi, A., Rodriguez-Muro, M., Rosati, R.: Ontologies and databases: the *DL-Lite* approach. In: Tessaris, S., Franconi, E., Eiter, T., Gutierrez, C., Handschuh, S., Rousset, M.-C., Schmidt, R.A. (eds.) Reasoning Web 2009. LNCS, vol. 5689, pp. 255–356. Springer, Heidelberg (2009). doi:10.1007/978-3-642-03754-2_7
8. Calvanese, D., Cogrel, B., Komla-Ebri, S., Kontchakov, R., Lanti, D., Rezk, M., Rodriguez-Muro, M., Xiao, G.: Ontop: answering SPARQL queries over relational databases. Semant. Web J. **8**(3), 471–487 (2017)
9. Calvanese, D., Kalayci, T.E., Montali, M., Tinella, S.: Ontology-based data access for extracting event logs from legacy data: the onprom tool and methodology. In: Abramowicz, W. (ed.) BIS 2017. LNBIP, vol. 288, pp. 220–236. Springer, Heidelberg (2017). https://www.springer.com/us/book/9783319593357
10. van der Aalst, W., Weijters, T., Maruster, L.: Workflow mining: discovering process models from event logs. IEEE Trans. Knowl. Data Eng. **16**(9), 1128–1142 (2004)
11. Leemans, S.J.J., Fahland, D., van der Aalst, W.M.P.: Process and deviation exploration with inductive visual miner. In: Proceedings of BPM Demo Sessions. CEUR Workshop Proceedings, vol. 1295, p. 46. CEUR-WS.org (2014). http://ceur-ws.org/
12. Eck, M.L., Lu, X., Leemans, S.J.J., van der Aalst, W.M.P.: PM^2: a process mining project methodology. In: Zdravkovic, J., Kirikova, M., Johannesson, P. (eds.) CAiSE 2015. LNCS, vol. 9097, pp. 297–313. Springer, Cham (2015). doi:10.1007/978-3-319-19069-3_19
13. Verbeek, H.M.W., Buijs, J.C.A.M., Dongen, B.F., van der Aalst, W.M.P.: XES, XESame, and ProM 6. In: Soffer, P., Proper, E. (eds.) CAiSE Forum 2010. LNBIP, vol. 72, pp. 60–75. Springer, Heidelberg (2011). doi:10.1007/978-3-642-17722-4_5
14. Dongen, B.F., Medeiros, A.K.A., Verbeek, H.M.W., Weijters, A.J.M.M., van der Aalst, W.M.P.: The ProM framework: a new era in process mining tool support. In: Ciardo, G., Darondeau, P. (eds.) ICATPN 2005. LNCS, vol. 3536, pp. 444–454. Springer, Heidelberg (2005). doi:10.1007/11494744_25
15. van der Aalst, W.M.P., Bolt, A., van Zelst, S.J.: RapidProM: Mine your processes and not just your data. CoRR Technical Report abs/1703.03740, arXiv.org e-Print archive, March 2017. http://arxiv.org/abs/1703.03740
16. Günther, C.W., Rozinat, A.: Disco: discover your processes. In; Lohmann, N., Moser, S. (eds.) Proceedings of the Demonstration Track of the 10th International Conference on Business Process Management (BPM). CEUR Workshop Proceedings, vol. 940, pp. 40–44 (2012). http://ceur-ws.org/
17. Günther, C.W.: XES Standard Definition Version 1.0. Technical report, Fluxicon Process Laboratories, November 2009. http://www.xes-standard.org
18. van Dongen, B.F., van der Aalst, W.M.P.: A meta model for process mining data. In: Proceedings of EMOI - INTEROP. CEUR Workshop Proceedings, vol. 160. CEUR-WS.org (2005). http://ceur-ws.org/
19. Günther, C.W., Verbeek, E.: XES Standard Definition Version 2.0. Technical report, Fluxicon Process Laboratories, March 2014. http://www.xes-standard.org
20. Günther, C.W., Aalst, W.M.P.: A generic import framework for process event logs. In: Eder, J., Dustdar, S. (eds.) BPM 2006. LNCS, vol. 4103, pp. 81–92. Springer, Heidelberg (2006). doi:10.1007/11837862_10
21. Bao, J., et al.: OWL 2 Web Ontology Language document overview, 2nd edn. W3C Recommendation, World Wide Web Consortium, December 2012. http://www.w3.org/TR/owl2-overview/

22. Baader, F., Calvanese, D., McGuinness, D., Nardi, D., Patel-Schneider, P.F. (eds.): The Description Logic Handbook: Theory, Implementation and Applications. Cambridge University Press (2003)
23. Calvanese, D.: Query answering over description logic ontologies. In: Fermé, E., Leite, J. (eds.) JELIA 2014. LNCS (LNAI), vol. 8761, pp. 1–17. Springer, Cham (2014). doi:10.1007/978-3-319-11558-0_1
24. Vardi, M.Y.: The complexity of relational query languages. In: Proceedings of the 14th ACM SIGACT Symposium on Theory of Computing (STOC), pp. 137–146 (1982)
25. Calvanese, D., De Giacomo, G., Lembo, D., Lenzerini, M., Rosati, R.: Tractable reasoning and efficient query answering in description logics: The DL-Lite family. J. Autom. Reasoning **39**(3), 385–429 (2007)
26. Calvanese, D., De Giacomo, G., Lembo, D., Lenzerini, M., Rosati, R.: Data complexity of query answering in description logics. Artif. Intell. **195**, 335–360 (2013)
27. Motik, B., Cuenca Grau, B., Horrocks, I., Wu, Z., Fokoue, A., Lutz, C.: OWL 2 Web Ontology Language profiles, 2nd edn. W3C Recommendation, World Wide Web Consortium, December 2012. http://www.w3.org/TR/owl2-profiles/
28. Calvanese, D., Lenzerini, M., Nardi, D.: Unifying class-based representation formalisms. J. Artif. Intell. Res. **11**, 199–240 (1999)
29. Berardi, D., Calvanese, D., De Giacomo, G.: Reasoning on UML class diagrams. Artif. Intell. **168**(1–2), 70–118 (2005)
30. Abiteboul, S., Hull, R., Vianu, V.: Foundations of Databases. Addison Wesley Publ. Co. (1995)
31. Antonioli, N., Castanò, F., Coletta, S., Grossi, S., Lembo, D., Lenzerini, M., Poggi, A., Virardi, E., Castracane, P.: Ontology-based data management for the Italian public debt. In: Proceedings of the 8th International Conference on Formal Ontology in Information Systems (FOIS). Frontiers in Artificial Intelligence and Applications, vol. 267, pp. 372–385. IOS Press (2014)
32. Gottlob, G., Kikot, S., Kontchakov, R., Podolskii, V.V., Schwentick, T., Zakharyaschev, M.: The price of query rewriting in ontology-based data access. Artif. Intell. **213**, 42–59 (2014)
33. Kontchakov, R., Lutz, C., Toman, D., Wolter, F., Zakharyaschev, M.: The combined approach to query answering in DL-Lite. In: Proceedings of the 12th International Conference on the Principles of Knowledge Representation and Reasoning (KR), pp. 247–257 (2010)
34. Rodriguez-Muro, M., Calvanese, D.: High performance query answering over DL-Lite ontologies. In: Proceedings of the 13th International Conference on the Principles of Knowledge Representation and Reasoning (KR), pp. 308–318 (2012)
35. Rodriguez-Muro, M., Rezk, M.: Efficient SPARQL-to-SQL with R2RML mappings. J. Web Semant. **33**, 141–169 (2015)
36. Syamsiyah, A., van Dongen, B.F., van der Aalst, W.M.P.: DB-XES: enabling process discovery in the large. In: Ceravolo, P., Guetl, C., Rinderle-Ma, S. (eds.) Proceedings of the 6th International Symposium on Data-driven Process Discovery and Analysis (SIMPDA). CEUR Workshop Proceedings, vol. 1757, pp. 63–77 (2016). http://ceur-ws.org/
37. Jiménez-Ruiz, E., Kharlamov, E., Zheleznyakov, D., Horrocks, I., Pinkel, C., Skjæveland, M.G., Thorstensen, E., Mora, J.: BootOX: Bootstrapping OWL 2 Ontologies and R2RML Mappings from Relational Databases. In Villata, S., Pan, J.Z., Dragoni, M. (eds.) Proceedings of the 14th International Semantic Web Conference Posters & Demonstrations Track (ISWC). CEUR Workshop Proceedings, vol. 1486 (2015). http://ceur-ws.org/

Author Index

Printed in the United States
By Bookmasters

Printed in the United States
By Bookmasters